Human Diversity in Education

An Intercultural Approach

Human Diversity in Education

An Intercultural Approach

Kenneth H. Cushner, Averil McClelland

Kent State University

Philip Safford

Case Western Reserve University

9

Mc
Graw
Hill
Education

HUMAN DIVERSITY IN EDUCATION: AN INTERCULTURAL APPROACH, NINTH EDITION

Published by McGraw-Hill Education, 2 Penn Plaza, New York, NY 10121. Copyright © 2019 by McGraw-Hill Education. All rights reserved. Printed in the United States of America. Previous editions © 2015, 2012, 2009, and 2006. No part of this publication may be reproduced or distributed in any form or by any means, or stored in a database or retrieval system, without the prior written consent of McGraw-Hill Education, including, but not limited to, in any network or other electronic storage or transmission, or broadcast for distance learning.

Some ancillaries, including electronic and print components, may not be available to customers outside the United States.

This book is printed on acid-free paper.

2 3 4 5 6 7 8 9 LWI 21 20 19 18

ISBN 978-1-25-991381-5
MHID 1-25-991381-3

Senior Vice President, Products & Markets: *Kurt L. Strand*
Vice President, General Manager, Products & Markets: *Michael Ryan*
Vice President, Content Production & Technology Services: *Kimberly Meriwether David*
Brand Manager & Managing Editor: *Penina Braffman*
Marketing Specialist: *Alexandra Schultz*
Director, Content Production: *Terri Schiesl*
Content Project Manager: *Heather Ervolino*
Buyer: *Susan K. Culbertson*
Cover Designer: *Studio Montage, St. Louis, MO*
Cover Image: Puzzle Pieces: ©*Design Pics/Kristy-Anne Glubish*; Children with Globe: ©*Jani Bryson/Getty Images*
Media Project Manager: *Jennifer Bartell*
Compositor: *MPS Limited*
Typeface: *10/12 STIX MathJax Main Regular*
Printer: *LSC Communications*

All credits appearing on page or at the end of the book are considered to be an extension of the copyright page.

Library of Congress Cataloging-in-Publication Data

Cushner, Kenneth, author. | McClelland, Averil, author. | Safford, Philip L., author.
  Human diversity in education : an intercultural approach / Kenneth H.
  Cushner, Averil McClelland, Kent State University, Philip Safford, Case Western Reserve University.
  Ninth Edition. | New York : McGraw-Hill Education, [2019] |
  Previous edition: 2014. | Audience: Ages: 18+
  LCCN 2017038922 | ISBN 9781259913815 (acid-free paper)
  LCSH: Multicultural education–United States. | Individual differences in children–United States. |
  Sex differences in education–United States.
  LCC LC1099.3 .C87 2019 | DDC 370.117–dc23 LC record
  available at https://lccn.loc.gov/2017038922

The Internet addresses listed in the text were accurate at the time of publication. The inclusion of a website does not indicate an endorsement by the authors or McGraw-Hill Education, and McGraw-Hill Education does not guarantee the accuracy of the information presented at these sites.

www.mhhe.com

Brief Contents

Contents

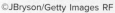

Chapter 3   Culture and the Culture-Learning Process 63

©Hill Street Studios/Blend Images LLC RF

Chapter 4   Classrooms and Schools as Cultural Crossroads 107

©Ingram Publishing RF

Chapter 5   Intercultural Development: Considering
the Growth of Self and Others 145

©KidStock/Getty Images RF

(2) Multicultural Teaching in Action 169

Chapter 6   Creating Classrooms That Address
Race and Ethnicity 171

©SolStock/Getty Images RF

Chapter 7   The Classroom as a Global Community:
Nationality and Region 205

©Corbis/VCG/Getty Images RF

Chapter 8 Teaching in a Linquistically Diverse Classroom: Understanding the Power of Language 245

©Paul Hawkett/Alamy Stock Photo RF

Chapter 9 Religious Pluralism in Secular Classrooms 271

©Mila Supinskaya Glashchenko/
Shutterstock.com RF

Chapter 10 Developing Gender Inclusive Schools and Classrooms: The Emergence of Gender and Sexual Diversity 303

©mrtom-uk/Getty Images

Chapter 11 Creating Developmentally Appropriate Classrooms: The Importance of Age and Developmental Status 333

©Caia Image/Glow Images RF

Chapter 12 Creating Inclusive Classrooms: The Ability/Disability Continuum and the Health Dimension 361

©Realistic Reflections RF

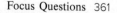

Chapter 13   Improving Schools for All Children: The Role of Social Stratification in Teaching and Learning 393

©Wavebreak Media ltd/Alamy Stock Photo RF

About the Authors

Kenneth H. Cushner is an Emeritus Professor of International and Intercultural Teacher Education, served as Executive Director of International Affairs, and has been Associate Dean at Kent State University (1987–2015). Prior to his university appointment he taught in schools in Switzerland, Australia, and the United States, and completed his doctoral studies at the University of Hawaii at Manoa while a degree scholar at the East-West Center. Dr. Cushner is a Founding Fellow and Past-President of the International Academy for Intercultural Research; has been a Fulbright Scholar to Sweden (2008) and Poland (2016); and has been a visiting professor at Shanghai International Studies University, the College of the Bahamas, University of Newcastle (Australia), Stenden University (the Netherlands), and the University of Nis (Serbia); has coordinated Semester at Sea's Teachers at Sea program (summers 2010 and 2011) and served as Intercultural Specialist for the Fall 2017 around the world voyage; and twice served as director of COST—the Consortium for Overseas Student Teaching. In addition to this text, he is author or editor of several books and articles in the field of intercultural education, including: *Intercultural Student Teaching: A Bridge to Global Competence, Beyond Tourism: A Practical Guide to Meaningful Educational Travel, International Perspectives on Intercultural Education,* and *Intercultural Interactions: A Practical Guide.* He has traveled with young people and teachers on all seven continents. Since retiring from Kent State University, Dr. Cushner has consulted with ECIS, a network of 400+ international schools in 90 countries; with NAFSA: Association of Intercultural Educators; and has instituted a professional development program for teachers in a Massai community school in northern Tanzania. In his spare time, Dr. Cushner enjoys playing music (guitar and percussion), travel, and photography.

Averil McClelland is retired from her position as Associate Professor and Coordinator of the Cultural Foundations of Education program in the College and Graduate School at Kent State University, from which she received her Ph.D. Dr. McClelland has had extensive experience in curriculum design and program evaluation, as well as experience with addressing issues of gender and education and cultural diversity in education. In addition to this text, she is the author of *The Education of Women in the United States: A Guide to Theory, Teaching, and Research* (Garland, 1992), as well as a number of articles in scholarly journals. She received the Distinguished Teaching Award from Kent State University in 1996, and has a long-standing relationship with the National First Ladies Library, where she develops Web-based curricula based on the lives of the nation's 44 First Ladies. Her special interests are the history, sociology, and politics of education, the reconstruction of teacher education, and internationalizing the college curriculum for preservice and practicing teachers.

Philip Safford, Adjunct Professor of Psychology at Case Western Reserve University, is Emeritus Professor and former chair of Special Education at Kent State University. Prior to earning his Ph.D. through the Combined Program in Education and Psychology at the University of Michigan, with specialization in special education and child development, he had been a teacher and administrator in residential treatment programs for children with emotional disorders. Dr. Safford has authored or edited six books and numerous articles dealing with special education history, early intervention for young children with disabilities, and related topics. He has directed or co-directed a number of training, research, and demonstration projects in special education supported by federal and state grants.

Preface

It is difficult to fathom the myriad changes that have occurred and that influence the content of this book in just three years since the previous edition. As this book goes to press, we have witnessed many nations in Europe as well as the United States that have made dramatic political shifts from open and liberal leanings to more populist, nationalistic and conservative ideologies. These shifts have been accompanied by an increase in xenophobia and stricter actions to reduce immigration, often accompanied by a rise in anti-immigrant, anti-Semitic and Islamophobic sentiment. The conflicts and struggles in Afghanistan, Iraq and Syria continue, as tensions between the United States and Russia fester. A questioning of Truth, with an onslaught of "fake news," has emerged, having a major influence on the 2016 U.S. presidential election. And we expect numerous changes to occur under the new U.S. Secretary of Education, Betsy DeVos.

And these challenges are in the political arena alone. Across the planet people continue to feel the stresses of the seemingly endless changes and challenges they confront on many fronts. Climate change continues to advance resulting in new and unpredictable weather patterns despite a vocal minority that appears to deny its existence. Although making gains, people continue to wrestle with questions surrounding same-sex marriage and gay rights; the question of health care, the accelerated identification of children with autism and other disabilities, as well as our aging population span cultural differences and cut across geographic, political, and social boundaries, continuing to impact us all at the local, national, and global levels.

Some people are eager to embrace innovation and change while others struggle through a variety of political and social means to retain older and more traditional ways of doing things. Such challenges continue to enter and impact our increasingly culturally diverse classrooms and communities. To effectively address and solve the multitude of issues we face it is incumbent upon teachers to provide young people with a foundation that will assist them to better understand the complex nature of the world in which they will live while developing the skills that will enable them to be proactive problem solvers in an interdependent, global society. This requires people who have the knowledge, skills, and motivations to reach beyond their own cultural boundaries and a willingness and ability to collaborate with others. If people are not willing and able to do so, these, and other future problems, simply will not be solved. Developing intercultural understanding and competence must be actively addressed throughout the school curriculum.

This ninth edition of *Human Diversity in Education: An Intercultural Approach*, continues to focus on the preparation of teachers and other human-service providers who can interact effectively with the wide diversity of people they are certain to encounter and who are able to transmit this knowledge and skill to the individuals in their charge.

New to This Edition

This book continues to receive overwhelmingly positive feedback from users around the world. Because of this we have maintained much of the familiar format. Regular users, however, will notice some changes in this edition. The book continues to provide a broad treatment of the various forms of diversity found in today's schools, including nationality, ethnicity, race, religion, gender, social class, language acquisition and use, sexual orientation, health concerns, and disability. The book also maintain its research-based approach, with an increased cross-cultural and intercultural emphasis. We continue to stress that it is both at the level of the individual teacher as well as the organizational structure of the school where significant change must occur with regard to how diversity is understood and accommodated. Little institutional or systematic change will occur until individuals fully understand the role that culture plays in determining peoples' thoughts and actions, and how they can go about altering its powerful influence. Culture learning of both teacher and student, along with intercultural interaction, remain central to this book. We also recognize that today's generation of young people continue to be exposed to greater diversity, both global and domestic, through the influence of global media, the demographic changes that have occurred in many local communities, as well as through the increased use of social media by individuals as well as in schools.

This ninth edition includes greater attention to the international aspects of curriculum. Chapter 2, for instance, has been expanded. In addition to addressing the historical foundations of multicultural education, this edition addresses the development of global education and explores some of the overlap between the two initiatives. Similarly, Chapter 7 continues to feature recent initiatives taken by such organizations as the Asia Society/EdSteps, the International Baccalaureate (IB) program PISA (the Programme for International Student Assessment), and others to significantly explore the inclusion of an international and intercultural dimension in teaching and learning. Chapter 4 introduces a new model exploring the Intercultural Learning Arena as a major means of illustrating some of the intercultural dynamics at play when teaching and learning across cultures.

We have maintained the inclusion of the Active Exercises and Classroom Activities at the end of each chapter. Case Studies and Critical Incidents continue to be integral teaching devices used throughout the book. Each chapter continues to open with a Case Study that introduces major concepts and sets the context for that chapter. A number of related Critical Incidents can be found at the end of most of the chapters. Each chapter also identifies an expanded number of updated references that students can access for more information. A teacher's guide and other online learning resources are also available that provide directions for instructors as well as classroom activities and test questions.

The general format of this edition remains similar to the previous one with a few modifications. Part One provides background to the broad social, cultural, and economic changes that confront society today (Chapter 1), with a historical overview of past multicultural and global education efforts (Chapter 2). We place particular emphasis on culture learning and intercultural interaction in Chapters 3 and 4. Chapter 5 explores the development of intercultural competence while providing a model that teachers can use to gauge their own growth as well as that of their students.

Part Two examines what teachers can do to make their classrooms and schools more responsive to diversity and more effective learning environments. In other words, how to structure classrooms that are collaborative, inclusive, developmentally appropriate, globally oriented, and religiously pluralistic. Each of the chapters in Part Two centers on a major aspect of diversity: race and ethnicity (Chapter 6), global understanding (Chapter 7), linguistically diverse classrooms, first and second language acquisition, and the power of language (Chapter 8), religious pluralism, with an updated statement on current law on religion and public schools (Chapter 9), gender and sexual diversity and a new focus on non-binary, gender non-conforming students (Chapter 10), age and development (Chapter 11), exceptionality and ability (Chapter 12), and social class and social status in relation to assessment (Chapter 13).

We hope you continue to find benefit from this edition, and we would welcome feedback from you.

Kenneth H. Cushner
Averil McClelland
Philip Safford

McGraw-Hill Connect® is a highly reliable, easy-to-use homework and learning management solution that utilizes learning science and award-winning adaptive tools to improve student results.

Homework and Adaptive Learning

- Connect's assignments help students contextualize what they've learned through application, so they can better understand the material and think critically.

- Connect will create a personalized study path customized to individual student needs through SmartBook®.

- SmartBook helps students study more efficiently by delivering an interactive reading experience through adaptive highlighting and review.

Connect's Impact on Retention Rates, Pass Rates, and Average Exam Scores

without Connect   with Connect

Using **Connect** improves retention rates by **19.8%**, passing rates by **12.7%, and** exam scores by **9.1%.**

Over **7 billion questions** have been answered, making McGraw-Hill Education products more intelligent, reliable, and precise.

73% of instructors who use **Connect** require it; instructor satisfaction **increases** by 28% when **Connect** is required.

Quality Content and Learning Resources

- Connect content is authored by the world's best subject matter experts, and is available to your class through a simple and intuitive interface.

- The Connect eBook makes it easy for students to access their reading material on smartphones and tablets. They can study on the go and don't need internet access to use the eBook as a reference, with full functionality.

- Multimedia content such as videos, simulations, and games drive student engagement and critical thinking skills.

Robust Analytics and Reporting

- Connect Insight® generates easy-to-read reports on individual students, the class as a whole, and on specific assignments.

- The Connect Insight dashboard delivers data on performance, study behavior, and effort. Instructors can quickly identify students who struggle and focus on material that the class has yet to master.

- Connect automatically grades assignments and quizzes, providing easy-to-read reports on individual and class performance.

©Hero Images/Getty Images

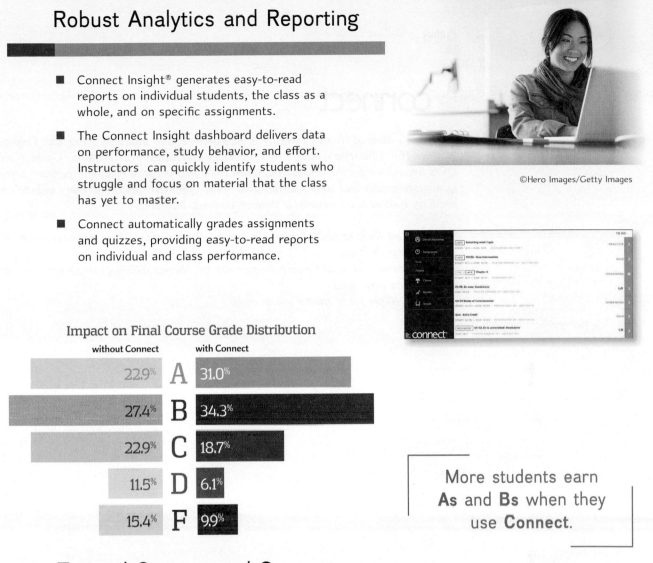

Impact on Final Course Grade Distribution

without Connect		with Connect
22.9%	A	31.0%
27.4%	B	34.3%
22.9%	C	18.7%
11.5%	D	6.1%
15.4%	F	9.9%

More students earn **As** and **Bs** when they use **Connect**.

Trusted Service and Support

- Connect integrates with your LMS to provide single sign-on and automatic syncing of grades. Integration with Blackboard®, D2L®, and Canvas also provides automatic syncing of the course calendar and assignment-level linking.

- Connect offers comprehensive service, support, and training throughout every phase of your implementation.

- If you're looking for some guidance on how to use Connect, or want to learn tips and tricks from super users, you can find tutorials as you work. Our Digital Faculty Consultants and Student Ambassadors offer insight into how to achieve the results you want with Connect.

McGraw-Hill **connect**®

The ninth edition of Human Diversity in Education, is now available online with Connect, McGraw-Hill Education's integrated assignment and assessment platform. Connect also offers SmartBook for the new edition, which is the first adaptive reading experience proven to improve grades and help students study more effectively. All of the title's website and ancillary content is also available through Connect, including:

- *A full Test Bank of multiple choice questions that test students on central concepts and ideas in each chapter.*
- *An Instructor's Manual for each chapter with full chapter outlines, sample test questions, and discussion topics.*
- *Lecture Slides for instructor use in class.*

1

Foundations for Teaching in an Increasingly Intercultural Context

Education in a Changing Society

Focus Questions

1. What is the rationale for attention to diversity and intercultural competence in education?

2. What are some of the fundamental changes influencing American society and the world, including issues such as globalization, our changing demographics, rapidly expanding technologies, environmental pressures, and consequent changing experiences, attitudes, and values among the generations? How do these changes impact teaching and learning?

3. What are some differences between schools designed to prepare students for an industrial age and schools designed to prepare students for an informational, global age?

4. Why do you think real, substantial change is so difficult? Or do you?

" Don't limit a child to your own learning, for he was born in another time. "

RABINDRANATH TAGORE

Case Study

Samantha Carter's Diversity Class

Samantha Carter wants to be a teacher. She has wanted to be a teacher for almost as long as she can remember. Called "Sam" by her family and friends, she has worked in local recreation programs, summer camps, and in neighborhood parks, sometimes coaching younger kids in volleyball and tennis. She has heard all the arguments against teaching as a career: It's a difficult, and sometimes even dangerous job; it's only moderately well paid; she could do more with her skills and abilities. But she really wants to be a teacher, and that's all there is to it.

Sam is also a volleyball player. She has a full athletic scholarship to the university and hopes to coach volleyball in the high school where she has already been hired to teach social studies in the fall. She has it all planned out: graduation in a few months, spend the summer using her new iPad (an early graduation present!) to design websites and interactive assignments and to record podcasts for the classes she'll be teaching, and finally, start her new job in a suburban school system just far enough from her parents' home to give her a real sense of independence. American history . . . World history . . . Economics . . . Government . . . and, of course, volleyball! She can hardly wait!

Except . . . except, here she is, sitting in a required diversity course, wondering why in the world everyone is making such a fuss about all this "diversity stuff." Haven't we gotten past all that? On the Internet, after all, no one knows what your color is, or your religion, or your gender. Indeed, she and her friends often use "alternate" personalities while surfing the Net, and clearly, people on Facebook, Twitter, and other social media can also give themselves "other" faces and personalities. The important thing is what people have to say, not what they look like!

Still, she recalls that the superintendent told her that the district she will be teaching in is changing rapidly in terms of race and social class—did he tell her that because it might be a problem? Well, it isn't as if she has never spent any time with people who are different from her. Her high school volleyball team looked like the United Nations, and they all get along fine. She knew all their parents and siblings, and they will be friends forever. And it certainly isn't as if she doesn't already know that some groups of people still suffer from discrimination— some of her college community service credits were spent working with kids in a low-income urban neighborhood, and she spent one whole summer volunteering in a community development project in Appalachia. She really liked the people she worked with and wished she could have done more to help them.

Why, Sam thinks to herself, she could probably teach this course! And anyway, she thinks, teaching social studies will give her great opportunities to introduce her students to issues of difference. Yet, she thinks with a little pang of doubt, the urban kids she worked with had zero interest in history. And some of the people in Appalachia spoke with such an accent she could hardly understand them. And she doesn't feel too well prepared to deal with children with disabilities either, and no doubt there will be students with both medical and developmental disabilities in her classes.

Sam is learning that society is changing—in lots of ways. If there is one thing she has found in the past few years, it's that schools aren't like they used to be, even when she was in school. Her older brother teaches sixth-, seventh-, and eighth-grade social studies in a school not too far from the district where she will be teaching, and one half of the students in his classes live in families headed by a single parent (some of them, fathers), one third are reading below grade level, and two thirds are eligible for free lunches. His classes are far from being all white or even all native-born: he has African American students, East Indian, Vietnamese, and Central American students, as well as students who are the children of immigrants and refugees from various countries in the Middle East and Africa. His students include fundamentalist Christians, some are Catholic, a growing number are Muslims, several are Jewish, and one is a Jehovah's Witness. He has one student in a wheelchair after surviving a bad automobile accident, two students with breathing apparatuses because of asthma, and at least six who are waiting (after 6 months) to be tested to determine their eligibility for

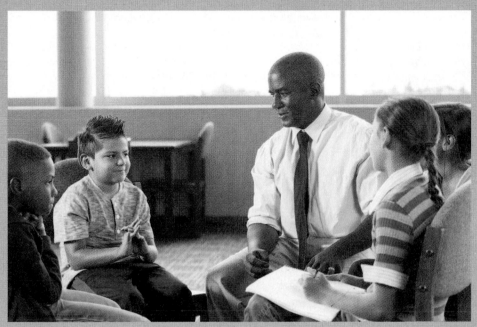
©asiseeit/Getty Images RF

the newly-created severe behavior disorders program, which is to be housed in a separate school on the other side of town.

Other changes are taking place as well, both for her brother and for herself in her new school. The principal of her new high school announced proudly that every teacher will have a Smart Board or SMART Board by fall. He also mentioned, though, that the needs and expectations of students seem to be changing, even from just a few years ago. Growing up with technology as they have, today's students seem easily bored, have shorter attention spans, want things done quickly, and don't like to read long assignments, even if they are good readers. What's going on here?

In addition, since the No Child Left Behind Act was replaced with the Every Student Succeeds Act in 2015, the performance of students, teachers, and school districts is being measured as never before. "The good news," says her professor, "is that the proponents of accountability really want all children to learn and all teachers to teach well. The bad news is that we have never before really tried to educate all children to the same standard, and we are still not altogether sure how to do that—nor can we all agree on what it means to be a good teacher!."

A classmate raises his hand. "What," he asks, "about kids with really bad family problems, kids whose parents aren't even there for them, or the growing number who are homeless? What about kids with attention-deficit/hyperactivity disorder (ADHD), or kids who just hate school? What about kids who are working 20 hours a week, or kids who just can't 'get it'? What about kids who don't speak English? What about kids who act out in violent ways?"

Another student, Joanne, raised her hand, asking, "How can teachers really go about preparing young students for a globally-connected future if they, themselves, have little knowledge or experience of the broader world in which we exist?"

She went on, "Last summer I was lucky enough to spend 4 weeks in Australia on a study abroad program designed especially for future teachers. This is something most teacher education students don't do, by the way, which I highly recommend! We spent a day with a group of Australian high school students who were part of a Global Futures Club in their school. One student in particular, a 15-year-old girl stood up and challenged us with some ideas I'd never thought about before. This really got me thinking. I was so impressed with what she had to say that I asked her if she could write it down. She had already done that as part of her club's activity, so she gave me a copy. I still carry it around with me, and if you don't mind I'd like to read it as I think there are some really important messages for us. Here's what she said . . ."

(continued)

"I want you to understand how I think about my future and my world. Wherever I live and work, I will certainly be mixing in a multinational, multifaith, multicultural setting. During my lifetime, a planetwide economic system is likely to operate. It will be controlled not so much by big nations but by big business networks and regional centers of trade like Singapore, Los Angeles, London, Tokyo, and Sydney. By the time I am 35 years old more people will live in Shanghai, just one city in China, than in the whole country of Austraila. Most people will be working across national borders and cultures, speaking more than one language—probably including an Asian language. That's the kind of job for which I need to be prepared. Because I am growing up in Australia, the Asia/Pacific area will be a strong focus of my world. There are three billion people in Asia alone, and that number will certainly continue to grow. The Asian continent (from India to Japan) already accounts for half of the world's population. The world's largest Muslim country is here, too, in Indonesia, just north of Australia. With a population of over 220 million, Indonesia's population is larger than that of Japan and Russia. People the world over will have to learn about Islam at school and to respect Muslims—even in the face of all the challenges present today."

"But it's not only happening to those of us in Australia. More than half of the population in many of the world's developing countries is under the age of 25. Think about the consequences of that! These are all potential partners and competitors of all of us young people around the world, and they'll all want the good things they see that life has to offer. It will not matter what nationality any of us have. Because our world is smaller, people move about, and most workplaces will be internationalized. Our world is likely to become borderless. We are more than likely to be employed by an internationally owned firm, and it is likely that in our homes someone will speak Japanese, Korean, Spanish, or Chinese."

"Our environment, too, will continue to be changed—and challenged. In the 1950s, when my grandparents were born, only two cities in the world, London and New York, had more than 8 million inhabitants. In 2015, there were 42 such cities—more than half of them in Asia. Environmentally what happens within the border of one country is no longer solely that country's business. Environmental responsibilities will be enforced internationally. By the time I am 50 years old, the world could be threatened by "green wars" or "water wars" unless my generation learns to do something to balance the unequal access to clean water, good soil, food distribution, and climate change."

Joanne continued. "The more that I think about it, all of our future students are like Sophie. A lot of our schooling, from the way people look at things, and even many of the textbooks used around the world, are Eurocentric in their thinking and orientation, and are really out of date. Schooling today must teach young people about living comfortably and successfully in a multicultural world. What skills and understandings will people living and working in the near future need? Do we know what an international curriculum looks like, and how it can be taught? Most schools today say that students need to be global citizens. But do they know *what* to teach? . . . And do they know *how* to teach? Are they confident that they can design and deliver a curriculum that will equip today's young people to live in a complex, intercultural world?"*

"Yes," says another classmate, "how are we supposed to teach everyone?"

"Perhaps," says the professor, "we'd be better off asking it another way: How are we to think about our practice of teaching so that everyone learns and that they learn what they need to learn given the times in which we live? The scene has shifted in schools today from an emphasis on teaching to an emphasis on learning. This change in focus makes it all the more important that we understand differences among students—all kinds of differences, visible and invisible, because those differences may influence a student's learning, and our job is to create classrooms in which everyone learns."

Sam sighs. She really does want to be a teacher, but it seems to be a lot more complicated than she thought it would be. As the world around her changes, perhaps she, too, will have to make some significant changes if she is going to be as effective an educator as she hopes to be.

* (Modified from Tudball, 2012).

The Reality of Social Change

As we get used to living in the 21st century, Samantha, along with all of us, is witnessing changing circumstances in many areas of life that have widespread importance for the future of our country, our schools, and the world-at-large. Taken together, these changed circumstances are resulting in profound shifts in the nature of some of our basic social institutions, such as the economy, politics, religion, the family, and, of course, education.

Institutions in Transition

The term **social institution** has been defined as a formal, recognized, established, and stabilized way of pursuing some activity in society (Bierstedt, 1974). Another way to define a social institution is to think of it as a set of rules, or **norms**, that enable us to get through the day without having to figure out how to behave toward others, or whether to brush our teeth, or if, in fact, we should go to school or to work. In this society, as in all societies, we have rules that pattern the way we interact with family members, friends, people we see often, such as neighbors, teachers, or doctors, and even strangers who fill certain roles—the bus driver, the clerk in the store, the server in a restaurant. We know these rules because we have internalized them as children, and in a stable society we can depend on the rules staying relatively the same over time. All societies, including nonliterate ones, create social institutions—or sets of norms—that govern at least five basic areas of social need: *economics* (ways of exchanging goods and services), *politics* (ways of governing), *religion* (ways of worshipping one or more deities), *the family* (ways of ensuring the survival of children), and *education* (ways of bringing up and educating the younger generation so that the society will continue to exist).

In our society, and indeed in most of the world, people are witnessing profound changes in the nature of these basic institutions; in other words, the rules—or norms—are changing, and more and more are feeling unsettled or unsure by what they are encountering. Many scholars who study the past as a way to understand the future assert that these changes are so fundamental as to constitute a shift in the very nature of our civilization. In his book *The Third Wave*, Alvin Toffler (1980) was among the first scholar-futurists to warn that our institutions (what is normative in society) are changing in specific and characteristic ways and to hint at the rise and the effect of globalization on us all. Many of today's changes, Toffler suggested, are neither random nor independent of one another. He identified a number of events that *seem* to be independent from one another—the "breakdown" of the nuclear family, the global energy crisis, the influence of cable television, the loss of manufacturing jobs in the United States, and the emergence of separatist movements within national borders of many nations. Today, we might add the ubiquitous use of new technologies, the Internet, and various social media that have dramatically changed the way we live our lives and interact across various boundaries—in many circumstances resulting in major social change. These and many other seemingly unrelated events are interconnected and may be part of a much larger phenomenon that Toffler described as the death of industrialism and the rise of a new civilization that he called "the Third Wave."

Toffler is not the only one to have perceived these changes before most people were aware of them. In the early 1980s, the book *Megatrends: Ten New Directions Transforming Our Lives* added a new word to the language. In this work John Naisbitt (1982)

accurately predicted the move toward globalization, the shift from an industrial economy to an "information" economy, and the growth of networks as a way of managing
information (although he didn't even mention the Internet or the World Wide Web!).
Later Naisbitt and Patricia Aburdene (1990) wrote *Megatrends 2000: Ten New Directions for the 1990s*, in which they discussed the evolution of telecommunications, the
rise of China as a competing power, and a growing need to "look below the surface"
to find the meaning of these changes for real human beings and real organizations.
More recently, *in The World Is Flat: A Brief History of the Twenty-First Century* Thomas
Friedman (2006) introduced the notion of the 'flat world' in which people from all
walks of life, almost regardless of their location, can engage in meaningful ways with
one another. Indeed, Patricia Aburdene (2005) revealed in her book *Megatrends 2010:
The Rise of Conscious Capitalism* that our society was reaching a new phase in which
the ideas of social responsibility, environmental values, and a spiritual dimension were
beginning to reshape capitalism in interesting ways. Although we cannot take all these
predictions as absolute fact (predicting the future is a precarious occupation), it is
worth thinking about our changing circumstances and the impact these changes are
having (and will continue to have) on the way we live, work, play, govern ourselves,
worship, and learn.

The Impact of Specific Changes on Basic Institutions

It is useful to think in terms of four different sets of specific changes that, taken together, seem to be reshaping our basic institutions. These areas, suggested by Willard
Daggett (2005) in *Successful Schools; From Research to Action Plans*, are *globalization,
demographics, technology,* and *changing values and attitudes among the generations.* New
circumstances in each of these areas are having an impact on the way we think about
and accomplish our purposes as a society. Also each of these areas provides a rationale
for greater intercultural knowledge and understanding. Let's take a closer look at how
each of these areas may be changing the basic social institutions in our society.

Factors Influencing the Institution of Economics

1. From National to Global   For much of our nation's history, the U.S. economy
has been based on manufacturing done by companies whose production could be found
within the borders of the country. Today, our economy is firmly global. Indeed, the
much-revered American corporation can hardly be said to exist any longer. In 2015,
General Motors sold more than 3.6 million vehicles in China compared to 3 million
in the United States in the same period. This represents the fifth year that sales in
China surpassed those in the United States. The acquisition of raw material, manufacturing processes, and distribution of goods by such giants as Ford Motor Company,
General Motors, or General Electric is done worldwide. In large measure because of
advances in computer technology and high-speed travel, we find ourselves looking more
and more often beyond our own borders for goods, services, and sales. *In The Work
of Nations: Preparing Ourselves for the 21st Century,* Robert Reich (1992), former Secretary of Labor, described this reality two decades ago in the following terms:

> Consider some examples: Precision ice hockey equipment is designed in Sweden,
> financed in Canada, and assembled in Cleveland and Denmark for distribution in
> North America and Europe, respectively, out of alloys whose molecular structure was
> researched and patented in Delaware and fabricated in Japan. An advertising

campaign is conceived in Britain; film footage for it is shot in Canada, dubbed in Britain, and edited in New York. A sports car is financed in Japan, designed in Italy, and assembled in Indiana, Mexico, and France, using advanced electronic components invented in New Jersey and fabricated in Japan. A microprocessor is designed in California and financed in America and West Germany, containing dynamic random-access memories fabricated in South Korea. A jet airplane is designed in the state of Washington and in Japan, and assembled in Seattle, with tail engines from Britain, special tail sections from China and Italy, and engines from Britain. A space satellite designed in California, manufactured in France, and financed by Australians is launched from a rocket made in the Soviet Union. Which of these is an American product? Which a foreign? How does one decide? Does it matter? (p. 112)

The effects of globalization are now increasingly encountered by each and every individual. Call the help desk with a problem with your computer, or have a question about your cable TV, and it is likely that the person you are speaking with on the other end of the phone is in India or Costa Rica. In your daily interactions, whether on campus or in your local stores, hospitals, and community in general, you are almost certain to encounter people who have immigrated to the United States and who speak a language other than English. While there are many positive aspects to globalization, this is not always the case; and certainly not so for everybody on the planet. While you may be able to buy your favorite fruits and vegetables almost any time of the year relatively inexpensively because they are flown in from countries around the globe, we also encounter the possibility of large-scale salmonella outbreaks, as was experienced across the United States in 2008 from contaminated jalapeño peppers imported from Mexico.

In fact, our often unquestioning behavior at home can often have some unanticipated consequences elsewhere. The recent addition of quinoa to the American health-conscious diet offers a good example of the potential negative impact globalization can have on traditional societies. Not too long ago, quinoa was a relatively unheard of Peruvian grain that could only be found in small health food shops. Nutritionists soon identified quinoa as the only vegetable source of all amino acids, giving it the biological food value equivalent of milk, meat, and eggs; this was viewed as a godsend to vegans and vegetarians alike. Sales of quinoa, now marketed as the "miracle grain of the Andes," skyrocketed. Consequently, the price shot up. It has tripled since 2006. The desire for quinoa in countries like the United States pushed prices for the grain so high that poorer people, who once depended upon it as a staple food in their diet, can no longer afford to eat it. In Lima, quinoa now costs more than chicken, and junk food is cheaper to buy than quinoa. Outside the cities, and fueled by overseas demand, the pressure is on now to turn land that once produced a diversity of crops into a quinoa monoculture.

Arguing that globalization was not new, Thomas Friedman (2006) wrote that, in fact, there have been three phases of globalization. The era he calls *Globalization 1.0* began at the end of the 15th century when Columbus opened trade between Europe and the Americas and lasted until around the beginning of the 19th century. This was the era of national competition—often incited by religion or the lure of conquest—that began the process of integrating the countries of the world. *Globalization 2.0*, he asserts, lasted from the beginning of the 19th century to the beginning of the 21st century and was an era characterized not by *national* entities in competition but by the formation of *multinational* entities—usually companies and corporations—driving global integration. He wrote:

These multinationals went global for markets and labor, spearheaded first by the expansion of the Dutch and English joint-stock companies and the Industrial Revolution. In the first half of this era, global integration was powered by falling transportation costs, thanks to the steam engine and the railroad, and in the second half by falling telecommunication costs—thanks to the diffusion of the telegraph, telephones, the PC, satellites, fiber-optic cable, and the early version of the World Wide Web (p. 9).

Beginning around the year 2000, Friedman claimed that *Globalization 3.0* emerged, a product of the convergence of three elements:

the personal computer (which allowed every individual suddenly to become the author of his or her own content in digital form) with fiber-optic cable (which suddenly allowed all those individuals to access more and more digital content around the world for next to nothing) with the rise of work flow software (which enabled individuals all over the world to collaborate on that same digital content from anywhere, regardless of the distances between them) (pp. 10–11).

The differences between the first two eras of globalization and Globalization 3.0 are striking. While the first two empowered national and multinational companies and corporations, Globalization 3.0 empowers *individuals* to "go global." Furthermore, while the first two eras of globalization were largely the product of European and American explorers, entrepreneurs, and companies, Globalization 3.0 is seeing the rise of individuals literally from everywhere, exercising their initiative in both competition and collaboration with other individuals around the planet, forming networks of communication and shared work that hold the possibility of competing effectively with—and sometimes superseding—both nation-states and national and multinational companies and corporations. While there are many examples of the benefits from globalization, such a transformation has also allowed organizations such as ISIS, or the so-called Islamic State, to recruit followers through a global reach.

2. *Growing Income Inequality.* The gap between the rich and poor has widened dramatically in the past few decades making upward mobility increasingly difficult for many low-income Americans. Wages for the wealthiest 1% of Americans more than doubled between 1979 and 2011 while wages of the median U.S. worker increased by only 6% over the same period. In 2015, in 34 OECD countries, the richest 10% earned 9.6 times more than the poorest 10% (the OECD, or Organisation for Economic Cooperation and Development, is a 35-member international agency founded in 1961 to stimulate economic progress and world trade).

Income inequality has significant impacts on many aspects of people's lives. There is a growing body of research, for instance, that demonstrates that despite huge advances in medicine, technology, and education, rich people tend to live longer than poor people. In the early 1970s, a 60-year-old man earning at the top half of the income ladder could expect to live 1.2 years longer than a man of the same age in the bottom half (*New York Times*, 2016). In 2001, that difference grew to 5.8 years longer than his poorer counterpart. Recent research has found that for men born in 1950, that difference had more than doubled, to 14 years. For women, the gap grew from 4.7 years to 13 years.

Discrepancies in income also have significant impact on educational attainment. College, for instance, has become virtually a necessity for upward mobility. Yet, the increasing cost of American higher education has resulted in it being out of reach for many. The children of college-educated parents are more than twice as likely to attend college as are the children of high school graduates and seven times as likely as those of high school dropouts. Only 5% of Americans aged 25 to 34 whose parents didn't finish high school have a college degree. This figure compared to 20% across 20 countries in the OECD.

The problem, of course, begins long before college. On the day children begin kindergarten, those from many low-income families are more than a year behind the children of college graduates in their grasp of both reading and math. Despite the efforts deployed by schools, this achievement gap will widen even more for many children by the time they reach high school.

3. A Change in the Work We Do   It will come as no surprise that manufacturing jobs in the United States have given way to so-called service jobs in recent decades. On the global scale, people around the world are increasingly divided by vast differences between rich and poor, and this discrepancy has widened in the past decade. The average U.S. citizen earns about $200.00 per day. This compares to those living in the poorest countries of the world (e.g., the Republic of Congo, Somalia, Haiti, Niger), who take home less than $2.00 per day. Services amount to approximately two-thirds of the U.S. domestic product, with financial services, such as banking, insurance, and investment leading the way followed closely by real estate services. Other growing service industries are transportation; health care; legal, scientific, and management services; education; wholesale and retail sales; arts; recreational services; hotels, restaurants, and other food and beverage services (U.S. Dept. of Labor, 2015).

Because service jobs—especially in sales, recreational services, hotels, restaurants, and so forth—do not generally pay as well as manufacturing jobs have in the past, these shifts in the economy disproportionately affect lower-income families. In his article, "Welcome to the Service Economy," Peter Rachleff (2006) noted that this was also the case in the first third of the 20th century, when the great mining and manufacturing companies had total control of workers. That situation changed when the labor movement of the 1930s and 1940s and "their contracts brought them not only improved wages and working conditions but also benefits including individual, family, and retiree healthcare coverage; paid vacations; and pensions. These benefits are not available to low-paid service workers in our economy today. Moreover, the idea of unionism is not popular in jobs where workers are encouraged to put their patients and customers first, to see themselves as 'unskilled,' and to expect little reward for their work" (Rachleff, 2006).

In the past, labor unions and the contracts they negotiated provided the scaffolding for working-class families to rise into the middle class; that "ladder" doesn't exist today in many service industries, which employ—probably disproportionately—many minority, immigrant, and poor individuals. One of the tasks ahead, then, is to create conditions in the service sector such that people can "move up" the social ladder into the middle class.

Recent trends in globalization, like the growth of China and India, have increased the number of U.S. jobs "outsourced" to other countries. Between 1984 and 2004 more than 30 million U.S. workers lost their jobs, mostly in high import-competing manufacturing industries such as clothing, autos, and electronics. These industries account for only 30% of all manufacturing jobs in the United States, but accounted for 38% of manufacturing job loss. Of those workers displaced, about one in three moved into new jobs with equal or better incomes, but one in four suffered earnings losses of more than 30%. This trend continued, with more than 2 million jobs being outsourced in 2011 alone. There are spin-off effects as well. Nearly 70% of Americans who have health insurance get their coverage through their employers, so losing a job can be extremely costly to families, with lost health coverage as well as lost wages (Children's Defense Fund, 2009).

An increased dependence on technology has also led to numerous changes in the way we work, with many jobs at risk of being lost due to increased automation, while at the same time new jobs emerging as a result of new technologies. The skills required in traditionally more "stable" jobs are undergoing change as one set of required skills is replaced by newer ones. This exacerbates the abilities and skills gap that many employees and employers face, thus creating uncertainty and insecurity for many workers—unless they are willing and able to rapidly reskill or upskill for their roles. In addition, technology is changing how work is organized, with new platforms connecting people in ways not possible just a decade ago. For example, websites such as HomeAway.com and Airbnb.com allow home owners to sublet all or part of their home to short-term guests in place of people using well-established hotel and motel chains. Similarly, companies like Uber and Lyft are connecting drivers with those who want rides, empowering individuals to assume new roles and responsibilities.

4. A Change in Generational Attitudes About Work   Until not too long ago, the norm was that folks went to work for a particular company and stayed there throughout their working lives. Indeed, as recently as 30 years ago, people who changed jobs too many times were considered quite undependable. Today, however, it's a different story. Although workers may frequently change jobs because their companies are moving production to another country, or eliminating jobs altogether, it is also the case that workers move to enhance their own prospects, and it is more likely today that workers will not work for the same company for 30 years.

Millennials are the 54 million adult Americans aged between 18 and 34, who, in 2015, make up one third of the U.S. workforce—the largest generation at work (most readers of this book fall into this category). These individuals are technologically-connected, grew up in the shadow of the September 11th terrorist attacks and the Great Recession, are well adapted to change, and highly innovative—when given the right environment, support, and autonomy.

As Raines (2002) noted, they have been bombarded with a unique set of messages since birth:

Be smart—you are special. They've been catered to since they were tiny. Think Nickelodeon, Baby Gap, and *Sports Illustrated for Kids.*

Leave no one behind. They were taught to be inclusive and tolerant of other races, religions, and sexual orientations.

Connect 24/7. They learned to be interdependent—on family, friends, and teachers. More Millennials say they can live without the television than without the computer. Many prefer chatting online, texting, Facebook or other social media to talking on the phone.

Achieve now! Some parents hired private agents to line up the right college; others got started choosing the right preschool while the child was still in the womb.

Serve your community. Fifty percent of high school students reported volunteering in their communities, many of their high schools requiring community service hours for graduation. On one Roper Survey, when Millennials were asked for the major cause of problems in the United States, they answered *selfishness.*

As a result of their upbringing, many young workers in this generation are looking for role models in the workplace. They want more learning opportunities, want to work with friends, have fun at work, get respect for their ideas, even if they are young, and have time flexibility to pursue family and interest activities.

Factors Influencing the Institution of Politics

1. International Agreements Changes affecting economics have their counterparts in the political sphere as well. As we increasingly interact with people from other nations in matters of trade, we also increasingly interact with them politically, and political events occurring in other countries have a much more profound effect on our own political agenda than they used to. For example, the realization of the North American Free Trade Agreement (NAFTA), the Central American-Dominican Republic Free Trade Agreement (CAFTA-DR), the General Agreement on Tariffs and Trade (GATT) Treaty—as well as its successor, the World Trade Organization—are political responses to the facts of international trade. The end of the Cold War and the dissolution of the Soviet Union in 1989 was a defining feature of international politics as the 20th century drew to a close (see Chapter 7). Today, the recurring ethnic and religious wars around the world, terrorist attacks on American soil and on Western interests around the world, and various uprisings throughout the Arab world during the 'Arab Spring' are expressions of new realities with which the United States must contend. In recent years a day does not go by without some news of opposition to one or more international agreements that is perceived to negatively impact the domestic economy. And as industrial growth and our growing dependence upon oil continue, new treaties addressing climate change, such as the Paris Climate Conference where 195 nations adopted the first-ever universal and legally-binding global climate deal, will be enacted. The norms have changed—we are doing politics differently. Yet, the increasing need to address the ever-growing array of global issues demands that people acquire new skills in intercultural understanding and collaboration.

2. Increasing Debate Between So-Called Conservative and Liberal Voters Over the past 20 years, conservative political ideas have come to the forefront on both economic and social issues. In part, this probably reflects a resistance to the very rapid change that characterizes the times in which we live.

In some ways, this may indicate a decline in the power of the two major political parties in the United States and provide some intriguing questions about the future. This was especially evident in the run up to the 2016 presidential election when none of the traditional Republican Party candidates were selected to represent the party, begging such questions as if we would see a rise in third parties? Will there be a greater emphasis on the difference between economic and social issues in the political marketplace of ideas? Will a new generation of voters be more interested in the electoral process than their parents have been? What will be the future of the Electoral College? How will the Democratic Party revise itself in light of the outcomes of the 2016 presidential race and the greater role that diverse groups play in the American electorate?

3. Political Participation Americans who voted in 2012 looked much more like what President Obama had envisioned—a multicultural array that reflected a changing nation. The 2016 election saw an unanticipated increase in the number of disenfranchised blue-collar workers take to the polls transforming the election and altering the direction the country would take on many fronts.

4. Change in Voting Technologies Another change in the political landscape with respect to voting is the advent of electronic voting machines, which have replaced voting with pencil or stylus and the hand-counting of ballots. Debates center around the following issues: security, lack of a paper trail of votes cast, interference with the transmission of results, inability to conduct an independent recount, vulnerability to tampering with the machines before the vote, and machine malfunction (Wang, 2004). The 2016 election saw widespread hacking of the computer systems by Russia at both the Republican and Democratic headquarters.

Given that younger generations of Americans are theoretically more likely to engage in civic affairs and are growing up accustomed to and trusting technological innovations, it will be interesting to see how long this debate continues. Clearly, there is going to continue to be a large role for education in giving young people both the knowledge and the judgment to support their involvement in civic affairs.

Factors Influencing the Institution of Religion

1. Increasing Diversity of Religious Ideas In times of transition such as we are experiencing today, organized religion can serve as a stabilizing influence. However, the institutionalized churches of all faiths are undergoing change as well. Once largely a nation steeped in the Judeo-Christian heritage, the United States is now home to a growing number of faiths that are unfamiliar to many people. Buddhism, Islam, and other religions of the East and Middle East are growing as new immigrants bring their religious ideas and practices with them, with Islam being among the fastest growing religions in the nation. Similarly, a wide variety of relatively small but active congregations built around scientific, philosophical, and psychological ideas are appearing to proliferate—the so-called New Age religious sects.

At the present time, religious affiliation in the United States is in the midst of a decline that appears to be twice as great as that which occurred in the 1960s and 1970s (Religion New Service, 2014). Roughly 80% of U.S. citizens identified with one of the major religions in the post-war baby-boom years of the 1950s. This was followed by the social upheavals and changes of the 1960s and 1970s that included a

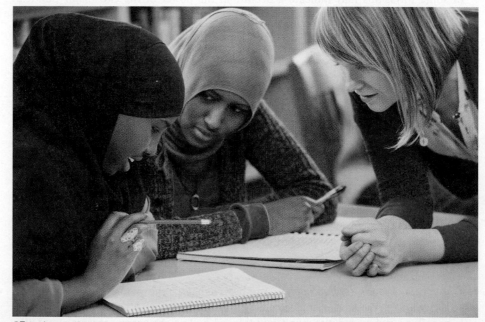

©Tetra Images/Shutterstock.Com RF

questioning of religious institutions and a subsequent decline in membership. This decline in religious identification leveled off by the end of the 1970s. Over the past 15 years, however, religious affiliation has been in a much steeper decline than that experienced in the 1960s and 1970s. Church attendance is down from 62% in 1994 to 53% in 2013, while church membership is down from 69% to 59%. At the same time, the number of people who say that religion is an important part of their life has dropped from 88% to 78%, with the percent who think religion is relevant to today's problems down from 80% to 70%.

2. The Rise of Fundamentalism in Many Religious Contexts   Conservative branches of mainline Protestant, Catholic, Jewish, and Muslim religions serve as havens for people for whom social change seems too rapid and too chaotic, and fundamentalist denominations (usually Protestant) are both the fastest growing religious organizations in the nation and, often, the most politically aware and active. Fundamentalism is not limited to Christianity but is also growing among young Jews and Muslims.

We see frequent reference to a rise of religious fundamentalism around the world today. Historically, at least in the United States in the late 19th and early 20th centuries, fundamentalism referred to a religious movement specific to the Protestant religion. This movement emanated primarily from the more traditional White Anglo-Saxon Protestants who felt displaced by the influx of non-Protestant immigrants from southern and eastern Europe that began to flood America's cities. The fundamentalists deplored the teaching of evolution in public schools, which they paid for with their taxes, sought to minimize the distinction between the state and the church, and resented the elitism of professional educators who seemed often to scorn the values of traditional Christian families.

In the 21st century, fundamentalism refers to a global religious response that aims to recover and publicly institutionalize aspects of the past that modern life has changed and obscured. Typically, fundamentalism views the secular state as the primary enemy, interested more in education, democratic reforms, and economic progress than in preserving the more traditional and spiritual dimension of life. This generally is evident in clear-cut and distinct roles for men and women, parents and children, clergy and laypersons.

3. The Marriage of Religion and Politics   The founders of the United States were firm in their belief that religion and politics, or church and state, should be separate. Indeed, the nature of the separation of church and state written into the First Amendment of the Constitution is there not so much to involve religion in public affairs but to protect religious groups from interference by the state.

Nevertheless, we have nearly always carried religious ideas into the public (or political) sphere. Organized religions have, at various times in our history, been more or less important in the carrying out of public business. Today, and for the past two decades or so, some religious groups—notably conservative Protestant Christian groups—have become important "players" on the political scene, not only by putting forth agendas for public policy, but also by systematically organizing and supporting their members in elections, from school boards to Congress.

This is not, however, just an American phenomenon, but a global one, as can be seen by the involvement of religiously backed political (and military) forces in eastern Europe and the Middle East in the past 20 years. The same technological revolution that has provided innovative individuals and groups with the means to author their own digital content and link to others around the world for very little money has also provided the mechanism for individuals and groups to organize and carry their message (sometimes based on religious ideas) to others who, without this technology, would be unreachable. As Friedman (2006) cautioned, "the playing field is not being leveled only in ways that draw in and superempower a whole new group of innovators. It's being leveled in a way that draws in and superempowers a whole new group of angry, frustrated, and humiliated men and women" (p. 8). Recent evidence of this can be seen in the rise of such extremist activities as the destruction and barbarism carried out by ISIS, the so-called Islamic State, which claims a religious identity that is not endorsed by any mainstream Muslims, and the Boko Haram kidnapping of young girls in Nigeria. These movements utilize various forms of social media and dramatic events spread across the global media to recruit disenfranchised young people to their ideology.

4. Generational Differences in Attitudes and Values, and the Role of Electronic Culture

Another shift that is having an impact on religion is the presence of a generation of young people who have been raised in a technologically rich environment. They are looking to all the major institutions, including religion, for new ways of understanding traditional messages and new forms of worship.

While issues and solutions vary, the younger generation of church-goers appears to be giving its elders pause for reflection. For example, a study of college students who identify as Jewish, sponsored by Hillel, the Foundation for Jewish Campus Life, shows that these students "are increasingly likely to be products of interfaith marriages, to have non-Jewish boyfriends and girlfriends, and to shun denominational labels" (Birkner, 2005). Indicating that this generation has a different understanding of identity, the director of the study's online student survey notes that

> they see their identity as a set of windows on a computer screen, and any number of screens can be open simultaneously. For them, it's not just a question of am I a Jewish American or an American Jew. They see themselves as American, Jewish, heterosexual and a volleyball player all at once. They don't feel the need for one of those windows to take over the whole desktop. (Birkner, 2005)

Similarly, two sociological studies of young Catholics note that this generation "is more individualistic, more tolerant of religious diversity and far less committed to the practices of their faith than older Catholics" (Heffern, 2007).

Recent surveys find that acceptance of homosexuality has grown rapidly, especially among young adults, even among religious groups that have traditionally been strongly opposed to it (Pew Research Center, 2015a). Among evangelical Protestants, for example, 51% of Millennials say homosexuality should be accepted, compared with about a third of Baby Boomers and a fifth of those in the Silent Generation. Similar patterns are seen among mainstream Protestants, in the historically black Protestant tradition, and among Catholics.

Compared with views on homosexuality, there has been little change in Americans' attitudes about abortion. Among the public as a whole, slightly more than half (53%) say abortion should be legal in all or most cases. Views on abortion have changed little across most major religious groups, although those who are unaffiliated and those who belong to historically black Protestant churches are somewhat more likely to support legal abortion than in the recent past. The survey also finds generation gaps within many religious groups in attitudes about a variety of other social and political issues. Young adults generally express more politically liberal opinions than older people when asked about the environment, the proper size and scope of government, and immigration.

Finally, Protestant Christian denominations are increasingly interested in framing the religious message in ways that the "wired generation" can understand. Typical of the language used by those who advocate meeting the religious needs of the newest generation by learning from the electronic culture to which they are so attuned is a passage from an exhortation on the Millennials from a youth ministry in St. Kitts and Nevis in the Caribbean:

> It's time to shift gears. The next generation is the net generation. They've grown up on the Internet. They've grown up networking. In my parents' generation they focused on buildings and institutions. Thank goodness, or we'd have nothing to stand on. . . . For the next generation, you must shift your emphasis from programs to relationships—from organization to networking—from committees to connecting—from boards to teams—from elections to spiritual gifts. (Youth-Impact Ministries, n.d.)

Factors Influencing the Institution of the Family

1. *Increasing Age of Men and Women at the Time of Marriage and Childbirth*
The age at which men and women marry in any society varies over time, and that is the case in the United States as well. In 1900, the average marriage age for men was 26 and for women, 22; by midcentury, it had fallen to 23 for men and 20 for women; but by 2010, it had reached the all-time high of nearly 29 for men and nearly 27 for women (U.S. Census Bureau, 2013).

Some researchers believe that this phenomenon bodes well for marriage and motherhood because marrying later in one's 20s often means that the partners have higher educational levels, which is, itself, a stabilizing factor in marriage. There is some evidence to support this. Mothers today are far better educated than they were in the past. In 1960, 18% of mothers with infants at home had any college experience; today that share stands at 67%. Moreover, since the overall life span is increasing—in 2003 the average life expectancy in the United States was 77.4 years (Arias, 2007)—ages for marriage and childbirth might be expected to rise. Debates still exist, however, about the relation between age of marriage and first children to divorce, health care, work life, religious affiliation, and other family and social issues. It is safe to say, though, that increasing the age at which typical couples marry will have some effects on the society as a whole.

2. *Increasing Diversity of Family Forms*
In the family, too, we are witnessing profound changes in structure and organization. For the first time in 150 years, the number of households headed by single adults and unmarried couples is greater than those headed by married couples (Coontz, 2006). Recent research on the changing demographics of our families graphically portrays the changing nature of family life. For instance, in 1942, 60% of families could be described as nuclear families consisting of two parents and their children. Furthermore, if one believes the images that until relatively recently were often portrayed in basal readers, this nuclear family includes a dog and a cat all living happily together in a white house surrounded by a neat picket fence. In these families, the father's role was to leave home every day to earn the money to support the family, and the mother's role was to stay at home and raise the children. Those were the norms. Today, fewer than 10% of American families match that picture and families are smaller due to both the growth of single-parent households and the drop in fertility. Not only are Americans having fewer children, but the circumstances surrounding parenthood have also changed. While in the early 1960s babies typically arrived within a marriage, today

fully four-in-ten births occur to women who are single or living with a non-marital partner. The norms, again, have changed.

It is estimated today that about half of all marriages in the United States will be disrupted through divorce or separation. More than 10 different configurations are represented by the families of children in today's classrooms; a most significant one is the single-parent family, often consisting of a mother and child or children living in poverty, which increased from 9% in 1960 to 26% in 2014, representing one-fourth of all children. Increasingly, this single parent is a teenage mother. We have seen a rapid increase in the number of children being brought up in "blended families"—a household with a stepparent, stepsibling or half-sibling, as well as raised by grandparents, with close to 5 million American children living in grandparent-headed households (Johnson and Kasarda, 2011). Another increasing family configuration, and a hotly debated topic, is one in which two adults of the same sex, committed to one another over time, are raising children who may be biologically related to one or the other adult, or who may have been adopted by them.

3. Increasing Intermarriage Across Racial and Religious Boundaries   There has also been a corresponding increase in the outmarriage rate, or intermarriage between individuals from different ethnic or religious groups in recent years, a rate that doubled from 6.7% in 1980 to 14.6% in 2008 (Johnson and Kasarda, 2011). Some racial groups are more likely to intermarry than others. Of the 3.6 million adults who got married in 2013, 58% of American Indians, 28% of Asians, 19% of blacks and 7% of whites have a spouse whose race was different from their own (Pew Research Center, 2015b). In some Asian American groups (Japanese Americans, for instance), more people marry outside the group than marry within the group (Cortes, 1999), and roughly 50% of American Jews marry outside their religion. The population of those identifying as members of two or more races continues to increase. The number went from 1.1 million in 2000 to an estimated 4.5 million in 2009, or roughly 4.5% of the total U.S. population. Percentage-wise, this increase (32.7%) was second only to the relative growth of the nation's Latino population (35.8%) (Johnson and Kasarda, 2011). Children of these mixed marriages will increasingly find themselves in our schools, as is evident in the 6.8% of young people under the age of 18 who claim similar multiple racial identities.

4. Increasing Effects of Poverty in a Globalized America   People living in poverty are a diverse group and reflect as wide array of values, beliefs, dispositions, experiences, backgrounds, and life chances as those in any other socioeconomic class. Although the poverty rate in the United States declined slightly from 15.0% in 2012 to 14.5% in 2013, the actual number of people living in poverty did not change with 45.3 million people living at or below the poverty line in 2013. In the United States, more women live in poverty than men. In 2013, 15.8% of women were poor compared with 13.1% of men. The difference between households headed by men or women in poverty is even more dramatic, with over 30% of female-headed households in poverty. For men in the same situation as head of household and no wife present that number is 15.9%. On the global scale, in 2012, 12.7% of the world's population, or roughly 900 million people, lived at or below $1.90 a day. Although a staggering number, this is down from 37% in 1990 and 44% in 1981. Poverty and its effects on children is not limited to the so-called Third World or developing societies. A recent report issued by United Nations Children's Fund (UNICEF), "Child Well-Being in Rich Countries," reports that the United States ranks among the lowest of wealthy countries for children, coming in 26th place of 29 countries, with only Lithuania, Latvia,

and Romania placing lower (UNICEF, 2013). The United States has the second highest percentage of children living under the relative poverty line, defined as 50% of each country's median income, and ranked 25th out of 29 in the percentage of people 15 to 19 years old who were enrolled in schools and colleges. One in five children in the United States lives at or below the poverty line. As educators, in order to be responsive to the needs of all students, it is helpful to consider the constraints that poverty may place on people's lives, particularly children's, and how such conditions might influence learning and academic achievement. Health and well-being, for instance, are often interrelated, and one factor can compound another. Substandard housing, inadequate medical care, and poor nutrition, for instance, can affect the rate of childhood disease, premature births, and low birth weights. All of these can impact a child's physical and cognitive development, thus influencing a students' ability to benefit from schooling.

Consider these facts about children collected by the Children's Defense Fund (2003, 2013): Each day in the United States, 2 mothers die in childbirth, 4 children are killed by abuse or neglect, 5 children or teens commit suicide, 7 children or teens are killed by firearms, 67 babies die before their first birthdays, 892 babies are born at low birth weight, 914 babies are born to teen mothers, 1,208 babies are born without health insurance, 1,825 children are confirmed as abused or neglected, 2,712 babies are born into poverty, 2,857 high school students drop out, and 4,475 babies are born to unmarried mothers. In addition, 1 in 5 was born poor, 1 in 3 will be poor at some point in childhood, and 1 in 6 is born to a mother who did not receive prenatal care in the first trimester of pregnancy. One in 5 is born to a mother who did not graduate from high school, 1 in 5 has a foreign-born mother, 1 in 3 is behind a year or more in school, 1 in 50 is homeless, 2 in 5 never complete a single year of college, 1 in 10 has no health insurance, 1 in 7 has at least one worker in their family but still is poor, 1 in 8 lives in a family receiving food stamps, 1 in 8 never graduates from high school, and 1 in 12 has a disability.

Clearly, the family pattern once considered the norm, that provided the image of the "right" and "proper" kind of family, and that guided the policies of our other institutions has changed.

Factors That Influence the Institution of Education

1. Changing Demographics of the School-Age Population and the Population as a Whole All the institutional changes discussed thus far are inevitably reflected in the institution of schooling—its purposes, policies, and practices. For example, demographic changes with respect to the total population of the United States are first seen in our schools. It is projected that by the year 2040, children of color will comprise more than half the children in classrooms, up from approximately one third at the beginning of the 21st century (U.S. Census Bureau, 2010). Startling changes are already occurring in a number of places in the country. For example, more than a decade ago, students from minority groups comprised more than 50% of the school populations in California, Arizona, New Mexico, Texas, and New York. In these states, minority children soon may find themselves in the uncomfortable position of being the majority in a world whose rules are set by a more powerful minority. Recent census figures for California show that there is currently no majority cultural group in the state!

Three factors are of primary importance in the shifting **demographics** of our population. First, immigration from non-European countries currently rivals the great immigrations from Europe that this country experienced at the turn of the 20th century. There is an important difference, however. In the early part of the 20th century, the majority of immigrants (87%) arrived from Europe. Except for language, it was relatively easy for these new immigrants to fit into the cultural landscape of the country; after all, many of these people looked similar to the majority of people around them. Today, 85% of the roughly 1 million immigrants who come to the United States each year come from Latin America and Asia (Cortes, 1999), resulting in what has been referred to as the "browning of America". Most of the new immigrants look somewhat different from the mainstream, which immediately sets them apart. Indeed, many communities are becoming increasingly international as the phenomenon of globalization extends its reach.

Second, while birthrates among Americans as a whole are just holding their own, birthrates among nonwhite populations are considerably higher than they are among whites. Among European Americans, for instance, birthrates have dropped to 1.4 for every 2 people, well below the 2.1 replacement level. Birthrates for all other groups have remained the same or increased slightly. When most current teacher education students were born (mid-1990s), approximately 1 in 4 schoolchildren was a child of color (traditionally referred to as minority students). By the year 2020, it is likely that this figure will increase to 1 in 2, and many of these children will be poor. By midcentury, people of color will become the majority of Americans. The census bureau, for instance, projects that by the year 2050 the percentage of European Americans will decline to 47% while more than one-fourth of the U.S. population will be of Hispanic origin. By 2056, the average U.S. resident will trace his or her descent to Africa, Asia, Central and South America, the Pacific Islands, or the Middle East—almost anywhere but white Europe (U.S. Census Bureau, 2010).

Third, the total population of children in relation to adults in the United States is changing as the public grows older. Although the number of school-age children will increase from now until the year 2025, the number of American youth compared to citizens age 65 and older will continue to shrink (U.S. Census Bureau, 2010). The Pew Research Center has predicted that if current immigration trends and birth rates continue, by 2050 virtually all (93%) of the nation's working age population growth will come from immigrants and their U.S.-born children (Pew Research Center, 2013). An increasing concern is that there will not be enough workers to support the aging baby boom population, who will be a tremendous drain on the nation's Social Security system at a time when the system itself may be in jeopardy. In addition, emerging medical technology is enabling people to live longer lives, and the health care needs of an aging population are projected to strain the government's Medicare program to its limits unless adjustments are made. Both of these concerns mean that public resources for school-age populations will be in direct and serious competition with the needs of older Americans.

2. Increasing Language Diversity Among Schoolchildren Along with ethnic and racial diversity often comes linguistic diversity. Increasing numbers of children are entering school from minority language backgrounds and have little or no competence in the English language. Nearly 1 in 5 Americans, some 47 million individuals age 5 and older, speak a language other than English at home, reflecting an increase of approximately 50% during the past decade. It is estimated that there are approximately 4.5 million Limited English Proficient (LEP) students, or 9% of the school-age population, in schools in the United States, many of whom speak Spanish as their primary language (National Center for Educational Statistics, 2016), making the United States the fifth largest Spanish-speaking country in the world. The majority of these students (67%) can be found in the five states of California, Texas, New York, Florida, and Illinois, with the greatest percentage of increases being in Kansas, Delaware, Kentucky, and South Carolina, but most school districts in the country have LEP students. Spanish is the most common second language spoken in

America's classrooms, spoken by 75% of English language learners, although an increasing number of students are entering the schools speaking Arabic, Chinese, Korean, Russian, Hmong, Khmer, Lao, Thai, and Vietnamese. More than 50% of LEP students are in grades K-4, with 77% coming from poor backgrounds. A relatively high dropout rate characterizes this group of children in spite of all our efforts at bilingual education. Since a person's language provides the symbols used to understand the world, children whose symbol systems differ from those of the dominant group are likely to see the world from a different perspective, to look for meaning in different ways,

©Ariel Skelley/Blend Images LLC RF

and to attribute different meanings to common objects and processes. Although these students may be perceived as a challenge to our educational system in the years ahead, one consequence of successfully accommodating this diversity is that all of us—students, teachers, and communities alike—will become more knowledgeable, more accepting, and better skilled at communicating with people from different backgrounds.

3. Increasing Concern About Gender Differences in School Outcomes   In the 1970s and 1980s, there emerged an increasing awareness in many classrooms of a difference among children that was so fundamental that it had been overlooked as a matter of inquiry throughout most of our history. That difference is gender. Because we have included both girls and boys, at least in elementary education, since the very beginning of the common school, and because our political and educational ideals assume that school is gender neutral, the effect of gender on children's education has not been analyzed until recently. In the past 35 years, however, considerable research has been done on differences in the social and educational lives and academic outcomes of boys and girls in school. In the earlier years, the focus was on girls—the "stereotypical" roles they saw themselves playing in textbooks, the way in which they were counseled away from math and science courses, the ways in which teachers interacted with them, and ways in which the "culture of the school" tended to channel them in certain directions, both socially and vocationally.

Today, there are some who are equally concerned with the educational lives and outcomes of boys—the fact that they are dropping out of school at a higher rate, that their success in literacy is lower, and that fewer are academically prepared for college (and, in fact, are attending college in reduced numbers). Whatever the case, it is true that gender roles have changed in our society and that these changes have an effect on all our institutions, including, of course, education.

4. An Increasing "Clash of Cultures" Between Teachers and Students   A considerable discrepancy continues to exist between the makeup of the student population in most schools and that of the teaching force. Most of our nation's teachers continue to come from a rather homogeneous group, with approximately 85% being European American and middle class (National Center for Education Information, 2011). Indeed, the profile of the teacher education student that emerged from Zimpher's (1989) study has not changed appreciably. Typically, the teacher education student is a monolingual white female from a low-middle- or middle-class suburban or rural home who wants to teach children who are just like herself. The percentage of women in the teaching force continues to increase, with 84% of current public school teachers being female (Feistritzer, 2011).

These figures contrast sharply with the student diversity that currently exists in schools and that will continue to increase in the years ahead. Although alternative routes to teaching have resulted in a slight increase in the representation of teachers of color in recent years (Feistritzer, 2011), a considerable number of children are still missing important role models who represent their background within the school setting—boys in the early years, and children of color throughout the educational experience in general. European America students as well miss having role models who represent groups other than their own.

Equally critical is the fact that teachers (like many other people) tend to be culture-bound, and to have little knowledge or experience with people from other cultures, thus limiting their ability to interact effectively with students who are different from them. Indeed, in Zimpher's study, 69% of white teacher education students reported spending all or most of their free time with people of their own racial or ethnic background. This, too, has not changed appreciably in recent years. More disturbing, this same study reported that a substantial number of teacher education students do not believe that low-income and minority learners are capable of grasping high-level concepts in the subjects they are preparing to teach. Finally, the traditional identification of teaching as women's work means that even multiculturally sophisticated teachers are usually powerless to make their school's culture more accommodating to female and underrepresented students because white males are often in key decision-making roles.

Rethinking Schools and Learning: The Effort to Reform Our Schools

In terms of traditional definitions of social order, it appears that most of our social institutions are not working very well in the beginning of this new millennium. Another way to state this observation is to say that the norms governed by our institutions have changed. In this context, the principle values of democratic equality, liberty, and community are once again called into question. What does equality mean when people from a variety of cultures around the world are competing for the same jobs? What does liberty mean when language barriers prevent common understanding? What does community mean when allegiance to one's group prevents commonality with people in other groups?

Some scholars have argued that the changes we are experiencing require a shift from the ideals of a Jeffersonian political democracy (in which democratic principles are defined by individualism) to the ideals of a cultural democracy in which democratic principles are defined by cultural pluralism (McClelland & Bernier, 1993). Such a shift involves a radical change in our beliefs about how we are to get along with one another, what kinds of information and skills we need to develop, and how we are to interpret our national ideals and goals. Among other changes, this cultural view of democracy requires a fundamental rethinking of our national goals and how we structure or organize schools in relation to those goals. Schooling is, after all, the institution charged not only with imparting necessary information and skills but also with ensuring that young people develop long-cherished democratic attitudes and values. Schooling alone cannot completely alter the larger society in which it exists, but schooling can influence as well as reflect its parent society. Since teachers can engender or stifle new ideas and new ways of doing things with their students, they are in a position to influence both the direction and pace of change in our society.

As Sam is learning in her teacher education program, one of the most significant results of rethinking schools and teaching is the testing and accountability movement. Although there is considerable debate about both the means and ends of the movement, taken at face value it signals a major change not only in the way we think about schools but also in the way we think about teaching and learning. It is no longer acceptable to eliminate certain children from the ranks of the educable. Nor is it acceptable to think that it's all right if some children don't measure up to standards, or that you just can't "teach everyone." Indeed, the emphasis is now squarely on learning outcomes for *all* children.

Fortunately, some teachers have accepted this challenge and are learning to think about their practice in more inclusive ways. They work in classrooms in all regions of the country, and, increasingly, in schools around the world—sometimes alone and sometimes with colleagues who are also excited about new possibilities. They work with students of all backgrounds: white and nonwhite, wealthy and poor, boys and girls, rural and urban, domestic and international. They work with students of varied religions and of no particular religion, with students who have vastly different abilities, and with students who have different sexual orientations. They work in wealthy districts that spend a great deal of money on each student and in poor districts that have little in the way of resources. But most important, their classrooms reflect their belief that all children can succeed. In 21st-century schools and classrooms, teachers see change as an opportunity rather than a problem and difference as a resource rather than a deficit.

The Difficulty of Change

Change is difficult, particularly when it deals with the fundamental beliefs, attitudes, and values around which we organize our lives. Attempts at such change often result in hostility or in an effort to preserve, at any cost, our familiar ways of doing things and thinking about the world around us. The universal nature of such resistance to change is illustrated in the following parable.

The Wheat Religion: A Parable

Once upon a time there was a group of people who lived in the mountains in an isolated region. One day a stranger passed through their area and dropped some wheat grains in their field. The wheat grew. After a number of years, people noticed the new plant and decided to collect its seeds and chew them. Someone noticed that when a cart had accidentally ridden over some of the seeds, a harder outer covering separated from the seed and what was inside was sweeter. Someone else noticed that when it rained, the grains that had been run over expanded a little, and the hot sun cooked them. So, people started making wheat cereal and cracked wheat and other wheat dishes. Wheat became the staple of their diet.

Years passed. Because these people did not know anything about crop rotation, fertilizers, and cross-pollination, the wheat crop eventually began to fail.

About this time, another stranger happened by. He was carrying two sacks of barley. He saw the people starving and planted some of his grain. The barley grew well. He presented it to the people and showed them how to make bread and soup and many other dishes from barley. But they called him a heretic.

"You are trying to undermine our way of life and force us into accepting you as our king." They saw his trick. "You can't fool us. You are trying to weaken us and make us accept your ways. Our wheat will not let us starve. Your barley is evil."

He stayed in the area, but the people avoided him. Years passed. The wheat crop failed again and again. The children suffered from malnutrition. One day the stranger came to the market and said, "Wheat is a grain. My barley has a similar quality. It is also a grain. Why don't we just call the barley grain?"

Now since they were suffering so much, the people took the grain, except for a few who staunchly refused. They loudly proclaimed that they were the only remaining followers of the True Way, the Religion of Wheat. A few new people joined the Wheat Religion from time to time, but most began to eat barley. They called themselves The Grainers.

For generations, the Wheat Religion people brought up their children to remember the true food called wheat. A few of them hoarded some wheat grains to keep it safe and sacred. Others sent their children off in search of wheat, because they felt that if one person could happen by with barley, wheat might be known somewhere else too.

And so it went for decades, until the barley crop began to fail. The last few Wheat Religion people planted their wheat again. It grew beautifully, and because it grew so well, they grew bold and began to proclaim that their wheat was the only true food. Most people resisted and called them heretics. A few people said, "Why don't you just admit that wheat is a grain?"

The wheat growers agreed, thinking that they could get many more wheat followers if they called it grain. But by this time, some of the children of the Wheat Religion people began to return from their adventures with new seed, not just wheat, but rye and buckwheat and millet. Now people began to enjoy the taste of many different grains. They took turns planting them and trading the seed with each other. In this way, everyone came to have enough sustenance and lived happily ever after.

This parable carries many metaphorical messages: It applauds diversity and recognizes that a society cannot function to its fullest when it ignores the ideas, contributions, efforts, and concerns of any of its people. The parable illustrates some of the consequences of unreasonable prejudice, but also recognizes the powerful emotions that underlie a prejudiced attitude. It also indicates the power of naming something in a way that is familiar and comfortable to those who are uncomfortable about accepting something new.

But perhaps most important, the parable recognizes the tendency people have to resist change. People are creatures of habit who find it difficult to change, whether at the individual level, the institutional level, or the societal level. People often work from one set of assumptions, one pattern of behavior. Because of the way in which people are socialized, these habits of thought and behavior are so much a part of them that they find it very difficult to think that things can be done in any other way. Some habits people develop are positive and constructive; others are negative and limiting. The story shows us that sometimes even a society's strengths can become weaknesses. And yet new circumstances and opportunities arise in each generation that demand that new perspectives, attitudes, and solutions be sought. Such circumstances are evident today in the changing face of the American classroom, and much of the responsibility for change must lie with teachers and teacher educators.

How prepared are *you* to accept the reality of change? How ready are *you* to examine some of your own beliefs and ideas about others? About yourself? About how *you* can interact with others? Are you at a point where, like Sam in the case study, you can begin to see how critical it is that you may have to change?

Ideological Perspectives on Multicultural Education

Attention to social differences among students has a relatively long history in this society, beginning at least with the arguments for the common school (which was intended to give students of different social class backgrounds a "common" educational experience that would enable the society to continue to be governed by "we, the people"). During some periods of our history, the focus was also on assimilation to a "common culture," by which was meant a dominant, largely Anglo society. During other periods—notably in the early years of the 20th century, when black scholars began to develop curricular materials on the African American experience in America, and in the 1940s, when the Intergroup Education movement had as its main objective the reduction of prejudice and discrimination in the U.S. population—various attempts have been made to perceive difference as a strength rather than as a problem.

The field known as multicultural education emerged in the aftermath of the civil rights movement in the 1960s, first with the ethnic studies movement and later with a somewhat broader "multicultural" education effort. Within that effort (and outside it as well), there are a variety of perspectives on both the definition and the goals of multicultural education, which will be discussed in greater detail later in the book. Essentially, **multicultural education** can be defined as a process of educational reform that assures that students from all groups (racial, ethnic, socioeconomic, ability, gender, etc.) experience educational equality, success, and social mobility. Today, as we continue to move closer to a truly global society, an education that develops intercultural competence becomes increasingly essential.

Some important questions emerge from what is in fact a healthy debate about our ability to provide educational opportunity and success for all children. Some of these questions have existed from the beginning; others have emerged as knowledge has increased and times have changed. Consider the following:

- Is intercultural education for everyone, or for minority students alone?
- Should intercultural education focus on the individual student, on the student as a member of a group, or on both?
- To what extent should intercultural education include the study of relationships of power along with the history and contributions of all people?
- Is intercultural education academic or political or both?
- Will intercultural or multicultural education, as an ideological movement, divide us as a people or bring us closer together?
- Are intercultural teaching practices good for everyone?
- To what extent should intercultural education have as a goal the reconstruction of the whole society?
- How are multicultural education, global education, and intercultural competence similar or different? Are there common areas where they all intersect?

All of these questions are important, in part because they are inexorably related.

Given the interdependent nature of the world in which we live, it is becoming less and less possible to think about purely American (or, to be more accurate, 'United Statesian') issues of difference. If the students being taught happen to belong mostly to one group or another, it is still the case that all of them, at some point in their lives, will need to learn how to understand and work with those who are different from themselves. If you think that local issues of inequality, poverty, and unequal access to education, housing, and jobs are central to Americans' work concerns, consider that well over half the world's population is struggling with the same issues (Cushner, 1998). Americans work to preserve and protect democratic institutions in this society while millions of people around the world try to understand what democracy really is.

Multicultural or intercultural education, both as fields of study and practice and as ideological perspectives, have experienced a continued broadening in scope and interests over the years. Increasingly, the fields and their ideologies are turning toward a more global sensibility. This change does not mean that local or national issues are no longer important; it means that what Americans have and continue to learn locally has important implications for global action. It also means that, inasmuch as we are not the only society struggling with issues of difference, there is much we can learn from others around the world. For instance, what can we learn from the French as they struggle with the question of whether or not to allow Muslim girls to wear the hijab, or head scarf, in public schools? What can we learn from the way Arabs and Jews are portrayed in textbooks in Palestinian and Israeli schools?

This book is based in part on a notion of intercultural interactions and their cognitive, emotional, and developmental aspects. An intercultural interaction can be domestic—that is, between two (or more) people within the same nation that come from different cultural backgrounds—or it can be international, between two (or more) people from different countries. The cultural identity of the parties involved in an interaction may come from a limited and mutually reinforcing set of experiences or from more complex and sometimes conflicting elements. The significant difference in an interaction may be race, class, religion, gender, language, or sexual orientation; it may be physical or attitudinal in origin; it may be age-related or status-related; or any combination of these.

Regardless of the kind of differences involved, all people tend to approach significant differences in similar, oftentimes negative, ways. That is, to understand the processes involved is a first step toward overcoming these differences; and both culture-specific knowledge and culture-general knowledge are prerequisites on the road to social justice.

Goals of This Book

This book is about change, especially as it relates to diversity. It is about teaching all children in a society that is growing more diverse each year. It is about changes in classrooms and in the act of teaching within those classrooms. It is about changes in schools and in the larger society in which these schools are embedded. It is equally about change within oneself, for change in the larger dimensions of society cannot occur without significant changes in one's own perception, attitudes, and skills. All these environments (self, classrooms, schools, and society) are connected, so that changes in any one of them produce disequilibrium and change in the others. Their connectedness, and the mutual influence that each one exerts on the others, is visually depicted in Figure 1.1.

As a teacher in the 21st century, you will spend your career in ever-changing schools, schools whose mission will be to help society make an orderly transition from one kind of civilization to another. Your ability to feel comfortable and operate effectively within such a changing environment will require a unique set of cultural understandings and interpersonal skills that go beyond traditional pedagogy. These skills, perspectives, and attitudes that you as a teacher must adopt in order to coalesce diverse students into an effective learning community must also be transmitted to the students in your charge, who will live their lives in the same kind of highly interconnected and interdependent world. You are thus walking both sides of a double-edged sword, so to speak. The process that you undergo to become more effective working across cultures must ultimately become content that you teach to students. This feat will not be easy!

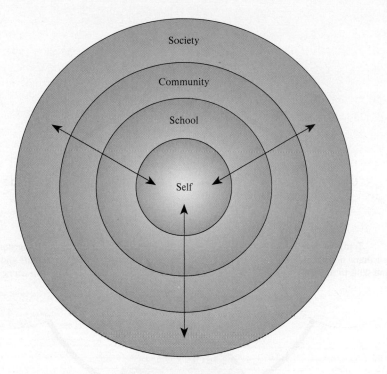

Figure 1.1
Interconnected
Environments

Figure 1.2 illustrates four basic goals of this book, which can be viewed as steps in understanding intercultural education and your role as an educator in an inclusive system. A word about each goal follows.

Goal 1: To Recognize Social and Cultural Change

The first step in providing an education that is truly intercultural is to improve students' understanding of the concept of pluralism in our global society. Pluralism in this context must consider such sources of cultural identity as nationality, ethnicity, race, gender, socioeconomic status, religion, sexual orientation, geographic region, health, and ability/disability, and must look particularly at how each of these identities has had an impact on the individual as well as the group. This step requires that teachers understand the social changes that have historically and are currently taking place in our pluralistic society; these social changes provide the underlying rationale for an intercultural education and are found in Chapters 1 and 2, as well as throughout the book.

Goal 2: To Understand Culture, Learning, and the Culture-Learning Process

After establishing the need for an intercultural education it is necessary to understand just what is meant by that term. What does the term *culture* refer to, and how do people come to acquire different cultural identities? With what knowledge do children already come to school? Too often schools do not legitimize the experiences children bring with them to the school; instead schools label some children as failures

Figure 1.2

Goals of This Book

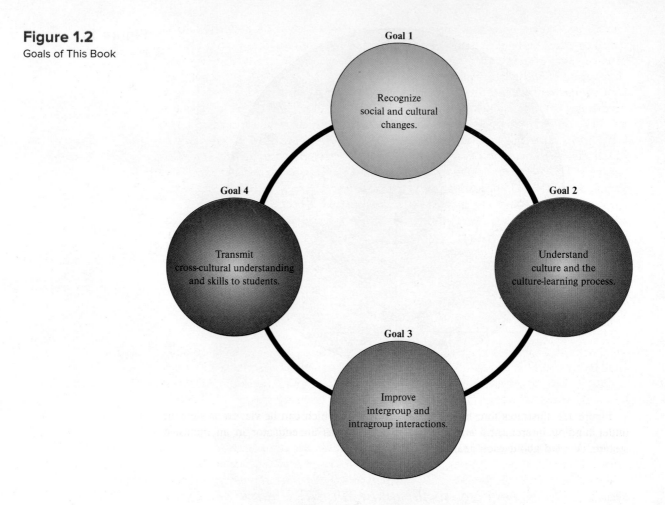

because their backgrounds, including their language and culture, are not seen as adequate or legitimate. Teachers must thus expand their knowledge base of culture and the different groups found in the United States as well as abroad. This means that curriculum content must be expanded and pedagogy adapted to include the experiences of all students. Chapter 3 examines these issues and in the process provides models of the sources of cultural learning and of the culture-learning process. An important recognition here is that differences within groups are often as important as differences between groups. Individuals belong simultaneously to many different groups, and their behavior can be understood only in terms of their simultaneous affiliation with these many groups. These models illustrate how culture filters down to the individual learner who actively engages with it, accepting and absorbing certain elements and rejecting and modifying others.

Goal 3: To Improve Intergroup and Intragroup Interactions

While Goal 2 is to examine how individuals come to acquire their particular cultural identity, Goal 3 is to show how culturally different people interact with one another and how these interactions can be improved. We must work to improve *intergroup* as well as *intragroup* interactions. We must also learn how individuals develop intercultural competence and improve their interactions with other cultures. Goal 3 demands attention to such issues as development of intercultural sensitivity and competence, cross-cultural understanding and interaction, attribution and assessment across groups, and conflict management. Teachers, in particular, must broaden their instructional repertoire so that it reflects an understanding of the various groups with whom they will interact. To help teachers understand the interaction between culturally different individuals (whether from different groups or from the same group), Chapter 4 presents a model of intercultural interaction that applies culture learning to ourselves as well as to our students and that develops a culture-general model of behavior. These models help us analyze the nature of intercultural interaction, and they show how key concepts can be applied to various types of school situations. Chapter 5 offers some useful models of development and synthesizes them with a new and somewhat more sophisticated model of intercultural development that helps increase the number of concepts as well as the language with which we can profitably understand and discuss these issues.

Goal 4: To Transmit Intercultural Understanding and Skills to Students

The book's final goal is to help teachers transmit to students the same understandings and skills that are contained in (1) the model for explaining cultural differences and (2) the model for improving intercultural interaction in order to prepare multicultural citizen-actors who are able and willing to participate in an interdependent world. That is, this book strives to empower action-oriented, reflective decision makers who are able and willing to be socially and politically active in the school, community, nation, and world. This book is concerned not only with developing the knowledge and skill of practicing teachers, but also with transferring this knowledge to the students in their charge. Thus, individuals become proactive teachers and reflective practitioners who can ultimately prepare reflective citizen-actors (their students) for an interdependent world. The content of these models is universal. It applies to all intercultural situations, not just those confronted by teachers in classrooms and schools. Teaching these understandings and skills to students can be accomplished both through teacher modeling and through explicit instruction, and both methods are illustrated in the remaining chapters of the book.

The Role of Stories, Cases, and Activities

Stories

This book contains many stories because stories help us visualize and talk about new ideas and experiences. Some stories are about real people and events, while others, like the story of the wheat people, are folktales and parables. Stories contain the power to speak about complex human experiences; in this book, stories speak about how people experience the fact of human diversity. Stories help us see the universals within the experience. Everyone, no matter what his or her cultural or biological differences, goes through similar stages of experience when confronted with change. Stories, like no other literary device, help us cut through the morass of individual and cultural differences that separate us and enable us to focus on the universals of the experience as we come to grips with those changes.

Case Studies and Critical Incidents

Because it is difficult to imagine situations with which you have had little experience, this book develops a series of Case Studies and Critical Incidents describing multicultural teaching situations that you might encounter. These scenarios are actual or synthesized real-life situations that have been described by a number of researchers and practitioners. Think of them as scenes in a play about schools with a multicultural student population. Most cases have been generated from multiple sources, each of which is noted in the list of references.

Because the cases cover a variety of communities and classrooms with diverse kinds of people in them, multiple issues are embedded in most of the cases. Although each case is designed to illustrate one or more particular issue related to the topic at hand, the portraits of people, places, ideas, and activities are rich enough that they can also be used to discuss topics in other chapters. Taken together, these cases illustrate a number of complex classroom realities that defy simple right-and-wrong solutions. They present small dramas in which a number of interpretations are possible and in which a number of ideas can be used to develop plans of action and fallback positions. Each chapter begins with a Case Study that introduces many of the concepts that will be further developed. Critical Incidents can be found at the end of many of the chapters that ask you to give further consideration to the topics presented.

Summary

This chapter provides an overview of some of the factors that are undergoing change in American society and that have an influence in the lives of children and teachers in schools. Such rapid social change has resulted in schools being caught in the transition from the Second Wave, an earlier factory model that offered a standardized curriculum for all, to the Third Wave, a more globally oriented dynamic model that attempts to address social change and prepare a citizenry that is more inclusive, integrative, and proactive. This book is designed to assist pre-service and in-service teachers to (1) recognize social and cultural change, (2) understand culture and the culture-learning process in self and others, (3) improve intergroup and intragroup interactions, and (4) transmit cross-cultural understandings and skills to students. The chapter also recognizes that change is difficult, yet is a force that we all must understand and accommodate—both as individuals and as institutions.

Chapter Review

Go to the Online Learning Center at www.mhhe.com/cushner9e to review important content from the chapter, practice with key terms, take a chapter quiz, and find the Web links listed in this chapter.

Key Terms

demographics 19	norms 7	social institution 7
multicultural education 25		

Reflective Questions

1. Identify three changes that American society is undergoing, and discuss how those changes are reflected in schools.

2. Think back to your experiences in elementary or high school. What indication do you have that your school was attempting to become a different kind of school? What indication do you have that your school was reflective of an information-age school?

3. In the case study, Sam questions why she needs to be in a diversity course. What experiences have you had that might lead you to say that you are well prepared for diversity? In what areas do you not feel as well prepared?

References

Aburdene, P. (2005). *Megatrends, 2010: The rise of conscious capitalism.* Charlottesville, VA: Hampton Roads.

Arias, E. (2007). Statistics from United States life tables, 2003. *National Vital Statistics Reports, 54*(14). Retrieved from http://www.cdc.gov/nchs/data/nvsr /nvsr54/nvsr54_14.pdf

Baca, L. (2000, November 15). *The status and future of bilingual education.* Paper presented at the 10th annual conference of the National Association for Multi-cultural Education, Orlando, FL.

Bierstedt, R. (1974). *The social order.* New York: McGraw-Hill.

Birkner, G. (2005, November 4). Millennials forcing big changes at Hillel. *The Jewish Week* [Electronic version]. Retrieved from http://www.jewishweek.org /news/newscontent.php3?artid=11622

Children's Defense Fund. (2003, 2013). *American children's yearbook.* Retrieved from http://www.childrensdefense.org/child-research-data-publications/each-day-in -america.html

Children's Defense Fund. (2009). Retrieved from http://childrensdefense.org.

Coontz, S. (2006, October 22). Marriage as a social contract. *The Philadelphia Inquirer* [Electronic version]. Retrieved from http://www.contemporary families.org/subtemplate.php?t=inTheNews&ext=marriageascontract

Cortes, C. (1999, May). The accelerating change of American diversity. *The School Administrator,* 12–14.

Cushner, K. (1998). *International perspectives on intercultural education.* Lanham, MD: Lawrence Erlbaum.

Daggett, W. R. (2005). Preparing students for their future [White paper]. Retrieved from http://www.icle.net/pdf/Preparing%20Students%20for%20Their%20Future%206-05.pdf

Feistritzer, C. E. (2011). *Profiles of teachers in the U.S. 2011.* Washington, D.C.: National Center for Educational Information.

Friedman, T. L. (2006). *The world is flat: A brief history of the twenty-first century, updated and expanded.* New York: Farrar, Straus, & Giroux.

Heffern, R. (2007, March 6). 'Bookend' generations—Studies point to much smaller U.S. church. *National Catholic Reporter Online.* Retrieved from http://www .catholic.org/national/national_story.php?id=23289

Johnson, J. H., & Kasarda, J. D. (2011). Six disruptive demographic trends: What census 2010 will reveal. Chapel Hill: University of North Carolina Kenen-Flagler Business School.

Maps and cartograms of the 2004 U.S. presidential election results. (2004). Retrieved from http://www.cscs.umich.edu/~crshalizi/election/

McClelland, A., & Bernier, N. (1993). A rejoinder to Steve Tozer's "Toward a New Consensus Among Social Foundations Educators." *Educational Foundations, 7*(4), 61.

Mirza, M., Senthilkumaran, A., & Ja'far, Z. (2007). *Living apart together: British Muslims and the paradox of multiculturalism.* London: Policy Exchange.

Naisbitt, J. (1982). *Megatrends: Ten new directions transforming our lives.* New York: Warner Books.

Naisbitt, J., & Aburdene, P. (1990). *Megatrends 2000: Ten new directions for the 1990s.* New York: Morrow.

New York Times (February 12, 2016). Retrieved from http://www.nytimes.com/2016/02/13/health/disparity-in-life-spans-of-the-rich-and-the-poor-is-growing.html?rref=collection%2Ftimestopic%2FSocial%20Security%20Administration&_r=0

National Center for Educational Information (2011). *Profile of teachers in the U.S. 2011.* Washington, D.C. Retrieved from http://www.edweek.org/media/pot2011final-blog.pdf

National Center for Educational Statistics (2016). The Condition of Education 2016 (NCES 2016-144), English Language Learners in Public Schools.

Pew Research Center (2013). "Second-Generation Americans: A Portrait of the Adult Children of Immigrants." Social & Demographic Trends (February 7, 2013), 2. Retrieved from http://www.pewsocialtrends.org/files/2013/02/FINAL_immigrant_generations_report_2-7-13.pdf

Pew Research Center (2015a). U.S. Public Becoming Less Religious. Accessed September 9, 2016 at: http://www.pewforum.org/2015/11/03/u-s-public-becoming-less-religious/

PEW Research Center (2015b). Interracial marriage: Who is marrying out? Accessed September 13, 2016 at: http://www.pewresearch.org/fact-tank/2015/06/12/interracial-marriage-who-is-marrying-out/

Rachleff, P. (2006). *Welcome to the service economy.* Retrieved from http://www.zmag.org/content/showarticle.cfm?ItemID=10876

Raines, C. (2002). *Managing millennials. Generations at work.* Retrieved from http://www.generationsatwork.com/articles/millenials.htm

Reich, R. (1992). *The work of nations: preparing ourselves for the 21st century.* New York: Vintage Books.

Religion New Service (2014). Graphs: 5 Sings of the "Great Decline" of religion in America. Retrieved from: http://religionnews.com/2014/08/01/five-signs-great-decline-religion-america-gallup-graphs-church/)

Sahadi, J. (2005, August 30). *CEO pay: The sky gets even higher.* Retrieved from http://money.cnn.com/2005/08/26/news/economy/ceo_pay/

Toffler, A. (1980). *The third wave.* New York: William Morrow.

Tudball, L. (2012) *Global perspectives on the internationalization of teacher education.* In B. Shaklee, & S. Baily (Eds.), *Internationalizing teacher education in the United States,* 93–111. Lanham, MD: Rowman Littlefield.

UNICEF (2013). Retrieved from http://www.unicef.org/policyanalysis/index_68637.html

U.S. Census Bureau. (2001). Retrieved from http://www.census.gov/population/ceb2000

U.S. Census Bureau. (2010). *American Fact Finder.* Retrieved from http://factfinder.census.gov, and http://www.census.gov/hhes/www/ioindex/reports.html

U.S. Census Bureau (2013). *American Fact Finder.* Retrieved from http://factfinder2.census.gov/faces/tableservices/jsf/pages/productview.xhtml?src=bkmk

U.S. Dept. of Labor (2015). Bureau of Labor Statistics. Accessed August 31, 2016 at http://www.bls.gov/emp/ep_table_201.htm

United States Election Project. (2006). Retrieved from http://elections.gmu.edu
/Voter_Turnout_2004.htm

Wang, T. A. (2004). Understanding the debate over electronic voting machines.
Reform Elections.org. Retrieved from http://www.reformelections.org/publications
.asp?pubid=475

Youth-Impact Ministries. (n/d). Retrieved from http://www.youth-impact.org
/millenials.htm

Zimpher, N. L. (1989). The RATE project: A profile of teacher education students.
Journal of Teacher Education, 40(6), 27–30.

©Jani Bryson/E+/Getty Images RF

Multicultural and Global Education
Historical and Curricular Perspectives

Focus Questions

1. As a matter of principle, do you think that differences in language, religion, country of origin, and culture should be recognized and taken into account in schools, or should schools be the central place in American society where all students are "made into" good Americans?

2. What do you think the phrase "good American" means?

3. Do you think it would be a good idea if all students in schools learned about people in other countries and cultures as a matter of course?

4. Do you think faith-based schools should receive support from federal and state tax funds?

5. On balance, do you believe that recent waves of immigration into the United States are a major problem or a major benefit to the society as a whole?

❝ Scholars describe the United States as one of history's first universal or world nations—its people are a microcosm of humanity with biological, cultural, and social ties to all other parts of the earth. ❞

NATIONAL COUNCIL FOR THE SOCIAL STUDIES

When Noah Webster observed that "our national character is not yet formed," he identified a central dilemma that still faces the United States, as well as many other multiethnic nations (as cited in Frost, 1942, p. 1.41.1). This land of immigrants is, indeed, a land in which it is not all that difficult for many people to feel like strangers in their own country.

In the United States, one major instrument for attempting to create unity out of diversity has been the public school system, which has been a powerful tool for socializing us into a common culture. Resistance to this attempt at socialization has also been a part of our history, either by those who have not wanted to be "melted," or those who believe their vision of the "American way of life" should be the model to which all others must be formed. Thus public schools have always been a battleground where various groups have sought to control the public school and its curriculum and, by so doing, shape our common culture. The way schools should address American pluralism has been publicly debated from the beginning of our Republic and continues unabated today, particularly in light of our position as one leading player in the global community of nations.

Educational literature over the past 175 years reflects profound disagreement about how to educate the young while forging a nation-state from a multiethnic population. Should differences of language and culture be recognized and taken into account? Or should we work as hard and fast as we can to assimilate newcomers to "the American way of life"? Indeed, as our nation becomes increasingly diverse and increasingly a part of an interdependent global community, many question whether or not there really is any longer something called the "American way of life." What *is* certain is that advocates on all sides of the debate have never been fully satisfied with the role played by the school and the way it carries out its socializing mission. There have been many times when dissatisfaction grew into violent action.

If, as we argued in the preceding chapter, fundamental changes must be undertaken in the way we "do school" for an increasingly diversified population, then it will be helpful for us to examine the history, not only of specific incidents in the struggle for equal educational opportunity, but also of the debate surrounding multicultural or intercultural education. What follows is a somewhat abbreviated but, we hope, clear account of how educators have reached their current place with respect to this debate and what the major issues are today.

Historical Perspectives on Diversity in the United States

We Have Been Different From the Beginning

One might argue that intolerance toward differences in the Americas began with the introduction of European culture in the 1490s. There is considerable evidence that the Native populations that lived in the Americas before European settlement exhibited far greater tolerance toward diversity of thought and lifestyle than did the arriving Europeans. The Taino people, for instance, greeted Columbus with food, shelter, and open festivity when the Spaniards first arrived on their small Caribbean island in 1492. At first intrigued with the Taino, Columbus wrote that "their manner is both decorous and praiseworthy" (as cited in Brown, 1970, p. 1).

Case Study

Learning from One Another's Common Global Problems

To: Rebecca Wilson (rwilson@unimail.edu)
From: Julianna Schneider (Schneiderjulianna@hamburg.edu.de)
Re: Reconnecting?
Date: October 4.

Dear Becky,

I hope this e-mail finds you well. It has been about a year since we communicated and four years now since my year studying abroad at your university in the United States. It's really surprising how quickly the time seems to go! Now that I am in my first real teaching position in a middle school in Hamburg I find myself reflecting more and more about what I learned and experienced in your public schools, communities, and college classrooms, as well as the many long talks we shared late into the night.

Things have changed in so many ways in Germany in the past few years with the recent influx of immigrants and refugees that have entered our country. I'm not sure if you know all the details, but in 2015 alone, just a couple of years ago, we took in more than 400,000 refugees! While some of us have responded with open arms and others feel really threatened, it has been quite a challenge for all Germans. I am struggling to find ways to engage my students in sensitive and meaningful ways around some of the issues we experience and face on an almost daily basis. I know that your country has a long history of welcoming immigrants and perhaps we could learn something from you as we share our experiences. I do realize, though, that this has presented a challenge for many Americans in recent years. Perhaps we can connect our students in a conversation around some of these issues so they can learn from one another.

Anyway, I hope you are well, that you are, in fact, teaching now, and that we might do something together around this issue. I still remember sharing those big family holiday traditions with you and your family, so give them my regards.

Hope to hear from you soon,
Your friend,
Julianna

To: Julianna Schneider (Schneiderjulianna@hamburg.edu.de)
From: Rebecca Wilson (rwilson@unimail.edu)
Re: Reconnecting?
Date: October 5.

Hello Julianna,

What a nice surprise waking up this morning to find your e-mail. I've been reading a little bit about what has been happening in Germany and wondered how it might be affecting you. I'm glad you wrote.

I have been teaching in the same middle school for two years now. My teaching team includes four content area teachers and one integration specialist who assists us with children who have special learning needs. My primary responsibility is language arts. You know that in the past few years, teachers have had many more requirements placed upon them and that quite a lot of our teaching seems to be preparation for the end-of-year tests that students must complete. I'm pretty sure I can work closely with our social studies teacher, and between the two of us develop something meaningful that would satisfy our requirements while linking with you and your students. I'll get back to you on that as soon as possible.

So yes, I would be eager to begin working with you and see how we might collaborate. In the meantime, give me and my team a little background about Germany's experiences with diversity and I'll put some thoughts together on our country's experience.

I look forward to hearing from you.

Becky

(continued)

©Ariel Skelley/Blend Images LLC RF

To: Rebecca Wilson (rwilson@unimail.edu)
From: Julianna Schneider (Schneiderjulianna@hamburg.edu.de)
Re: Reconnecting?
Date: October 6.

Dear Becky,

Our experiences in Germany are rather different from your experiences in America. Ethnic diversity is a relatively new phenomenon in Germany. Up until the 1950s, most Germans lived in predominantly homogeneous cultural communities, and few people traveled overseas or had contact with foreign visitors. Speaking a foreign language or experiencing a different lifestyle seemed to be something that was reserved for the educated and wealthier middle and upper classes, and just not a part of the everyday life for most Germans.

The situation began to change rather dramatically in the 1960s when Germany, together with several other European countries, began to recruit workers from southern and southeastern Europe. Waves of predominantly male migrants from Italy, Spain, Greece, Yugoslavia, and Turkey came to work in the factories of the then booming industrial centers. We referred to them as "guest workers." After some time, many of these "guests" were ultimately given permission to remain in the country, and by the late 1970s they had turned into residents, raised families, and were beginning to settle into their new environment. In accordance with German immigration law, migrants could be granted permanent work and residence permits without becoming naturalized German citizens. In addition to these new immigrants, in the 1970s there was a sizable group of ethnic Germans and Jews who came here from Russia for a better life and were granted German citizenship status on the basis of specific legal provisions concerning the repatriation of the descendants of ethnic Germans and the compensations for Jews. A lot of our attention to these new faces in our schools, something we referred to as intercultural education, began during these times. Our attention then was focused on accepting and working with students who speak a different language, something, I believe, was rather different from the way you approached multicultural education in the United States.

Today, a growing number of refugees leaving war-torn regions have entered Germany, again under special circumstances. The majority of these people come from across the African continent as well as from such countries as Afghanistan, Iraq, and Syria. Germany has agreed to accept about one million of them—more than any other nation in Europe! These new arrivals really emphasize the differences that exist between the more traditional German-born locals and the non-German-born immigrants, thus setting the stage for significant discrimination and conflict. Immigration policy and bureaucracy differs sharply between those who have always been here and the newcomers.

More people with backgrounds different from the dominant culture now live in Germany than ever before. The result is a dramatic increase in the diversity within our classrooms—and in the pressures on most teachers who are from the mainstream and have little understanding of how to teach in a multicultural setting. Intercultural education that now focuses on much more than simply language differences is suddenly a very important topic for us to consider. Your country has a long history of addressing domestic diversity in schools. We, on the other hand, are dealing with more international diversity than you seem to have.

I wonder how you deal with recent immigrants and refugees, and what we might learn from the experiences of multicultural educators as we address a newer global reality. What do you think?

Julianna

To: Julianna Schneider (Schneiderjulianna@hamburg.edu.de)
From: Rebecca Wilson (rwilson@unimail.edu)
Re: Reconnecting?
Date: October 9.

Dear Julianna,

Sorry for the delay in getting back to you, but I wanted to talk more with my teaching team while doing a bit of background research myself. This issue is certainly one that our entire team is interested in pursuing, and there is a lot of interest in doing this with you. We see lots of opportunities to compare the way our two countries have addressed diversity in the past, and then how we are addressing the very real concerns and issues that face so many nations today. We began brainstorming possible ways we might approach this in our various content areas. Although these are just some preliminary ideas, we could look at the historical experiences of our respective pasts as well as what's happening today through social studies. Since in the United States almost all of us have immigrant pasts, we might do a family tree exercise with each of our students and see what we could learn about the challenges our own ancestors faced (see the Active Exercise at the end of this chapter). We could discuss issues related to acculturation, or how cultures change as a result of long-term contact with others. I don't know if you have many books in the German language about immigrants and refugees, but we have many books that we could read in language arts that address these issues. We could also do things such as writing letters to newspapers or social service agencies, or uploading blog posts about what we are learning. In math, we might generate and compare both historical and present-day data as well as survey and collect data on people's opinions on various topics related to immigration. We could do this in both of our countries and compare the similarities and differences. In science, we might look at other pressures that might cause people to move away from their homes—anything from climate refugees, those forced to leave their homes because climate change has made some parts of the planet uninhabitable, to looking at famine today and in the past, like the Irish Potato Famine. Suffice it to say that there are many ways we might address these issues and we are really excited to begin doing so.

You are correct when you say that America has a long history of immigration; our country was founded by immigrants looking for a better life. But it wasn't always easy—either for the newcomers or for those who had been here for several generations. Many people, of course, came from Europe and didn't look all that different from "Americans." But for the poor among them—the Irish, Italian, Slavic "huddled masses yearning to breathe free"—it was always a struggle. This was not so much the case for Germans, however. Did you know that nearly 50 million Americans trace their heritage to Germany? It's the largest of any immigrant group in the United States! Today,

(continued)

however, immigrants and refugees come from all over. Fewer and fewer are from Europe, mostly coming instead from Central and Latin America, the Middle East, Africa, and Asia. The unrest over immigration is happening again. While we are a nation founded by immigrants and all Americans, except for our native populations can claim heritage from somewhere else, many people seem to feel threatened and are beginning to push back against this. I'm not sure where this will end, but it certainly is an issue people here are beginning to talk about.

The bottom line in all of this is how our various societies and institutions, like schools, respond to difference and the sometimes sudden and unexpected influx of new people. You mentioned that society in general, and schools in particular in Germany, have only recently begun addressing issues related to what we call "diversity." We, in the United States, have a somewhat longer history of trying to integrate a multicultural perspective into our schools. In our country, we began to really understand and address these issues in earnest in response to the civil rights movement in the 1950s; this was about the same time that your country began to experience demographic shifts. It has not always been an easy task.

It seems as if we are beginning to experience an issue that is as much a domestic concern as it is a global issue. I wonder if there are similarities between our historical experiences and the issues we currently face, and how our respective nations will respond. I look forward to our journey together.

More soon,
Becky

The Taino's hospitality, however, was soon met with severe cruelty by the Spaniards. Within 20 years of Columbus's landing, the Taino were extinct as a people. In fact, this tendency toward intolerance for both religious and cultural diversity on the part of the Spaniards may have prevented them from becoming the dominant culture in North America. So much energy was spent repressing and fighting the native populations that the northern spread of Spanish culture was halted in the Southwest.

The emergence of the English as the dominant force in the new lands may be partially attributed to their somewhat greater tolerance, born, perhaps, of their own need for religious freedom. However, even though the English government allowed, even encouraged, immigrants from a variety of ethnic backgrounds to settle in America, it was the white, English-born Protestants who, by the time the United States became a nation in 1776, had emerged as the dominant group. This group, too, was fearful of "different" kinds of immigrants. In 1698, for example, South Carolina passed an act exempting Irish and Roman Catholics from new bounties (Dinnerstein & Reiners, 1975). In 1729, Pennsylvania placed a duty on all servants of Scotch-Irish descent. One official at the time wrote, "The common fear is that if they continue to come, they will make themselves proprietors of the province" (p. 2). Ironically, the very people who originally had come to the New World to escape religious persecution were among those who actively engaged in the persecution of others for their beliefs, values, and lifestyles.

Industrialization, Immigration, and Religious Pluralism

In the early years of the 19th century, an influx of European immigrants followed the Industrial Revolution across the Atlantic. At the same time, the United States was developing the idea of the "common school," heralded in part as a way to give all children, no matter what their cultural, religious, or economic backgrounds, a common experience that would help them understand one another and provide a common basis for citizenship in a democracy. Despite a growing network of public elementary schools, the increasing diversity within the United States began to be viewed as a "problem" for public schooling. The first battles within these pluralistic common schools were not waged around the issue of race or ethnicity, as is common today, but around the issue of religion.

Many new immigrants in this period were Catholic and, to native-born Protestants, represented a threat to the stability of the republic—as well as competition for newly created industrial jobs. Many suspected that immigrant Catholics owed a greater allegiance to the Pope in the Vatican than to the U.S. government, an issue that was not finally settled until the election of John F. Kennedy to the presidency in 1960. Second-, third-, and fourth-generation Protestants also opposed the emergence of Catholic schools, believing that they were intended to instill undemocratic values in Catholic children. Catholic parents, on the other hand, felt that a Catholic education was necessary to preserve their children's religious faith and an important vehicle for maintaining Catholic communities.

Opposition to Catholic schooling often became violent both in word and deed. Political cartoonists had a field day with caricatures of the pope as an ogre attempting to "swallow" the United States. More serious, however, were physical attacks on Catholic schools, exemplified by the burning of the Ursuline convent in Charleston, Massachusetts, by a Protestant mob in 1834 (Provenzo, 1986, pp. 90–91).

In the 1830s, The Common School Movement, which was supposedly nonsectarian but was largely Protestant driven, came into dramatic conflict with those who wished to educate their children in religious-based schools. If the emphasis in Catholic schools was toward a religious faith, the emphasis in the common school was toward a secular government that would maintain the new forms of democracy being developed in the United States. The democracy that was taking shape was rapidly becoming a kind of civil religion, and the development of loyalty to that idea was one of the foundations of public schooling. Thus, Catholics had some justification for the belief that the common school might socialize their children away from their religious faith. As the number of Catholic immigrants increased, and the network of Catholic schools grew, Catholic parents began to insist that public funds raised through taxation to support public schools should also be used to fund private Catholic institutions. That debate continues to this day.

Catholics were not the only group who were feared and persecuted. In 1835, the Indian Removal Act saw the last vestige of Native American culture in the eastern United States swept westward across the Mississippi River in the tragic roundup known today as the Trail of Tears. In the case of Jews, the last barrier to their voting rights was not abolished in New Hampshire until 1877. In 1882, the immigration department passed an act that prohibited the entry of Chinese into the country.

The Civil War: Freedmen's Schools and the Issue of Race

Issues of race in *public* education became important only after the Civil War. In the pre–Civil War South it was against the law to educate black slave children, so no racial *educational* problem existed in southern schools. In the North, blacks who had bought or had been given their freedom achieved some education in the common schools, in African American church communities, and through abolitionist efforts. After the Civil War, the education of black children was still not perceived to be a "national problem" by most whites because, where African Americans were educated at all, they were educated in separate schools.

Southern states, notably resistant to providing public education for blacks, were not above taxing them for white schools. In some places—Florida, Texas, and Kentucky, for example—black schools were built only after black citizens paid a second tax to build their own schools (Webb & Sherman, 1989, p. 524).

In 1865, Congress established the **Freedmen's Bureau** to help freed slaves with the transition to citizenship. In 1866, the law was amended to assist in the provision of black schools. Many of the teachers in these schools were northern white women, often daughters of abolitionist families. Indeed, the story of the women, both black and white, who taught in the "Freedmen's Schools" is among the proudest in the history of teaching. By 1870, nearly 7,000 white and black "schoolmarms" were teaching 250,000 black students, and learning to cross the barriers of race and class that have characterized American history. The legacy of these teachers was enormous. Not only did they educate the children who later became the teachers in segregated schools, but they educated a generation of free black leaders who are too seldom talked about today (Hoffman, 2003).

Violence characterized the development of black schools after the Civil War as it had the development of Catholic schools earlier. Burning buildings and harassment of black teachers and students were commonplace. However, passage of the Fourteenth Amendment to the Constitution in 1868 made responsibility for civil rights a federal rather than a state function and, as a result, African Americans began to gain more access to public education. Fully aware that education was a way out of poverty, black parents saw that their children got to school, one way or another. When they were needed on the farm, they alternated between school and work, as this Alabama boy describes:

> I took turns with my brother at the plow and in school; one day I plowed and he went to school, the next day he plowed and I went to school; what was learned on his school day he taught me at night and I did the same for him (Weinberg, 1977, p. 46).

Black children remained in segregated schools that were funded at minimal rates and often open for only part of the year. Indeed, despite efforts through the courts to equalize the rights of blacks in all spheres of public life, in 1896 in the *Plessy v. Ferguson* decision, the Supreme Court held that segregation was not prohibited by the Constitution. *Plessy v. Ferguson,* which upheld the doctrine that "separate but equal" facilities for blacks and whites were constitutionally permissible, justified separate (usually inferior) education of African American children in both the North and South until 1954, when *Brown v. Board of Education* made such unequal facilities illegal.

Very few African American children with disabilities received any schooling at all in the 19th century, but the tiny number who did, mainly those with visual impairments, experienced double segregation. Among the 30 public and private residential schools for blind pupils established in the United States between 1832 and 1875 was the first school for "the colored blind," in North Carolina (Wallin, 1914). By 1931 there were five such separate schools for black children and youth. Ten other black schools maintained separate (inferior) departments for blind students, most of which used secondhand materials such as badly worn Braille books that were virtually impossible to read. Moreover, "segregation not only kept black children in separate schools staffed by black teachers, but prevented those teachers from attending courses given at white southern colleges" (Koestler, 1967). Their lower salaries made attendance at northern colleges prohibitive.

Historical Perspectives on Approaches to Diversity in U.S. Schools: Anglo-Conformity and Assimilationist Ideology

The issue of diversity as a problem for public schools is not a new phenomenon. During the earlier years of massive immigration, from about 1870 to perhaps 1920, the "problem" of diversity in the schools was largely perceived as a problem of how to assimilate children of other nationalities. In short, it was thought to be the school's task to make immigrant children as much like white, middle-class, Anglo-Saxon Protestants as possible in as short a time as possible.

Interestingly, a key strategy employed by public schools to accomplish this goal involved establishing the field of speech therapy (formally termed speech/language pathology). Immigrant children placed in New York's "vestibule" or "steamer classes" were instructed in the proper use of English by speech teachers, who very soon, at parents' requests, were also assigned to work with children who had medically impaired articulation or fluency. Described as **Anglo-conformity,** or the assimilationist model, the rationale for this strategy was typified by these words of Ellwood Cubberly, a prominent educator at the turn of the 20th century:

> Everywhere these people settle in groups or settlements to set up their national man-
> ners, customs, and observances. Our task is to break up these groups or settlements, to
> assimilate and amalgamate these people as part of our American race and to implant in
> their children so far as can be done, the Anglo-Saxon conception of righteousness, law
> and order, and our popular government and to awaken in them a reverence for our
> democratic institutions and for those things in our national life which we as a people
> hold to be of abiding worth (as cited in Trujillo, 1973, p. 21).

The assimilationist strategy was applied to each new ethnic group as immigrants poured through Ellis Island and other ports of entry. Jews, Poles, Slavs, Asians, and Latin Americans all became the "raw material" from which the "new American" would be made. Between 1860 and 1920, 37 million immigrants became naturalized citizens. Their sheer numbers changed the ethnic makeup of America. By 1916, for example, only 28% of San Francisco's population claimed English as its first language.

Yet despite the high number of immigrants, the *dominant* American culture retained its English, Protestant identity. The nation's public schools, staffed largely by white, middle-class, Protestant women, did little or nothing to encourage the expression of ethnicity or address the special needs of an increasingly diverse student population. Indeed, in the eyes of the nativist population, the schools were supposed to prevent such expression. Taken from the industrial process used in making steel in which iron ore and a number of other ingredients are melted down and combined to produce a "new" metal—steel, the metaphor of a melting pot was used to describe the process of helping immigrants shed their native languages, learn English, and assimilate into the dominant American culture.

The term *melting pot* actually came from the name of a play written by Israel Zangwill (Zangwill, *The Melting Pot,* 1909). The goal of creating one homogeneous culture from the many that arrived on the shores of the United States is captured in the following speech from that play:

> America is God's Crucible, the great Melting Pot where all the races of Europe are
> melting and reforming! Here you stand, good folk, think I, when I see them at Ellis
> Island, here you stand in your fifty groups with your fifty languages and histories, and
> your fifty hatreds and rivalries, but you won't be long like that, brothers, for these are
> the fires of God. A fig for your feuds and vendettas! Germans and Frenchmen, Irish-
> men and Englishmen, Jews and Russians—into the Crucible with you all! God is mak-
> ing the American. . . . The real American has not yet arrived. He is only in the
> Crucible. I tell you—he will be the fusion of all races, the coming superman (p. 37).

James Banks (1988) suggested that assimilationists believe that one's identification with an ethnic group should be short-lived and temporary as it presents an obstacle to an individual's long-term interests and needs. Assimilationists believe that, for a society to advance, individuals must give up their ethnic identities, languages, and ideologies in favor of the norms and values of the larger, national society. The goal of the school, from an assimilationist perspective, should be to socialize individuals into the society at large so all can function in an "appropriate" manner; that is, in a manner that supports the goals of the nation as expressed through its leaders. Ethnic group identification, if it is to be developed, should be confined to small community organizations. In short, the goal for assimilationists has been to make it possible for everyone to be "melted" into a homogeneous whole.

The assimilationist view, sometimes called a *monocultural* perspective, shares an *image* or *model* of American culture. In this view there is a core "American" culture composed of common knowledge, habits, values, and attitudes. For people who think of American culture this way, these common characteristics might include the following: "real" Americans are mostly white, middle-class adults (or are trying to be); they are heterosexual, married, go to church (mostly Protestant but sometimes Catholic). They live in single-family houses (which they own, or are trying to); they work hard, eat well, stand on "their own two feet"; they expect their children to behave themselves; they wash themselves a good deal, and generally try to smell "good"; they are patriotic and honor the flag; they are often charitable and, in return, expect only that those receiving their charity will try to "shape up"; and they are not very interested in "highfalutin" ideas found in books written by overly educated people; instead they believe in "good, old-fashioned common sense."

Of course, this is a composite picture. Not all monoculturalists fit neatly into this view of "real" Americans. But most share many of these characteristics, and divergence from some of them (for example, heterosexuality) almost automatically disqualifies a person even if that is the only way in which he or she differs. For people who see American culture in this narrow way, those who do not share these characteristics are clearly not "real" Americans, whether they happen to have been born here or not. Moreover, their difference makes them dangerous to the maintenance of America as it is "supposed" to be. It is therefore a primary role of schooling to make the children of the culturally different into "American" children; that is, to teach these children those ways of thinking, behaving, and valuing that will help them fit harmoniously into the monoculturalists' culture. Children of monoculturalists, of course, do not need such help because they already match the model.

Although exceptional individuals, those who have disabilities and those who are intellectually or otherwise gifted, may be considered "real" Americans, they too have been viewed in some sense as "others." Beginning in the 1870s, large urban school districts formed separate classes for "unrulies" and for "backward" or "dull" pupils. In actuality, most such classes were repositories for children who, for one reason or another, "didn't fit" the regular program. From these beginnings, special education emerged as a separate, smaller system within the public school.

Multiculturalism and Pluralist Ideology: The Civil Rights Movement and the Schools

Those who believed strongly in the idea of the melting pot have been both bemused and angered by the fact that the contents of the pot never melted. Eventually, in opposition to the **assimilationist ideology**, came the call for **cultural pluralism** by a small group of philosophers and writers who argued that a political democracy must also be a cultural democracy (Banks, 1988). To these pluralists, immigrant groups were entitled to maintain their ethnic cultures and institutions within the greater society. The analogy they used was that of a salad bowl, and in order to have a rich, nutritious salad

Source: Library of Congress Prints and Photographs Division [LC-DIG-ppmsca-03119]

(society), it was necessary to include a variety of cultures. In short, American society would be strengthened, not weakened, by the presence of different cultures.

Pluralists view one's social group as critical to the socialization process in modern society. The group provides the individual with identity, a sense of belonging or psychological support, particularly when faced with discrimination by the larger society. It is through one's group, usually the ethnic group, that one develops a primary language, values, and interpersonal relationships, as well as a particular lifestyle. Pluralists believe the identity group (racial/ethnic, religious, and so forth) to be so important that the schools should actively promote their interests and recognize their importance in the life of the individual. Because pluralists assume a "difference" rather than a "deficit" orientation, they stress the importance of a curriculum addressing different learning styles and patterns of interaction, and fully recognize students' cultural histories. The assumption is that the more congruent the school experience is with the other experiences of the child, the better the child's chance of success.

Six decades after *Plessy v. Ferguson*, diversity in American society and in its schools again became the subject of major social turmoil. During the 1960s and 1970s, fueled by the general social ferment of the civil rights movement and the war in Vietnam, educational reform legislation was enacted in the following areas: desegregation, multicultural and bilingual education, mainstreaming students with special needs into regular classrooms, and gender-sensitive education. These programs recognized the pluralistic nature of this society in a positive rather than a negative sense. Each one attempted to help some educationally disadvantaged group of students to receive a better education within a pluralistic framework.

It is important to realize that these educational mandates were not achieved in isolation but as part of the larger human and civil rights struggles of the 1960s and 1970s. During this period, Congress passed a number of antidiscriminatory statutes: the *Voting*

Rights Act (1963), dealing with voter registration; the *Equal Pay Act* (1963), requiring that males and females occupying the same position be paid equally; the *Civil Rights Act* (1964), which ended discrimination in public places and banned employment discrimination on the basis of race, color, religion, sex, or national origin; the *Bilingual Education Act of 1968* (Title VII of the *Elementary and Secondary Education Act*), which established programs for children whose first language was not English; *Title IX of the Education Amendments* (1972), prohibiting sex discrimination against students and employees of educational institutions; and the *Education of All Handicapped Children Act* (1975), requiring schools to assume the responsibility for educating all children in the least restrictive environment possible. It was, in the words of one partisan observer, a period of "intensity of concern and commitment to do something about the problems in America stemming from the continued growth of its pluralistic character" (Hunter, 1975, p. 17).

In education the chief concerns were for access and equity: access to public education for excluded groups and a guarantee that such education would be equitable, that is, that it would be commensurate with the best that public education could offer. All these efforts rested on the belief that previously excluded groups had an inherent *right* to educational equity. Why was it important to emphasize the *rights* of racial and ethnic minorities, women, and persons with disabilities? Why was it important to enact legislation that protects their rights? Quite simply, because these rights had not been recognized in the past, and large numbers of people had experienced discrimination and unequal opportunity in a society that rests on the principle that *all* citizens are equal under the law. The civil rights movement was a reaffirmation of beliefs that form the very basis of American society and an insistence that we live up to our ideals in education as well as in other aspects of social life. Specifically, Spanish-speaking Americans in the Southwest, Puerto Ricans on the East Coast, Asian Americans on the West Coast, Native Americans on reservations and in urban settlements, and African Americans throughout the United States began to seek their fair share of what America had to offer and demand that the nation live up to the ideals it professed. The powerful buildup of unrest and frustration born of the discrepancy between American ideals and American practices sought an outlet.

The start of these events is usually marked by the 1954 Supreme Court decision in *Brown v. Board of Education.* This landmark decision stated that segregated schools were inherently unequal and that state laws that allowed separate schools for black and white students were unconstitutional.

In 1967, the U.S. Commission on Civil Rights was established primarily to investigate complaints alleging the denial of people's right to vote by reason of race, color, religion, sex, or national origin. About the same time (1966), the National Education Association issued a study supporting the teaching of Spanish to Mexican Americans in Tucson and the American Association of Colleges of Teacher Education produced a policy statement on pluralism entitled, "No One Model American." These and other investigative, judicial, and legislative moves were directed toward ending educational discrimination and the comfortable middle-class perceptions about cultural assimilation that supported discrimination. Together, these reports and judicial proceedings began to dim the embers under the American melting pot.

In the 12-year period from 1963 to 1975, private and government studies and hearings and a series of lawsuits regarding rights to native language instruction, placement of children with disabilities, and desegregation produced many mandates for the schooling of minority students. Concurrently, new educational strategies and curricula, especially in bilingual and bicultural education, appeared in districts across the nation.

The Civil Rights Act of 1964 made it illegal for public schools that received federal or state funds to assign students to schools based on their color, race, religion, or country of origin. The Bilingual Education Act was passed in 1968 as Title VII of the Elementary and Secondary Education Act. President Lyndon Johnson clarified the intent of this law in the following words:

> This bill authorizes a new effort to prevent dropouts; new programs for handicapped children; new planning help for rural schools. It also contains a special provision establishing bilingual education programs for children whose first language is not English. Thousands of children of Latin descent, young Indians, and others will get a better start—a better chance—in school (Tiedt & Tiedt, 1990, p. 9).

In 1970, the Office of Civil Rights Guidelines tried to make special training for non–English-speaking students a requirement for public schools that receive federal aid. The office stated:

> Where inability to speak and understand the English language excludes national origin-minority group children from effective participation in the education program offered by a school district, the district must take affirmative steps to rectify the language deficiency in order to open its instructional program to these students (Tiedt & Tiedt, 1990, p. 9).

Also during the 1960s and early 1970s, members of the women's movement began to pressure Congress to enact legislation that would guarantee equitable educational experience for girls and women. The result was Title IX of the Education Amendments of 1972. Intending to prohibit discrimination in elementary and secondary schools on the basis of sex, the preamble to this statute reads, in part:

> No person in the United States shall, on the basis of sex, be excluded from participation in, be denied the benefits of, or be subjected to discrimination under any education program or activity receiving federal financial assistance (U.S. Department of Education, Title IX, 2015.)

It was not until 1975, however, that the rules and regulations enforcing Title IX were published and sent to state departments of education and to school districts. In the interim, there was heated controversy, as well as 10,000 written comments from citizens (Carelli, 1988, p. 85).

Similarly, the Education of All Handicapped Children Act of 1975 (P.L. 94-142) became the basis for the educational rights of children and youth with disabilities. Like other educational equity efforts, P.L. 94-142 was not enacted in a vacuum but was the culmination of a long-lived movement. In 1948, for example, prior to the *Brown v. Board of Education* decision, Congress prohibited discrimination against people with disabilities by the U.S. Civil Service Commission. In 1968, the Architectural Barriers Act prohibited the use of government funds to construct facilities that were inaccessible to the handicapped. With enactment of amendments to the Vocational Rehabilitation Act of 1973 (P.L. 93-112) and amended by P.L. 93-516, even more far-reaching policies were established. The most familiar part of this legislation, Section 504, specifically prohibits any form of discrimination against persons with disabilities on the part of any agency receiving government funds. Enactment of the Americans with Disabilities Act of 1991 extended that prohibition to the private sector.

The Emergence of Global Education in the United States

In the case study at the beginning of this chapter, Julianna, in Germany, and Becky, in the United States, are having different, yet related, experiences. Julianna is confronting a sudden influx of students from widely different countries as a result of decisions made by her government to accept refugees fleeing war-torn regions in North Africa and the Middle East. Their presence, thus, makes Julianna's classroom a multicultural one, something that is new to her as well as to her colleagues, students, and community-at-large.

Becky, on the other hand, is probably accustomed to the idea of a multicultural classroom, and has probably had some experience teaching in one. She is now working with her colleagues to bring a global perspective into her classroom through adopting ideas and methods from intercultural education to her U.S. curriculum. Both Becky and Julianna could use a primer on global education due to the rapidly changing realities occurring in many parts of the world.

The term "global education" was coined by French-born, American microbiologist René Dubos in 1969 (Peters, 2009). It is Dubos who is also responsible for popularizing Jacques Ellul's admonition to "think globally, act locally." Over the next few decades, global education became one of a number of terms which refers to the beliefs and practices of those who promote and study education that has a global focus. Global education developed in the United States in a different but somewhat parallel track to multicultural education, and at about the same time—the decades of the 1960s and 1970s of the 20th century. The basic idea, however, can be found much further back in time, to ancient Greece, when Diogenes called himself "a citizen of the world." Or, perhaps we might look to the 17th century in Europe, when Erasmus, the Dutch priest, wrote satirically about those who view their own national origins as quite the best of all. Or, we can listen to the Czech theologian, Comenius—also in the 17th century—who was the first to promote the idea that schools had a role in furthering international understanding (Peters, 2009, pp. 12–16). While **multicultural education** has directed its attention to issues of equity among domestic populations, global education looks to the world and asks how education can make the *whole* world better.

In the United States, interest in educating for world-wide perspectives goes back at least to John Dewey (1916) and his idea that education should result in a society in which citizens can democratically engage with one another, can disagree and debate, but, in the end, find solutions to common problems. Schools should be the catalyst where students learn about the world around them and practice democracy in their classrooms. As Cushner (2018) notes, [Dewey] saw education as inclusive, participative, and experiential, laying the foundation that cultural diversity should be considered fundamental in education.

In the 1930s, Hilda Taba (1932), responding to increasing racism and anti-Semitism prior to World War II, investigated attitudes toward race, class, and ethnicity in the social studies. After the war, in the late 1940s and 1950s, while the United States was engaged in helping rebuild Europe and Japan, progressives concentrated on studies about other parts of the world, racial interactions, and ethnic studies. In the 1960s, along with major protests about America's involvement in Vietnam, peace and conflict studies, as well as human rights education, international studies, and intercultural studies were added as areas of study in many schools. In the late 1960s and 1970s, the women's and civil rights movements helped generate multicultural education, environmental education, and global education (Xanthopoulos, 2017).

By 1969, when the term **global education** was coined, there were a number of efforts already at work trying to respond to population and other changes around the world. Thus, defining this effort became a major interest of its proponents. It is the case that definitions of global education differ, but not by much. For example, the following are representative of many:

- Global education . . . is an interdisciplinary approach to learning concepts and skills necessary to function in a world that is increasingly interconnected and multicultural" (Xanthopoulos, 2017).

- Global education begins with raising awareness of global challenges such as poverty or the inequalities caused by the uneven distribution of resources, environmental degradation, violent conflicts or human rights, thus creating deeper understanding of the complexity of the underlying causes. It aims to change people's attitudes by them reflecting on their own roles in the world. Global education motivates and empowers people to become active, responsible global citizens (Global Education Network, 2009).

Global education, thus, involves learning about those problems and issues that cut across national boundaries as well as the interconnectedness of systems—ecological, cultural, economic, political, and technological. Global education involves *perspective taking*—seeing things through the eyes and minds of others—and it means the realization that while individuals and groups may view life differently, they also have common needs and wants (Tye, 1991, p. 5).

Comparing these definitions offers some insights into the field.

First, global education is *interdisciplinary*; that is, its content can come from all or nearly all disciplines. But the global perspective can also be *applied* to all or nearly all disciplines.

Second, it is an *approach* (hopefully, a creative one); that is, it is not a subject area like mathematics or foreign language, but rather it is an approach to teaching and curriculum design based on an idea. Yet, the global perspective can be used in many disciplines—mathematics, foreign language, chemistry, and history.

Third, it is meant to both participate in and direct change in societies through perspective taking (what it means to walk in their shoes)—learning about other people and places and their histories, problems, attitudes, and values.

Fourth, it tries to solve problems through stressing inclusiveness, tolerance, justice, cooperatio3n, and non-violence.

Rationales for global education vary, as do definitions. In 1991, the journal *Educational Leadership (EL)* published an article citing the 1991 American Society of Curriculum and Development (ASCD) in which the following rationale was given:

. . . our increasing worldwide interdependence is demonstrated by the expansion of technological, political, cultural, economic, and ecological networks connecting different peoples, cultures, civilizations, and regions (Tye & Kniep, 1991, p. 47).

In 2006, the U.S. Council of Chief State School Officers (CCSSO) issued a Global Education Policy Statement in which it said:

CCSSO and its members believe that in order to address the challenges of the 21st century, our education system must reflect knowledge and understanding of global perspectives and dimensions as well as the multifaceted perspectives within our own country; therefore, we believe certain core areas must be addressed in order for American students to thrive in and contribute to the global society. Our students must learn about many cultures as an integrated part of their study of literature, history, social studies, natural sciences, the arts, and other courses throughout the curriculum. Only by learning about other cultures, faiths, and ways of living will they be able to better their understanding of the various perspectives that frame our world and the people who inhabit it. More than ever before, students from around the globe are learning to adapt to change and to capitalize on expanding opportunities to become multilingual and learn to use mathematics, science, and technological skills in ways that meet or exceed the levels of current American students. We must take a constructive, positive, and innovative approach to preparing our children in a similar fashion, increasing the rigor of our academic standards, and thereby ensuring that all students are prepared to succeed in a global society (CCSSO, 2006; Peters, 2009, p. 35).

In 2016, the National Council for the Social Studies (NCSS) Board of Directors wrote:

Global education and international education are important because the day-to-day lives of average citizens around the world are influenced by burgeoning international connections. The goods we buy, the work we do, the cross-cultural links we have in our own communities and outside of them, and increased worldwide communication capabilities all contribute to an imperative that responsible citizens understand global and international issues (McJimsey, Ross, & Young, 2016).

As the world has gotten smaller, through technology, travel, and international cooperation and competition, the world has also found itself with shared issues and problems. The securing of human rights and social justice are some of these problems. Others have been listed by the National Council for the Social Studies as evidence of the global nature of societies today:

- the technical developments of global systems of communication and transportation;
- the change from local, regional, and national economies into a global economy;
- the increased interaction among societies, resulting in a need for understanding the distinctiveness as well as commonalities of world cultures that coexist with an array of distinctive local, national, and regional cultures;
- the worldwide political interdependence that is altering traditional boundaries between domestic and international politics;
- the impact of human activity upon the planet's ecosystem and the constraints on human activity imposed by limits of the system;
- the power of art and popular culture to communicate common affective and cognitive experiences around the globe;
- the perspective consciousness that expands our daily awareness that we are members of the global human species, with the world as our community; and
- the changes in land use (McJimsey, Ross, & Young, 2016).

Global education has emerged as one response to these issues.

Multicultural and Global Education: Differences and Similarities

As both multicultural and global education developed, over time they have often been compared and sometimes even used each other's terminology. It is important to note, however, that they have major differences. First, they have different legal and philosophical justifications (Kirkwood-Tucker, 2009). Multicultural education, for instance, is rooted in democratic theory and thus can be mandated by law. As Heilman (2009) wrote:

Multicultural education is justified as necessary to assure justice, liberty, and freedom of expression, which are foundational to democracies and central to individual lives and micropolitics. Because democracy requires the just distribution of public goods and opportunities and equal treatment under the law, multiculturalism and diversity are perennial issues in our debates about our largest policy concerns (p. 28).

Global education, on the other hand, does not ordinarily have the legal grounding that multicultural education has, but must depend for its justification on ethical arguments and organizations like the United Nations Human Rights Council (UNHRC), the Organization for Economic Cooperation and Development (OECD), the World Trade Organization (WTO), and others (Kirkwood-Tucker, 2009). Indeed, the Paris Agreement of 175 nations to reduce carbon emissions, signed in New York in April 2016, represented a milestone of global cooperation on the issue of climate change. All of these organizations have plans for advancing global outlooks and collaboration through education.

Another way in which multicultural and global education differs is that they have different constituencies, different supporters, different antagonists, and different scope. Although both movements find support in progressivism and challengers among conservatives and nationalists, because multicultural education has a basis in a series of laws and court decisions, its work is often the product of public debate. It, thus, has a high profile. Global education, on the other hand, does not. According to Heilman (2009),

> Global education tends to engage in issues in nations that are external to a student's country of residence; thus, it lacks a public focus on understanding and problematizing cultural diversity and national multiculturalism (p. 3.2)

While these differences are important, they are also becoming less and less sharp, especially as global issues such as climate change, water shortages, migration, food insecurity, and war grow more critical. Both multicultural and global education are interested in helping students understand other people and other cultures; both focus on equity; both desire to improve students' sense of civic responsibility and citizenship; and both work toward the goal of solving problems.

Approaches to teaching in these fields are also held in common, particularly insofar as they are learner-centered, participatory, reflective, experiential, and empowering. They share values of tolerance, solidarity, justice, empathy, equality, responsibility, cooperation, inclusion, and diversity (Global Education Network, 2009). The American Council on Education's (ACE) publication, *At Home in the World* (Olson, Evans, & Shoenberg, 2007), while asserting the differences between multicultural and global education programs, also cited Cortés (1998) in making a strong statement on ways in which they can work together:

> Multicultural education becomes enriched when it consciously incorporates global perspectives into the examination of American multiculturalism, as well as comparing multiculturalism in the United States with multiculturalism in other societies. Similarly, global education reveals more when it consciously includes the consideration of racial, ethnic, religious, linguistic, and other kinds of diversity as critical elements of the global experience.

With much in common, and proponents of both looking to build bridges between them, the future for multicultural and global education continues to look promising.

Challenges to Multicultural and Global Education in American Schools

Nevertheless, there are significant challenges to the work of both multicultural and global education. A number of shifts in contemporary thinking around the world pose difficulties for education systems that have been or are thinking of becoming engaged in work requiring changes in the way we think about each other and the broader world around us. Three of these are the difficulty of change itself, as presented in Chapter 1; the ideological assumptions about schooling and identity that create resistance to change; and the worldwide shift in governmental politics from liberal to conservative.

The Difficulties of Change

As noted above, there is a very strong element of social change in the definitions and rationale for both multicultural and global education. At the same time, institutions within societies, such as schooling, are composed of what some call "deep structures," are values and assumptions widely shared and expected by members of the society (Tye & Tye, 1992, p. 8). **Deep structures** do not change easily; indeed they only change when the society in which they are embedded changes, demanding new directions for schools and other institutions. Thus, for example, the one-room schoolhouse of early Massachusetts became the large building modeled on a factory under the influence of industrialization. Similarly, science entered the curriculum in the late 19th century, as curricular materials based on Protestant Christianity faded away. As more and more children went to school in the 20th century, schooling became mandatory up to the age of (usually) 16, the curriculum grew, students were organized into grades by age, and we began to divide students by what we defined as ability. Tye and Tye (1992) described some of the deep structures of schooling in existence at the end of the 20th century this way:

> A classroom means a space approximately thirty feet by thirty feet, with four walls, windows, rows of individual desks, blackboards, etc. Curriculum consists of separate subjects, taught in little or no relationship to each other. The school day is divided into six or eight approximately equal periods of time. The teacher is in charge. . . . There are other regularities which have to do with the norms of the teaching profession, the role of parents and community members, and the hierarchical nature of the educational bureaucracy. These are the characteristics of schooling . . . . which are assumed to be right and thus seldom seriously questioned (p. 8).

In the second decade of the 21st century, largely as a result of the Digital Revolution in the larger society, we have added technology to our classrooms (though unevenly); we have tweaked the number of and length of class schedules to some degree—one semester courses instead of those lasting a whole year, double periods during the day; courses offered on only two or three days a week. But in general, if someone who went to school in 1930 visited any of our schools today, he or she would probably feel at home; he or she would know where the Principal's office might be, recognize the bathrooms, and know where the teacher usually stood in the classroom. These are some of the regularities of schooling.

However, there is more to it than that. While each school reflects the deep structures of schooling in any society, individual schools have unique personalities of their own, based on who their students are, who teaches there, who leads the school, who the parents are, and, sometimes, where the school is located. Schools have histories, as well, and these differences help give each school its own identity within the school system in which it exists. Because each school is to some degree unique, changes can happen more easily, which is one reason why education for cultural diversity and global citizenship can occur in some schools at all.

©Hill Street Studios/Blend RF/Glow Images RF

Ideological Resistance to Broader Perspectives

At the same time, however, no school can become too different from its home school system unless the system as a whole also changes. It is important to understand the challenges those who undertake change toward a more global education may face:

- With some exceptions, educators and policymakers concerned with education, however well-meaning, have not themselves had the opportunity to think much about education for a truly global era. Even if they have, their own education has rarely prepared them to undertake such education seriously and effectively.

- Despite scattered calls for 21st-century skills and knowledge, there is no deep desire for such innovative education on the part of most families, or most citizens. We have nearly all been to school, we think we know what it should be like, and school approaches appearing markedly different from the "known" rarely find a favorable response in the community. At most, innovations are tolerated as long as they lead to adequate performance on traditional measures.

- Even when there is both the desire and the policy for a 21st-century education, our assessments are almost all geared for the classical subject matter knowledge and almost never offer the means to assess the flexible, cooperative thinking that is the hallmark of interdisciplinary thought.

- Perhaps most perniciously in the United States—but alas, not only in the United States—there is a deep distrust of education that attempts to transcend borders and to take seriously the customs, values, and priorities of nations and regions very different from one's own. Such provincialism and exceptionalism grows more fervent in times of crisis. Cosmopolitanism, internationalism, and globalism are often considered dangerous concepts or even "fighting words" (Gardner, 2011, p. x).

Despite the negative tone of these words, it really is the case that all national schooling is designed to raise up the next generation of people to "belong" to their own society.

Thus, schooling has a socialization function—to make Americans, or Brazilians, or Chinese, or Russians, or Nigerians out of its children and youth. Today, we find ourselves in the same peculiar position as did the people living in the United States at the end of the 19th century and the beginning of the 20th: how to identify as belonging to the nation rather than a state or region of the country. Remember that during the Civil War, soldiers tended to belong to units like the Connecticut Volunteers, the Indiana Swamp Hogs, the Scandinavian Regiment from Wisconsin, General Turner Ashby's Cavalry from Virginia, or General C. R. Wheat's Louisiana Tigers. This is because, as soldiers, they identified with their ethnic backgrounds or their states, or sometimes, their leaders. Even the two major armies were often thought of regionally as the northern or southern armies. To think of oneself first as an American was not the norm.

At present, while we have come to think of ourselves both regionally and nationally, we are just beginning to think of ourselves as citizens of the world (Grimley, 2016). Indeed, a familiar question is, "How do I become a global citizen while remaining an American?" This question underlies another challenge to broader thinking and that is the belief that experience in multicultural or global classrooms will result in social conflict and the loss of national unity. Indeed, the very notion of "America First," which is a major slogan today, reflects this belief.

Ideological Shifts in Governmental Politics from Liberal to Conservative

A third challenge to both multicultural and global education in the United States today is the governmental shift in political attitudes from liberal to conservative. This is not confined to the United States; it is, in fact, a world-wide phenomenon. Owing largely to anxieties brought about by the very same phenomena that created the rationales for multicultural and global education—that is, rapid social, economic, technological, cultural, and religious change—many people are responding by wanting to "go back" to a time when they felt safer, more "at home," more able to negotiate their lives. In the West, this generally means a belief in individual rights, free markets, private property, and limited government. Although conservative ideas do not necessarily lead to antagonism toward the ideas of multiculturalism and globalism, in practice today there is also a sharper distinction between "us" and "them," as well as a distrust of anything perceived to be "un-American."

We have experienced these shifts before. The "Know-Nothing" Party in the 1850s was the result of strong anti-immigrant feelings in the country, as well as antipathy toward Roman Catholics that emerged in the 1840s during the Irish immigration following the Great Famine in Ireland. In the 1930s, an isolationist "America First" movement opposed intervention in World War II, called for a buildup of American military, and defended the anti-Semitic priest, Father Charles Edward Coughlin, who had a huge following on his weekly radio program. The "America First" group also defended fascists and supporters of Nazi Germany. This movement lasted until the Japanese attacked Pearl Harbor, and then vanished. Again, in the 1950s, Senator Joseph McCarthy initiated what some would call a "witch hunt" to discover hidden Communists in government, popular culture (notably movies), the military, and even education. *McCarthyism* is defined as the practice of making accusations of disloyalty, especially of pro-Communist activity, in many instances unsupported by proof or based on slight, doubtful, or irrelevant evidence, or, the practice of making unfair allegations or using unfair investigative techniques, especially in order to restrict dissent or political criticism (Dictionary.com). In this particular era, individuals, including teachers and professors, were often required to sign pledges that they were not, nor had ever been members of the Communist party. The House Un-American Activities Committee and the Federal Bureau of Investigation (FBI) under J. Edgar Hoover, also sought to find "closet" Communists, largely in the movie industry; many were blacklisted, unable to get work, and their lives ruined. Eventually, Senator McCarthy went after the military, many of them heroes of World War II, and the country turned against him. Even so, including subsequent Supreme Court cases, the movement lasted for most of the 1950s.

To what extent our current political environment really mirrors similar shifts in the political winds is still unknown. Suffice it to say that it may not be the most conducive climate in which to make progress in either multicultural or global education. Recent changes in state and federal ideas about the nature of schooling, particularly those involving academic achievement as nearly the sole purpose of school-based education, also present certain challenges. Quite often, one is more likely to hear a discussion of assessment in a teacher's meeting than the fact that some Illinois 8th graders, under the auspices of the Pulitzer Center, are investigating hope, courage, and resilience in "fractured lands" (Pulitzer Center, 2017). However many challenges there are to the adopting of global as well as multicultural perspectives, these areas of teaching and learning are here to stay. It is incumbent upon those who are leading the way toward new ways of grappling with widely-shared human problems to know the challenges and work to overcome them.

Internationalization in Higher Education

Having an international or global component in colleges and universities is not a new phenomenon. Study abroad programs, cross-cultural experiences of various kinds for students, curriculum enrichment, strengthened foreign language instruction, and encouraging international students to enroll on campus all have been part of what Altbach and Knight (2007) call "traditional internationalization." It is the case, however, that internationalizing higher education has expanded widely in the past 20 years or so for many of the same reasons that global perspectives have burgeoned in schools and elsewhere. The term most often used in higher education for these activities is *internationalization*.

There has come to be a steady stream of students from many countries on all continents who desire an international academic and/or cultural experience and satisfy that desire by enrolling in institutions of higher education in a country other than their own. American colleges and universities are perhaps the largest host institutions, but certainly not the only ones.

Another popular imperative for planners in higher education is the development of international knowledge and experiences for American students on their own campuses. One way of doing that is to internationalize the entire college or university curriculum. The American Council on Education (ACE) Center for Internationalization and Global Engagement (CIGE) lists six plural areas of interest for those wishing to internationalize their campus in a comprehensive way:

1. *Articulating global strategy.* making plans with all stakeholders on the campus; developing an internationalizing mission statement, and, in general, making the case for internationalization;

2. *Faculty global engagement.* providing incentives for faculty to engage in international travel and work: developing their own international competence so that they may

pass their knowledge and experience to students; encouraging faculty to engage with colleagues in other countries on international research.

3. *Global partnerships.* taking advantage of opportunities to expand global reach through various kinds of partnerships, including student and faculty exchanges, dual degree programs with institutions across borders, and dual research programs.

4. *Internationalizing student learning.* weaving a global focus into most learning outcomes; building student global competence are goals for students who cannot study abroad.

5. *Leading internationalization.* Putting an emphasis here is on those administrators, including the President of the institution and usually an internationalization officer, and the responsibility they share for the success of the internationalization program.

6. *Student mobility.* Developing orientations, re-entry programs, and other supports for the flow of students who leave the campus for study abroad or who are coming from abroad to study on the American campus.

While many colleges and universities are internationalizing their campuses slowly rather than comprehensively, it is the case that more and more opportunities for global/international education will be available in the coming years. More and more undergraduate students have had experiences abroad in high school or with families, and these students will look forward to integrating more such experiences into their college education. Also, as the world gets smaller, increasing numbers of jobs and professions will include international work, thus making international/global education part of a large number of college majors. Indeed, it is probably not too much to say that:

> As the context is increasingly characterized by global competition in which knowledge is a prime factor for economic growth, internationalization has also become more market oriented, aiming to attract talented students and highly skilled workers as key resources for the knowledge economy (van der Wende, 2011).

Intercultural Education and the Preparation of Teachers in Higher Education

One area of higher education in which attention to internationalization is gaining momentum is the professional preparation of K-12 teachers. The vehicle, or type of teaching-learning relationship often used in this regard is intercultural education, a set of ideas that falls somewhere in between multicultural and global education. Like multicultural education, it has its place in the classroom, and is concerned with day-to-day interactions among people with different cultural backgrounds. Like global education, it is also concerned with larger issues such as the universality of human rights and justice in the context of cultural difference. And the need is strong. As Cushner (2018) notes:

> Teachers, today, must be able to develop a new set of interculturally grounded knowledge, skills, and dispositions in their students. Thus, teachers and teacher educators alike must not only enhance their own intercultural competence, but must also understand the concepts as well as nuances of intercultural interaction sufficiently so they can transfer this through a range of curricular experiences to the students in their charge. Ironically, all these skills are grounded in concepts of intercultural understanding and communication (p. 1).

UNESCO's International Commission on Education for the Twenty-First Century (1996) provided a set of Guidelines in which are contained four "pillars" for the role and objectives of intercultural education:

Learning to know, by combining sufficiently broad general knowledge with the opportunity to work in-depth on a small number of projects. The Commission further states that "a general education brings a person into contact with other languages and areas of knowledge, and . . . makes communication possible;" these results of a general education represent some of the fundamental skills to be transmitted through intercultural education.

Learning to do, in order to acquire not only an occupational skill but also, more broadly, the competence to deal with many situations and to work in teams. In the national and international context, learning to do also includes the acquisition of necessary competencies that enable the individual to find a place in society.

Learning to live together, by developing an understanding of other people and an appreciation of interdependence by carrying out joint projects and learning to manage conflicts in a spirit of respect for the values of pluralism, mutual understanding, peace and cultural diversity. In short, the learner needs to acquire knowledge, skills, and values that contribute to a spirit of solidarity and cooperation among diverse individuals and groups in society.

Learning to be, so as to better develop one's personality and be able to act with ever greater autonomy, judgment, and personal responsibility. In that respect, education must not disregard any aspect of a person's potential such as his or her cultural potential, and it must be based on the right to difference. These values strengthen a sense of identity and personal meaning for the learner, as well as benefiting their cognitive capacity (UNESCO, 1996).

Currently, there is increasing interest in international elements of K-16 education in the United States. A number of policy documents have been released from various professional education associations, including NAFSA: Association of International Educators, the Asia Society, and the National Council for Curriculum and Assessment in Ireland (NCCA). The Asia Society/EdSteps book, *Education for Global Competence: Preparing Our Youth to Engage the World* stressing global competence has been well received in the field. In addition, the nation has seen the rapid growth of International Baccalaureate (IB) programs in public schools. The Longview Foundation has produced a document called *Teacher Preparation for the Global Age: The Imperative for Change*, AACTE: American Association of Colleges for Teacher Education has created an international TAG (Topical Action Group), and the comprehensive Global Teacher Education website (www.globalteachereducation.org) has been established to "internationalize teacher preparation so that U.S. teachers are better prepared to educate globally competent citizens."

A key concept in intercultural education is the notion of *global competence*. As defined by Mansilla and Jackson (2011), global competence is "the capacity and disposition to understand and act on issues of global significance" (p. xiii). Further,

Globally competent individuals are aware, curious, and interested in learning about the world and how it works. They can use the big ideas, tools, methods, and languages that are central to any discipline (mathematics, literature, history, science, and the arts) to engage the pressing issues of our time. They deploy and develop this expertise as they investigate such issues, recognizing multiple perspectives, communicating their views effectively, and taking action to improve conditions (p. xiii).

PISA, the Programme for International Student Assessment, from the OECD, will begin assessing global competence in secondary education beginning with the 2018 assessment. They define global competence as the capacity to analyze global and intercultural issues critically and from multiple perspectives; to understand how differences affect perceptions, judgments, and ideas of self and others; and to engage in open, appropriate, and effective interactions with others from different backgrounds on the basis of a shared respect for human dignity (OECD, 2016, p. 4).

The Impact of Global Perspectives on American Education

Regardless of the issue, problem, site, or nature of the teaching and learning, it is clear that multicultural and global perspectives have gained a foothold in the American school and college curricula, as well as in professional associations here and abroad. It is also clear that its proponents are currently better equipped to deliver it and that the need for it continues to expand. As noted by The New Commission on the Skills of the American Workforce (2007):

> The best employers the world over will be looking for the most competent, most creative, and most innovative people on the face of the earth and will be willing to pay them top dollar for their services. . . .Beyond [strong skills in English, mathematics, technology, and science), candidates will have to be comfortable with ideas and abstractions, good at both analysis and synthesis, creative and innovative, self-disciplined and well organized, able to learn very quickly and work well as a member of a team and have the flexibility to adapt quickly to frequent changes in the labor market as the shifts in the economy become ever faster and more dramatic.

Those students who have had the benefit of multicultural and global education will be well prepared to qualify for the work of the 21st century. The characteristic elements of innovation, collaboration, flexibility, diversity, empathy, and inclusion that are the hallmarks of this kind of education will serve them well—in a new economy and a more just and sustainable society.

Summary

The history of multicultural education has its roots in a debate between those who think that American schooling should provide a common education to all children based on the history and culture of European Americans and Western civilization, and those who think that American schooling must recognize and affirm the rich historical and cultural backgrounds and perspectives of a population that has always been diverse and is becoming ever more so. Global/international education developed at nearly the same time as multicultural education, but in a different track, from different sources, and with different purposes and scope. Nevertheless, multicultural and global education have enough commonality that they can profitably enhance one another in order to provide answers to common problems faced by all the world's peoples.

Chapter Review

Go to the Online Learning Center at www.mhhe.com/cushner9e to review important content from the chapter, practice with key terms, take a chapter quiz, and access active workbook activities.

Key Terms

Anglo-conformity 43
assimilationist ideology 45
cultural pluralism 45

deep structure 52
Freedmen's Bureau 42
global education 48

global partnerships 56
multicultural education 48

Active Exercise

Additional Active Exercises are available online at www.mhhe.com/cushner9e.

Family Tree: Tracing One's Roots and Family Experiences

Purpose: To discover your family's experiences in past generations and compare them to immigrants and refugees today.

Instructions: Most of us in the United States can trace our family history, or roots, to someplace other than where we currently reside. Speak with family members and look through old family photographs (if you have any) to trace your family's heritage as far back as possible. If you are adopted or do not know your ancestors, respond in terms of an adoptive or foster family, or one to which you closely identify. Respond to the following questions as best you can, and share your responses with others.

1. From what parts of the world did your family (or families) originate?

2. What motivated your ancestors to leave their homeland for a new world? When did they leave? If your ancestors were always in North America, what was their life like prior to European contact?

3. What hardships did your ancestors face in previous generations, either when they first arrived or soon after they made a contact? What did they do to overcome any hardships? Do they recall any prejudice that was experienced?

4. What did your ancestors do in the previous two to three generations? How did this influence what the family does today?

5. What languages did your ancestors speak? What has happened to these languages in your family today?

6. What family traditions or practices have been carried out over the years that are special or unique to your family?

7. What do you know of the meaning behind your family name? How, if at all, has it changed over the years? Do you know the reason for any changes?

8. How are the experiences of your family similar to, or different from, those faced by various immigrants or refugees today?

9. In what ways was this exercise easy or difficult for you to do? Under what circumstances might an exercise like this be difficult for a student to do? What might you do as a teacher to modify it in special circumstances?

Reflective Questions

1. This chapter suggests that the experiences encountered during the civil rights movement remains in the public mind. Do you agree that this is, in fact, the case? If so, why? If not, why?

2. This chapter presents the histories of both multicultural and global education. How do you think those histories are similar and how are they different? What are some similarities between the objectives and after practices in multicultural and global education? What commonalities can you identify? What might be an advantage of looking for similarities between the two types of education?

3   If major societal changes in the 19th century such as industrialization and immigration changed the "deep structures" of our society, what deep changes have occurred in recent decades that seem to call for a more global education?

4.   What challenges—geographical, cultural, religious, political, or economic—do we face as we attempt to incorporate a global perspective into the curriculum of public education? What do you think are possible outcomes if we succeed? Or, if we fail?

References

Altbach, P. G., & Knight, J. (2007). The internationalization of higher education: Motivations and realities. *Journal of Studies in International Education, 11*, 290–305.

American Council on Education: Section on International Education and Global Engagement. (2017). Retrieved from http://www.acenet.edu/higher-education/Pages/Internationalization.aspx.

Banks, J. A. (1988). *Multiethnic education: Theory and practice* (2nd ed.). Boston, MA: Allyn & Bacon.

Brown, D. A. (1970). *Bury my heart at Wounded Knee.* New York: Holt, Rinehart, & Winston.

Carelli, A. O'B. (1988). What is Title IX? In A. O'B. Carelli, (Ed.), *Sex Equity in education: Readings and strategies.* Springfield, IL: Charles C. Thomas.

Cortés, C. E. (1998). Global education and multicultural education: Toward a 21st-century intersection. In Swartz, L., Warner, L., & Grossman D. (Eds.), *Intersections: A Professional Development Project in Multicultural Education and Global Education, Asian and American Studies* (pp. 114–133). Boston: The Children's Museum.

Council of Chief State School Officers (CCSSO) Washington, D.C. (2006). Global education policy statement. In Peters, L. (2009). *Global education using technology to bring the world to your students* (p. 35). Washington, DC: International Society for Technology in Education.

Cushner, Kenneth. (2018). Intercultural training for educators. *The international encyclopedia of intercultural communication.* New York: John Wiley & Sons.

Dewey, John. (1916). *Democracy and Education.* New York: Macmillan.

Dictionary.com. (2017). *McCarthyism.* Retrieved from http://www.dictionary.com/browse/mccarthyism?s=t.

Dinnerstein, L., & Reiners, D. M. (1975). *Ethnic Americans: A history of immigration and assimilation.* New York: Harper & Row.

Frost, R. (1942). The gift outright. In *The witness tree* (p. 1.41.1). New York: Henry Holt.

Gardner Howard. (2011) Preface. In Mansilla, V. B. & Jackson, A. *Educating for global competence: Preparing our youth to engage the world.* Washington, D.C. Council of Chief State School Officers (CCSSO) and New York, NY: The Asia Society.

Global Education Network. What is global education? Retrieved from http://glen-europe.org.

Grimley, N. (2016). Identity 2016: "Global citizenship rising, poll suggests," BBC News. Retrieved from http://www.bbc.com/news/world-36139904.

Heilman, Elizabeth E. (2009). Terrains of global and multicultural education: What is distinctive, contested, and shared? In Kirkwood-Tucker, Toni Fuss, (Ed.) *Visions in global education: The globalization of curriculum and pedagogy in teacher education and schools* (pp. 2.5–4.6). New York: Peter Lang.

Hoffman, N. (Ed.) (2003). *Women's "true" profession: Voices from the history of teaching* (2nd ed.). Cambridge, MA: Harvard Education Press.

Hunter, W. A. (Ed.) (1975). *Multicultural education through competency-based teacher education.* Washington, DC: American Association of Colleges of Teacher Education.

Kirkwood-Tucker, Toni Fuss, (Ed.) (2009). *Visions in Global Education: The Globalization of Curriculum and Pedagogy in Teacher Education and Schools—Perspectives from Canada, Russia, and the United States.* New York: Peter Lang.

Koestler, F. (1967). *The unseen minority: A social history of blindness in the United States.* New York: David McKay.

Mansilla, V. B. & Jackson, A. (2011). *Educating for global competence: Preparing our youth to engage the world.* Washington, D.C.: of Chief State School Officers (CCSSO) and New York, NY: The Asia Society.

McJimsey, M., Ross, B., & Young, S. (2016). Global and international education in social studies. Board of Directors, Silver Spring, MD: National Council for Social Studies (NCSS). Retrieved from http://www.socialstudies.org/positions /global_and_international_education.

OECD (2016). Global competency for an inclusive world. Paris: Organisation for Economic Co-operation and Development (OECD) (p. 4). Retrieved from https://www.oecd.org/education/Global-competency-for-an-inclusive -world.pdf.

Olson, C., Evans, R., & Schoenberg, R. (2007). *At home in the world: Bridging the gap between internationalization and multicultural education.* American Council on Education. Retrieved from https://bookstore.acenet.edu/products/home-world -bridging-gap-between-internationalization-and-multicultural-education.

Peters, L. (2009). *Global education using technology to bring the world to your students.* Washington, D.C.: International Society for Technology in Education.

Provenzo, E. F., Jr. (1986). *An introduction to education in American society.* Columbus, OH: Charles E. Merrill.

Pulitzer Center. (2017). Eighth graders investigate home, courage, and resilience in 'fractured lands.' Retrieved from http://pulitzercenter.org/blog/eighth-graders -investigate-hope-courage-and-resilience-fractured-lands.

Taba, H. (1932). *The dynamics of education.* New York: Harcourt Brace.

Tiedt, P. L., & Tiedt, I. M. (1990). *Multicultural teaching: A handbook of activities, information, and resources* (3rd ed.). Boston: Allyn & Bacon.

Trujillo, R. (1973). Bilingual-bicultural education: A necessary strategy for American public education. In National Bilingual Bicultural Institute, *A relook at Tucson, '66 and beyond.* Washington, DC: National Education Association.

Tye, K. A. (Ed.) (1990). *Global education: From thought to action. 1991* Yearbook of the Association for Supervision and Curriculum Development. New York: ASCD.

Tye, K. A. & Kniep, W. M. (1991). Global Education Around the World. *Educational Leadership*, April, 47–49.

Tye, B. B. & Tye, K. A. (1992). *Global education: A study in school change.* Albany, NY: State University of New York Press.

UNESCO (1996). International Commission on Education for the Twenty-first Century.

van der Wende, M. (2011) Internationalization of higher education. Retrieved from https://www.mysciencework.com/publication/show/03acd4dc37a5707f068ea0a6cc cc0ece.

U.S. Department of Education, Office of Civil Rights, Title IX and Sex Discrimination, 2015. Retrieved from https://www2.ed.gov/about/offices/list/ocr/docs/tix_dis.html.

Webb, R. B., & Sherman, R. R. (1989). *Schooling and society* (2nd ed.). New York: Macmillan.

Weinberg, M. (1977). *A chance to learn: A history of race and education in the United States.* New York: Cambridge University Press.

Xanthopoulos, J. A. (2017). Global education. *New dictionary of the history of ideas.* Retrieved from http://www.encyclopedia.com/history/dictionaries-thesauruses -pictures-and-press-releases/global-education.

Zangwill, I. (1909). *The melting pot.* New York: Macmillan.

©Hill Street Studios/Blend Images LLC RF

Chapter

3

Culture and the Culture-Learning Process

Focus Questions

1. How is it that you became the cultural being that you are today?

2. How have different individuals and institutions you have come into contact with influenced you?

3. How has the media influenced your cultural identity? Your religion? Your community? What other forces operate to influence your cultural identity?

4. What do you know about your own culture that you can use to better understand another culture, or that will enable you to talk intelligently about cultural differences with someone who is different from you?

"The first month or two in class I was always saying, 'Look at me when I talk to you,' and the (Navajo) kids simply wouldn't do it. They would always look at their hands, or the blackboard, or anywhere except looking me in the face. And finally, one of the other teachers told me it was a cultural thing. They should warn us about things like that. Odd things. It makes children seem evasive."

TONY HILLERMAN,
The Skinwalkers

The word *education* is derived from the Latin word *edu-care,* meaning "to lead forth." If we are to seriously engage in the education of students who will be contributing, collaborative, and proactive citizens in a multicultural, multilingual, and multi-faith society, we must lead our students in such a manner that they understand the cultural basis of their own as well as others' behavior; are cognizant of the conditions, both present and past, that affect people around the world; and are able to take the necessary steps to adjust to change, both in themselves and in the world around them.

Clearly, *education* is a broader term than *schooling.* Indeed, one of the difficulties we all encounter in talking about education is that it is pervasive in human life. Not often emphasized, however, are the actual settings, apart from schools, in which education occurs and the precise nature of teaching and learning in those settings. Yet it is in these settings—particularly in the home, the neighborhood, our houses of worship, and increasingly through various forms of media—that we acquire the language, knowledge, attitudes, and values that enable us to engage in the dramatic conversation called "culture." It is in these settings that people develop the cultural identities they bring to their interactions with others, both within as well as outside of school. And it is through these settings that we must work to lead our students forward into the future.

Giroux and Simon (1989) wrote about the importance of teachers understanding their own cultural identities and those of their students:

> By ignoring the cultural and social forms that are authorized by youth and simultaneously empower and disempower them, educators risk complicity in silencing and negating their students. This is unwittingly accomplished by refusing to recognize the importance of those sites and social practices outside of the schools that actively shape student experiences and through which students often define and construct their sense of identity, politics, and culture (p. 3).

These ideas can be clarified through the use of a "thought experiment"—a community you can enter in your imagination, so as to consider the educational implications of living there. In this experiment, imagine a medium-sized suburban city of about 100,000 people that is a first-ring suburb of a major city of about half a million people. The entire metropolitan area has a population of about 1.5 million people and is an hour or so from two other midsized cities. Let's call this city Beechland Heights. Now, conditions in such a city will vary depending on its ethnic and religious composition, its economic base, and its location (Is it in New England? The deep South? The Midwest? The mountain states of the West? The Southwest? The Northwest?). The size of Beechland Heights is also a factor to consider. If it were a city of several million, or a village of several hundred (or thousand) people, conditions might be different. In this thought experiment, Beechland Heights may assume a variety of characteristics. Read on and see what you can surmise.

Exploring the Concept of Culture

One of the greatest difficulties people have when they begin to explore concepts related to culture and culture learning is that of agreement on what it is they are talking about. This chapter looks closely at the concept of culture and the culture-learning process; that is, how we acquire a cultural identity. The chapter begins with some definitions of culture and with some of the analytical concepts devised by social scientists in their attempts to understand cultural similarities and differences among groups of people as well as individuals. This discussion sets the stage for subsequent analysis of intercultural interaction and intercultural development that occurs in the context of schools.

Case Study

Beechland Heights: A Thought Experiment

The imaginary city of Beechland Heights is clearly a geographical community that has a rather wealthy residential section, a number of middle-class neighborhoods, and a few neighborhoods that are rather poor. It has some manufacturing industries, a number of churches, two synagogues—one conservative and one reform—as well as a mosque. Throughout the area are numerous day-care centers, a number of quality museums, a relatively large public library system, one daily newspaper, and two smaller community weekly papers. There are numerous hospitals in the area, department stores, discount stores, bars, neighborhood convenience stores, and several commercial and service businesses. It has a municipal park, a large YM/YWCA as well as a Jewish Community Center, a welfare department, a children's services department, and a juvenile detention center. It has a professional theater, a dance company on the brink of collapse due to lack of funding, several malls, and a downtown business district. It has an adequate number of lawyers, doctors, dentists, accountants, architects, and other professionals. It has both public and private elementary, middle, and high schools. There are a few Catholic schools as well as one small Jewish day school. There are three well-established, well-endowed private schools in neighboring suburbs just outside the city limits. Beechland Heights has one large private university and a community college, both of which interact well with the community.

Within the geographical community that is Beechland Heights, there is also a set of educational communities—groups of people who are actively engaged in instruction and learning (formal and informal) as well as those organizations and settings in which deliberate and systematic teaching and learning occurs. It is in these educational communities that the dramatic conversations of culture take place in particular ways—in families, neighborhoods, businesses, religious settings, and voluntary associations. So the particular combination of settings in Beechland Heights sets the tone, so to speak, of the community itself and of the educational messages—both coherent and conflicting—available to its people.

Say, for the sake of the experiment, that Beechland Heights is in upstate New York and is a largely Protestant city (of all denominations, including three good-sized black churches). It also has a considerable number of Catholic families, enough to support several churches, as well as a few Catholic schools, 13 public elementary schools that feed into six middle schools, and four comprehensive high schools. There is a significant Jewish community that supports one K–8 Jewish day school, and relatively small groups of Islamic and Buddhist families.

Say, further, that for the most part, Beechland Heights is a historically white, working- and middle-class city that has undergone significant ethnic changes due to the migration of people from the inner city over the past 20 years. The African Americans who live in the neighboring city have been there for at least 75 years, and they comprise about 40% of the population, most having migrated from the deep South between the World Wars to work in the city's factories. Let's further suppose that the area industries are suffering from severe competition, both domestic and foreign. Business is not good, and the residents of Beechland Heights are fearful that many jobs could be lost, thus creating a depressed economic situation for all income-producing businesses.

As in all communities, the cultural conversations of Beechland Heights have their roots in the economic, religious, socioeconomic class, and family life of the town. The particular education received by an individual growing up in Beechland Heights depends, in large part, on the ethnic, religious, social class, and occupational character of the individual's family and the character of the housing and neighborhoods in which the individual lives, works, and plays. These factors—as well as others, such as the age of the individual, the individual's health, and the size and composition of the family of which the individual is a member—also have a great deal to do with the access the individual has to a broad or narrow range of educational resources and experiences available both within and outside the school.

(continued)

Take a look, now, at six 16-year-old high school students who live in Beechland Heights. What cultural conversations do you think have meaning for them?

Michael Williams is an African American young man who has lived his entire life with his grandmother and grandfather (retired and at home), his mother (an assembly line worker at a nearby factory), his aunt (who works evenings cleaning at the museum), two brothers, and a sister in a house on the northeast side of the city. He doesn't know who or where his father is. His older brother never went to college after he graduated from high school, and, like his mother, works in a local factory—although he is thinking about joining the army. The family regularly attends the local Baptist church. As a child, Michael played basketball at the community house near his home and continues to help out there with younger children. He attends the public high school and is in the college prep academic program where he earns excellent grades. He has a steady girlfriend; is a member of the high school golf team, which practices at the local golf course; is on the school newspaper staff, which is advised by an editor of the Beechland Heights newspaper; and works after school and weekends at the golf course.

Dinorah Rodriguez lives in a small but pleasant ranch house on a cul-de-sac on the south side of town. She is the youngest of a large, extended Mexican family; her parents having come to the United States initially as migrant workers before she was born. Although she attended Catholic parochial school through the eighth grade, she currently attends the public high school, where she is taking business-related subjects and is planning to become a secretary—perhaps in one of the local banks. Her family has always been very involved in the local Mexican community as well as in the church, and Dinorah gained a considerable amount of attention (not all of it positive) when she became the first altar girl at St. Mary's. Her family keeps in close contact via e-mail with the extended family members who remain in Mexico, and still sends money to support one of her aunts who is a nun. At home, the family speaks a fair amount of Spanish, something that Dinorah finds rather embarrassing when her friends are around. In school, she earns reasonably good grades, is on the cheerleading squad, and is a scorekeeper for the wrestling team. She dates a number of boys, mostly athletes, and works on weekends at a department store in a local shopping mall. Many in the family have been feeling somewhat anxious since the 2016 election, unsure of how all the rhetoric about sending immigrants and refugees home might impact them, their family, and others in their small but rather tight-knit community.

Steven Wong lives in a large, comfortable house on The Hill, on the west side of town, with his parents and a younger sister. His father is a successful businessman, and his mother, an artist, is in charge of the adult volunteers (called docents) at the museum where Steven sometimes works as a guide for special exhibits. His family does not belong to any religious group. He attends a private high school located in a neighboring community, where he struggles a bit for average grades, and is a member of the tennis and debate teams. As a child, Steven played Little League baseball, belonged to the Boy Scouts, and traveled extensively in the United States and to Hong Kong to visit family. He doesn't date much, and when he does it is usually with non-Asian girls who are children of his parents' friends. He is not certain that he wants to go to college, much to his parents' dismay.

Jacob Goldsmith lives with both of his parents in the same neighborhood as Steven Wong on The Hill. When Jacob was younger, he attended the one small Jewish day school that drew children from Beechland Heights as well as three or four other nearby communities. Jacob's father is a pediatrician with a fairly successful practice in town. His mother is a professor of English literature and teaches at a small private college located about half an hour away. Jacob is an avid reader, plays tennis and golf on the school teams, and one day hopes to be a doctor like his father. His family is affiliated with Temple Israel, a reform synagogue near the school, but is not highly observant. For Jacob's Bar Mitzvah, his family took him on his first international trip—a 2-week trip to Israel. Since then he has remained active with a small group of Jewish high school students that meet Wednesday afternoons at the Temple. He hopes to return to Israel one day—perhaps to study for a year during college.

Susan McArthur lives with both of her parents, also on The Hill not far from Steven Wong and Jacob Goldsmith. Susan is new to the area, having moved from Switzerland just a few months ago. Although born in Michigan, her family has lived in Switzerland, Argentina, and Japan since she was two years old. Her father, an executive with a large multinational company, has assumed positions of leadership and management in each of these nations, primarily responsible for the company's expansion and integration into these overseas markets. Susan's mother completed her Ph.D. in English Literature not long ago and obtained a position at the nearby university. This, in addition to the fact that her father has decided to retire from the company, prompted the family to move back to the United States. Growing up in so many different places has enabled Susan to be comfortable speaking a number of languages; she speaks English, French, and Spanish rather fluently and understands a bit of Japanese. She also has the rather unique experiences of adjusting to new cultures as well as saying goodbye to friends every now and then. Although she never really likes leaving her friends and schools behind whenever she has to move away, this is something that many of her friends have had to do over the course of their lives. She and her friends in the international schools refer to themselves as global nomads, or **Third Culture Kids** (TCKs for short). TCKs share the unique experience of growing up outside of their passport culture, often in a community with other **expats** (persons temporarily living outside of their country of citizenship), thus developing a set of skills and dispositions that make them distinct from many others of their age who do not share similar experiences. Susan worries if she will fit in, how she will make friends with others who do not understand her background, and what it will be like living within the borders of the United States after being outside the country for so many years.

Shameka Collins lives with her parents, an African American mother who works as a bookkeeper for a local department store, and a European American father, who spends much of his time working out of state. She sees him only occasionally—perhaps once or twice a month. Her family is one of only three African American families on her street, which is on the south side of town. Shameka is the only biracial student in her school, although most other students are not aware that her father is white. She has an older brother who is stationed on a nuclear submarine presently on duty in the Persian Gulf. As a child, Shameka was a Girl Scout for a while but dropped out. She has gone to Sunday school at the local Presbyterian church all her life. After school and on Saturdays she works at the main branch of the public library downtown, saving most of the money she makes for college. Since Shameka and her mother are generally alone, they spend as much time together as possible. Her mother has taught her to sew, and she makes almost all her own clothes. She worries about leaving home when she goes to college and is trying to decide whether to attend the local community college for two years before actually leaving home. Because she takes advanced placement courses in high school, she will be eligible for courses at the college in her senior year and will probably become a student there. She thinks perhaps she will become a doctor.

Each of these students, residents of Beechland Heights, participates in a particular pattern of educational life, out of which has emerged a cultural identity. The cultural knowledge, beliefs, attitudes, and values of these students, like those of most Americans, are multiple—none identifies with a single cultural group. Yet their cultural and educational patterns are different and sometimes surprising. How do you see their various cultural influences affecting their lives? What aspects of their upbringing do you think influences them most today? In what ways are they similar to or different from one another? In what ways are they similar to or different from you? Can you put yourself in Beechland Heights? A series of related critical incidents can be found at the end of this chapter.

Defining Culture

Culture is studied by many different disciplines, including anthropology, sociology, education, psychology, health, business, and the military. If you were to peruse the literature of these various disciplines looking for the concept of culture, you would find literally hundreds of definitions. Some of these definitions are more useful than others in an examination of how culture influences the teaching-learning process. What all these definitions seem to have in common is the idea that culture refers to a human-made part of the environment as opposed to aspects that occur in nature. Culture determines, to a large extent, people's thoughts, ideas, patterns of interaction, and material adaptations to the world around them.

Coon (2000) referred to culture as "the totality of socially transmitted behavior patterns, arts, beliefs, institutions, and all other products of human work and thought characteristic of a community or a population" (p. 53). He likens culture to the act of cooking. When cooking, you begin with some basic ingredients, but then you add a few condiments, include a little bit more or less of certain items, adjust the cooking time, and so forth.

The criteria by which cultures define themselves, and differentiate themselves from one another, vary a great deal. The basic ingredients that determine a culture are geography, ethnicity, language, religion, and history. The factors that divide cultures can consist of any combination of these elements plus the "condiments" of the local scene. In Iraq, for instance, the population is divided religiously between Muslims and Christians; among Muslims between Shia and Sunni Muslims; and ethnically between Arabs and Kurds, as well as a number of other, smaller ethnic and religious groups. The situation is similar in India, where religion divides Muslims and Hindus; however, the Hindu majority is further split according to the caste to which one is born. In the United States and other modern nation-states, group loyalties based on cultural differences exist, but more or less as subsets of an overarching group loyalty called nationalism or patriotism. Ethnicity further divides these groups.

A culturally defined group can be as small as a group of Aborigines in the outback of Australia or as large as a nation-state. It can exist in a small, defined territory, or its members can share a territory with other culturally defined groups. It can be a closed system, or it can be open to new ideas introduced from other cultures. The only real requirement is that people who share the culture sense that they are different from those who do not belong to their group.

Culture in Everyday Use

Sociologists, who study culture in terms of various competing social groups within a society, have developed a number of concepts that are useful in discussions of cultural pluralism. Some of these terms are used interchangeably and often can cause confusion. Five terms commonly used to describe social groups that share important cultural elements but that are smaller than a whole society are subculture, microculture, ethnic group, minority group, and people of color.

Subculture

The term **subculture** refers to a social group with shared characteristics that distinguish it in some way from the larger group in which it is embedded. Generally, a subculture is distinguished either by a unifying set of ideas and practices, such as the corporate culture or the drug culture, or by some demographic characteristic, such as the adolescent culture (Bullivant, 1993). Subcultures can be defined by age-cohorts, such as Millennials or Generation Y (those born roughly between 1980–1994) or Generation Z (those born roughly between 1995–2012). Such subcultures share certain characteristics, beliefs, and common experiences that set them apart form other cohorts.

Microculture

The term **microculture** also refers to a social group that shares distinctive traits, values, and behaviors that set it apart from the parent macroculture of which it is a part. Although the terms *microculture* and *subculture* are often used interchangeably, *microculture* seems to imply a greater linkage with the parent culture. Microcultures often mediate— that is, interpret and transmit—the ideas, values, and institutions of the larger political community (Banks, 1989). Thus, for example, the family, the workplace, or the classroom can each be thought of as a microculture embedded in the larger culture of the neighborhood, the business, or the school. These larger macrocultures are themselves embedded in larger professional, regional, or national cultures. Thus a particular entity, such as the school, may be simultaneously both a macroculture (the culture of the school as a model of society) and a microculture (the culture of the particular school).

Minority Group

The term **minority group** refers to a social group that occupies a subordinate position in a society. In 1978, Wagley and Harris defined a minority group as one that experiences discrimination and subordination within a society, is separated by physical or cultural traits disapproved of by the dominant group, shares a sense of collective identity and common burdens, and is characterized by marriage within the group (as cited in Bennett, 1990, p. 42). However, characterizing minority groups based on these criteria sometimes leads to confusion and inaccuracy. For example, women are often referred to as a minority group because they are thought to be oppressed, even though they constitute more than half the general population and do not, as a rule, marry within their group. Similarly, when students who are African American, Native American, or Latino constitute a majority of the population in a particular school, the school is often referred to as a "majority-minority school." The term *minority* can also be used in different ways in different countries. In the Netherlands, for instance, *minority* refers to immigrant groups that occupy a low socioeconomic status. Chinese, for instance, are considered minorities in the United States and Canada, but not in the Netherlands because they do not have low socioeconomic status (Cushner, 1998).

Ethnic Group

The term **ethnic group** refers to groups who share a common heritage. When asked to complete the statement, "I am _____" using as many descriptors as possible to define yourself, those statements that reflect identification with a collective or reference group are often indicative of one's ethnic identity. When people respond that they are African American, Jewish, or Polish, they are identifying with a group of people who share a common heritage, history, celebrations, and traditions, who enjoy similar foods, and who might speak a common language other than English. A sense of peoplehood, or the feeling that a person's own destiny is somehow linked with others who share this same knowledge, reflects identification with an ethnic group. Thus people can live in one nation and claim one nationality, yet maintain ancestral ties to another.

People of Color

The phrase **people of color,** a phrase often used within the United States, refers to nonwhite minority group members, such as African Americans, Mexican Americans, Puerto Ricans, and Native Americans, but reflects recent demographic realities of the United States. This phrase is preferred over *ethnic minority* by many people because these groups are, in many schools and communities, the majority rather than the minority.

As the United States and its schools grow increasingly complex with respect to cultural plural differences, many voices are beginning to criticize the use of collective terminology like *people of color*. These voices call for awareness and understanding of specific ethnic, racial, religious, and other groups. In this effort, it is recognized that the terms *Hispanic* or *Latino,* for example, are only umbrella terms for a number of Spanish-speaking ethnic groups, including Puerto Rican, Spanish, Salvadoran, and Mexican. Similarly, the term *Native American* is an umbrella term for an enormous variety of tribal or ethnic identities (over 400 officially recognized by the Bureau of Indian Affairs), including the indigenous people of Alaska and Hawaii. Clearly, these groups can be as different from one another as they can be from the mainstream society.

Commonalities in Definitions of Culture

Many definitions of culture ask the question, "What do all cultures have in common?" Some try to answer this question by examining the functions or purposes of culture. Webb and Sherman (1989), for example, described culture in a functional way:

> Cultures solve the common problems of human beings, but they solve them in different ways. . . . Each provides its people with a means of communication (*language*). Each determines who wields power and under what circumstances power can be used (*status*). Each provides for the regulation of reproduction (*family*) and supplies a system of rules (*government*). These rules may be written (*laws*) or unwritten (*custom*), but they are always present. Cultures supply human beings with an explanation of their relationship to nature (*magic, myth, religion,* and *science*). They provide their people with some conception of time (*temporality*). They supply a system by which significant lessons of the culture (*history*) can be given a physical representation and stored and passed on to future generations. The representation usually comes in the form of dance, song, poetry, architecture, handicrafts, story, design, or painting (*art*). What makes cultures similar is the problems they solve, not the methods they devise to solve them (pp. 49–50).

Culture can also be understood in terms of the assumptions or ideas inherent in the concept itself. Four of these assumptions seem particularly important.

Humans Construct Culture

Human beings are born with certain genetically determined predispositions, some of which underlie behavior and others that direct physical features. Although these predispositions are not precise, they do help determine the parameters under which humans develop. Humans have fewer biological instincts (e.g., breathing, swallowing) than any other species does, which means that we are born relatively helpless and remain so for a considerable amount of time, longer than any other organism in the animal kingdom.

Unlike most members of the animal world, people are not biologically programmed so that they automatically know how to utilize the environment to find food and shelter. In short, we do not know how to survive without other people to care for us and to teach us. Therefore, humans must discover ways of effectively interacting both with their environment and with each other. They must learn how to *construct* the knowledge, including rules of living, that will enable them to survive. This knowledge, the manner in which it is presented (in the family, in the neighborhood, in literature, art, school lessons, etc.), and the meaning it has for us is called *culture*. Culture, then, is the one factor that determines the kinds of guidelines to which the individual is exposed.

The concept of culture usually refers to things (both physical and mental) that are made or constructed by human beings rather than to things that naturally occur in the environment. When you look out over a body of water, for instance, neither the water itself, the undeveloped beachfront, nor the horizon is considered culture. These items are naturally occurring components of the environment. How we *think about* and what we *do* with the natural environment, however, is usually dependent on our culture. Thus, a beachfront along Miami Beach in the United States has been viewed as a good place to build condominiums, hotels, piers, a boardwalk, and a marina. Similarly, in Sharm el Sheikh, located along the Red Sea on the Sinai Peninsula in Egypt, one of the world's greatest beach resorts can be found in this otherwise parched desert region. In another culture, this same beachfront might be regarded as a sacred space with little human intervention allowed.

The physical artifacts of any culture are expressions of people's underlying knowledge, attitudes, and values toward a part of the natural environment. Other expressions of culture include behavioral patterns—for example, people's tendency to litter the oceans and beaches with various kinds of waste. Traditional societies in many parts of the world, on the other hand, have an entirely different view of the natural environment. Rather than seeing themselves as controllers of nature, many Native Americans, for instance, believe strongly that human beings are an integral part of the natural world. Since in their view we live within rather than outside nature, they believe we should not interfere with it too much.

This example is interesting because it not only shows that different sociocultural groups perceive the world in very different terms but also that cultural beliefs and attitudes can and do change. Western peoples are now beginning to see the damage they have caused to the environment and to consider not only ways to clean it up but also ways of rethinking the very basis of the relation of human beings to nature.

Culture Is Shared

Culture is not only constructed, it is *socially constructed* by human beings in interaction with one another. Cultural ideas and understandings are shared by a group of people who recognize the knowledge, attitudes, and values of one another. Moreover, they agree on which cultural elements are better than others, arranging these in a hierarchy of value that may change over time. Mainstream American attitudes about children's place in the economy provides a good example. Before the middle of the 19th century, children in the United States were regarded as economic assets to their families and to the community. That is, they worked not only on the farm or in the shop but also often outside the family for money that went to help support the family. Zelizer (1985) made a distinction between the "useful" and the "useless" child in talking about the change that occurred during the last half of the previous century:

> By 1900 middle-class reformers began indicting children's economic cooperation as unjustified parental exploitation, and child labor emerged for the first time as a major social problem in the United States.... By 1930, most children under fourteen were out of the labor market and into schools (p. 61).

This example illustrates the changing nature of cultural ideas. The notion that children do not belong in the labor market and that parents whose children bring income into the family may be exploiting them has become a highly valued idea in our society, but it is one that is relatively new. In contrast to early-19th-century families, we believe that children should be in school when they are young. Moreover, when we encounter families that do send their children out to work, whether it be in the United States or elsewhere, we have a sense that they are doing something wrong. Thus, in contemporary mainstream U.S. culture, until our children are in midadolescence, we place a greater value on the "useless" (nonworking) child than we do on the "useful" one who works. Indeed, although many people find ways around it, in this country there are legal restrictions on the age at which children can be employed. In some parts of the world, however, many families are still highly dependent upon their children to generate income—even in the face of strong criticism from outsiders.

In nearly all instances, shared cultural identification is transmitted from one generation to the next. One exception to this cultural transmission process, however, can be seen in the case of deaf persons whose primary language is a manual system, ASL (American Sign Language) in North America. Although most deaf persons have hearing parents, the Deaf normally form strong ties to their own community and tend to marry a deaf partner. Thus, cultural transmission in this instance is deferred until entry into the Deaf community occurs through instruction in schools for the Deaf and through a network of social clubs, theater, political organizations, and publications. For some young people, their first enculturation into the Deaf community may come through enrollment at the world-famous Gallaudet University and its related centers and school, which provides schooling from preschool levels through college.

Culture Is Both Objective and Subjective

A third common feature of culture is that it is comprised of two components: objective elements and subjective elements (Triandis, 1972). The **objective** components of culture, sometimes referred to as "big C," consist of the visible, tangible elements of a group; that is, the endless array of physical artifacts the people produce, the institutions they create, the language they speak, the clothes they wear, the food they eat, and the unending stream of decorative and ritual objects they create. These elements are relatively easy to pick up or observe, and all people would describe them in a similar manner. It is the objective elements of culture that are most commonly thought of when cultural differences are considered. **Subjective** components of culture, sometimes referred to as "little c," are the invisible, less tangible aspects of culture, such as the attitudes people hold, the values they defend, their norms of behavior, the manner in which they learn,

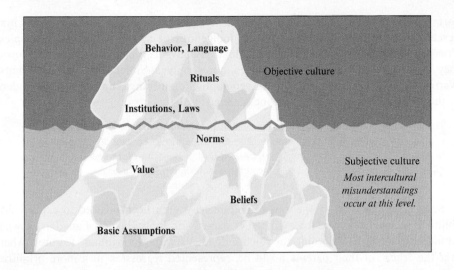

Figure 3.1
Iceberg Model of Culture

and the hierarchy of social roles—in short, the *meaning* that the more objective components of culture have for individuals and groups.

In this respect, culture can be likened to an iceberg: only 10% of the whole is seen above the surface of the water (see Figure 3.1). It is the 90% of the iceberg that is hidden beneath the surface of the water that most concerns the ship's captain who must navigate the water. Like an iceberg, the most meaningful (and potentially dangerous) part of culture is the invisible or subjective part that is continually operating at the unconscious level and shapes people's perceptions and their responses to those perceptions. It is this aspect of culture that leads to most intercultural misunderstandings, and that requires the most emphasis in good multicultural or intercultural education. When teachers focus on such things as food, festivals, and fashion, or when tourists mainly visit museums, monuments, and mansions, they are emphasizing the objective or surface aspects of culture. Good intercultural education and/or tourism focuses on the subjective, or hidden dimensions of a culture, thus helping people gain an understanding of the more meaningful and important aspects of culture.

Culture Is Nurtured

A final assumption about culture is the idea that it involves nurturing and growth, similar to the nurturing of plants. In the case of humans, however, the growing process involves teaching the young, both formally and informally. Thus, to **enculturate** a child is to help that child become a member of her or his social groups. In the United States, as elsewhere, enculturation may mean helping a child negotiate the different cultural perspectives found among the various social groups in which he or she participates.

Culture is also related to growth through the fine arts (music, dance, literature, and the visual arts) as well as through social behavior. A "cultured" person is one who has been nurtured (helped to grow) by participation in such activities. However, observation tells us that it is people of comfortable circumstances who most frequently have the time, energy, and inclination to devote to such pursuits. Thus is born the notion of an elite (high-status) group.

The idea that culture "belongs" to an elite group also carries with it the notion that this kind of "high culture" has more value than what we might call "folk" culture. In part, this idea has its roots in the late 19th century, when Western anthropologists first developed their ideas from the study of indigenous or so-called 'primitive' peoples. Comparing other and usually less technologically advanced civilizations to their own, they saw differences that were perceived not simply as differences but as deficits. Warren's (1873) textbook on physical geography, for instance, introduced its readers to the "races of man" in the following manner:

> The Caucasian race is the truly cosmopolitan and historical race. The leading nations of the world, those who have reached the highest state of civilization and possess a history in the true sense of the word, belong to it. It has, therefore, not improperly been called the active race; while the others, embracing the uncivilized or half-civilized peoples, have been termed the passive races (p. 86).

Such quasi-evolutionary theories of culture have even been invoked to explain disabilities. Down syndrome, for example, is named for John Haydon Langdon Down's ethnic classification, according to which individuals with "mongolian" features, whatever the "race" of their parents might be, represented regression to a more primitive state of evolutionary development. Tragically, before the discovery of its chromosomal basis in the 1950s, a newborn with Down syndrome was often described as a "throwback," as were infants with a variety of congenital anomalies.

Western anthropologists' notion of cultural evolution was directed mainly at other (non-Western) societies. At the top of the cultural hierarchy were the highly "civilized" peoples, mostly the Europeans and Americans who popularized the concept. At the bottom were the more primitive "savages" or "natives." Everyone else was placed somewhere in between and thought of as having the potential to climb up the cultural ladder. Inherent in this and other cultural models was the anthropologists' assumption that the natural progression of culture is upward. Indeed, the idea of a hierarchy of cultures existed well before anthropology was even accepted as a scientific discipline. In 1824, half a century before Warren wrote his textbook, Thomas Jefferson wrote:

> Let a philosophic observer commence a journey from the *savages* of the Rocky Mountains, eastwardly towards the seacoast. These he would observe in the earliest stages of association, living under no law but that of nature, subsisting and covering themselves with the flesh and skins of wild beasts. He would next find those on the frontiers in the *pastoral stage,* raising domestic animals to supply the defects of hunting. Then succeed our own *semi-barbarous* citizens, the pioneers of the advance of *civilization,* and so in his progress he would meet the gradual shades of *improving* man until he would reach his, as yet, most improved state in our seaport towns. This, in fact, is equivalent to a survey, in time, of the progress of man from the infancy of creation to the present day (as cited in Pearce, 1965, p. 155).

Jefferson's categories foreshadow those of the early anthropologists. In many ways our thinking has not moved very far beyond this framework. Books with such titles as *Affable Savages* (Huxley, 1957) and commonly used terms such as *underdeveloped* and *developed nations,* or *Third World* versus *First World* perpetuate the idea of cultural movement toward something perceived as more ideal or better or more civilized. Moreover, the direction of this movement is generally toward a culture that looks a great deal like our own. While these ideas are largely discredited among modern anthropologists, they continue to exist in the minds of many Americans when contrasting U.S. society with other societies, particularly those that are less technological. And this is increasingly becoming a dangerous idea to sustain because, in the past 30 years or so, other nations have made great strides in the world marketplace—economically, socially, and educationally. As Fareed Zakaria (2008) noted, this is:

> not so much about the decline of America but rather about the rise of everyone else. It is about the great transformation taking place around the world, a transformation that, though often discussed, remains poorly understood.

Traditionally, Americans have expected their schools to socialize all students into traditional European American, upper- and middle-class culture, generally referred to as "the best of Western civilization." Although it is true that great art, beautiful music, and meaningful literature have been given to the world by Western peoples, it is equally clear that Western contributions do not represent all that is great and beautiful in the world.

Applying the Concept of Culture

When school programs are instituted to increase awareness and understanding of specific groups, they are called group-specific or **culture-specific approaches** and stress information about a particular group of people, usually identified by a single characteristic such as race, ethnicity, religion, or gender. Although these approaches have much to offer, several problems are associated with them. First, while they attend to differences *between* one group and another, these approaches do not attend to important differences *within* groups. Consequently, they tend to give the impression that all people identified as belonging to a group (all Latinos or all Jews, for instance) are alike, which is clearly not the case. Second, because these programs usually rely on students of certain *samples* of the larger group (e.g., *urban* African Americans, *white* middle-class girls, Navajo *who live on reservations*), they may promote stereotypes. Third, group-specific programs, because of their intentionally narrow focus, cannot attend to the wide array of differences that collectively control the teaching–learning process.

In contrast to the group-specific approach to understanding diversity is another, more inclusive approach that attempts to deal directly with the complex nature of

©Hill Street Studios/Getty Images RF

cultural phenomena. Called a **culture-general approach,** it derives mainly from principles developed in the fields of cross-cultural psychology and training, intercultural communication, and social psychology. Professionals working in these fields are mostly interested in the effect of culture on the *individual* and on the interface or interaction between individuals of different groups. In addition to describing how culture affects an individual, these psychologists have also been developing a variety of educational and training strategies to help individuals anticipate and deal effectively with problems that may arise in intercultural interaction.

Culture-Specific Versus Culture-General Frameworks

It is important to understand the distinction between culture-specific and culture-general knowledge. A culture-general concept is one that is universal and applies to *all* cultural groups, as seen in the following example.

The way an individual "learns how to learn" depends on the socialization processes used by his or her culture. That is, learning style is related to socialization processes. This very general statement can be regarded as a cultural universal, or culture-general concept. It doesn't tell us anything about an individual's preferred learning style, but it does tell us that everyone has one and that it is formed by socialization experiences. Thus, knowing that socialization experiences vary from culture to culture, it follows that learning styles will also vary among cultures. Such a culture-general concept is valuable to teachers in that it warns them of the possibility that there will be many variations in learning style among their students. So informed, a teacher presiding over a multicultural classroom would be alert for signs of learning style differences and would attempt to develop alternative lesson plans or instructional approaches that address those differences.

A culture- or group-specific concept, on the other hand, is one that applies to a specific cultural group. For example, both Hawaiian and Native American children have historically acquired most of their knowledge, values, and attitudes about the world through direct participation in real-world events. Traditionally, their teachers were usually other members of their family or ethnic group who were also participating in those events. Thus direct participation, or **in-context learning,** became their familiar and preferred learning style.

Contrast in-context learning with the more formal schooling given to most children in the majority of schools. Most children are sent to a captive learning environment (schools) where specially trained teachers who are usually total strangers use books and other abstract learning tools to provide indirect participation, or **out-of-context learning,** about real-world events. In a classroom where both cultural groups are present, the teacher should anticipate learning style differences (culture-general knowledge), try to assess the culture-specific learning styles that are present, and then adapt instruction accordingly.

In short, teachers in multicultural classrooms need to have both culture-general and culture-specific knowledge. That is, they need to know that certain cultural universals (e.g., learning style differences, patterns of communication, value orientation) are at work in every multicultural classroom, and then they need to gather—through observation, inquiry, and study—the particulars of those variations so that they can plan and deliver instruction that is appropriate for *all* their students. To focus solely on culture-specific knowledge, which is always based on *samples* taken from some target culture, is to ignore not only individual differences within that group but also the cultural universals that cut across groups. Likewise, to focus solely on culture-general knowledge is to ignore the very real differences that separate groups and that provide a map for assessing and adapting instruction.

The Culture-Learning Process

Individuals tend to identify themselves in a broad manner and in terms of many physical and social attributes. For example, a young man might identify himself as an attractive, athletic, Asian American who intends to be a doctor and live in upper-class society. Other people also identify individuals according to these attributes, and interactions among individuals are often shaped by such identifications. Figure 3.2 shows 12 sources of cultural identity that influence teaching and learning. Who learns what, and how and when it is learned, is briefly described here and is further illustrated and discussed in later chapters.

What Is Learned: The Sources of Cultural Knowledge

1. Race is a very amorphous term. Biologically speaking, it refers to the clustering of inherited physical characteristics that favor adaptation to a particular ecological area. However, race is culturally defined in the sense that different societies emphasize different sets of physical characteristics when referring to the same race. In fact, the term

Figure 3.2
Sources of Cultural Identity

is so imprecise that it has even been used to refer to a wide variety of categories that are not physical, for instance, linguistic categories (the *English-speaking race*), religious categories (the *Jewish race*), national categories (the *Italian race*), and even to somewhat mythological categories (the *Teutonic race*) (Yetman, 1991). Although race has often been defined as a biological category, it has been argued that race as a biological concept is of little use because there are no "pure" races. Evidence from the analysis of the human genetic code reveals that more than 99% of human genetic characteristics are common to all people, meaning that there is much more similarity among people than there are differences (National Human Genome Research Institute, 2016).

The use of the term *race* is not based on biology; rather, it is socially defined on the basis of physical criteria such as skin color. Historically, the term has its roots in classifying groups of people by class inequalities, not skin color, with the British referring to the Irish as a "lower race." Then, during European colonial expansion, race began to be defined in terms of skin color in reference to those populations brought together in colonial America: the English and other European settlers, the conquered Indian peoples, and people from Africa brought in as part of the slave trade. Thus, race is an important social characteristic not because of its biology but because of its cultural meaning in any given social group or society. In the United States, race is judged largely on the basis of skin color, which some people consider very meaningful and use as a criterion for extending or withholding privileges of various kinds. Through subtle yet effective socializing influences, group members can be taught to accept as "social fact" myriad myths and stereotypes regarding skin color, stature, facial features, and so forth. This is not limited to the colonial situation in the United States, however. In the latter part of the 19th century it was employed by Europeans to rank one another and to justify social, economic, and political inequalities among their peoples. During World War II, the Nazis under Adolf Hitler enjoined the expanded ideology of "race" and "racial" differences and took them to an extreme end: the extermination of 11 million people they considered as "inferior races" (e.g., Jews, Gypsies, Africans, homosexuals, and so forth) and other unspeakable brutalities of the Holocaust (American Anthropological Association, 1998).

The use of the term *race* continues to change, even from one census to another. The U.S. Census Bureau, for instance, uses the federal government's definitions of race when performing a census. The question asking about race in the 2000 census, for instance, was different from the one used in the 1990 census in several ways. Most significantly, for the first time, respondents were given the option of selecting one *or more* race categories to indicate their racial identities.

Racism results from the transformation of race prejudice and/or ethnocentrism through the exercise of power against a racial group defined as inferior by individuals or by institutions, with the intentional or unintentional support of an entire culture. Simply stated, racism is preference for, or belief in, the superiority of one's own racial group over any other.

Institutional racism can also exist when either an individual in authority or an organization that harbors negative race prejudice (or any other prejudice for that matter) puts practices or procedures in place that actively discriminate toward a particular group.

Affirmative action initiatives were established by the federal government in the 1960s as an attempt to counteract historic discrimination faced by ethnic minorities, women, and other underrepresented groups to compensate for the ways such groups have historically been excluded in the employment, education, and government sectors of society.

2. Sex/gender is also culturally defined on the basis of a particular set of physical characteristics. In this case, however, the characteristics are related to male and female reproduction. Cultural meanings associated with gender are expressed in terms of socially valued behaviors (e.g., nurturing the young and providing food) that are assigned according to sex. Such culturally assigned behaviors eventually become so accepted that they are thought of as natural to that sex. Thus, gender is what it *means* to be male or female in a society, and gender roles are those sets of behaviors thought by a particular people to be "normal" and "good" when carried out by the assigned sex. In brief, sex refers to male and female while gender refers to masculine and feminine.

In all sociocultural groups, gender includes knowledge of a large set of rules and expectations governing what boys and girls should wear, how they should act and express themselves, and their "place" in the overall social structure. Beardsley (1977) noted that any social or psychological trait can be "genderized" in favor of one sex or the other. Thus, in the dominant society of the United States, active traits such as aggressiveness are genderized in favor of males and against females, whereas more passive traits such as submissiveness are genderized in favor of females and against males. Culture is dynamic, however. In early 2013, Sheryl Sandberg, the COO of Facebook, published *Lean In: Women, Work, and the Will to Lead*, that challenged these very assumptions when she urged women not to shy away from ambition and leadership, and to take a more active role in determining the direction that their lives and careers might take.

Like cultural definitions of race, the specific set of traits assigned to males and females may vary by society. And within a society, these traits may vary by ethnicity, class, or religion. For instance, on a continuum of submissiveness to males (a norm in U.S. society), many African American females might be located closer to the less submissive end of the scale, many Hispanic females might be located closer to the more submissive end, and many European American females would probably be located somewhere in between.

Geert Hofstede (2001), who conducted the world's largest investigation into cross-cultural differences on a global scale, named one of the five dimensions he identified as Masculinity versus Femininity, referring to the distribution of societal roles between the genders. His studies revealed that (a) women's values differ less among societies than men's values, and that (b) men's values from one country to another contain a dimension from very assertive and competitive and maximally different from women's values on the one side, to modest and caring and similar to women's values on the other. The assertive pole has been called "masculine" and the modest, relationship or caring pole "feminine."Nations high on masculinity include Austria, Hungary, and Switzerland. Those high on femininity include the Scandinavian countries of Sweden, Norway, and Denmark. The United States falls close to the middle.

3. Health is culturally defined according to a particular group's view of what physical, mental, and emotional states constitute a healthy person. The expert opinion of the medical profession usually guides a society's view of health. Although a medical model has dominated cultural definitions of health, most disabilities (mental retardation, deafness, blindness, etc.) are not judged in terms of this model's norms. Thus, just as a person with cerebral palsy would not be considered sick, it is possible to be a healthy blind person or person with mental retardation.

In the United States and most of the industrialized world, the prevailing health system is almost totally biomedical. However, alternative systems such as acupuncture, holistic medicine, homeopathy, chiropractic, and faith healing are available, and the acceptance of alternative systems varies widely both within and between social groups. In other societies (e.g., China or India), what we deem alternative medicine may in fact be the dominant model, and our ideas of biomedicine may be operating at the fringes. The cultural meanings associated with health depend on which model, or which combination of models, an individual or family group accepts. For example, a four-year-old Russian child, who had recently immigrated with her family to the United States, suddenly suffered a high fever and flu-like symptoms. The child's middle-class European American preschool teacher wanted the family to take the child to the doctor immediately for an antibiotic. The child's grandmother, on the other hand, who was the family expert on medical matters, prescribed a traditional treatment: the child should be put to bed, surrounded by lit candles and family members engaged in prayer. In this case, the grandmother was the final authority, and the child got better.

4. Ability/disability, like the term *health,* is culturally defined according to society's view about what it means to be physically, emotionally, and mentally "able." The categories of ability and disability refer to a wide variety of mental and physical characteristics: intelligence, emotional stability, impairment of sensory and neural systems, and impairment of movement. The social significance of these characteristics may vary by setting as well. For example, the terms *learning disability* or *learning disabled* are primarily used with reference to schooling and are rarely used outside of school. Indeed, it may be that the current emphasis on learning disability in American schools is primarily a reflection of a technologically complex society's concern about literacy. In other nations, specific learning disabilities among people who are otherwise unimpaired are of little concern. In fact, this "condition," as a category of exceptional individuals, is nonexistent in most of the world.

The cultural meaning of *ability* and *disability* is related to both the needs and the public perception of the ability or disability itself. For example, the culture of the Deaf "needs" a shared, rule-bound system of communication (sign language) as well as shared traditions and values among its members. However, the public acceptance of deaf individuals is far less positive than for those who are gifted. This lack of acceptance can be seen in the privileges accorded each group in schools. School experience might enhance the self-esteem of a gifted student while it threatens that of a student who is deaf. In the United States, the reaction to **ability/disability** hovers closely around a socially defined norm: We favor bright individuals but often exclude those who show evidence of extreme intelligence; we favor individuals who "overcome" their disabilities but often exclude those who, for one reason or another, cannot.

5. Social class is culturally defined on the basis of those criteria on which a person or social group may be ranked in relation to others in a stratified, or layered, society. There is considerable debate about the criteria that determine social class. Some criteria identify class membership primarily in terms of wealth and its origin (inherited or newly earned). Other commonly used criteria include education, power, and influence over others. Class structures vary widely among societies and social groups in terms of their rigidity and their importance to an individual's life chances. In some societies, such as Britain and India, for example, the class structure is fairly rigid and determines to a large extent the opportunities that are available to each person. In these societies, a person is truly born into a particular social class and tends to remain there. In other societies, the structure is not so rigid, and although individuals may be born into a particular social class, it is expected that they may move up by virtue of their achievements. Societies also vary according to the value placed on leaving one's social class. In the United States, upward mobility is a value; in Britain it is not so highly valued. The consequences of these attitudes are not always salutary. In the United States, for example, if individuals do not succeed in moving up, the perception may be that something is wrong with them.

©SuzanaProfeta/Getty Images RF

Social class differences are also tied to a person's social expectations and cultural tastes. For example, individuals who exhibit the child-rearing practices, speech, and general tastes of the upper classes in matters such as dress, food, and housing can affect their social image and thereby their chances for upward mobility.

6. Ethnicity/nationality are culturally defined according to the knowledge, beliefs, and behavior patterns shared by a group of people with the same history and perhaps the same language. Ethnicity carries a strong sense of "peoplehood"—that is, of loyalty to a "community of memory" (Bellah, Madsen, Sullivan, Swidler, & Tipton, 1985). It is also related to the ecological niche in which an ethnic group has found itself and to adaptations people make to those environmental conditions.

The category of *nationality* is culturally defined on the basis of shared citizenship, which may or may not include a shared ethnicity. In the contemporary world, the population of most nations includes citizens (and resident noncitizens) who vary in ethnicity. Although we are accustomed to this idea in the United States, we are sometimes unaware that it is also true in other nations. Thus we tend to identify all people from Japan as Japanese, all people from France as French, and so forth. Similarly, when American citizens of varying ethnic identities go abroad, they tend to be identified as "American." A tragic example of this misconception is the recent history of ethnic warfare in the former Yugoslavia and Iraq. The post-election violence in Kenya in 2007–2008 was ethnically based, as is the ongoing violence in such nations as South Sudan, Myanmar, Nigeria, and India. Americans in general are unaware of the role that ethnicity may play in dividing people. Most of the conflicts that occur across the planet are the result of long-held ethnic strife and do not cross national boundaries.

7. Religion/spirituality are culturally defined on the basis of a shared set of ideas about the relationship of the earth and the people on it to a deity or deities and a shared set of rules for living moral values that will enhance that relationship. A set of behaviors identified with worship is also commonly shared. Religious identity may include membership in a worldwide organized religion (e.g., Islam, Christianity, Judaism, Buddhism, Taoism) or in smaller (but also worldwide) sects belonging to each of the larger religions (e.g., Catholic or Protestant Christianity, or Orthodox,

Conservative, Reformed, or Hasidic Judaism). Religious identity may also include a large variety of spiritualistic religions, sometimes called pagan or "godless" religions, that are often but not always associated with indigenous peoples in the Americas and other parts of the world. Like ethnicity, religious affiliation can engender intense loyalty, as witnessed through the actions of members of the Al Qaeda or ISIS (Islamic State) networks found throughout the Middle East and North Africa, or among the Taliban in Afghanistan in their attempts to live out their perceived religious missions (even though most would agree that these so-called Islamic fundamentalist groups do not adhere to any of their true religious principles). Religion also engenders a sense of belonging or community and pride in a people's shared history. Because religious identity involves individuals' relationship with the earth and with forces perceived to be greater than themselves, the cultural meaning of religion is often expressed in terms of a rigid sense of righteousness and virtue that is linked to a belief in salvation or the possibility of an eternal life after death. It is thus often an extremely powerful determiner of behavior.

8. Geographic location/region are culturally defined by the characteristics (topographical features, natural resources) of the ecological environment in which a person lives. Geographic location may include the characteristics of a neighborhood or community (rural, suburban, urban) and/or the natural and climatic features of a region (mountainous, desert, plains, coastal, hot, cold, wet, dry). It has been argued that, in the United States, people's regional identity functions in the same way as their national heritage. Thus, southerners, westerners, and midwesterners are identified and often identify themselves as members of ethnic-like groups, with the same kinds of loyalties, sense of community, and language traits.

The cultural meanings of geographic location are expressed in terms of the knowledge a person has of how to survive in and use the resources of a particular area. This knowledge may include what foods are "good" (and how to grow and harvest them), how to protect oneself from the natural elements and common dangers of the locality, even how to spend leisure time. This kind of knowledge also applies to the type of community a person lives in. It is commonly acknowledged, for example, that "city people," "country people," and "suburban people" can be quite different from one another. The nature of that difference stems in part from their familiarity with, and knowledge about, how to live in a particular kind of community with its particular resources and dangers.

9. Age is culturally defined according to the length of time an individual has lived and the state of physical and mental development that individual has attained. Chronological age is measured in different ways by different social groups or societies. Some calculate it in calendar years, others by natural cycles such as phases of the moon, and still others by the marking of major natural or social events.

Mental and physical development is also measured differentially, in much the same way and under many of the same circumstances that health is determined. Most humans view such development as a matter of stages, but the nature and particular characteristics of each stage may differ widely. In most Western societies, for example, age cohort groups are usually identified as infancy, childhood, adolescence, adulthood, and old age. "Normal" development markers include the acquisition of motor and language skills (infancy and childhood), the ability to understand and use abstract concepts (childhood and adolescence), and the ability to assume responsibility for oneself and others (adolescence and adulthood). In other societies, these cohort groups may differ. For example, in many non-Western societies, the cohort group we define as adolescents may not exist at all, and the classifications of childhood and old age may be longer or shorter.

The cultural meaning of age is usually expressed in terms of the abilities and responsibilities attributed to it. Thus, in the United States, childhood is prolonged (hence the category of adolescence), and adult responsibilities are not expected until at least age 18, if not age 21 or beyond. In other societies (and indeed in the United States prior to the 20th century), childhood is shorter, and adult responsibilities are assumed at younger ages.

10. Sexuality is culturally defined on the basis of particular patterns of sexual self-identification, behavior, and interpersonal relationships (Herek, 1986). Different from sex (male and female) and gender (masculine and feminine), sexuality refers to who one is attracted to. There is growing evidence that a person's sexual orientation may be, in part, a function of that person's innate biological characteristics (LeVay & Hamer, 1994). Culturally speaking, sexuality is tied to a number of factors, including sexual behavior, gender identity (both internal and external), affiliation, and role behavior. Like health, sexuality has a variety of orientations, including lesbian, gay, straight, and bisexual. Traditionally, those who deviate from socially approved norms are often socially ostracized, bullied, and sometimes physically abused or even killed, as was the case of the Matthew Shepard murder in 1998. In traditional mainstream U.S. culture, the prevailing view of sexuality is bimodal: only male and female are identified as possibilities. In other societies, additional possibilities are available. The Lakota Sioux, for example, approve four sexual orientations: biological males who possess largely masculine traits, biological males who possess largely feminine traits, biological females who possess largely feminine traits, and biological females who possess largely masculine traits. The female-identified male in Lakota society is called *berdache* and is accorded high honor because he possesses multiple traits and characteristics. Berdache tend to be teachers and artists, and if a berdache takes an interest in one's child or children, it is considered to be an advantage. In contemporary U.S. society, as well as in many other nations around the world, acceptance of same-sex marriage and transgendered individuals is becoming more frequent and increasingly accepted.

11. Language is often defined as a system of shared vocal sounds and nonverbal behaviors that enables members of a particular group to communicate with one another. Language may be the most significant source of cultural learning because it is through language that most other cultural knowledge is acquired. Indeed, some researchers consider language and the category systems available in language to be *the* determiner of culture (Sapir, 1949; Vygotsky, 1962; Whorf, 1968).

Considerable research on the relation of brain function to language gives evidence that human beings are hardwired for language development at a particular stage in brain development (Chomsky, 1966). That is, children who are in the company of other people appear to be programmed to learn whatever spoken language or sign system is used around them. Children even appear to invent their own language systems, complete with syntactical structures, if no other language is available (Chomsky, 1966). Language is meaningful in terms of both its verbal properties (what we name things, people, ideas) and its nonverbal properties (its norms regarding interpersonal distance, meaningful gestures, and so forth). Because language literally represents reality, the types and meanings of verbal and nonverbal behavior in any society or social group will reflect people's experience with their surroundings and the ways in which they interact with it. More than any other characteristic, language is a window into another person's life.

12. Social status is culturally defined on the basis of the prestige, social esteem, and honor accorded an individual or group by other social groups or by society (Berger & Berger, 1972). Social status cuts across the other categories. Every social group or society appears to construct hierarchies of honor, prestige, and value with which to "sort out" its members, often on the basis of such attributes as race, age, gender, ability, and so forth. In some cases, social status varies with social class; in many other cases, however, social class does not explain a person's status in a social group or society. Thus persons may occupy a high place in the class system in terms of income and power but not be accorded prestige or honor. The children of a newly wealthy family who can well afford to send them to Harvard, for example, may have little prestige among the sons and daughters of inherited wealth. Similarly, there may be people accorded high status in the society who occupy relatively low-class positions. In U.S. society, many entertainers and sports figures fit this description. Social status is normally expressed through social roles. Thus, status assigned to a person's gender may determine the role that person plays in any situation; an individual's health status may determine the role he or she plays as a "sick" person; an individual's social class status may determine the role that person plays as a member of the upper, middle, or working class; and so forth.

While there is some overlap among these 12 attributes of culture, the important point to remember is that a particular society or social group culturally defines each of them. The cultural identity of all individuals (i.e., their knowledge, attitudes, values, and skills) is formed through their experience with these 12 attributes. Such experience is gained through contact with socializing agents such as family, house of worship, workplace, peer group, and the various forms of mass media. These socializing agents can be thought of as transmitters of cultural attributes. It is through these socializing agents (depicted in Figure 3.3) that individuals acquire the cultural knowledge that is defined by race, ethnicity, gender, language, and social class.

Figure 3.3

Socializing Agents That
Transmit Culture

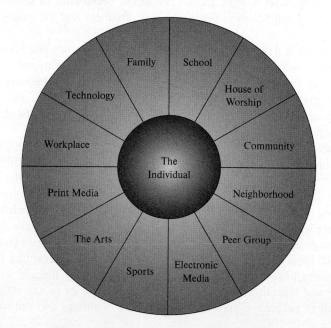

How Culture Is Learned: The Socializing Agents

We acquire the specific knowledge, attitudes, skills, and values that form our cultural identity through a variety of socializing agents that mediate the sources of cultural identity and give them a particular "cultural spin." Thus a person's understanding of race, gender, social class, disability, age, sexuality, and so forth depends in part on how that socializing agent is interpreted by those particular families, schools, neighborhoods, peer groups, workplaces, houses of worship, and communities that the person affiliates with at a particular time. Each of these socializing agents has its own slightly different interpretation of a particular cultural attribute, which it passes on to its members.

In contemporary social life, some socializing agents, such as families and peer groups, operate face-to-face, while others, such as the mass media, use technology to operate from a distance. Television, films, the Internet, various social media, and the music industry, for example, exert significant influence on the self-perceived identity of many young people. Referred to by some researchers as the "third educator" (following family and school), television influences young people's acquisition of basic language and visual and aural skills. It also influences their ideas of "appropriate" dress, language, attitudes, and values.

Cortes (2000) suggested that the media functions much like the school curriculum, serving as a powerful teaching medium. Especially with regard to intercultural understanding and the school curriculum, he said, "the media curriculum is chaotic, inconsistent, multivocal, in many respects unplanned and uncoordinated, laden with conflicting messages, and offering myriad perspectives" (p. 19). In addition, the media often blurs information with entertainment, creating confusion in the minds of the many people. For example, a survey of viewers of the television show *America's Most Wanted* revealed that 50% considered it to be a news program while 28% considered it entertainment (Rosenstiel, 1989). Where do we draw the line on many of the more popular reality shows broadcast almost daily? How much of them are, in fact, reality, and how much is scripted entertainment? These media lessons not only may affect young people's picture of themselves and others, but also may affect the picture that adults have of them.

The media also teaches about older people, and again with conflicting messages. The visual image of the woman who has "fallen and can't get up" describes older people as weak, helpless, and slightly hysterical—and in need of a product that will alert some caregiving agency that she needs help. Conversely, commercials for vitamins for older adults often depict them as active people—hiking, swimming, traveling—no doubt as a result of taking the promoted vitamins. Because we live in a nation that is growing older, we can expect more commercials defining older people as active rather than passive.

Other technological tools, such as computers, microwave ovens, and smartphones appear to exert significant influence on our notions of time. Teachers and other human service providers have noticed, for example, that over the last 30 years or so both children and adults have exhibited shorter attention spans. People seem to have become accustomed to receiving information and accomplishing tasks in shorter periods of time and are thus less likely or unable to persevere in tasks that take a long time.

Other socializing agents of note include the performing and visual arts and, in the United States at least, sports. These widely available carriers of cultural messages help shape people's attitudes, values, and behavior. The aesthetic value of design, language, music, dance, and theatre, as well as ideals of moral and ethical behavior, are presented through the arts. Likewise, behavioral ideals such as fair play, personal achievement, and competition are taught through sports. It is also true that other qualities may be taught through these media; violence, for example, is an increasing part of movies, television, and sports. The contemporary nature of national sports teams as bottom-line businesses comes increasingly into competition with our cultural interest in providing a level playing field for all competitors.

Figure 3.3 provides a visual overview of how cultural knowledge is filtered by a variety of socializing agents to individuals through experience. Although sources of cultural knowledge (race, language, sexuality, etc.) are universal and appear in all cultures, the socializing agents (family, schools, media, etc.) that transmit them vary considerably from one culture to another. In most industrialized societies, for example, a wide variety of socializing agents bombard people daily, often with contradictory messages. In agriculturally oriented societies, on the other hand, a few primary socializing agents (e.g., family and gender group) may share the bulk of the culture-filtering process. As a result, individuals in different cultures develop very different worldviews.

When Culture Is Learned: The Process of Socialization

One way to begin to understand how individuals acquire cultural knowledge, attitudes, values, and skills from the social groups with whom they have meaningful contact is to look closely at the concept of **socialization.** Socialization is the process by which people learn the norms that are expected of them by a particular group. These patterns may include the acquisition of a particular language, knowledge of social roles and role behavior, and particular understandings of all aspects of the physical and social environment and normative behaviors toward it. Berger and Berger (1972) noted that "the socialized part of the self is commonly called identity" (p. 62).

There is some consensus that the processes of socialization can occur at three stages of life: (1) *primary socialization*, which involves the socialization of infants and young children by families and other early caregivers; (2) *secondary socialization*, which in most contemporary societies involves the neighborhood, the religious affiliation, the peer group, and the school as well as various media and other influences that surround and come into the home; and (3) *adult socialization*, which involves the socialization of adults into roles, settings, and situations for which they may have been unprepared by primary and secondary socialization. Some examples of adult socialization include taking a new job, marrying, moving to a new area, or becoming a parent (Sheehy, 1994).

These stages of the socialization process are not entirely discrete but rather interact with one another throughout our lives. What we learn as children can be reinforced or modified, for good or ill, by what we learn as we grow up and have more experiences. In each of its three stages, the purpose of socialization is to teach the learner those habits of mind and action that will make him or her a loyal and functional member of a particular group. The use of the word *habits* in this context is important, for it points to another aspect of socialization, which is that the learner should internalize socially approved patterns of behavior so that he or she will voluntarily—and with little thought or effort—think and behave in an appropriate manner.

One important aspect of the internalization of particular knowledge, beliefs, attitudes, values, and behaviors is that the process by which they are acquired is, in a sense, a secret. Most people remember very little about their own socialization, the assumptions they make about the world, what has conditioned them, and the various cultural patterns that have become so ingrained in their makeup as to become nearly invisible.

Primary Socialization and Cultural Similarities

Most people share some aspects of primary socialization that are common to all or most of the people of their primary group. The primary group "Americans," for instance, traditionally would include those who have been born in the United States and speak English as a native language. Consider, for example, the rules they have learned about eating. When food is put before most Americans, they expect that it will be placed on a plate or in a bowl on a table at which they expect to sit on chairs. Once seated, the American automatically reaches for utensils called forks, knives, and spoons; cuts meat with the fork in the left hand and the knife in the right hand (except for left-handed folks); and then switches the fork to the right hand to carry the food to the mouth. In the same situation, a British person expects the plates, bowls, table, and chairs; cuts meat with the fork and knife in the same hands as an American; but then does *not* switch the fork to the right hand but continues to use it in the left hand. In the same situation, a Japanese person may expect the food to be placed on a low table, at which he or she will kneel, and the utensils used to carry food to the mouth will be two long, slender wooden or plastic implements that many Westerners call chopsticks. And in yet other cultural contexts, the hand and fingers (particularly the right hand) would be used to pick up or scoop food. On a global scale, it is thought that roughly one third of people prefer to eat with knives and forks, one third with chopsticks, and one third with their hands. In all cases, the people eating will not consciously think about these expectations and behaviors, they will simply expect and do them because they are "right," "appropriate," and "proper." Friedman's (1984) book *How My Parents Learned to Eat* is an interesting children's story that discusses Japanese and American eating customs and can be used to introduce such similarities and differences to children.

Within this general "American" set of rules for eating (as within any large nation-state), however, there are many variations. How formally we set our tables, how many utensils we use, whether our plates are served for us or we serve ourselves (and how many different plates we use), what kinds of food we eat, what we commonly use as a beverage (water, milk, wine, soda or pop, coffee, tea), and whether we bring the beverage to the table in its original container or in a pitcher, all depend somewhat on the region in which we live; the ethnic, social class, and religious origins of our parents; our ages; and so forth. No matter what the particulars are of our personal and family rules for eating, however, we believe they are "normal" in part because we have internalized them.

Here is another example of both the secret nature of primary socialization and the degree to which knowledge acquired through primary socialization is internalized: the way people learn to speak. Do you remember how you learned to talk? If you have taken another language in school, perhaps it was difficult for you—but your *own* language, now that was easy! Or so it seems. It might, however, be very difficult for you to teach a non-English speaker to correctly pronounce the sentence "Can you tell me the time?" when that person might more easily say "Can you dell me the dime?" What might you tell this person about English that would correct his or her pronunciation? Go ahead; try it. How would you teach someone to make the correct sounds?

Most people begin to play with their tongue, noting supposed differences in where it is placed in relation to the teeth. But that is not where the distinction lies. If you have determined that a little puff of air passes out of the mouth when the *t* sound is made in such words as *tell* and *time* that is not passed in words beginning with the letter *d,* you are on the right track to discovering the secret. Correct speakers of English aspirate their stops; that is, some air passes out of the mouth when such letters as *t, p,* or *k* are spoken. This aspect of pronunciation is considered a secret because even though most of us differentiate these sounds quite regularly and easily, you probably were not able to describe the difference to others. This practice has become so much a part of your behavior that you take it for granted; you must consciously think about it in order to describe it to others. This is not the end of the secret, however. If you think about it some more, you will realize that English speakers aspirate their stops only at the beginning and in the middle of words, not at the end. We do not aspirate the *t* in *hit, bit,* or *cat.*

That you have learned these rules is quite clear; you use them all the time. How these rules were learned, however, is considerably less clear. They were probably not taught in formal sessions with your parents or by reading appropriate language texts. Indeed, you may not have been able to talk about them at all because you did not have the language to use words such as *aspirate* or *stops.* Rather, you probably learned these rules through trial and error and with much reinforcement while you learned to speak your native language. This particular language pattern is often hidden, as are its results. The same is true for other aspects of cultural learning; they, too, can be conceived as patterns that are hidden from our conscious thought and behavior.

Few people receive formal instruction in how to be an appropriate member of any particular cultural group. Rather, people are culturally socialized by observing others, by trial and error, and by continuous reinforcement. In other words, cultural knowledge such as the rules for speaking and eating are learned experientially, not cognitively. Consequently, it becomes difficult for many people to speak comfortably about the cross-cultural problems they might encounter. One of the difficulties people often face in their intercultural encounters, then, is that while they may feel uncomfortable or unsure in a given situation, they may be unable to talk about the problem with any specificity. Thus, as is natural to most, people may try to avoid situations in which they feel discomfort—certainly *not* one of the long-term goals of multicultural or intercultural education. A reasonable goal is for people to become more knowledgeable and thus conversant about the issues at play in cross-cultural interaction so that when problems or misunderstandings arise, we have the cognitive and linguistic tools, as well as the comfort level, to inquire into and talk about our differences.

Secondary Socialization

Perhaps the most important source of secondary socialization in most people's lives is the school. It is in school that individuals are often introduced to ideas and values that differ from those they acquired at home. In fact, one of the purposes of education is to "lead forth" or "liberate" individuals from the narrow confines of their primary socialization—in a sense, to expand their cultural identities. The difficulties of this process of alteration, however, should not be minimized, especially in situations where the cultural knowledge, beliefs, values, and skills required by the school may be in conflict with those of the home. Still, teachers often find themselves attempting to serve as "change agents" of their students' cultural identities.

The main goal of most school socialization in the United States has traditionally been to teach the rules of middle-class attitudes, values, and behavior. This cultural socialization to the middle class is no less a secret than the varied cultural socialization of individual families. The school, like the family, does not make cultural socialization explicit; it is simply taken for granted as "normal." Few people ever take a formal course in the variations of cultural knowledge that exist, and they almost never examine their own cultural patterns in contrast to others. Few ever learn why they behave the way they do, or why they think many of the things they think. Fewer still ever evaluate the assumptions they make. People thus generally lack the concepts and vocabulary with which to talk about these things. Yet cultural patterns that are a given, along with the assumptions, beliefs, and behavior associated with them, often do guide us along whether we are aware of it or not.

There is yet another aspect of socialization that must be analyzed: the power of early socialization when viewed from the inside. It is certainly true that as we grow up and meet people outside our childhood social groups, we learn that there are a variety of ways to interact with the physical and social environment. As children, however, we experience the imposition of patterns of socialization as absolute (Berger & Berger, 1972). There are two simple reasons for this absoluteness: (1) the power of adults in relation to young children, and (2) ignorance of any other possibilities. Berger and Berger described the nature of this experience in the following way:

> Psychologists differ in their view as to whether the child experiences the adults at this stage of life as being very much under his control (because they are generally so responsive to his needs) or whether he feels continually threatened by them (because he is so dependent upon them). However this may be, there can be no question that, objectively speaking, adults have overwhelming power in the situation. The child can, of course, resist them, but the probable outcome of any conflict is a victory on the part of the adults. It is they who control most of the rewards that he craves and most of the sanctions that he fears. Indeed, the simple fact that most children are eventually socialized affords simple proof of this proposition. At the same time, it is obvious that the small child is ignorant of any alternatives to the patterns that are being imposed upon him. The adults confront him with a world—for him, it is *the* world. It is only much later that he discovers that there are alternatives to this particular world, that his parents' world is relative in space and time, and that quite different patterns are possible (p. 51).

Some Consequences of Socialization

Ethnocentrism

Because of the absoluteness with which the child experiences socialization, he or she begins, early on, to share the human tendency to view the world from his or her own perspective and to begin to believe that his or her way is, if not the only way to view the world, certainly the *best* way. This perspective, called **ethnocentrism**, refers to the tendency people have to evaluate others according to their own standards, and it is an almost universal result of socialization. Think again about the example of eating behaviors: When confronted by someone from Bangladesh who may eat with his or her hands, most Americans would consider such behavior not as simply different but as *beneath* their own, and may make negative judgments about the person. While a certain degree of ethnocentrism serves to bind people together, it can also become a serious obstacle when those who have internalized different ideas and behaviors begin to interact with one another.

One major expression of ethnocentrism is a strong *resistance to change*. People have a tendency to resist change, even under the best of circumstances, as illustrated in the story of the Wheat Religion people in Chapter 1. If people believe that their way of doing things is best and if they have the power to choose to continue in familiar ways, why should they change? Consider the case of the United States and the adoption of metrics. At this time, all countries of the world have adopted the metric system as their primary means of measurement except the United States, Liberia, and Myanmar. We continue to resist this change despite the difficulties it causes travelers, manufacturers, and others who must interact in a variety of ways with people from other nations. Failure of a Lockheed Martin engineering team to convert English measures to metric values used by NASA scientists was the cause of the September 1999 loss of the Mars planet orbiter, a spacecraft that smashed into the planet Mars instead of reaching a safe orbit. This oversight resulted in the destruction of a $125 million spacecraft and jeopardized the entire Mars program.

While this example comes from life outside of schools, other examples of ethnocentric behavior do not. There is, for example, continued insistence on the part of some educators and politicians that we need to strengthen a Eurocentric curriculum in our schools on the grounds that a curriculum based on "the best of Western civilization" is the most valuable preparation any student could have. However, there is increasing interest among some educators to consider alternative perspectives. Consider this response to American educators in the 1700s about sending Native American children to American schools:

> You who are wise must know that different Nations have different Conceptions of things and you will therefore not take it amiss if our Ideas of this kind of Education happen not to be the same as yours. We have had some Experiences of it. Several of our Young People were formally brought up at the Colleges of the Northern Provinces: they were instructed in all your Sciences, but when they came back to us they were bad Runners, ignorant of every means of living in the woods . . . neither fit for Hunters, Warriors, nor Councellors, they were totally good for nothing.
>
> We are, however, not the less obliged by your kind Offer, though we decline accepting it. And to show our grateful Sense of it, if the Gentlemen of Virginia will send us a Dozen of their Sons, we will take Care of their Education, instruct them in all we know, and make Men of them (as cited in Blaisdell, 2000).

More recently, the debate over Afrocentric curriculum efforts is, for example, one that should be examined quite closely. Can a school experience that embraces an African perspective effectively reach African American children better than the standard Eurocentric curriculum? Is this curriculum worth embracing and evaluating? After years of emphasis on common curriculum content, evaluated by standardized tests that are close to national in scope, and increased pressure and movement toward the adoption of Common Core curriculum standards across the nation, American policymakers (and many educators) are increasingly less open to variations in curriculum driven by differences in the cultural backgrounds of American students. Yet, if culturally driven curricula are to continue to be a part of our educational system, expressions of ethnocentricity on the part of all sides in that debate must become more aware of ways in which their ethnocentric attitudes become a barrier to finding the "good" in diverse approaches to knowledge and skills.

Perception and Categorization

Another result of socialization is that we learn to *perceive* the world and to *categorize* information about people and things in our environment in particular ways. Perception and categorization are both cognitive processes that are shaped by socialization. People receive millions of bits of information each and every day through their senses. To think that people can respond to each individual piece of information is expecting too much; a person's physical and emotional systems would be overwhelmed. Because of the need to simplify things, people organize their world into categories; into each category they put items that share similar characteristics. People then generally respond to the category to which an individual item belongs.

Perception refers to the stimulation of the sense organs; that is, to what people immediately report seeing, hearing, feeling, tasting, and smelling. While no two people have exactly the same physiological structure and therefore no two people perceive stimuli identically, those with healthy nervous systems tend to perceive similar things in the environment in similar ways. Physicists, for example, tell us that the human eye can discern more than 8 million colors as distinguished by variations in wavelength. There is no practical reason, nor is it humanly possible, even to consider all these fine variations of shade and hue let alone to react to each individual color. Individuals, therefore, need some schema with which to group colors, the most familiar probably being the one based on the spectrum in which red, orange, yellow, green, blue, indigo, and violet are the major colors. When asked about the color of the sky, a Westerner's response typically is "blue." A sapphire is blue, oceans depicted on a map are blue, and robin's eggs are blue. Grass, however, is green, as are the leaves of most trees and the inside of a kiwi fruit.

In traditional Japanese language, however, the term *aoi* refers to colors that span blue and green wavelengths. When asked the color of the sky, a Japanese individual's response would be "aoi." When asked the color of grass, the response would again be "aoi." How would you explain these responses? Certainly the entire Japanese population is not color-blind! Rather, whereas European Americans have learned to place these particular stimuli into different schemata, traditional Japanese have learned to place them in the same one.

Clearly, sense perception alone is not sufficient. We also need to make sense out of the busy world around us, and to do so, we utilize schemata. Another term for such schemata is *category*. **Categorization** is the cognitive process through which human beings simplify their world by putting similar stimuli into the same group. What kind of categories we use, how narrow or broad they are, and what meanings are attached to them are all shaped by culture and acquired through socialization. A good example of the relation between perception and categorization is the dog: how people perceive the animal, and how they have learned to respond to the stimuli. All people will see, or perceive, the dog in a similar way, but they will certainly think about it differently. Most Westerners think of dogs as pets, as companions, and in some cases, as important members of their families. A traditional Muslim, confronted by the same creature, might consider the dog filthy, a lowly animal, and something to be avoided at all costs—similar to the reaction a North American might have to a pig. People in some Asian or Pacific Island nations might place a dog in the category of food. It is not uncommon to find dog meat as part of the human diet in many parts of the world.

The concept of a *prototype image* is critical in the analysis of categories. For most categories that humans create, there is one set of attributes or criteria that best characterizes the members of that category. In other words, there is a clear example of what the category encompasses. This example becomes a "summary" of the group and is the image most often thought of when the category is mentioned. If you were asked to think about a bird, for instance, you might conjure up an image of a creature about 8 or 9 inches long (beak to tail feathers), brown or perhaps reddish in color, that has feathers, flies, and nests in trees. You probably did not think of a turkey, penguin, ostrich, or even a chicken. For someone socialized in or near the jungles of South America, the prototypic image of a bird might be larger and more colorful because those birds that we call exotic (e.g., parrots) are part of their everyday world. Yet robins, parrots, and penguins have all the critical attributes that characterize members of the bird family; they all have feathers, beaks, and hollow or lightweight bones, and they all lay eggs. Teachers must examine what their own prototype image of a student is and how they will respond to those who do not fit neatly into this image.

Stereotypes

Categories help people to simplify the world around them. That is, people put stimuli that have common characteristics into one category and then respond to the group. People do not, for instance, respond to each and every chair or table when they walk into a room but refer to them in their broader context of chairs, tables, or furniture.

People respond in a similar manner in their interactions with people. **Stereotypes** are examples of categories of people. Socially constructed categories designed to simplify the identification of individuals who are in some way "other" frequently become negative stereotypes associated with groups. Here we find that the processes of perception and categorization along with ethnocentrism combine to create a potentially harmful situation. Although any cultural group may teach its members to categorize other groups either positively or negatively, most stereotypes end up as negative labels placed on individuals simply because they are members of a particular group.

In the most general sense, the word *stereotype* refers to any sort of summary representation (or prototypic image) that obscures the differences *within* a group (Brislin, 1993). Stereotypes obtain their power by providing categories that appear to encode a significant amount of information in a concise manner and that help us avoid having to pay serious attention to all the sensory data that is available. Negative stereotypes also enable us to keep our ethnocentric ideas intact by preventing us from seeing contradictory evidence before our very eyes. For example, it is much easier and quicker for us to think of all girls as stereotypically weak or passive than it is to notice that at least some of the girls in our classroom are stronger and more aggressive than the boys. Indeed, if we do notice such a thing, we tend to label those particular girls as "unfeminine," which helps us avoid the larger task of accurately differentiating one girl from another and also allows us to maintain a cultural value that teaches that boys are supposed to be strong and aggressive while girls are not. Stereotypic conceptions of others can be acquired through both early and later socialization and are powerful insofar as they promote group solidarity and ethnocentric beliefs.

Some Limits on Socialization

Although perception and categorization both depend in part on the cultural knowledge and meanings associated with the physical and social environment in which a child is socialized, and although early socialization is a powerful factor in the development of identity, it is also true that the power of socialization has limits. Three of these limitations are particularly important to educators.

First, socialization is limited to some extent by the nature of the child's physical organism. For example, it is true that an infant or very young child can learn any language and any particular pattern of living, but it is not true that any child can be taught beyond his or her biological limits. Socialization to color wavelength categories, for example, may be limited by color blindness to red and green. Similarly, socialization to musical sounds will not necessarily produce an operatic singer. However, sensory limits in one area may be, and often are, compensated for by increased attention to other senses, as in people with hearing limitations.

Second, because socialization is an unending process that is never completely finished, its powers of control are never absolute. Because a child is socialized according to one set of patterns (language, situational behavior, understanding of role, categorization) does not mean that he or she cannot learn new patterns. Indeed, the extension of socialization beyond childhood knowledge is one of the chief purposes of formal schooling.

Third, socialization is limited in its power because human beings are not simply passive recipients of socialization; they always act on that socialization in some way. Individuals resist or reject accepted norms, they reinterpret accepted norms, and they create new kinds of normative behavior. Thus socialization can be seen not as an all-powerful force that totally molds the human creature but rather as a transactional process through which individuals are shaped but not totally determined. Your future students might become Nobel Prize winners, shuttle astronauts, or famous inventors.

Each of these limits on socialization is a resource on which educators can build. However, as Dewey (1916/1966) noted repeatedly, the most effective learning takes place when it begins with what the child already knows and moves on from there. It is important for teachers to understand not only the nature and purpose of cultural socialization in general but also the specifics of the cultural patterns to which they and their students have been socialized.

Understanding Cultural Differences

Variations in Cultural Environments: Returning to Beechland Heights

Figure 3.4 summarizes the discussion of the culture-learning process and points out its complexity in such multicultural societies as the United States, Canada, Australia, or England. Although the sources of cultural identity are the same for all societies, each society—indeed, each community—varies considerably in the number and character of its socializing agents. Thus, in a technologically less complex and relatively homogeneous society like the traditional Maasai of Kenya or Tanzania, the sources of cultural identity shown in Figure 3.4 may be transmitted through fewer socializing agents, most notably the family and the members of other families in the community. Because these families have nearly every aspect of life in common, there is likely to be little conflict in the way the various attributes of culture (e.g., age, sexuality, social status) are transmitted to the individual in such a society. The same, by the way, may be said of small towns and villages anywhere in the world, although much of this is changing due to the ubiquitous presence of technology and social media that is rapidly bringing people the world over into closer contact.

In complex societies like the United States and many other industrialized nations, however, most individuals interact daily with a vast array of socializing agents, each of which puts a slightly different spin on each of the cultural attributes. For example,

Figure 3.4
The Culture-Learning
Process

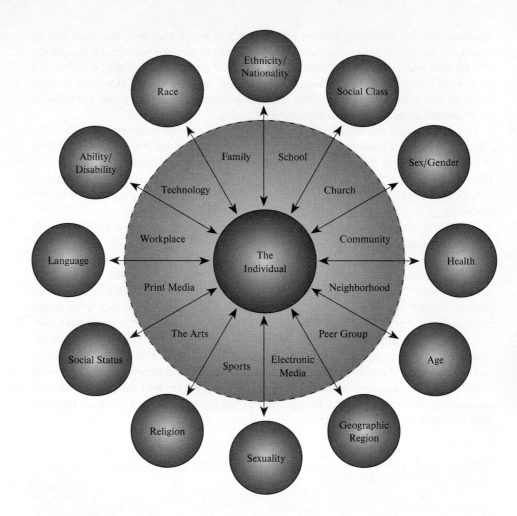

your place of worship is likely to have a significantly different view of sexuality than your peer group or your favorite television program. Do you think, for instance, that in Beechland Heights, Dinorah Rodriguez finds a discrepancy between the teachings of her Catholic upbringing and the sexual ideas she views on music videos or television's sitcoms or soap operas? This daily interaction with a variety of socializing agents, each of which may have a unique interpretation of cultural attributes, means that individuals are bombarded with a variety of conflicting cultural messages.

Furthermore, individuals are not simply passive recipients of incoming messages. Once a message is received, each individual interprets and acts (or not) on its content according to his or her own personality and prior experiences. This interactive aspect of culture learning is depicted in Figure 3.4 by the directional arrows that connect the individual to various socializing agents and through them to the universal cultural attributes. In short, culture learning is a two-way process in which individuals are both forming and being formed by incoming cultural messages. And in many ways, no two individuals construct their world in the same manner.

Perhaps another example would be helpful. Gollnick and Chinn (2002) described two hypothetical women who live in Chicago and who are both 30 years old, white, middle class, Polish American, and Catholic. One woman identifies very strongly with her Polish American heritage and her church in the context of living in Chicago, which has a large Polish American population. She does not identify very strongly with her age group, her class status, or her gender. The other woman defines herself as a feminist, is equally interested in her urban life, and is conscious of her age but does not pay too much attention to her ethnic background, her religion, or her social class. The significance of these patterns lies not in each woman's self-definition but in the attitudes, values, knowledge, and behavior that such definition entails.

The first woman may well spend more time with family than with nonrelated friends, may be a member of a right-to-life group, might choose wine rather than Perrier, may be knowledgeable about and participate in Polish ethnic organizations, and is likely to understand, if not speak, Polish.

The second woman may find her most intimate companions among women's groups, be pro-choice in her stand on abortion, choose to live in the city despite the possibility of living in a small town or the country, and—if she does not have children—hear her biological clock ticking.

This example illustrates how individuals operating in relatively similar settings with relatively similar environmental demands and socializing agents can develop distinctly different cultures. Perhaps you can begin to imagine how different groups and individuals operating in different settings with differing environmental demands and using different sets of socializing agents can develop distinctly different cultures. Figure 3.4 can help you recognize the multitude of factors that enter into the cultural identity equation.

In addition, consider that each of the two outer circles in Figure 3.4 can spin, so that every cultural attribute can be filtered differently by each of the socializing agents, which might combine differently with a variety of personality types. For instance, a passive-reflective individual would interact with the many incoming cultural messages differently than a volatile, nonreflective person might. You can begin to see how complex culture learning can be; how variable individuals can be in the manner in which they receive, process, and output the various influences they encounter; and how these messages can be transformed into differing behavior and belief patterns. Although you might think that in reality an infinite number of cultural formations is possible, the three parts in Figure 3.4 can be used with a little practice as a diagnostic tool for analyzing any multicultural or intercultural situation.

Despite this enormous potential for variation among individuals and within groups, similarities or generalizations can be made about groups of people, and these generalizations are referred to throughout this book. People have a tendency to use information that may or may not be reflective of all individuals within a given group. We must always be cautious when using culture-specific information to discuss whole groups because there will always be individuals who do not fit. Individual differences between two people who belong to the same group may be greater than between two people who belong to different groups.

Generalizations differ from stereotypes about people, and this point must be kept in mind. **Generalizations** refer to the tendency of a majority of people in a cultural group to hold certain values and beliefs and to engage in certain patterns of behavior. Thus this information can be supported by research and can be applied to a large percentage of a population or group. Stereotypes refer to the application of a specific piece of information (which may be a generalization or possibly an inaccurate piece of information) to *every* person in that group. Thus, unsupported information blurs specific knowledge about other individuals. Such **stereotypes** would, for instance, say that Steven Wong *must* get very good grades because he is Chinese and male, and Shameka Collins *ought* to be more interested in a secretarial job because she is African

American and female. We must keep in mind, however, that these stereotypes are typically the kind made by some white European Americans about Chinese people and African Americans. They are not what Chinese people and African Americans think about other Chinese people and African Americans. Clearly, such stereotypes are in error, as life in Beechland Heights demonstrates. A generalization, on the other hand, would suggest that U.S. European Americans are more individualistic when compared to the Chinese. We can document this in the research literature and apply it in the majority of cases when we are comparing the two cultures. It would be a stereotype, however, to say that Americans are individualistic all of the time. Certainly they exhibit collective behavior; for instance, when the traffic signal turns red most will stop. But the majority of the time the majority of European Americans will respond more individualistically when compared to the more collectively-oriented Chinese.

Variations in Cultural Attributes, Socializing Agents, and Cultural Learners

Building a positive attitude toward differences requires a more sophisticated way of looking at diversity. Much of the educational research on individual differences related to culture rests on three assumptions.

First, it is assumed that there is a standard or ideal against which difference can be seen, measured, or understood. In American society, people who are white, middle class, Protestant, English-speaking, healthy, physically and mentally typical, heterosexual, and male are said to make up the dominant cultural group. This "ideal" is, of course, a stereotype, much like the stereotypes of other cultural groups. It is important to note, however, that in the United States this particular stereotype refers to people who are socially privileged by virtue of birth characteristics over which they have little or no control (Howard, 1993; McIntosh, 1992). They are also educationally privileged in that their preschool socialization tends to prepare them for schooling, which is based on middle-class attitudes and values. One unfortunate consequence of belonging to this model group is that its members don't have to think of themselves as just one of many groups, each with its particular pattern of characteristics. Because they are the model group, they fit into perceived societal norms and thus do not have to think about their cultural patterns much at all (see the discussion of "white privilege" in Chapter 6). It also must be recognized that many of the nation's institutions have been built with this stereotypical model group as their foundation—the very framework that is in conflict with an increasing number of Americans.

The second assumption is that any deviation from this normative group is the very definition of difference. If a person speaks only Spanish rather than English or is Asian rather than European American; Jewish rather than Protestant; female rather than male; homosexual rather than heterosexual; working class rather than middle class; chronically ill or with a physical, emotional, or mental disability rather than healthy or typical, that person is likely to be perceived as different, and this difference is seen as a deficit to be overcome.

Finally, research on difference assumes that studies of large groups of children with certain characteristics will tell us a great deal about *all* children who possess some or most of these characteristics. This assumption has at least two serious problems, however. One is that while most research looks at only one characteristic at a time (e.g., gender or social class), no one ever belongs to just one group. Every individual simultaneously belongs to a number of groups: gender, social class, ethnic, and so forth. What these "single-characteristic" studies look for are central tendencies, ways in which each particular group of children is the same. This tendency to focus on one narrow point may be problematic and may encourage stereotypes. In and of themselves, such stereotypes are oversimplifications that tend to ignore the diversity of behavior differences that exist within a group.

While this single-characteristic research has taught us much, it does not enable us to focus on differences within groups, only on differences between groups. Furthermore, it compares groups according to only one characteristic. Thus, it does not help us understand how various characteristics (gender, social class, ethnicity, disability, etc.) combine with one another to form individual personalities and learning styles. For example, to be a deaf American who uses American Sign Language with other deaf people but uses English in interacting with hearing persons, as Humphries (1993) noted, is "to be bicultural and bilingual. This is just for starters. To be a deaf sign language user *and* African American, Hispanic, Asian/Pacific Islander, or American Indian in the United States is to be multicultural" (p. 15).

The second serious problem is that such research is most often statistical and tends to be interpreted by practitioners (and the public) in more global terms than its results warrant. If, for example, 65% of a given group of girls are found to be less successful at math than a comparable group of boys, the tendency is to believe that *all* girls are less successful at math. Although this generalization is not warranted by the research, it tends to become "true" in the minds of many people and thus to influence their behavior toward girls. Similarly, educators' attitudes and practices regarding students with disabilities have too often been based on broad labels or classifications such as *mental retardation, learning disability,* and *behavior disorder,* all of which obscure wide individual differences.

This book tries to avoid this problem of group stereotyping by looking at the universal connections between culture and learning. These connections are universal in the sense that they seem to apply to all people no matter what their various group affiliations. Figure 3.2 illustrates the sources of cultural knowledge that, when mixed together, form the cultural identity of *all* groups and individuals. These attributes are, for the most part, societal designations that have little meaning for the individual except as experienced through various socializing agents such as the family, house of worship, neighborhood, and peer group. In other words, individuals acquire a cultural identity within the larger society through their experiences with a variety of daily socializing agents.

What teachers must understand is that cultural-learning patterns vary considerably both between and within various cultural groups. Subsequent chapters describe in more detail some of the ways in which differences in cultural learning may lead to misunderstanding and conflict in schools and classrooms. This book also shows how these same differences can be used as a positive resource in learning-community classrooms. For now, play with the model in Figure 3.4. Ask yourself what the universal attributes mean to you in view of your own life experiences and which socializing agents have accounted for your understanding of them. Do the same for others who are close to you, such as family members and friends.

This book will ask these same questions about students, teachers, parents, and school administrators. With the help of the stories incorporated in this book for illustrative purposes and the cases presented for analysis, you will gradually become a sensitive and skillful teacher of *all* children, not just those whose cultural background matches your own. For, as you have seen in Beechland Heights, although a person may *seem* to be quite different from you by virtue of membership in a different race or class or religion, that person may also share some important cultural aspects with you. Even when an individual *seems* to have many cultural aspects in common with you, they may in fact be quite different in some important ways.

Critical Incident

Definitely College Material

Steven Wong is the child of a rather well-to-do professional family. Compared to many students in his community, he is well traveled, having had the opportunity to visit Hong Kong as well as other countries throughout Asia in order to maintain family and cultural connections. He has also had exposure to many different opportunities as he was growing up. To his parents' dismay, Steven is not excited about attending college, sometimes saying he would rather study the martial arts as a professional and at other times saying he would like to leave the area, perhaps move out west, and "find" himself.

- How might you explain Steven's apparent ambivalence toward college?
- How would you explain the fact that at times he wishes to pursue the martial arts and at other times he is seemingly uncommitted to anything?
- What factors in his school and community might contribute to his confusion? If he were to come to you, a teacher, asking for guidance, how would you advise him?

Critical Incident

Who, Exactly, Am I?

Dinorah Rodriguez is a first-generation immigrant to the United States; her parents are recent immigrants. Dinorah's father works in a local factory and has learned to speak English rather well. Her mother, however, has never worked outside the home and, as a result, has not had as strong a reason to learn English. Thus, at Dinorah's home, more Spanish is spoken than English, most meals reflect the family's Mexican tradition, and most interactions are restricted to family or others from the Latino community. Dinorah feels as if she is under great pressure, caught between two worlds, torn between the expectations and demands of her own family and culture and those of her American classmates. She is embarrassed to have friends over to her house and has always been uncomfortable when her parents attend school functions as well as parent-teacher conferences.

- What cultural factors can you identify that are immediately responsible for her conflicts?
- If Dinorah came to you, her teacher, asking for advice, what would you focus your attention on?
- If you were Dinorah, what would you want from your friends? From your teachers? From your parents?

Critical Incident

What's Wrong With a Golf Scholarship?

Michael Williams, who comes from a working-class family and was raised by his grandparents and mother, is planning to go to college, although he does not have a particular major in mind. He is, however, pretty certain that he would like to continue with his golf and hopes to obtain a college scholarship through the sport. Many people in his community would have expected him to play basketball rather than golf.

- To what would you attribute the expectations others have of him?
- To what would you attribute his love of golf?

- What obstacles might Michael encounter as he pursues his goals?
- If he came to you, his teacher, troubled because many people did not seem to support his wishes, what advice might you give him?

Critical Incident

Am I Black or White?

Shameka Collins lives a life many people could not imagine. Being biracial in American society has presented her with both numerous opportunities and many challenges. Many doors were open to her, especially when she was young, but since her father began working away from home, she feels as though things have changed.

Shameka identifies herself as African American now, not because of what she thinks but because of what everybody else thinks. It's just become easier, she says. In seventh and eighth grades, soon after her father left, Shameka saw a counselor on a regular basis. She told her counselor that sometimes she doesn't feel like a black person because in many ways she was raised white. When she was younger, she would tell the counselor, she used to wish that she was just one race, because then she could say that's what she was and it was less confusing for people. But that wish created a dilemma for her. She felt that if she just said she was black, then she was denying her white side. And if she said she was white, she was denying her black side.

- How might you help Shameka understand her internal conflicts?
- If you were Shameka's classroom teacher, what might you do to make things easier in the classroom for her, or others like her?

Critical Incident

Where Do I Fit In?

Growing up in Beechland Heights, Jacob Goldsmith knew there were people from a variety of backgrounds. But because he attended the Jewish day school until eighth grade, he spent most of his time with other Jewish children from the local communities. It was, unexpectedly, quite an adjustment when he moved to the local high school, where he suddenly found himself a minority and with many other young people whom he did not know. He found it especially difficult in ninth grade, his first year in the school, around the winter holidays when most of his classmates were busy preparing for Christmas. Jacob was reluctant to bring many peers home because his home was not extensively decorated for the holidays—his family had a small menorah on the dining room table. He was uncomfortable going to holiday parties, especially ones that had a gift exchange. And he was surprised and a bit embarrassed that, on occasion, he wished his family could have a Christmas tree like everyone else. He often wondered why his parents just didn't move to another part of the state where there were more Jews.

- If you were Jacob's teacher, how would you help him understand his situation? What would you suggest he do?
- What other children do you think might be having similar experiences as Jacob?
- If you were on a school diversity committee, what would you suggest the school consider doing to better understand the experiences students like Jacob were having?

Critical Incident

Spending much of her young life growing up in many different countries overseas has meant that Susan McArthur has had very different experiences than most, if not all, of her classmates in Beechland Heights. She can test out of the two foreign language courses offered at the high school, Spanish and French. She would like to study Japanese or perhaps Mandarin while in high school at the university where her mother will be teaching. Although she found it challenging to move from country to country and school to school so frequently, she sees this as valuable experience and the probable reason she would like to pursue university studies in translation or international relations. She worries, however, that she will have a difficult time fitting in and meeting new people here because they have not shared common experiences.

• If you were Susan's teacher, what would you suggest that might help ease her integration into her new school?

• How might you help others in the school understand and begin to benefit from Susan's rather unique experiences?

Summary

All people, regardless of the culture in which they were raised, share certain common experiences. This chapter presented the dynamics of culture and the culture-learning process that all people, students as well as teachers, experience and bring with them to the school context. Of particular interest to educators are the primary and secondary socialization processes and the 12 sources of cultural knowledge that represent the diversity of knowledge and experiences to which people are exposed. Critical to educators concerned with improving people's skills in intercultural understanding and communication is the recognition that some of the results of the socialization process present barriers to cross-cultural interactions. Effective intercultural education understands and addresses such issues as critical process as well as content.

Chapter Review

Go to the Online Learning Center at www.mhhe.com/cushner9e to review important content from the chapter, practice with key terms, take a chapter quiz, and access active workbook activities.

Key Terms

ability/disability 80
affirmative action 78
age 82
categorization 91
culture 68

culture-general approaches 76
culture-specific approaches 75
enculturate 73
ethnic group 69
ethnicity/nationality 81

The Nature of Culture and Culture Learning

Purpose: To identify qualities that characterize the concept of culture.

Instructions: Read and review the following material. Respond accordingly in the space provided using examples from your own life.

The process by which people come to believe that there is a "right" way to think, express themselves, and act—in other words, how people learn their culture—is called **socialization**. It is the process by which individuals learn what is required of them in order to be successful members of a given group, whatever that group may be. Socialization is such a potent process that people are hardly aware that other realities can exist. This results in the presence of **ethnocentrism**, the tendency people have to judge others from their own culture's perspective, believing theirs to be the "right" or "correct" way to perceive and act within the world.

Most people in today's industrialized societies can be considered to be multicultural because they have been socialized by a number of different individuals or groups that influence their behavior and thought patterns (e.g., gender, nationality, ethnicity, social class, religion, and so forth). At this point, it may be helpful to look at how culture, in the broadest sense, influences people's behavior. Brislin (2000) and Cushner and Brislin (1996) offer a discussion of features that are helpful in understanding culture's influence on behavior and that can be applied to the multiple influences suggested previously. This list is summarized below. You should consider each, and then apply it to your own lives and experiences with the various groups with which you interact. First, individually identify examples from your own past that reflect *each* of the aspects of culture. Then share your responses in small groups. Be ready to share an example of each aspect with the larger group.

1. Culture usually refers to something that is made by human beings rather than something that occurs in nature. Thus, sand along a beach may be a natural occurrence, but the condominiums along the beachfront are not.

   My example of something made by human beings:

2. Culture concerns itself with people's assumptions about life that are often unspoken or hidden from consciousness. Thus, most Americans, when putting a hand out to greet someone new, assume they will do likewise and then they can shake hands. This may not be the case when meeting someone from Japan.

   My example of an aspect of my culture that I believe is "hidden" or a "secret":

3. Culture is a collective creation that most members of the group practice. In the United States, as well as many other countries, it is common for people

to unconsciously walk on the right side of a hallway or sidewalk. In other countries, such as Britain, Australia, or New Zealand, it is common for people to walk on the left side of hallways and sidewalks.

My example of something most people from my cultural group practice that might be different from another group:

4. Clear childhood experiences that individuals can identify exist that help develop and teach particular values and practices. For instance, the American value of individualism is often introduced to young people through early jobs they may have had (babysitting, saving an allowance for something I want, etc.).

My example of something I did in my childhood that teaches a cultural value or practice:

5. Because culture is often a secret and most people do not share a common vocabulary and understanding, people are often unable to comfortably discuss cross-cultural problems with others. Cultural differences, thus, become most evident in well-meaning clashes.

My example of a culture clash that occurred because people did not understand the differing cultural perspectives that were operating at the time:

6. Culture allows people to fill in the blanks so they do not have to repeat the rules for every action to other members of the group. Thus, when someone is invited to a happy hour after work, it is clear to most people that they should expect to spend no more than a couple of hours at the bar or pub, and not plan to make a night of it.

My example of a common behavior that seems mostly automatic and commonly understood:

7. People experience strong emotional reactions when their cultural values are violated or when a culture's expected behaviors are ignored. Thus, recent rulings in France that student's heads must remain uncovered in school has drawn strong criticism from the Islamic community.

My example of a strong emotional response I have observed when people's cultures clash:

8. When changes in cultural values are contemplated, like legalizing same-sex marriages or outlawing the right of citizens to carry handguns, the reaction that "this will be a difficult uphill battle" is likely.

My example of a major cultural change that is or was difficult for people to make:

Reflective Questions

1. Look back at Webb and Sherman's definition of culture on page 70. Compare two different cultures or ethnic groups that you are familiar with in terms of the categories to which they refer. What categories are similar and which ones are different? How would you explain the differences and similarities?

2. Differentiate between objective culture and subjective culture. Can you provide two examples of each from the cultures or ethnic groups you identified in the first question?

3. Consider the 12 sources of knowledge described in the chapter. Complete an inventory on yourself. How might your inventory differ from one of your parents? Compare your inventory to that of a classmate. How are they similar? Different? How would you explain some of the differences?

4. How does the way your parents or community socialized you to understand your social class differ from the way the popular media does? How about your understanding of your gender? How about your understanding of sexual relations?

References

AAA (1998). American Anthropological Association Statement on Race adopted May 17, 1998. Retrieved from http://www.aaanet.org/stmts/racepp.htm

Banks, J. A. (Ed.)(1989). Multicultural education: Characteristics and goals. *Multicultural education: Issues and perspectives* (pp. 3-32). Boston: Allyn & Bacon.

Beardsley, E. (1977). Traits and genderization. In M. Vetterling-Braggin, F. A. Elliston, & J. English (Eds.), *Feminism and philosophy* (pp. 117-123). Totowa, NJ: Littlefield.

Bellah, R. N., Madsen, R., Sullivan, W. M., Swidler, A., & Tipton, S. M. (1985). *Habits of the heart: Individualism and commitment in American life.* New York: Harper & Row.

Bennett, C. L. (1990). *Comprehensive multicultural education: Theory and practice.* Boston: Allyn & Bacon.

Berger, P. L., & Berger, B. (1972). *Sociology: A biographical approach.* New York: Basic Books.

Blaisdell, B. (2000). *Great speeches by Native Americans.* New York: Dover.

Brislin, R. (1993). *Understanding culture's influence on behavior.* Fort Worth, TX: Harcourt Brace Jovanovich.

Brislin, R. (2000). *Understanding culture's influence on behavior* (2nd ed.). Fort Worth, TX: Harcourt Brace Jovanovich.

Bullivant, B. M. (1993). Culture: Its nature and meaning for educators. In J. A. Banks (Ed.), *Multicultural education: Issues and perspectives* (2nd ed., pp. 29-47). Boston: Allyn & Bacon.

Chomsky, N. (1966). *Cartesian linguistics.* New York: Harper & Row.

Coon, C. (2000). *Culture wars and the global village: A diplomat's perspective.* Amherst, NY: Prometheus.

Cortes, C. (2000). *The children are watching: How the media teach about diversity.* New York: Teachers College Press.

Cushner, K. (1998). Intercultural education from an international perspective: An introduction. In K. Cushner (Ed.), *International perspectives on intercultural education* (pp. 1-14). Mahwah, NJ: Lawrence Erlbaum.

Cushner, K., & Brislin, R. (1996). *Intercultural interactions: A practical guide.* Thousand Oaks, CA: Sage.

Dewey, J. (1966). *Democracy and education.* New York: Free Press. (Original work published 1916)

Friedman, I. (1984). *How my parents learned to eat.* Boston: Houghton Mifflin.

Giroux, H., & Simon, R. (1989). *Popular culture: Schooling and everyday life.* Granby, MA: Bergin & Garvey.

Gollnick, D. M., & Chinn, P. C. (2002). *Multicultural education in a pluralistic society* (6th ed.). Upper Saddle River, NJ: Merrill/Prentice Hall.

Herek, G. M. (1986). On heterosexual masculinity: Some physical consequences of the social construction of gender and sexuality. *American Behavioral Scientist, 29*(5), 570.

Hofstede, G. (2001). *Culture's consequences: Comparing values, behaviors, institutions, and organizations across nations* (2nd ed.). Thousand Oaks, CA: Sage.

Howard, G. R. (1993). Whites in multicultural education: Rethinking our role. *Phi Delta Kappan, 75*(1), 36-41.

Humphries, T. (1993). Deaf culture and cultures. In K. M. Christensen & G. L. Delgado (Eds.), *Multicultural issues in deafness* (pp. 3–16). White Plains, NY: Longman.

Huxley, F. (1957). *Affable savages.* New York: Viking Press.

LeVay, S., & Hamer, D. H. (1994). Evidence for a biological influence in male homosexuality. *Scientific American, 270,* 44–49.

McIntosh, P. (1992, January–February). White privilege. *Creation Spirituality,* pp. 33–35, 53.

NHGRI (National Human Genome Research Institute, 2016). Retrieved from: https://www.genome.gov/

Pearce, R. H. (1965). *The savages of America: A study of the Indian and the idea of civilization.* Baltimore: Johns Hopkins University Press.

Rosenstiel, T. B. (1989, August 17). Viewers found to confuse TV entertainment with news. *Los Angeles Times,* p. A1.

Sandberg, S. (2013). *Lean in: Women, work, and the will to lead.* New York: Alfred A. Knopf.

Sapir, E. (1949). *Culture, language, and personality.* Berkeley: University of California Press.

Sheehy, G. (1994). *New passages: Mapping your life across time.* New York: Ballantine Books.

Triandis, H. (1972). *The analysis of subjective culture.* New York: Wiley-Interscience.

Vygotsky, L. S. (1962). *Thought and language.* Cambridge, MA: MIT Press.

Warren, D. M. (1873). *An elementary treatise on physical geography.* Philadelphia: Cowperthwait.

Webb, R. B., & Sherman, R. R. (1989). *Schooling and society* (2nd ed.). New York: Macmillan.

Whorf, B. L. (1968). Science and linguistics. In Alan Dundes (Ed.), *Everyman his own way: Readings in cultural anthropology.* Englewood Cliffs, NJ: Prentice Hall.

Yetman, N. R. (Ed.). (1991). *Majority and minority: The dynamics of race and ethnicity in American life* (5th ed.). Boston: Allyn & Bacon.

Zakaria, F. (2008). *The post-American world.* New York: W.W. Norton, p. 1.

Zelizer, V. A. (1985). *Pricing the priceless child: The changing social value of children.* New York: Basic Books.

Classrooms and Schools as Cultural Crossroads

Focus Questions

1. How might the cultures of students and teachers be similar or different? How might they be in support of one another? In conflict with one another?

2. What cultural characteristics might people who appear to be different from one another share? How can teachers begin to understand the culturally determined traits and behaviors of students and families?

3. How might teachers become better prepared for the cross-cultural differences they are certain to encounter among students? How can they begin to help their students understand and appreciate these differences, thus preparing them better for the increasing number of intercultural interactions they are certain to encounter in a global society?

"It is often hard to learn from people who are just like you. Too much is taken for granted. Homogeneity is fine in a bottle of milk, but in the classroom it diminishes the curiosity that ignites discovery."

VIVIAN GYSSIN PALEY

Case Study

Melinda's Induction Year Dilemma

Melinda had just completed a degree in science education at a large northern university and was excited about the prospects of teaching in one of the area high schools. All through her education she had been encouraged to pursue the STEM (science, technology, engineering, and math) subjects as areas of specialization. She had often heard about the shortage of science teachers, especially women in the sciences, and thought she might have an edge in terms of employment as well as be a model for other young girls. Melinda felt confident that she would obtain a position in a high school not too far from where she had grown up and gone to school. She had held this dream ever since her own high school years.

When Melinda finally graduated, however, the employment situation in the area close to her home had changed. Many of the schools had fallen on difficult financial times, and in most districts, school levies had failed year after year. When school districts from the South came to recruit teachers at her university, Melinda found herself seriously considering the possibility of relocating. After all, she did want to teach, and she felt well prepared for any classroom situation.

When offered a position at Wake Central High School, Melinda gladly accepted and eagerly made plans to move to North Carolina. Wake Central High is an urban school of approximately 2,200 students in grades 9 through 12. Approximately 25 percent of the students are black, 6 percent are Latino representing Mexico as well as a number of different nations throughout Central and South America, 5 percent are of Asian descent, 60 percent are European American, and about 4 percent represent other parts of the world. A majority of students come from families at or below the poverty level with an increasing number of students uncertain of where they will sleep when the school day is finished due to the increasing number of homeless families in the county. The school has a large vocational program in which more than half the juniors and seniors are enrolled. Approximately 20 percent of the faculty are Latino or African American; the rest are European American.

Wake Central High has an aging faculty, with an average age of 46. Last year the principal, Mr. Henderson, was unable to hire any teachers of color. This year he was able to attract one new Latino and two new African American faculty members among the new teachers. Melinda was one of three European Americans hired in the same year. She was excited about her first teaching situation and confident that she would be successful. She had, after all, taken a course in multicultural education in her undergraduate teacher education program, and at least knew some of the basic concepts and theories.

A few months after the start of the school year, Melinda knew that she was confronting a reality far different from the one she had originally imagined. She felt unprepared for the student diversity that she faced each and every day, and she had no idea how to help students

Schools, in particular, are cultural crossroads in a society where distinct but overlapping student, teacher, parent, community, and school cultures intersect. This chapter examines what occurs when people from different cultures come together, as they increasingly do in globally oriented pluralistic societies. We then take an in-depth look at a culture-general model for understanding intercultural interactions. We introduce an intercultural perspective, which draws from the work of cross-cultural psychologists and trainers who, more than any other group of scholars and practitioners, have been developing practical strategies to help people understand and navigate the oftentimes tricky waters of intercultural transition and interaction. Finally, we present this model in action and provide opportunities for you to apply this model to the analysis of some common cross-cultural situations found in school settings.

address what she felt were basic educational needs. She was unaccustomed to the variety of languages and dialects spoken by students, had little understanding of what went on in students' lives outside school, and struggled daily to present class lessons that motivated and engaged students. And to top everything off, Melinda found herself in the middle of significant racial strife.

It seems that in January of the previous year, Mr. Henderson had met with the African American teachers at their request. They had many concerns, ranging from insufficient minority representation on the teaching and coaching staffs to the way white teachers were interacting with many of the African American and other students of color. They felt that most white teachers did not appreciate the need for the proposed Martin Luther King recognition activities; they were disappointed at the lack of white response to a request for donations to the United Negro College Fund; and they felt a negative response to Black History Month activities and other efforts to make the curriculum more culturally relevant.

As a result of this meeting, a Human Relations Committee was formed. This volunteer group planned and organized a two-day race relations institute. The results of the workshop were disastrous. Instead of improving race relations in the school, the situation became worse. A group of white teachers sent around a list of possible themes for the coming school year, a few of which were perceived as racist by the African American teachers. A group of concerned black teachers and parents sent letters to community leaders and upper-level administrators voicing their concern. Once parents of the Latino students became aware of the situation they started demanding equal attention to address the needs of their children, many of whom became increasingly alienated from school-related activities. Students formed a group they called "Students Against Racism" as a means to express their concerns and frustrations.

In March of last year, Mr. Henderson had met with the equal opportunity officer in the district and with a racially mixed group of teachers. While concerns were aired, none of the problems were solved. A discussion was begun, but as Mr. Henderson puts it, "We have a long way to go. We definitely have some white teachers who are insensitive to the needs and experiences of others, as well as some teachers of color who perceive the white teachers as racist. I'm not quite sure how to begin addressing the students' needs, except to say that we will continue to bring the various parties together to address whatever needs arise. I only hope people will stay with me for the long haul."

Melinda was quite uncomfortable attending faculty meetings, and the spin-off was affecting her classroom interactions. She was frustrated, unsure of what was really going on, and uncertain if she could remain in such an environment. She began to seriously question how anyone could teach in such a stressful situation, and if she should just go back home where she at least understood the lay of the land.

Schools and Classrooms: Where Cultures Intersect

Within the important limitations of economic circumstance, most people choose the neighborhoods they live in, the places they work and shop, and where they spend their leisure time. In schools, however, as nowhere else in American society, people of many different backgrounds are forced to come together in close quarters for significant periods of time. In this section, we first examine the various cultures (student, teacher, parent, and school) that come together in the context of the school. Second, we examine the role of the teacher as a cultural mediator who is responsible for developing a cooperative learning community within this complex and potentially chaotic setting.

Student Culture

Students make up by far the largest percentage of people in a school community. Roughly 50.4 million students were enrolled in public schools in the year 2016, with an additional 5.2 million attending private institutions (NCES, 2106). In addition to those students in domestic schools, an increasing number of students are attending schools outside of their home country or receiving an internationally-focused education in international schools. Although there are approximately 6,000 such international schools around the world today that serve approximately 3 million students, this number is expected to increase to more than 10,000 schools by the year 2020 serving more than 5 million students (Hallgarten, Tabberer, and McCarthy, 2015). Perhaps more than most social groups, as discussed in Chapter 1, students represent and exhibit the greatest diversity in American society. Of the 50.4 million public school students in pre-K through grade 12 in the fall of 2016, 24.6 million were of European American descent. The remaining 25.9 million included 7.8 million African American students, 13.3 million Latino/a students, 2.7 million Asian/Pacific Islander students, 0.5 million American Indian/Alaska Native students, and 1.5 million students of two or more races (NCES, 2016). The percentage of students enrolled in public schools who are European American is projected to continue to decline as the enrollments of Latino/a and Asian/Pacific Islander students increase. Add to this the alarming increase of homeless children in public schools that during the 2013–14 school year numbered more than 1.3 million. Like the experience of many minority students, homeless students experience significant academic, social, and socio-emotional challenges. Homeless youth, for instance, are ill four times as often as other children; experience three times the rate of emotional and behavioral problems; are four times as likely to show developmental delays; are twice as likely to exhibit learning disabilities; and 83 percent of homeless youth are exposed to at least one serious violent incident (NEAHCY, 2017). Not only do students reflect the cultural identities of their families (ethnicity, religion, social class, etc.), they also define themselves by creating their own particular in-school groups.

It is a cultural universal that all people categorize others into one of two major divisions: those with whom they identify and wish to spend their time (called *ingroups*), and those with whom they may interact in the workplace or hallways yet keep a respectable distance from (known as *outgroups*). Ingroup formation in school can be based on many different criteria, from the more potent cultural identities already discussed (e.g., ethnicity, race, religion, gender) to the relatively fluid but no less important unifying features of academic groups (e.g., biology club, French club), special interest or skill groups (e.g., choir, football), or groups that are, from the point of view of most adults, less desirable but nonetheless purposeful, such as gangs. Stop for a moment and think of the many varied student cultures that can be found in schools, some to which you belonged and some which you may have even shunned. Typically, individual students gain a certain school identity from participation in these groups. These microcultures within the school operate in ways similar to the macroculture outside it. Individuals learn appropriate rules of interaction, modes of communication, expression of values, and so forth. And as with larger groups such as nation-states, membership in these in-school microcultures (gangs, chess club, choir) often brings exclusion from other microcultures (other gangs, sports teams, band).

Teacher Culture

Teachers make up the other dominant social group within the school community, with more than 3 million teaching in public schools and another 500,000 in private institutions (NCES, 2016). And just as the presence of international schools worldwide will continue to grow, the number of teachers in these schools is also expected to increase, from the current number of about 300,000 to the anticipated need for up to half a million teachers by the year 2020 (Hallgarten, Haberer, and McCarthy, 2015). An increasing number of teachers are finding employment in these international schools – either for their entire career or for a short-term experience. But unlike the diversity found within the student population, teachers are a relatively homogeneous group. Indeed, a disturbing reality, given the increasing diversity of students in public schools, is the relative cultural homogeneity of the teaching force. In the United States, about 82% of the teaching force are European American and three fourths are female. Despite recent efforts to recruit underrepresented groups into the teaching profession, it is projected that well into this century the majority of new teachers will continue to be female and white. This statistic is not surprising. Teachers in the United States have always been mostly female and white, at least since the early part of the 19th century. However, this statistic raises interesting issues about the cultural and economic backgrounds of teachers in contrast to that of students.

The fact that a large proportion of our teachers are female is related to the power structure of schools. Teachers have a good deal of authority in their classrooms, but it is not true that they have much authority in the schools. For example, teachers are just beginning to have something to say about school policy or about the curriculum they are expected to teach. Reasons for this lack of authority may vary, but an important one has to do with the way in which large numbers of women entered the teaching profession in the 1830s and 1840s. Prior to that time, the person behind the schoolroom desk was a schoolmaster, a man. However, after about 1830, the growth of industry began providing more and more lucrative jobs for men, leaving teaching vacancies in the classroom. At the same time, the common school movement was evolving across the United States, opening up additional teaching positions. Conveniently, it was determined that women, who were "natural mothers" and therefore possessed the knowledge, skills, and talents needed to deal with young children, must also be "natural teachers." The elementary school was projected as an extension of the home and the teacher an extension of the mother. The fact that women would work for about one third the wages paid to male teachers was also a significant factor in their employment in American schools.

Given the history of their entry into the profession, female teachers have never had the status that male teachers once had. Unfortunately for all teachers, the low status of women teachers has become associated with teachers more generally. Administrators, who have greater authority, higher pay, and higher status, still tend to be mostly European American men. Thus, in our society, schools have become organized in such a way that leadership and policy are very often the exclusive province of white, male administrators.

Parent Culture

It is increasingly recognized that parents play a critical role in the academic success of their own children as well as in building a sense of community within the school. Yet it may sometimes be difficult to encourage all families to be active participants in the classroom. New immigrant and refugee families may come from cultures where the status of the school was such that parents had little say, or were actively discouraged from contributing and participating in school life, leaving all decisions and actions to the "professionals" in charge. Language facility may be another barrier that keeps many

©Comstock Images/Jupiter Images/Alamy Stock Photo RF

parents from contributing fully in school life. Sometimes socioeconomic and perceived status differences may discourage parents from feeling welcomed in the school. Sara Lawrence Lightfoot (Lightfoot, n.d.) has been quoted as saying, "For those parents from lower-class and minority communities [who] have had minimal experience in negotiating dominant, external institutions or have had negative and hostile contact with social service agencies, their initial approaches to the school are often overwhelming and difficult. Not only does the school feel like an alien environment with incomprehensible norms and structures, but the families often do not feel entitled to make demands or force disagreements." Effective teachers and other school officials then must seek ways to invite and otherwise encourage participation from a wide range of families who may not have much direct exposure and experience in schools. This may include such things as meeting in various community centers, sending communications home to families in multiple languages, employing bilingual teachers and other staff, and having translators available for parent-teacher conferences.

School Culture

Both schools and the teachers who inhabit them are, to a large extent, culture-bound, and the culture most are bound to is the dominant culture of European American, middle-class society. This, however, is only one of the many culture groups in the United States. One purpose of public schooling has always been to transmit the cultural beliefs, values, and knowledge affiliated with the dominant group to those in the next generation. The danger, of course, is the ethnocentric tendency of most people, teachers included, to believe that their own cultural tradition represents the "best" way. Too often, the perception of both power and virtue combine to lessen the chance that white, middle-class teachers will make a real effort to understand the cultural differences that direct the lives of many of their students. At best, many of these teachers are predisposed to regard diversity as interesting; at worst, they are likely to regard it as a deficit. Teachers seldom come to their classes with the notion that diversity is an exciting and enriching phenomenon. Lightfoot (1989) described many good teachers as wishing that the diversity they see in September will somehow fade away as the class becomes a group.

Teachers as Cultural Mediators

The cultural interplay between teachers, students, parents, and their school produces a context within which significant culture learning can occur. In a sense, teachers must become cultural mediators in their classrooms and must walk both sides of a double-edged sword. Teachers must become more knowledgeable about the role of culture in teaching and learning while becoming better able to address the educational needs of students and families from a variety of backgrounds. At the same time, teachers must turn this knowledge and skill into content that actively engages students in learning about and more effectively accommodating cultural differences. Students need to learn how culture is formed and how to understand and handle the many intercultural interactions they are certain to encounter.

Throughout this process, it is imperative that teachers and students understand that a certain amount of adjustment and discomfort may occur. It is useful to remember that when we as individuals are confronted by someone who looks, behaves, or thinks differently from ourselves, we suddenly become aware that our way of doing things may not be the only one. Such a confrontation often affects us at an emotional level—we may feel anxiety, uncertainty, and discomfort. Lacking a vocabulary to describe most cross-cultural differences and wishing to avoid discomfort, people may choose to avoid further interaction with those who are different from them. Such avoidance behavior perpetuates the cycle of discomfort, mistrust, and ignorance and confounds our efforts to improve intergroup relations.

These same feelings often characterize teachers whose students are different from them and perhaps different, as well, from the value and behavior norms of the school. From the school's point of view, such students are often perceived as having deficits that need to be overcome through some type of remedial action. Sadly, such actions are often punitive to students, involving exclusionary practices such as tracking and negative labeling (e.g., at-risk students, learning disabled). Because most of us do not have a wide variety of experience with cultural patterns other than our own, deliberate instruction in culture, including acquiring a vocabulary in order to talk about its patterns, its substance, and its behavioral results, is one way to create a dialogue concerning differences. Such strategies help us truly understand ourselves and others.

Cross-Cultural Adaptation

It would be easy for teachers to give in to discouragement and try to find a school where the students were like them. The reality, however, is that such schools do not exist in today's world. Teachers will have to adjust to the fact that they will continue to find themselves in significantly diverse settings.

Early studies of cross-cultural transitions suggested that people experience a predictable pattern of adjustment when undergoing significant, long-term encounters in new cultural settings (Lysgaard, 1955; Oberg, 1960; Trifonovitch, 1977). These early models, although brought into question in recent years, presented a visual representation that plots people's experiences on a graph, with emotional experiences along the vertical axis and time across the horizontal axis. The resulting image appeared as a U, hence this process of adjustment to living and working in another culture, often referred to as the "U-curve hypothesis", was meant to characterize the experience of what is commonly referred to as *culture shock*.

A term that is more accurate and useful than culture shock—*transition stress*—captures the variety of ways that individuals may experience the challenges that accompany major transitions. Within the course of a day, a week, or a month, for instance, an individual in a new setting may experience transition stress as a result of many things: changes that occur in his or her identity and/or role; confusing or misunderstood communication styles and interactions; the energy required to learn new ways; coping with the fact that one's normal behavior does not produce the expected results; the perception of being judged or stereotyped by others; the need to build new relationships; as well as managing the sheer emotional complexity of going through many of these simultaneously (Berardo, 2012).

Early in an intercultural experience, for instance, people may be eager and enthusiastic, as Melinda was in the case study. However, people can equally be anxious and uncertain, encountering an array of emotions from anxiety, uncertainty, and ambiguity, to excitement and enthusiasm—in other words, a range of situations and contexts that may bring on stress. The list of possible reactions to transition and intercultural interaction can go on and on, and will vary depending on the role of the individual (e.g., teacher, student, business professional, tourist), as well as the location (e.g., encountering domestic diversity within one's own country; interacting overseas in a culture relatively similar to one's own; interacting with people from a culture vastly different from one's own).

There are many examples of similar transition stress in the psychological literature (e.g., newlyweds, retirees). Beginning teachers and new students moving into the culture of a particular school face a double challenge. Teachers new to the profession must simultaneously adapt to the culture of the surrounding community and to that of the teaching profession, which, of course, has a culture of its own. In the school context, new teachers must integrate themselves into the norms and attitudes of both a well-established teaching staff and their students, who bring with them the norms of their own communities. After some time, new teachers, like new arrivals in any new culture, may become so frustrated by their inability to make sense of their new world that they begin to react in an aggressive, regressive and perhaps hostile manner. At the same time, new students must also adjust not only to the school culture, which may be very different from their home and neighborhood cultures, but also to the behavioral and academic expectations of schooling and to the many possible student microcultures within the school. If their school experience is too stressful and anxiety-provoking, students can become so frustrated that they may give up, act up, or drop out.

At this point the individual must make a critical choice: remain, and learn how to function effectively within the new setting; or allow the frustrations to build, and eventually retreat from the unpleasant situation. Those individuals most likely to succeed in their new setting begin to confront their new cultural environment. They learn to cope with embarrassment, disappointment, frustration, anxiety, and identity problems at first, and then begin the process of culture learning by focusing on the subjective culture of the new environment.

Eventually, people who succeed in altering their own cultural identity to include the new experience are able to interpret the world and interact with others both from their own perspective as well as from the perspective of that which had been alien to them before. A major change occurs in an individual's ability to process information and to understand the world in ways similar to those in the other group. The individual now shows indications of becoming more genuinely appreciative of differences because the world now seems reasonable and acceptable from more than one point of view. This is the point where one begins to become bicultural or intercultural.

Most individuals require a significant amount of time before they can develop the in-depth understanding that is required for them to live and work effectively and comfortably with people from other cultural backgrounds. Some researchers suggest that this period may be as long as two years—and that with the individual experiencing full immersion and speaking the local language.

A related experience is often encountered by bilingual learners whose primary language is not English (see Chapter 8). Such children often encounter two levels of linguistic adjustment (Cummins, 1979). On one level, children may acquire Basic Interpersonal Communication Skills (BICS) relatively quickly and within two or three years appear to be quite fluent—on a surface, or objective, level. That is, non-English speakers may quickly be able to communicate effectively with other children on the playground, during their free time, and during informal interactions in the classroom. Yet when these children are given standardized tests of educational achievement, they do not do as well—a secondary, deeper level of linguistic competence is at play. Students may need between five and seven years to attain Cognitive Academic Language Proficiency (CALP)—the level of linguistic competence in a second language that is typically required in schools. Clearly, if acquiring a cultural identity through primary socialization requires full immersion in a culture over a long period of time, it stands to reason that reshaping a cultural outlook as a result of secondary socialization will also take considerable time.

In Chapter 3, Figure 3.4 provided a visual overview of how the various sources of cultural identity are acquired by individuals through interaction with the many socializing agents they encounter. Although the sources of cultural identity (e.g., race, language, sexuality) are universal and appear in all societies, the socializing agents (family, school, media, and so forth) that transmit them vary considerably from one society to another. In most industrialized societies, a wide variety of socializing agents bombard people daily, often with contradictory messages. In agriculturally oriented societies, on the other hand, a few primary socializing agents (e.g., family and gender group) may share the bulk of the culture-transmission process. The result is that individuals with different cultural patterns develop very different worldviews.

Acculturation and Identity

Extended intercultural contact can have a significant impact on individuals as well as groups. **Acculturation** refers to the changes that take place as a result of continuous firsthand contact between individuals of different cultures (Berry, 1990, 2004; Redfield, Linton, & Herskovits, 1936). Such contact not only produces changes in people's attitudes, values, and behaviors, but may also significantly affect their cultural identity. At least theoretically, long-term contact between people of different backgrounds should impact both the individual experiencing the transition as well as the larger host or receiving culture. Historical as well as present-day experiences of different groups, however, may determine, to a great extent, the outcome. For instance, immigrants and refugees who enter a new culture with long-standing, distinctive cultural norms may have very different experiences from members of established ethnic minority groups (Ward, Bochner, & Furnam, 2001). Newcomers, for example, may have come from relatively homogeneous countries such as Japan, where cultural identity is rarely challenged, and may have had no experiences with the new host culture. Under such conditions, the pressures for cultural change are often intense, immediate, and enduring. For successive generations, the pressures may take on a different form as the groups evolve into established ethnic communities.

John Berry (1990) addressed two issues that are at play when differentiating among acculturating groups. Comparing the degree of mobility and the degree of choice (or voluntariness of contact), he identified four distinct groups of interest to educators: (1) those people with a high degree of mobility and who voluntarily made the contact are referred to as **immigrants** (relatively permanent) or **sojourners** (temporary visitors); (2) those with a high degree of mobility who may have little or no choice related to their contact, like those fleeing the recent conflict in Syria or other war-torn regions, are considered **refugees;** (3) those with a low degree of mobility but a high degree of voluntary contact with others are known as **ethnic groups;** and (4) those with a low

Figure 4.1
Acculturating Group
Types

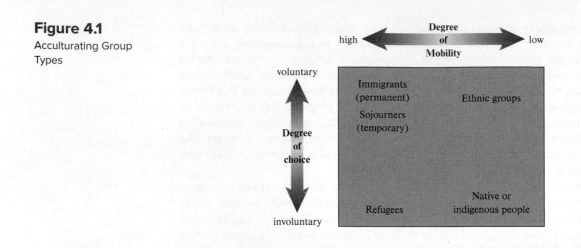

degree of mobility and a low degree of voluntary contact reflect the native people, or
indigenous people, of a nation (see Figure 4.1). Members of each of these groups can
have distinct needs and experiences within the school community.

People also differ in the degree to which they wish to retain or are willing to change
their cultural identity. Here, people's acculturation attitude can be determined by their
responses to two distinct questions: "Is it of value to me to maintain my own cultural
identity and characteristics?" and "Is it of value to me to maintain relationships with
other groups?" As shown in Figure 4.2, four distinct outcomes are possible in response
to these questions. In **integration,** people maintain relationships with other groups
while at the same time maintaining their own cultural identity and characteristics. Such
people retain their own unique cultural identity while functioning fairly well within a
mainstream culture. They can, in a sense, walk in two worlds and are well on the way
to being bicultural. American Jews are often cited as an example of a well-integrated
group in U.S. society; there are many well-established Jewish agencies, educational
offerings, and community organizations that people can interact with while they maintain relatively positive interactions and involvement within the mainstream.

In **assimilation,** people maintain relationships with other groups but generally do
not consider it of value to maintain their own cultural identity. An assimilation decision
that is freely chosen is often referred to as the "melting pot." However, when assimilation is forced, a situation more akin to a pressure cooker might develop. Although

Figure 4.2
Acculturation Strategies
of Ethnocultural Groups

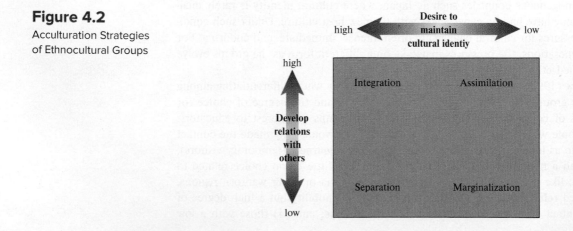

American society has often been referred to as a melting pot, some people contend that significant social and cultural barriers prevent many people from achieving assimilation and that many people simply do not wish to give up their heritage in favor of a mainstream culture. The pot, some would say, never melted.

In situations where people value their own cultural identity but do not value relationships with other groups, two possible outcomes exist. When the situation is by choice for both groups, it is referred to as **separation.** When such a scenario is forced on one group by another, more dominant group, the situation is called **segregation,** as was prominent in the American South in the first half of the 20th century or under apartheid in South Africa until 1994.

Finally, a unique situation occurs when people do not value their own identity nor do they value relationships with other groups. In such a scenario, **marginalization** may occur, and individuals may experience extreme cases of ethnocide or deculturation.

Members of each of these four groups have distinct needs, experiences, and expectations of the school community. It is possible to observe each of the four acculturation attitudes within a given family unit. Imagine a family of four from a small village in Guatemala who recently immigrated to the United States. The father may lean toward integration for job prospects. He may work hard to learn English so he can fit in at work yet may still remain quite active with local Guatemalan/Latino community affairs. The mother, unable to enter the host society, may work hard to retain her Spanish language and her local social interactions. She then becomes a separatist. Hearing the Spanish language at home and eating Guatemalan food all the time may bother the teenage daughter. She may prefer assimilation, so she works hard to speak only English and to blend in through school activities. The brother, on the other hand, may not want to accept his Guatemalan heritage but may be rejected by his classmates. He may retreat and thus become marginalized.

Themes From Cross-Cultural Psychology

The fields of cross-cultural psychology and intercultural training offers teachers the following set of themes or principles that can be used to study intercultural interactions in the classroom (Pederson, 1988).

1. *People tend to communicate their cultural identity to others in the broadest possible terms.* For instance, on meeting someone for the first time, you may communicate many different things about yourself—your age, nationality, ethnic group, religious affiliation, where you grew up, and the nature of your family. At other times you may describe your status at work or in the community, your health, your social class, or the way you have come to understand your gender. Each of these sources of cultural identity carries with it associated rules for behavior. When offering such information to new acquaintances, we give them cultural clues regarding what to expect from us and how to interact with us. Multiple "cultures" influence us at various times, so every one of us may be considered multicultural.

2. *We are all multicultural, and our cultural identity is dynamic and always changing.* As our environmental circumstances and group associations change, we adapt our cultural identity and behavior accordingly. For example, in certain circumstances our gender-related knowledge and beliefs may be predominant; at another time our religious beliefs may stand out; and at still another, our

ethnicity may be most important. Thus, our multicultural nature leads to behavior variations that are sometimes difficult to understand and appreciate.

3. *Although culture is complex and variable, it is nevertheless patterned.* Culture helps individuals make sense of their world and thereby to develop routinized behavioral patterns to fit different contexts and circumstances. Common phrases such as the "culture of the organization," the "culture of the community," or the "culture of the society" refer to the fact that culture is not simply patterned for an individual but also for a setting, a community, or a society as a whole. When viewed from the outside, these patterns can appear quite complicated and difficult to understand. Yet each of us moves quite easily among the cultural patterns with which we are familiar. When confronted by someone whose behavior is *not* familiar, it is the responsibility of the outsider to listen, to observe, and to inquire closely enough so that the patterns of that person (or social group or society) become evident and understandable. To do so decreases the possibility of misunderstanding and conflict and increases the likelihood of acquiring new and useful understanding and appreciation.

4. *Interactions with other cultures can be viewed as a resource for understanding.* In this case, complexity can be an asset. The more knowledge and experience we have with other groups, the more sophisticated we can be in our interpretation of events. The more complex our thinking is the more lenses or insights we can bring to help understand a given situation. Culturally different encounters help prepare us to deal more effectively with the complexity that is increasingly a part of our lives. In short, the number of cultural variables we learn to accommodate will determine our ability to navigate within a fast-moving, ever-changing society.

5. *Behavior should be judged in relation to its context.* Observable behavior cannot be understood apart from the context in which it occurs. Seen outside its context, another's "different" behavior can, at best, seem meaningless and, at worst, be profoundly misinterpreted. Contextual inquiry enables us to be more accurate in our judgments of others. Consider this real-life example of an 11-year-old boy shared with one of the authors. This child would become rowdy and disruptive in the classroom every day about 2:00 in the afternoon. Inevitably, the teacher sent the child to the office, where he was promptly sent home. Defined in terms of the middle-class cultural context of the school, this child was definitely a troubled child, and he was so labeled by nearly all the adults in the building. Eventually, however, an astute counselor recognized a pattern and did some inquiry. It turned out that the mother's boyfriend would come home every day about 2:45, often quite drunk and abusive. In his rage, the boyfriend frequently abused the mother. The boy, quite accurately understanding the cultural pattern of the school, figured out that his misbehavior would result in his being sent home and that if he was sent home by 2:30, he would arrive before the boyfriend did and thus be able to protect his mother. Suddenly this so-called troubled boy's behavior makes sense, and he becomes something of a hero because he had found a way to protect his vulnerable mother. Without full knowledge of the context, behavior is often meaningless or badly misinterpreted. Culture, thus, provides a context from which to view and judge others.

6. *Persons holding an intercultural perspective continually strive to find common ground between individuals.* In a sense, we must strive to be bifocal. That is, we

must be able to see the similarities among people as well as their differences. While it is the differences that tend to stand out and separate people, it is precisely in our similarities where common ground, or a common meeting point, can be found. An intercultural perspective permits disagreement without anyone necessarily being accused of being wrong. If culture in all its complexity is understood as an individual's attempt to navigate the river of life, then cultural differences can be understood simply as pragmatic acts of navigation and judged accordingly. In this view, cultural differences become tolerable and the "we-they" or "us-them" debate is avoided. There are no winners and losers. We are all in this together. Either we all win—or we all lose. The International Baccalaureate® (IB), for instance, in its mission statement states that it aims to develop inquiring, knowledgeable, and caring young people who help create a better and more peaceful world through intercultural understanding and respect. To this end the organization works with schools, governments, and international organizations to develop challenging programmes of international education and rigorous assessment. These programmes encourage students across the world to become active, compassionate, lifelong learners who understand that other people, with their differences, can also be right. More about the IB and other global or international initiatives can be found in Chapter 7.

A Model of Intercultural Interaction

Researchers in the field of cross-cultural psychology have developed a variety of methods that can be used to analyze, understand, and improve intercultural interactions. Cushner and Brislin (1996) developed a framework for understanding the dynamics of any intercultural encounter between individuals with different cultural patterns. The approach is grounded in the recognition that people have similar reactions to their intercultural encounters regardless of the setting or the person they are interacting with, the role they adopt, or their own cultural background. Research suggests that because these phases are experienced universally, they can serve as the basis of an analytical model that anyone participating in an unfamiliar intercultural encounter can use as a tool for better understanding and anticipating the cultural nuances they might encounter (see Figure 4.3). Although most people assess informally, using whatever bits and pieces of relevant experience they may have, employing a general model provides a more systematic and effective means of assessment.

Because this model is deliberately general, its usefulness lies in its adaptability to a broad range of intercultural encounters. This captures the experience of cultural differences from a variety of perspectives (emotional, informational, and developmental), while offering frameworks within which specific problem situations can be addressed. However, it does not go beyond its diagnostic purpose. That is, the model does not offer prescriptive courses of action for dealing with difference. Such approaches are

Figure 4.3
Stages of Intercultural Encounters

not only impossible, they are unethical given the complex realities of today's classroom. It is the individual student or teacher, empowered with cross-cultural knowledge, who must inquire into the causes and then propose solutions to the specific problems and issues that arise. The discussion that follows provides an examination of each stage in the culture-general framework and describes each of the 18 themes encompassed by this model. The critical incidents, or scenarios, found later in the chapter will give you an opportunity to apply this framework.

Stage 1: Understanding Emotional Responses in Intercultural Interaction

In any intercultural encounter, people's emotions are quickly aroused when they meet with unpredictable behavior on the part of others or when their own behavior does not bring about an expected response. The nature and strength of these emotional reactions quite often surprise the people involved, especially in the case of students who do not anticipate the differences between their own cultural patterns and those of the school. Strong emotions can also be experienced by teachers, like Melinda in the case study, who find themselves in a school or classroom context that is significantly different from what they expect. Recognizing and accommodating the strong emotional responses that people are certain to have when they become involved in intercultural interactions is critical to successfully negotiating those interactions. Figure 4.4 identifies the emotional responses most commonly experienced by persons confronting an unfamiliar culture. A brief description of these responses follows.

Anxiety

As individuals encounter unexpected or unfamiliar behavior on the part of others, they are likely to become anxious about whether their own behavior is appropriate. Children and teachers in new schools, individuals in new jobs, and families in new communities will all experience some degree of anxiety as they attempt to modify their own behavior

Figure 4.4

Emotional Responses in Intercultural Interaction

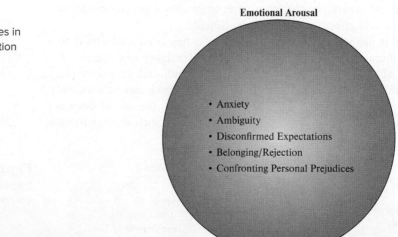

Emotional Arousal

- Anxiety
- Ambiguity
- Disconfirmed Expectations
- Belonging/Rejection
- Confronting Personal Prejudices

to fit new circumstances. Such feelings may be powerful, while their cause, if it is due to cultural differences, may initially be unidentified. Feelings of anxiety may result in a strong desire to avoid the situation altogether, and individuals sometimes go to great lengths to do so, all the while rationalizing their avoidance behavior on other grounds. Such a response should be avoided as this does not serve to improve one's understanding nor the relationship.

Ambiguity

When interacting with those who are culturally different, people may often receive messages that are not quite clear—yet they must make decisions and somehow produce appropriate behavior. Most people, when faced with an ambiguous situation, try to resolve it by applying culturally familiar criteria. For example, it is quite common, when giving instruction to individuals who are just beginning to speak English to ask them if they understand what has just been said. In an attempt not to seem ignorant or impolite people will often respond in the affirmative but then act in ways that suggest they do not fully understand. Because the new intercultural situation may not fit familiar criteria this strategy is often ineffective.

The uncertainty of ambiguous situations may be the most critical element in the development of anxiety and is one of the more important factors in intercultural misunderstandings. People who are effective at working across cultures are known to have a high tolerance for ambiguity. That is, in situations where they do not have full understanding of what is going on, they can tolerate a certain degree of uncertainty and discomfort, are skilled at asking appropriate questions, and are able to modify their behavior accordingly.

Disconfirmed Expectations

Individuals may become upset or uncomfortable not because of the specific circumstances they encounter but because the situation differs from what they expected. Despite the recognition that differences are all around, people have a tendency to expect others to think and behave in ways similar to themselves. Thus, when involved in intercultural interactions, most people are surprised and disconcerted when others do not respond in expected ways. For example, a child may consistently look at the floor when being spoken to by an adult rather than looking the adult in the eye. This reaction sets up a cycle in which unexpected behavior is attributed both negatively and inaccurately according to preconceived notions of what is right, or correct (this student isn't paying attention and is disrespectful). Further actions, such as the student being scolded for showing disrespect based on such negative or inaccurate attributions, also do not produce the intended result (the student continues to look at the floor). This situation is often very upsetting for all parties involved. For another example, teachers, especially new ones, want to succeed and do well in their classrooms. If the reality of the classroom does not meet the new teacher's expectation, significant discomfort may result. Think back to Melinda's initial expectations of her move to North Carolina and the reality she ultimately encountered.

Belonging/Rejection

People have the need to fill a social niche, to feel that they belong and are at home in the social milieu in which they find themselves. When they are immersed in an

©STOCK4B-RF/Jupiter Images RF

intercultural situation this sense of belonging may be difficult to achieve because they do not know the rules of behavior in the new situation. Instead, people may feel rejected as outsiders, and when this sense of rejection is strong enough, they may become alienated from the situation altogether. Students, for example, who feel alienated from the classroom or school are more likely to become discipline problems and have difficulty paying attention to classroom work. Similarly, teachers who work with youngsters very different from themselves may feel alienated from their students and their students' families, and may respond with undue exercise of power or with burnout.

Confronting Personal Prejudices

Finally, a person involved in intercultural interactions may be forced to acknowledge that previously held beliefs about a certain group of people or certain kinds of behaviors may be inaccurate, inappropriate, or without foundation. Such a revelation may result in embarrassment or shame. It may also require a basic change in attitude and behavior toward others. For instance, it is not uncommon for young college students who grew up hearing from parents or other adults that certain groups of people were lazy or unintelligent to suddenly confront contradictory evidence when they encounter people from that group in their residence halls, classrooms, or the workplace. People confronting personal prejudices must decide to question their earlier beliefs and change their subsequent behavior, or maintain those beliefs even in light of their new information. Since change is difficult even in the best of circumstances, people often continue to harbor their prejudices even when faced with contradictory evidence. Making the cognitive shift can be very demanding, but it is essential. Similarly, it is also possible that people may experience being the target of prejudice exhibited by others for the first time and have to confront this new reality.

Stage 2: Understanding the Cultural Basis of Unfamiliar Behavior

In addition to accommodating their feelings, the parties in an intercultural encounter need to understand the impact of the particular cultural influences that have shaped one another's knowledge about the world. Individuals typically try to understand another person's behavior according to their own cultural knowledge base. Put another way, since most people do not have extensive experiences with people who think and act differently from them, they tend to interpret another's behavior in terms of their own cultural frames of reference. This tendency is the basis of ethnocentrism. In brief, people see what they expect to see, and with incomplete information or inaccurate knowledge, they may make inappropriate judgments about a given situation.

Consider the student referred to earlier who consistently looked at the floor when being spoken to by an adult. *Some* children from certain ethnic groups (e.g., some Mexican Americans, African Americans, or South Pacific Islanders) *may* be taught to demonstrate respect for elders or persons in authority by avoiding eye contact. Hence, a child who is being spoken to by an adult would avoid gazing into that person's eyes. On the other hand, *most* European American children (who become the majority of teachers) are socialized to look a person of authority directly in the eye. Imagine the outcome of an interaction involving a Mexican American, African American, or South Pacific Island child being addressed by a European American teacher. The child, as she or he may have been taught, looks away from the gaze of the teacher, thereby from their perspective, demonstrating respect. The teacher, expecting eye contact as a sign of respect, may interpret the child's behavior as "He is not listening to me" or "She does not respect me." This incorrect judgment may result in a reprimand, in response to which the child attempts to show respect by continuing to look away. Without understanding the cultural basis for this behavior, future interactions between this particular teacher and student may be in serious jeopardy. Such incorrect judgments might also be what prompts the strong emotional responses discussed above.

The individual skilled in intercultural encounters learns to suspend judgment and seek alternative explanations of unexpected behavior rather than to simply interpret such behavior according to his or her own cultural framework. The question "Why is this behavior occurring?" precedes the question "What is the matter with this child?"

There are many aspects of cultural knowledge, each of which reaches the individual through a network of socializing agents (see Chapter 3). Regardless of the complexity of this socialization process, the resulting knowledge base functions to give us satisfactory explanations of our world and to tell us how best to interact with the people around us. Within this cultural knowledge base, however, the following kinds of knowledge are likely to differ across cultural patterns (see Figure 4.5).

Communication and Language Use

Communication differences are among the most obvious issues that must be confronted when crossing cultural boundaries. Language issues exist whether the languages involved are completely different (e.g., Japanese, Kiswahili, English, American Sign Language), are similar in root but not in evolution (e.g., French, Italian, Spanish), or are variations or dialects of the same language (e.g., French, French-Canadian; English, Ebonics). In any case, it is not always easy to learn a second or third language, although it is increasingly becoming a necessity. In addition, nonverbal communication customs

Figure 4.5
Analyzing Unfamiliar
Behavior

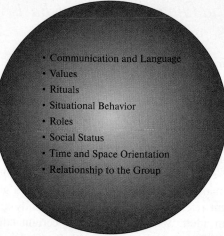

- Communication and Language
- Values
- Rituals
- Situational Behavior
- Roles
- Social Status
- Time and Space Orientation
- Relationship to the Group

such as facial expressions, gestures, and so forth also may differ across cultures, so that what a particular gesture means to one person may be very different from what it means to someone with another cultural pattern. The familiar head nod up and down that means "yes" to you may indicate "no" in Bulgaria, Macedonia, Albania, and Greece.

Values

The development of internalized values is one of the chief socialization goals in all societies. Values provide social cohesion among group members and are often codified into laws or rules for living; for example, the Ten Commandments for Christians and Jews, the five pillars of Islam, or the Hippocratic Oath for doctors. The range of possible values with respect to any particular issue is usually wide, deeply held, and often difficult to change. For example, in the dominant culture of the United States, belief in progress is highly valued and seemingly religious in character. A teacher holding that value may have a very difficult time interacting with parents who seem not to value their daughter's academic potential. The young woman's parents may believe that she should assume the traditional role of wife and mother after high school rather than seek a college education. The teacher, on the other hand, may believe that the young woman should "look to the future" in another way, "change with the times," and "make progress" for herself. These differences are not small and can be the cause of tremendous tension.

Rituals and Superstitions

All social groups develop rituals that help members meet the demands of everyday life. Such rituals vary in significance from rubbing a rabbit's foot before a stressful event to the intricate format of an organized religious service. The difficulty, however, is that the rituals of one social group may be viewed as silly or superstitious by members of other social groups. Increasingly, children from a wide variety of religious and cultural backgrounds bring to school behaviors that are often misunderstood and labeled "superstition." Traditional Native American spirituality, for example, often includes rituals involving the personification of natural objects such as trees, rocks, and animals.

People who have been brought up with a scientific and technological mindset usually view such personification as superstition.

Situational Behavior

Knowing how to behave appropriately in a variety of settings and situations is important to all people. The rules for behavior at home, school, work, sporting events, and so forth are internalized at an early age and, of course, vary with the given context. Such rules can be easily broken by an individual who has internalized a different set of rules for the same setting or situation. A child, for example, who has learned that learning is best accomplished by quiet and intense observation is likely to run afoul of a teacher who believes that learning is best accomplished by active participation with others in class.

Roles

Knowledge of appropriate role behavior, like that of situational behavior, may vary from role to role and from group to group. How an individual behaves as a mother or father, for example, may be different from how that person behaves as a teacher. Similarly, the role of mother, father, or teacher may vary among sociocultural groups. Furthermore, role patterns change over time. For example, middle-class mothers now are increasingly also working mothers, which necessitates considerable alterations in the role of mother. Indeed, this change in middle-class motherhood brings it into closer correspondence with the pattern that has long been established by working-class mothers.

Social Status

All social groups make distinctions based on various markers of high and low status. Both social class and social status are the result of stratification systems whose role assignments may vary considerably from group to group. The role of grandmother, aunt, or other family member may be more flexible among some African American, Latino, or Asian cultures with these individuals assuming different responsibility and greater importance than it does in middle-class, European American society. Often the aunt of an African American child bears considerable responsibility for the well-being of that child. Middle-class, European American teachers who are unaware of this status and relationship may, when confronted by a proactive aunt, believe that the child's mother is somehow shirking her responsibilities.

Time and Space

Differences in conceptions of time and space may also vary among social groups. In addition to differences in the divisions of time (e.g., a week, a crop harvest), groups vary in the degree to which time is valued. It is common for many European Americans, for example, to value punctuality because it is seen as an expression of respect. Because time is so highly valued, such people pay much attention to its use—time is seen as money, something to be spent or saved, or in some circumstances, to be wasted. Measures of time and their value may be much more elastic in some societies where work is less synchronized. Similarly, the ease and comfort of a person's position in

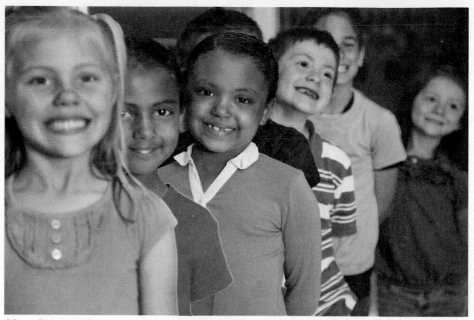

©Steve Debenport/Getty Images RF

space vis-à-vis other people may vary. How close one person stands to another when speaking and the degree to which people should stand face-to-face with another are both subject to cultural variation.

Relationship to the Group Versus the Individual

All people sometimes act according to their individual interests and sometimes according to their group allegiances. The relative emphasis on group versus individual orientation varies from group to group and may significantly affect the choices a person makes. In the dominant culture of the United States, for instance, individualism is highly valued. Schools have traditionally reinforced this value through emphasis on "doing one's own work," the ability to "work independently," and the recognition of "individual responsibility." However, other social groups, such as the Japanese or some American ethnic groups, place much greater emphasis on group behavior, group solidarity, and group helpfulness and well-being. These social groups often consider it wrong to stand out, to be independent, or to "rise above" the group. In a major study comparing national cultures on this dimension, the United States, Australia, and Great Britain stood out among the top nations on individualism (Hofstede, 1983). Guatemala, Ecuador, Panama, Indonesia, and Taiwan ranked among the highest on collectivism.

Stage 3: Making Adjustments and Reshaping Cultural Identity

Finally, as a result of prolonged intercultural interaction, individuals may experience personal change. That is, people may alter the way they perceive others and themselves, as well as how they process those perceptions. Typically, for example, individuals who have had significant intercultural experiences become more complex thinkers. This

Figure 4.6
Ways of Processing
Information

- Categorization
- Differentiation
- Attribution
- Ingroups/Outgroups
- Learning Style

accomplishment is, of course, one of the central goals of multicultural or intercultural education because it enables people to handle more culturally complex stimuli, to be more accurate in their interpretations of others' behavior, and thus to deal more effectively with the differences they encounter. As individuals continue to have intercultural experiences, they become less culture-bound and more understanding of how others perceive the world. Such individuals can now see from another's point of view; they are more complex thinkers and can handle a greater variety of diverse information. They are also less likely to make inaccurate judgments or attributions because they are more likely to inquire into puzzling beliefs and behavior, thereby improving their understanding.

Think back to the gaze-avoidance behavior in the interaction between the European American teacher and the Mexican American, African American, or South Pacific Island child. The interculturally knowledgeable teacher understands the meaning that underlies the child's gaze-avoidance and more accurately judges the child to be listening and demonstrating respect. Although even people who have considerable intercultural experience may have limited knowledge of the content of a particular cultural knowledge base, they do know that all people process information in similar ways, and they are willing to investigate the outcomes of such processes. Several important ways of processing information are listed in Figure 4.6, each of which can be investigated by the participants in intercultural exchanges.

Categorization

Because people cannot attend to all the information presented to them, they create categories for organizing and responding to similar bits of information. Cultural stereotypes, for example, are categories usually associated with particular groups of people. People involved in intercultural interactions often categorize one another quickly according to whatever category systems they have learned. Examples of this kind of categorization might be old/young, rich/poor, native/foreigner, and typical/disabled. The context within which people categorize each other also influences the categorization process. Recall the earlier example of the boy who was sent home from school before the end of each day. From one perspective, the boy was categorized as a troublemaker. Once the context of the situation was better understood, the boy was seen as a hero, doing whatever he could to help protect his mother. Of particular importance is the fact that category systems and their meanings not only differ from group to group but also are rarely neutral in value. Thus, "placing" another person in a particular category may also "place" that person in a more or less valued position (e.g., many people place being learning disabled in a less valued position than not to be learning disabled).

Differentiation

Information related to highly meaningful categories becomes more refined or differentiated. As a result, new categories may be formed. Such refinement or differentiation is usually shared only among people who have had many experiences in common (e.g., doctors) and thus may be unknown even to those whose background, apart from occupation, is similar. A good example of this process is the way in which people in Asia might differentiate rice. Because it is an extremely important part of their diet and thus their way of life, rice can be referred to by many different terms and can have many different uses. For most European Americans, rice is not as important, and thus fewer references are made to it. A school-based example of differentiation might be found in the manner in which students in a particular high school differentiate their peers into groups such as brains, nerds, jocks, and so on. Although a similar type of differentiation may occur in most high schools, the particular categories and their meaning may differ considerably from one school to the next.

Ingroups and Outgroups

People the world over divide others into those with whom they are comfortable and can discuss their concerns (ingroups) and those who are kept at a distance (outgroups). Based on initial categorization and differentiation as well as on continuing interaction, individuals may identify one another as potential members of their own ingroup or as members of an outgroup. People entering new cultural situations must recognize that they will often be considered members of an outgroup, will not share certain ingroup behavior and communication, and thus will be kept from participating in certain ingroup activities. A really good, if somewhat mundane, example of this process is the situation experienced by a substitute teacher who is, by definition, an outsider in the culture of the classroom and school.

Learning Style

Sometimes called cognitive style, **learning style** refers to a person's preferred method of learning. Learning styles are partly the result of strengths and weaknesses in sensory perception (one's hearing may be more acute than one's vision, for example). However, cultural patterning may teach a child to attend to certain kinds of stimuli rather than others, as when children from collectivist societies learn better in cooperative groups. How (and what) an individual perceives, the categories into which that person places sensory stimuli, and whether that person prefers to learn through observation, listening, or action can all be based on cultural patterns. For example, some Native Hawaiian or Native American children, as they are growing up, learn from a variety of individuals, both adults and other children. Such children may also participate more in group learning; that is, they may learn and practice a skill with other children, not necessarily on their own. These children's preferred learning style (the way in which they have learned how to learn) may be more group oriented than the learning style of the majority of their European American counterparts, who have a tendency to learn how to learn in a more individualistic manner. Such children may not achieve as well in a more traditionally oriented classroom as they might in a cooperative learning situation.

Attribution

People not only perceive others according to familiar categories, they also make judgments about others based on the behavior they observe and its meaning in their own social milieu. People judge others, for example, to be competent or incompetent, educated or naive, well-intentioned or ill-intentioned. Psychologists call these judgments *attributions* and tell us that within about 7 seconds of meeting someone new, initial judgments are made. These initial "sizing-up" judgments, once made, are usually quite resistant to change. Human judgments, however, are fallible, and certain judgment errors occur repeatedly in human thought. One of these, called the *fundamental attribution error* (Ross, 1977), describes the tendency people have to judge others on different sets of criteria than they apply to themselves, particularly with respect to shortcomings. Thus, if I fail at a given task, I am more likely to look to the situation for an explanation—it was too hot, someone else was unfair to me, the task was well beyond my capabilities. If I observe someone else fail at a task, I am more likely to explain the failure in terms of the other person's traits—she is lazy, he is uneducated, she is uncaring. This tendency is even more prevalent when individuals with different cultural patterns interact because there is likely to be unfamiliar behavior in such situations. Given the speed with which people make judgments and the probable lack of intercultural understanding, attribution errors abound in intercultural situations. Couple this with the tendency people have to form categories (and thus, sometimes, negative stereotypes about people) and you can quite easily see how a very detrimental, complex situation can evolve.

Applying the Culture-General Model

At this point, you may appreciate the potential of the culture-general model but not know how it can be applied in your daily interactions. The main value of such a model is that it allows people to build a common, culture-related vocabulary that can be used to analyze intercultural interactions in a variety of contexts. That is, it provides a tool whereby people can more accurately judge the nature of the interactions in which they are reading about, witnessing, or participating.

We can apply this to the traditional model used to explain the communication process, for instance, to show how the attribution process may be operating in an intercultural dialogue between a teacher and student from different cultures. The following four diagrams illustrate this.

In the traditional communication model (see Figure 4.7), Person A, the sender, has a message he wishes to communicate to Person B. The sender encodes the message in a form he believes the receiver, Person B, will understand. The channel refers to the medium in which the message is transmitted (e.g., print, spoken, electronic). Person B then decodes the message, hopefully attributing the same meaning that was intended by the sender.

Figure 4.7
Traditional
Communication Model

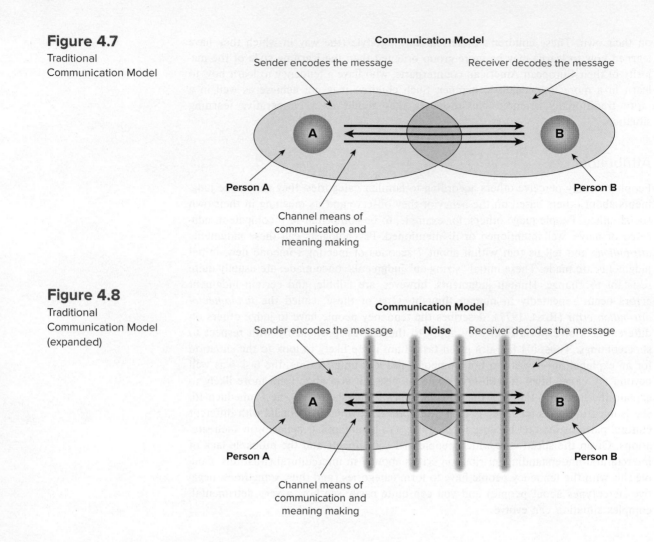

Figure 4.8
Traditional
Communication Model
(expanded)

In the traditional communication model, noise (see Figure 4.8) refers to interference that may occur in the interaction between the Sender and Receiver. Such noise can be a physical disruption like loud background noise; a physiological impairment, such as deafness; psychological interference, such as one's emotional state that may distract her from focusing on the message; or cultural difference, such as using different languages or having different meanings attributed to words.

The traditional communication model can be modified to explain the interaction that may occur between a teacher and student in an Intercultural Learning Arena model (see Figure 4.9). In this case, we understand that teacher A, socialized within her or his culture, perceives the world from her or his own culture's perspective and orientation. The student, B, has similarly been socialized within her or his culture to view the world from her or his own perspective or cultural point of view. The channel, here, may be expanded to include the instructional approach used by the teacher, including both the verbal as well as the nonverbal language used.

The noise in the Intercultural Learning Arena model (see Figure 4.10). can be expanded to include the subjective or silent messages both student and teacher may be making to themselves throughout their interaction or learning encounter. For example,

Figure 4.9

Intercultural Learning Arena Model

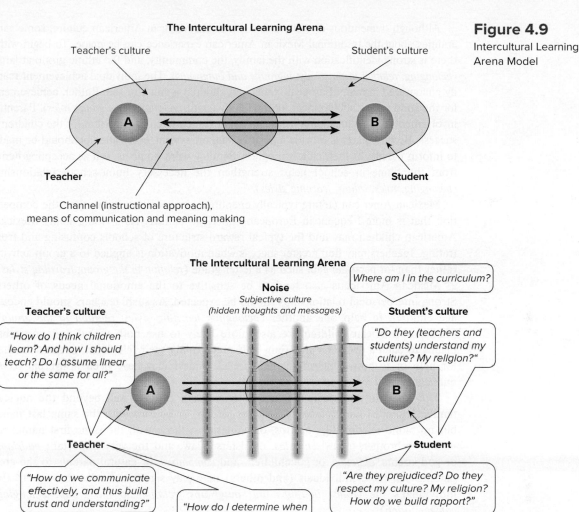

The Intercultural Learning Arena

Teacher's culture

Student's culture

A

B

Teacher

Student

Channel (instructional approach),
means of communication and meaning making

The Intercultural Learning Arena

Noise
Subjective culture
(hidden thoughts and messages)

Teacher's culture

Student's culture

Where am I in the curriculum?

"How do I think children learn? And how I should teach? Do I assume linear or the same for all?"

"Do they (teachers and students) understand my culture? My religion?"

A

B

Teacher

Student

"How do we communicate effectively, and thus build trust and understanding?"

"How do I determine when and if students learn?"

"Are they prejudiced? Do they respect my culture? My religion? How do we build rapport?"

Figure 4.10

Intercultural Learning Arena Illustrating Possible Subjective or Silent Thoughts

the student may be wondering if the teacher may be prejudiced, if she or he truly understands and values their culture, or how their group or experience is portrayed in the curriculum. The teacher, likewise, may be wondering if her or his instruction is reaching the student, how she or he may develop effective rapport with the student, or how the teacher will know if the student has achieved the instructional objectives. This internal dialogue, which can also include the various attributions each is making about the other, is going on silently all the time within the minds of all participants in an intercultural instructional event as it is in any dialogue.

The following discussion of Mexican Americans, paraphrased from Farris and Cooper's book, *Elementary Social Studies: A Whole Language Approach* (1994), can be used to illustrate how the culture general framework can be applied to enhance one's understanding of the cultural differences about a specific group. In the discussion, specific themes of the culture-general model are designated in italics. Following this discussion are a few cases for you to analyze.

Although tremendous diversity exists within the Mexican American culture, some generalities about the traditional Mexican American experience can be made. To begin with, there is strong identification with the family, the community, and the ethnic group at large (*belonging; relation to the group; ingroups and outgroups*). The individual achievement readily encouraged in many European American children is not stressed. Rather, achievement for the child means achievement for the family (*status; relation to the group; roles*). Parental involvement in the education of Mexican American children is important for the children's success. Because parents provide a positive support system, every attempt should be made to inform parents of their child's progress. Sending work home as well as accepting items from the home in school helps strengthen the necessary home-school relationship (*belonging; roles; values; learning styles*).

Mexican American culture typically encourages cooperation rather than the competition that is more frequent in European American culture. As a result, many Mexican American children may find the typical reward structure of schools confusing and frustrating. Teachers may find greater success when motivation is applied to a group activity rather than for personal gain such as a letter grade (*relation to the group; learning styles*).

Mexican Americans also tend to be sensitive to the emotional needs of others. Strong interpersonal relationships should be expected. As such, teachers should encourage children to help one another (*belonging; learning styles; relation to the group*). Mexican American children are also more likely to use both verbal and nonverbal means to elicit a teacher's attention. This may explain their reluctance to ask a teacher for help or to pose a question; their actual request may have been nonverbal (*communication and language use; attribution*).

The Mexican American humanistic orientation extends well beyond the nuclear family. Extended family actively includes *primos*, or cousins with the same last name but no blood relationship; *tocayos*, or namesakes, those with the same first name; *cuñados*, or brothers-in-law; *cuñadas*, or sisters-in-law; and the very important *padrinos*, or godparents, *ahijados*, or godchildren, and *compadres*, or natural parents to the godparents. All these individuals (and others) may play significant roles throughout the individual's life (*roles; ingroups and outgroups; relation to the group; belonging; categorization*).

In such an extended family, status and role relationships are rigidly defined. Younger children defer to older children, and females often defer to males. Respect for parents is expected, regardless of one's age. Sexual roles are well defined, with females having responsibility for the condition of the home and the raising of children. Males, having higher status, are primarily the wage earners (*roles; class and status; categorization*). There is also a strong obligation to the family. Teachers should keep these roles and obligations in mind when hearing that students have responsibilities such as caring for younger children after school or working in the family business (*values; relation to the group; roles*).

Finally, among Mexican American families there exists a strong orientation and identification with Mexican Catholic ideology. This powerful force reinforces their value system, many of their daily actions, and their respect for parents, family, and tradition (*rituals and superstitions; values; belonging*).

Identifying Commonalities Among Groups

In the brief example about Mexican American culture, at least 11 culture-general themes were evident; perhaps you have identified others. Used in this manner, the culture-general model can help both students and teachers find commonalities among the cultural differences they encounter. For example, some aspects of the Mexican American experience are similar to those in other ethnic experiences, and some are different. Some may be similar to your own experience, and others will be different.

Viewed in the broadest terms possible, the goal of this model goes beyond simply negotiating intercultural interactions or adapting one's teaching to accommodate culturally diverse learning styles. Its search for commonalities among people of all cultures offers the possibility that all individuals in a pluralistic society will feel sufficiently similar that they can confront differences. In short, awareness of similarities—kinship feelings, for example—can motivate people to learn about and appreciate differences. This model offers a way to go beyond tolerance, which often means "letting people alone," to begin to build a truly intercultural society.

Identifying Differences Within a Group

The Mexican American discussion presented in this chapter has at least two dimensions in which the cultural-general model is useful: (1) in building a common vocabulary around differences between groups, and (2) in using those concepts to analyze culture-specific information. The information about traditional Mexican American culture provided an example of using the model across ethnic/nationality boundaries—differences that are most commonly thought of as cultural differences—and of looking for commonalities among specific cultural ideas and practices. A third dimension of difference is also made more visible through the use of the culture-general model, and that is in identifying and analyzing differences within a specific cultural group. Such differences as social class, geographical location, sexual orientation, or religion, for example, are not always easy to "see" but may in fact be important differences in the way individuals perceive the world, interact with one another, and approach learning.

Questions raised by a consideration of these kinds of differences can lead to inquiry about, for instance, whether particular Mexican American children are Catholic, whether particular Mexican American children have learned to operate in a cooperative manner, or whether particular Mexican American children identify strongly with their extended families. Research has shown, for example, that some of these cultural attributes may diminish in successive generations of Mexican American families. Indeed, to automatically assume that such characteristics will occur in all children and adults of Mexican American descent is unwisely to stereotype all individuals who "belong" to a particular ethnic group, and to run a grave risk of misinterpreting observable behavior.

Critical Incidents at Wake Central High

The next step in understanding the culture-general model is to apply it in the analysis of some school-based intercultural encounters. Only by doing so is it possible to understand the degree to which culture influences teaching and learning in schools. This section examines the kinds of incidents that might occur in the fictitious Wake Central High School described in this chapter's Case Study (see p. 108). You should realize, however, that the incidents reported here could easily occur in most schools in the United States.

Go back to the Case Study and take a close look at Melinda's induction year. Stop at this point and consider some of the culture-general themes that may be at play. It seems obvious that this situation is highly charged and emotional for many of the people involved. To begin with, Melinda must reconcile the reality of this situation with her early expectations. Thus, Melinda is clearly experiencing a case of disconfirmed expectations. Melinda must begin to understand the real situation and adjust her behavior according to what is, rather than to what she expected.

Melinda is also faced with a considerable amount of ambiguity in her new situation. Although she is enthusiastic about the challenge of an urban teaching experience, she is quite unprepared for its specific dimensions. Such a situation promises to elicit a high degree of uncertainty or ambiguity. Melinda is aware that certain actions are expected, but unsure of what those actions are or how to begin to learn them. At another level, Melinda is certainly experiencing a high degree of anxiety as she strives to integrate into the faculty of the school. Such ambiguity and anxiety, though common, must eventually be negotiated if Melinda is to be effective in her new setting. As Melinda begins to build closer relationships with other teachers and gain a better understanding of her students, her emotions will come under control and she can begin to feel as if she belongs in this setting.

Melinda's situation represents only one of many interculturally complex and oftentimes ambiguous situations that might arise in such a diverse setting as Wake Central High. The Critical Incidents describe some other situations that could conceivably occur. Read each incident and consider responses to the questions that follow, or discuss these in small groups. You will find some discussion at the end of the Critical Incidents section.

Critical Incident

Andre's Role Dilemma

Andre is a 23-year-old, first-year social studies teacher hired at the same time as Melinda. African American and from a middle-class background, Andre has always prided himself on knowing a lot about people at all socioeconomic levels and from many different ethnic groups. Andre began the year with the intent of relating especially well to the African American students. He intends to show them that he is really one of them and understands their needs.

While walking down the hall on his first day in school, Andre sees a group of young African American males standing near a wall of lockers. They are wearing typical casual clothes—low-slung pants, T-shirts, and sneakers. Andre is dressed in slacks, shirt, tie, and sport coat. Andre greets the group with a hearty "What's happening, bro?" The students look at him and continue with their own conversation. Andre tries to strike up a conversation by asking about any good rap groups in the school, saying that he has done some "bad rappin'" himself. The boys eye him up and down, then slowly move on down the hall. Andre is puzzled, thinking that they would respond to his approach and would see him as a "brother."

The next day, Andre sees the same group again and begins to approach them. Seeing him coming, one of the group steps forward and quite sarcastically says, "Hey, bro! You be down in Room 104 (the teachers' lounge), not in my face!" Then the group walks away. Andre does not understand the group's obvious hostility and rejection.

- Why do you think the students rejected Andre's attempts to be friendly?
- What culture-general themes do you see operating in this scenario?

Critical Incident

Rosita's Alientation Problem

Rosita Gomez had been in the United States for two months, arriving as an orphan from El Salvador, and sponsored by a European American, middle-class family. Before her arrival, her American parents went to Wake Central High School and provided the administrators and faculty with information about her situation. To make her adjustment easier, a number of teachers organized a group of students to act as sponsors for Rosita. The students were to teach her about the school and community and help her with transition problems as well as to offer friendship.

During these two months, the appointed students have indeed helped Rosita in school and have been friendly to her. They have encouraged her to become involved in student council and to attend after-school extra-help sessions whenever needed. Rosita, though, is often left out of students' social activities such as parties, group movie dates, and volleyball games, and she thinks she is being treated as an outcast. She feels lonely and afraid and complains to her parents and school counselor about her feelings. Her complaints confuse the other students and teachers very much because they have tried hard to make Rosita feel at home.

- How might you explain this situation?
- What culture-general themes do you see operating here?

Critical Incident

Joao's Identity Crisis

Joao is a teenager from Providence, Rhode Island, who has been sent to live for two years with his aunt and uncle in North Carolina. This is the first time that Joao has been away from his immediate family, who immigrated from Brazil when he was a child. His family is strongly united and feels a deep pride in their Brazilian heritage. Joao had heard that Wake Central has a reputation as a place where students from different backgrounds get along well together, so he has not been worrying about being the only Brazilian in the student body. He has looked forward to attending his new school.

During Joao's first week in school, he discovered that several members of the faculty viewed him as belonging to a group of students who spoke Spanish. A few teachers greeted him in Spanish, and one suggested that he join a club for mainly Central American students. Joao was surprised and resentful that these teachers just assumed he was Hispanic. During his second week, a teacher gave him a notice to take home to his uncle, and it, too, was in Spanish. Joao startled the teacher by breaking into tears and loudly protesting, "Please try to remember—I'm Brazilian. I speak Portugese not Spanish!"

- How would you explain Joao's reaction?
- What culture-general themes may be operating here—from all perspectives?

Critical Incident

Rema's Classroom Concerns

Rema is a 16-year-old girl from Syria who came to the United States as one of just a few Syrian refugees. She was fortunate to have family already living in the country who eagerly welcomed her. Although she still has some difficulties in speaking and writing

English, her language skills are sufficient for her to be academically successful in Wake Central High. Midway through the 11th grade, Rema was achieving B's and C's in all her classes, including Andre's social studies class.

Actually, social studies is Rema's favorite subject, and Andre continually remarks to others on the breadth and depth of her reading. Rema reads voraciously and does not limit herself to that which is studied in class. She keeps up on international news and reads literature in two languages.

Andre is concerned, however, about Rema's test scores. When the class takes a multiple-choice, true-false, or fill-in-the-blank test, Rema's grades are usually among the highest. When the class is assigned an interpretive essay, however, Rema's grade is always much lower. Andre has said many times, "Rema just never really gets to the point; she tries to talk about everything at once." Despite repeated efforts to remedy this writing problem, Rema continues to write confusing analyses.

- How might you best explain this situation?
- What culture-general concepts do you see in this situation?

Critical Incident

Lack of Communication With Kaye

Issues of communication affect dialogue among teachers as well. Kaye Stoddard is in the middle of her first year as assistant principal at Wake Central High. She is an energetic person who seeks out staff input concerning school policies and curriculum. She encourages staff participation through periodic surveys and group discussions at staff meetings. Lately, however, Kaye has been disturbed about the dearth of input she is receiving from the two Latino teachers. She is particularly interested in their ideas because so many of the school's students are Latino. Although she has solicited feedback through weekly questionnaires in each teacher's mailbox, most of her replies come from the European American teachers.

- How might this situation be explained?
- What culture-general concepts may be at play?

Discussion of Critical Incidents

Andre's Role Dilemma

There are many possible explanations for Andre's situation. First, the group may feel that Andre's clothes are too different. They can't relate to this different-looking adult (*outgroup; categorization*). Second, Andre's use of Ebonics or Black English may be incorrect in this particular time and place and thus may label him in their eyes as a "phony"— someone who can't be trusted (*communication; outgroup*). Third, it is possible that Andre came on too hard to these particular students and that he was seen as pushy and was rejected because of it (*role; situational behavior; communication*).

Using the culture-general framework to analyze the situation suggests another possible explanation. The group may not accept Andre because they see him as an outsider regardless of his race or his language. Andre is still a teacher in the eyes of these students (*role; status*) and one that they do not yet know. Andre has been categorized by the students in a different way than he would categorize himself; that is, as an outgroup member rather than as the ingroup member he expected to be (*categorization; ingroup versus outgroup*).

It is important to differentiate the particular criteria that others use to form categories and thus the meaning attributed to those groups. Although Andre may have been fairly close to their age and talked their talk, he is still seen as an adult teacher, an authority figure who perhaps cannot be trusted, at least at the outset. As a teacher, he should not expect to be included as one of their group. Their response told him that he should be in Room 104, that he is a teacher and should act like one. New teachers are usually eager to be accepted by students. This desire is normal, especially because teachers may not be far removed from the lives and concerns of high school students themselves. Given time, Andre can establish the rapport he wants, but he must do so in his role as a teacher.

Rosita's Alienation Problem

It is possible that Rosita, having had a major transition in her life recently, is magnifying the situation. Perhaps the circumstances are such that she is experiencing what is commonly referred to as culture, or adjustment shock. However, *culture shock* is a very generalized term that refers to an overall reaction to a complex series of events; the term isn't very useful when analyzing specific situations. There is something more specific going on here.

It is also possible that the students do not really like Rosita and are trying to have as little to do with her as possible. The appointed students may feel put upon by their teachers and are thus taking it out on Rosita. However, the students are having what appears to be extensive contact with Rosita in school. If they did not like her, they would probably forgo school contact as well.

Viewed through the culture-general model, it is possible that Rosita's predicament can be understood in terms of *ingroup and outgroup* behavior. In every culture there exist ingroups, people who are comfortable with one another, share similar values and casual language, and seek each other's company. Ingroups allow people to share their concerns, laugh and joke about problems as a way to reduce tensions, and generally just let their hair down. The students in this situation represent such an ingroup. Rosita has left her own ingroup behind in El Salvador and needs to reestablish herself as part of a new ingroup. The students, however, do not see Rosita as being part of their ingroup, at least not yet. She would not understand most of their jokes, does not share their intimate and extensive knowledge of other students and teachers, and could not easily enter into their conversation. The students thus do not invite Rosita to share in their social activities. Not belonging to an ingroup, Rosita feels like an outcast (*belonging*) and is missing the support system so needed during her difficult transition to a new culture.

Joao's Identity Crisis

Many different issues may be at play in Joao's situation. First, Joao might have felt some dislocation at being sent to live with his aunt and uncle in the first place. His sense of unity with his family in Providence was very strong, and it is reasonable to suppose that he missed them very much (*belonging*). Second, in Providence Joao had been attending schools where many other students were native Brazilians. The idea of going to school with students from other ethnic and cultural groups—but not Brazilian—although initially interesting, might also have been somewhat frightening (*ingroup and outgroups*). It is also possible that Joao's parents had kept him under such tight discipline that he never learned much self-discipline. Thus, his first experience of living away from home may have been so demanding that he was unable to control himself.

At another level, Joao was obviously upset about being identified as a member of a cultural group other than his own (*categorization*; *values*). Proud to be a native Brazilian and having shared this pride with other Brazilian students back in Providence, he couldn't adjust to being viewed as a Spanish speaker from Mexico or Central America. In addition, he was used to teachers who recognized the Portuguese language and culture, and he was perhaps shocked to find teachers who did not (*disconfirmed expectations*).

The teachers meant to be helpful to Joao, of course. They no doubt thought he came from one of the Spanish-speaking countries because they needed to quickly fit him into one of the ethnic and cultural categories already familiar to them. Because the Portuguese language is similar enough to Spanish that Joao could understand the teachers when they addressed him in Spanish, they found it convenient to *categorize* him with the other Spanish-speaking students.

Rema's Classroom Concerns

There are many ways to explain Rema's writing performance. It is possible that she lacks the basic writing skills and vocabulary necessary to write lengthy compositions of this kind. However, her overall academic performance indicates that she is competent in English vocabulary and writing. Her problems with written expression are probably not due to technical deficiencies.

It is also possible that Rema has misunderstood or misinterpreted the main elements of the work she is studying. But having read works of equal breadth and depth on her own, it is unlikely that Rema is unable to analyze and appreciate what she is reading.

Alternatively, Rema may not be able to think clearly under the pressure of tests. However, she doesn't seem to exhibit this problem in objective tests; she shows no particular "test anxiety." So Rema's problem seems to lie elsewhere.

Analyzed from the standpoint of cultural differences, however, it is possible that Middle Eastern and North American preferred *learning modes, cognitive styles, and communication patterns* are very different. In many cultures, communication is accomplished through associations. Everything that is associated with an idea is considered relevant when thinking about or communicating a concept. Such communication may seem highly indirect to a European American, who typically gets right to the point and reasons in a systematic, step-by-step fashion. In contrast, a Middle Easterner may make many loops while communicating a particular point. In short, when viewed in terms of her native Syrian culture, Rema's highly associative compositions demonstrate both her knowledge of the subject and her overall intellectual ability. Once Rema and her teacher are aware of these culturally different writing styles, they can take some practical steps to improve the situation.

Lack of Communication With Kaye

One simple explanation for Kaye's dilemma might be that the Latino teachers do not want to interact with Kaye because she is not Hispanic. However, there is no justification for this explanation. The entire school population is mixed, thereby making it difficult for the Latino teachers to limit their interactions with non-Latinos. Also, there is no indication that Kaye feels that she is the target of hostility.

It is also possible that the European American teachers dominate the Latino teachers, giving them little chance to express their opinions. Again, however, there is no indication that domination is the problem. Nor is there any indication that the Latino teachers are indifferent concerning the subjects Kaye includes in the surveys and meetings. Like other professionals, most teachers have strong opinions about many issues in their workplace.

A more probable explanation can be found in culturally different *communication* styles. Kaye has taken an impersonal approach to eliciting opinions, whereas the Latino teachers may favor a more personalized approach. Latino culture strongly emphasizes the affective side of interpersonal relationships. Personalized contact is thus very important to many Latino teachers. Although Kaye is genuinely interested in the opinions of all her teachers, she has approached them impersonally through her written surveys and large-group staff meetings. The Latino teachers might respond more easily if approached individually or addressed personally at a meeting. At the same time, many Latinos feel strong affiliation with the group (*relationship to the group*; *individualism versus collectivism*), and the Latino teachers might respond even more enthusiastically if they were asked for their ideas and opinions together in a small group.

Each of these Critical Incidents has explored several of the many possible cultural issues at work in diverse settings like Wake Central High School. They illustrate ways in which classrooms and schools function as cultural crossroads, as places where people with infinite variations of cultural knowledge, beliefs, values, and skills meet and are forced to interact. In this chapter we have presented a culture-general model that offers a language and concepts that provide a common framework for all such interactions, no matter what their variation. Perhaps you would like to analyze experiences you have had that might be understood in light of the culture-general model. See if you can think of some.

Part 2 of this book presents longer Case Studies in which teachers, students, administrators, parents, and others also experience various cross-cultural interactions in the context of evolving ideas of good practice in schools. Remember as you read on that there is never any "one best answer" to the issues that arise. Indeed, an understanding of the complexities of cultural diversity suggests that in many instances the idea of a single "best solution" is not only impossible but is also inimical to a culturally pluralistic environment. In short, teachers must learn to feel comfortable with, appreciate the possibilities of, and negotiate effectively in ambiguous situations.

Summary

In no other social setting in society does such a diverse gathering of people come together for a prolonged period of time than in the school. Thus, the potential for a wide range of intercultural interactions between students and teachers is great. This chapter introduced the 18-theme culture-general framework for understanding intercultural interactions between people, regardless of their cultural backgrounds, who they are interacting with, or the roles that they adopt. Such a framework provides an opportunity for people to better understand their emotional reactions to intercultural situations, the knowledge base that people bring with them as a result of being socialized within any given culture, and the manner in which people's cultural identity may be reformed. Such a framework also provides a vocabulary and categories with which people can discuss cross-cultural issues with others.

Chapter Review

Go to the Online Learning Center at www.mhhe.com/cushner9e to review important content from the chapter, practice with key terms, take a chapter quiz, and access active workbook activities.

Key Terms

acculturation 115	indigenous people 116	segregation 117
assimilation 116	integration 116	separation 117
ethnic groups 115	marginalization 117	sojourners 115
immigrants 115	refugees 115	

Observing Cultural Differences

Purpose: To apply the 18-theme culture-general framework to casual observations made during interactions with others.

Instructions: Make extended observations of yourself as well as others over the course of about a week. The focus of your observations should be on potential misunderstanding or miscommunication between people of different cultural backgrounds (remember that we define culture rather broadly). Record your observations as precisely as possible, identifying any and all of the culture-general themes that you believe apply. Finally, propose alternative explanations or attributions for the behavior you have observed from two (or more) perspectives. Use the following as a guide, but do not necessarily limit yourself to the space provided. You should make *at least* five different relevant observations. Make additional copies of this form if needed.

Example

Interaction as I Observed It	Cultural-General Theme(s)	Possible Attributions
Two girls, one Mexican and the other European American, discuss plans of what they will do Friday night. Mexican girl insists upon asking her parents' permission before making commitment to her friend.	Family roles Individualism vs. Collectivism	Collectivist orientation (tendency for Mexican). May require approval from others before taking action, whereas European American (individualistic tendency) is more comfortable making her own plans.

Observation 1

Interaction as I Observed It	Cultural-General Theme(s)	Possible Attributions

140

Observation 2

Interaction as I Observed It	Cultural-General Theme(s)	Possible Attributions

Observation 3

Interaction as I Observed It	Cultural-General Theme(s)	Possible Attributions

Reflective Questions

1. Reflect on the 18-theme culture-general themes introduced in this chapter. These themes are meant to identify issues that people are likely to encounter when interacting with people different from them. Using the following sentence as a starting point, fill in the blank with each of the 18 themes and answer the questions accordingly.

   "Can you think of a time when _____ was evident in your life or in interactions with others? How might this have interfered with your ability to function effectively? When might it be an asset to you?"

2. Interview a student or a family who has come from another country. What experiences can they recall about their cultural adjustment to a new land? What have you learned from them about their experience that would assist you as a teacher?

3. Reflect on the acculturation groups discussed in the chapter. What are some needs that would be similar and different among students who were immigrants, refugees, minority group members, members of an indigenous group, or short-term sojourners (such as year-abroad foreign exchange students)?

4. Locate a newspaper article that discusses a cultural conflict in a school or community. How can you apply the 18-theme cultural-general framework to better understand the dynamics at play?

References

Berardo, K. (2012). Framework: Four key components of transition planning. In K. Berardo and D. Deardorff (Eds.), *Building cultural competence: Innovative activities and models,* (pp. 183–189). Sterling, VA: Stylus Publishing.

Berry, J. (1990). Psychology of acculturation: Understanding individuals moving between cultures. In R. Brislin (Ed.), *Applied cross-cultural psychology* (pp. 232–253). Newbury Park, CA: Sage.

Berry, J. (2004). Fundamental psychological processes in intercultural relations. In D. Landis, J. Bennett, & M. Bennett (Eds.), *Handbook of intercultural training* (3rd ed.). Thousand Oaks, CA: Sage.

Cummins, J. (1979). Cognitive/academic language proficiency, linguistic interdependence, the optimum age question, and some other matters. *Working Papers on Bilingualism.* No. *19*, 121–129.

Cushner, K., & Brislin, R. (1996). *Intercultural interactions*: *A practical guide* (2nd ed.). Thousand Oaks, CA: Sage.

Farris, P. J., & Cooper, S. M. (1994). *Elementary social studies*: *A whole language approach.* Madison, WI: Brown & Benchmark.

Hallgarten, Tabberer & McCarthy (2015). 3rd Culture schools: International schools as creative catalysts for a new global education. Royal Society for the Encouragement of the Arts, Manufacturers and Commerce, London (www.thersa.org)

Hofstede, G. (1983). Dimension of national cultures in fifty countries and three regions. In J. Deregowski, S. Dzuirawiec, & R. C. Annis (Eds.), *Expiscations in cross-cultural psychology* (pp. 335–355). Lisse, The Netherlands: Swets & Zeitlinger.

Lightfoot, S. L. (1989). Interview with Bill Moyers. *The World of Ideas* [Television series]. American Broadcasting Corporation.

Lightfoot, S. (n.d.). AZQuotes.com. Retrieved from AZQuotes.com Web site: http://www.azquotes.com/quote/1264797

Lysgaard, S. (1955). Adjustment in a foreign society: Norwegian Fulbright grantees visiting the United States. *International Sociol Science Bulletin*, *7*, 45–51.

NAEHCY (2017). National Association for the Education of Homeless Children and Youth. Retrieved from http://www.naehcy.org/legislation-and-policy/legislative-updates-news/us-department-education-releases-homeless-guidance

National Center for Educational Statistics (2012). *Back to school statistics: Fast facts.* Retrieved from https://nces.ed.gov/fastfacts/display.asp?id=372

Oberg, K. (1960). Culture shock: Adjustments to new cultural environments. *Practical Anthropology*, *7*, 177–182.

Pedersen, P. (1988). *A handbook for developing multicultural awareness.* Alexandria, VA: American Association for Counseling and Development.

Redfield, R., Linton, R., & Herskovits, M. J. (1936). Memorandum for the study of acculturation. *American Anthropologist*, *38, 149–152.

Ross, L. (1977). The intuitive psychologist and his shortcomings: Distortions in the attribution process. In L. Berkowitz (Ed.), *Advances in experimental social psychology* (Vol. 10). New York: Academic Press.

Trifonovitch, G. (1977). Culture learning-culture teaching. *Educational Perspectives*, *16*(4), 18–22.

Ward, C., Bochner, S., & Furnam, A. (2001). *The psychology of culture shock.* East Sussex, England: Routledge.

©KidStock/Getty Images RF

Intercultural Development

Considering the Growth of Self and Others

Focus Questions

1. Have you ever said to yourself something like, "I certainly wouldn't have thought that way a few years (or months) ago. I've changed and see things much differently now"? As a teacher, you expect students to learn, to grow, and to change as a result of certain experiences or encounters. What benchmarks might you use to determine if your students are becoming more sophisticated in their understanding and analysis of culture and intercultural effectiveness? What benchmarks might you use to determine if you are becoming more sophisticated in your understanding and analysis of culture and more interculturally competent?

2. What differences can you identify in people who are more effective working across cultures in comparison to those who exhibit more ethnocentric or mono-cultural behaviors?

3. How might you help students as well as yourself to become more interculturally competent—that is, to advance from an ethnocentric orientation to one that is more ethnorelative?

" One of the higher callings for young people in the coming century will be working to increase intercultural understanding. Such people will be the missionaries of the age, spreading light among groups . . . by giving them a modern vision of the new global community. "

CARL COON

This book aims not only to help you develop an understanding of how individuals are socialized into their immediate social and individual identity groups (i.e., family, ethnic group), but also to address your subsequent ability to accept and interact more effectively with people different from yourself. In this chapter we look at what it means to become more interculturally competent, to develop greater awareness and sensitivity to your own culture as well as your ability to interact effectively with cultures other than you own.

The Case Study in this chapter presents multiple perspectives and viewpoints on issues related to culture and intercultural interaction in a school and community. As you read the Case Study, try to identify the variety of points of view. The Critical Incidents at the end of the chapter will bring you back to the Case Study as you explore the development of intercultural sensitivity.

Intercultural Competence

Just what does it mean to have an intercultural mind-set and skill-set? What are the attitudes and behaviors of people who are not only comfortable but effective working across cultures? How would you recognize such an orientation in teachers and students? In yourself? How can we assist people to develop such an orientation?

Early studies in intercultural competence attempted to identify the specific behaviors that were evident in individuals who were effective at living and working across cultures. Such studies suggested that interculturally effective people have three qualities in common:

(1) They are able to manage the psychological stress that accompanies most intercultural interactions.
(2) They are able to communicate effectively across cultures—verbally as well as nonverbally.

©FatCamera/E+/Getty Images RF

Case Study

Dissent at Maplewood School

Sue Murray (fifth-grade math and science team teacher): It didn't begin with Mr. Jameson's letter to the editor in the local paper late in February, but that was when it did gain momentum and draw an increasing number of people into the issue. And now, just two months from the end of the school year, all kinds of people are angry and hurt, many are confused, teachers are getting anxious, and the students don't know what to think. Mr. Goodwin, the principal, seems to be doing all that he can to bring the various parties together, and as I understand it, they are making considerable progress. Let's see if I can piece together all that has happened. I'll begin with the letter I just referred to. Then there are a few other letters to the editor that show the range of responses.

Dear Daily Record Editor,

As a taxpayer and citizen of this fine city, I resent what I see going on in the schools. As I know them, schools are meant to prepare young people for the future. If students are to go to college, then they should have the prerequisite courses they need to succeed. If they are to learn a trade, then the school is to provide them with the skills they will need to do their job. A student who is undecided on what the future will hold should be given an opportunity to try many different things. This is all well and good, and is as it should be. It is the way schools have operated since I went to them many years ago.

But since when have the schools become responsible for addressing all the demands of any group that comes along and claims they have been mistreated or ignored in society? I do not think the schools should be teaching multicultural education. What is it anyway? No one has shown me a book on multicultural education that students study from. It's not a part of the state assessments, the SAT, nor has it ever been discussed in any way with the Common Core. We used to have good schools here that worked for everyone. Now they don't seem to be working at all. Why should teachers and students spend their time having so-called cultural festivals and potluck dinners, and paying good money to invite some cultural dance group in to perform for kids? Let's get it straight, schools have a responsibility to prepare people for life, not to teach everyone about other groups' problems. With so many different people now living in America, there would be no more room in the school day if that were all teachers taught. Besides, aren't we all supposed to be Americans anyway? If people don't like the way things are, they should go back to where they've come from. After all, they came to America—they should do it the American way!

But perhaps it is not all the teachers' fault. Perhaps there is a lack of leadership in the schools—from the administrators to the board of education. And while I cannot stop paying my taxes, I can vote "NO" for the next school levy and vote to replace the current members of the board. I think many others would agree with me and follow my lead.

John Jameson, a disgruntled citizen
February 27

Editor, Daily Record,

I am writing in reference to Mr. Jameson's letter about issues in the schools. I agree. It's time we take a stand and stop pandering to every group that comes along. My son returned from serving in the Army in Afghanistan and has been out of work for six months now, and he can't seem to get a job because of such things as affirmative action and job-outsourcing. Yet I see many other people working in jobs that could go to real Americans who support our country in very real ways. I've traveled to other countries and each time I do I am reminded about how much better we have it here in America. I think the schools are part of the problem, and they'd better shape up soon.

Rebecca Reynolds
March 5

To the Editor of the Daily Record,

I wish to disagree with the letters written by Mr. Jameson and Ms. Reynolds who complained about the schools addressing multicultural education. As someone who works in the business community, I know how fast the world is changing—much faster than many people in this city seem to be—and our children must be prepared for these changes. School may be the only

(continued)

place where children can learn about other people—about other cultures, about how different people think and act, and about how to learn to get along with those who are different. Most parents are too busy or not experienced enough to tackle such a difficult task; therefore, we need the schools to do this for us. After all, it is in the school, like nowhere else in society, that children of different backgrounds come together for long periods of time. What better place is there for children to learn about diversity? I am in full support of our schools doing all they can to address diversity, and I hope others in this community come forward with their support as well.

Joyce Maples
March 8

Sue Murray: As I already said, it wasn't the letters to the editor that started everything, but they do give you a sense of the variety of people's reactions. Ever since the start of the school year tensions have continued to mount. It seems as if no one is happy with the way things are, and I don't understand why. I was excited to begin teaching in the fifth-grade team after teaching for 5 years in a fourth-grade self-contained classroom. But with all the developmental changes the children are going through and all the ethnic and racial tensions that have emerged, I don't know if I can take another year. We have parents who are angry that we are not addressing what they think are critical issues. We have had a number of parent meetings involving all the teachers as well as the principal where we attempted to discuss their concerns, but nothing seemed to help. And many parents and other local citizens have been showing up at school board meetings to voice their concerns.

I think the problems began back in October at the school Halloween party. We have been concerned about violence in general and the increase in the number of violent movies that influence many of the children's choices of costume. Rather than have children dress in whatever costume they might if they went out trick-or-treating, we encouraged them to come dressed as some historical, political, or social figure. I was really surprised when two boys, Tom and Daniel, came dressed as Native Americans and three others, Keenan, James, and Troy, came dressed as sports mascots—two as Cleveland Indians and one as an Atlanta Brave. What a social commentary they were making, and quite sophisticated, I might add, for a group of young students. They had placards that challenged people's stereotypes: some demanded changing the team logos and some argued to maintain them out of tradition. Even the imbalance of power was evident in the three-to-two mix they presented. Many of the children were oblivious to the messages these students were trying to make, but not all. Some, in fact, were quite taken by their statement. Their presence even caused a stir among some of the parents who came to observe the annual Halloween march around the school. Mrs. Marks, the president of the PTO, took a photo of them for the school newspaper. The paper was printed just before Thanksgiving. I think it was this incident, in combination with some of the Thanksgiving plays and classroom activities, that really set things off. Some parents of the younger children in the school started complaining that putting on a traditional Thanksgiving play was perpetuating stereotypes. I do agree with them on that account. It was soon after we came back to school after the winter break that I really began to be bothered by all this attention to diversity. Some of the African American parents started complaining that not enough was being done to present their struggles and that we shouldn't be doing things only during February for Black History Month. The PTO was asked to form a multicultural committee, and aside from Mrs. Marks, it seemed that there were mostly minority parents involved.

And then, what really got me was when Mr. Goodwin, the principal, called me in to his office. He said one of the African American parents complained that I wasn't a good teacher. The father said that his son wasn't learning from me and that I was treating some of the kids differently. I don't treat any of my students any differently. And I really think the parents would accuse me of playing favorites if I did start doing things differently for different groups. After all, we all want the kids to learn what's best for them. And we've been pretty good about being able to make that happen in this school—for everybody. I think the diversity is an asset for us. The more differences we have here, the better. More difference equals more creative ideas in the classroom, and I certainly wouldn't want all the kids to be the same around here.

It's bad enough that most of the teachers are pretty much the same. If everyone were the same, it would be boring. The more cultures people can know about, the better off we'd all be. I have my master's degree with a specialty in math, and I'm pretty good at science. I'm a good teacher. I can't help it if some of the kids don't catch on as quickly as the others or don't all learn in the same way. I work hard at what I do, and I resent being accused of playing favorites or not treating all kids the same. Some of these parents should try to teach a room full of kids who are overloading on hormones. It's not easy work, you know.

I asked Mr. Goodwin to let me know which of the parents complained, but he wouldn't tell me. I told him that I'd rather meet personally with the parents to discuss the issue instead of them hiding behind the principal. He said he was arranging a parents' meeting soon and that would be the time for people to discuss their feelings. He said he was considering bringing in a facilitator to help keep the discussion in a positive light.

I wonder how my teaching team feels?

(3) They are able to develop and maintain new and essential interpersonal relationships (Brislin & Yoshida, 1994).

Other conceptualizations of intercultural effectiveness and sensitivity consider the interplay between the cognitive, affective, and behavioral domains (Bennett, 1993).

People with an intercultural mind-set, for instance, move from an avoidance or a tolerance of difference to a respect and appreciation of difference. They move from an unconscious ethnocentrism to a more conscious awareness of their own and others' cultures. And instead of being conscious of what not to do to avoid racism, sexism, and other prejudices, they understand what to do to create respectful, productive intercultural relationships. Interculturally effective people are proactive in nature and seek out diverse perspectives and contributions when making decisions and taking actions.

Different from such terms as multicultural or international, the term "intercultural" refers to a penetration at the interpersonal level, implying an exchange between individuals of different groups with a focus on building trust, understanding and thus interpersonal relationships so people can begin to collaborate across cultural boundaries. Intercultural sensitivity refers to the ability to perceive cultural context, recognizing both cultural similarities and differences. *Intercultural competence*, then, refers to the enactment of intercultural sensitivity through the acquisition of an expanded repertoire of culturally appropriate behavior that is suitable for the time, place and circumstances (Cushner, 2014). *Intercultural competence* is comprised of an open-mindedness and genuine interest in other cultures; being observant and knowledgeable about cultural differences and similarities; an ability to resist stereotypes and anticipate complexity; and, being able and willing to modify behavior so people can interact and communicate effectively with those different from themselves (Deardorff, 2009). In essence, this equally reflects a mind-set, a heart-set, and a skill-set.

Interculturally competent individuals thus are able to listen empathically, perceive others accurately, maintain a nonjudgmental approach, gather appropriate information about another culture, shift their frame of reference as required, take appropriate risks, and thus recognize and respond appropriately to cultural differences. In real-life outside the classroom as well as within, such skills are critical when people engage in decision making, negotiation, or problem solving across cultures; when subordinates and authority figures from different backgrounds interact extensively; or when individuals or families make major transitions. The school and classroom provide an ideal context in which to practice and develop these skills.

Intercultural competence may be as much a tool for survival in today's world as is the development of literacy, mathematics, and technological skill. Educators today must strive to fully integrate an intercultural education and perspective while carrying on with the traditional educational needs of communities and nations. Yet these are not easy issues to adequately address. Intercultural education and training is a delicate and difficult endeavor that must be approached with the greatest of sensitivity. Bennett (1993) pointed out that intercultural interactions among human populations have typically been accompanied by violence and aggression:

> Intercultural sensitivity is not natural. It is not part of our primate past, nor has it characterized most of human history. Cross-cultural contact usually has been accompanied by bloodshed, oppression, or genocide. Education and training in intercultural communication [and we might say intercultural education] is an approach to changing our "natural" behavior. With the concepts and skills developed in this field, we ask learners to transcend traditional ethnocentrism and to explore new relationships across cultural boundaries. This attempt at change must be approached with the greatest possible care (p. 21).

In addition to the intense reactions identified by Bennett, evidence for the unnaturalness of intercultural contact can be seen in people's everyday behaviors. Many people, including those who do not harbor intense prejudices, admit that interactions with culturally different others tend to be more anxiety provoking than are interactions with very similar people (Cushner & Brislin, 1996). For a smaller number of people, this anxiety leads to a strong preference for interactions with similar others (a small ingroup) and an active avoidance of intercultural interactions. Such people, however, will not fare well in today's world, where intercultural interaction is increasingly commonplace.

Developing Intercultural Sensitivity

So how do people develop intercultural sensitivity? Of great concern is the relative lack of information most teachers and teacher educators have about intercultural development and sensitivity. Just what is meant by this concept? How do we know when we "have it"? What are the benchmarks that teachers should strive for with their students? If we are to aid people's intercultural development, where do we begin to understand how people move from an ethnocentric perspective to one that is more ethnorelative in orientation? These are all legitimate questions and issues to consider.

The manner in which people develop intercultural competence, in general, is similar to the way people learn anything that is new and different (see Figure 5.1). The general

Figure 5.1
Stages of Intercultural Learning

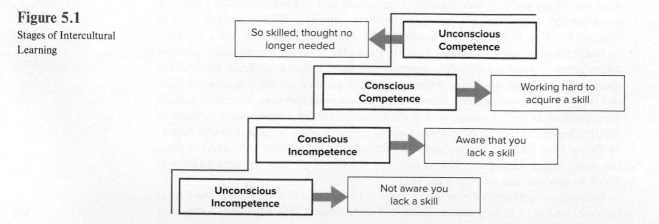

stages one would experience in culture learning begin with the stage of *Unconscious Incompetence*—that is, not even being aware that one lacks a certain knowledge or skill set; slowly moving toward *Conscious Incompetence,* where one becomes aware that he or she lacks a skill; to *Conscious Competence*, where one actively works hard to learn a skill; and ultimately reaching a stage of *Unconscious Competence*, where one has become so skilled that conscious thought about how to act is no longer needed.

While no single study can be cited that lists all of the essential qualities of intercultural competence, researchers and practitioners in such fields as intercultural communication and training have something concrete to offer teachers and teacher educators when it comes to understanding how people become interculturally competent. Deardorff's Pyramid Model of Intercultural Competence (2006) identified the need for individuals to exhibit certain motivational attitudes—such as respect, openness, and curiosity—that subsequently lead to the acquisition of knowledge, comprehension, and skill (see Figure 5.2).

Bennett's (1993) developmental model of intercultural sensitivity (DMIS) provided a framework for understanding intercultural development and awareness along

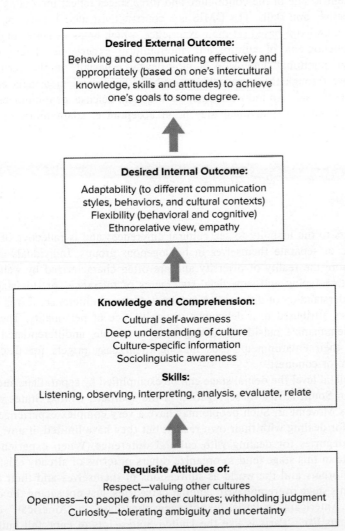

Figure 5.2
Pyramid Model of
Intercultural Competence
(Deardorff, 2006)

Figure 5.3

Developmental Model of
Intercultural Sensitivity
(Bennett, 1993)

a continuum from highly ethnocentric (a monocultural mind-set) to highly ethnorelative (an intercultural mindset).

In explaining the DMIS, Bennett noted that an increase in cultural awareness is accompanied by improved cognitive sophistication. Specifically, as people's ability to understand difference increases, so does their ability to negotiate a variety of worldviews. As a six-stage model that describes the experience of cultural difference, the DMIS is linear to the extent that it allows us to address the question, "So, what do we do next?" Such a model provides a valuable tool to educators of both young people and adults as they struggle to achieve greater intercultural sensitivity.

The developmental model of intercultural sensitivity is based on the observations of thousands of subjects who appeared to develop in similar ways. Three stages lie on the ethnocentric side of the continuum, and three stages reflect increasingly ethnorelative perspectives and skills. The DMIS is a constructivist model, meaning that people build their knowledge based on their experience, which helps us better understand the complex phenomena of culture and intercultural experience. There is a strong affective, or emotional dimension at most levels, especially in the early stages. As people move through the stages, their worldview becomes increasingly complex. On the ethnocentric side, an individual may be at denial, defense, or minimization. On the ethnorelative side, an individual may be at acceptance, adaptability, or integration (see Figure 5.3).

Ethnocentric Stages of the DMIS

Denial

Denial refers to the inability to see cultural differences and is reflective of individuals who isolate or separate themselves in homogenous groups. Individuals at this stage tend to ignore the reality of diversity and are often characterized by well-meant, but ignorant, stereotyping and superficial statements of tolerance. At this stage, an individual's understanding of difference is minimal. Cultural difference, if it is considered, is sometimes attributed to a deficiency in intelligence or personality. There is a tendency to dehumanize outsiders, viewing them as simple, undifferentiated aspects or objects of their environment, thus making them easy targets for discrimination, exploitation, or conquest.

At a societal level the denial stage can be exemplified by separatists, such as under apartheid in South Africa or segregation in the southern United States prior to the Civil Rights Movement. Such people may have a very complex experience and many categories for dealing with their own reality, but they have limited, if any, experience and few categories for dealing with cultural difference. When experiencing difference, people in this stage tend to organize others in terms of already existing categories, seeing others and the world as subversions of themselves and their own world. People in this stage overemphasize familiar categories; just not seeing the differences. If they are Americans in Paris, for instance, they have an "American" experience, and say things like, "Paris is like the United States—lots of cars, tall buildings, and

McDonald's." If thinking about immigrants, a person in denial sees major issues rather simplistically. Because they have the category of language differences (a general understanding), but not of assimilation or adjustment (a specific and more complex issue), they may support language development programs as a means to deal with the problem. While such efforts may be helpful on the surface, they tend to ignore other, more fundamental aspects of the groups' problems (such as racism and discrimination).

Bennett called this stage the "stupid questions syndrome," suggesting that people in denial tend to have a few, perhaps four, ideas or pieces of stereotypic knowledge about a given country or culture. Consider Africa, the only continent that many people refer to as a country. The stereotypic knowledge many European Americans have about Africa might include wild animals, poverty, disease, and jungle. Everything about Africa, then, is thought of in terms of these four ideas. When an individual at this stage meets an African, all these images come to the forefront. Such a person may think or ask, "So, when you leave your hut in the morning, aren't you afraid the wild animals from the jungle will attack you?"

Stop for a moment and think about the categories many people around the world might have of Americans. Do they tend to see Americans as overweight (lovers of fast food), lazy, rich, and all driving big cars? If so, a person from overseas who is in the denial stage, when meeting an American, might ask, "So, when you leave your big house in the morning, do you get in your big car and drive to McDonald's for your big breakfast?" They are bringing forth all their stereotypic information in their judgment of an American. Is this a true and accurate characterization of American people? Of course not. Nor is it a true and accurate characterization of people who live in the many different countries found on the African continent.

Outside of one's own context, things are rather fuzzy. People in denial see others as living in a different reality and, without having much knowledge of those people, may say such things as:

"Live and let live! That's what I say. Mixing just causes trouble."

"Business is just business the world over."

"As long as they all speak English, there will be no problem."

"Technology doesn't care about culture."

"They were born here, so they should know how to do it the American way."

"With my experience, I can be successful in any culture without any special effort."

"I never experience culture shock."

Denial has profound consequences, and when people at this stage are brought together with others, unpleasant things can sometimes occur. Because such people have many categories for dealing with their own culture, but few, if any, for dealing with other cultures, they may have only one single category for foreigners—"people of culture." The title of a book on the Cambodian war experience, *To Destroy You Is No Loss: The Odyssey of a Cambodian Family* (Criddle, 1996), captures an extreme sentiment of someone in this stage. An orientation such as this can lead to atrocities like the Holocaust, the wave of sectarian violence recently experienced in Iraq, or the "ethnic cleansing" recently witnessed in Darfur. People begin to believe that other people do not have feelings like they have, and they then treat those people as less than human.

Children in this stage are socialized that theirs is *the* view of the world, instead of learning that theirs is *one* view of the world. Although the thinking of people at this stage isn't necessarily evil, it is ignorant, and their behavior can become evil. Individuals at this stage are not capable of thinking about difference and must discover commonalities among people before they can progress to more sophisticated levels. Moving individuals from this stage to the next involves helping them to develop better skills of category discrimination and to become more sophisticated in their thinking and more complex in their cognitive processing.

Defense

Defense is the next stage of the developmental model of intercultural sensitivity. Movement into this stage is driven by the inadequacies of the existing rudimentary categories. This stage is characterized by a recognition of cultural difference coupled with negative evaluations of those whose culture is different from one's own and superior judgments of one's own culture. The greater the cultural difference observed, the more negative the accompanying evaluation. Strong dualistic us–them thinking is common in this stage that is often accompanied by overt negative stereotyping. When forced into contact with others, individuals in this stage often become defensive feeling that they are losing out on something they deserve. People at this stage prefer to separate themselves from others because they often don't have categories for dealing with difference. Although people at this stage are beginning to develop a more differentiated view of others, they tend to have a "hardening of the categories" and a narrow focus on a small, typically elite sample of a society. Such people defend their way as the one best way.

Three areas of defense are typically found: denigration or derogation, superiority, and sometimes reversal. *Denigration* or *derogation* refers to belittling or actively discriminating against another person. *Superiority* assumes extreme ethnocentrism to the point where one looks down on another believing that others are beneath them. People exhibiting superiority may act on their belief in a harsh, negative way rather than simply avoiding others as they might do in Denial. *Reversal* refers to changing sides or evaluating one's own culture as inferior to another. In an intercultural context, reversal is often referred to as "going native" and is evident when people return home from an overseas experience, identifying more with their host culture and criticizing their own. Individuals who exhibit reversal tendencies may avoid contact with fellow citizens and associate solely with host nationals.

Defense protects an individual's own worldview of the possibilities of other realities. No longer hidden away, other (meaning different) people suddenly become a force that must be reckoned with. Individuals at this stage tend to develop a polarized worldview. They put up a fence and raise their own flag, so to speak, and keep others at a distance. Such a scenario often results in an us–them scenario and may lead to the formation of militia groups or gangs. Both sides, the dominant group as well as the minority group, act to protect their own position. In reversal, nothing changes in one's worldview; one just changes sides and acquires the prejudices of the other group.

People in the defense stage may make statements such as the following:

"Genetically, they just don't have the capability to understand these things."

"The only way I can live around them is to spend most of my time at the expatriate (or country) club."

"We invented this stuff, and we're really the only ones who can make it work."

"These are American schools, and they've worked really well for us. Others should just learn to do it our way."

"I am so embarrassed by my fellow citizens that I spend all my time with the locals." (This statement is an example of reversal.)

"Women are naturally passive, so they wouldn't fit at this level."

"Asians are not assertive, hence they are poor leaders."

It's not uncommon for people to be in the defense stage, but they must be encouraged to move on. Because defense is a heavy affective state, people need to be supported in this stage. Developmental tasks require supporting people affectively while stressing the commonalities among people. People moving from this stage begin to say such things as "We're all in this together" and "We all came in different boats—but we're now in this one together." A good place to begin when considering how to move people from this stage is to point out such differences as learning style (using learning style inventories) and communication patterns that demonstrate that all individuals and groups have different ways of approaching common concerns. The 18-theme culture-general model also works well here.

Minimization

Minimization is entered with the discovery of commonality. In this stage, people begin to recognize and accept superficial cultural differences such as eating customs, money, and so forth (the tip of the iceberg in Figure 3.1), yet continue to hold the belief that all human beings are essentially the same. The emphasis at this stage is on the similarity of people and the commonality of basic values, with the tendency to define the basis of commonality in ethnocentric terms (thinking such things as "since everyone is essentially the same, they're really pretty much like me"). This perceived commonality could exist around physical universalism (with people saying such things as "We are all the same—we all eat, sleep, breathe, bleed red, and die." or "We are all people of color after all.") or around spiritual universalism (saying things as "Deep down we are all children of the same God, whether we know it or not.").

Minimization is a very profound stage. There is evidence to suggest that most teachers, for instance, are at this stage—and they are pleased to be here because they have transcended defense (Mahon, 2003; Cushner, 2011). It is difficult to move people from this stage because they think they are doing okay. This stage, for instance, can become official institutional policy, which can be problematic as people tend to be "nice but color blind." Individuals at the minimization stage see people as basically the same, with little recognition of the differences that in fact do exist. People at this stage tend not to make reference to physical characteristics (race, for instance), believing that such traits are not important as long as they just treat all people the same. In minimization, people ignore the influence of culture and lived experience that may be quite different among people, believing that all people have the same needs—but in reality they don't.

In this stage, although recently considered a transition stage from the ethnocentric to ethnorelative side of the continuum, an ethnocentric assumption that everyone should share the same reality—usually *my* own—continues to exist. People say and believe such things as, "If everyone knew of my religion, they'd all want to follow it." In schools, people might say, "They came to this country, so they know we must have the best education system." Internationally you might hear people say, "Australia is just like the United States, only 20 years behind." But you must keep in mind, as is becoming increasingly clear on the global scale, that everyone in the world does not aspire to be American.

At the minimization stage people may say things like the following:

"The key to getting along in any culture is to just be yourself—authentic and honest."

"Customs differ, of course, but when you really get to know them they're pretty much like us."

"I have this intuitive sense of other people, no matter what their culture."

"Technology is bringing cultural uniformity to the underdeveloped world."

"No matter what their culture, people are pretty much motivated by the same things."

"It's a small world after all."

"I don't see any difference—race, gender, or culture. We're all just people."

The developmental task to move people out of this stage is cultural self-awareness. Pointing out aspects of an individual's own culture and showing how it might differ from another person's is a good place to begin. However, resistance among people might develop around such things as strongly held values. Cultural awareness does not mean that people must like and accept everything; it is not a case of "anything goes." People can maintain a sense of morality about them by contextualizing another's behavior and beliefs. Take nudity, for example. Is it appropriate to take off your clothes? Well, it matters—the context is critical. In certain circumstances it is appropriate to take off your clothes (as in the shower), but in other situations (out in public), perhaps not. The context is the key to legitimizing the behavior. Culture, thus, becomes the context from which to explore another's values. Once the context is set and understood, then individuals can decide how they will behave. Once cultural awareness is achieved, the person can move from minimization to acceptance.

Bennett asserted that a paradigmatic shift in thinking must occur for an individual to move from the ethnocentric stages of the continuum into the ethnorelative side. Movement into the ethnorelative stages represents a significant change in one's view of difference, from something to be avoided to something that is sought out. Individuals in the ethnorelative stage search for ways to adapt to difference and begin to recognize that people live in culturally different contexts. The notion of context is not understood in ethnocentric stages.

Ethnorelative Stages of the DMIS

Acceptance

Acceptance of difference is the first stage on the ethnorelative side of the continuum. This stage represents an individual's ability to recognize and appreciate cultural difference in terms of both people's values and their behavior. Acceptance of cultural differences is seen as understanding that there are viable alternatives to the way people organize their existence and experience. At this stage, the individual is beginning to demonstrate the ability to interpret phenomena within a cultural context and to analyze complex interactions in culture-contrast terms. Categories of difference are consciously expanded and elaborated, with people understanding that others are "Not good or bad, just different." Later, the individual can see those beliefs, values, and other general

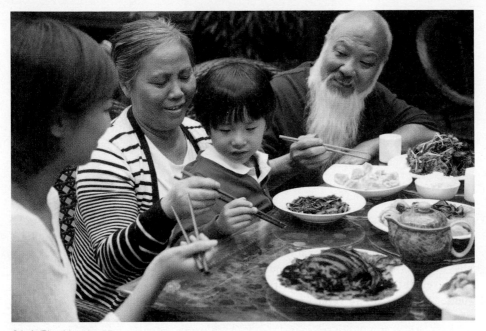

©Jade/Blend Images RF

patterns of assigning "goodness" and "badness" to ways of being in the world that exist in a variety of cultural contexts. People in this stage also begin to seek out cultural difference.

Acceptance of another's difference does not necessarily mean agreement nor necessarily how to adopt to those differences. People may have respect and value for cultural differences, but not necessarily agree with all they see. It is here that people begin to discriminate—people do have individual tastes and preferences, and not all cultures or cultural practices will be liked or valued by all people (the cultural belief that the role of all women should focus on home and family, for instance, is not universally accepted). The more sophisticated knowledge you possess in a category, the more personal preference you can bring (as a wine connoisseur is able to do). This behavior is not ethnocentric as long as you assume that the other is equally complex and acceptable within a given context. Even though people find that they may not necessarily agree with all they see practiced within another culture, they can, at least, understand what they witness. Teachers at this stage, for instance, might understand that family or other collective influences may be greater for a Latino or Asian child than for an Anglo counterpart, and this understanding may temper their expectation that students make their own independent choices on major life decisions. They may then seek out ways to work more closely with a student's family.

People in this stage may say things like the following:

"The more difference the better—more difference results in more creative ideas."

"You certainly wouldn't want to be around the same kind of people all the time—the ideas get stale, and besides, it's boring."

"I always try to study about a new culture before I go there or interact with the people."

"The more cultures you know about, the better comparisons you can make."

"I know that my African American students and their families, and I, a European American man, have had very different life experiences, but we're working together as a learning community."

"Our new student is from Mexico. Where can I learn about Mexican culture so I can be more effective in the classroom?"

But acceptance alone is not sufficient to drive effectiveness with another culture. It is necessary to develop new skills to be more effective teachers or businesspeople.

Adaptation

Adaptation is the stage during which people begin to see cultural categories as more flexible and become more competent in their ability to communicate across cultures. Individuals are able to use empathy effectively, shift frames of reference, and are better able to understand others and be understood across cultural boundaries.

Movement into this stage from the previous one is driven by a need for action (better teaching, more profit) and cognitive empathy—the ability to change frames of reference. A significant amount of groundwork must be laid before a shift can occur and people are ready to learn new skills. The greater the cultural gap, the more difficult it will be to make the shift. The individual begins to experience reality in a more "other" way and can understand and feel about the world as the other would.

Two forms of adaptation exist: cultural adaptation and behavioral adaptation. *Cultural adaptation* refers to the ability to consciously shift perspective into alternative cultural worldview elements and to use multiple cultural frames of reference in evaluating phenomena. *Behavioral adaptation* refers to the internalization of more than one complete worldview, enabling people to shift into different frames without much conscious effort and then act in culturally appropriate ways. It is at this stage that we say that people are becoming bicultural or intercultural. A teacher at this stage, for instance, would be able to modify his or her responses to and expectations of students from lower versus middle socioeconomic groups as necessary when it comes to students' ability to participate in after-school extracurricular activities. Fellow students may understand that the needs of refugee students are quite distinct from those of international exchange students—even though they may both be from abroad—and will, in turn, respond differently to them.

But at this stage people are not simply acquiring skills. Nor are they simply regurgitating lists of dos and don'ts; this type of reaction creates emulation, not empathy. Knowledge and behavior here are linked by conscious intention, with category boundaries becoming more flexible and permeable, and intentional perspective taking and empathy being evident.

In the adaptation stage, people may say things like the following:

"To really help this student learn, I'm going to have to change my approach."

"I know they're really trying hard to adapt to my style, so it's only fair and right that I try to meet them halfway."

"I interact with my male and female colleagues somewhat differently to account for differences in the way respect is communicated."

"I can maintain my values and also behave in culturally appropriate ways."

"I interact with my Latino families from Central and South America differently to account for differences in the way respect and authority are communicated."

Integration

Integration is the final stage of the developmental model of intercultural sensitivity. Although it is rarely achieved, it reflects those individuals who have multiple frames of reference and can identify and move freely within more than one cultural group. *Integration* refers to the internalization of bicultural or multicultural frames of reference, with individuals at this level being able to mediate between multiple groups. People at this level are able to facilitate constructive contact between cultures and tend to become cultural mediators or cultural bridges.

People at this stage may say things like the following:

"Everywhere is home, if you know enough about how things work there."

"I feel most comfortable when I'm bridging differences between the cultures I know."

"Whatever the situation, I can usually look at it from a variety of cultural points of view."

Understanding that intercultural development is an evolutionary and not a revolutionary process should greatly influence the manner in which we educate both children and teacher education students. Intercultural competence is not achieved in one course or one single experience. Rather, it comes about after recognizing where one is on the developmental continuum, and then engaging in systematic, oftentimes repetitious, and well-planned exposure to intercultural interactions that are designed to nudge one to increasingly complex levels. Think back to the discussion of adjustment in Chapter 4, which emphasized the rather long time required before individuals become fully adjusted to another cultural setting—and that came after full immersion in a new place.

Where are You, and Most Teachers, on the Intercultural Continuum?

As implied by the DMIS, acquiring intercultural competence is developmental, comprehensive, and therefore, takes time. That is, it is a process that is more evolutionary, than revolutionary, and cannot be achieved quickly nor with a cognitive-only approach. Significant first-hand experience, or encounters with difference over a sustained period of time, is essential if people are to advance to more complex intercultural thinking and behavior.

Enhancing intercultural competence comes about after recognizing where one is on the developmental continuum, and then while providing both support and challenge, engaging in systematic, oftentimes repetitious and well-planned exposure to intercultural interactions that nudge one toward increasingly more complex levels. Moving too quickly along the continuum is akin to the scuba diver plunging immediately to a depth of 100 feet without taking the requisite time to equalize pressure and accommodate to the new environment—the shock can just be too great for the system to accept. Alternatively, gradual movement or immersion enables the diver to adjust to the changing circumstances and thus to function more effectively in the new environment. So, too, should it be with intercultural development. Understanding and integrating what we know about intercultural development and sensitivity into the education of young people, as well as ourselves as teachers, will result in a more culturally effective and culturally competent citizenry. Where do you think you fall on the intercultural continuum? Where do you think most teachers fall?

The Intercultural Development Inventory (Hammer & Bennett, 2003), or IDI, is an assessment instrument designed to determine where on the intercultural continuum an individual, or an organization, lies. As educators, if we know where individuals fall on the continuum, we can be mindful of the particular strategies and experiences that can be used to move them from one stage to another. The particular needs and approaches we might use when moving someone from Denial or Defense to Minimization are significantly different than those that we would use when moving someone from Minimization to Acceptance.

When considering how to enhance our own intercultural competence we must consider the prior experiences, or lack thereof, that most bring to the profession as well as where most fall on the intercultural continuum. Most teachers, as reported earlier, are middle class, live in small- to medium-sized suburban communities, and have limited experience with people different from themselves. This is certainly in contrast to the increasing percentage of students of color and the rise in immigrant and refugee populations in American public schools, and the fact that an increasing number of students live in poverty. The picture is not much different in many other nations, by the way, except that the predominant ethnic background of teachers may vary from nation to nation (Cushner, 1998).

Recent research using the IDI provides us with some evidence that the majority of today's teachers and teacher education students encounter others from an ethnocentric orientation, or at best, are on the cusp of Minimization. Mahon's (2003) study of 155 teachers from the American Midwest placed all of them at Minimization or below. Her follow-up study (2009) of 88 teachers in the American West found 84% to be in Minimization or below. Bayles (2009) found 91% of 233 teachers in a U.S. urban, southern school district at Minimization or below. Such findings are not limited to the United States. Grossman and Yuen (2006) found that of 107 teachers in schools in Hong Kong, 55% were in Denial or Defense and 43% were in Minimization, with only 2% fully on the ethnorelative side of the continuum. Yuen's (2009) survey of 386 teachers in nine schools in Hong Kong revealed the majority to be in Denial/Defense, with minimal recognition given to cultural differences.

Two studies that look at the intercultural sensitivity of students show some surprisingly differences between young people and their teachers, and present what has been referred to as an 'intercultural conundrum' (Cushner, 2012). Pederson (1998) used a modified version of the IDI with 145 12-year-old 7th graders, and found 35% to be in high Minimization and 35% in Acceptance. Among 336 high school students in an international school in Southeast Asia, Straffon (2003) found 71% to be in Acceptance and 26% in Cognitive Adaptation, with/only 3% on the ethnocentric side. Both of these studies showed that the greater the amount of exposure to difference (city versus suburban and rural schools in the Pedersen study and the amount of time in international schools in the Straffon study), the higher the level of intercultural sensitivity.

So, herein lies an intercultural conundrum. The majority of teachers—those responsible for advancing knowledge, skill, and attitude of young people—appear to be stuck on the ethnocentric side of the continuum, while their students show evidence of being more sophisticated in terms of intercultural development.

- How might you explain the findings that young people may be further along the intercultural continuum than their teachers?

- What are some things you might do to enhance your intercultural competence?

- What are some things you can do as a teacher to help develop the intercultural competence of your students?

Critical Incidents at Maplewood

The Case Study introduced at the beginning of the chapter ended with Sue Murray asking, "I wonder how my teaching team feels?" This chapter's Critical Incidents are perspectives from other teachers in Maplewood School. At the end of each, you will be asked to categorize the teacher's orientation according to where you think they fall on the DMIS.

Critical Incident

John Reading, Fifth-Grade Social Studies and Language Arts Teacher

I'm in "seventh heaven," you could say. I came into the teaching field after spending 2 years as a Peace Corps volunteer teaching English in Kenya. It was the best 2 years of my life. I learned to speak Kiswahili fairly well and had a chance to teach in both a secondary school and a local teachers' college. I spent weekends working with younger children in the village in which I lived. We did general maintenance around the village, started all kinds of community action projects such as building a small community center, and organized a variety of local artists to showcase their work.

That experience changed my life. I grew up in a community not far from where I now teach. In many ways it was quite similar to Maplewood—there were few minorities, although that has changed somewhat over time. I didn't have too many friends who were different from me—we were all pretty much the same. Not much diversity, they'd say now, although that wasn't a term we used back then. We were all just "normal," I guess you'd say.

I became interested in the Peace Corps after many years of learning about different people in general. As a little kid I remember looking at *National Geographic* magazine at my uncle's house. He was a geologist and taught at a local community college. I was interested in the pictures—the different ways people dressed, or didn't dress. I was also quite intrigued by the various ways people decorated themselves—from their jewelry to tattoos and body painting to body piercing. I guess even people in this country today, when you think about how they pierce or tattoo their bodies, have much in common with some of the people I would read about then. But most kids probably wouldn't see the similarity.

In high school, I was active in the Exchange Student Club. I could never afford to be an exchange student myself, but I was always interested in other people. Then, I had one teacher, Mr. Philips, my 11th-grade English teacher, who had spent 2 years in Thailand as a Peace Corps volunteer. I was really intrigued by him and his experience. It was then that I began thinking about doing that myself. I applied during my student teaching semester and was accepted to the program in Kenya.

What an eye-opener that 2-year experience was for me. I changed more in that time than I ever could have imagined. I'm sure the experience had more of an influence on me than I had on those in my village, who I became really attached to, by the way. I'm now trying to arrange to have a more formal link between the village school and our school, but I haven't yet been able to raise enough money to do anything substantial.

I would like all of my students to have experiences like those that I had. But you know, it's hard to do. When I returned from Kenya, most of my family and friends weren't very interested in hearing about my experiences—they wanted me to just fit right back into how I used to be and the way they were. But I couldn't. I had changed too much. Many of the things they were interested in seemed rather unimportant to me. This created some friction between my friends and me for a while. The Peace Corps tried to warn us about this problem when we returned. They said we would experience a reverse culture shock, that coming back home would be difficult because we had changed so much and most others at home had not. Boy, were they right! I keep in closer contact with many of my old Peace Corps friends now than I do my older friends from home.

Perhaps here in the school I can do something that can make a difference in the way young people view others. That's why I'm kind of glad all this discussion about diversity is happening now. I think it's a wake-up call that, if we're not prepared for it, will bring all kinds of trouble. There is a place for us as teachers to work with young people on these issues. Not only can I share some of my experiences, but perhaps I can create experiences for the students themselves that will help to introduce them to others in their world in a more personal and substantial way. I think it's critically important that people learn how to view the world from more than one perspective, and I hope to be able to develop this ability in my students. They have to begin to understand the plight of the world's indigenous peoples, understand the experiences of the African Americans and Native Americans in this country, and show greater concern for the environment. Teaching is a great vehicle from which to do this. I'm beginning to feel most comfortable when I'm helping people see the world around them from another perspective—kind of as a bridge builder. I can now look at most situations from at least two cultures' points of view. I think young people today need this mind-set as well.

- Where on the continuum of the DMIS would you place John? Justify your thinking.
- What kinds of activities might John do with his current students that would build on his experiences in Kenya?

Critical Incident

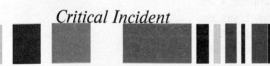

Fran Violet, Fifth-Grade
Language Arts Teacher

I'm really getting tired of all the commotion, although I won't come out and say it to too many people. I feel like an outsider during some of the teachers' meetings we've had. There seem to be two camps developing among the staff. There are those who are in favor of making changes to address the so-called needs of other groups, and others, like myself, who are rather quiet and in the background continuing to do a good job, or so we believe, just teaching kids.

I've been teaching in the district for 25 years now and have seen all kinds of educational fads come and go. I'm pretty sure this attention to culture will just do the same. After all, we only have so much time in the day to teach all that we are supposed to teach. There's such an emphasis today on competency tests, which don't even measure multicultural education. It's probably only a matter of time until all the hoopla dies down. It even angers me when I think that I've had to attend after-school workshops on diversity and multicultural education. They really didn't teach me anything I could use. They were more of a gripe session presented by some people who had a bunch of complaints to make. Then they handed us a list of multicultural books we should have the kids read. Come on. Give me a break. Do they really expect me to become motivated by that?

And the kids! I've seen quite a few changes since I began teaching here. That's what I think the problem is. It's not about culture. Yes, it's true that there are more minority children in the school now than there were a number of years ago. But the problem, as I see it, is about kids and their families. It doesn't matter what a child's cultural background is. I look at kids pretty much the same. Sure there are some differences, like some just pick things up quicker than others do. Some are better in certain subjects than others. Some are better in sports or art or music. But all in all, kids are basically the same. I want them all to succeed in school, and I do my best to teach them all. While people's cultures may differ, once you get down to it, kids are kids, and all people are pretty much the same. All people, after all, have the same basic needs. I have a general sense of other people; no matter what culture they are from, I can usually read them pretty well. If kids don't have a solid, stable family, then that's where there's going to be trouble. There has been such an increase in the number of children coming from broken families. Why, one year I had 20 out of 28 kids who came from some sort of rearranged family. If you ask me, that's where the problem lies.

- Where on the continuum of the DMIS would you place Fran? Justify your thinking.
- What suggestions might you make to Fran to help her advance along the DMIS continuum?

Critical Incident

Steven Goodwin, Principal

Ever since I became principal of this school 6 years ago, I have been on a continuous learning curve. I had no preparation in college for issues of diversity. It wasn't even talked about when I first went to school 25 years ago. It's kind of been "trial by fire," you might say. As our community changed and as I became more involved in school administration, I suddenly had so many new things which I had to understand. I had training to be a school principal at a nearby university, but most of that training focused on leadership, finances, and management from a dominant-culture perspective. My professors were from, I guess you would say, the "old school," where everything was supposed to fit one particular orientation. But I quickly learned that things are different in the real world. Ever since our community demographics began to change and people began moving from the city to our suburb, the rules have never quite been the same. I think I'm beginning to understand it quite well—although it still requires a lot of work on my part. I'm not sure I always get it right.

Take this recent dispute, for instance. This community has always supported the local sports teams. Even our high school mascot is an Indian, and no one had questioned it since it became part of our culture some 60 years ago. That is, until this year. I'm beginning to understand the other side of the coin now. I guess the more time I spend with people from other groups and learn about their cultures, the more I begin to understand their point of view, their language, and their way of interacting. For so many years, all people have been forced to adapt to one mainstream point of view—like it or not! I guess for the most part, at least for so many years, people tried pretty hard to adapt. Some might say they were forced to adapt. For many years we called it the "melting pot"; all people were to become like the majority culture. For some it worked. As I understand it, and it makes sense to me, it was fairly easy for most European immigrants to fit into the mainstream culture in the early part of the 1900s. Most of these immigrants came from similar language backgrounds—at least they were all European—and shared relatively similar ways of life. Once they learned the English language, their physical features allowed them to pretty much fit right into the mainstream. And then their foods became part of the national diet, like Italian, Polish, or German influences.

Many other immigrants, however, had quite different experiences. African Americans were forced to come to this country—some call them "involuntary immigrants," never wanting to be here in the first place. And today, most immigrants come from countries whose languages, ethnicity, religion, skin color, and general way of life are significantly different—not only from the mainstream but from one another as well. This alone makes it very difficult for people to "just fit right in."

I guess I look at it this way. So many people have been struggling to adapt to our way of life for so long that it's only fair that we now try to make some changes. I guess for me that means that so many people in the schools have been trying hard to adapt to my style that it's only fair that I try to meet them halfway. To solve some of the problems we face in our school and community, I'm going to have to change my approach. I'm beginning to understand that I can maintain my own culture's values, but at the same time I can learn to behave in ways that are appropriate for another culture. Now it's getting easier for me to say that about my behavior. But I recognize that for many others in the school community, including parents as well as some of the teachers, the situation is not so clear. Many of them are threatened and are not sure how to make the changes—nor want to make any changes. I'm working real hard, in addition to all the other things I have to stay on top of, to encourage this school community to face these issues and address them in positive ways. I also recognize that I will have to continue to be a role model for others to demonstrate how this diversity can be accomplished. I constantly try to learn about other people and account for cultural differences in my interactions with them and to help our school community do the same.

- Where on the continuum of the DMIS would you place Steven? Justify your thinking.

- What are some things Steven might do to encourage development among his school community, especially among the more resistant teachers and families?

Summary

Fundamental to effective intercultural education is an understanding of the manner in which people develop their ability to understand and interact more effectively with people different from themselves. The developmental model of intercultural sensitivity (DMIS) was introduced as one means to understand how people can grow from being ethnocentric to becoming more ethnorelative in their orientation.

Chapter Review

Go to the Online Learning Center at www.mhhe.com/cushner9e to review important content from the chapter, practice with key terms, take a chapter quiz, and access active workbook exercises.

Key Terms

acceptance 156   defense 154   integration 159
adaptation 158   denial 152   minimization 155

Learning About Others

Purpose: To learn about cultural differences by interviewing someone from a different culture or ethnic group while applying concepts from the culture-general framework.

Instructions: Find someone from a culture different from your own to interview (preferably someone outside your immediate and known peer group). Try to choose someone you think will have different attitudes, opinions, and experiences than you have. Choose some questions from the list that follows, or develop some of your own. Before you interview the person, answer the questions for yourself. For each of the questions, follow up with "Why?" in order to explore underlying values and reasons for peoples' behavior or beliefs. Take notes of the responses. Discuss the questions and the "why" with the other person until you have found at least five major areas where there are clear differences between your answer and the other person's. Also be sure to identify five major areas where you are in agreement with one another. Prepare a short paper or presentation that summarizes your findings.

a. What people in your life are the most important to obey? Why?

b. Who makes final decisions in your life at home and school? Why?

c. Who do you think determines your fate—the individual, the family, or God? Why?

d. Whom should you respect? How do you show respect? Why?

e. Who should help determine your identity? Why?

f. What does it mean to be successful in life? Why?

g. Whom should you trust? Why?

h. What are the signs of success? Why?

i. What provides "security" in your life? Why?

j. Who should your friends be? Who decides? Why?

k. Where, and with whom, should you live? Why?

l. Whom should you marry? At about what age? Who decides? Why?

m. What is expected of children when they are young? Why?

n. What should you depend on others for? Why?

o. When should you be self-sufficient, if ever? Why?

p. What should you expose to others, and what should be kept private? Why?

q. How should you plan for your future? Why?

r. What should be remembered from your heritage? Why?

s. What was better when you were younger or during your parents' youth? Why?

t. What do you wish for your children that you could not have? Why?

1. What did you learn about the other person that is significantly different from you? How might this knowledge affect the interviewee as a learner? You as a teacher?

2. What did you learn about the other person that is similar to you? Were you surprised by this? How might this knowledge affect you as a teacher?

Reflective Questions

1. Return to the case study introduced at the beginning of the chapter. Where on the continuum of the DMIS would you place each of the individuals: Sue Murray, John Jameson, Rebecca Reynolds, and Joyce Maples? Justify your decisions.

2. Draft a brief response to each of the three who wrote letters to the editor: John Jameson, Rebecca Reynolds, and Joyce Maples. As a teacher, what would you emphasize in your response?

3. Where on the DMIS would you place yourself? What criteria are you using to make your judgment?

References

Bayles, P. P. (2009) Assessing the intercultural sensitivity of elementary teachers in bilingual schools in a Texas school district. (Doctoral dissertation, University of Minnesota). Retrieved from: http://proquest.umi.com/pqdweb?did=1684138321& Fmt=7&clientId=4653&RQT=309&VName=PQD

Bennett, M. J. (1993). Towards ethnorelativism: A developmental model of intercultural sensitivity. In M. Paige (Ed.), *Cross-cultural orientation* (pp. 27-69). Lanham, MD: University Press of America.

Brislin, R., & Yoshida, T. (1994). *Intercultural communication training: An introduction.* Thousand Oaks, CA: Sage.

Criddle, J. (1996). *To destroy you is no loss: The odyssey of a Cambodian family.* Providence, UT: East/West Bridge Publishing House.

Cushner, K., & Brislin, R. (1996). *Intercultural interactions: A practical guide* (2nd ed.). Thousand Oaks, CA: Sage.

Cushner, K. (1998). *International perspectives on intercultural education.* Lanham, MD: Lawrence Erlbaum.

Cushner, K. (2011). Intercultural research in teacher education: An essential intersection in the preparation of globally competent teachers. *Action in Teacher Education,* 33:5-6, 601-614.

Cushner. K. (2012). Intercultural Competence for Teaching and Learning. B. Shaklee, & S. Baily (Eds.) *Internationalizing Teacher Education in the United States,* 41-59. Lanham, MD: Rowman Littlefield.

Cushner, K. (2014). Strategies for Enhancing Intercultural Competence across the Teacher Education Curriculum. In J. Phillion, S. Sharma and J. Rahatzad (Eds.), *Internationalizing Teacher Education for Social Justice: Theory, Research, and Practice* (139-162). Charlotte, NC: Information Age Publishing, Inc.

Deardorff, D. (2006). Identification and assessment of intercultural competence as a student outcome of internationalization. *Journal of Studies in International Education, 10*(3), 241-266.

Deardorff, D. (2009). *Sage handbook of intercultural competence.* Thousand Oaks, CA: Sage.

Grossman, D., & Yuen, C. (2006). Beyond the rhetoric: A study of the intercultural sensitivity of Hong Kong Secondary School Teachers. *Pacific Asian Education, 18*(1), 70-87.

Hammer, M., & Bennett, M. J. (2003). Measuring intercultural sensitivity: The Intercultural Development Inventory. *International journal of intercultural relations*, *27*, 403–419.

Mahon, J. (2003). *The intercultural sensitivity of practicing teachers: Life history perspectives.* Unpublished dissertation, Kent State University, Kent, Ohio.

Mahon, J. (2009). Conflict style and cultural understanding among teachers in the western United States. *International Journal of Intercultural Relations*, *33*(1), 46–56.

Pederson, P. V. (1998). Intercultural sensitivity and the early adolescent. Doctoral dissertation, University of Minnesota. *Dissertation Abstracts International*, 9826849.

Straffon, D. A. (2003). Assessing the intercultural sensitivity of high school students attending an international school. *International Journal of Intercultural Relations*, *27*: 487–501.

Yuen, C. (2009). Dimensions of diversity: Challenges to secondary school teachers with implications for intercultural teacher education. *Teaching and Teacher Education*, *26*(3), 732–741.

2

Multicultural Teaching
in Action

Creating Classrooms That Address Race and Ethnicity

Focus Questions

1. Do you believe all people are prejudiced? If so, in what ways do you display prejudice?

2. Did you hear messages about certain groups of people as you grew up that you no longer support? How did you come to change your beliefs or point of view?

3. How are factors of racism and prejudice evident in schools? In your community? In your nation?

4. What behaviors are effective when dealing with people who hold extreme prejudices? What actions might teachers take to reduce prejudice in their students?

" Prejudice is a great time saver. You can form opinions without having to get the facts. "

E. B. WHITE

Case Study

The Chameleon

The school board meetings were generally not as heated as they were that night in October when the issue of bilingual education was brought up for discussion. More than 600 residents showed up for the meeting; so many that a new location had to be found and six police officers had been called into the auditorium as a precautionary measure. What had started a couple of weeks earlier when a few students accused some teachers and administrators of prejudice and discrimination had now developed into a districtwide debate about the purpose and success of multicultural and bilingual education. The current state of affairs had certainly come a long way from the initial problem, which developed when a few Mexican American and Vietnamese students had not been chosen for the cheerleading squad. Some people were saying, in no uncertain terms, that students who were just learning to speak English could not be understood well enough to be on the cheerleading squad. One of the adults in the community was overheard to say, "If small groups of individuals had a difficult time under-standing these particular students, how could a crowd of already screaming sports fans?" Over the past two weeks, majority students throughout the school began repeating these arguments. There had even been some fights between a group of Spanish-speaking boys and a group of African American football players.

Jane Myers, who has been teaching in this school for seven years, had never experienced such heated debate and outright antagonism before. To top it off, the administration seemed to be dragging its feet and not quite sure how to address the issue.

Ms. Myers located the phone number of a presenter she had seen a year earlier and arranged a time for him to come to the school and meet with the junior and senior classes. She knew that something rather dramatic, but real, had to be done to get people talking with one another. John Gray could certainly facilitate that!

John Gray arrived on the planned day with plenty of time to have a cup of coffee, meet the principal, and arrange the auditorium for his needs. He had agreed to do the program, but only if persons in positions of authority would also attend; this group included Mr. Johnson, the principal; the two assistant principals; and even two of the school board members.

Ms. Myers welcomed the more than 500 students once they settled into their seats in the auditorium. "This morning we have a speaker who will use a teaching approach known as psychodrama to help us explore issues related to prejudice and racism. Mr. John Gray is a former personnel manager with a major Fortune 500 company and holds an MBA from Harvard University. Please join me in welcoming him to our school."

John Gray approached the stage as the students applauded. He was quite distinguished looking, really the picture of a rather successful, polite, white business executive. He stood more than 6 feet tall and wore a gray business suit, white shirt, and red tie. His hair was straight and graying, and he had rather angular and prominent facial features.

He began in a pleasant manner, smiling and stating that he had not come with any kind of prepared speech. He would, instead, just share some ideas with the students and allow for some open discussion. But he did make some rather pointed comments. "I'll begin this morn-ing by saying that if you are silent with me, I will be making three assumptions about you and the silence. One, if you are silent, that tells me that you understand everything I am saying. Two, silence tells me that you agree with whatever I am saying. And three, silence tells me that you support what I am saying. Is this clear?" He paused.

"The only way I'll know anything different is if you break the silence. You see, silence, to me, is very critical. Silence suggests inaction, and the inaction, in a sense, becomes a form of action." He waited again and took in the audience's silence. "So, you all just sent me the message that you understood what I just said, that you agreed with what I said, and you sup-ported me by your silence."

There was some light laughter and apparent nervousness among the audience. A crucial contract had just been entered into with the group.

"Like any good teacher," Gray began, "I use three instructional approaches. You might think of these in terms of how you learn to do complex things, let's say learning to ride a bike. When

I use the lecture method, I tell you about riding. Now this approach may transfer a significant amount of useful information, but it does not provide you with the opportunity to practice the appropriate actions. Would you learn how to ride the bike? Probably not! The second approach I call the 'show-me' approach. I can demonstrate for you how to ride a bike. This approach may enable you to see what is expected, but once again, it probably will not result in you learning how to ride. There just is no opportunity to practice the skill. Now the third approach I call the 'involve-me' approach. Once you are involved, you really do begin to learn."

Gray went on to introduce the concept of prejudice and gave example after example of how people's preferences, or prejudices, can become problematic if they are extended and expected from all people. Whereas, he said, he had a prejudice toward apple pie, but he did not think that all people should have only apple pie. At the same time, other people had no right to tell him what flavor pie to consume. But if Mr. Johnson, as the principal, went around and told all the students that they could eat only apple pie in school or they would be punished, then Mr. Johnson would be combining his prejudice for apple pie with his power and would be discriminating against a certain group of people—cherry pie eaters, for instance. Then, Gray said, we get into a thing called 'pie-ism.' That, he explained, was when people and institutions, like schools, got into conflict, and then the silence had to be broken.

Gray posed a question to students. "How many of you think you are prejudiced?" Only a few hands went up. "Well, I for one think you are all prejudiced and that you are ignoring the reality in yourself. I think it's important that we all recognize that we have certain information about other people that we have been taught that may not be accurate, but yet we continue to support."

There was silence in the room.

"So, if I go by the silence, you are all agreeing with me. See, you are all prejudiced, you just weren't willing to admit it earlier."

Suddenly a hand went up from the middle of the auditorium. Gray called on the student, and he rose to speak.

"I don't think you can get away with calling me prejudiced," said the student. "I have many black and Hispanic friends, and I'm not alone. Many others in this school have friends from different backgrounds."

"Oh, I know where you are coming from," replied Gray. "You're just showing off in front of your friends to let them know how liberal you are. You can't fool most of us—we know your kind."

The student sat down quietly. Others in the room began to fidget in their seats. A female student then jumped up to defend the boy.

"How can you say that about him, you don't even know him? I think you're being prejudiced!" she challenged.

"You may be partially correct," replied Gray, "but I also know where you're coming from. Tell me," he asked, "are you Jewish?"

"No, I am not," she answered. "And why is that important?"

"Because I am a Christian; a good Christian; and I think if Jews want to believe in a God other than Jesus Christ, they should go back to Israel where they belong."

The students grew restless and agitated.

"How can you say such a thing? What does that have to do with anything?" another girl blurted out.

"What, may I ask, do you want to be when you grow up?" asked Gray.

"A politician," she replied.

"Oh, I don't think I'd spend my time doing that if I were you," he quickly responded. "Women can never really hold positions of authority and power because they are generally much more emotional than men. And there are many studies that prove that. In fact, a recent research study undertaken at the University of California at Berkeley—you know of it, I assume—stated that without a doubt women are more prone to tears and cry more when under pressure. No one can be a successful leader when their emotions get in the way, and women have that problem all the time—just look at how you are acting with me. Now you wouldn't want a leader

(continued)

to behave like this, would you? And I know that some of you in the audience will differ with me, but that's all right. That's your choice."

A few members of the audience laughed. Two students who were close to the back got up to walk out, and Mr. Johnson approached them and quietly asked them to return to their seats.

"You know what really bothers me?" Gray continued without seeming to miss a beat, "is that affirmative action order. That order told me that I had to hire a certain number of minorities and women in my organization, and I resented that. I didn't like being forced into anything, especially having to hire people who could not do the job."

An African American male student jumped in. "What do you mean by people who couldn't do the job?"

"Well, you know," replied Gray. "Your people have trouble passing certain competency tests. Take teacher tests, for instance. Your people just can't pass those tests at the same rate that white teachers do. And you want to be teachers and teach my children? I think there's something terribly wrong with affirmative action. It's getting to the point where my children had to have a card saying they were minority or female before they could be considered for a job. That's just not right."

The students were silent.

"So I felt that I had to break the silence and fight back. I thought that if I could reach young people like yourselves in schools—because you are our future—I want to encourage you to speak out. Young man, may I ask you where you are from?"

"I'm from Africa. Nigeria to be exact. I was not born as an African American, although my family is working on getting our American citizenship."

"Well, let me suggest something to you. You're in a good school. When you learn to speak like a good American, then I can look to you as a good American who can understand what I'm trying to say. Why don't you solve the problems that you have in Africa before coming here and getting so upset with me? I see why your school is having such a debate about bilingual education. How many of you speak English as your first language, might I ask?"

The students—boys and girls, whites and blacks, Latinos and Asians—as well as teachers and administrators sat silently as most of the hands went up.

"And what is this school doing to promote diversity?" Gray asked.

Mr. Johnson jumped in. "Mr. Gray, I promised you academic freedom. But please try to keep your comments from being personal in nature. Students, if you have questions to ask of Mr. Gray, you can do that now. You don't have to wait for a question-and-answer period, but do ask one at a time."

"Well, I think that as a group you're showing disrespect for me," Gray continued, directing his comments toward Mr. Johnson. "Maybe I'm wasting my time with you. I really resent the way I've been treated. I don't know if you planted people in the audience to attack me, but I resent the laughter I've heard as well as some of the putdowns from those of you who may have a view that differs from mine. I've got better things to do than to stay here with you. No wonder you're having all these troubles about bilingual education in your school. I really resent the way I've been treated."

And with that, John Gray picked up his materials and walked off the stage. The students applauded as he left.

After Gray left the stage, Mr. Johnson approached the microphone. "I guess the lecture is over, and by the sounds of it, there are many people who have many things they'd like to say. I suggest we go back to our homeroom classes for a while and discuss what we have all just experienced. Then we can all come back together and meet here in the auditorium right after lunch."

Note This case study concludes with some very important additional information contained in the critical incidents at the end of the chapter. It is based on the video program *Chameleon* by John Gray and Associates; and on a section from the book *A Country of Strangers: Blacks and Whites in America,* by David K. Shipler (New York: Vintage Books, 1997).

Lay Versus Scientific Understanding of Race and Ethnicity

This chapter's Case Study vividly illustrates issues of racism and prejudice in action. It also provides a context in which to apply some of the 18 culture-general themes introduced in Chapter 4. For instance, in addition to raising the issue of prejudice, what attributions do you think the students were making about John Gray? What judgments were you making about John Gray as you read the Case Study? How would you react in the presence of someone like him? Would you be experiencing some anxiety? How would you communicate with such a person?

Pedagogies: Old and New

Teachers and school administrators who understand the deep-seated influence that race and ethnicity play in people's lives do not shy away from confronting these issues. On the contrary, they understand the historical significance and current state of affairs that this sensitive and controversial experience assumes in people's lives, and they believe they have an obligation to address these issues in their teaching. Such teachers understand the role that race plays, both in the lives of individuals and in society at large. Such teachers, especially those working primarily with children from the majority culture, understand that their students may be quite unaware of the impact that race can have on others' as well as their own lives. These teachers provide significant guidance, support, and structure to classroom and school environments that encourage new interactions and opportunities to openly discuss and learn about race and ethnicity. Increasingly, there are a number of school programs and curriculum guides that have proven effective at improving relations between individuals and groups (see Stephan & Vogt, 2004, for a review of many of these).

Roles: Old and New

In classrooms that actively address issues related to race and ethnicity, teachers understand their role as active agents of change and they are not afraid to openly discuss race and racism, thus making it an important topic for conversation. These teachers reach out to individuals as well as to community organizations that represent various ethnic and racial groups' perspectives and experiences. Such an approach provides for authentic voices while building necessary bridges between young people and the community. Not only are children exposed to alternative perspectives, they also interact with community representatives who are actively working to change the status quo. Such activities model for young people and others the desired outcomes of an effective multicultural curriculum, principally the skills and attitudes needed to become proactive agents of change. These approaches get young people engaged in change efforts that affect their own school and community, helping to guide them to become bridge builders—reflecting aspects of the developmental level of Adaptation discussed in Chapter 5.

Place of Content Knowledge: Old and New

In recent years, race, like ethnicity, has been viewed less as a biological reality and more as a cultural construct, both of which are functions of the categorization process

(Kottack & Kozaitis, 1999). Americans, like all people, categorize things in numerous ways, and the use of the term *race* is no exception. People may categorize themselves, or be categorized by others, according to such factors as language, religion, geography, history, ancestry, or physical traits. Think back to the range of socializing agents discussed in Chapter 3. When people assume that an ethnic group has a biological basis, they are referring to that group as a race. But there is increasing evidence that race has no biological basis. For instance, Hispanics or Latinos, referred to by some people as the Hispanic race, are quite a diverse group, with members tracing their heritage from Central and Latin America, the Caribbean, and Spain. Hispanics, or Latinos, are an example of a linguistically based ethnic group (Spanish speaking), not a biologically based race. Thus, not only is the term *race* used rather loosely, but it is also often used incorrectly.

The concept of race is intended to reflect the shared genetic material, or **genotype,** within a group of people. Most people, however, scholars included, tend to use **phenotype** traits, visible traits such as skin color, to classify people according to a given race. There are many problems with using the phenotypic approach to race. For one, cultures vary in the importance given to a particular trait, and there is no agreement on which phenotypic characteristics should be emphasized. Skin color, the most apparent difference to early scientists, thus became the criterion most often used. Arbitrary cultural value was attached to skin color, which subsequently became the basis for discrimination.

As discussed in Chapter 3, although more than 99% of human genetic characteristics is common to all people, it is not uncommon to still find textbooks that present the three great races as distinct from one another—white, black, and yellow. This rather simplistic and inaccurate categorization scheme used race as a power mechanism by keeping white European colonizers separate from their Asian and African subjects. Attempts to make these groupings sound more scientific—by using such terms as *Caucasoid, Mongoloid,* and *Negroid*—cloud the reality that white people are really various shades of pink, beige, or tan; black people are various shades of brown; and so-called yellow people are really various shades of tan or beige. Another problem with such a categorization occurs with such groups as Polynesians, Native Americans, and Australian Aborigines. Then there is the phenomenon of racial mixing, accelerated by European expansion, that occurred on a global scale as people, labor, and goods were increasingly exchanged between nation-states. No such clear-cut categorization of people based on skin color is sound.

Race as a cultural construct, however, is quite alive. But again, cultures vary in the manner in which race is construed. In the United States racial identity is acquired at birth as an ascribed status, not based on simple biology or ancestry. Consider the child of a racially mixed couple involving one African American and one European American parent. It is obvious that half the child's genetic material comes from each parent. However, American culture classifies the child as black, although it makes just as much sense to classify the child as white, and former President Barack Obama provides a good example. In such a case, heredity is being overlooked. To confound the situation even more, racial categorization can vary from state to state. For instance, in some states, any person known to have any African American blood in his or her heritage will be classified as black. Such a situation is referred to as **hypodescent** (where *hypo* means "lower") because it automatically places the child in the minority group (Kottack & Kozaitis, 1999).

A case from Louisiana vividly illustrates the role that the government can play in legalizing or inventing racial classification. Susie Guillory Phipps, a light-skinned woman with European facial features and straight black hair, discovered that she was black only when she was an adult. When she ordered a copy of her birth certificate, she found that her race was listed as "colored." She had, however, been brought up white and was twice married to white men. Phipps challenged a 1970 Louisiana law that classified as legally black anyone with at least one–thirty-second "Negro blood." The state insisted that her racial classification was correct even though the state's lawyer admitted that Phipps looked like a white person (Yetman, 1991). The critical incidents at the end of this chapter refer to this.

Assessment: Old and New

Assessment across cultural, racial, and ethnic boundaries has historically been a sensitive issue. The traditional cross-cultural research literature is filled with numerous studies that report the unfortunate but common practice of taking an assessment instrument developed and normed on one cultural group and using it with little or no modification in another cultural setting. Such use more often than not results in inaccurate judgments of people because:

(1) Certain concepts that are important in one culture may be missed by some assessment instruments.

(2) Procedures developed in one country or culture may not be appropriate for use in another cultural setting.

(3) It may be assumed that all people share in certain experiences that are not, in fact, universally practiced.

Assessment that is sensitive to the role of race, ethnicity, and culture considers the sociocultural context of the learner and the learner's family as well as that of the examiner, and addresses such issues as biases, stereotypes, and prior experience as well as the selection of appropriate testing instruments or interview procedures. Awareness of such issues enhances the possibility of more relevant and culturally sensitive assessments. In addition, issues related to language and its complexities must also be considered when selecting and conducting assessments. The teacher who is sensitive to racial and ethnic concerns also struggles to understand that people display strengths and talents in many different ways.

Understanding Prejudice and Racism

Discussions of categorization and stereotyping (see Chapter 4) inevitably lead into a discussion of issues surrounding prejudice and discrimination. People have a tendency to surround themselves with others who provide social acceptance and help in time of need. As a result, people spend a considerable amount of time and energy learning the norms of the groups to which they wish to belong. One consequence of this is that individuals begin to think that the familiar behaviors of their group are good and natural and that those of others are less good and less natural. Recall that *ethnocentrism* refers to the tendency people have to make judgments based on their own standards and to apply those standards to others. When people make nonreflective judgments about others, these judgments are called *prejudicial*. The word **prejudice** implies a lack of thought or care in making a judgment (or attribution); prejudicial responses are quick, narrow in scope, and based, oftentimes, on negative emotions rather than accurate information. Prejudice appears to be a cultural universal; that is, people around the world tend to behave in similar ways toward certain other groups.

Although racial and ethnic prejudice can be expressed in both positive and negative ways, in the United States it has primarily negative connotations. Prejudice is often defined as a dislike based on a faulty and inflexible generalization that can be directed toward a group as a whole or toward an individual simply because she or he is a member of that group (Allport, 1979). The fact that prejudicial beliefs are rooted in inflexible generalizations means that educators will meet with great resistance to their efforts at change.

The Functions of Prejudice

It is easy to judge others' prejudices (and even our own) rather harshly, but it is equally important to understand that if prejudice did not have a psychological function it would quickly disappear. Just as fear encourages people to prepare for danger and pain makes people aware of some problem, prejudice also serves an adaptive purpose. We defined the concept of *categorization* in Chapter 3 as the cognitive process through which people simplify their world by putting similar stimuli into the same group. In our evolutionary past, this process served us well and aided our survival. Rather than having to determine if each bear or lion we encountered was dangerous, we generalized and quickly classified all of them as dangerous. We constantly categorize aspects of our environment—it happens automatically and simply helps us to function in a complex world. It served as a survival mechanism—we did not have to question each time we encountered a lion or bear to consider that it might not be hungry. We simply considered them all a potential hazard, avoided them as much as possible, and remained safe. The problem arises when we use the same process to develop negative ideas about groups of people and then act with that knowledge. Among the early researchers studying prejudice, Katz (1960) suggested that prejudice serves at least four functions: an *adjustment function*, an *ego-defensive function*, a *value-expressive function*, and a *knowledge function*.

Adjustment Function

People need to adjust to the complex world in which they live, and if holding certain prejudicial attitudes aids that adjustment, they will be maintained. For instance, a teacher who believes that members of certain ethnic groups or people with disabilities are incapable of achieving at a high level then has an excuse for not finding alternative methods of reaching them. This attitude reduces the work-related responsibilities of the teacher, thus making one's life a bit easier. However, it obviously prevents these students from achieving their full potential.

Ego-Defensive Function

People may hold certain prejudicial attitudes to protect their own self-concept. If less successful students want to think of themselves as on equal terms with higher achieving students, they may be inclined to view the comparison group as cheaters. Holding this attitude protects the self-image of these individuals without any painful self-examination of the reasons for their own lack of success. The ego-defensive function also protects a positive view of one's ingroup. Rejection of others then becomes a way of legitimizing one's own viewpoint as well as a way of avoiding the possibility that others may have an equally legitimate point of view. This is similar to the level of Defense on the developmental model of intercultural sensitivity (Bennett, 1993) discussed in Chapter 5.

Value-Expressive Function

People use prejudicial attitudes to demonstrate their own self-image to others. If people believe they are custodians of the truth about the role of education, for instance, or that the god of their religion is the one true god, then other groups must be incorrect or inferior in their thinking. If one's group has attained success through the use of highly valued technology, then those who do not have this technology must be backward. The value-expressive function presents a certain image to the world whereas the ego-defensive function protects that image by blaming others when things go wrong.

Knowledge Function

Some prejudicial attitudes make the stereotypical knowledge of one's ingroup the basis of one's personal judgments and actions. Our interactions with others, for instance, may be directly dependent upon the internal images and messages we carry in our minds. Thus, if a teacher believes that a certain group of people are inferior or have inherent deficiencies, that teacher's interaction with students will reflect his or her beliefs. Holding these attitudes allows individuals to make quick (usually negative) decisions when faced with choices involving individuals from the outgroup. There is often a close relationship between the knowledge and adjustment functions. The former has to do with the information that one's ingroup believes is important; the latter has to do with how people use that information in making decisions.

Such behaviors may have a profound impact on the relationships and interactions children have with their teachers, significantly impacting educational achievement. Interviews of Maori children in New Zealand, for instance, report time and again that negative, deficient beliefs and behaviors on the part of teachers were central to developing negative relations and avoidance behavior of students (Bishop & Berryman, 2006).

Prejudice Formation: The Components of Prejudice

Three components of prejudice can be identified: cognitive, affective, and behavioral. The *cognitive component* refers to the need people have to simplify the world around them, considered as the process of categorization discussed above as well as in Chapters 3 and 4. Recall that stereotypes are merely categories of people, and narrowly constructed categories may result in negative stereotypes. The *affective component* refers to the feelings that accompany a person's thoughts about members of a particular group. The affect attached to any concept can, of course, be positive or negative. This is the component most often thought of when people think of prejudice. The *behavioral component* is the discriminatory behavior that people who harbor negative prejudices are capable of directing toward others, especially when that person possesses both prejudice and power. Power differentials are often evident between differing racial and ethnic individuals and groups.

Educators can work with each of these components in different ways. In Chapters 3 and 4, we learned that the *categorization process* is a cultural universal that helps all people simplify the multitude of stimuli they confront each day. As educators, we must recognize this fact, make a point of informing others about it, and work to broaden our students' (and our own) categories. One long-term goal of both intercultural and global education is for individuals to become broader, more complex thinkers. That is, as educators we should strive to help people develop the ability to perceive and evaluate situations from a number of perspectives, not just their comfortable, native orientation. In addition to this cognitive dimension, the affective and behavioral components are also under the control of educators. Strategies and programs that have successfully reduced negative affect and behavior toward others will be discussed in the following sections.

How Children Learn Prejudice

We have known since the 1940s that children as young as age 3 or 4 are aware of their own racial or ethnic background and tend to have prowhite/antiblack bias (Augoustinos & Rosewarne, 2001; Clark & Clark, 1947; Katz, 1983). It is in the early childhood and elementary school years that children's attitudes toward members of other groups are being formed and crystallized. Thus, a critical role of schooling should be to provide positive experiences that cause children to rethink their beliefs about group differences because on their own they are unlikely to do so. The literature on prejudice formation identifies a number of ways in which children may learn to be prejudiced: observation, group membership, the media, and religious fundamentalism (Byrnes, 1988; Hofheimer-Bettman & Friedman, 2004; ADL, 2013).

Observation and Passive Learning

Children learn negative prejudice by observing the behavior of others, particularly respected elders. If those who surround a child display racist, sexist, homophobic, anti-Semitic, or other negative attitudes, children may be inclined to follow suit. Although children often learn much unconsciously from the subtle messages given by others, some learn prejudice from more blatant efforts by parents and community. This learning typically occurs unconsciously and early in one's life, thus making the unlearning of such beliefs a tremendous challenge.

In a similar manner, school also plays a powerful role in the lives of children. Aspects of school culture can inadvertently promote and reinforce negative racial prejudice by having relatively homogeneous administrators, staff, and student body; a curriculum that emphasizes the perspectives and experiences of the dominant culture; and a learning environment that emphasizes only one value system.

Group Membership

Children, like other individuals, want to feel that they belong to a group. If the group that the child identifies with excludes or devalues certain others, the child is likely to adopt that behavior and those attitudes. Thus children may learn prejudice simply as a survival technique, as a way to fit into a group. Some children, for instance, are actively prepared from a very early age for adult roles in various religious cults or in secular organizations like the Ku Klux Klan.

The Media

Exposure to media is another way in which children learn prejudice. Although the media may not actively teach prejudice, it sometimes reinforces stereotypes or in some cases introduces stereotypes where they may not already exist. Portraying minority group members in stereotypic or negative roles, or being invisible, especially in positions of leadership and authority, are examples of how media influence children's thinking. Cowboy and Indian films, for instance, have had a significant impact on children's views of Native Americans (Cortes, 2000). Both electronic and print media, through children's stories, often equate beauty with goodness and ugliness with evil. The symbolic association with evil of physical disabilities such as hunchbacks, peg legs, eye patches, and hooked arms have been shown to encourage a negative attitude toward disabilities (Bicklin & Bailey, 1981).

Religious Fundamentalism

The more orthodox or fundamental a person's religious beliefs are, the greater the prejudice toward other religious and cultural groups is likely to be. People's strict adherence to certain religious practices may actively encourage them to believe that all other doctrines, as well as the individuals who believe in them, are at best "wrong" and at worst dangerous.

Extreme Cases of Prejudice

Racism

The concept of race and the practice of racism have always been intertwined in the United States. The term *racism,* as discussed in Chapter 3, refers to the transformation of negative race or ethnic prejudice through the use of power that is then directed toward individuals or groups thought of as inferior. Although overt racism, as displayed by John Gray in the case study, seems to have declined over the years, a rise in anti-Semitic and anti-Muslim incidents across the United States occurred in the aftermath of the 2016 election. It is important to understand that both individuals and institutions can display racism. *Individual racism* is evident when a person who harbors negative prejudice discriminates against another individual. *Institutional racism* reflects intentional or unintentional institutional policies that unfairly restrict the opportunities of specific groups. Policies or practices that make it difficult for certain groups to participate in certain activities, for example, by charging fees for services that are out of the range of some groups, are examples of institutional racism.

Hate Groups

The term *hate group* refers to any organized body that denigrates select groups of people based on their ethnicity, race, religion, nationality, gender, gender identity, or sexual orientation or that advocates the use of violence against such groups or their members for purposes of scapegoating. The term, as used in the United States, is generally applied to white supremacist groups such as the Ku Klux Klan, the White Aryan Resistance, and the Church of Jesus Christ Christians/Aryan Nations. Local chapters of hate groups tend to target racial or ethnic minorities in their immediate area, but all of the groups are anti-black and anti-Semitic.

It is difficult to obtain accurate figures on the number of hate groups or individual membership in such groups, but estimates suggest that more than 900 groups, representing some 20,000 to 200,000 members, now exist in the United States. The number of hate groups in the United States has increased since the start of the century, thought to be in response to the anticipated surge in immigrants and minority groups in the country and the projection that White Americans will be in the minority in the coming decades. Similar activity is happening in some European nations as well. Some of these groups limit their activities to producing and distributing literature, actions that would be most typically observed in schools; others are known to commit acts of violence, including vandalism, intimidation, assault, and murder.

White Privilege

People can in many ways unknowingly contribute to the existence of prejudice. A particular situation, referred to as **white privilege**, exists when white people, who may have been taught that racism is something that puts others at a disadvantage, are not taught to see the corresponding advantage that their color brings to them.

Peggy McIntosh (1992) referred to white privilege as "an invisible package of unlearned assets that I can count on cashing in each day, but about which I was meant to remain oblivious. White privilege is like an invisible weightless knapsack of special provisions, maps, passports, codebooks, visas, clothes, tools, and blank checks" (p. 33).

White privilege, like its counterpart male privilege, remains largely unconscious for most perpetrators and may lead to white racism (Sleeter, 1994). This may be due to a number of factors such as that whites have traditionally been in the majority, have accumulated greater power and wealth on the backs of others, and control much of the nation's resources and media, making it possible to insulate themselves from the plight and rage of others. As Sleeter (1994) contends, this is perpetuated by having tacit agreement among whites to continue to reap the benefits of the past, and not to talk about it except in ways that continue to present current race relations as legitimate. In addition, at the individual level, people generally do not recognize their own behavior and how it may oppress others. Rather, people typically attribute success and status to personal traits (e.g., I work hard or I am smart) rather than to situational factors (such as institutional racism or socioeconomic capability; recall the fundamental attribution error discussed in Chapter 4), believing that they have "earned" or otherwise are worthy of what they have acquired.

McIntosh identified numerous instances where whites in general are at an advantage over people of color. For instance, most whites can arrange to be in the company of people of their own race most of the time, can find a home in an area they can afford and in which they would want to live, can go shopping alone most of the time without being followed or harassed, will find examples of their own race as the foundation of the school curriculum, and will not be asked to represent their entire race whenever the issue of race or ethnicity is broached. In what ways can you see that you or others around you may have been privileged?

Racial Profiling

Although there is no single, universally accepted definition of *racial profiling*, it generally refers to the law enforcement practice of targeting someone for investigation while passing through some public space (public highways, airports, etc.) where the reason for the stop is a statistical profile of the detainee's race, ethnicity, or national origin (especially prevalent in times of national crises and war). In such instances, race may be used to determine which drivers to stop for minor traffic violations (sometimes referred to as "driving while black"), which motorists or pedestrians to search for contraband, and more recently, which travelers to single out for more extensive security clearance before boarding an airplane.

Racial profiling has increased in frequency in the United States in recent years, both for traditional domestic groups, such as African Americans, and among more recent immigrants, such as Arab Americans. Despite the civil rights victories of 40 years ago, official racial prejudice is still reflected throughout law enforcement practices as well as the criminal justice system. Although some observers claim that racial profiling doesn't exist, there is an abundance of stories and statistics that document the practice. Soon after the 2016 presidential election, President Trump issued an executive order initially banning travel to the United States from seven predominantly Muslim countries—a clear example of racial profiling.

Strategies for Prejudice Reduction

It is in schools, perhaps more than in any other social setting, where people have intimate and regular interactions with a wide diversity of people. But we cannot simply assume that just because people are in close proximity to those different from themselves that positive outcomes and cross-group friendships necessarily develop. Close analysis of many school desegregation studies has demonstrated some rather surprising and counterintuitive effects. For one, greater diversity does not necessarily lead to an increase in cross-racial friendships, either in the short term or the long term. The opposite, in fact, can be the case. Moody (2001), for instance, found that the more diverse the school, the greater the tendency of students to self-segregate into ingroups based on race and ethnicity.

Some of this may be attributed to a U.S. emphasis on individuality as opposed to a collective orientation (Bronson & Merryman, 2009). Americans, in general, define their ingroup preferences according to their individual likes and dislikes. Thus, individuals may learn to see differences, and then, as a result, form subgroups based on their individual likes and similarity to others (e.g., they join organized sport and recreation groups with others like themselves). Although singular, individual identity is a long-term goal for many U.S. citizens, it is ultimately achieved by joining many distinct subgroups—especially in the high school years. On the contrary, in a highly collectivist culture like Japan, which values and seeks social harmony over individualism, young people are discouraged from seeking individual preferences. In a rather ironic way, it seems that the more the culture emphasizes individuality, the greater the tendency for young people to form subgroups in school as young people search to find their own identity.

It is thus essential that educators at all levels take the opportunity to become proactive in understanding and improving intergroup relations. This should take place on two levels—through teacher (and parent) talk as well as through formal curriculum efforts.

Parent and Teacher Talk

In their book, *Nurture Shock: New Thinking about Children,* Bronson and Merryman (2009) pointed out some other surprising research that challenges the assumptions many parents and educators have made about behavior and its impact on racial attitudes of young people. Many parents and teachers, for instance, assume that children will only see and

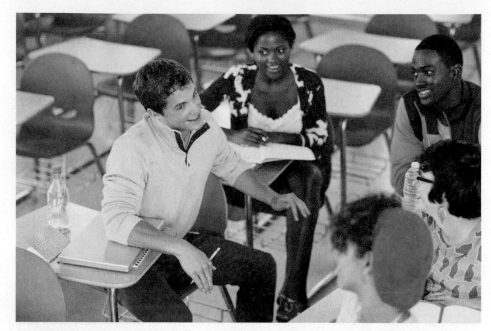

©Paul Bradbury/age fotostock RF

be interested in race when it is pointed out to them, and thus go to great lengths to ignore the concept. A number of studies report a high percentage of parents who are uncomfortable talking about the topic of race in any meaningful manner. A 2007 study of 17,000 families with children in kindergarten (Brown et al., 2007), for instance, reported that 75% of European American parents and 45% of African American parents never, or almost never, discussed issues of race with their children. But racial differences, as gender, *are* evident to children. If the topic is not discussed openly and intelligently, children will be left to their own devices to make meaning, or vulnerable to the influence of others (e.g., peers, the media), which may result in misinformation, or worse, racist notions. As discussed above, U.S. children and young people rather spontaneously develop ingroup preferences, often based on similarity of appearance such as skin color (Bigler, 1999). This preference then extends to a belief that those who look like me are similar in other aspects as well—and the things I do not like belong to those who look dissimilar.

Teachers and parents may assume they are creating a color-blind environment for children when they avoid discussing issues of difference related to race (or other categories for that matter). Recall the concept of Minimization discussed in Chapter 5. People find this a comfortable place to be, saying such things as, "I don't see differences, I just see children," or, "I treat everyone alike." It is, thus, essential that parents and teachers not only develop a knowledge base about issues related to race and racism, but a comfort level as well so they can lead or enter such conversations on a regular basis with ease.

Curriculum Transformation

Critical to reducing prejudice and establishing an interculturally sensitive classroom is the teacher's understanding of, and ability to integrate, intercultural awareness and prejudice reduction activities into the curriculum. We are fortunate that the educational research literature supports our efforts to reduce prejudice. Indeed, there is some indication that if we are proactive and mindful, we may even be able to decrease the likelihood that prejudiced attitudes will develop (Byrnes, 1988).

Educational strategies that have demonstrated the ability to reduce prejudice generally fall into four categories: (1) improving social contact and intergroup relations; (2) increasing cognitive sophistication; (3) improving self-esteem; and (4) increasing empathy and understanding of other groups. These categories all have curricular implications, which are discussed in the following sections.

1. Improving Social Contact and Intergroup Relations

Research by organizational psychologists, sociologists, economists, and others repeatedly demonstrate that groups that are diverse in terms of race, ethnicity, gender, and sexual orientation are more innovative than homogeneous groups, and in surprising ways (Phillips, 2014). Collaborating with people from different backgrounds, it seems, not only provide exposure to new information and ideas, but when interacting with people who are different, group members tend to prepare better, anticipate alternative viewpoints, and expect that reaching consensus will take time and effort. From a programmatic standpoint, the most promising of all change efforts stems from the work of researchers interested in intergroup interaction. Allport (1954), in proposing the *contact hypothesis*, suggested that one way to reduce negative prejudice is to bring representatives of different groups into close contact with one another. Sometimes this method proves helpful, but not always; it is sometimes possible that negative prejudice is reinforced or, in fact, formed where it did not previously exist.

After considerable research it has been found that it is the conditions under which groups come together that are critical. Certain characteristics of the contact situation seem to be essential to ensure positive outcomes. Considerable efforts under many different circumstances (e.g., bilingual classrooms, integrated housing and schools, conflict management programs, summer camp programs) have led to recommendations concerning the best conditions under which social contact can be improved. These conditions relate to equal status contact, superordinate goals, encouragement, and personal familiarity.

Equal Status Contact

Amir (1969), working in integrated school settings in Israel, found that if individuals coming together have equal status, or equal access to any rewards available, conditions are set for improved relations. In Switzerland, for instance, French, German, and Italian are all recognized as official languages of the country, with all documents made available in all three languages. Speakers of diverse languages, therefore, are all valued, well informed, and provided with the tools that enable them to participate in the society at large. This seems to be completely the opposite of the current movement under way in many states in the United States to make English the official language, even though this country boasts the fifth largest Spanish-speaking population in the world. Currrently 31 states have made English the official language. Although English-only laws are largely symbolic and non-enforceable, they have been interpreted by some to mean that English is the required language for day-to-day life. In one example, when the law was passed in Colorado, a school bus driver reportedly prohibited students from using Spanish on their way to school (Zentella, 1997). And in Kansas City, a student was suspended for speaking Spanish in the hallways (Reid, 2005).

In the school context, equal access to rewards can be understood to mean equal access to knowledge, grades, or extracurricular offerings. For all students to have equal access to knowledge and grades, culturally relevant and responsive teaching through appropriate curricula and instructional strategies must be employed (Gay, 2000; Ladson-Billings, 1995). Culturally relevant or responsive teaching reflects a wide range of practices that places culture at the core of teaching and learning. This involves many of the elements explored throughout this book, including such things as acknowledging the cultural heritage of various ethnic groups; building bridges between home, community, and school; employing a range of instructional strategies that are responsive to varying student learning styles; and integrating diverse content and resources into all subject areas.

Enabling all students to gain all the benefits schools have to offer includes encouraging their participation in extracurricular offerings, which may not occur in the "natural" course of events. Social class status, for instance, has a significant impact on the kinds of school experiences in which a child may participate. Children from lower socioeconomic groups, for instance, tend to participate in fewer after-school activities than do their middle-class counterparts, and thus may not reap the potential benefits of such participation. For example, the development of skills related to group and team thinking and acting that have been shown to be associated with successful managerial or other higher-level employment are often learned through extracurricular activities rather than in formal classrooms (Brislin, 1993). Likewise, developing the ability to engage in a wide array of interpersonal interactions is greatly enhanced through participation in the nonformal side of the curriculum. Legislation regarding equal rights for disabled persons is also intended to bring equal access to children with disabilities, as is Title IX of the Education Amendment that is designed to eliminate discrimination based on gender.

Superordinate Goals

Achieving equal status contact in and of itself, however, is not sufficient. Individuals who come together and work toward achieving some superordinate goal or common task that could not be satisfied without the participation of all involved are more likely to learn to get along. This concept stems from the work of Sherif (1958), who found that although it was relatively easy to create hostility and aggression between two groups of boys at summer camp, it was far more difficult to bring them back together again as one larger, cooperative group. He was finally able to bring both groups back together by staging an incident in which a bus got stuck in the mud while on the way to a camp outing. For the bus to continue on its way, and for the young people to continue on to their outing, they all had to work together to push the bus back onto the road. This superordinate goal, which could not have been achieved without everyone's participation, required all the campers to work together for overall success.

In the school context, superordinate goals are readily available in the form of team sports, drama productions, and music performances and through cooperative learning activities that can be easily integrated in the classroom setting. When students with disabilities participate in the mainstream of school life (extracurricular as well as academic activities), such co-participation with nondisabled peers in pursuit of common goals is possible. Similarly, students who have opportunities to work with others across racial and ethnic boundaries in activities like sports, plays, and concerts tend to develop more positive attitudes toward one another. Educators who work in schools that are more homogenous will need to put more effort and imagination into planning activities that involve diverse groups. Such activities may teach students to "see" invisible differences, such as differences in learning style, differences in religious attitudes, or differences in knowledge and perceptions related to gender roles. Activities might also involve cooperative efforts with other communities and schools or efforts to encourage the implementation of international exchange student programs on a regular basis. Educators could encourage integrated activities between students with disabilities and without disabilities, across traditional age barriers, between high school and elementary school students, or between older people in the community and students of all ages.

Encouragement of Intergroup Interaction

To be effective, efforts to reduce prejudice must be seen as important at all levels of the school—from the classroom to the lunchroom to central administration. Such efforts cannot be seen entirely as the whim or "cause" of an individual teacher or particular group. Teachers, school administrators, and as many other adults as possible must actively encourage and show support for such efforts. Do not interpret this caveat, however, to mean that an individual teacher cannot initiate such changes. Innumerable teachers acting independently or with a small group of colleagues have demonstrated that the initial efforts of a single individual can have broad effects, especially in curricular decisions. Although the school system controls much of a teacher's ability to make significant and permanent change partly in the way it controls available resources, it by no means controls everything. Indeed, many, if not most, school systems today are eager and willing to support a teacher who is trying something new in the way of curricular revision. Careful documentation of the revision process and its results are needed to institutionalize the changes that are effective and to refine the teacher's initial work.

Personal Familiarity

A high acquaintance potential must exist during intergroup contact situations, encouraging close contact between individuals in a given situation. In other words, people must have the opportunity to get to know the "other" person in ways that render the stereotypic image clearly inappropriate. It is very difficult, for instance, for a student to believe that all people on welfare are lazy when that student knows firsthand that Susan and her mother are both working as much as they are allowed to within the welfare rules and that if Susan's mother took an available job that did not include health benefits, she would lose the health card she is using to treat Susan's chronic asthma.

Informal activity, perhaps even structured into the day or on weekends, must occur. Students can be placed in different heterogeneous groups for a variety of purposes, or they can be encouraged (or required) to participate in mixed team sports—any situation that will enable them to get to know others on a personal basis.

Some Cautions in Applying the Contact Hypothesis

Although application of the contact hypothesis generally proves beneficial, applying it in the real world of school settings has always been problematic due to a variety of factors. Many schools, for example, are relatively monocultural and appear to be homogeneous, providing little opportunity for intergroup contact to occur. In such situations it might be best to stress the diversity that is evident within a group, such as socioeconomic, religious, or gender differences.

But even when cultural, ethnic, racial, and socioeconomic diversity is evident in the school, other factors often mediate against regular, meaningful intergroup interaction. Problematic issues of applying the contact hypothesis in schools may center on the criterion of equal status contact. Although equal status contact provides much of the foundational structure that underlies many group activities in the classroom, including cooperative learning strategies, it may be difficult to bring this about in the somewhat artificial setting of the school primarily because groups do not have equal status outside the school. Students do not leave their social status at home when they come to school. Social contact efforts, therefore, may lead to increased stereotyping among groups.

Some schools continue to experience patterns of racial and ethnic segregation, often as a result of the neighborhoods they serve or by segregated housing patterns, which reduces the possibility of intergroup contact, certainly out of school. In many instances, integrated schools may end up resegregating themselves through the practice of ability or achievement tracking. Grouping students by academic ability has long been, and continues to be, practiced in many schools and may result in the unintended segregation of students by ethnicity or race (Stephan, 1999). Tracking, or segregation by group, may relegate a disproportionate number of low-income students and students of color to lower-tracked classes in which they receive inferior education, thus perpetuating the problem. Tracking can occur for a variety of reasons and in many different contexts, not only by achievement nor only in the classroom; tracking also may occur as a result of participation in extracurricular activities, on the playground, or in the lunchroom.

Another problem with the equal status concept is that it may not generalize beyond the immediate context in which an intervention occurs. That is, while intergroup relations may appear to improve among individuals who come into contact in the school setting, such attitude change may not transfer to other contexts. Equal status between two groups may not generalize to other outgroups or when status is not equal, as in a community context.

Community-level factors may also play a role. Blau, Lamb, Stearns, and Pellerin (2001) looked at the relationship between equal-status contact in neighborhoods and subsequent achievement in school. They found that all students, regardless of their race, achieved at lower levels in their social studies courses when they lived in homogeneous communities in which race and socioeconomic status were closely related. That is, neighborhoods that were homogeneous with regard to race and class did not provide a favorable context for the challenges of learning about key social science concepts such as social differentiation.

2. Increasing Cognitive Sophistication

Strategies designed to increase cognitive sophistication or complexity have been shown to have a positive impact on prejudice reduction (Hofheimer-Bettmann & Friedman, 2004). *Cognitive complexity* refers to the degree to which an individual differentiates or makes distinctions between discrete aspects of an event, and/or makes connections or relationships among these elements. Persons high in cognitive complexity are able to analyze or differentiate a situation into many constituent elements, and then explore connections and potential relationships among those elements. Complex people tend to be more open to new information and to form more accurate impressions of others than less complex persons. People of high complexity, for instance, are attracted to a broader variety of people, are more flexible in their thinking, use fewer stereotypes, tend to search for more information when faced with a decision, tend to be more creative, and are less influenced by the persuasive communication of others (Streufert & Swezey, 1986).

A considerable amount of research points to the fact that individuals who think in narrow terms are more likely to have a high degree of prejudice. Strategies that are designed to help individuals avoid stereotypes and overgeneralizations and become aware of the biases in their thinking and behavior do help them become less prejudiced (Gardiner, 1972; Boyd-MacMillan, 2016). This research suggests that we will see positive change in this dimension when we focus our teaching efforts on improving students' critical thinking skills. Thinking in a critical manner is antithetical to prejudicial thinking. Rather than reacting quickly because of an emotional response, students must search for and examine the reasons or motivations behind their thoughts and actions. People who think critically tend to question, analyze, and suspend judgment until all available information is collected and examined.

Teachers should work hard to create the kind of classroom environment that encourages critical thought. In such classrooms, students feel respected and have a certain degree of trust. Students cannot function at higher levels of cognitive activity when their anxiety level is high. Feelings of safety and trust are thus a corollary of student risk taking. Recall the role that the culture-general themes of anxiety, belonging, and status play in people's sense of emotional stability.

The classroom should also reflect, as Lipman (1980) stated, a "community of inquiry," or as described later in this book, a "learning community." Such an environment is characterized by questions of all kinds—those for which there are "right" answers and those that have more than one right answer. Indeed, some educators feel that to prepare students for the real world outside school, teachers' questions must force students to consider all sides of the problem, some of which may, in fact, be conflicting.

A balance should be maintained between teacher talk and student talk. Students must believe that their ideas are important and that what they have to say is critical. It is through discussion with others and through the sharing of ideas and problems that critical thinking develops. Within the context of a safe, open classroom discussion, all students should be allowed to participate and to feel that their contributions are welcomed. This is behind the notion of 'belonging' that was introduced as one of the 18 culture-general themes in Chapter 4. Students should be taught to think about their thinking and should be able to justify their reasoning with evidence. An emphasis should be on *metacognition,* or becoming aware of how one has come to a decision. Students who are aware of how they arrive at defensible positions are on their way to becoming independent, self-regulated learners.

To think critically means to think broadly, to take all sides of a problem into account, and to weigh the resulting evidence. In short, to think critically is to avoid simplistic approaches. Too often, students are encouraged to "learn what is in the book," which frequently means to avoid "thinking" altogether. Teachers who create an environment in which risk taking is encouraged, in which cooperation in problem solving is stressed, and in which mistakes are not perceived as sins or personal faults are more likely to engender achievement in students. In such classrooms, an emphasis on thinking skills is not seen as an addition to an already overcrowded school day. It does not require a special course or time of day. Rather, critical thinking is a goal that permeates each and every lesson and all teacher-student contact.

3. Improving Self-Confidence and Self-Acceptance

Pettigrew (1981) established a clear inverse relationship between the degree of prejudice a person harbors and the individual's sense of self-worth. That is, the more confident a person is in his or her own sense of identity and competence, the lower is that person's degree of prejudice, and vice versa. Although the relationship is not necessarily cause and effect, there are strong indications that self-acceptance is critical to mental, physical, and emotional health. Children with high self-esteem tend to be open and respectful of other people and maintain their sense of self without having to denigrate others.

©Blend Images/Alamy Stock Photo RF

Classroom activities designed to increase self-confidence also tend to bring about a decrease in levels of prejudice. Children can develop confidence in themselves when they are in educational environments in which they feel secure and accepted, in which their participation is valued, and in which they know the boundaries or limits. Involving children in lessons in which they can see themselves or their culture reflected in a variety of ways helps to create a solid sense of self as well as a classroom that is respectful and understanding of others. Creating such environments should be of prime concern to educators.

4. Increasing Empathy for and Understanding of Others

Although prejudice reduction is enhanced through social contact, cognitive sophistication, and an increase of self-esteem, long-term gains require educational activity that actively engages the emotions. Activities designed to help students see the world from another's perspective and thus develop **empathy,** or an understanding of the thoughts and feelings of another, are effective in reducing prejudice and improving intergroup relations (Garcia, Powell, & Sanchez, 1990). Classroom dramatizations and skits, reading narratives from another's perspective, and simulations are excellent tools for helping children become sensitive to others who act or look different.

Shaver and Curtis (1981), for example, offered a simulation to help children understand what it is like for those with speech difficulties. They suggested students put something in their mouths (such as a small clean rubber ball or dental cotton—something large enough that it won't be swallowed) and then make a telephone call to a store and ask for information. Students can then discuss how it feels to be unable to communicate effectively.

The classic cross-cultural simulation Bafa Bafa, or the children's version Rafa Rafa, provides an excellent way for students to gain an understanding of what it is like to move between cultural groups (Shirts, 1977). In this experience, individuals learn "proper" behavior associated with the creation of two distinct cultural groups. After some time, members of each group have the opportunity to interact with one another. They very quickly experience feelings of anxiety, rejection, apprehension, and confusion—those feelings often referred to collectively as *culture shock*. Most individuals who have made a significant transition from one country or culture to another encounter such feelings. This simulation allows students (and teachers or parents) to explore the feelings and experiences of immigrant, migrant, or refugee students; international exchange students; students in newly desegregated schools; newly mainstreamed children with disabilities; or just about anybody cast in the role of "new kid on the block."

Students may also write stories or act out plays and dramatizations of situations that characterize acts of prejudice and discrimination. In this manner, students "step into the shoes" of another, thereby gaining an insider's perspective of what it is like to be discriminated against.

Comprehensive Programs That Improve Intergroup Relations

In addition to the efforts that individual classroom teachers and large-group activities can make (e.g., team sports, school plays), a number of educational programs have been developed that demonstrate a positive effect on students' attitudes, values, and behaviors (Stephan & Vogt, 2004). Brief descriptions of some successful programs designed for K–12 children are presented next.

Antibias Education for Young Children

In 1989, the National Association for the Education of Young Children (NAEYC) published *Anti-Bias Curriculum: Tools for Empowering Young Children*. This approach aims to help children develop the knowledge and skills they will need to work together in diverse, inclusive schools and communities. The four interacting goals of culturally relevant antibias education for young children are: (1) nurturing every child's construction of knowledge, confident self-identity, and group identity; (2) promoting each child's comfortable, empathetic interaction with people from diverse backgrounds; (3) fostering each child's critical thinking about bias; and (4) cultivating each child's ability to stand up for her- or himself and for others in the face of bias (Derman-Sparks & Olsen Edwards, 2010). The antibias approach is under development and influencing practice currently in a number of countries.

Cooperative Learning

Cooperative learning strategies refer to a set of approaches that modify standard academic topics in such a way that the materials are learned in small, oftentimes interethnic, cooperative learning groups. Applying the criteria discussed in the section titled

"Improving Social Contact and Intergroup Relations," students work with one another in cooperative groups in pursuit of the common goal of achieving the objectives of the lesson at hand. Eight different cooperative approaches have been studied, with a considerable amount of research demonstrating that when the conditions outlined by Allport (1954) are met in the classroom, students are more likely to have more friends across racial and ethnic groups than they would when compared to students in the traditional classroom (Cooper & Slavin, 2004).

A World of Difference

The Anti-Defamation League's *A World of Difference* program is one of the largest and best-established efforts developed for schools to address issues of prejudice and racism. Teachers receive training in the use of specially designed curriculum materials that not only sensitize students to the existence of prejudice, bigotry, and discrimination but help them develop the skills needed to respond effectively to others. The instructional approach through the program is highly interactive, with an emphasis on students' everyday concerns related to issues of identity, the prevalence of bias, examining instances of exclusion in their own schools, and ways of developing more positive intergroup relations (Hofheimer-Bettman & Friedman, 2004). *A World of Difference* programs have grown over the years to include four distinct programs: *A Classroom of Difference,* offering anti-bias training in K-12 contexts for children, teachers, and administrators; *A Campus of Difference*, providing similar training on college campuses for young adults, faculty, and administrators; *A Community of Difference*, offering programs for social service workers, staff of community organizations, and civic leaders to develop skills designed to improve peoples' ability to collaborate more effectively; and *A World of Difference Institute International Programs* designed to offer their various programs in countries around the world.

Facing History and Ourselves

Started more than 40 years ago, *Facing History and Ourselves* has explored issues of prejudice, racism, and anti-Semitism by examining the unique circumstances surrounding Nazi Germany and the Holocaust and other examples of genocide. The work has grown to consider additional topics: Democracy and Civic Engagement, Race in U.S. History, Justice and Human Rights, Anti-Semitism and Religious Tolerance, Bullying and Ostracism, Global Migration, and Genocide and Mass Violence. The program emphasizes the development of critical thinking skills while concerning itself with the moral issues of justice, human rights, and concern for the welfare of others. Students develop skills in the use of inquiry, analysis, and interpretation while learning about hatred, stereotyping, scapegoating, ethnocentrism, power, and obedience (Tollefson, Barr, & Strom, 2004).

Critical Incidents

The Case Study introduced at the beginning of the chapter ended with John Gray leaving the school assembly and Mr. Johnson sending students back to their homeroom classes for some discussion of what had just occurred. This chapter's Critical Incidents extend the encounter and raises a series of questions for you to consider.

Do You Know Anyone Else Like John Gray?

There was much discussion among the students as they went back to their classes. When Jane's group reconvened in the classroom, it took her a few minutes to calm them down.

"Was he for real?" one of them asked.

"How could he be? Someone would kill him on the street if he went around talking like that to everyone!" another replied.

Jane jumped in. "How many of you know someone like John Gray?" she asked. The room quieted down. About six hands went up.

"So," Jane continued, "it seems that some of you know someone pretty similar to Mr. Gray. Who might that person be?"

"My uncle Pete's a lot like him," a boy offered from the back of the room. "Whenever we're together at family gatherings he just rants and raves about 'those people' this and 'those people' that. He really seems to resent it when someone from another race appears to do well. He once moved out of a neighborhood that was becoming integrated. He gets so loud and forceful at times that we all just want to leave . . . but we can't . . . he's a close relative, you know. Boy, it really bothers me."

Sue picked up from across the room. "My sister has changed quite a lot since she got married a few years ago. I don't ever recall her being prejudiced at home. I'm not, and my parents don't seem to be. But ever since she married George she's become quite racist. I don't understand it. She has a college education, but her husband doesn't. She just seems to have adopted whatever he thinks. I've gotten into a few arguments with her, but not when her husband is around. I'm kind of afraid to speak up when he's in the room."

"What are you most afraid of, Sue?" asked Ms. Myers.

"Well," Sue continued, "he's quite loud when he gets upset. I've seen him insult other people, and I'm just afraid I couldn't take his tirade. And besides, I don't want to upset my sister, so I just keep quiet. I don't know if that's the best thing to do."

"Sometimes my father gets like John Gray," Samantha added. "I've fought with him a few times when I've heard him say some rather negative things about people, especially about some of my friends at school. He gets quite upset with me when I challenge him, but it really bothers me that he can be so close-minded—and insult my friends at the same time!"

- Does John Gray remind you of anyone you know?

- When you are with this person, or a person like him, what feelings does it generate in you?

- What do you do when you have those feelings?

- How do you interact with this individual? Is this an effective strategy to employ?

Reflections From John Gray

After the classroom discussions the students gathered back in the auditorium. As they settled into their chairs, Mr. Johnson walked onto the stage, took the microphone, and reported that there had been some very lively discussions in each of the homerooms.

Mr. Johnson went on to report that he had been able to convince Mr. Gray not to leave because he thought it would be good to have Mr. Gray join them as they talked about their experiences and their various discussions.

There was quite a bit of talking and movement among the students when Gray returned to the stage. He took the microphone from Mr. Johnson and sat on a stool on the right side of the stage.

"I'm glad Mr. Johnson talked me into staying," Gray opened. "I understand you had quite lively discussions in your homerooms. That's good, because it is only after we begin talking about some of these issues that we will ever be able to solve them. In this case you were breaking the silence, and I applaud you for that. I'd like to talk with you now about your reactions to me. I wonder if any of you have any questions for me now?"

There was nervous commotion throughout the room until one student stood up.

"Are you for real? How would you deal with a person like yourself?" he asked.

"That's a very good question," replied Gray. "Let me tell you a few things about me, and then we can look at a few things about you. Would that be all right with you? And, by the way, what differences do you notice about me now?"

"Well, for one thing," a student replied, "You seem much more relaxed. You are not confronting us; you are sitting, and you seem to be listening to what we are saying."

"How do you know I am listening?" asked Gray.

"Well, for one, you are responding to what I just said. You asked me a question and waited for my response."

"Yes, I will admit that sometimes I get to the point that I do not listen nor respond to the things you might say to me. But when I am doing that, I must tell you, I am not acting. I am not role-playing with you. What I am doing is what I call 'role-taking,' and let me define that. I did not memorize a script and come in here to play the role of a bigot. That's what happens in role-playing. But I was role-taking here with you this morning. I was sharing with you many messages that I heard when I was growing up—perhaps some of the messages you, too, have heard while you were growing up and perhaps still hear today. Maybe some of you shared that in your group discussions. Now while I may have heard those messages when I was younger, I do not support them today. But I do hear them in my head every now and then. I have to stop and remind myself that those are old messages, often prejudices, and I do not believe them anymore. They are like tapes that suddenly turn on in my mind when I'm in certain situations. But now that I am aware of them and now that I have more sophisticated knowledge and experience today, I know how to turn them off. So, in role-taking I was sharing messages that I grew up hearing and I was playing them all back for you. Do you recall what was said to you at the beginning of the session? You were told that you would participate in a psychodrama that would illustrate racism and prejudice in action. How many of you heard that? While you were told up front what was to happen, most of you were still personally drawn into the experience."

"I was also searching for your buttons with the hope that you would begin to feel what it might be like to be discriminated against for no other reason except being placed in a category based on some outward characteristic. That's in part what a prejudice is—it's making judgments about an individual based on some preconceived knowledge you may have about a group, even if that knowledge is incomplete or wrong. And, by the way, I apologize if I forgot 'your group.' Perhaps I neglected to talk about gays or the elderly or overweight people. All of us belong to a variety of groups that can be stereotyped and discriminated against. And that statement I made about research and women in leadership? That was not accurate. You have to be careful about how messages are presented. Sometimes they may sound quite authoritative, yet may not be truthful."

"What I'd like to do now is give you some feedback on how I saw you dealing with me so that when you are in a similar situation you can better evaluate what it is you would like to do. Is that all right?"

Many students signaled that that would be useful information.

- Reflect on the earlier interaction between John Gray and the students. What kinds of reactions and responses did the students have to John Gray?

- What are some possible consequences when people respond in such situations with laughter or silence?

Critical Incident

John Gray Shares an Important Part of Himself

John Gray reflected upon the encounter in the auditorium and offered to give some feedback to the students.

"One thing I recall," Gray continued, "was hearing quite a lot of laughter in the group. I remember in one group asking a man why he was laughing. He replied that he was laughing to prevent himself from coming up on stage and carrying me out the door—and that I better hope he kept on laughing. But consider the consequences of laughter in such a situation. Think of a young child, perhaps a brother or sister or niece or nephew. And think of when someone might laugh when they hear an ethnic joke or when they are watching a show on television like the Archie Bunker *All in the Family* show. Is it possible that through the laughter we create stereotypes that may not have existed before? The child, seeing people laugh at ethnic jokes, may think, 'I like to see people laugh. Telling that joke makes people laugh.' Then he or she goes into the classroom and tells that ethnic joke and begins the whole process over again. So, it's important to think about the consequences of laughter and the role we play."

"So, what can people do in a situation like this?" one student asked.

"I think it's important that we take a stand, tell others that we do not appreciate or support the telling of ethnic jokes, so others hear an alternative voice," said Gray. "You may not be the most popular person at the moment, but I can guarantee you that someone in the group will appreciate your sensitivity and your efforts."

"Now, related to this, let's talk about silence. Many of you were silent this morning. You may not have agreed with everything I was saying, and some of you may have actually agreed with some things you heard, but very few of you made your feelings known. Oh, you may have nudged someone sitting next to you and said something like, 'he can't be real.' But let me remind you that I am real. There are people all around you, people who, while they may not be as vocal as I was, believe and act in such a manner in their neighborhoods and homes."

"But let's think about the consequences of silence. I think about Hitler. He got into power because people around him were silent and didn't challenge him. When you are silent, you are giving tacit approval of the messages you hear around you. So, my challenge to you is to break the silence. When you see an act that you know is wrong, or when you hear someone say something that you know is damaging, make yourself known. Even by simply standing up and stating something like, 'You know that state-ment you just made, I disagree with you and think it is wrong.' You will do wonders at drawing the attention away from the bigot and will make those around you know that there is at least an alternative point of view. Your simple comments can go quite far at making change."

It was becoming obvious that the students had spent quite a bit of time talking about these difficult topics throughout the day. Gray sensed that it was time to bring the day to a close. The students had had quite an experience. Little did they know that they were about to be challenged once again.

"I know it's been a long day for us all, and I believe we've learned quite a lot. And if you think about it, you did most of the teaching here today. I think I spent less than an hour with you this morning, yet you have been engaged in this topic for most of the day."

"There is another part of myself that I have a need to share with you," he went on. "Sit back for a moment and think about me now. What images come to your mind? What judgments do you make about me now?" He paused a minute or two.

"Let me share something else with you. For over 20 years I have been using my physical appearance to illustrate the myth of race and the impact of color. Perhaps by sharing a little bit about myself I can make people stop to think about the judgments they make about others, as well as about the myth of race and the impact of color. You see, under the definition of race in this country, I would like you to know that I am black, or African American, my parents are black, both sets of my grandparents were black, I am married to a woman who is black, and I have five children of various shades."

There was silence and disbelief around the room. Students and teachers were look-ing back and forth at one another and at Gray, who still, by anyone's determination, looked as European American as could be. Then he showed some slides on the screen. One was of his family, showing the range of colors that were represented. Then there was one of his parents—obviously black, but light-skinned, with Gray, appearing white, among them.

"For many of you, your heads will be spinning right now. But I want you to know that what you see may not always be what you get. I am for real, and my experiences are real. Many of you may be confused because none of the visual cues about my ethnic identity are evident. Your judgments are now in question. I ask you to question all the judgments that people are so quick to make. And perhaps in your classes tomor-row you can further discuss issues related to color, race, and racism. I'd be interested in knowing what you do as a school and as individuals around these issues as the year progresses."

And with that, John Gray left the school.

- What do you think John Gray means when he asks the students to reflect upon the "myth of race and the impact of color"?

- How does skin color influence people's judgments or attributions?

- Can you recall a time when you or someone you know made a judgment that was premature and the reality turned out to be different from what was expected? What were the consequences of the quick judgment?

- What suggestions might you offer to others that will help them to avoid the temp-tation to make quick judgments or attributions?

Summary

Prejudice and racism have both been rampant in many forms throughout American society. In this chapter, we provided an overview of issues related to prejudice and racism, beginning with a historical perspective and then tracing some of the major developments in efforts designed to address its occurrence in society. We then explored the concept of prejudice, prejudice formation, and prejudice reduction, emphasizing that various actions taken by teachers, schools, and communities can go a long way toward reducing, and in some instances preventing, its occurrence.

Chapter Review

Go to the Online Learning Center at www.mhhe.com/cushner9e to review important content from the chapter, practice with key terms, take a chapter quiz, and access active workbook activities.

Key Terms

empathy 190	hypodescent 176	prejudice 177
genotype 176	phenotype 176	white privilege 182

What Does It Feel Like to Be Excluded?

Purpose: To develop empathy by imagining what it might be like to be excluded or discriminated against, and to propose possible responses.

Instructions: Developing an understanding of the experience of others in a pluralistic society is critical if teachers and students are to develop a fuller knowledge of culture and its various forms. One way to develop such a skill is to listen to the voices of individuals who have felt excluded from the mainstream for one reason or another—perhaps due to overt racism; subtle, institutional racism; general ignorance; subtle pressure; or genuine dislike. Read the following quotes and try to identify one or two feelings associated with them. Then, consider what you as a teacher might say and do in response (adapted from an exercise developed by Beth Swadener).

Low-income mother: "My son understands that we have no money the last week of each month, and yet he was pressured by his teacher to have a new workbook by the next class. When we could not afford it that week, he was made to sit out of class. The teacher said, "Everyone else remembered to get their book, why not you?"

As the mother, I feel _____

_____

_____.

As a teacher, I might _____

_____

_____.

Jewish parent: "Last year our daughter asked me, 'Could we have a Christmas tree and just not use it?'"

As the parent, I feel _____

_____

_____.

As a teacher, I might _____

_____

_____.

Chinese parent: "My daughter asked me, 'Can I have blonde hair? It's better to be blonde.'"

As the parent, I feel _____

_____

_____.

As a teacher, I might _____

_____

_____.

Native American parent: "The schools continue to miseducate my son. The images he has of native people are limited, and there is virtually no relevant Native American history taught in his school."

As the parent, I feel _____

_____

_____.

As a teacher, I might _____

_____

_____.

Islamic parent: "My child's school has many Christian-based activities and has never even recognized that some of the students are not Christian."

As the parent, I feel _____

_____

_____.

As a teacher, I might _____

_____

_____.

Single parent: "I feel that all my son's behavior at school is blamed on the fact that I'm a single parent, and that many judgments about our family are made based on no other evidence than our 'single parent family' status."

As the parent, I feel _____

_____

_____.

As a teacher, I might _____

_____

_____.

Vietnamese parent: (translated from Vietnamese) "My children speak and read better English than I do. It is so hard when lots of letters and information come home from school in English. I also feel that my children are losing respect for their parents and the elders in this country."

As the parent, I feel _____

_____

_____.

As a teacher, I might _____

_____

_____.

Extend this activity by collecting some of your own quotes from statements by children, parents, and other community members that represent diverse groups and who have felt excluded. Record three of your own examples.

Classroom Activities

1. Review sample elementary textbooks from various content areas (social studies, science, etc.) and across grade levels. In what topic areas would you find it easiest to integrate concepts related to race, ethnicity, and prejudice? How might you do this in a 3rd-grade classroom? A 6th-grade classroom? A high school science class?

2. It is very common in elementary schools to reserve part of each day or week to current events. Review a week's worth of newspapers from your local area. Identify two to three news events or other items from the newspaper that would lend themselves to discussion of race and prejudice for children in grade 3 or 4, or grade 10 or 11. How might you integrate this into your classroom?

3. Recall the surprising finding that greater diversity in a school does not necessarily on its own lead to an increase in cross-racial friendships. What are some suggestions that you might offer a local high school that would increase the likelihood that more meaningful cross-racial relationships might develop among students?

4. It is important to help young people understand the power and pervasiveness of stereotypes, both of those they hold of others as well as how others may stereotype them. Propose a lesson you might develop for high school students that helps them explore how the stereotypes they hold may influence their actions in a negative way. How can you help them understand the stereotypes those outside of their own country may hold of them, and to explore their validity?

Reflective Questions

1. What are some ways in which Jane and the other teachers could continue to educate themselves about new methods related to prejudice reduction while simultaneously keeping up with student needs and school requirements, especially when time is such a problem?

2. Not every teacher and administrator in the school appreciates the direction Jane and some others are taking toward antiracist education. How might Jane continue to broaden her students' perspectives in the face of criticism from her colleagues?

3. What experiences have you had in educational institutions that were effective at developing positive intergroup relations? What aspects of the contact hypothesis were evident?

4. If a close friend or family member were to make a prejudiced comment or tell an ethnic joke, would you protest? Why or why not? What about if it was a stranger who said the same thing? What if it was about a group of which you were a member?

References

Allport, G. (1954). *The nature of prejudice*. Reading, MA: Addison-Wesley.

Allport, G. (1979). *The nature of prejudice* (25th anniv. ed.). Reading, MA: Addison-Wesley.

Amir, Y. (1969). Contact hypothesis in ethnic relations. *Psychological Bulletin, 71*(5), 319–343.

Anti-Defamation League (2013). Accessed July 5, 2013 at: http://www.adl.org/assets/pdf/education-outreach/How-Do-Children-Learn-Prejudice.pdf

Augoustinos, M., & Rosewarne, D. L. (2001). Stereotype knowledge and prejudice in children. *British Journal of Developmental Psychology, 19*, 143–156.

Bennett, M. J. (1993). Towards ethnorelativism: A developmental model of intercultural sensitivity. In M. Paige (Ed.), *Cross-cultural orientation* (pp. 27–69). Lanham, MD: University Press of America.

Bicklin, D., & Bailey, L. (1981). *Rudely stamp'd: Imaginal disability and prejudice*. Washington, DC: University Press of America.

Bigler, R. (1999). The use of multicultural curricula and materials to counter racism in children. *Journal of Social Issues, 55*(4), 687–704.

Bishop, R., & Berryman, M. (2006). *Culture speaks: Cultural relationships and classroom learning*. Wellington, New Zealand: Huia Publishers.

Blau, J., Lamb, U., Stearns, E., & Pellerin, C. (2001). Cosmopolitan environments and adolescents' gains in social studies. *Sociology of Education, 74*, 121–138.

Boyd-MacMillan, E. M. (2016). Increasing cognitive complexity and collaboration across communities: Being muslim being scottish. *Journal of Strategic Security* 9, no. 4 (2016): 79–110.DOI: http://dx.doi.org/10.5038/1944-0472.9.4.1563

Brindley, R., & Laframboise, K. L. (2002, May). The need to do more: Promoting multiple perspectives in pre-service teacher education through children's literature. *Teaching and Teacher Education, 18*(4), 405–420.

Brislin, R. (1993). *Understanding culture's influence on behavior*. Fort Worth, TX: Harcourt Brace Jovanovich.

Bronson, P., & Merryman, A. (2009). *Nurture shock: New thinking about children*. New York: Hachette Book Group.

Brown, T. N., Tanner-Smith, E., Lesane-Brown, C. L., & Ezell, M. E. (2007). Child, parent, situational correlates of family ethnic/race socialization. *Journal of Marriage and Family*, 69(1), 14–25.

Byrnes, D. A. (1988). Children and prejudice. *Social Education, 52*(4), 267–271.

Carim, N., & Soudien, C. (1999). Critical anti-racism in South Africa. In S. May (Ed.), *Critical multiculturalism: Rethinking multicultural and antiracist education* (pp. 153–171). London: Routledge Falmer.

Clark, K., & Clark, M. (1947). Racial identification and preference in Negro children. In T. M. Newcomb & E. L. Hartley (Eds.), *Readings in social psychology*. New York: Holt, Rinehart & Winston.

Cooper, R., & Slavin, R. E. (2004). Cooperative learning: An instructional strategy to improve intergroup relations. In W. G. Stephan & W. P. Vogt (Eds.), *Education programs for improving intergroup relations: Theory, research, and practice* (pp. 55–70). New York: Teachers College Press.

Cortes, C. (2000). *The children are watching: How the media teach about diversity*. New York: Teachers College Press.

Derman-Sparks, L., & Olsen Edwards, J. (2010). *Anti-Bias education for young children and ourselves*. Washington, DC: National Association for the Education of Young Children.

Garcia, J., Powell, R., & Sanchez, T. (1990, April). Multicultural textbooks: How to use them more effectively in the classroom. Paper presented at the annual meeting of the American Educational Research Association, Boston. (ERIC Document Reproduction Service No. ED320262)

Gardiner, G. S. (1972). Complexity training and prejudice reduction. *Journal of Applied Social Psychology*, 2(4), 326–342.

Gay, G. (2000). *Culturally responsive teaching: Theory, research, and practice*. New York: Teachers College Press.

Hemson, C. (2006) *Teacher education and the challenge of diversity in South Africa*. Cape Town, South Africa: Human Sciences Research Council.

Hofheimer-Bettman, E., & Friedman, L. J. (2004). The Anti-Defamation League's A World of Difference Institute. In W. G. Stephan & W. P. Vogt (Eds.), *Education programs for improving intergroup relations: Theory, research, and practice* (pp. 75–94). New York: Teachers College Press.

Katz, D. (1960). The functional approach to the study of attitudes. *Public Opinion Quarterly, 24*, 164–204.

Katz, P. A. (1983). Developmental foundations of gender and racial attitudes. In R. H. Leahy (Ed.), *The child's construction of social inequality* (pp. 41–78). New York: Academic Press.

Kottack, C. P., & Kozaitis, K. A. (1999). *On being different: Diversity and multiculturalism in the North American mainstream*. Boston: McGraw-Hill.

Ladson-Billings, G. (1995). But that's just good teaching! The case for culturally relevant pedagogy. *Theory into Practice, 34*(3), 159–165.

Lipman, M. (1980). *Philosophy in the classroom*. Philadelphia: Temple University Press.

McIntosh, P. (1992, January–February). White privilege: Unpacking the invisible knapsack. *Creation Spirituality*, 33–35, 53.

Moody, J. (2001). Race, school integration, and friendship segregation in America. *American Journal of Sociology, 107*(3), 679–716.

National Association for the Education of Young Children. (1989). *Anti-bias curriculum: Tools for empowering young children*. Washington, DC: Author.

Pettigrew, T. F. (1981). The mental health impact. In B. P. Bowser & R. G. Hunt (Eds.), *Impacts of racism on white Americans* (pp. 97–118). Beverly Hills, CA: Sage.

Phillips, K. W. (2014). How Diversity Works. *Scientific American, 311*(4), 42–7, October 1, 2014. Retrieved from https://www.scientificamerican.com/article/how-diversity-makes-us-smarter/

Reid, T. R. (2005). Spanish at school translates to suspension. *Washington Post*, December 9, 2005. Retrieved from http://www.washingtonpost.com/wp-dyn/content/article/2005/12/08/AR2005120802122.html

Shaver, J. P., & Curtis, C. K. (1981). *Handicapism and equal opportunity: Teaching about the disabled in social studies.* Reston, VA: Council for Exceptional Children.

Sherif, M. (1958). Superordinate goals in the reduction of intergroup tension. *American Journal of Sociology, 63*(4), 349–356.

Shirts, R. G. (1977). *BAFA BAFA: A cross-cultural simulation.* Del Mar, CA: SIMILE II.

Sleeter, C. (1994, Spring). White racism. *Multicultural Education, 1*(4), 5–8, 39.

Southern Poverty Law Center (2017). Accessed March 9, 2017 at: https://www.splcenter.org/hate-map

Stephan, W. G. (1999). *Reducing prejudice and stereotyping in schools.* New York: Teachers College Press.

Stephan, W. G., & Vogt, W. P. (2004). *Education programs for improving intergroup relations: Theory, research, and practice.* New York: Teachers College Press.

Streufert, S., & Swezey, R. W. (1986). *Complexity, managers, and organizations.* New York: Academic Press.

Tang, C. (2007). *Diversity in education assignment.* Unpublished manuscript, School of Education, University of Cape Town.

Tollefson, T., Barr, D. J., & Strom, M. S. (2004). Facing history and ourselves. In W. G. Stephan & W. P. Vogt (Eds.), *Education programs for improving intergroup relations: Theory, research, and practice* (pp. 95–110). New York: Teachers College Press.

Vally, S., & Dalamba, Y. (1999). Racism, 'Racial integration' and desegregation in South African public secondary schools. *A report on a study by the South African Human Rights Commission.* Unpublished Report.

Yetman, N. (1991). *Majority and minority: The dynamics of race and ethnicity in American life* (5th ed.). Boston: Allyn & Bacon.

Zentella, A. C. (1997). The hispanophobia of the official English movement in the U.S. *International Journal of the Sociology of Language, 127*, 71–86.

Chapter

7

The Classroom as a Global Community

Nationality and Region

Focus Questions

1. What is globalization, and what does it mean to be a globally connected society?

2. What does it mean to be a globally competent individual? How does this develop in people, and how can teachers facilitate this development?

3. How have recent conflicts and the interdependence of nations altered what we do in schools?

4. What are some powerful concepts that underlie a global perspective? What are some practical strategies that can be used to prepare students to better understand and interact with others around the world so they might prevent or solve problems that are global in nature?

" The love of one's country is a splendid thing. But why should love stop at the border? "

PABLO CASALS, *Spanish Cellist, Wrote music for UN Anthem for world peace, 1963 Presidential Medal of Freedom; 1876-1973*

" People of different religions and cultures live side by side in almost every part of the world, and most of us have overlapping identities which unite us with very different groups. We can love what we are, without hating what—and who—we are not. We can thrive in our own tradition, even as we learn from others, and come to respect their teachings. "

KOFI ANNAN, *Former Secretary-General of the United Nations*

Case Study

A Global Classroom

It was 8 o'clock on a Tuesday morning in early February when Nate Kozlowski rushed into the front office with good news. Yesterday, Samir's uncle had returned from India with the package his class had been anxiously awaiting—a collection of artifacts to complement the story writing project they had initiated with a small school in southern India. Now he would be able to share its contents with the class and make this project even more meaningful and real. Nate was eager to tell his principal, Mrs. Lewis, because she had seemed so certain that this project would fail and that the children would be let down. Well, it hadn't, and Nate was delighted.

Nate's first year as a teacher had started with many challenges in the world-at-large that, in many ways, found their way into the classroom. In the year before he began teaching in his current position, the conflict in Syria had supposedly come to an end; the debate surrounding immigration had escalated in his own community as the refugee crisis continued to accelerate in Europe; questions about Russian involvement in the outcome of the 2016 presidential election continued to emerge; the Black Lives Matter movement and questions about police-community relations were frequent in the news; and the nationwide increase in Islamophobic and anti-Semitic attacks had occurred; while many people in this Michigan community still had not found good-paying jobs even eight years after the Great Recession; a range of new health scares and possible pandemics emerged across the globe; and the environment seemed to be wreaking havoc all around the world with warmer winters, oppressive heat waves, violent storms, and an increasing frequency of forest fires.

Nate felt a need to try and help his students see how many of these critical issues affecting others around the world also impacted them, and to consider how these issues would continue to do so in the future. He wanted to connect his students in firsthand ways with others in the world but was unsure at first how to do this in the most effective way. Nate knew he had to attempt something; that it was time to alter the course of events at least in his own classroom. He had taken some workshops in multicultural education, global education, and cooperative learning over the past few summers and was eager to try some of the strategies he had heard about. He was also beginning to integrate various parts of his curriculum, and saw many opportunities to link language arts, social studies, science, and the arts. He was even willing to try to integrate other areas of the curriculum while exploring how he might add a global perspective to the classroom.

Several of his students were first-generation American families whose parents had immigrated to the United States in recent years. Many of them, as well as many of the long-term residents, had lost their jobs in the manufacturing sector as a result of increasing globalization. Tensions rose at times between various groups in the community over the loss of jobs and recent immigration. Nate thought that working to develop an international perspective might provide his students with concepts and activities that would cut across the various ethnicities, nationalities, and experiences found in his class. An international approach could also help his students better understand the circumstances faced by many people in different parts of the world, how their own family's past experiences might be similar, and how their own local community was interconnected with others.

Nate began with a unit on immigration that he hoped would develop empathy in his students for newcomers to this country. He also hoped this sense of empathy would be applied to the relatives and ancestors of students with deep roots in the United States. An activity on immigration might also serve to bring the group together as they explored both the similarities and differences in their backgrounds. He asked his students to go home and interview family members about their own or their ancestors' experiences coming to this country, asking them to inquire specifically about the following topics:

1. From what country did your ancestors come?

2. When did they leave their country of birth?

3. Why did they leave that place?

4. What was their experience when they first came to this country? Do people remember experiencing any hardships? Were any stereotypes and prejudice directed at them?

5. Where did they first arrive in this country?

6. How did they come to live in Michigan? When did they come here, and why?

7. Are there any traditions from the home country that are still practiced?

8. What makes our people unique in this country today?

A week later, Nate had students come to the front of the room, share their stories, and locate their family's place of origin on the world map. He gave them each a piece of yarn, and as they located their country of origin, he asked them to attach it to the map at that country and extend the yarn to Grand Rapids. He was surprised by the results of this exercise. The discussion that followed the presentations was enlightening for both Nate and his students. He was not surprised to see many of the students stand up and talk about their family history with a sense of pride. For many of them, this was the first time anyone had asked them about their ancestry. It seemed to Nate that this was also the first time that the students had listened intently to one another's stories. There seemed to be a real sense of contribution for most of the students. They were especially interested in Guy's and Hannah's stories. Some of Guy's ancestors had arrived in the country in the 1600s. He shared stories of people jumping ship off the New England coast and ending up in Vermont. Hannah shared stories of her grandparents' escape from Hitler's armies and how lucky most of her family had been to get out of Germany alive before the Holocaust had really taken hold. She did know, however, that two of her relatives had perished in the Holocaust.

What surprised Nate, however, was the difficulty that some students had with the exercise. For instance, at first, Steve avoided participating in the exercise by offering the excuse that he had left his notes at home. The next day, when urged again to participate, Steve stood in front of the class and mumbled something like, "I'm adopted and I don't know anything about my parents." There was complete silence. An awkward moment or two followed, until Nate quietly said, "My father was adopted too, and he didn't know much about his background either. His adopted family helped him learn about their Polish background, and he grew up in that tradition. Perhaps there are some traditions that your adopted family follow that you can take for your own. What background is your adopted family?"

Steve began to relax when he replied, "Well, I guess they're all German. I mean, my grandparents speak a little German when they visit, and my parents make it a point to go to the Oktoberfest every year. My father really likes it when he has his German beer. They're even talking about visiting Germany in the next couple of years and plan on taking me and my sister. I guess I'm really German, but I'm not sure what it means to be German. I feel very much American, if you know what I mean."

Nate asked how many others felt more "American" than affiliated with their ethnic ancestry. Almost all the students raised their hands. "Well," said Nate, "it is good that we all feel American, because we are, but I want you to think about what being American means."

Nate led a discussion with the class as they all reflected on the experiences they and their families had encountered in recent years. When all the presentations were finished, students were asked to identify generalizations in people's experiences and to pose hypotheses to explain what they observed. Peter noticed that most people seemed to come to the United States for better job opportunities, or for more money, as he put it, both in the past and today. A few people came for religious freedoms. Jeremy used this point as an opportunity to discuss religious freedom today, and especially what it might mean for many of the Muslims who had immigrated to Michigan over the years, and now comprised the largest Arab community in the United States. Kathy noticed that everyone, except for one of David's relatives, came from somewhere else. When encouraged, she went on to suggest that almost everyone was an immigrant at least once in his or her past. Mark, an African American child in the class, reminded everyone that his ancestors didn't come here by choice and perhaps that explained

(continued)

many of the differences that exist between African Americans and many other groups. Nate took this opportunity to discuss with the class the differences between voluntary and involuntary, or forced, immigration.

Nate then began to probe into students' feelings about the immigrants they read about in current events. Most were familiar with stories of Haitian refugees, the situation in Cuba, and the constant debate about Mexicans crossing the border into the United States. A few were aware of immigrant and refugee groups from Southeast Asia, the fact that many refugees had left Iraq, Syria, and other nations in the Middle East in recent years in response to the conflict. Nate was hoping that a discussion about the plight of today's refugees and immigrant groups would enable students to identify with their situation and to compare it to that of their own ancestors. A few were able to make this leap, but most only nodded in half-hearted agreement. Nate was content that perhaps he planted a few seeds for future discussion and activity, which he promised himself he would develop. Anyway, tomorrow he would follow up with an internationally cooperative writing assignment with a classroom in India that he was sure would address some of the issues that had been raised in their discussion while at the same time building bridges with others living in other parts of the world.

Nate had read about a particular project, a partnership story project that was designed to integrate language arts, social studies, and cooperative learning (Cushner, 1992). Through *small group activity*, students in one country decide on a topic or problem, develop the main characters as well as a setting, and write the first half of the story. This first half is then sent to children in another country who are asked to complete the story and translate it into their own language. When completed, the classrooms have an internationally developed story translated in two languages that can also be co-illustrated by the children. In addition to collaborating on the story, classrooms can exchange a variety of artifacts, photos, letters, and so forth. It was the package of artifacts that Samir's uncle had brought from the school that had excited Nate and the children so much.

The project began when Nate had asked Samir's uncle, someone who had recently immigrated to the United States from Madurai, India, if he would be willing to connect his class with another in India for a collaborative writing project. Nate's class would break up into three groups, each writing the beginning of a story. Because they had been studying the environmental crisis in social studies, Nate asked them to build their story line around this topic. Each group started a story. One was an adventure story involving a school of fish in a polluted lake. Another was a mystery involving a missing mineral. The third focused on abuses of the world's wildlife. When they were finished with the first half, they sent all three unfinished stories to the class in India when Samir's uncle had returned to visit family.

Although it was six weeks later, Nate's students were nevertheless very excited the morning he told them that the completed stories had been returned. Rather than just share the endings that had come back, Nate decided to turn the activity into a real culture-learning experience by rereading his own students' unfinished stories and then asking them to imagine how they thought the Indian students would complete each story. After Nate finished reading the first half of each story to his class, he showed them the beautifully written Tamil script and the pictures that the Indian students had created to complete the stories. An example of one of the stories follows:

Part One (The United States)

Once in a circus there was a tiger who would not perform because he was lonely. The circus owner sent his daughter, Maryetta, to the jungle to find a friend to perform with the lonely tiger. Maryetta's father gave her $1,000 to purchase a tiger. Her father told her to spend the money wisely.

The next day on a boat trip to the jungle, Maryetta met a trapper named Toby. Toby asked Maryetta why she was going to the jungle. Maryetta told him that she needed to purchase a tiger for her father's circus. "What a coincidence," Toby remarked, all the while trying to figure out a way he might obtain Maryetta's money before the real trapper could reach her. "I am meeting a girl from a circus tomorrow."

"You are?" Maryetta asked, looking puzzled. "Do you know what circus she is from?"

(continued)

"No," replied Toby, "but it must be yours. How many girls could there be going to the jungle tomorrow to buy a tiger?"

"I guess you're right. I'll meet you by the river at 10:00 tomorrow morning."

Toby wanted to get there before the real trapper did, so he said, "Why don't we meet at 9:00 and get an early start?" They agreed to this and then went their own ways. The next day was a beautiful summer day, perfect for trapping tigers. Toby rented a boat and met Maryetta precisely at 9:00.

"I'll need to collect my fee of one hundred dollars each morning before we begin," Toby told Maryetta.

"I thought you told my father your fee was one hundred and fifty dollars per day," Maryetta said, wondering why he had lowered his fee.

"Oh, well, I guess I forgot what I said before. One hundred and fifty dollars it is then," said Toby.

"Alright, but I don't have a lot of money. Do you think we'll be trapping for a long time?"

"Probably only two or three days," Toby reassured.

"Well, then, let's get going!" exclaimed Maryetta.

At first, the boat trip down the river was pleasant. About noon, however, the boat struck a huge rock which punctured its side. Maryetta and Toby spent the rest of the day repairing the boat. As a result, they had to spend the night on the river bank. During the night, Maryetta thought she heard voices. When she peeked out of her tent she saw Toby talking to a wolf. She couldn't believe her eyes or ears!

Although she had been raised around the circus and always knew that animals were special, she had never talked to one! She listened intently.

"Go make friends with the tiger and bring him back here," Toby told the wolf.

"When do you want me to bring back that stupid tiger?" asked the wolf.

"Five days from now will be good. Then I will have enough money to buy the secrets I want from the old wizard."

"Okay, I'll see you then," said the wolf, and he crept away.

Maryetta silently closed the flap of her tent and slumped to the ground. Something was very, very wrong. How was she going to get back to the circus safely with the tiger and not let Toby know that she knew he was a fake?

The next morning Toby told Maryetta the boat was fixed. Toby then said, "I don't want to be rude, but where is my money?"

Maryetta answered, "I'll pay you later." She thought to herself, I have no intention of paying Toby. Toby said, "I want my money now!"

Maryetta said that because the boat accident was not her fault she should not have to pay for the first day. Toby replied, "Well, it's not my fault either, and besides, we had an agreement."

They argued for a while, and Toby finally agreed that Maryetta could pay him later. He told her he would begin to look for the tiger today.

They boarded the boat together to begin the search for the tiger. Along the way they spotted a beautiful tiger being chased by a wolf.

Maryetta said, "Toby, I know you sent the wolf after the tiger and you better make sure the wolf doesn't harm him or you won't be paid!" They anchored the boat and went ashore. Toby and Maryetta began to chase after the tiger and the wolf. Suddenly, Maryetta tripped over a vine and broke her leg. Toby came along, grabbed Maryetta's money, and ran off with it!

At this point Nate stopped reading. He asked how many students remembered this half of the story. All hands were raised. He then asked them to write down a few sentences about how they thought the story would end. How do *you* think the story will end?

Of the 26 students in Nate's class, 11 completed the story in a way that Maryetta's task is fulfilled. In these stories, Maryetta catches the tiger and takes it home, and it performs as desired in the circus. Three students resolved the story by creating a new character who saves Maryetta from her injury and from Toby. In 6 stories, the tiger frees Maryetta from her crisis, and in 3 of these stories, the tiger goes on to catch Toby. In 2 stories, Maryetta escapes, finds the wizard, and seeks revenge on Toby. In 1 case each, the wolf helps Maryetta first catch the tiger and then Toby; Toby steals the money from Maryetta and does not catch the tiger; Maryetta is cured in a hospital and becomes friends with Toby; and Toby spontaneously recognizes and reconciles his evil ways.

Nate could sense the excitement of the students as they waited to hear how their Indian colleagues had completed the story. He sat on the edge of his desk and continued with the second half.

(continued)

Part Two (India)

The wolf who was chasing the tiger stopped after hearing Maryetta's cries and ran toward her. He finally reached her. He felt sad when he saw the flow of blood from her leg.

"Don't be afraid. I shall help you," said the wolf.

The wolf then ran into the forest and brought rare herbs and placed them on her leg. At once, Maryetta felt relief from the pain and felt pleasant again. Maryetta looked at the wolf with love and gratitude.

The wolf asked Maryetta, "How did you fall?"

She explained everything to him. The wolf felt bad when he heard of Toby's treacherous deeds. The wolf told Maryetta that he would get the money from Toby. Maryetta saw the birds, trees, and other creatures around her. Suddenly she didn't feel lonely any more. She felt happy that she was a part of an endless creation of nature. She felt the encouragement and nourishment given by the surrounding birds and trees.

Toby went straight to the old wizard with the money he robbed from Maryetta. After getting the money from Toby, the wizard taught him the mantras (magic phrases) that he could use to conquer the animals and humans. Toby then quickly left, greedy to make more money.

Then Toby saw a tiger running towards him in a frenzy. He tried to conquer the tiger with the mantras he had learned from the wizard. But the tiger pushed him down and tried to attack him. At that time, the tiger heard the voice of a wolf and he ran away.

The wolf and Maryetta saw Toby struggling for his life. The wolf did not like to help the treacherous Toby. He thought that this was the right punishment for his terrible deeds. But Maryetta was deeply moved by Toby's suffering. She felt sad that she did not have the money to admit him to a hospital.

Maryetta pleaded with the wolf to help Toby. The wolf halfheartedly ran and brought rare herbs. Maryetta made a bandage with the herbs for Toby's wounds. She also gave him some juice from the herbs. He then recovered and could breathe easy again.

Toby slowly came to consciousness and appreciated the gentle qualities of Maryetta and apologized to her. He revealed that he had given the money to the old wizard. He felt sorry that he was spoiled by his own greed.

In the meantime, the wolf went to the tiger. He asked the tiger, "Why did you try to kill Toby?"

The tiger angrily replied, "It is but natural that we are angry towards men who prevent us from living independently in the forest and who try to hunt us. Toby is trying to destroy us totally by violence, tricks, and mantras. For him, money is bad."

The wolf said, "Toby not only cheats the animals, but also the humans. For this greedy fellow, money is everything."

Toby was truly sad. He felt ashamed of himself and asked to be pardoned.

Then the wolf, the tiger, Toby, and Maryetta danced together in joy in a circle. Then Maryetta told the tiger, "In my father's circus there is a male tiger suffering without a companion. If you can come with me, he would be very happy."

Maryetta looked at the female tiger with love and affection. The female was moved to tears. She began to wonder if that male tiger was the one that had been taken away from her long ago. She agreed to go with Maryetta.

All four returned to the circus. The male tiger was happy to see the female tiger that he had been separated from so very long ago. Soon they were able to identify one another. What a pleasure it is when separated ones come together again!

Maryetta was very happy. She had learned to talk with the animals. Her love toward them grew many times over. She looked after the tigers with special care.

One day, Maryetta fell asleep while playing with the tigers. She listened to the conversations of the tigers as she woke up. She pretended as if she was sleeping and continued to listen to them.

The female tiger said, "Maryetta is a wonderful girl. But she does not realize the fact that the forest is our heaven. Even this golden cage is still a cage."

Maryetta was deeply moved. The next day Maryetta's father called her and said, "Maryetta, I have grown old. I am retiring from the circus as of today. Hereafter, you should run the circus."

Maryetta said, "I shall free those wonderful animals from this sorrowful, tortuous caged life, and I will go and live in the forest." And that she did.

Nate followed this reading with a discussion. To begin the discussion he asked each student to respond, in writing, to the following questions.

(continued)

- In what ways is the ending different from what you expected?
- What surprised you as you heard the end of the story?
- What do you think you learned about Indian culture?
- What might reading this story tell you about American culture?

The discussion that followed was lively. Most of the children thought that good would prevail over evil. What seemed to surprise them, however, was that the bad characters also changed for the good. On further probing, some of the children questioned whether human nature could be modified so quickly, as if through sudden insight or experience, and wondered if it might be possible with terrorists. Many students were also struck by the use of herbs and mantras in the story as well as the apparent reverence for nature and living things.

While the children were discussing what they thought they had learned about Indian culture, Karl suggested that Indians seem to care about nature in general and animals in particular. He also asked about the possibility of humans really talking to animals. He remembered watching a television show about how researchers were trying to communicate with dolphins, whales, and gorillas. Kathy seemed particularly moved by Maryetta's change of heart toward Toby and thought that Indians might care that other people are safe and peaceful. Kamal said he was learning about some of the ways African healers treated their patients and the fact that the Indians used herbs and mantras reminded him of this.

It was a bit more difficult, however, for the group to discuss what they might have learned about their own culture. With probing, Nate was able to get something of a discussion going. Some students thought that both countries were alike in many ways. Others were surprised that, while most of the American students would let the characters in the story die, the Indian children seemed to have compassion for them.

The discussion of violence in the world in general as well as in American society, toward both people and animals, was the most lively. Finally, Maria pointed out that the way the story was completed showed that the Indian students believed that people's labels can change, whereas in the United States, she thought, a label might remain with a person for quite a long time. She was even bold enough to ask how many in the class still felt uncomfortable with Arabs and Muslims in the community. Nate thought that Maria raised a good question, and he allowed it to develop into a whole-class discussion about prejudice and racism in their classroom and in the community. At the end of the discussion, the children explored the box of artifacts sent by the school that included personalized letters from each student, colorful decorations and artwork that could be hung around the classroom, and a collection of recipes of local favorite foods. All of Nate's students agreed with the Indian class that the two classrooms should continue a long-term friendship and an exchange of ideas, resources, and letters.

Education in a Global Society

It is the purpose of schools to prepare students for life in the larger societies in which they live. In a democratic society this responsibility means preparing students not only to know about democracy in a civil society, but also to be able to put it into practice. In a globally interdependent world, this responsibility means preparing students for a future in which they will come into increasing contact with people different from themselves. It means a reality in which an increasing number of American firms have offices in overseas locations, an increasing number of international firms have offices within the United States, or people in many parts of the world are connected electronically while working for the same organization or on the same project. It means political boundaries that are constantly shifting and rapidly changing, thus creating opportunities and challenges not imagined in recent decades. Moreover, it is no longer necessary to leave one's own community to come into regular contact with people from other nations or to be significantly influenced by the actions of others from far away.

Compared to young people in other nations, American students typically spend less time studying global topics and score low in terms of knowledge of and interest in international affairs or geography (Lutkus, Weiss, Campbell, Mazzeo, & Lazer, 1999; Niemi & Junn, 1998; GSF, 2013; CFR, 2016). The Global Studies Foundation (2013) reports that the United States finished 11th out of 12 countries when comparing the international knowledge of students. They report that a significant number of 18-24 year olds cannot locate significant places on a world map, including the United States (11%), the Pacific Ocean (29%), China (37%), Russia (39%), India (56%), Japan (58%), UK (69%), and Saudi Arabia (76%), to say nothing of Iraq and Afghanistan (both 87%). Nor are they well versed in current events, with 43% unable to identify Mexico as the largest source of American immigrants today. Only 25% can identify India and China as countries with 1 billion people, while 30% estimate the U.S. population to be between 1-2 billion. Perhaps even more of a concern is that 17% do not know that the United States has nuclear weapons; roughly two of five Americans believe that world population growth does not affect them; that global climate change will be gradual so we can deal with it gradually; and that because the world is so big and complex the United States should solve problems like terrorism and the environment on its own. A similar study of geographic knowledge of U.S. students undertaken in 2014 showed that about three-quarters of eighth grade students scored below the proficient level, indicating partial or less than partial mastery in geography (GAO, 2015). This should not come as a surprise. Analysis of teacher survey data in the same assessment showed that 50% of eighth grade teachers reported spending only 3 to 5 hours per week of classroom instruction time on social studies—the vehicle through which geography is taught. Similarly, as of 2013, only 17 states required a geography course in middle school and 10 states required a geography course for students to graduate from high school (GAO, 2015).

In response to this, educators are beginning to seek out concepts, skills, and strategies that will help students understand what is happening in other parts of the world so they can function more effectively in a globally interdependent world. A central focus of this effort is to develop an understanding of globalization and to attain an education that is international and intercultural in scope.

What Is Globalization?

Globalization, referring to an increase in the scope and magnitude of human contact with its subsequent escalation of interaction and interdependence, seems to be the defining, and sometimes controversial, concept of the 21st century. Yet, globalization is not a new phenomenon. In his book, *The World Is Flat*, Thomas Friedman (2006) traced the start of this phenomenon back to the time when Columbus traversed the globe more than 500 years ago. As Friedman and others have pointed out, recent advances in communication and transportation technologies have resulted in a rapidly shrinking world, which has increased and sometimes forced contact among people from diverse cultures.

Some examples of globalization in economics include: multinational corporations that operate on a global scale, with satellite offices and branches in numerous locations; outsourcing that can add to the economic development of a struggling country, bringing much needed jobs, but at the same time resulting in a loss of jobs at home;

establishment of the World Trade Organization (WTO) which supervises world trade; the European Union as an economic and political union of 28 countries that are located primarily in Europe; and the North American Free Trade Agreement (NAFTA), a trade bloc in North America. Globalization in technology is evident in such ventures as: global news networks, like CNN or the BBC, which contribute to the spread of knowledge; military cooperation between countries, such as the Strategic Arms Reduction Treaty (START) or anti-terrorism agreements; and environmental cooperation designed to address problems that cross national boundaries. Globalization in the blending of cultures is evident in: Greek culture that spread across Africa, Europe, and Asia; the Silk Road that was a trade route between China and the Mediterranean Sea area, which allowed for the exchange of not only goods, but culture and knowledge; Christian missionaries from Europe, which allowed for the globalization of Christianity; colonization all over the world, which was a major cause of globalization; and food, where you can find people eating sushi in Peru or Indian food in Europe. Other examples of globalization include: the Olympics, which started in ancient Greece and continue today; the FIFA World Cup, which has more viewers than any other sporting event from around the world; the United Nations, which acts as an intergovernmental organization aiming to promote cooperation in many areas including human rights, peace, and economic development; and organizations such as the Red Cross, which respond quickly to disasters around the world.

Living in the "flat" world that Friedman depicted poses many challenges that transcend cultural, ethnic, and national boundaries. We increasingly find ourselves in a world characterized by an interconnectedness in our economic, environmental, political, and social systems that brings about increasingly complex intercultural interactions, conflicts, and change. The world comes closer together through global terrorism, diseases such as AIDS and worries about Zika or Ebola pandemics, struggles for peace, drug trafficking, the threat of environmental decay, and the interdependence of our economic systems. The distinctions between what is local and what is global have been blurred, and many people find it difficult to comprehend the new scenario in which they find themselves. Life in the 21st century requires that those who are striving to work together in various endeavors around the globe develop understanding of and sensitivity to the views of others as well as a sense of connectedness that taps into common values and goals. In today's world, global citizens must be able to communicate and collaborate with those whose attitudes, values, knowledge, and ways of doing things differ significantly from their own. Building bridges across cultural boundaries requires a high degree of flexibility, a tolerance for ambiguity, and an understanding of the role culture plays in shaping thinking and behavior. Because these traits are not necessarily innate and consequently need to be developed, education can and must play a key role in facilitating the bridge-building process. How can we begin to understand the phenomenon of globalization, and how does it affect teaching and learning? In an earlier book, Friedman (2000) provided one of the clearest descriptions of globalization and its impact on society, and we discuss this in the following section.

©Emily A. White RF

Characteristics of Globalization

Globalization replaced the Cold War in the late 1990s, and with it came many distinct changes in the way in which people around the world interact with one another and their immediate, as well as distant, environment. Friedman used the Lexus and the olive tree as symbols to differentiate the two extremes. He said,

> the Lexus and the olive tree were actually pretty good symbols of this post–Cold War era: half the world seemed to be emerging from the Cold War intent on building a better Lexus, dedicated to modernizing, streamlining, and privatizing their economics in order to thrive in the system of globalization. And half of the world—sometimes half the same country, sometimes half the same person—was still caught up in the fight over who owns which olive tree (p. 5).

Although the Lexus characterizes everything that is modern, fast-paced, and dynamic, the olive tree represents everything that keeps people rooted to a particular location, idea, or way of life, with many seeing the conflict as between fundamental religions and societies and the more progressive West (typically referring to the countries of Europe and European origin like the United States) as the epitome.

Globalization is characterized by integration; the world has become an increasingly interwoven place, and a person's opportunities are determined by the connections that person has with others. Another feature of globalization can be summarized in a single word—the Web. We have gone from a Cold War system built around division and walls with one of two superpowers in charge to a system built around integration and websites. During the Cold War we knew that at least two people or nations were in control of events. In the globalization system we reach for the Internet, which is a symbol that we are all increasingly connected and nobody is quite in charge—unlike the Cold War.

Globalization is a dynamic, ongoing process. It is the inexorable integration of markets, nation-states, and technologies to a degree never witnessed before, with a powerful backlash from those brutalized or left behind by the new system. Globalization has its own dominant culture that tends to create a homogenizing set of circumstances. In previous eras this sort of cultural homogenization happened on a regional scale—the Romanization of Western Europe or the Islamification of Central Asia, North Africa, and the Middle East by Arabs. Today, globalization has tended to involve the spread, for better or for worse, of Americanization and commercialization—from Big Macs to iMacs to Mickey Mouse. While the Cold War was a world of friends and enemies, the globalization world tends to turn all friends and enemies into competitors.

The Cold War system of power was built around nation-states. Today, the globalization system is built around three balances that overlap and affect one another:

(1) The traditional balance of power is now in the hands of one nation, the United States, which is the sole and dominant superpower and has tremendous influence over much of what happens in many nations around the world although China, Russia, and India are fast becoming increasingly important.

(2) There exists a balance between nation-states and global markets, made up of millions of investors around the world who Friedman referred to as the "electronic herd," able to, with the click of a mouse or sending a Tweet, influence financial markets around the world.

(3) There exists the sensitive balance between individuals and nation-states.

Because globalization has brought down many of the dividing walls and because it simultaneously wired the world into networks, the individual suddenly has more power to influence both markets and nation-states than at any time in world history—as was evident with the impact Russia had on the 2016 U. S. presidential election. As a result, in addition to superpowers and supermarkets, we now have super-empowered individuals, some of whom are quite angry and powerful. In more recent years, we have seen the actions of such people as Bradley Manning, accused of giving classified files to WikiLeaks; and Edward Snowden, who has admitted to releasing classified material about the government's collection of cell phone and Internet data, as further examples of super-empowered individuals challenging the superpowers.

Teaching With a Global Purpose

How can educators begin to respond to such changes in the social order, begin to understand the current state of affairs, and still empower their students with the knowledge and skills to be more effective with their international counterparts? The fact is that Americans (and others) are increasingly engaged with other people, thus demanding greater intercultural sensitivity, understanding, and a recognition of the shared values and challenges as well as differences among populations. We must begin asking ourselves questions such as these:

- When is the best time to begin addressing an international perspective?
- How do we learn about one another in ways that span boundaries and enlarge our understandings?
- How do we accomplish this learning in a way that respects the sacred while promoting the secular?
- How do we interact with others in a socially responsible way so as not to exploit but to grasp the essence of other peoples and their important contributions to a clearly global society?

The lack of barriers and walls that globalization brings presents its own set of new challenges. The concept of learning communities is discussed in other chapters, but those contexts are concerned mostly with integrating domestic diversity. This chapter discusses learning communities that are true global communities in which members are committed to thinking, growing, and inquiring with people who cross cultural as well as national boundaries. We are thus faced with new and significant challenges. For instance, how can we build the trust and intimacy that is essential to community with those who live in distant countries? Technology may be one tool that empowers us to reach further into the world, but we must be careful that we do not neglect the work that is needed to develop and maintain true interpersonal relationships and community. This issue is of grave concern because we may have a tendency to look to people in other countries as new customers or competitors and, thus, may interact with them at only a surface level. We may impose our own standards, for our own good, on other people and thereby neglect the impact our presence might have on them. We are then surprised when they resent our presence.

Education for a Global Perspective

A number of professional educational associations have addressed issues related to global and international education over the years. The National Council for the Social Studies (NCSS, 2016) defines a *global perspective* as the development of the knowledge, skills, and attitudes needed to live effectively in a world possessing limited natural resources and characterized by ethnic diversity, cultural pluralism, and increasing interdependence. Teaching toward a **global perspective** emphasizes the following ideas (NCSS, 2016):

1. The human experience is an increasingly global phenomenon in which people are constantly being influenced by transnational, cross-cultural, and multicultural and multiethnic interaction.

2. The goods we buy, the work we do, the cross-cultural links we have in our own communities and outside them, and increased worldwide communication capabilities all contribute to an imperative that responsible citizens understand global and international issues.

3. There is a wide variety of actors on the world stage, including states, multinational corporations, and numerous voluntary nongovernmental organizations, as well as individuals.

4. Humankind is highly interdependent with the state of the global environment.

5. Citizen participation is critical at both local and international levels.

Education for a global perspective helps individuals better comprehend their own condition in the community and world, and make more accurate and effective judgments about other people and about common issues. It emphasizes the study of nations, cultures, and civilizations, including our own pluralistic society, and focuses on understanding how these are interconnected, how they change, how one has influenced another, and what each individual's roles and responsibilities are in such a world. An education with a global perspective provides the individual with a realistic, balanced perspective on world issues and an awareness of how enlightened self-interest includes concerns about people elsewhere in the world. The catchphrase "Think Globally, Act Locally" has served the field of social studies education well. Making global concerns concrete, immediate, and meaningful to students is difficult yet critical.

How Do We Achieve the Cognitive Demands Required for a Global Mind-Set?

The process of international socialization lies at the intersection of cognitive, affective, and behavioral processes. It does not, however, come automatically with cognitive development or physical maturity. Rather, like many developmental processes, certain experiences at critical times seem essential to alter attitude and knowledge formation in this domain. Some characteristics of intellectual development, for instance, may prohibit an international perspective from emerging until an individual has reached a certain age or stage of development. Thus, critical periods may exist for the international socialization of young people, thus becoming bookmarks for educators (Cushner, 2008).

Educators make frequent reference to *Piaget's stage theory of development* to ground their understanding and explanation of developmental opportunities of young learners. Piaget proposed four stages of cognitive development: *the sensorimotor period,* from birth to 2 years of age; *the preoperational period,* from 2 to 7 years of age; *the concrete operational period,* from, age 8 to 12; and *the formal operational period*, beginning at around age 12. The preoperational and concrete operational periods are of most interest with regard to the international socialization of young people.

Characteristic of the preoperational period is that children begin to internalize mental representations of the world around them. Until this ability is perfected, children do not seem capable of taking the perspective of another and are said to be egocentric, with the world being viewed as if the child was the center of the reality. A child at this stage is generally incapable of cooperative play (Bybee & Sund, 1982), providing evidence of this egocentricity. Rather, two children tend to play independently, with little or no concern for the actions of others.

We've used the term ethnocentrism to refer to how people tend to view and/or explain the world from their own cultural perspective or point of view. There is a gradual shift away from cognitive egocentrism as children progress to concrete operations in the middle childhood years. Children at the age of 7 or 8 are able to correctly identify the right and left hand of a person standing opposite them. This partial relativism becomes a more true relativism around age 10 or 11, when children can correctly identify that an object in the middle can be both on the right and left of something. Flavell, Botkin, and Fry (1968) applied this in their work on perceptual role-taking ability by demonstrating that children in this age period have an increased ability to communicate with others by comprehending the perspective of the listener. They thus begin to understand that others may have a viewpoint that is different from their own.

Related to this is a process Piaget termed *perceptual* or *cognitive centration*, referring to the tendency children have of being so overwhelmed by one aspect of a visual experience that they are unable to attend to other aspects of a situation. This helps explain why young children often are unable to acknowledge conflicting or contradictory points of view on social issues, often seeing things as black or white, right or wrong. As children progress from the preoperational stage to concrete operations, they begin the process of decentering, especially if provided guidance and practice, and can accommodate shades of gray and alternative points of view. Selman and Schultz (1990) reported that between 9 and 15 years of age children acquire the skill of third-person perspective taking.

Children's thought processes, too, shift from being static to dynamic. That is, the preoperational child is generally unable to conceive of change upon an object—what is perceived is assumed to have always been, and unlikely to change. As the child progresses to the next stage, the world is seen as more dynamic and changeable. In addition, as children become older, they become increasingly capable of demonstrating concern for the needs of others in the community at large. This may help explain the shift from a present, concrete orientation to a more future, abstract, and general orientation noted by Adelson and O'Neill (1966) in their study of the growth of political ideas in early adolescents.

In support of using developmental theory to explain international socialization, studies indicate that political understanding and learning are initiated at a relatively early age as children begin to interact with authority roles, make decisions, and deal with interpersonal and intergroup cooperation and conflict. The types of experience encountered affect subsequent attitudes regarding national and international identity and perception. Remy, Nathan, Becker, and Torney (1975) concluded that children in the intermediate grades (grades 4 to 8) have a sense of their national identity and are beginning to develop attitudes, values, and beliefs of their own nation and others as international beings and actors, as well as gaining knowledge about such issues as war and peace.

The middle childhood years (ages 8 to 12) may represent the critical period in the development of an international or intercultural perspective in children, especially considering the existence of attitude flexibility that is later followed by attitude rigidity. This age period seems to be characterized by rapid cognitive development, especially related to the area of perspective and role-taking ability, low rejection of groups, high attitude flexibility, development of more differentiated intergroup perceptions, and is a time when one is beginning to be able to perceive another's point of view. For those of us concerned with the role of experience in the attainment of intercultural sensitivity, this represents an ideal time to begin traveling with young people and having them participate in significant intercultural experiences. Educational efforts to develop an international and intercultural perspective should, therefore, begin during these years.

Is Technology Facilitating a Global Mind-Set?

As we pointed out in Chapter 5 that, based on the results of numerous studies using the IDI, the majority of teachers fall on the ethnocentric side of the Intercultural Continuum. Two studies looking at the intercultural sensitivity of young people showed some surprisingly unexpected results. Pederson (1998) used a modified version of the IDI with 145 12-year-old seventh graders, and found 35% in high Minimization and 35% in Acceptance. Among 336 high school students in an international school in Southeast Asia, Straffon (2003) found 71% to be in Acceptance and 26% in Cognitive Adaptation, with only 3% on the ethnocentric side. Both of these studies showed that the greater the amount of exposure to difference (city versus suburban and rural schools in the Pedersen study and the amount of time in international schools in the Straffon study), the higher the level of intercultural sensitivity.

Herein lies the conundrum: the majority of teachers—those we make responsible for advancing the knowledge, skill, and attitude of young people—appear to be on the ethnocentric side of the continuum, while their students show evidence of being more sophisticated in terms of intercultural development. How might this be explained? It is possible that we do not have sufficient tools to assess intercultural sensitivity in young people. It is also conceivable that any intercultural sophistication people may acquire when they are young diminishes as they age and are socialized into adulthood. It's also possible that something else is going on—perhaps even a confluence of powerful and fundamental changes in both society in general as well as within the field of education more specifically, all with intercultural overtones, which are converging at this time that may accelerate the rate and frequency at which young people are exposed to new experience, new people, and new ideas. This is especially important when viewed in terms of the developmental readiness of acquiring an intercultural perspective.

The United States employed about 3.7 million teachers in 2016 (NCES, 2016), more than half of whom are above age 40. The experiences of children growing up, interacting, and learning about the world today, are significantly different from the experiences of most teachers. Although we have no data on the intercultural sensitivity of people in earlier generations, recall the conundrum: young people appear to be more culturally sensitive than those in older generations. A multitude of factors may be coming together suggesting that the seeds of change may be sown and that we may be on the verge of something we have not witnessed in the past. This confluence of factors includes:

- an increase in the number of children attending school worldwide;

- an increase in overall exposure of young people to cultural diversity through increased movement of people across national borders as tourists, immigrants, and refugees, and greater global media exposure;

- a slow but nonetheless concerted effort in some schools to provide more culturally relevant content, including increased attention to second language learning;

- greater understanding and attention to intercultural concepts as they relate to the instructional process itself; and

- a growing desire on the part of young people to travel and study outside their home countries.

Perhaps the shift in intercultural competence is beginning to take place as a result of the increased integration and ubiquitous nature of digital technologies in schools around the world. Millennials, the most technologically savvy generational group so far, are more proficient with technology than most of their teachers and parents. In 2012, 78% of teens had a cell phone, with almost half (47%) of them owning smartphones. That translates into 37% of all teens who have smartphones, up from just 23% in 2011. Also, 95% of teens use the Internet, 80% regularly use social networking sites, most commonly Facebook, with 16% using Twitter (Pew Research, 2013). Technology is also much more pervasive, and Internet penetration rates are increasing worldwide—especially in Africa where it has increased 3,606%; the Middle East where it has increased 2,639%; and in Latin America where it has increased 1,310% since 2000 (Miniwatts Marketing, 2013).

International linkages in education have existed at least since the 1920s when a number of global learning networks began in Europe and the United States. Such efforts made use of available technologies and modes of communication that enabled classrooms to exchange cultural artifacts such as letters, photos, and flowers from their local area with children in other parts of the world. Today's technology makes it increasingly easy to bring children into more frequent and regular interaction with one another—and oftentimes in very meaningful ways. A number of engaging Internet-based school linkage initiatives exist and they will be reviewed at the end of this chapter. Suffice it to say for now that there is a flurry of activity and a world of opportunity that is just beginning to unfold for children around the world that may explain the intercultural conundrum presented earlier.

Curriculum Transformation: The International Perspective

The foundation of a framework for integrating a global perspective across the curriculum was made practical by Robert Hanvey in his 1978 paper, "An Attainable Global Perspective." In this work, Hanvey identified five elements of a global perspective that can be transformed into teachable skills and perspectives that cut across academic disciplines and grade levels. Each of these elements is examined in the discussion that follows.

Perspective Consciousness

Perspective consciousness refers to a person's awareness that he or she has a view of the world that is not universally shared, that this view is shaped by unconscious as well as conscious influences, and that others may have profoundly different views. This dimension especially differentiates opinion from perspective. Opinion refers to the surface layer of a person's thoughts. It is the tip of the iceberg, so to speak, showing only a small portion of its totality. Underneath the surface lie the generally hidden, unexamined assumptions and judgments people make about life, about others, and about right and wrong (think back to the iceberg analogy of culture in Chapter 3). The assumption that human dominance over nature is both attainable and desirable is an example of a perspective that lies deep in many Western minds. It was not until this traditionally unexamined assumption surfaced that many philosophical choices that previously had escaped our attention were raised. As a result, debate involving our relationship with the environment ensued and stimulated considerable thought, activity, and discussion. Today, some still struggle to understand our role in both the cause and correction of global warming. Similarly, the feminist movement raised the consciousness of women and men regarding the role of women in society. In the process, deep layers of chauvinism inherent in much of our thinking about male and female roles were revealed. Likewise, concerned parents, addressing the unmet needs of their exceptional children, pointed out how the educational system (and society in general) discriminated against a large segment of society, and as a result, were the cause behind many of the current practices related to exceptionality (see Chapter 12).

Children can develop perspective consciousness in a number of ways. Ethnocentrism suggests that most individuals have a tendency to overemphasize their own culture's perspective, importance, and point of view. Children can be encouraged to question their own cultural perspectives and to consider how others might view them, and social studies curricula can help students examine their own culture's behavior from another point of view. When studying people in other parts of the world, for instance, students can be asked to explore why most people prefer to live in their native habitats despite what may appear to be rather difficult conditions. Why, children in your classrooms might ask, would anyone want to live in the Arctic, where people have to contend with extremes in temperature and have to hunt for their food? Or why would the Munduruku people of the Amazon River in South America want to live where the temperature is extremely hot year-round; where there are poisonous animals and annoying insects to contend with; and where the food staple, the poisonous manioc, has to be boiled and pounded over hot fires in the sweltering heat just to make it eatable? Likewise, children growing up in those regions of the world might ask the same of our young students: how can anyone live in an environment where the air is polluted, where the water is trapped in pipes and treated with chemicals, and where food is not freshly hunted and prepared but is packaged and loaded with preservatives so its shelf life can be extended? It can be quite enlightening and engaging to help students see how strange their own behavior looks to others as others' might appear to them.

Children can also develop perspective consciousness by reading some of the numerous books that have been written either from another's perspective or from an insider's point of view. Children's books such as *The True Story of the Three Little Pigs as Told by A. Wolf* (Scieszka, 1989) or, *The Wolf's Story: What Really Happened to Little Red Riding Head* (Forward, 2005), for instance, are good ways to help children see that other points of view exist around most topics. In addition, teachers can use common optical illusions to help children see how the same image can appear differently when viewed from alternate perspectives. Even young children can recognize that others may interpret events in quite different ways, making comments such as, "He says I'm not big enough to play."

State of the Planet Awareness

The awareness of prevailing world conditions and trends includes such aspects as population growth and migration; economic conditions; resources and the physical environment; political developments; advancements in science and technology, law, and health; and various forms of conflicts. Most people, even from highly mobile societies like the United States, spend the majority of their time in their local area. However, developments in communication technology have brought the world, if not into most people's homes, certainly within most people's reach. Extensive global media coverage via television news is making its impact felt at the diplomatic and war tables as well.

The liberal weekly *Die Zeit* of Hamburg, Germany, relates two incidents that capture the extent of the impact made by the aggressive CNN news broadcasting team relatively early in its existence:

> In the summer of 1989, when the U.S. government was searching for a response to threats that hostages in Lebanon would be killed, a White House advisor was asked where President George Bush was spending the day. "He is in his office, watching CNN," the advisor said. "CNN is interviewing Middle East experts; maybe one of them will have an idea that the president can use." And when the Americans marched into Panama in December, 1989, Soviet leader Mikhail Gorbachev made use of the medium. CNN's Moscow correspondent was called to the Kremlin in the middle of the night. There, a press aide read a condemnation of the invasion for the camera. The official note to the U.S. ambassador was not delivered until hours later. The Kremlin's excuse was that it was counting on Washington getting the Kremlin's reaction immediately via CNN (CNN, 1990, p. 34).

Another illustration of the media's educational role can be seen in its coverage of the first Gulf War in the winter of 1991. The U.S. military, knowing that Iraq was watching coverage of the war on CNN, actually planned their movements differently from those they were reporting to the American public so as to confuse the enemy. Thus, while the media makes **state of the planet awareness** a possibility as never before, it also makes the spread of misinformation easier and faster than ever before. Today, we might hear this referred to as "fake news." A recent example of this experience was created during the 2016 U. S. presidential campaign when false news items were generated by numerous sources which people believed and acted upon. Also, if we are not careful, we may find it very easy to believe that the real world consists only of televised images according to CNN. Sometimes referred to as the CNN effect, this refers to the notion that compelling images on television, such as those viewed during a humanitarian crisis, cause policymakers to intervene in situations where they might not otherwise be in the best interests of the nation. Schorr (1998) suggested that this is "the way breaking news affects foreign policy decision. Neuman (1996) described the CNN effect in the following way: "It suggests that when CNN floods the airwaves with news of a foreign crisis, policymakers have no choice but to redirect their attention to the crisis at hand. It also suggests that crisis coverage evokes an emotional outcry from the public to 'do something' about the latest incident, forcing political leaders to change course or risk unpopularity" (pp. 15–16). Or recall the story line in the successful film *Wag the Dog,* which portrays a media-produced war created to divert public attention from unethical presidential behavior.

General public awareness of the state of the planet must become a priority. Children must be taught to reflect on national and world conditions and to ask questions that go beyond the obvious. For example, they should be aware that despite all of the United

©Ariel Skelley/Blend Images LLC RF

Nations' accomplishments, conditions for most of the world's people show serious deterioration (Childers & Urquhart, 1994; UNHCR, 2016). For instance:

1. The world's population has grown more in the last 50 years than in the previous 4 million years and is the single biggest threat to our planet and its resources. World population is projected to increase from 7.5 billion in 2017 to a projected 11–12 billion, meaning there will be 4 billion more mouths to feed. This number alone is equal to what the total world population was in 1975.

2. Four hundred million people are unemployed in the "south" (the preferred term for those countries once referred to as undeveloped or third world). Forty million new jobs are needed each year just to maintain the present world condition. Under present north-south imbalances, there is not the remotest chance that these jobs will materialize.

3. Over 1 billion people live in poverty today, 40% more than in 1980. In 1960, the wealthiest one fifth of the world's population were 30 times richer than the poorest one fifth. Today, the wealthiest one fifth of the world's population are 60 times richer than the poorest one fifth. Viewed from the perspective of a single country, such conditions represent the classic condition for a massive and violent revolution.

4. Through television, radio, film, and the Internet, poor countries of the south have acquired knowledge of the affluent lifestyles of the minority in the north and of some southern elites, permitting angry comparisons with the desperate poverty of the vast majority in the south.

5. In 1951, when the United Nations High Commission on Refugees (UNHCR) was founded, there were some 1.5 million legally classified refugees worldwide. Today, more 65 million people around the world have been forced from their homes as a result of conflict or persecution—nearly 34,000 a day! Among them are nearly 21.3 million refugees, over half of whom are under the age of 18. There are also 10 million stateless people who have been denied a nationality and access to basic rights such as education, healthcare, employment, and freedom of movement, as well as an increasing number of climate refugees— people leaving their homelands due to the life-altering impact the climate change has had on their immediate environment.

6. World grain production per capita has shrunk by half since 1950. In Africa, grain production has dropped 28% since 1967 due to the effects of drought, desertification, erosion, and population growth. Every day, more than 16,000 children die from hunger-related causes. This is one child every 5 seconds.

7. The rate of environmental deterioration continues unabated despite the best intentions of the activists and policymakers. The problems posed by global warming, ecosystem destruction, and ozone depletion demand urgent attention. Currently, 1 in 5 people in the world survive on less water per day than is used to flush a toilet.

8. On a global basis, only $1.90 is spent, per person per year, on the United Nations. This figure compares to $150 spent per person worldwide on weapons.

Most people do not know that within the United States, nearly 57 million Americans or 19% of the population, were considered disabled or handicapped in 2010. Nor do most people know how many Americans go hungry or are homeless, or how many children are born addicted to cocaine or suffer from AIDS-related complications.

Students must be actively encouraged to expand their knowledge base, to review international news sources, and to inquire into the knowledge and perspective of international visitors. Such actions, incidentally, would also help students develop the first dimension of global education, perspective consciousness.

Understanding one's place relative to others in a global society is critical. If the world population were reduced to 100 people while maintaining existing human ratios, there would be 60 Asians, 12 Europeans, 13 from North and South America, and 14 Africans; 49 would be female and 51 would be male; 82 would be nonwhite and 18 would be white; 67 would be non-Christian and 33 would be Christian; 89 would be heterosexual and 11 would be gay or lesbian; 32% of the entire world's wealth would be in the hands of only 5 people and all 5 would be citizens of the United States; 80 would live in substandard housing; 67 would be unable to read; 50 would suffer from malnutrition; and only 1 would have a college education and 1 would own a computer (Family Care Foundation, 2008).

Cross-Cultural Awareness

The cross-cultural dimension of global education includes an awareness of social and cultural diversity around the world and at least a beginning awareness of how one's own culture and society might be viewed from other vantage points. Hanvey suggests that this dimension may be the most difficult to attain because people typically do not have the time or expertise needed to truly understand those who are different from themselves. We also know that understanding about others does not necessarily follow from simple contact. Lengthy, structured, and intimate contact under certain conditions is required to gain an insider's understanding of those in another culture (see Chapter 6 for a more in-depth discussion of intergroup relations and the contact hypothesis).

How can schooling best develop **cross-cultural awareness** in young people? To define what schools might reasonably hope to accomplish in this direction, it may be helpful to recall the iceberg model of culture as you consider four levels of cross-cultural awareness posited by Hanvey.

The first level involves awareness of superficial or extremely visible cultural traits, the kind that often become the basis for stereotypes: skin color, dress, language patterns, ceremonies, and so on. Much of this information is obtained through textbooks, television, and tourism. At this level, the individual outside a given culture typically interprets observed actions of others as exotic, or worse, bizarre. This level is most like the denial and defense stages of the DMIS discussed in Chapter 5.

The second level involves awareness of significant but more subtle cultural traits that contrast markedly with one's own. Such information is often gained as a result of culture conflict situations and is often interpreted as unbelievable. The reaction here, however, is more on an emotional level. Interactions are considered frustrating, irrational, and against "common sense," similar to those encountered at the DMIS stage of defense.

The third level also includes an awareness of significant and subtle cultural traits that contrast markedly with one's own. However, this level is characterized by more intellectual emphasis and analysis. Others' behavior is better understood and seen as more like one's own. This level might be likened to the minimization stage on the DMIS.

The fourth level involves awareness of how another culture feels from the perspective of an insider. People attain this perspective through cultural immersion: that is, from living the culture. Information is perceived as believable not simply because it is understood at the cognitive level but because of its familiarity at the subjective or affective level. This level might be likened to reaching the state called "home" on the U-curve or the DMIS stages of acceptance, adaptation, and integration.

Effective culture learning is more of an affective and behavioral process than a cognitive process. A person truly learns about another culture by living it, not by being told about it. Development of intercultural competence may be, as Hanvey and others have noted, the most difficult, yet the most critical, of the five dimensions to achieve. However, strategies do exist that can assist people on their way to becoming interculturally competent. The culture-general framework introduced in Chapter 4, for instance, can have a significant impact on cognition, affect, and behavior in cross-cultural settings (Cushner & Brislin, 1996). It is a cognitive tool that engages the emotions and may be just the tool for the school context.

Knowledge of Global Dynamics or World Systems

Attaining this fourth dimension of a global perspective, knowledge of global dynamics or world systems, requires a modest understanding of how world ecosystems operate. Educators can stress the interconnectedness of things by asking students to consider the impact one particular decision or action will have on another. The following examples illustrate interconnectedness.

In southeastern Australia, an increase in female fish populations discovered in area river basins was found to be caused by an increase in estrogen in the water. Following an extensive investigation, it was determined that this hormone found its way into area waterways by being flushed out in toilet wastewater. Women using birth control pills eliminated higher-than-usual levels of estrogen in their urine. This increase of estrogen in the wastewater directly affected the development of fish downstream! This is a good example of an unanticipated, unintended outcome. And, we are now learning that fish caught in many U.S. waters contain pharmaceutical residues, including medicines to treat high blood pressure, bipolar disorder, and depression—another unanticipated consequence!

Now consider an example of the vulnerability of ecological systems to changes in distant parts of the world. The recent increase in mosquito populations across the United States can be directly tied to our tremendous appetite for inexpensive fast-food hamburgers. Stop for a moment and consider some of your own hypotheses to explain this phenomenon. What have you proposed as the cause? Not so surprisingly, many people know that an increasing proportion of the meat we eat comes from cattle raised on land that was once rain forest in Central and South America. But most would still not see the connection. We have come to understand that these rain forests provide the winter nesting sites for many of the Northern Hemisphere's migrating bird populations. As an increasing percentage of the rain forest is destroyed, so too are the winter nesting sites for these birds, resulting in a greater than normal death rate for the species. The decline in bird population has resulted in fewer songbirds returning north each year, and consequently, an increase in the mosquito population that forms a major part of the birds' diet. This is a vivid example of the impact that individual choice, in this case eating habits, can have. The global educator's catchphrase, "Think Globally, Act Locally" again becomes paramount.

When a new element is introduced into any system, it can often have unanticipated effects. Hanvey suggested that there are no side effects, only surprise effects. Thus, when we intervene in any system, we should be prepared for some surprising consequences. Think of a spider's web. Although the web is composed of multiple strands, when one is touched in even the slightest manner, it vibrates and affects the entire web. We confront numerous other examples of this principle in action almost every day. Global warming caused by the carbon dioxide buildup in the atmosphere, depletion of the ozone layer, the greenhouse effect, the poisoning of groundwater, and the weakening of the eagle's egg as a result of the pesticide DDT moving up the food chain are all examples of these surprise consequences, which we are now trying to correct. We must learn, as Hanvey suggested, to look for the "concealed wiring," the hidden functions of elements in a system.

Awareness of Human Choice

Hanvey's fifth dimension, awareness of human choices, represents the final critical step in attaining a global perspective. The problems of choice that confront individuals, nations, and the human species as they increase their knowledge of the global system are addressed in this dimension. Until recently, people were generally unaware of the unanticipated outcomes and long-term consequences of their actions. This is no longer the case as a global consciousness or cognition is emerging. People now must consider the implications of an expanded knowledge and communication base. Negligence, or even making an unwise choice out of ignorance, may set the stage for countless problems at some future time.

Fortunately, we know a great deal more than we used to, and choices do exist. Consider the use of chlorofluorocarbons (CFCs) and the growing problem of ozone depletion. We have two choices: we can continue to use CFCs because at the present time they make refrigeration and propellants possible, or we can stop using them because of their effect on the environment, while actively seeking a replacement product. The simple substitution of pump spray mechanisms for propellant sprays on a variety of products is a good example of a successful alternative. It is awareness of the problem, however, that often makes the difference in the success of alternatives.

Children can make remarkable strides toward realizing their power and ability to bring about change. Many years ago, Israeli elementary schoolchildren went on a campaign to protect some of their nation's threatened wildflower populations. They raised the awareness of adults to such an extent that the adults stopped indiscriminately picking the flowers. Many of the threatened flowers have since been removed from the endangered species lists.

Likewise, a number of years ago one of the authors of this text initiated a school exchange program between fifth- and sixth-grade children in northeast Ohio and schoolchildren in the Yucatán peninsula of Mexico and in Belize. Seventeen children went on the first trip from Ohio to Belize. One gesture of appreciation the Ohio children made to their host community was to present the village school with a world atlas signed by everyone at the visitors' school. The gift seemed to be the first book the Belize school actually owned. This discovery made such an impression on the students from Ohio that on their return home they decided to do something about the situation. All the fifth- and sixth-grade students in the school became involved in operating an after-school snack bar, collecting usable books from the community, and packaging them for shipment overseas. With the proceeds from their snack bar and their collection efforts, students were able to send more than 500 books to their peers in this small village in Belize. Needless to say, the children felt tremendous pride, realizing that they, personally, could have such an impact on individuals so far away. This lesson was one that no textbook could teach them and that they will never forget.

©Blend/Image Source RF

What, Specifically, Should Students Study?

The American Forum for Global Education (AFGE, 2004), one of the nation's first educational organizations devoted to helping educators understand how best to develop a global understanding in their students, identified three major areas on which a global education curriculum should focus: global issues, problems, and challenges; culture and world areas; and the United States and the world. Within these three larger themes, 10 specific topics of study are recommended:

1. Conflict and its control, including terrorism and national security
2. Economic systems and international trade
3. Global belief systems, including the study of differing philosophies and religions
4. Human rights and social justice, including gender equity issues as well as health, education, and food security
5. Management of the planet's resources, including the study of energy and environmental degradation
6. Political systems, including a study of the United Nations, negotiations and treaties, and nongovernmental organizations
7. Population, including population control and immigration and emigration concerns
8. Human commonality and diversity through the study of race and ethnicity, thus working to reduce prejudice and ethnocentrism
9. The technocratic revolution, looking at the increasing roles that science, technology, and communication play in people's lives
10. Sustainable development, including studies of urban growth and the disparities that exist between countries of the north and those in the south

Characteristics of a Global Classroom

Most schooling is an ethnocentric activity, with most national systems of schooling addressing the needs of the nation they serve and transmitting the "proper" attitudes and beliefs thought to be necessary to maintain the society. Long-term goals in most schools, however, reflect some of the ideals of a global perspective. If you were to closely examine the philosophical goal statements of most schools, you would find statements such as these: to appreciate people from other cultures; to develop sensitivity to the needs of people different from themselves; to increase knowledge about people around the world.

The philosophical stage has been partially set, but the methods for implementing such goal statements have created a problem. Schools in the United States, as well as most parts of the world, typically present curricular experiences through a predominantly cognitive approach and from a rather narrow ethnocentric point of view. In addition, until recently, curriculum development efforts have had little input or interaction from people of different backgrounds. Such assumptions and practices are presently being called into question. To build true professional global communities in which teachers and students can begin to collaborate in real-world problem solving, we will need to help students learn firsthand about cultures of other countries, share what they are learning locally and globally with others, collaborate on common projects across national boundaries wherever possible, study and live in other countries with students from those countries, welcome global career opportunities, and develop capacities for success in a global village. But how can these goals be achieved?

Broadly speaking, a globally competent student has knowledge and genuine curiosity about the state of the world that includes an understanding of the historical experiences of other people, their cultural practices, environmental and economic concerns; sufficient cross-cultural skills that enable her or him to communicate effectively with people from other countries and cultures; and a commitment to inclusive ethical citizenship and social action. Teachers, too, must exhibit similar knowledge, skills, and dispositions if they are to effectively guide their students toward global competence. Teachers should know the international dimensions of their subject matter; have the pedagogical skills to assist their students to analyze primary sources from other nations; and a willingness to guide students to become responsible global citizens.

In a classroom with a global perspective, global education is not merely an add-on to an already overcrowded curriculum. Rather, relevant concepts and activities that develop a global perspective are woven throughout the curriculum. Most important, global classrooms seek to help students develop such critical cognitive skills and attitudes as empathy, interconnectedness, perspective taking, cross-cultural understanding, action orientation, and prejudice reduction. In such classrooms, students are active in building connections with others. They may have pen pals, or e-pals, with children in other parts of the world. In addition to communicating through writing with others and thus developing their language skills, students may be sharing audiotapes, videotapes, photographs, classroom materials, and other artifacts that reflect their own and each other's cultures. Children may read books about people's lives in other communities, which helps develop a global perspective while simultaneously achieving the goals and objectives of a language arts curriculum. Students may work on collaborative writing projects with peers in other countries, as Nate's class was doing with students in India. In short, students go about developing their language arts and other skills with other people in mind.

Pedagogies: Old and New

All the pedagogical techniques discussed in this book also apply to the global classroom. Indeed, the use of developmentally appropriate practice, collaborative and cooperative groups, and student involvement in planning takes on a new and richer dimension when placed in the context of an international perspective. However, a global perspective can also be introduced in more traditionally oriented classrooms. What is important here is the notion of a broader perspective. In addition, students in global classrooms may use technology in creative ways. Classroom computers can be connected to networks that enable children to communicate on a regular basis with others from around the world. Joint activities may develop whereby classes in two or more countries collaborate in real time, on some global issue, as is being done in an increasing number of schools that use video teleconferencing technologies such as Skype to motivate young people in social studies and foreign language education (Roberts, 2007). Schools may also use digital technologies to link classes, enabling them to transfer artwork, poetry, essays, and other student work to other schools. Rather than simulate a French café in a traditional French language class, some schools have had video teleconferences or Skype calls in French cafés, thus allowing students to see and interact directly with students overseas in a real-life setting. Or young people from around the world can come together via technology to discuss a global current event.

Roles: Old and New

In global classrooms, local members of the international community are considered to be an integral part of the school. As events unfold around the world, representatives from the various communities are invited into classrooms to share their experience and perspectives. These presentations may occur at regular times in certain classes (e.g., social studies, language arts) or during regular school assemblies devoted to world events. Such involvement serves to break down some of the personal barriers that tend to develop between people. Not only are students introduced to different perspectives, they are also introduced to various cultures and languages firsthand. Such activities add a personal element to the content under study that a textbook cannot while serving to build bridges of understanding in the local community. Thus, when a natural disaster occurs somewhere in the world or when a conflict breaks out, children can associate it with real people; it is no longer an abstract event unfolding in some far-off, abstract corner of the world. Finally, having adults from other parts of the world serve as teachers helps students understand that teaching and learning can occur in a variety of ways.

Place of Content Knowledge: Old and New

Globally oriented classrooms, like collaborative classrooms, integrate subject matter from various academic disciplines. Often these integrated curricula are jointly developed by educators from many countries. This collaboration, of course, helps ensure the accuracy of the content being studied. For example, the Pacific Circle Consortium developed educational materials that integrate the perspectives and contributions of educators from the United States, Canada, Australia, New Zealand, and Japan as well as some Pacific Island nations. One of their products, *The Ocean Project,* used the Pacific Ocean as a curriculum vehicle for students located in countries on the Pacific Rim. Two such projects have been developed. One provides fifth- and sixth-grade students in two different countries with an integrated look at the culture, environment, economics, and cultural interaction of the other group's region. At the beginning of the unit, each group of students studies local conditions (environment, culture, economics, etc.). Next, a simulated transoceanic voyage brings the students to the other country, where they study similar concepts in that location. Students in Honolulu, Hawaii, and Hiroshima, Japan, for instance, thus learn about one another's way of life and local environment. A similarly developed unit for upper secondary school students looks at the use of the world's oceans, treaties, and international law. An international project on Antarctica has also been developed. Additional collaborative projects that can engage your students are discussed later in the chapter.

Assessment: Old and New

Assessment in global classrooms may generally be described as global and comprehensive as well. That is, because of the wide variety of activities and the emphasis on cross-disciplinary or interdisciplinary studies, global classrooms can easily use both traditional and alternative forms of assessment. If technology is used in global classrooms to stimulate curricular activities, it can also be used in evaluation. Everything from computer-generated assessments in which students receive immediate feedback to the production of videos, PowerPoint or Prezi presentations, Webquests, and other technology-based activities can be assessed for how they demonstrate what students know and can do. Increasingly, the assessment of many internationally collaborative activities has proven to have a significant impact on knowledge attainment. The central point to remember in the assessment of global classrooms, as well as of other kinds of classrooms described in this book, is that when a wide variety of activities enhances the curriculum, they can be evaluated in a wide variety of ways.

Teaching the Global Perspective

Development of a global perspective should be integrated throughout the school curriculum, not just in the social studies. Although large-scale infusion is desirable, an international perspective can be integrated into the curriculum by individual teachers offering international focus courses, by internationalizing instructional methods and materials, by encouraging international travel as an important part of one's education, and by internationalizing the disciplines.

International focus courses exist in such areas as anthropology, regional history, geography, global or world studies, foreign language study, art and music, world religions, ethnic group studies, and international business. Such courses seem most appropriate at the middle and secondary level and quite readily emerge from the disciplines themselves.

Internationalizing instructional methods and materials might emphasize intercultural interaction in the classroom using the special experiences of immigrant and international students as resources. Teachers should employ culturally appropriate instructional and assessment strategies, and textbooks should be reviewed for balance. Partnership programs with other schools and countries, such as those with the schools in India and Belize referred to earlier, can also be developed.

Well-developed international travel experiences can also be an integral part of many classes, from eco-tourist ventures in Central American rain-forest regions to language experience or arts opportunities in foreign countries. Such programs, if designed to go beyond the typical tourist experience and into the local culture, can provide that experiential dimension that is so critical to effective culture learning (Cushner, 2004).

Internationalizing the disciplines involves infusing key elements of a global perspective across the entire curriculum. There are numerous ways this infusion can be accomplished at all levels and in all content areas. For instance, in reading and language arts, students might study how non-American and non-British writers use the English language. World literature courses should strive to include numerous examples from a non-Western origin. And literature should be integrated with the social sciences as a way to introduce multiple perspectives on abstract concepts. Children's literature can also be used to present concepts of interest in international education. Classic Dr. Seuss books, such as *The Lorax* and *The Butter Battle Book,* can be used in a study of the environment and the nuclear arms race, respectively. Students might also analyze the portrayal of minorities and internationals in basal textbooks.

In science education, teachers might help students observe and understand the natural world and study the problems created as a result of increased technology and innovation. Students should be encouraged to ask questions about global warming, about water shortages, or about growing threats of extinction. Then, students should be encouraged to propose solutions to many of these problems, solutions that require knowledge and input from diverse peoples and cultures, all of whom "own" the problems and will ultimately have to come together to solve them. Although technology may be universal, as proposed for possible solutions to problems, its application is quite specific. The study of what constitutes "appropriate" technology in a given situation demands sensitivity to such aspects as local environment, culture, history, and language. The topic of unplanned change can be introduced through the study of biology and evolution. Inequities of energy consumption across the planet can be explored. Finally, the global nature of such systems as the water cycle, the mineral cycle, and the energy cycle can be studied.

In foreign language education, cultural studies can be expanded beyond the mother country to include colonized people as well as immigrant and refugee populations. The role of translators in world diplomacy can be studied. Foreign languages can be taught through folk songs, and English as a Second Language or English as a Foreign Language can be introduced to foreign language teachers and students.

Mathematics education should stress the metric system. The United States is the only industrialized nation in the world not actively using metrics. Math concepts can be illustrated through problems that simultaneously teach about world trends and global issues. Traditional numeration systems from other cultures can be studied. The mathematics and possible computer application of Islamic art can be analyzed. Likewise, the impact of women on the development of mathematics (as well as other topics) can be introduced.

Finally, history and social studies should look at various perspectives on similar issues. The American Revolution, for instance, certainly looked different through British eyes. Studying other nation's textbooks, maps, or discussing current events with international students can go far in helping students develop perspective consciousness. Issues of population growth, personal family migration, history, and cultural diffusion can become the focus of historical inquiry, as can the interaction between geography, culture, and the environment.

The bottom line is that students should be encouraged to ask difficult questions and to explore possible reasons and solutions from a variety of points of view. Why, for instance, does one fifth of the world's population (in the north or developed countries) use two thirds of the world's natural resources, and what might be done to counterbalance this? What does it really mean to be an overpopulated nation when an individual from the United States has the same impact on the earth in terms of pollution and utilization of resources as 24 or 25 individuals from a country such as Malawi? And why should soybeans, for instance, be exported from Brazil to feed cattle in the Western nations, to the detriment of the small farmers in South America and the benefit of wealthy corporations in North America? These questions are difficult to explore, but are ultimately ones that have to be addressed if the people of the world are ever to live in true balance.

Comprehensive International Education Frameworks

Programs for the K-12 Context

Many have recognized that in order to have the greatest influence developing an international education, rather than approaching it in a piecemeal manner, a more comprehensive, all-inclusive approach has the greatest chance of achieving lasting impact. The following organizations offer comprehensive curricular frameworks and/or policy documents that can serve to guide such a process at the school and/or district level.

International Baccalaureate Organization (IBO)

The International Baccalaureate, referred to as the IB, consists of four high-quality international education programs currently in more than 5,000 schools reaching more than 1.3 million students in 45 countries. The IB continuum offers four distinct programs (IBO, 2017):

- the IB Primary Years Programme (PYP), designed for students aged 3 to 12, focuses on developing the whole child as an inquirer, both in the classroom and in the world outside;
- the IB Middle Years Programme (MYP), for students aged 11 to 16, provides a framework of academic challenge encouraging students to embrace and understand the connections between traditional subjects and the real world, and become critical and reflective thinkers;
- the IB Diploma Programme (DP), for students aged 16 to 19, offers an academically challenging and balanced program with rigorous, externally-evaluated final examinations designed to prepare students for success at university and beyond; and
- the IB Career-Related Certificate (IBCC), for students aged 16 to 19, the newest offering from the IB, incorporates the vision and educational principles of the IB Programmes into a unique offering specifically designed for students who wish to engage in career-related learning.

As stated in the IB literature (IBO, 2017), the aim of all IB programmes is to develop internationally minded people who, recognizing their common humanity and shared guardianship of the planet, help to create a better and more peaceful world. Common to all of its programmes is how the IB organization defines international education; stating that the various programmes aim to develop citizens of the world in relation to culture, language, and learning to live together while building a sense of identity, cultural awareness, and development of universal human values. This is achieved by stimulating curiosity and inquiry in order to foster a spirit of discovery and enjoyment of learning; equipping students with the skills to learn and acquire knowledge, individually or collaboratively, and to apply these skills and knowledge accordingly across a broad range of areas. IB programmes also aim to provide international content while responding to local requirements and interests, encourage diversity and flexibility in teaching methods, and provide appropriate forms of assessment and international benchmarking.

The IB learner profile is the IB mission statement translated into a set of learning outcomes for the 21st century. The learner profile provides a long-term vision of education, serving as a set of ideals that can inspire, motivate, and focus the work of schools and teachers, uniting them in a common purpose. The IB has incorporated the learner profile into all of its programmes so that it is the common ground on which all IB World Schools stand, and contains the essence of what they, and the programmes, are about. Thus, the Learner Profile guides all students to strive to be Inquirers, Knowledgeable, Thinkers, Communicators, Principled, Open-Minded, Caring, Risk-Takers, Balanced, and Reflective. Although the IB is focused on K-12 education, in an effort to expand the range of IB professional development experiences and to offer additional professional learning opportunities to prospective and current IB practitioners, the IB has forged partnerships with a growing number of prestigious universities and institutions from around the world to offer IB certificates in teaching and learning and IB certificates in leadership. A few select universities have begun to integrate IB principles across their teacher education curriculum. Graduates of these programs are thereby authorized by the IB Organization to teach in any IB World School.

Asia Society/EdSteps

The Asia Society, in conjunction with the Council of Chief State School Officers, published the document, *Educating for Global Competence: Preparing our Youth to Engage the World* (Boix Mansilla & Jackson, 2011). The document introduces a definition of global competence as the capacity and disposition to understand and act on issues of global significance, stating that globally competent individuals are aware, curious, and interested in learning about the world and how it works. Globally competent individuals can use the big ideas, tools, methods, and languages that are central to any discipline (mathematics, literature, history, science, and the arts) to engage the pressing issues of our time. They deploy and develop this expertise as they investigate such issues, recognizing multiple perspectives, communicating their views effectively, and taking action to improve conditions.

Applicable at all age levels and content areas is the framework presented in this document. Globally competent students should be able to perform the following four competences:

1. Investigate the world beyond their immediate environment, framing significant problems and conducting well-crafted and age-appropriate research.

2. Recognize perspectives, others' and their own, articulating and explaining such perspectives thoughtfully and respectfully.

3. Communicate ideas effectively with diverse audiences, bridging geographic, linguistic, ideological, and cultural barriers.

4. Take action to improve conditions, viewing themselves as players in the world and participating reflectively.

The document presents numerous vivid examples of this in action in a variety of classroom contexts.

Programs for Teacher Education

The Longview Foundation

The Longview Foundation for World Affairs and International Understanding (www .longviewfdn.org) has been helping young people in the United States learn about world regions and global issues since 1966. The foundation recognizes the critical role that teachers play in preparing young people for a new global reality while at the same time understanding that few teachers begin their careers with the deep knowledge and skills necessary to bring the world into their classrooms. A major focus of their work has been to facilitate the building of purposeful partnerships between state government, Nongovernmental organizations (NGOs), colleges of education, and communities to integrate global competence into teacher and student experiences.

In 2008, the Longview Foundation brought together leaders in education, government, and other sectors to examine what was being done in schools, colleges, and departments of education to prepare future teachers for the new global reality and to generate momentum to do more. The result was the commissioning of a new report and funding stream for Longview. *Teacher Preparation for the Global Age: The Imperative for Change*, was published and made available as one means to highlight promising practices and to suggest a framework for internationalizing the education of all pre-service teachers and increasing the number of world language teachers, especially in less commonly taught languages (Longview, 2008).

World Savvy–Global Competence Certificate

World Savvy (www.worldsavvy.org) is a national education nonprofit founded in the aftermath of the September 11 attacks that works with educators, schools, and districts to integrate global competence into teaching and learning in K-12 classrooms so young people can be prepared to engage, succeed, and meet the challenges of 21st century citizenship. World Savvy has reached more than half a million students and 3,500 teachers, in part, through their *Global Competence Certificate* program (GCC), the first-of-its-kind, graduate-level certificate program in global competence education for teachers. Developed in collaboration with leading experts in global education from Teachers College of Columbia University and the Asia Society, the GCC is designed specifically for in-service educators who are interested in embedding global learning into their teaching practice and preparing their students for the global reality beyond the classroom. The program combines online classes, an international field experience, and a capstone project.

Programs That Link Schools

In addition to the many global education activities and projects in which individual schools and classrooms can participate, a number of projects and networks have been formed that are designed to better inform and connect schools around the world. Following are summaries of a few of these programs in which students from around the world may participate.

Associated Schools Project Network of UNESCO

The Associated Schools Project Network (ASPnet), boasting the largest international program for schools in the world, provides a network for more than 7,900 schools from 176 nations to engage in a variety of collaborative activities (www.unesco.org/education/asp). The Baltic Sea Project, for example, begun in 1998, works with 200 schools in nine countries that border the Baltic Sea, raising awareness of environmental issues in the region while helping students understand the science, social, and cultural aspects of human interdependence. Other projects include Breaking the Silence–The Transatlantic Slave Trade Educational Project (TST), World Heritage Education Project, the Educational Toolkit on Dolphins, an online 24-hour student conference on globalization, a UNESCO antiracism campaign, and the innovative Mondialogo Intercultural Dialogue and Exchange initiative.

Global Nomads

Global Nomads Group (www.gng.org) fosters dialogue and understanding among more than 1 million of the world's youth who reside in over 60 countries. Since fewer than 3% of the world's young people travel during their school years, Global Nomads uses technology to facilitate conversations between middle school and high school students who otherwise would not meet.

GLOBE

GLOBE (Global Learning and Observations to Benefit the Environment, www.globe .gov) is a worldwide hands-on, primary and secondary school-based science and education program. GLOBE's vision promotes and supports students, teachers, and scientists to collaborate on inquiry-based investigations of the environment and the Earth system, working in close partnership with NASA and NSF Earth System Science Projects (ESSPs) in study and research about the dynamics of Earth's environment. Started on Earth Day 1995, today the international GLOBE network has grown to include representatives from 111 participating countries and 140 U.S. partners coordinating GLOBE activities that are integrated into their local and regional communities. Due to their efforts, there are more than 50,000 GLOBE-trained teachers representing over 20,000 schools around the world. GLOBE students have contributed more than 20 million measurements to the GLOBE database for use in their inquiry-based science projects.

LinkTV

LinkTV (www.linktv.org) is the first television channel and website dedicated to providing global perspectives on news, events, and culture, connecting viewers with people and organizations in the forefront of social change and the cultures of an increasingly global community. YouthNoise.org, a component of Link's Engagement division, is composed of 158,000 registered users from all 50 states and 176 countries, creating a virtual meeting place for the next generation of global social activists.

Peace Corps World Wise Schools

Peace Corps World Wise Schools (www.peacecorps.gov/wws) has assisted more than 3 million U.S. students to communicate directly with Peace Corps volunteers all over the world, many who facilitate school linkage programs.

International Children's Digital Library

International Children's Digital Library (www.icdlbooks.org) is an online collection of books that represents outstanding historical and contemporary books from throughout the world. The ultimate goal is to have every culture and language represented so that every child can know and appreciate the riches of children's literature from the world community.

iEARN

iEARN (www.iearn.org) is the world's largest nonprofit global network that enables young people to use the Internet and other new technologies to engage in collaborative educational projects that both enhance learning and make a difference in the world. More than 30,000 schools representing more than 140 nations engage more than 50,000 teachers and 2 million students each year in a variety of activities that work across national boundaries. While the use of technology is often the main focus, the fact that students engage across cultures makes this an ideal global education experience itself. In addition to the technology-based format, annual conferences enable teachers to meet face-to-face to exchange ideas and build relationships.

Global Classrooms

Global Classrooms (www.unausa.org/global-classrooms-model-un) is the home for Model United Nations (UN) an innovative United Nations–based educational program that engages middle school and high school students in an exploration of current world issues through interactive simulations and curricular materials. Global Classrooms cultivates literacy and leadership as students explore important topics such as peacekeeping, sustainable development, and human rights. Model United Nations is an authentic simulation of the UN General Assembly, UN Security Council, or other multilateral body, which introduces students to the world of diplomacy, negotiation, and decision making.

At Model UN, students step into the shoes of ambassadors of countries that are members of the United Nations, from Argentina to Zimbabwe. The students, better known as "delegates," debate current issues on the organization's vast agenda. They prepare draft resolutions, plot strategy, negotiate with supporters and adversaries, resolve conflicts, and navigate the UN's rules of procedure—all in the interest of resolving problems that affect the world.

Perspectives on a Globally Oriented Curriculum

Reflect upon the Case Study at the beginning of the chapter. What Nate attempted to do in the first part of the school year was to integrate into his curriculum three types of knowledge that will help his students evaluate their interpersonal experiences both inside and outside school. First, he integrated knowledge and understanding of prejudice formation and prejudice reduction (see Chapter 6). Second, he tapped into the growing body of knowledge related to the development of an international perspective. Third, he is applying cooperative learning strategies, thus providing students with necessary practice in developing the skills needed for collaborative living and working.

Nate's classroom activities reflect a number of strategies related to global or intercultural education.

1. Nate has demonstrated that it is possible to combine global education with the development of traditional curriculum skills in such areas as language arts, social studies, and art.

2. He has not shied away from real but sensitive issues such as prejudice and interpersonal conflict that greatly affect the lives of his students. Rather, he has acknowledged these issues as real problems that are worth confronting and analyzing. And he has done this in a subtle, creative manner that will set the stage for subsequent activity once everyone has a common foundation.

3. By integrating traditional content areas, the day is not broken into brief time slots during which content and curricular experiences are segregated from one another. Rather, classroom activities are designed to be meaningful and relate to the lives and experiences of the students. Through the partnership story, for example, students have an opportunity to develop their language arts skills while they learn valuable social studies concepts about culture, specific countries, and interpersonal interaction. At the same time, students work in cooperative groups and develop linkages with others around the world.

4. He has actively sought to reduce prejudice, not by simply telling students that it is wrong but by enabling them to learn, firsthand, about similarities and differences among at least two groups of people.

These examples represent just the beginning of what is possible in a globally oriented classroom.

Ethical Concerns

Clearly, there are a variety of ethical issues involved in developing a global classroom. Among them are the fair allocation of available resources (including computers and other technology), the need to consider families and communities when discussing global concerns, and perhaps most important, the need to balance advocacy with inquiry. Although it is tempting for educators to become advocates when discussing the world's problems, the role of schooling remains one of inquiry. Assessing students on the degree to which they are able to use the tools of inquiry, on the breadth and depth of their research, on their analytical skills, and on their creativity in proposing solutions is more appropriate than assessing them on the degree to which they subscribe to a particular point of view.

Similarly, there are ethical considerations involved in the length of time given to newer ideas such as global education. Its emphasis on attitude and behavior change may require educators to allocate large amounts of time to achieve even modest gains. Social psychologists have had a difficult time demonstrating that significant, long-lasting behavior change follows from short-term attitude change efforts. Although it may be possible to demonstrate a change in attitude as a result of a short-term intervention (efforts at a summer camp program, for instance), there has been little evidence to demonstrate either that the attitude change persists or that it leads to a subsequent long-term change in behavior.

The converse may in fact be true, as seen in research concerning attitudes toward people with disabilities. An individual who has had little contact with persons with disabilities may initially react with discomfort or pity and be acutely aware of the disability. In one study, for example, teachers participating in an intensive five-week summer training institute on teaching young children with disabilities initially demonstrated a negative change in attitude, as measured by the Attitudes Toward Disabled Persons scale (Stahlman, Safford, Pisarchick, Miller, & Dyer, 1989). Positive attitudes, as defined by this scale, are those that regard a person with disabilities as essentially like everyone else, not as someone special. For many of the teachers in this study, this workshop was their first exposure to children with disabilities, and as a result, they had difficulty not being overly solicitous and eager to help. Later follow-up experiences with students with disabilities gradually led to more "normalized" attitudes.

Critical Incident

A Delayed Response

A couple of days after Nate's class received the completion of their partnership story, Nate overheard Lenny and Paul giggling and talking about how silly it seemed that people in India would use rare herbs as medicines. The boys thought it even more unusual that Indians would consider using mantras to control people and animals, and the two began referring to Indians in derogatory ways.

- Why do you think Lenny and Paul would, after two days, begin to ridicule the people they had spent time studying about?
- How would you handle the immediate situation?
- What might you do to prevent this reaction from happening?

Summary

This chapter takes as its starting point the reality that we live in an interconnected, interdependent, global society and that it is the responsibility of teachers and schools to prepare students to live within it in a productive manner. Globalization has many meanings for many different people. In this chapter it means actively introducing students to people and ideas from around the world, helping students learn to think in terms of whole systems (economic, political, social), and acquainting students with global issues that are certain to have an impact on their lives. International education should help students learn to participate with other students from all over the planet in thinking through hard questions involving not only intercultural competence but also the ability to span all kinds of social as well as geographical boundaries.

When people encounter situations that induce or require them to behave in new and different ways for an extended period of time, there is a real possibility for long-term attitude and behavior change. If, for instance, school organizational structures can be modified to encourage or require intergroup interaction over an extended period of time, the likelihood that everyone may learn to regard themselves as tolerant, understanding, and able to get along with people increases. Government legislation that provides mandates for altering organizational structure on a national level is based on this idea. Official support and status for bilingualism in Canada or multilingualism in Switzerland are promising examples of this policy in action. Never believe, however, that mandates alone will do the job. What is required is persistent face-to-face activity and a good deal of trial and error!

Chapter Review

Go to the Online Learning Center at www.mhhe.com/cushner9e to review important content from the chapter, practice with key terms, take a chapter quiz, and access active workbook exercises.

Key Terms

cross-cultural awareness 223

globalization 211

global perspective 215

perspective consciousness 219

state of the planet awareness 220

Future's Window

Purpose: To project the needs of individuals and society in the years ahead, and to examine what this means for educators.

Instructions: In this activity you are to become a futurist and project into the future—both your own as well as that of the world. Divide a page into quadrants, with the top half representing your "Self" and the bottom half representing the "World." The left side of each half represents "5 years," and the right half represents "20 years" into the future. You are to make at least five entries in each quadrant; things you expect to have accomplished or to be dealing with in 5 years and in 20 years, and things you expect the world to be confronting, both in 5 years as well as 20 years. Do not record what you wish will happen but what you predict will occur based on what you see happening today. Do this activity alone at first. If you are doing this in a group setting, after a short while, share your responses with others and compile a group list.

Self—5 years	Self—20 years
World—5 years	**World—20 years**

1. Look closely at what is on your list, or, if you have done this activity in a group, look closely at the compilation. What messages seem to jump out at you as you look closely at the response patterns? Do not be surprised if quick responses do not emerge. Take some time to analyze the similarities as well as the differences in the columns. What generalizations seem to emerge?

2. What questions do you have as a result of the generalizations you observed?

3. As people analyze their responses, it is not uncommon to say something like, "It seems as if things will be quite nice and easy for individuals, but there will still be problems in the world." This is a critical observation. If you have not already made this observation yourself, please consider it for a moment. Does such a statement hold true for your responses to the above task?

4. Let's assume that you can safely make the same observation and statement given the responses on your list. What is the responsibility one has to others? Why do you think it is that, in general, people project their own future to be fine even when the rest of the world continues to face problems and challenges?

5. Discuss your responses to the above with others in a group. Do not be surprised if there is much disagreement over people's responses.

6. Next, look closely at your projections for the world. What generalizations seem to stand out as you analyze this information?

7. Which of the following statements can you agree with given the projections you have made for the world? Check one.

    The issues that the world will face seem quite pessimistic and insurmountable.

    The issues that the world will face seem complex but generally will be resolved.

8. It is often said that each individual can and must do her or his own part to help improve the bigger picture. All of the problems the world will face, whether they are in fact solved or not, will require the coordinated efforts of many different people from many different career and cultural backgrounds who are able to work together. The problems of the world are such that they will be solved by the coordinated efforts of many different people and nations, or they will not be solved at all.

9. What is the role of education in helping people develop the ability to solve the problems that you believe the world will face?

10. What are some things you can do through your teaching that will help your students develop the awareness, knowledge, and skills necessary to collaborate with others whose ways of interacting and values may be quite different from their own?

Classroom Activities

1. A common activity in primary and middle school is to introduce students to the media and the world around them by having them report on current events from local newspapers and other sources. This activity extends the traditional current events activity, asking students to utilize the global media and report on a current event from multiple perspectives. Identify a current-events topic of global significance, such as an event that crosses national boundaries or an activity occurring in one nation that has direct impact elsewhere. Locate the

same news story from *at least* three nations (at least one from a non–English-speaking nation). A few good places to find such sources include: www.inkdrop.net/news; www.newspaperindex.com.

2. Children's literature is an exceptional way to introduce multiple perspectives to young people. Identify a topic of concern to children worldwide. Then, seek out children's books that address the topic or concept from multiple experiences. Develop an annotated bibliography of your recommendations and share it with others.

3. Film is another ideal way to introduce multiple perspectives and intercultural conflict to middle and secondary school age students. A number of films have been produced that display people interacting in a variety of intercultural contexts—some humorous and others more serious in nature, but all providing visual examples of effective as well as ineffective cross-cultural encounters. Some example of films addressing this include: *Mr. Baseball, Mosquito Coast, Moscow on the Hudson, Coming to America, Planet of the Apes, Karate Kid, My Big Fat Greek Wedding, Slumdog Millionnaire, The Joy Luck Club, Lion,* and *Fiddler on the Roof.* Seek out additional films useful for this purpose. Foreign films also provide an exceptional opportunity to look closely into the lives of others. With this, you can do a comparative analysis by focusing on elements that reflect cross-cultural similarities and differences in behavior, value, or belief.

4. Knowledge of global systems, as Hanvey proposed, is really about understanding global interconnectedness. High school students can research innovations in a range of contexts (e.g., science, technology, agriculture, medicine) and explore the "downstream" unanticipated impact of that innovation. The introduction of DDT, for example, while increasing crop yield many times over, had an unanticipated detrimental impact on other life forms once it entered the food chain. This was first noted in the late 1950s when spraying to control the beetles that carry Dutch elm disease resulted in early deaths of robins in Michigan and elsewhere. Researchers discovered that earthworms were accumulating the pesticide and that the robins eating them were being poisoned. Other birds later were impacted as well, including the eagle whose egg shells were weakened as a result of the chemical. What other systemic impacts can be identified?

Reflective Questions

The Case Study teacher, Nate Kozlowski, developed a number of activities and curricular redesigns that infused global awareness into his sixth-grade curriculum. Still, he is bothered by several aspects of his work.

1. How can he continue to educate himself about new methods of global education while simultaneously keeping up with student needs and school requirements? Time is definitely a problem.

2. He knows that the United States is a widely diverse country with many unsolved problems regarding race and ethnicity. How can he justify moving to a global perspective when the problems at home remain so critical?

3. Although he has been relatively successful in incorporating a global perspective into social studies, language arts, and some of the arts, how can he do the same with such seemingly culture-neutral subjects as mathematics and science?

4. He has found that many students do not relate at all to the idea of ethnicity. Rather, they think of themselves as Americans and have neither knowledge of nor emotional ties to their own ethnic roots. How can he encourage these students to appreciate and value ethnic and racial diversity without seeming to denigrate the American way of life?

5. Not every teacher and administrator in his school appreciates the direction Nate is taking toward a global perspective. How can he continue to broaden his students' perspectives in the face of criticism from his colleagues?

References

Adelson, J., & O'Neill, R. P. (1966). Growth of political ideas in adolescents: The sense of community. *Journal of Personality and Social Psychology, 4,* 295–306.

American Forum for Global Education. (2004). Retrieved from http://www.globaled.org/

Avery, P. G., & Hann, C. L. (2004). Diversity and U.S. 14-year-olds' knowledge, attitudes, and experiences. In W. G. Stephan & W. P. Vogt (Eds.), *Education programs for improving intergroup relations: Theory, research, and practice* (pp. 195–210). New York: Teachers College Press.

Boix Mansilla, V. and Jackson, A. (2011). *Educating for global competence: Preparing our youth to engage the world.* New York: Asia Society.

Bybee, R. W., & Sund, R. B. (1982). *Piaget for educators* (2nd ed.). Columbus, OH: Charles E. Merrill.

Council on Foreign Relations (2016). What college students know about the world: A survey of global literacy. Council on Foreign Relations, Sept. 13, 2016. Retrieved from http://www.cfr.org/society-and-culture/college-aged-students-know-world-survey-global-literacy/p38241

Childers, E., & Urquhart, B. (1994). *Renewing the United Nations system.* Geneva, Switzerland: United Nations.

CNN. (1990, December). Television for the global village. *World Press Review, 37*(12), 34.

Cushner, K. (1992). Creating cross-cultural understanding through internationally cooperative story writing. *Social Education, 56*(1), 43–46.

Cushner, K. (2004). *Beyond tourism: A practical guide to meaningful educational travel.* Lanham, MD: Scarecrow Education.

Cushner, K. (2008). International socialization of young people: Obstacles and opportunities. *International Journal of Intercultural Relations, 32*:2,164–173.

Cushner, K., & Brislin, R. (1996). *Intercultural interactions: A practical guide* (2nd ed.). Thousand Oaks, CA: Sage.

Family Care Foundation. (2008). *If the world were a village of 100 people.* Retrieved from http://www.familycare.org/news/if_the_world.htm

Flavell, J., Botkin, P., & Fry, C. L. (1968). *The development of role taking and communication skills in children.* New York: Wiley.

Forward, T. (2005). *The wolf's story: What really happened to Little Red Riding Hood.* Somerville, MA: Candlewick Press.

Friedman, T. (2000). *The Lexus and the olive tree: Understanding globalization.* New York: Anchor Books.

Friedman, T. L. (2006). *The world is flat: A brief history of the 21st century.* New York: Farrar, Straus & Giroux.

Global Studies Foundation, 2013. GSF Fact Sheet 1: The State of Global Studies in the United States. Retrieved from http://www.globalstudiesfoundation.org/publications.cfm?id=2

Government Accountability Office (2015). K-12 education: Most eighth grade students are not proficient in geography. Retrieved from http://www.gao.gov/assets/680/673128.pdf

Grossman, D., & Yuen, C. (2006). Beyond the rhetoric: A study of the intercultural sensitivity of Hong Kong secondary school teachers. *Pacific Asian Education, 18*(1), 70–87.

Hammer, M., and Bennett, M. (1998). *The Intercultural Development Inventory (IDI) Manual.* Portland, OR: Intercultural Communication Institute.

Hanvey, R. (1978). *An attainable global perspective.* New York: Center for Global Perspectives.

International Baccalaureate Organization, 2017. Retrieved from www.ibo.org

Longview Foundation. (2008). *Teacher preparation for the global age: The imperative for change.* Silver Springs, MD: Longview Foundation for World Affairs and International Understanding.

Lutkus, A. D., Weiss, A. R., Campbell, J. R., Mazzeo, J., & Lazer, S. (1999). *The NAEP civics report card for the nation.* Washington, DC: National Center for Education Statistics.

Mahon, J. (2003). Intercultural sensitivity development of practicing teachers. *Dissertation Abstracts International, 64*(7), 2353A (UMI No. 3097199).

Mahon, J. (2006). Under the invisibility cloak? Teacher understanding of cultural difference. *Intercultural Education, 17*(4), 391–407.

Mahon, J. (2009). Conflict style and cultural understanding among teachers in the western United States: Exploring relationships. *International Journal of Intercultural Relations, 33*(1), 46–56.

Miniwatts Marketing (2013). Internet World Stats Usage and Population Statistics. Retrieved from http://www.internetworldstats.com/stats.htm

National Center for Educational Statistics Fast Facts, 2016. Retrieved from https://nces.ed.gov/fastfacts/display.asp?id=372

National Council for the Social Studies (2016). Global and international education in social studies. Position statement revised and updated 2016. Retrieved from http://www.socialstudies.org/positions/global_and_international_education

Neuman, J. (1996). *Lights, camera, war: Is media technology driving international politics?* New York: St. Martin's Press.

Niemi, R., & Junn, J. (1998). *Civic education: What makes students learn.* New Haven, CT: Yale University Press.

Pappamihiel, E. (2004). Hugs and smiles: Demonstrating caring in a multicultural early childhood classroom. *Early Childhood Development and Care, 174*(6), 539–548.

Pederson, P. V. (1998). Intercultural sensitivity and the early adolescent. Doctoral dissertation, University of Minnesota. *Dissertation Abstracts International,* 9826849.

Pew Research (2013). Pew Internet & American Life Project. Retrieved from http://www.pewinternet.org/Reports/2013/Teens-and-Tech.aspx.

Remy, R. C., Nathan, J. A., Becker, J. M., & Torney, J. V. (1975). *International learning and international education in a global age.* National Council for the Social Studies, Bulletin 47, pp. 39–40.

Roberts, L. (2007). *Harnessing information technology for international education.* Retrieved from http://internationaled.org/PDKroberts.htm

Schorr, D. (1998, November 27). CNN effect: Edge-of-seat diplomacy. Christian Science Monitor, p. 11.

Scieszka, J. (1989). *The true story of the three little pigs as told by A. Wolf.* New York: Viking.

Selman, R., & Schultz, L. (1990). *Making a friend in youth: Developmental theory and pair therapy.* Chicago, IL: University of Chicago Press.

Stahlman, J., Safford, P., Pisarchick, S., Miller, C., & Dyer, D. (1989). Crossing the boundaries of early childhood special education personnel preparation: Creating a path for retraining. *Teacher Education and Special Education, 12*(1), 5–12.

Straffon, D. A. (2003). Assessing the intercultural sensitivity of high school students attending an international school. *International Journal of Intercultural Relations, 27,* 487–501.

UNHCR (United Nations High Commission on Refugees). (2016). Retrieved from http://www.unhcr.org/en-us/figures-at-a-glance.html

Teaching in a Linquistically Diverse Classroom

Understanding the Power of Language

Focus Questions

1. Do you remember learning to talk? If not, why not?

2. Think of occasions when you were speaking to someone and that person seemed not to understand what you meant. How many different reasons can you think of for this phenomenon?

3. What is the difference between an accent and a dialect?

4. Have you ever been speaking to someone who was standing too close to you for your comfort? Why do you think you felt uncomfortable?

5. How do you learn best? If faced with the need to learn something new, what would you do (e.g., read about it, talk to someone about it, have someone show you)?

6. What do you think about bilingual education? Is it necessary for some children? Does it hinder or help English language learners?

" Language is never neutral. "

SONIA NIETO

Case Study

Emma Lansing Learns to Listen to Language[1]

Emma Lansing was a student teacher at an elementary school in a southern university town and the first thing she learned in Mrs. McCord's first grade classroom was that she had to listen very carefully to the language spoken by everyone. More than anything else, this classroom held a really close-knit group of people—children and adults—who paid attention to language.

The reason for this was an approach to teaching language arts researched, developed, and tested by Mrs. McCord, called "language study," a way of teaching standard English in a linguistically diverse classroom that *at the same time* honors a wide variety of English accents and dialects by including them in classroom "talk." This also applies to languages other than English, such as those that her Spanish-speaking students brought with them into the classroom. It is a way of helping children learn to code-switch between language used at home or with friends, and language spoken in school and other more formal settings. In order to do this, you have to learn to *listen.*

When Emma arrived for her first day in late-August, she found a school in which 99% of the children received free and reduced breakfast and lunch. Other social differences were present as well: students from Mexican and South American families (70%) usually lived in brightly painted trailers where they and their families raised chickens and grew vegetables in backyard gardens. Students from African American families (25%) and white families (5%) were more likely to live on shady streets without sidewalks, where they played in large grassy areas.

In Mrs. McCord's classroom, Emma learned how the language study approach had been developed:

"Young children come to school steeped in their home language, lullabies, jokes, and family stories from infancy," explained Mrs. McCord. "It is hard to tell a 5- or 6-year-old that the language spoken by his or her mother, father, grandmother, grandfather, aunt, or uncle is 'wrong.' Casting doubt on the words used by a family to speak, to think, to dream either disconnects children from everything they already know, or may very well disconnect them from school itself."

"But the school requires them to learn standard English," protested Emma. "All the tests are in standard English!"

"That's right," responded Mrs. McCord. "And that's part of the problem. The children *need* to learn how to speak the language of power, the language spoken on television, in most books, and in the workplace in most places around the country. Linda Christensen, a white European American who spent 30 years teaching in the inner city of Portland, Oregon, was passionate about this. She said:

"We must teach our students how to match subjects and verbs, how to pronounce lawyer, because they are the ones without power and, for the moment, have to use the language of the powerful to be heard. But, in addition, we need to equip them to question an educational system that devalues their life and their knowledge. If we don't, we condition them to a pedagogy of consumption (Christensen 1996, 212)."

"Wow!" breathed Emma. "I never thought of it that way!"

"If we're to do both parts of that prescription," Mrs. McCord went on, "we must also include students' family dialects and languages in school. Those words, that grammar, that syntax, must have high status, too."

---

[1] This case study is an adaptation of the work of Dr. Jen McCreight in her first grade classroom, chronicled in McCreight, Jen. (2016). *Celebrating diversity through language study: A new approach to grammar lessons.* Portsmouth, NH: Heinemann. The new approach to teaching language arts in a linguistically diverse classroom, called Language Study, was researched, developed, and tested by Dr. McCreight. It has proved to be an effective way of engaging even very young students in understanding and negotiating the ways that they, and others, listen, speak, and respond.

"How do you do that?" asked Emma, thinking this was going to be a real challenge.

"Well, this approach that I call language study, in its simplest form, is a student-centered approach to grammar study. It has two main components: (1) to teach students how to negotiate the language they use based on context and (2) to build on *background knowledge* to make the study of words relevant for all children."

"How do you know student's background knowledge?" Emma asked.

"From the students, themselves, and from their families," answered Mrs. McCord. Indeed, the earliest goal of language study is to bring together children's home and school backgrounds. Actually, we're starting tomorrow."

Explaining that the first building block in language study is the language invitation, Mrs. McCord said, "The purpose of the invitation is first, to *engage* students in studying language by beginning conversations about how they use words daily, and second, to give you a chance to *assess* their prior knowledge and determine appropriate next steps. You'll see. I'm ready to extend the invitations."

Emma was a little dubious.

When Emma walked into the class the next morning, she saw that tables in the room had been rearranged; on one table were photographs of children on playgrounds; various kinds of houses of worship which with the children might be familiar; and pictures of sports, especially soccer, which is very popular with both Mexican and U.S. children. On a second table were children's story books that told about children in various places and circumstances, including *Flossie and the Fox*.[2] On a third table were clippings of newspaper stories and advertisements from magazines. And on a fourth table was a laptop and various videos of linguistically diverse read-aloud stories.

Seated at two of the tables were classroom volunteers, one of whom had a lilting Irish accent and sat at the newspaper clipping and advertisement table; the other was at the table with children's books. Mrs. McCord motioned Emma to the table containing photographs, and she, herself, took the laptop and story read-aloud table. The students were invited to select a table and begin examining the pictures, books, etc.

---

[2] *Flossie and the Fox*, by Patricia McKissack and Rachel Isadora, (New York, NY 1986). Dial Books. Read by Superbrashert1. https://www.youtube.com/watch?v=XIz5B0LgkG8

(*continued*)

As children explored the materials, adults asked questions. Emma, at the photo table, noticed that several of the children were engrossed in a picture of multiracial children at a playground.

"How are these kids speaking?" she asked. "What might they be talking about?" "Do you speak differently in different places?"

Looking at a picture of soccer teams from Mexico and the United States, two students had a long discussion about which language each team spoke. These students, Maria and Jorge, were from Guatemala and Mexico: both came from Spanish-speaking homes and lived next door to one another. Both also felt comfortable using Spanish in school. Eventually, they came to an agreement on the language of the teams: those players that had the Mexican flag on their uniforms probably spoke Spanish, while the players whose uniforms were red, white, and blue probably spoke English.

Later, Mrs. McCord told Emma that this had been a very important conversation because it showed that the students were thinking of *context*, choices in language use by relying on the *place-* and *person-based* considerations people make when they use words to communicate.

When the table conversations had kind of petered out, Mrs. McCord called the whole class together to discuss their impressions. Students spoke about language they used with family and language they used with friends. They noticed that people speak in different languages (e.g., Spanish or Chinese), and different media (newspapers, magazines, books, movies) for different purposes. They also wanted to learn about other languages and about dialects. "Why do some English words sometimes sound different?" asked several students.

"All in all," enthused Emma, "I think the kids learned a lot, and so did I!"

"That's good," Mrs. McCord smiled. "Because there are many more stages to this process. In a week or two, we'll start creating 'translation charts' with the students—sheets of paper with three columns drawn vertically so that students can study what different words we use at different times and for different occasions. For instance, in one column are words we use with family; in the second column, words we use with friends; and in the third column, words we use with other grown-ups, like teachers and principals. So, upon meeting people, we might say, "Hi! I'm home!" to family; "Dude, what's up?" to friends; and "Hello, how are you?" to other adults.

"After that," went on Mrs. McCord," we try to identify a language problem, such as not having many books in other languages or in multiple languages in our library. Then we create a plan to solve that problem, and then take action to remedy the problem. Then, we have a big celebration of language—a kind of party to which we invite our parents and other community folks. Finally, we meet together several times to reflect on what we've learned and where we go from there."

Emma had no more doubts. "This is great!" she said. "I can hardly wait to start making translation charts!"

Case Analysis

As the world "shrinks," American schools are increasingly seeing children coming into classrooms with dialects and languages other than standard English. Indeed, native-born children speak many different dialects of English, including African American Vernacular English (sometimes called Ebonics, or urban English), Mountain English (usually children from Appalachia), Cajun Vernacular English (mostly southern Louisiana and Eastern Texas), Hawaiian Creole English (sometimes called Pidgin), Latino Vernacular English (Chicago and Miami English), Pennsylvania Dutch English, Yeshiva English, and many more. This diversity of language forms is also the case in all English-speaking countries such as Canada, Australia, New Zealand, the United Kingdom, the Republic of Ireland, and many English-speaking island and continental countries in Central and South America. Nevertheless, students whose home languages are either dialects of English or another language altogether need to learn standard American

English in addition to their home languages because standard English is the language of power in the United States—it is used in school, in testing, on radio and television, on websites, and in workplaces.

Typically, such students are "taught" standard English by *correcting* inaccurate vocabulary and grammar both in speech and in writing, as well as through a great deal of *practice* in standard English. There are some fairly elaborate strategies for teaching English as a Second Language (ESL) students, and there is a brisk debate about the context in which they are used (there will be more about that later in the chapter). Since all languages, including dialects, have a particular structure, and often particular vocabulary and pronunciation, in Mrs. McCord's class students are taught standard English by *observation*, *study*, and *comparison*. Moreover, they are taught in a classroom community that honors all language differences and makes all language differences part of the study process. The fundamental idea is to learn where and when to use which language and with whom. Thus, the translation charts include family, friends, and other adults (or more formal situations), because the relationship between the speaker and the person spoken to matters as much as the place and the situation.

This process and skill is called **code-switching**, defined as the ability to shift between dialects or languages depending on the context of a situation (Genishi & Dyson, 2009). It is clearly a major goal in language study.

Characteristics of a Linguistically Diverse Classroom

Classrooms that are linguistically diverse are also usually culturally diverse. This is the case regardless of whether the classroom has students from other countries or students from different places in the United States, or both. Therefore, what is good practice in culturally diverse students is also good practice for those who are linguistically diverse because language is an important element of culture. Always remember that all students—whose first language is not English, those who speak an English dialect, and those that are standard English speakers—need to have lots of opportunities to learn words that may not be required in an ordinary conversation. Thus, the best classrooms for all these students will have a look, a feel, and sounds of a particular kind of classroom life that is easily discernable.

First, linguistically diverse classrooms are organized for activity. Student work covers the walls of halls and classrooms. Arrangements of classroom furniture and equipment vary according to the work being done in them: easy chairs or sofas for reading and conversation, tables for assembling books and newspapers, tables and counters for scientific work, computer corners, and open spaces for gathering people together. There is a sense of "purposeful clutter in these schools and classrooms. They are places to do things in, not places to sit and watch" (Wood, 1992, pp. xiii–xiv).

Second, everyone present in the classroom participates in this activity-oriented environment. Young children are eager to show off the books they have written; older students are engaged in activities that range from interviewing older community members to completing a scientific inventory of nearby plants and animals. Parents and teachers are often found working together to develop and implement instructional goals (McCaleb, 1994). Principals, teachers, parents, and students often work collaboratively on joint projects, such as publishing a newspaper or refurbishing the library. Because of all this ongoing activity, such schools and classrooms are rarely quiet, at least in the traditional sense of a school where adults talk and children listen.

©Getty Images/blue jean images RF

Third, in linguistically diverse classrooms, there is a sense that everyone belongs to the community: students, teachers, parents, administrators, support staff, volunteers, and other members of the broader community outside the school. Relationships among all people are collaborative, and each individual perceives all others as both teachers and learners. In a learning community, each individual is valued: cultural and linguistic identity is affirmed by using what each person brings to school as starting points and building blocks (McCaleb, 1994, p. xii).

The Need for Effective Linguistically Diverse Classrooms

So far, the image of effective linguistically diverse classrooms has been those in elementary schools, but they can be found in all levels of schooling, from pre-schools to high schools, and colleges as well. Between the 2003–2004 school year and the 2013–2014 school year, the number of English language learners (ELLs or ELs) in the United States grew from 4,217,026 to 4,460,956, an increase of nearly a half million students. And the numbers are growing (NCES, 2015).

Each of these students comes to the classroom with a first language; younger students may not have had schooling in their native languages, but most will have some. Older students, for the most part, will have been schooled in their first language and it will be foremost in their minds when they begin. Some students, particularly those who have come from active war zones, may be of an age (perhaps ages 6 to 12) to have been in school, but have not because there were no schools to go to, or their families were on the run or in refugee camps.

While there is a need to teach English to linguistically diverse students, it is important to remember that they also need to maintain and develop their first languages. This is because if a student knows content in one language, it is easier to identify words and ideas in another. At the beginning level, if one can read, even a few words, in one's first language, it is easier to learn to read those words in another language (Levitan, 2015).

It is also because "there is no more personal tool that bridges the gap between home and school than language." (McCreight, 2016, p. xvii). Again, this is the case whether the language is not English or is a dialect of English. School is strange enough when a 4- or 5-year-old first encounters it; if the language that child has spoken since babyhood is not found in school, it is all the more disconcerting.

Pedagogies: Old and New

Much has been written lately about new ways of teaching that are presumed to benefit a wider variety of students. Included in these new ways of teaching are labels such as interactive learning, engaged learning, inquiry learning, emancipatory curriculum, critical pedagogy, discovery learning, and collaborative learning. There are indeed some "new" aspects contained in these ideas, but in general they can all be grouped into the much more traditional category of good teaching. Moreover, most of them have been around for a long, long time.

Dialogue, for example, or what is sometimes known as interactive teaching and learning, is Plato's dialectic in contemporary dress. Discovery learning, or the use of teaching techniques that present students with questions and materials that impel students to active investigation, was the centerpiece of Abelard's teaching in the 12th century (Broudy & Palmer, 1965). Critical pedagogy, inquiry learning, and collaborative learning all hearken back at least to John Amos Comenius in the 17th century. He believed that understanding was more important than rote learning, that demonstration was more effective than listening to experts, that education should follow the natural development of the student, that students should teach and learn from one another, and that both text material and learning activities should incorporate the student's own experience as a starting point.

What is relatively new in linguistically diverse classrooms is not that such varied methods of instruction should exist, but that they should exist more or less simultaneously and be exercised by both children and adults. Their emphasis depends on the age of the student, the nature of the subject matter, and the kind of learning activities used. In a linguistically diverse classroom there is plenty of room for all the old methods of dialogue: telling, demonstrating, modeling, and problem posing. In addition, several relatively new ideas about teaching are often incorporated. One is that teaching strategies should attend to the development of "voice" among students. That is, teaching should encourage the expression of distinctive beliefs and experiences based on biological, sociocultural, and linguistic differences. In multilingual classrooms, teachers try to include all students in a wide variety of conversations and encourage all students to participate.

Roles: Old and New

As with pedagogy, traditional roles of adults and children in linguistically diverse classrooms are not so much changed as they are expanded. Thus, the role of teacher as teller is expanded to teacher as guide, as coach, as learner, and sometimes as cheerleader! The role of teacher is also expanded to include other adults—parents, administrators, and community members—who provide various types of specialized assistance to the regular classroom teacher. Similarly, the role of teacher is also extended to students, who serve as teachers and critics to one another. The role of learner, like that of teacher, is expanded in learning-community classrooms. Because everyone (teachers, students, administrators, parents, and community members) has unique experiences and specialized knowledge to share, it follows that everyone (adults included) will be a learner as well as a teacher.

Place of Content Knowledge: Old and New

In a linguistically diverse classroom, the place and function of content knowledge also varies, although it is certainly no less important than in traditional classrooms. Thus mathematics, language, history, science, and the arts serve in dual capacities. Sometimes such knowledge is learned as an end in itself, which is the more traditional approach to content. At other times, content knowledge serves as a means to another end, such as solving a problem or constructing a new way of looking at the world, which is the newer approach to content learning. More often than not, subject matter knowledge is acquired in the service of other goals. For example, if students need to produce a newspaper, they must know how to use language in intelligible ways. If students are going to measure the amount of rainfall during a storm, they must know about fractions and forms of measurement. Conversely, in traditional classrooms, it is likely that such subjects as language and mathematics are taught as ends in themselves, with applications of that knowledge coming later (or maybe not at all). In linguistically diverse classrooms, the project or activity often comes first, and the acquisition of English language knowledge and skills needed to accomplish the activity become necessary tools in the service of that activity. In this way, students come to appreciate the relevance of subject matter knowledge, and practice standard English at the same time.

Assessment: Old and New

In traditional classrooms, assessment or evaluation of student achievement is largely accomplished through the practice of paper-and-pencil testing. Moreover, the results of such assessment are often used to separate (track) students into homogeneous groups, presumably for their own benefit. Standardized commercial tests indicate to administrators and the community how "well" or "poorly" an individual student or teacher or class or school is doing in relation to other students, teachers, classes, and schools.

In linguistically diverse classrooms, such traditional paper-and-pencil forms of assessment are also used, especially in the now-almost-universal standards-based environment generated by the No Child Left Behind Act and its successor, the 2015 Every Student Succeeds Act. However, in a linguistically diverse classroom, these same tests are used for some additional purposes. For example, proficiency and unit tests are used for instructional feedback to individual students as well as for the purpose of grouping students or to provide interim or final grades. In addition, other forms of assessment including peer evaluation, portfolios, group tests, and self-evaluation are used. Teachers combine these various measures when judging what grade a student has earned.

At this point, you might be wondering how these ideas are related to the issues of individual biological, psychological, sociocultural, and linguistic differences discussed in the earlier chapters of this book. As an example, look at the ways in which one important source of cultural identity—language—might play out in a particular classroom.

Perspectives on First Language Acquisition

It is often said that language is what makes us human. Certainly, language is the primary means for socializing us into our families and our social groups and, through them, to acquiring our cultural identity. How humans developed the power of language and speech in the beginning has been a topic of great interest and even greater debate for several centuries. Since Alfred Russell Wallace and Charles Darwin developed the theory of evolutionary development, it has been widely accepted that the ability to create syntax (word order) to vocalize that word order (to speak), and to think or produce thought (using, of course words), must have developed in humans over a long period of time. Recent research, however, indicates that on the contrary, the faculty (or mechanism) of language appeared from a small mutation in one individual, and that all languages in the world are descended from a stone-age, East African dialect (Derbyshire, 2011). As the theory goes, about 100,000 years ago the mechanism of language appeared as a biolinguistic unit, in a small African population a bit prior to the large exodus of African populations to the rest of the world (Derbyshire, 2011).

Furthermore, human beings have the capacity to learn any language at all, which probably means that the *faculty* of language came before language itself. So, diversity of language is a testament to both the commonality and the variety of human beings. As Berwick and Chomsky (2016) recently wrote:

> We are born crying, but those cries herald the first stirrings of language. German babies' cries mirror the melody of German speech; French babies mirror French speech—apparently acquired *in utero* (Mampe et al., 2009). Within the first year or so after birth, infants master the sound system of their language, then, after another few years have passed, they are engaging their caretakers in conversation.

While debates about the origin of language go on, we can be a bit more down-to-earth and think about these linguistic commonalities and differences in a more practical way. For example, how did we experience language when we were just learning to talk?

Language and the Family

A number of scholars have referred to language as the first institution encountered by the individual (Berger & Berger, 1972; Boroditski, 2009; Port, 2010; Sinha, 2009). This conclusion may surprise you if you think of the family as being the first institution, the one that introduces us to language. Infants, however, can't know what a family is until they have acquired some form of language. Language objectifies, interprets, and justifies reality for the child, thus structuring the child's environment (Berger & Berger, 1972, pp. 68-69). It puts labels on roles (mommy, police officer, teacher) and permits the child to extend those roles into the wider community. It also brings the meanings and values of the wider community onto the small stage of the immediate family. Consider the case of the father in the act of punishing the child:

> As he punishes, he talks. What is he talking about? Some of the talking may just be a way of giving vent to his own annoyance or anger. But, in most cases, much of the talking is a running commentary on the offending act and the punishment it so richly deserves. The talking interprets and justifies the punishment. Inevitably, it does this in a way that goes beyond the father's own immediate reactions. The punishment is put in the vast context of manners and morals; in the extreme case, even the divinity may be invoked as a penal authority. . . . The punishing father now represents this system (pp. 69–70).

Institutional Aspects of Language in the Family

Language has several characteristics in common with other social institutions (Berger & Berger, 1972). First, *language is external*. It is experienced as "out there," in contrast to the individual's private thoughts or feelings (which, incidentally, are also structured by language and its meanings). Further, when an individual hears language spoken by another person, that person is speaking according to a particular language system that was created neither by the speaker nor the listener. It is external to them both.

Second, *language has objectivity*; that is, everyone who shares it agrees to accept the norms and conventions of its particular symbol system. Berger and Berger noted that "the objectivity of one's first language is particularly powerful" (p. 72). They wrote:

> Jean Piaget, the Swiss psychologist, tells the story somewhere of a small child who was asked whether the sun could be called anything except "sun." "No," replied the child. How did he know this, the child was asked. The question puzzled him for a moment. Then he pointed to the sun and said, "Well, look at it" (p. 72).

Third, *language has the power of moral authority to direct us*. As children learn to speak their native language, they are usually excused small lapses in pronunciation and usage. As they grow up, however, inappropriate use of language may very well expose them to ridicule, shame, and guilt. Consider the child who speaks a language or dialect different from that of the school, the working-class college student who is expected to engage in polite conversation at a formal reception, and the adult who tries to speak in the rapidly changing vernacular of her teenage children. Not only are these individuals often misunderstood, they are also often the objects of considerable disdain.

Finally, *language is historical*. It was there before we were born and will continue after we are gone. Its meanings were accumulated over a long period of time by myriad individuals now lost forever. Furthermore, language is a living, changing tool, with new words and meanings constantly being added, some for a few days, others for much longer. Some regard language as a "broad stream flowing through time" (p. 75). Berger and Berger wrote:

> An Austrian writer, Karl Kraus, has called language the house in which the human spirit lives. Language provides the lifelong context of our experience of others, of self, of the world. Even when we imagine worlds beyond this one, we are constrained to put our intimations or hopes in terms of language. Language is the social institution above all others. It provides the most powerful hold that society has over us (p. 75).

Given the power of language to shape us in many ways, it is well to keep in mind that it is not only our "own" language—formal or informal—that has such power. As Gonzalez (1974) noted,

> There is no such thing linguistically speaking as a good language or a bad language, a superior language or an inferior language. Each language is appropriate for its time, place, and circumstances. All languages are complete in this respect (p. 565).

Perspectives on Language Variation

A number of Mrs. McCord's classroom activities are designed to show how language varies from one group to another, as well as between individuals within the same group. Likewise, teachers and students sometimes speak different heritage languages, but more often, they speak the same language in different ways. Moreover, teachers and students use both verbal and nonverbal means to communicate significant messages to one another.

Verbal Communication

Whether over thousands of years or suddenly, 100,000 years ago, humans have developed the ability to produce, receive, store, and manipulate a variety of symbolic sounds. Human beings, more than any other creature, depend on the production of sound in the form of verbal language as their primary means of communication.

Within any given language, however, vocabulary, pronunciation, syntax (grammatical structure), and semantics (the meaning of words) may differ widely. Furthermore, the form in which language is conveyed may also differ, as, for example, in sign language where syntax is composed of a combination of specific movements of the fingers, hand, and arm as well as facial expressions. Most people are fascinated to watch this kind of speech, made public in recent years by signers who accompany performances on television or talks by public officials. As Mrs. McCord's students interviewed one another they were able to hear other variations in language, such as accents and dialects, as well.

Accents

An **accent** differs from the standard language only in the way words are pronounced, and it often results from pronunciation habits shared by people from a geographical region. People with a typical New England accent, for example, may pronounce the words *car, far,* and *bar* as if they were spelled caaa, faaa, and baaa. Similarly, people who have learned to speak English in Appalachia, the South, or the West may have significant differences in the way they pronounce the same words. People whose first language is not English may have difficulty pronouncing certain English words. Japanese speakers, for example, often have trouble with the letter *l,* and Russian speakers may have difficulty with the letters *w* and *v* as they are used in English words. Note that such speakers may be speaking quite proper standard English, but with an accent (Gollnick & Chinn, 2005).

Dialects

A **dialect** is a variation of some standard language form that includes differences in pronunciation, word usage, and syntax. Such differences may be based on ethnicity, religion, geographical region, social class, or age. Dialects differ not only in their origin but also in the specifics of their expression. Regional differences, for example, usually involve variations in the pronunciation of vowels (recall the example of people from New England). Similarly, people from southeastern Ohio, West Virginia, Kentucky, and Tennessee may have both Appalachian accents and also speak a dialect of English sometimes referred to as **mountain English.** Social dialects, on the other hand, are most often distinguished from one another by variations in the pronunciation of consonants, particularly the *th* sound and the sound of the consonants *r* and *l.* Regional and social dialects and accents may vary together or be a combination from a number of sociocultural origins, depending on the life experiences of the speaker. Although a variety of dialects are spoken in the United States, the three most widely known are **African American Vernacular English (AAVE), rural (or mountain) English,** and **standard English.**

African American Vernacular English is a dialect spoken primarily but not exclusively by urban African Americans. Although it is often associated with those who live in low-income communities, it is also spoken by African Americans from a variety of social classes and can serve, in part, as an expression of cultural identity. The influence of social class on African American Vernacular English is seen mainly in the ability of black English speakers to switch back and forth between their home language and standard English. One explanation for the origin of AAVE is that it is derived from Gullah, a Creole dialect developed by Africans brought to the United States as slaves, which puts English words into a syntax similar to many African languages. Another explanation sees it as a version of a regional English dialect spoken by early English settlers on the East Coast. Gullah is still spoken by some residents of the Sea Islands off the Carolina coast, and while many of the distinctive features of AAVE are similar to Gullah, it is also similar to other dialects spoken by European whites in some rural areas of the United States. Indeed, some scholars have found that similarities outweigh differences when comparing African American Vernacular English with standard English (Wolfram, Adger, & Christian, 1999).

Rural English, sometimes called mountain English, is a dialect spoken primarily in Appalachia and is derived from the language of early English settlers in the area. People from Appalachia are often ridiculed for their speech, but some linguists say that mountain English is the "purest" English spoken in the United States and the closest to the English spoken in Shakespeare's time. It has been preserved, in part, because of the isolation of mountain people, in the same way that Gullah has been preserved off the coast of the Carolinas.

Finally, middle-class European Americans may be surprised to learn that so-called standard English is also a dialect of the English language. Although the term "standard English" is usually taken to mean that version of the English language most acceptable or most "correct," there are, in fact, many varieties of standard English. Gollnick and Chinn (2005) noted that "the speech of a certain group of people in each community tends to be identified as standard" (p. 253). Moreover, standard English as it is spoken in countries such as Australia, India, Nigeria, and England differs significantly from standard English as it is spoken in the United States (Tiedt & Tiedt, 1995). Standard English, as the term is used in U.S. schools, usually refers to that dialect spoken by educated middle and upper classes and to the formal written and oral English that dominates print and broadcast media.

Bidialectalism

Bidialectalism refers to the ability to speak two (and sometimes more) dialects and to switch back and forth easily. Examples of people engaging in bidialectalism are the country boy who has become an executive in a large city and switches dialects when he goes back to his hometown, or the African American woman who has become a professor and speaks standard English but switches to AAVE when speaking informally to African American colleagues, students, or friends. The ability to "code-switch," which is so important in Mrs. McCord's class is often encouraged in schools as a way of enabling youngsters to both broaden their language horizons and receive the perceived economic and social benefits of speaking standard English. Although research does not support the belief that it is necessary to speak standard English in order to read or write it, it is often the case that prejudice against those who speak nonstandard dialects may lead to economic and social discrimination (Grossman, 1995).

Sign Language

Although sign language is often thought of as nonverbal communication, it is also a form of verbal expression. One form of sign language is the language of signs spoken by the deaf. Several varieties of signed communication exist, notably **American Sign Language** (ASL), which is the only sign system recognized as a language in the United States (sign languages also exist in other countries); signed English, which translates oral or written English into signs; and finger spelling (sometimes called the manual alphabet), which literally spells out English words letter by letter. Very young children acquired ASL in infancy in the same way that their hearing classmates learned oral language. Like other languages, ASL has its own syntax and rhythms. Young deaf children learn to think in it and translate other sign languages and lip reading into ASL. Closely associated with the culture of the deaf, ASL is the subject of often-heated debate in educational circles. Some educators believe that all deaf or hearing-impaired children should learn to speak orally; others believe that signed communication is not only sufficient but that these individuals—both hearing and hearing-impaired—are bilingual in ASL and English.

Nonverbal Communication

Nonverbal communication, used by both hearing and hearing-impaired individuals, refers to body movements, facial expressions, and a variety of word replacement strategies. It has been estimated that nonverbal communication accounts for 50% to 90% of the messages we send and receive (Barnlund, 1968). In 1973 Leubitz identified four functions of nonverbal communication: (1) to convey messages; (2) to augment verbal communication; (3) to contradict verbal communication; and (4) to replace verbal communication. For purposes of analysis, three aspects of nonverbal behavior are usually studied: **proxemics** (the culturally determined comfortable distance between people when they are speaking with one another), **kinesics** (the study of body movements), and **paralanguage** (sounds made by the voice that are not words such as crying, sighing, and word substitutes such as "Shhh") (as cited in Gollnick & Chinn, 2005, pp. 218–219). It is well to remember, however, that these nonverbal aspects of communication are seldom used or experienced individually; rather, they combine in various ways with one another and with verbal language to produce the innumerable nuances we take for granted in ordinary communication.

Perspectives on Second-Language Acquisition

With increasing immigration to the United States in recent decades, schools are being faced with the challenges of large numbers of children for whom English is not their first language. This is not a new phenomenon for American schooling. Contrary to popular belief, **bilingual education** is not a creation of the 1960s, although the civil rights movement gave it renewed emphasis. Indeed, Ohio was the first state to pass a bilingual education law in 1839—allowing German-English instruction if parents requested it. Similar laws were enacted in Louisiana for French and English in 1847 and in the New Mexico territory for Spanish and English in 1850. By the turn of the 20th century, many local districts and nearly a dozen states were providing bilingual education in languages including Norwegian, Italian, Polish, Czech, and Cherokee (History of Bilingual Education, 1998). At that time, at least 600,000 children in primary schools (public and parochial) received part or all of their instruction in German—about 4% of all American elementary students.

Bilingualism and the Law: 1960-2015

Nativist fears stemming from World War I changed the political winds, however, and by the mid-1920s bilingual education provisions were replaced by English-only laws in a majority of states. The ferment surrounding civil rights in the 1960s brought renewed interest in bilingual education. In the 12-year period from 1963 to 1975, private and governmental studies and hearings and a series of lawsuits regarding rights to native language instruction, placement of children with disabilities, and desegregation produced many mandates for the schooling of minority students. Concurrently, new educational strategies and curricula, especially in bilingual and bicultural education, appeared in districts across the nation. The Bilingual Education Act was passed in 1968 as Title VII of the Elementary and Secondary Education Act. President Lyndon Johnson clarified the intent of this law in the following words:

This bill authorizes a new effort to prevent dropouts; new programs for handicapped children; new planning help for rural schools. It also contains a special provision establishing bilingual education programs for children whose first language is not English. Thousands of children of Latin descent, young Indians, and others will get a better start—a better chance—in school (as cited in Tiedt & Tiedt, 1995, p. 6).

In 1970, the Office of Civil Rights Guidelines tried unsuccessfully to make special training for non-English-speaking students a requirement for public schools that receive federal aid. The office stated:

Where inability to speak and understand the English language excludes national origin–minority group children from effective participation in the education program offered by a school district, the district must take affirmative steps to rectify the language deficiency in order to open its instructional program to these students (as cited in Tiedt & Tiedt, 1995, p. 6).

A significant case in the development of multicultural and multilingual education was *Lau v. Nichols,* decided by a 1974 Supreme Court ruling. This decision declared that a San Francisco school district violated a non-English-speaking Chinese student's right to equal educational opportunity when it failed to provide needed English language instruction and other special programs. An important consequence of the *Lau* decision was the declaration that school districts across the country must provide students an education in languages that meet their needs. Other cases followed, making the same arguments for African American and Latino students.

In 1981, a pedagogically sound plan for **limited English proficient** (LEP) students was set by the Fifth Circuit Court in Texas in *Casteñada v. Pickard.* The plan required a sufficient qualified staff to implement the plan, including hiring new staff and training current staff, as well as the establishment of a system to evaluate the programs. It is important to note that a formal "bilingual education" program was not required; however, it did require that "appropriate action to overcome language barriers" be taken through well-implemented programs.

The debate on the requirement that schools provide special programs for English language learners, and the degree of that provision, is still a matter of debate today, although as a matter of policy, the nation has once again reverted to preference for English-only programs. In the fall of 2009, for example, the Supreme Court ruled, in *Horne v. Flores,* that Arizona's funding for programs that serve English language learners does not violate the terms of the Equal Educational Opportunities Act, and that states are free to develop their own funding plans for such programs. This case, fought in the courts since 1992, is an example of the debate about "how much funding is enough" to provide sufficient resources for teaching English language learners. In *Flores,* the Supreme Court overturned two lower courts, which had found in favor of those who asserted that, in fact, state funding was insufficient.

The Current Debate on How to Teach English Learners (ELs)

When the **No Child Left Behind Act** (NCLB)—the 2001 reauthorization of the Elementary and Secondary Education Act (ESEA)—was signed, several things happened to the Bilingual Education Act. First, it was moved from Title VII of ESEA to Title III of NCLB. Second, it was renamed *The Language Instruction for Limited English Proficient and Immigrant Students*. Third, it did not make any distinctions between bilingual (learning two languages at once) and non-bilingual programs (usually English immersion programs, often called ESL or English as a Second Language programs). Because of the accountability (testing) measures central to NCLB, the issue of how and when to test English language learners in English rather than in their native language became a point of dispute. Particularly concerned with "making" annual yearly progress mandated under NCLB, school districts began instituting addition time on learning English, thus interrupting (and sometimes ruining) dual language programs in which students were making progress in both their native language and English, which is the kind of program undertaken by Mrs. McCord.

With the passage of the **Every Student Succeeds Act (ESSA)** in December 2015, responsibility and funding for English learners remains in Title III, plus funding has increased due to the increase in the numbers and percentage of English learners in the United States. Further, measures for accountability have softened somewhat into the following two choices:

- For one year, exclude the student from taking the reading/English language arts test and from counting results of either or both the math and English language arts tests; OR

- For the first year of the student's enrollment in a U.S. school, report on but exclude from accountability system the results on these tests; for the second year of enrollment, include a measure of student growth on both tests; and for the third year of enrollment, include proficiency on both tests in the accountability system.

Here we still see an "English-only" bias, associated with legislators' sense of urgency that these students learn to speak English as rapidly as possible so that they can be tested and not be left too long outside the call for accountability. But the measures allowed in ESSA do recognize that students' first language is a very important element in the transition to English.

Understanding Terminology

One of the difficulties in discussing second language acquisition is the terminology that has developed as more research has been done and the laws have changed. Judie Haynes (2010) noted that:

All of the following terms are used to refer either to programs or "students: who are learning to understand, speak, read, and write in English."

Programs

- **ESL** (*English as a Second Language*). This term generally refers to programs in the United States.

- **EFL** (*English as a Foreign Language*). This term refers to students learning English in a foreign country. For example, Chinese students studying English in China are in an EFL program.

- **ESOL** (*English to Speakers of Other Languages*). This term is used to describe programs in different parts of the United States, primarily in the South.

- **ENL** (*English is a New Language*). This term is used by the National Board for Professional Teaching Standards.

Students

- **ELL or El** (*English Language Learner, or English learner*). This is the term most often used to describe students who are learning English in the United States.

- **LEP** (*Limited English Proficiency*). This term is used to describe ELLs by laws and government documents. Many consider it a pejorative term.

- **Bilingual.** This term refers to the fact that students speak more than one language. It can also refer to a program where students receive content information in their native language.

Just as there are many different ways to discuss English learners and their programs, so there are a number of different kinds of programs. The following are a sample of the most frequently found kinds of ESL programs:

- *Two-Way Immersion/Dual Language.* A native English-speaking group and a non-English group (e.g., Spanish speakers) are both taught academic content in both languages for an extended period of time. Both groups develop academic proficiency in both languages.

- *Transitional Bilingual Education.* ELLs receive academic instruction in their first language for part of the day. For the remainder of the day, they receive ESL taught traditionally, with the focus on language, plus some mainstream classes. As English proficiency increases, instruction through the first language decreases. The program lasts 2 years to 4 years.

- *ESL Pullout.* Students attend mainstream classes for much of the day and also meet separately for about 3 hours to 10 hours a week in small groups with an ESL instructor who focuses on language development.

- *Content-Based ESL.* ELLs receive ESL instruction, taught by an ESL licensed teacher, in preparation for grade-level content instruction in English. The emphasis is still on language development, but augmented with academic subject matter vocabulary and beginning concepts.

- *Sheltered English Instruction.* ELLs are taught academic content in English by a content licensed teacher. However, the English language used for instruction is adapted to the proficiency level of the students. While the instruction focuses on content, sheltered English instruction also promotes English language development.

- *Structured English Immersion.* ELLs are taught subject matter in English by a content licensed teacher who is also licensed in ESL or bilingual education. The teacher is proficient in the first language of the student. Students may use their native language for clarification, but the teacher uses only English. No ESL instruction is provided in this model.

- *Heritage Language.* A program where ELLs are taught literacy in the language the student regards as his or her native, home, and/or ancestral language. This covers indigenous languages (e.g., Arapaho and Shoshone) and immigrant languages (e.g., Spanish). The intent is to provide literacy skills that can then transfer to English language acquisition.

- *Specially Designed Academic Instruction in English (SDAIE).* A program of instruction in a subject area, delivered in English, which is specially designed to provide ELL students with access to the curriculum.

- *Native Language Literacy.* Language arts instruction focuses on developing oral language, reading, and writing skills in the student's first language. Teachers fluent in the students' native language provide instruction utilizing techniques, methodology, and special curriculum in the students' primary language.

- *Parental refusal students.* Districts that have students whose parents have refused the ELL services offered by the district must still provide the ELL student with the services necessary to acquire English fluency and access the academic content of the curriculum. This places the burden of ELL services on the mainstream classroom teacher who must provide appropriate accommodations and adjust teaching to the student appropriately in order for the student to access the content and acquire English. (Dept. of Ed., State of Wyoming n/d).

Stages in Second Language Acquisition

Years of research on the factors involved in learning a second language have produced agreement that second-language learners will move sequentially through these six predictable stages of language acquisition (Robertson & Ford, n/d).

1. *The silent/receptive or preproduction stage.* This is also called "the silent period," when the student takes in the new language but does not speak it. ELLs need time to listen to others talk, to digest what they hear, to develop receptive vocabulary, and to observe their classmates' interactions. This stage can last from 10 hours to 6 months.

2. *The early production stage.* In this stage the individual begins to speak using short words and sentences, but the emphasis is still on listening and absorbing the new language. There will be many errors in the early production state. This stage can last an additional 6 months.

3. *The speech emergence stage.* In this stage, lasting up to another year, speech becomes more frequent, words and sentences are longer, but the individual still relies heavily on context clues and familiar topics. Vocabulary continues to increase and errors begin to decrease, especially in common or repeated interactions. This can take 1 year to 3 years.

4. *The beginning fluency stage.* In this stage speech is fairly fluent in social situations with minimal errors. New contexts and academic language are challenging and individuals will struggle to express themselves due to gaps in vocabulary and appropriate phrases.

5. *The intermediate language proficiency stage.* In this stage communicating in the second language is fluent, especially in social language situations. The individual is able to speak almost fluently in new situations or in academic areas, but there will be gaps in vocabulary knowledge and some unknown expressions. There are very few errors, and the individual is able to demonstrate higher order thinking skills in the second language such as offering an opinion or analyzing a problem. This stage may take another year.

6. *The advanced language proficiency stage.* In this stage the individual communicates fluently in all contexts and can maneuver successfully in new contexts and when exposed to new academic information. At this stage, the individual is essentially fluent and comfortable communicating in the second language. To achieve this stage often takes 2 years to 5 years.

Because students go through these stages in different time periods, it is usually understood that it takes 5 years to 7 years to fully acquire a second language. No school district in the United States allows that much time. Ordinarily, students in classes in English as a second language are expected to be in all-English classes after 3 years at the most.

Understanding the Difference between Social and Academic Language Acquisition

The expectation that school districts have about the length of time it takes ELLs to become fluent in English often ignores the important distinction between social language and academic language. As Haynes (2007) described it,

> **"Basic Interpersonal Communication Skills (BICS)** are language skills needed in social situations. It is the day-to-day language needed to interact socially with other people. English language learners (ELLs) employ BIC skills when they are at the playground, at lunch, at parties, playing sports, and talking with friends. Social interactions are usually context embedded. They occur in a meaningful social context. They are not very demanding cognitively. The language required is not specialized. These language skills usually develop within 6 months to 2 years. Problems arise when teachers and administrators think that a child is proficient in a language when he or she demonstrates good social English."
>
> **"Cognitive Academic Language Proficiency (CALP)** refers to formal academic learning. This includes listening, speaking, reading, and writing about subject area content material. This level of language learning is essential for students to succeed in school. Students need time and support to become proficient in academic areas. This usually takes from 5 years to 7 years."
>
> **"**Academic language acquisition isn't just the understanding of content area vocabulary. It includes higher-level skills such as comparing, classifying, synthesizing, evaluating, and inferring. Academic language tasks are context reduced. Information is read from a textbook or presented by the teacher. As a student gets older the context of academic tasks becomes more and more reduced. The language also becomes more and more cognitively demanding. New ideas, concepts, and languages are presented to the students at the same time."

Research on the difference between BICS and CALP tends to show that schools should enable teachers and ELLs to have more time devoted not only to social language learning but to academic language learning as well. Rushing students through a language support program, no matter how good it is, will not develop academic language skills to the extent needed. It would also be well to provide more support for upper elementary and middle school students who have been unschooled in their native language. In addition, maintenance (and growth) of students' first languages should be encouraged, in the home and in school. As you may have noted, Mrs. McCord would approve of all these recommendations!

Other Important Concepts in Second Language Acquisition

Considerable agreement has also been achieved on several contextual factors involved in acquiring a second language. One of these is the "affective filter hypothesis" (Krashen, 1981; Krashen & Terrell, 1983), which suggests that emotions are a factor in the ease or difficulty in learning another language. In particular, negative emotions such as anxiety, embarrassment, or anger produced by early attempts to speak a second language can produce a kind of filter that gets in the way of the learner's ability to process new or difficult words.

Other important contextual factors are: (1) the linguistic distance between two languages (how different they are from one another); (2) the student's level of proficiency in his or her first language (including not only speaking but also reading and writing); (3) the dialect of the first language (whether it is standard or nonstandard); (4) the relative status of the student's first language in the community; and (5) social attitudes toward the student's first language (Waiqui, 2000).

Of particular importance in English language acquisition is the need to build upon the child's knowledge of his or her *first* language. Research on the role of the first language demonstrated the relationship between language acquisition and the overall personal and educational development of children (Baker, 1988; Cummins, 2000). This research has resulted in the following findings:

- Developing abilities in two or more languages throughout the primary school years provides a deeper understanding of language and how to use it effectively.

- The level of development of children's first language is a strong predictor of their second-language development.

- School acceptance and promotion of various first languages helps develop not only the first language but also the majority school language.

- Instructional time taken in a child's first language does not inhibit development in the majority school language.

- First languages are fragile and easily lost in the early years of school.

- To reject a child's language in the school is, in large measure, to reject the child.

Instructional approaches or strategies in teaching children who are English language learners is available from a variety of sources, but one of the most complete is from the Education Alliance at Brown University. Strategies discussed focus on listening, making connections between what the child is reading and what the child already knows, modeling language use for the child, daily sharing as a part of the school day, having regular conversations with students about their reading and writing, and providing lots of opportunities for students to practice speaking, reading, and writing (Teaching Diverse Learners, n.d.)

As Cummins (2000) noted,

> In short, the cultural, linguistic and intellectual capital of our societies will increase dramatically when we stop seeing culturally and linguistically diverse children as "a problem to be solved" and instead open our eyes to the linguistic, cultural, and intellectual resources they bring from their homes to our schools and societies.

Ethical Issues: Local and Global

Teaching linguistically diverse students also entails ethical and moral issues. Mrs. McCord, for example, is aware that students who speak another language, or who speak dialects of standard English, are likely to be stigmatized by other students as well as by school policies, particularly in schools without well-developed programs for English language learners.

Most U.S. schools, and a majority of the general public, are committed to the proposition that all students learn and perform effectively in standard English, which is the language of choice by the dominant social group. Therefore, debates about bilingual education and English as a second language revolve as much around issues of cultural domination and subordination as they do around what is best for individual students. In short, the debate about bilingual education is part of a larger debate about who controls the school curriculum and for what purposes.

Another ethical issue is the degree to which assessment of student progress is measured by culture-biased tests that favor students who are already fluent in standard English. It is likely, for example, that a student may be quite knowledgeable about a subject matter but cannot express his or her knowledge in the manner required by certain kinds of tests. Similarly, most traditional assessment instruments tend to favor students who are field independent rather than global learners, who are visual learners rather than auditory or kinesthetic learners, and who prefer to work alone rather than in cooperative groups. In recent years, alternative forms of performance-based assessment have been designed that enable teachers to accurately assess progress for those students who do better with other styles of learning. However, such assessments are relatively slow in being incorporated into statewide, government-mandated tests. In the meantime, teachers like Mrs. McCord must find ways to demonstrate that their students are, in fact, learning effectively according to current, proficiency-based assessment strategies.

A third ethical issue is a global one and concerns the degree to which language provides the keys to understanding other people in an increasingly interdependent world. Globalization, worldwide television (especially cable news networks such as CNN), and the Internet have tended to make English a worldwide standard language. Indeed, more than 60 countries now use English in an official capacity. Moreover, globalization of communication, a growing world urbanization, the spread of Western cultural and media products, and a disdain for the traditional all contribute to the loss of small, community-based languages (Wallmont, 2003).

Critical Incident

Mrs. McCord's Dilemmas

Many of the students in Mrs. McCord's classroom speak a second language or a dialect other than standard English—especially at home. She also realizes that many of them are likely to be stigmatized by other students as well as by school policies, particularly in schools without well-developed programs for English language learners.

• What should she do given this reality in her classroom?

• What should she do for her students as individuals?

• What would you do?

Increasingly, especially since the No Child Left Behind legislation was enacted, children are faced with demonstrating their competence and achievement using standardized tests, which may not be as effective at accurately assessing children from some backgrounds. In the meantime, teachers like Mrs. McCord must find ways to demonstrate that their students are, in fact, learning effectively according to current, proficiency-based assessment strategies.

• How might she approach this dilemma?

Summary

Classrooms that are linguistically diverse seem to typify the need for effective teaching and learning in the 21st century. Of particular importance in this regard is attentiveness to the language or languages of students and teachers and to the ways in which all individuals naturally approach teaching and learning. Clearly, language structures the very thoughts and ideas we have as human beings. Not only do we have particular vocabularies that have meaning for us, but we also structure our sentences and pronounce our words in particular ways that we have learned as part of our primary socialization as young children and that therefore seem comfortable and "right" to us.

In classrooms where children of diverse backgrounds attempt to learn a prescribed curriculum, teachers must pay attention to the students' linguistic backgrounds so that they can be certain that all children are effectively understanding and participating in all learning activities. Teachers who are working with children whose first language is not English must remember that each child's language is an integral part of that child's personhood, and must make every attempt to regard that personhood with respect. Both the proponents and opponents of bilingual education want children to learn; they disagree—sometimes profoundly—on the best means (and the best language) to achieve that goal. Because of the history of the bilingual education debate and because of the increasing interconnectedness of today's world, teachers must be clear in their own minds about the relative merits of bilingual education.

Chapter Review

Go to the Online Learning Center at www.mhhe.com/cushner9e to review important content from the chapter, practice with key terms, take a chapter quiz, and access active workbook activities.

Key Terms

accent 255
American Sign Language 256
bidialectalism 256
bilingual 260
bilingual education 257
code-switching 249
dialect 255
English as a foreign language (EFL) 259

English as a new language (ENL) 259
English as a second language (ESL) 259
English language learner (ELL or EL) 260
English to speakers of other languages (ESOL) 259
Every Student Succeeds Act (ESSA) 259

kinesics 257
limited English proficient (LEP) 258
mountain English 255
No Child Left Behind Act (NCLB) 258
paralanguage 257
proxemics 257
rural English 255
standard English 255

Interviewing Non–Native English Speakers About Their Experiences in This Country

Purpose: To raise awareness and sensitivity and learn about the problems faced by new speakers of English.

Instructions: Interview a person who first came to the United States speaking limited or no English. This person might be an international student on campus, or a student or parent who came to the United States speaking minimal English (feel free to adjust the following questions accordingly to accommodate the person you are interviewing).

1. Describe some of the initial difficulties or problems you encountered when you first arrived in this country. To what would you attribute the problems?

2. What significant cultural differences did you encounter in the early stages of your adjustment to this country? How did you overcome these?

3. What primary language did you speak before coming to the United States? Describe your competency as a speaker of your home language. Describe your competency as a speaker of English today.

4. What communication problems did you experience when you first came to this country? How did you handle these?

5. What kinds of communication difficulties, if any, do you or your children currently face?

6. What might people (or schools and/or teachers if interviewing a child or parent) in the United States do that would help to reduce adjustment and communication difficulties for new immigrants?

7. What messages do you have for other non-English speakers that might make their adjustment and communication easier?

8. What can you conclude about communication, culture shock, and adjustment that would be useful for teachers?

Classroom Activities

1. In the elementary classroom, experiment to see what the "comfort zone" is for each student. Draw a circle with a diameter of about 3 feet on the floor with chalk, and ask students to take turns standing in the middle of the circle. Then, ask another student to stand with his or her toes on the outside of the line. Does the student in the circle feel comfortable with another student standing this close to him or her? Can the "outside" student move closer (cross the line) without making the "inside" student uncomfortable? Do this until all students have had a chance to be "inside" and "outside." Keep track of the results. Discuss with students the importance of *proxemics* and whether or not their experience with this activity can be in any way attributed to cultural ideas.

2. Another nonverbal form of communication is called *kinesics*, and relates to the way in which human beings communicate with body movements. Ask for six volunteers to stand in front of the class and try to communicate the following ideas to the rest of the class without saying anything: anger, sadness, excitement, disgust, sympathy, boredom. Give each student a piece of paper with the feeling or idea he or she is to demonstrate. As each student adopts the stance, facial expression, or other body movement for his or her term, ask the rest of the class to describe what they see in the demonstrator's body movement. When each feeling or idea has been expressed and noted, discuss with the class how they "knew" what the student was demonstrating.

3. a high school classroom, students can be assigned to research the way or ways in which their school district deals with English language learners. Ask students to find out the history of the program or policy in that district, how many ELL students there are, how successful the program appears to be, and any debates surrounding the program or policy. If there is no program or policy, ask students to interview a school board member, or someone in the superintendent's office to find out why there is no program or policy.

4. Another activity for high school students is to ask a faculty member or parent or community member who speaks another language fluently to come to class and begin speaking to the students in that language. Teachers might provide a

little more stress by first telling the students that the visitor will be giving them instructions on a project that will be a part of their unit grade. Ask the speaker to speak for at least 5 minutes. When he or she is finished speaking, ask all students to write a short essay on how the experience affected them, and what it might be like to be an English language learner in their school.

Reflective Questions

Clearly, establishing a linguistically diverse classroom like Mrs. McCord's first grade class is fraught with both difficulties and possibilities. Put yourself in Mrs. McCord's place, at this early point in the school year, and answer the questions she is asking herself:

1. How am I going to create a democratic, linguistically diverse classroom culture when my students come from such different backgrounds? and speak so many different languages and dialects?

2. How am I going to discourage standard English speakers from stigmatizing those students whose language differences are often rejected in American schools?

3. How am I going to provide ways in which all my students can participate fully in the life of the classroom?

4. How am I going to create a classroom environment in which students can teach each other effectively?

5. How am I going to organize instruction so that all students can have equal access to the material at hand?

6. How many of my students' parents are able and willing to come into the classroom to assist in teaching? How do I find that out?

Endnote

This case study is an adaptation of the work of Dr. Jen McCreight in her first grade classroom, chronicled in McCreight, Jen. (2016). *Celebrating diversity through language study: A new approach to grammar lessons.* Portsmouth, NH: Heinemann. The new approach to teaching language arts in a linguistically diverse classroom, called Language Study, was researched, developed, and tested by Dr. McCreight. It has proved to be an effective way of engaging even very young students in understanding and negotiating the ways that they, and others, listen, speak, and respond.

References

Anderson, L. (2001, May 29). Bilingual debate reaches boiling point. *Chicago Tribune.*

Baker, C. (1988). *Key issues in bilingualism and bilingual education.* Clevedon, UK: Multilingual Matters.

Barnlund, D. (1968). *Interpersonal communication: Survey and studies.* Boston: Houghton Mifflin.

Berger, P., & Berger, B. (1972). *Sociology: A biographical approach.* New York: Basic Books.

Berwick, R. C., & Chomski, N. (2016). *Why only us? Language and evolution.* Cambridge, MA: The MIT Press.

Boroditski, L. Lost in translation. *The Wall Street Journal* (July 23, 2010). Online at http://online.wsj.com/article/SB10001424052748703467304575383131592767868.html#printMode

Broudy, H., & Palmer, J. R. (1965). *Exemplars of teaching method.* Chicago: Rand McNally.

Castañeda v. Pickard, 648 F2d 989 (1981).

Christensen, Linda. (1996). Whose standard? Teaching standard English. In Power, Brenda M. and Hubbard, Ruth S., Eds. *Language development: A reader for teachers.* Upper Saddle River, NJ: Prentice-Hall.

Cummins, J. (2000). *Bilingual children's mother tongue: Why is it important for education?* Retrieved from http://www.iteachilearn.com/cummins/mother.htm

Department of Education, State of Wyoming, n/d. Types of ELL programs. Retrieved from https://edu.wyoming.gov/...programs/EMM_ELL_program_type_definitions.pdf.

Department of Statistics of Georgia (2004). *Statistics on population of Georgia.* Retrieved from www.statistics.ge

Derbyshire, David. (2011). Is this how Eve spoke? Every human language evolved from 'single prehistoric African mother tongue.' Daily mail. com. Retrieved from http://www.dailymail.co.uk/sciencetech/article-1377150/Every-language-evolved-single-prehistoric-mother-tongue-spoken-Africa.html.

Digital Chalkboard. (2009–2015). *Culturally and linguistically diverse students.* Retrieved from https://www.mydigitalchalkboard.org/portal/default/Content/Viewer/Content?action=2&scId=100051&sciId=1458

Genishi, C., & Dyson, A. H. (2009). *Children, language and literacy in diverse times.* New York: Teachers College Press.

Gonzalez, G. (1974). Language, culture, and exceptional children. *Exceptional Children, 40,* 8.

Grossman, H. (1995). *Teaching in a diverse society.* Boston: Allyn & Bacon.

Haynes, Judie. (2007). Explaining BICS and CALP. Retrieved from http://www.everythingesl.net/inservices/bics_calp.php.

Haynes, J. (2010). Understanding second language terminology. Retrieved from http://www.everythingesl.net/inservices/essential_vocab.php

History of bilingual education. (1998, spring). *Rethinking Schools, 12,* 3. Retrieved from http://www.rethinkingschools.org/archive/12_03/langhst.shtml

Hogan-Brun, G., & Ramoniene, M. (2004). Changing levels of bilingualism across the Baltic. *Bilingual Education and Bilingualism, 7*(1), 62–77.

Hornberger, N. (2000). Bilingual education policy and practice in the Andes: Ideological paradox and intercultural possibility. *Anthropology & Education Quarterly, 31*(2), 173–201.

Hornberger, N., & Ricento, T. (1996) Unpeeling the onion: Language planning and policy and the ELT professional. *TESOL Quarterly, 30*(3), 401–428.

Horne v. Flores 129 S.C. 2579 (2009).

Krashen, S. D. (1981). *Second language acquisition and second language learning.* New York: Pergamon Press.

Krashen, S. D., & Terrell, T. D. (1983). *The natural approach: Language acquisition in the classroom.* Englewood Cliffs, NJ: Prentice Hall.

Lau v. Nichols, 414 U.S. 563 (1974).

Leubitz, Lois. (1973). *Nonverbal communication: A guide for teachers.* Lincolnwood, IL: National Textbook Company.

Levitan, J. (2015). Bilingual students need support in their native language." *Education Week*, May 13, 2015. Retrieved from http://www.edweek.org/ew/articles/2015/05/13/bilingual-students-need-support-in-their-native.html?qs=bilingual+students+need+support+in+their+native+language+.

McCaleb, S. P. (1994). *Building communities of learners: A collaboration among teachers, students, families, and community.* New York: St. Martin's Press.

Mampe, B., Friederici, A. D., Christophe, A. & Wermke, K. (2009). Newborns' cry melody is shaped by their native language. *Current Biology 19* (23): 1194-1997.

Mejia, A., & Tejada, H. (2003). Bilingual curriculum construction and empowerment in Colombia. *International Journal for Bilingual Education and Bilingualism, 6*(1), 37-51.

NCES, (2015). Digest of Education Statistics. and percentage of public school students participating in programs for English language learners, by state: Selected years, 2003-04 through 2013-14. Retrieved from https://nces.ed.gov/programs /digest/d15/tables/dt15_204.20.asp, March 24, 2017.

Nieto, S. (2005). Public education in the twentieth century and beyond: High hopes, broken promises, and an uncertain future. *Harvard Educational Review, 75*(1), 1-20.

Neito, S. (2016). Foreword. In McCreight, J. *Celebrating diversity through language study: A new approach to grammar lessons.* Portsmouth, NH: Heinemann, p. ix.

Perna, L. W., & Swail, W. S. (2000). A view of the landscape: Results of the national survey of outreach programs. *Outreach program handbook 2001* (pp. xi-xxix). New York: The College Board.

Port, R. F. (2010). Language as a social institution: Why phonemes and words do not live in the brain. *Ecological Psychology 22*, 304-326. Online at http://www.cs.indiana .edu/~port/pap/port%20lg%20as%20social%20intstn%20EcoPsycg2010.pdf.

Senge, P. (1990). *The fifth discipline: The art and practice of the learning organization.* New York: Doubleday.

Sinha, C. (2009). Language as a biocultural niche and social institution. In V. Evans & S. Pourcel (Eds.), *New directions in cognitive linguistics.* Amsterdam: John Benjamins Pub. Co.

Spellings, M. (2006). Letter to chief state school officers announcing an LEP initiative of the U.S. Department of Education. Retrieved from http://www.ed.gov /policy/elsec/guid/secletter/060727.html

Stone, E. (1989). *Black sheep and kissing cousins: How our family stories shape us.* New York: Viking Penguin.

Teaching Diverse Learners, The Education Alliance, Brown University, n.d. (2017) Retrieved from http://www.aliance.brown.edu/tdl

Thompson, G. (2009). Where education and assimilation collide. *New York Times Series,* online at http://www.nytimes.com/2009/03/15/us/15immig.html? pagewanted=1.

Tiedt, P. L., & Tiedt, I. M. (1995). *Multicultural teaching: A handbook of activities, information, and resources* (4th ed.). Boston: Allyn & Bacon.

Trillos, M. (1998). Conclusiones. In M. Trillos (Ed.), *Educación Endógena Frente a Educación Formal.* Bogotá, Universidad de los Andes: Centro Colombiano de Estudios de Lenguas Aborígenes.

Varghese, M. M. (2004). Professional development for bilingual teachers in the United States: A site for articulating and contesting professional roles. *Bilingual Education and Bilingualism, 7*(2/3), 222-238.

Waiqui, A. (2000). Contextual factors in second language acquisition. *CAL Digests.* Retrieved from http://www.cal.org/resources/digest/0005contextual.html

Wallmont, M. (2003). Extinction fear for languages. *CNN online.* Retrieved from http://www.cnn.com/2003/TECH/science/05/22/extinct.language

Wolfram, W., Adger, C., & Christian, D. (1999). *Dialects in schools and communities.* Mahwah, NJ: Prentice Hall.

Religious Pluralism in Secular Classrooms

Focus Questions

1. Do you remember a time when you attended a religious service with someone of a different denomination or faith? What was it like? Did it feel strange to you? Why?

2. Do you know anyone who attended, or did *you* attend, a parochial school? How did it differ from a secular public school?

3. How and in what ways do you think religious knowledge should be a part of public schooling?

4. Do you believe public funds should be used in support of parochial schools?

5. Why do you think the framers of the Constitution prohibited the establishment of a state religion and also guaranteed the free exercise of religious beliefs?

" Without knowledge, the people perish. "

BOOK OF PROVERBS

Case Study

Religion in a Secular Classroom

Melissa Morgan had been teaching fifth grade in a small town in her home state of Georgia for 4 years, and she loved it. She had been married for 2 years, lived only five blocks from the school, and walked to work most mornings, passing on her way the principal's house, the local Baptist church, and the drugstore on the town square. Two evenings a week she attended classes at the local university where she was almost finished with her master's degree in reading. On Sundays she and her husband sang in the Methodist church choir, where many of her students' families also attended. It was a peaceful life in a town known primarily for the neatness of its surrounding farms, the beauty of its old magnolia trees, and the computer technology developed at the university where her husband taught English. Or, at least, it had been a peaceful life until last year.

It all started during the spring semester a year ago when she took a children's literature course taught by a colleague of her husband's, a woman who, prior to becoming a professor, had been a youth minister in Chicago. One of her assignments had been to select several books written at the upper elementary level that could be used to introduce common themes from several of the world's major religions. From subsequent class discussions on ways in which children's literature could be used for a variety of purposes, Melissa had begun to develop an idea that seemed to solve one of her recurring problems. Because her school was in a university town, her students often represented a greater variety of cultural and religious backgrounds than one would normally expect to find in a small southern town. In the past 4 years, she had had students from Japan, South Africa, and Ireland as well as a number of students from various parts of this country; all were the children of university faculty or graduate students. As a result, her own classroom sometimes reflected the same split between local people and newcomers that now and then caused misunderstanding and strife in the community. For the most part, she had been able to help students who were new to the town (and, indeed, the country) adjust to life in Georgia. But there was one element of the cultural differences in her classroom that had stumped her, and that was the difference in religion that had created a number of overt conflicts in the past.

Armed with some new insights about using literature for purposes in addition to reading instruction, Melissa spent the summer developing a series of lessons. They were designed to take advantage of the religious diversity in her class by not only using books and other materials about different religious faiths but also by planning activities that would lead children to discover more about their own religious backgrounds.

When school began in the fall, she was ready—convinced that it would be a wonderful year. She was doubly excited because students in her class represented a wider variety of religious backgrounds than had been the case the year before. Along with the usual Southern Baptists, Methodists, and Presbyterians were a Catholic student who had come to the United States from Brazil 3 years ago, three local Jewish students, five African American students who attended the African Methodist Episcopal church in town, four Muslim children from Iran whose parents were professors at the university, and two children who had been schooled at home until this year by parents who belonged to a conservative evangelical church. She also had students whose families were part of a small Unitarian Universalist congregation made up almost entirely of university faculty and their families.

The year began calmly enough, and her initial efforts to weave information about various religions into class discussions seemed to go well. During the month of September she had made home visits to each of her students' families, some of whom she already knew. In the course of these visits she was able to talk informally with parents and other family members, interact with her students in their home settings, and learn something about the cultural and religious backgrounds of those she did not know well. The father of one of her Iranian students turned out to be a professor of architecture and promised to come in to her class one day to talk about both the mathematics and the art in Islamic mosque architecture. She was thrilled!

Near the end of October, the school held its annual open house for parents and community members. Her class was eager for everyone to see the exhibit they had been working on since the beginning of school—models of houses of worship from around the world that included an Islamic mosque, a Hindu temple, a Buddhist temple, a Jewish synagogue, a stone Gothic cathedral, a Greek Revival Congregational church, a brick African Methodist Episcopal church, a clapboard Southern Baptist church, and a Quaker meeting house. Each model stood against a map of other parts of the world where such a building might be found, and each display was surrounded by pictures and books related to that particular place of worship.

About a week after the open house, Melissa's principal asked her to stop in the office after school. After a little small talk, the principal got to the point: "We've had some complaints about the fact that you're dealing with religion in your class."

She was astonished. "Who's complained?" she asked. "And what about?"

"It seems," continued the principal, "that there are two kinds of complaints. Some parents object to their children talking about religion in school at all, and others believe their children are being exposed to ideas that they believe are not Christian. One family wants to come in and look at the books we have in the library to see if there are any offensive materials there."

©Hill Street Studios/Blend Images LLC RF

"Well," said Melissa, "you know what the children and I have been doing; you've seen the models and maps. Did you explain our project to the parents who called? I really didn't intend to upset anyone, you know."

"Yes, I do know," said the principal, "but I'm afraid we've got something of a problem here. At least one of these families has a history of suggesting that the school might not be 'purely' Christian. They're part of the small group of parents in this school who objected so strenuously to celebrating Halloween because they felt it encouraged pagan beliefs and devil worship. As you know, several years ago we did away with the Halloween Party in favor of a 'Dress Up As Your Favorite Book Character' Day every fall."

"What do you think I should do?" Melissa asked.

"I'm not sure," replied the principal. "Perhaps you should put your models away and let it just die down."

"What will I tell the students? They have been so interested in this project and learned so much!"

"Perhaps you could just say that you all need the space in the classroom," answered the Principal, looking somewhat aggrieved.

A little shaken, Melissa went home that evening wondering if all her ideas about building on religious diversity would be stalled. She certainly hadn't intended to find herself in the middle of a battle over religion! She also didn't want to stop the discussions and activities in class that had led to such a good project as the models; her students were learning a great deal and seemed to be loving it. On an impulse, she called her own minister to talk about the problem. She asked if Rev. Thomas could suggest anything.

"Indeed I can," said Maggie Thomas. "The clergy in the area all belong to a regional clergy council that meets next week. Let me bring this up and see what they say. Perhaps you'd like to attend and tell us about what you're doing in class so everyone can hear it at the same time."

Melissa agreed, and the next week she met with the clergy council, where she carefully explained that although she wasn't teaching any particular religious beliefs, she did think that learning about other religions was a good thing for students. She told them that the idea for building the models had come from the students, and that she had been able to bring art, mathematics, and geography as well as both reading and writing into the project, and she told them how proud the students were of their work. At the end of the meeting, each member of the council agreed that what she was doing was a good thing, even if it had never been done before. Several expressed a desire to see the models for themselves, and Melissa promptly issued an open invitation to all. She was pleased that one of those who wanted to see the exhibit was the pastor of the church attended by several of the families who had complained. "Perhaps," she thought as she drove home, "there is an ecumenical spirit in this town after all." And then she found herself thinking about the coming holidays. "I wonder if we should talk about the many December religious celebrations in addition to Christmas that are held around the world?"

Rationale for Attending to Religion in Public Schools

Citizens of the United States have, since our national beginnings, been deeply concerned with the role of religion in matters of state. Some of our earliest settlers came to this continent to escape religious prejudice, and all who have come in the years since have brought with them their religious ideas, beliefs, rituals, and habits of mind. Even those who profess to be agnostic or atheist have formed their spiritual values in express rebellion *against* varieties of formalized religion that exist or existed in their particular cultural worlds.

In addition, much of the **cultural capital** of human societies emerges from philosophical, literary, musical, and artistic attempts to answer fundamentally religious questions: Who are we? Where did we come from? What is our purpose on earth? and What happens when we die? Thus, whether individuals see themselves as "religious" or not, religious references and allusions permeate their lives. In most if not all societies, religious references are used in everyday language; families, schools, and other institutions organize time around religious observances; and places of worship exert influence in community affairs. Even money often has religious symbols and language on it.

In part, this connection to religious ideas and symbolism emerges from a seemingly universal human need to be associated with a spiritual dimension. In some societies that connection permeates not only the ways in which the society is organized but also nearly every minute of daily life. When religion plays a large role in society, as it did in our own history in the Massachusetts Bay Colony and as seen recently in such places as Afghanistan and Iran, the society is called a **theocracy.** In other societies, the connection is looser, with some degree of separation between secular and religious life. That was the intention of the founders of the United States, who wrote such a separation into the Constitution in the First Amendment, which reads:

> Congress shall make no law respecting an establishment of religion [**establishment clause**], or prohibiting the free exercise thereof [**prohibition clause**]; or abridging the freedom of speech, of the press; or the right of the people peaceably to assemble, and to petition the Government for a redress of grievances (1791).

Notice that while the writers of the Constitution did not *establish* a religion as a dimension of the state, they also were careful to ensure that religion could be freely practiced by individuals, that religious speech (as well as other forms of speech) was protected by the Constitution, and that peaceable assembly to practice religious beliefs (as well as for other purposes) was guaranteed. It was, however, passage of the **Fourteenth Amendment** in 1868, which granted to citizens of the states all the rights they had as citizens of the nation, that caused the issue of separation of church and state to have a direct influence on schooling (Uphoff, 1993, p. 95).

Definitions of Religion

Uphoff (1993) noted that religion is a concept that seems easily definable until one actually tries to define it. We have available to us definitions of religion that are both universal (those that apply to all religions) and sectarian (those that apply only to a specific denomination or sect). Yinger (1970), for example, defined religion broadly as "a system of beliefs and practices by means of which a group of people struggle with . . . the ultimate problems of human life" (p. 7). The sociologist Durkheim (1969) defined it a bit more concretely but still in a universal manner when he said, "A religion is a unified system of beliefs and practices relative to sacred things, that is to say, things set apart and forbidden—beliefs and practices which unite into one single moral community called a church [*sic*], all those who adhere to them" (p. 46). Similarly, Berger and Berger (1972) viewed religion as "an overarching view of reality concerned with ultimate meanings which provides a cohesive view of the world, explains evil and prosperity, and offers guidelines for social action in the secular realm" (pp. 348–352). Most broad definitions of religion encompass concepts of a deity, of shared values and an orientation toward the sacred, and of a sense of community.

On the other hand, narrower, sectarian definitions of religion (e.g., Presbyterian, Catholic, Muslim, Jewish, Buddhist, Seventh-Day Adventist, Mormon) will have relatively different answers to the following questions:

1. What theological outlook or point of view does this religion acknowledge?

2. What kinds of religious practice do the people who belong to this religious denomination accept as expressive of proper worship and devotion?

3. What kind of religious experience—feelings, perceptions, and sensations—ensures that some contact will be made with ultimate reality (i.e., a supernatural agency)?

4. What knowledge about the basic tenets of faith, scriptures, and traditions are necessary to the practice of this particular religion?

5. What are the consequences of this religious belief, practice, experience, and knowledge on an individual's daily life?

6. What are the consequences of falling away from the practice, experience, and knowledge of this particular religion?[1]

Answers to these questions in large measure determine the differences between one religious group and another. Furthermore, it would be a mistake to regard these differences as simply "interesting" variations on a theme. Rather, a person's very identity and relationship with one or more deities and other human beings are vested in these beliefs, which are generally regarded by members of a particular faith as true in some ultimate sense. Thus, for example, religious beliefs about the proper kinds of food to eat, the proper way to prepare and eat it, the relative place of males and females in society, and the kinds of rituals required to receive the deity's blessing as well as the number and relative importance of deities themselves, all have a bearing on how an individual conducts his or her daily life. These ideas are so strongly held and so central to a religious person's sense of individual and collective identity that conflicts of belief among different religious groups can—and often have—led to war.

As is clear from today's news, going to war for religious beliefs is just as likely to happen now as it has been throughout history. Indeed, for some contemporary Muslim extremists, terrorist actions are based on and justified by long-remembered people and the battles they fought during the Crusades 700 years ago, as well as by perceived injustices perpetrated more recently. Indeed, it is not unusual for some extremists to refer to all modern Westerners as "Crusaders." Similarly, historically violent insurgencies in Northern Ireland based on centuries-old disputes between Catholics and Protestants, and the torture and horrific murder of thousands of Muslims by Serbian Christians in Kosovo, speak to the potential depth and danger of religious identity. Sadly, religious persecution by members of one religion against members of another religion is an old, old theme in the story of humanity.

The experiences of religious pluralism in the United States are not new, but some things have changed over time. First, the degree to which religious belief has been deemed a necessary part of *public* life has changed. In periods of fundamental social change, such as we are living in today, human beings often turn to the comfort and security of an organized faith and set of absolute values, and many believe that these values should be actively incorporated into the larger society. Second, the advent of technology—especially computer technology—means that it is no longer necessary to actually *attend* a religious service other than your own to obtain knowledge of it. Most faiths, and many individual synagogues, mosques, and churches, have numerous websites on which they can display and promote their religious ideas. Third, the increasing interdependence of the world's social systems means that what happens in one part of the world quickly affects what happens in another part of the world. This connectivity is no less true of religious systems than it is of economic ones.

Religious Pluralism in the United States

Religious pluralism in the United States is so great that a complete accounting is not possible in a short chapter, but it is possible to describe major religious groups that flourish here and to give a brief summary of their histories. Prior to colonization by Europeans in the 16th century, the Americas were home to a wide variety of religious practices by native peoples. Although Native American societies differed widely in various aspects of culture, in language, and in appearance, all shared a fundamentally religious outlook that emphasized the centrality of a Creator, a reverence for the natural world, and a belief that human beings were a part of nature and were obligated to preserve and protect it. Interestingly, this focus on the human condition as a part of nature, and the importance of living in such a way that our natural world is both preserved and conserved, is, at the beginning of the 21st century, being adopted by a number of contemporary religious groups, including many members of evangelical denominations.

European Influences on Religion in the United States

As Europeans began to explore and colonize the Americas, they brought with them another set of religious variations—Christianity and Judaism—as well as a belief quite contrary to the native religions: that human beings were *apart from* nature and were intended to conquer and control it. This difference in worldview with respect to the place of human beings in the natural world is perhaps the most significant and profound difference between so-called Western religions and most indigenous or "native" ones.

In New England, a puritan form of Protestantism took hold as a dominant theme; in the middle colonies, greater diversity of religious belief, including Catholic, Quaker, and Anabaptist, as well as others, meant that no particular denomination prevailed; in the South, the dominant religion stemmed from the Anglican Church of England. Jews also were among the earliest immigrants: first came Sephardic Jews from Spain and Portugal and then German Jewish immigrants; by the American Revolution, there were about 3,000 Jews in the colonies (Sowell, 1980, p. 77). Religious diversity continued to expand in the late 18th century. In the 19th century, large numbers of Catholics from Ireland and Italy and Jews from Russia and eastern Europe immigrated to the

United States, each group containing within it great diversity of belief and practice. In the 20th century, particularly since the 1960s, the United States has experienced increasing Catholic immigration from Cuba, the Caribbean, Mexico, and Central America.

African Influences on Religion in the United States

In the 17th, 18th, and 19th centuries, large numbers of Africans were brought to the United States as slaves, and they brought with them not only a large set of their own **African religions,** but Islamic influences as well. As noted in the Amherst College Documentary History Project on African-American Religions:

> Working its way down from the Sahara long before Christianity began to touch the West African coast, Islam like Christianity interacted in complex ways with the traditional religions of Africa. Brought to the Americas by enslaved African Muslims, Islam struggled with difficulty to preserve itself in an inhospitable, Christian-controlled environment. Meanwhile, ordinary believers of all sorts, eager to mobilize any resources that might aid them in coping with life's daily hardships, everywhere tended to borrow freely from one another's traditions of religious practice. In sixteenth-century Mexico, for example, there was a complex intermingling of African, Mesoamerican, and European practices of divination (AARDOC, 2006).

Indeed, the creativity with which Africans interpreted and utilized Protestant scriptures and music to make their daily lives more bearable and to further the cause of freedom produced a unique contribution to American religious and political life. Negro spirituals, for example, were very often used as a form of clandestine communication to spread news of slave activities. After slavery was finally abolished in the middle of the 19th century, African American churches continued to have an immense influence on the cultural and educational lives of their members and are today still central to African American culture and African American social and political struggles.

Middle Eastern Influences on Religion in the United States

Although the importation of Muslim African slaves brought Islam to the Americas very early, it was in the late 19th and 20th centuries that a growth in the Muslim faith in the United States reached influential proportions. This was the case in part through conversion and in part through immigration. In fact, Islam is presently one of the fastest growing religions in the United States.

The converted Muslim population is primarily African American and often identifies itself as the Nation of Islam, a group whose history in the United States goes back to the 1930s and grew out of the works of W. D. Fard and Elijah Muhammad. The Nation of Islam was, and in some respects still is, a separatist group that emphasizes freedom, justice, and equality for African Americans and actively discourages intermarriage with whites. Perhaps its best-known leader was Malcolm X, the converted son of a Baptist minister who, as a result of his experience during a pilgrimage to Mecca (a hajj) and shortly before his assassination in 1965, began to shift his beliefs away from separatism and toward kinship among all human beings (Al-Ani, 1995).

The earliest Muslim immigrants—largely rural, poor, and uneducated—came to the United States between 1875 and 1912 from what was known as Bilad ash-Sham, or Greater Syria—an area that after World War I became Jordan, Lebanon, Palestine, and Syria-and also from Turkey, Albania, India, and elsewhere. The second wave, that immigrated after World War II, particularly from the Middle East and North Africa, were primarily educated professionals uprooted by political changes including the creation of the states of Israel and Pakistan.

The third wave, which continues today, began in the 1960s with the liberalization of American immigration laws (Al-Ani, 1995). These individuals came not only from the same areas as their earlier counterparts, but also from the former Yugoslavia. In addition, beginning in the 1970s, the oil-producing countries of the Middle East have sent many Muslim students to study in the United States, and these students have played an active role in Muslim communities. Like their European counterparts, many Muslims have come to the United States as a result of social and political unrest in their native countries.

Today, Islam in the United States—like Christianity and Judaism—has a global face. Highly educated Sunni and Shi'ite Arab Muslims comprise a large proportion of the Islamic community. In addition, however, Muslims from Turkey, Eastern Europe, and many African nations continue to enrich the Islamic community, and serious challenges continue to face Islamic residents. Life for Muslim Americans has never been particularly easy, but the attacks on the World Trade Center in September 2001 and the wars in Iraq and Afghanistan have increased both attention and a backlash of negative feelings toward Muslims in general. Jane I. Smith (n.d.), professor of Islamic Studies at the Hartford Seminary in Connecticut, wrote about other challenges facing American Muslims:

> Questions of identity, occupation, dress, and acculturation are particularly significant for many American Muslims. Other major issues include the relationships among different racial and ethnic Muslim groups as well as with other American Muslims; how and where to provide an Islamic education for one's children; and appropriate roles and opportunities for women. Many are moving from a phase of dissociation from mainstream American life to much more active participation in political and social arenas. American Muslims appear to be moving into another stage of identity in which these kinds of issues are being confronted and resolved in new and creative ways. The result may well be that a truly American Islam, woven from the fabric of many national, racial, and ethnic identities, is in the process of emerging.

In the United States, any discussion of religion must include a willingness to concede the complexity of American religious ideas and practices. In the introduction to a report on their recent national survey on religion conducted by the Baylor Institute for Studies of Religion, Bader et al. (2006) stated:

> In fact, under the surface American religion is startlingly complex and diverse. Americans may agree that God exists. They do not agree about what God is like, what God wants for the world, or how God feels about politics. Most Americans pray. They differ widely on to whom they pray, what they pray about, and whether or not they say grace. A vast majority of Americans are Christians, but attitudes amongst those Christians regarding the salvation of others, the role of religion in government, the reality of the paranormal, and their consumption of media are surprisingly diverse.

Clearly, while the United States has always been a religiously pluralistic country, today that pluralism is greater than it has ever been. Along with ethnic and racial pluralism, to which it is closely related in a variety of ways, religious pluralism has become a daily experience in classrooms all over the country—a fact that has educational implications in terms of curriculum materials, subject matter, school rules and customs, student services, school calendar decisions, scheduling of student activities, cafeteria offerings, holiday celebrations, teaching methods, and school financing (Uphoff, 1993). Rather than looking at these educational implications as problems, however, some teachers and schools are finding that such diversity of religion offers unique opportunities for teaching and learning.

Characteristics of a Classroom That Attends to Religious Pluralism

How, then, might an educator design a classroom not only to affirm religious pluralism but also to build on it?

Pedagogies: Old and New

Good teaching in a classroom that is sensitive to religious diversity, like good teaching in any classroom, is in large measure a matter of getting to know the students with whom you are working, their families, and the communities in which they live. Most teachers quickly learn the individual idiosyncrasies of their students with respect to psychological issues and traits: attention span, motivation, perceived intelligence, and so on. What is often less well known is the sociocultural background of students. Yet we know very well that the best context for learning is when students are able to build on what they already know. Knowing as much as possible about your students' backgrounds is also central to everything else that happens because you will be designing your classroom around *your* students and the experiences they bring with them to school.

Because formal religious teachings and values may or *may not* be a part of each of your students' lives, it is important to know something about the religious composition of your class. Chances are good that you will not have an overwhelming number of different religions represented in one room, so you need to know something about only those that are represented at any given time. However, you do need to know something about the worldview of those particular religions as well as the worldview of those students who do not subscribe to any religious tenets, particularly with respect to issues of gender and to the relationship between young people and elders. It is also wise to know whether a particular religious group values such skills as critical thinking and questioning for their children because some do not. In some religious contexts, a child simply does *not* question authority, religious doctrine, or their elders.

Knowledge about religious groups does not, of course, mean that you must design a classroom to match each child's unique experience. Indeed, one of the purposes of schooling in a democracy is to help students expand their experience beyond the relatively small world in which they live. However, it is important that you know something about the religious values of your students so that you can know how to approach new learning, where conflicts may develop, and when you can intercede to help students (and often parents) bridge the gap between their own experience and what they are learning in school. At the same time, you must understand and respect the community's primary values so that you do not go too far beyond the readiness level of community members.

Teachers who want to build on religious diversity must vary the instructional methods used in the classroom. The culture of the traditional American public school stresses certain teaching methods, patterns of instructional interaction, and assessment strategies. For example, teachers talk while students listen; individual students answer teacher-directed questions; individual students give oral reports to their class; students follow detailed, teacher-given instructions on how to carry out a task; and teachers issue paper-and-pencil tests. In the United States, these patterns emerge from a Western cultural worldview that emphasizes individualism, middle-class values, and a generally Protestant Christian belief system that stresses the importance of the minister as teacher and the individual's direct relationship with a deity. These teaching patterns may be relatively or totally unfamiliar to some students. Native American students, for example, whose religious worldview emphasizes communal patterns of interaction and individual choice, may be more interested in the activities of their peers than of the teacher and may feel that the teacher must earn their respect rather than simply get it by virtue of his or her position. That is, these students may believe that they should follow a teacher's directions because they have chosen to rather than because they are compelled to do so. Another example is African American students whose churches use an emotive "call and response" or a choral pattern of interaction; these students may respond to teachers' questions with emotion, with hand gestures, with changes in vocal tonality, or in chorus because those are patterns they have learned. In general, what may be *new* about pedagogy for a classroom that pays attention to religious diversity is the subtle but important ability of the teacher to vary and alter instructional patterns so that all students find both familiar and new ways of learning.

Roles: Old and New

Sensitivity to potential and real areas of conflict among students of different religious backgrounds requires that teachers adopt the role of interpreter and, sometimes, mediator. Once again, teachers must learn as much as they can about the religions represented in the classroom not only so that they can help students find the commonalities among different religious beliefs but also so that they can help students interpret differences. Parents and community members are often helpful in this regard, so long as they understand that their role is to explain rather than to convert. Indeed, perhaps more dissension regarding religious tenets has been caused by the failure of teachers to communicate closely with parents about what they are trying to accomplish in class than by any other single factor. Generally speaking, if parents understand that their children will not be deprived of either respect or affirmation because of their religious beliefs, most will be happy to help teachers in any way they can. Students, too, if they are old enough, can serve as teachers to their peers, as can other school staff and members of the community.

Another set of issues to consider in a religiously sensitive classroom is the role of school rules and customs. Attendance, for example, should be flexible for students involved in religious celebrations and/or duties, and policies such as dress codes should take account of religiously based regulations and customs. Dress codes that stipulate that students cannot wear hats in school must exempt the Orthodox Jewish boy who wears the yarmulke as a token of respect to his deity or the Amish girl who wears a dimity bonnet and long dress as a gesture of modesty.

Similarly, the fact that the school calendar conveys the importance of religious diversity is significant. For example, vacation times scheduled on traditional school calendars, as well as celebrations usually held in schools, tend to be based on the Christian holidays of Christmas and Easter. Moreover, common practices such as scheduling games on Friday nights (when many Jewish families begin the celebration of the Sabbath) or homecoming activities early in the autumn (which may fall on the Jewish High Holidays) should also be seriously reconsidered. Later in the school year, teachers need to be sensitive to the demands placed on older Muslim students who observe Ramadan and refrain from eating and drinking during the daylight hours. The customs involved in these special cases must be discussed openly in terms of their religious significance so that other students both learn about different traditions and come to respect the reasons for them. Much of this kind of discussion can take place in the context of learning about religious beliefs and customs as a part of more general curricular study.

Place of Content Knowledge: Old and New

When religion is the cultural focus of your thinking, it is well to remember that religion, unlike some other kinds of difference, has a powerful element of "truth" built into it. That is, it may be more difficult for a student to stand apart from his or her religious worldview and look at other religions because religious "truth" is often linked to fundamental ideas of the relationship between individuals and a supernatural power. Nevertheless, religious history and traditions, architecture, art, music, and ideas can become the basis for an enriched and affirming classroom. Although in recent years educators have been reluctant to consider teaching about religion in public schools, the study of the contributions of various religions to world civilization is worthwhile. Indeed, in 1964 the American Association of School Administrators published a book called *Religion in the Public Schools* in which the authors asserted that:

> a curriculum which ignored religion would itself have serious implications. It would seem to proclaim that religion has not been as real in men's lives as health, or politics, or economics. By omission it would appear to deny that religion has been and is important in man's history—a denial of the obvious. In day by day practice, the topic cannot be avoided. As an integral part of man's [sic] culture, it must be included (as cited in Uphoff, 1993, p. 95).

The study of religion generally can be incorporated into a variety of places in the curriculum; often the best place is the most obvious. Religious dietary regulations might be included in a home economics class, for example, or the intricate, geometrical designs of an Islamic mosque might be part of a math or art class. Because religion is and has been so fundamental to human life and history, locating its study in the context of a variety of subject matters is not difficult. At the same time, separate courses in the study of comparative religion or interdisciplinary courses that study the impact of religion on history, law, and art can be instituted, particularly at the secondary level.

Regular curriculum materials and resources in a religiously sensitive classroom should be carefully screened for bias of various kinds, including omission, not so much in order to exclude those materials as to point out the bias to students and let the bias, itself, become the subject of inquiry, discussion, and debate. At the same time, curricular resources—including books, articles, paintings, music, sculpture, maps, and artifacts such as wearing apparel and icons—that represent various religions can be made available for examination by students. Similarly, students who belong to particular religious groups can educate their classmates about their own religious beliefs and values. In all cases, the basis of study and discussion should be inquiry, not evangelism.

Assessment: Old and New

When you are teaching or learning about a belief system like religion, you must focus not only on assessing the knowledge that has been acquired but also on the form of that assessment. Uphoff (1993) offered a good example of religious sensitivity when he wrote about creating exam questions having to do with the concept of evolution. As you may be aware, the teaching of evolution is the subject of much controversy in some communities, with many people calling for balancing the curriculum by including the study of so-called intelligent design in biology and other classes. The following test questions illustrate the difference between showing respect for those families who accept as fact the story of creation as it is written in the Bible and giving the impression that those families are wrong:

> *Poor.* It took millions of years for the earth to evolve to its present state. (True/False)
> *Better.* Evolutionists believe that it took millions of years for the earth to evolve to its present state (True/False) (Uphoff, 1993, p. 104).

In the first question, the student must agree with a factual statement, while in the second, the student can agree that one group (not necessarily one to which he or she belongs) asserts that something is the case. You might agree that this makes a subtle but powerful difference.

Another issue concerns such assessments as psychological testing and health screening and care. Some families believe that psychological assessment by school personnel is an invasion of family rights, a corruption of values based on strict adherence to scriptural teaching, or an attempt on the part of school officials to alter or interfere with the religious beliefs of students. These families tend to think that psychological interventions to raise self-esteem or encourage self-expression—such as classroom games or the use of puppets as a way to enable children to speak freely—are suspect, sometimes in the extreme.

Similarly, health screenings and assessments, especially when they involve somewhat invasive procedures such as tine or PPD (purified protein derivative, or Mantoux) tests for tuberculosis, are often the focus of parental objections on a variety of religious grounds. Some parents also may have religious reasons for objecting to their children giving blood in high school blood drives. As schools increasingly become a source of health and social services for children, the number of objections raised by families from a variety of religious backgrounds may increase as well.

Pang and Barba (1995) noted that culturally affirming instruction should include culturally familiar interaction patterns, culturally familiar strategies, a culturally familiar environment, culturally familiar content, culturally familiar materials, and culturally familiar analogies, themes, and concepts. The next section explores some of the ways Melissa Morgan's classroom followed these guidelines with respect to religious sensitivity and appreciation.

Case Analysis

Educators who have been involved in school disputes about religion might think that this Case Study has an improbably positive resolution. Certainly, many schools have become the center of highly emotional and long-lasting acrimony about issues such as using counseling techniques to build self-esteem in children and have experienced major attempts at censorship of library and other materials.

Yet Melissa demonstrates several attributes of a good teacher in a religiously sensitive classroom. First, she takes advantage of her students' idea to build models as a way to get them to cooperate in a hands-on activity and to encourage individual students from different religious backgrounds to bring their own specialized knowledge to their classmates. Second, she skillfully integrates several aspects of the curriculum into the project so that students can see that knowledge is interrelated. Rather than listening to dry lectures about different religions, the students learned about various religious beliefs by studying the meaning that underlies different parts of the place of worship itself.

When objections come, Melissa does not try to withdraw, nor does she get angry, nor does she dismiss the objections as unreasonable. Rather, she goes to her own minister as a way to perhaps create linkages with the religious leaders of the community. That there happened to be a clergy council meeting the next week and that she happened to be a persuasive speaker might be viewed as fortuitous. However, many communities have organizations to which various clergy belong, and the notion of enlisting help from community members is always a good one.

As diversity of all kinds is increasingly prevalent in schools and as teachers like Melissa learn to appreciate and build on those differences, experiences like Melissa's will also increase. Thus future teachers will want to consider both the opportunities and possible implications of being an educational leader in the classroom and in the community.

Perspectives on Religion and Schooling in the United States

Because a religious or spiritual dimension is so close to the cognitive and emotional lives of human beings and because the founders of the United States believed that religion was so important that it should be addressed in the Constitution, the few words in the First and Fourteenth Amendments have been both the source of religious freedom and the source of educational battles around religion in the schools ever since. In schooling, the fundamental problem has been—and continues to be—how to resolve the tensions created by seemingly opposing principles: (1) the need for schools, as an arm of the state, to support a basic freedom guaranteed by the Constitution, and (2) the need for schools, also as an arm of the state, to uphold the **separation of church and state.** Throughout our history, these tensions have resulted in continually shifting opinions about a number of issues, and because ours is a nation of laws, the courts have been a decisive element in defining the relationship between religion and schools.

In an analysis written many years ago, Butts (1978) cast these issues into two broad categories that help sort out the confusion that often results when people begin to talk about the role (or absence) of religion in public education. The first category is education's role in protecting *private freedoms,* or "those that inhere in the individual, and therefore may not be invaded or denied by the state." He wrote:

> In the most general terms, freedom was sought for parents and their children on the grounds that every human being has the right, and should have the opportunity and the ability, to live one's own life in dignity and security. Further he or she is entitled to a chosen cultural or religious group without arbitrary constraint on action or coercion of belief by the state or by other community pressures (p. 272).

"Most often," he noted, "appeal was made to the free exercise of religion guaranteed by the First Amendment of the Constitution (and as applied by the Fourteenth

Amendment to the states) as a protection against coercion of belief or action by school or government authorities" (p. 272).

Butts's second category was education's role in guaranteeing *public freedoms,* "that is, those that inhere in the welfare of the democratic political community and which the . . . state is obligated actively to safeguard, protect, and promote whether threatened by a majority or minority in the community" (p. 272). He described the ground for public freedoms for teachers and students as the belief that every person in his or her capacity as a teacher, learner, and citizen had the right and should have the opportunity to speak, to read, to teach, to learn, to discuss, and to publish without arbitrary constraint on action or coercion of belief by the state or by other pressures.

This approach to protection of public freedoms has run into opposition by people who see it as a threat to the established order, in other words, a threat to the dominance of Protestantism as the foundation of public schooling. It has also been opposed by people for whom the protection of private freedoms is paramount; that is, those who see in the protection of *public* welfare a threat to *private* freedoms of parents to control the education of their children.

Several of the more important concrete issues over which these debates have raged are compulsory attendance, freedom to practice religious beliefs with respect to the Pledge of Allegiance, salutes to the flag, prayer and Bible reading in schools, released time for religious instruction, and the use of public funds for religious schools. Each of these issues has reflected the tension between private and public freedoms.

Private Freedoms: Religion and Compulsory School Attendance

The history of schooling in the United States is characterized by a continually expanding effort to include all children. One way in which this has been accomplished is by requiring all children to go to school until a certain age. This requirement was little regarded in the early years of the country; indeed, for much of our history, schooling was not only not required but also not really necessary to earn a living and develop a good life.

Beginning in the 19th century with the advent of industrialization and the major waves of immigration, compulsory schooling gained acceptance largely as a way of protecting young children from exploitation in factories and keeping children off the urban streets. In general, however, the move toward compulsory schooling can be seen as part of a larger movement toward the establishment of a social institution (the common school) that would provide the means to ensure a common citizenship and loyalty to the state among diverse individuals. Thus, early on the issue of compulsory schooling was seen by some Americans as an issue of the rights of parents versus the rights of the state.

In 1922, the state of Oregon narrowly passed an initiative requiring that all children between age 6 and 18 must attend a *public* school, or be granted permission to attend a private school by the county superintendent of schools. Fearing that such a law would destroy parochial schools, a Roman Catholic teaching order filed suit to have the law declared unconstitutional. In 1925, the Supreme Court did just that in *Pierce v. Society of Sisters,* saying:

> The fundamental theory of liberty upon which all governments in this Union repose excluded any general power of the State to standardize its children by forcing them to accept instruction from public teachers only. The child is not the mere creature of the State; those who nurture him and direct his destiny have the right, coupled with the high duty, to recognize and prepare him for additional obligations.

Although affirming the right of parents to send their children to private religious schools, the Court also stipulated that the state had a right to require children to go to *some* school and that the state could also regulate all schools. Thus the precedent was set for the development of a protected parochial school system alongside the public schools.

As is often the case, however, support for compulsory schooling ebbs and flows. By the 1960s and 1970s, many educators had doubts about requiring attendance of all children to the age of 16 or 18. Again, religious beliefs provided the means for the Supreme Court to further the cause of private freedoms and parental rights. In *Wisconsin v. Yoder* (1972), the Court upheld the decision of the Wisconsin Supreme Court that stipulated that Old Order Amish parents could disobey Wisconsin's compulsory schooling laws and remove their children from school at the end of the eighth grade. The Court held that:

> a state's interest in universal education, however highly we rank it, is not totally free from a balancing process when it impinges on other fundamental rights and interests, such as those specifically protected by the Free Exercise Clause of the First Amendment and the traditional interest of parents with respect to the religious upbringing of their children so long as they, in the words of *Pierce*, "prepare [them] for additional obligations."

Today, interest in compulsory schooling is once again on the rise, in part because of the perceived interest of the state in a new kind of workforce that can compete economically with other nations and in part because of the requirements of the No Child Left Behind reauthorization of the Elementary and Secondary Education Act of 2001. Although there is some debate on the actual number of high school completions, 2010 data from the National Center for Education Statistics indicates that high school dropout rates have declined among all populations since 1990, dropping overall from 12.1% to 7.4% (National Center for Education Statistics, 2010). Since more states have established graduation tests, however, there is increasing debate about how many students actually graduate on time, and about how such rates are measured.

Private Freedoms: The Practice of Religious Beliefs in Classrooms

Public sentiment regarding the role of religion in public schools, like public opinion on other issues, is often easier to understand when it is seen in a historical context. In the decisions cited in the previous section, for example, the right of parents to foster religious beliefs in their children versus the right of the state to compel school attendance was part of the larger questions of child labor and the development of schools as the primary socialization agents of citizenship in a democracy.

Similarly, the debates over the practice of religious beliefs in classrooms have often been part of the larger question of loyalty to the United States and the debate about the role of the state to protect a citizen's rights to equality. In the beginning of the Common School Movement, there was little question that religious practice—and indeed, religious sources of instruction—was a fundamental part of public schooling. Such practices as school prayer and the reading of the Bible on a daily basis were common, if not universal, and curricular materials such as the widely used McGuffy readers taught moral values derived from Christian Protestantism along with vocabulary and grammar. Although the influence of particular religious ideas and values on schooling has always been (and continues to be) partly a matter of the religious composition of the community in which a school is located, the basic structure of public schooling in the United States emerged from an allegiance to a Judeo-Christian heritage as much as it did from the development of an economically capitalist state. Indeed, the Judeo-Christian deity has been (and is) a more or less involuntary party to a wide variety of legislative and judicial meetings, deliberations, and decisions at the federal, state, and local levels. Note that although Americans say they separate church and state, it is still common practice for the president of the United States to place his hand on some version of the Bible when taking the oath of office.

The question of loyalty to the government usually arises in times of major political disagreement or war. In 1919, for example, in the wake of World War I and fears of involvement with world affairs, Nebraska passed a law requiring that all instruction in the public schools be given in English and prohibiting the teaching of any foreign language to children younger than the ninth grade. In *Meyer v. Nebraska* (1923), however, the Supreme Court ruled that such a law was unconstitutional, stating that the right of parents to guide their children's education is a constitutional right.

Similarly, during World War II, the Minersville, Pennsylvania, board of education enacted a policy that required all teachers and students in the public schools to incorporate the Pledge of Allegiance and a salute to the flag on a daily basis. One set of parents, who were Jehovah's Witnesses and prohibited by their religion from worshiping images, objected that the requirement set aside their First Amendment rights to free exercise of religion. In *Minersville v. Gobitis* (1940) the Supreme Court ruled in favor of the state's right to impose the flag salute rule. The dissent to this ruling was written by Justice Stone, who, on becoming chief justice 3 years later, reversed the *Gobitis* decision in *West Virginia State Board of Education v. Barnette* (1943), saying, in effect, that while the state could require the study and teaching of civic matters, it did *not* have the right to impose an ideological discipline that "invades the sphere of intellect and spirit."

The debate about the role of the state in providing equality of opportunity, on the other hand, has influenced other decisions regarding religion in the public schools. For example, a widely known and still heatedly debated controversy revolves around the issue of prayer and Bible reading in public schools. In a widely referenced case in 1963—*Abington v. Schempp*—the Supreme Court ruled that *requiring* student participation in sectarian prayers and reading from the Bible, particularly the New Testament, violated the First Amendment prohibition of separation of church and state. The argument here was that school prayers were fundamentally Christian (and usually Protestant), that all students were not Christian, that so-called nonsectarian prayers satisfied no one, and that therefore the removal of all religious practice from public school classrooms was necessary. The Supreme Court has ruled that sectarian prayers at high school graduations (*Lee v. Weisman,* 1992) and on the football field before a game (*Santa Fe Independent School District v. Doe,* 2000) are also unconstitutional. Still, because religious beliefs are so much a part of the identities of many people, the law and the practices of individual schools and people may be somewhat far apart.

Unfortunately, many people, including the national and local media, confused the argument in *Abington* with the actual decision, which did not "ban" prayer in schools but only said that *requiring* students to participate in sectarian prayers and Bible reading was unconstitutional. Indeed, in the majority opinion written by Justice Clark, the Court strongly supported the study of religion in public schools:

> It might well be said that one's education is not complete without a study of comparative religion or the history of religion and its relationship to the advancement of civilization. It certainly may be said that the Bible is worthy of study for its literary and historic qualities. Nothing we have said here indicates that such study of the Bible or of religion, when presented objectively as part of a secular program of education, may not be effected consistent with the First Amendment (1963).

Uphoff (1993) suggested that it was the self-censorship of educators and publishers based on both an inadequate reading of the Court decisions and a desire for equal representation for non-Christian religions that was responsible for the relative removal of religion from public schools in recent years. The vacuum created by this removal has enabled a strong challenge from the so-called religious right to reinstate religious practices into classrooms.

In 1993, Congress passed the Religious Freedom Restoration Act, which laid down several principles about the exercise of religion in schools and elsewhere. In part, the act stated that the government cannot "burden" an individual's exercise of religion unless that exercise conflicted with a compelling government interest and/or if that burden was the

©Design Pics/Don Hammond RF

least restrictive means of furthering such compelling interest. However, in 1997, the Supreme Court declared at least part of the law unconstitutional, with the result that it no longer applies to states and localities, but does apply to federal jurisdiction (Ackerman, 1998).

Public Freedoms: Public Funding for Religious Schools

Arguments for public funding for religious schools stem from the doctrine contained in the *Pierce v. Society of Sisters* decision previously discussed. As Butts (1978) noted:

> If parents have a private *right* to send their children to religious and private schools to meet the compulsory attendance requirements of the state, then distributive justice requires that the state provide parents with public funds to enable them to do what they have the private right to do (p. 286).

Arguments against public funding for religious schools, on the other hand, stem from the Establishment Clause of the First Amendment on the grounds that the taxpayer has a right to be free of taxation that promotes a religious doctrine.

Until about the middle of the 20th century, the American public in general, was inclined to believe that both national and religious interests were better served if public funds were not used for religious schools. The debate arose again, however, at midcentury, with Americans taking positions about both *direct* and *indirect* aid. Proponents of direct aid argued that since compulsory attendance laws served the state and since parochial schools contributed to the ability of those laws to be enforced, parochial schools should also benefit from public financial support. Further, they argued that since all citizens were required to pay taxes to support public education, those parents who wished—*and had a right*—to send their children to religious schools would have a double financial burden. In addition, they argued that the provision of separation of church and state in the Constitution said nothing about the ability of public and parochial schools to *cooperate* with one another.

A more moderate view favored *indirect aid* to religious schools. As early as 1930, precedent was set for such aid when, in *Cochran v. Louisiana State Board of Education,* the Supreme Court upheld a Louisiana law that affirmed the purchase of texts for use in private sectarian schools on the grounds that the books benefited the children and thus the state. After World War II, however, a variety of religious groups began to push the limits of *Cochran* by asking for public support for health and medical services and school lunches as well as for books. The greatest demand was for help with transportation of parochial students to their schools.

Perhaps the most cited and argued-over case regarding religion and public education, *Everson v. Board of Education* (1947), was the landmark case with respect to busing parochial schoolchildren. Emerging from a New Jersey case in which the state allowed public funds to be used to transport Catholic children to parochial schools, the Court ruled that payment for such transportation essentially benefited the children (and thus the state, as it had said in *Cochran*) rather than the school. The vote was 5 to 4, however, with the minority arguing that such support did, indeed, help children and parents maintain religious instruction at public expense.

A third position, generally taken by Protestant, Jewish, and civil libertarian supporters of the public school, as well as by many professional educators, argues that both direct aid and indirect aid to parochial schools are unconstitutional. Those who take this position base their argument on a strict separation of church and state. At the middle of the 20th century, both the National Education Association and the American Association of School Administrators adopted this position, asserting that although religious schools had every right to exist, they should be supported entirely by those who use them.

Over the next three decades, the action regarding federal aid to private schools moved from the courts to the legislature. At the federal level, the School Lunch Act of 1948, the National Defense Education Act of 1958, the Higher Educational Facilities Act of 1963, the Higher Education Act of 1965, and the Elementary and Secondary Education Act of 1965 provided financial support for school lunches in parochial schools; massive funding in a variety of areas for private, often sectarian, colleges; and funds for school libraries, textbooks, and secular instructional materials for private as well as public schools. Courts, however, continued to cut down state statutes supporting direct and indirect services to parochial schools, although they did create some conditions under which such aid would be permissible. Thus, in *Zorach v. Clauson* (1952) the Supreme Court ruled that schools could release students during public school hours to attend religious instruction off the school premises.

Charter Schools, Home Schooling, and Voucher Programs

Today, the debate about tax support for parochial education continues, made perhaps even more strident because of current efforts to provide competition for the public education system. Charter schools, home schooling, and voucher programs are often promoted by those who have religious reasons for wanting their children educated by alternative means. While these initiatives are often cyclical, it is the case that over the past few years there has been an increasing demand for and support of faith-based initiatives in many areas of public life.

Children who receive school vouchers, especially in urban areas where voucher programs are most likely to occur, quite often attend parochial schools. Although many have objected that redirecting public school funds to private, religious schools is a violation of the First Amendment's Establishment Clause, in 2002 the U.S. Supreme Court found that this was not the case with respect to the Cleveland, Ohio, school voucher program. In this case, the Court reversed a lower court decision that struck down the program on the grounds that nearly all students receiving vouchers attended parochial schools. But in a 5 to 4 decision, the majority found that Cleveland parents had a "sufficient range of choices among secular and religious schools that Ohio's voucher plan does not violate the First Amendment prohibition against the establishment of religion" (Frieden, 2002).

Clearly, a growing number of citizens in the United States appear to want to "blur" the boundaries between church and state. Indeed, the current Secretary of Education, Betsy DeVos, has campaigned for most of her adult life for the right of parents to select the best school for their children, or to teach them at home, regardless of the public school available in their district, and to have taxes which currently support public schools go with the child to whatever educational situation the child's parents think will be best. This would include charter schools, private schools, magnet schools, other public schools, religious schools, virtual schools, and home schools. About this funding proposal she says:

> Let me say it again: we must change the way we think about funding education and instead invest in children, not in buildings (DeVos, 2017).

Critics argue that such choice would destroy our long tradition of public education by defunding public schools, since Mrs. DeVos does not believe that current public schools, especially those in urban areas, can be made better. With regard to religious schools, whether sponsored by organized entities such as religious denominations, or set up by a group of like-minded religious parents, this funding plan would go all the way to completely underwriting private religious schools with public taxes. Whether or not this would violate the First Amendment Establishment Clause of the Constitution is an open question. If it were not to destroy traditional public education, it would certainly increase the education budget in communities, counties, and states.

Public Freedoms: The Provision of Religious Instruction

Current charges that public schools are too secular and lack the moral tone that will help children grow up to be better citizens are not new. At the end of the 19th century, a consensus had developed that religious instruction should not be a responsibility of public schools; but after World War I and II, many citizens thought that the schools were "godless" and that some sort of religious instruction should be returned to public classrooms. Throughout the 1940s and 1950s, efforts were made to get around Court decisions regarding the separation of church and state, but those efforts were largely unsuccessful. Two arguments were offered.

Some people—mostly Protestants and Catholics—sought a revival of sectarian instruction, usually through the demand for released time in the school day so that students could receive religious instruction from teachers of their own religious faith. Most often, this instruction was to be offered apart from the school building, usually in a nearby church. Others—primarily Protestants—urged that more attention be paid to a nonsectarian religious instruction through daily reading of the Bible and recitation of nonsectarian prayers in school. Both propositions were denounced by many people as an infringement of the separation of church and state. While a number of states and the U.S. Supreme Court had ruled in various ways on the issue of released time for religious instruction, the Supreme Court finally decided in *Zorach v. Clauson* in 1952 that students leaving the school building for religious teaching was permissible under the First Amendment because the school did not actively promote a sectarian form of instruction and because no public funds were expended for the effort.

The issue of Bible reading has also been decided variously. By the 1970s, a number of states had decided it was *not* religious instruction. At least six state courts, however, ruled that the Bible *was* a sectarian document, at least to Catholics, Jews, and nonbelievers. For Catholics, the King James version of the Bible was thought to be Protestant sectarianism. For Jews, reading the Bible does not hold the same significance that it does for Christians. Families of unbelievers objected to any religious practices at all. Nonsectarian prayers were usually objected to by everyone on the grounds that they watered down any real religious belief in an effort at compromise among belief systems and also on the grounds that such prayers nevertheless promoted religion against the Establishment Clause of the First Amendment. In 1963, the Supreme Court did away with most of these arguments in the previously discussed cases that declared *required* prayer and Bible reading to be unconstitutional even while they affirmed the value of teaching *about* religion in public schools.

In the past 30 years, new issues have arisen that bring religious pluralism in the classroom once again into sharper focus. First, immigration from various parts of the world by people whose religious structures and beliefs are very different from Christianity and Judaism has populated public school classrooms with students from a wide variety of religious backgrounds. Second, changes in the institutions of the family and the economy have weakened the social cohesion that normally helps bind communities together and provide the common socialization processes necessary to raise the next generation. In such circumstances, young people often feel rootless, answerable to no one, and alienated from a system that no longer really exists except in the minds of their elders. Indeed, as noted in Chapter 1, numbers of religiously unaffiliated in the United States have grown appreciably, especially among younger people (Pew Forum on Religion and Public Life, 2015). One result of these societal conditions may, in part, account for the increase in violence we are now witnessing in all segments of society, but particularly among our youth. Finally, the growth and importance attached to science and technology in our society tends to mask the smaller, more human dramas that contain the very essence of religious questions and meaning. It is small wonder that, in response, the call for religious instruction and moral values in public schools has become a widespread demand.

Perspectives on Religious Identity

Religion as a Form of Personal Identity

Still, of all the groups to which a person can claim loyalty, religion is perhaps the most common. Indeed, some researchers suggest that Americans are more likely to identify themselves as members of a religious community than as a member of any other group. People who identify themselves as members of a religious group often associate themselves closely with an ethnic group as well. For example, an Irish Catholic may consider her- or himself substantively different from an Italian Catholic, and a Russian Jew may feel quite different from a German Jew. We are reminded in this regard of a story related by a colleague who was teaching about diversity at an urban university in a highly ethnic city. After several class sessions on the subject, a student came up after class to tell her that she (the student) could, indeed, relate to the lesson. "You know," the student said, "I went all through Catholic school in my own Irish neighborhood, and it wasn't until I got to college that I met some Italian Catholics. You're right, they sure are different!"

This differentiation results in part from differences in ethnic histories and in part from differences in the development of religious practices among members of the same general faith. An individual has only to attend services at churches of three or four different Protestant denominations (e.g., Presbyterian, Southern Baptist, high Episcopalian) to know that there is great diversity *within* the same religious tradition. This diversity is even more true for the world's major religions. The diversity within Christianity, or within Islam, or within Judaism is in many respects far greater than the diversity among them. Moreover, people who identify themselves with a particular religious group also usually have placed themselves in a particular social as well as geographical location. The very term *Southern Baptist,* for example, says a great deal about the geographical roots of a person's religious identity, and the term *high Episcopalian* may indicate something about the social class to which a person belongs.

Religious identity has its strongest roots in the family, and many families not only encourage but also demand that their children follow in their religious traditions. Indeed, some families will go so far as to deny the existence of a child who breaks with the faith, and some religious groups, such as the Old Order Amish, will occasionally invoke the practice of "shunning" (never speaking to or acknowledging the presence of the person being shunned) when a community member strays from the fold. The belief that a person's religious identity is an integral part of that person's essential self can be seen in the reaction of parents whose children join a cult of some kind. Such parents believe that their child has been brainwashed and often will hire an expert to "deprogram" their child.

Religious identification also places a person in a particular relationship with the deity (e.g., Catholics as part of a community of believers, Protestants in a one-to-one relationship with their deity). That relationship may determine a person's view of the possibility of a life after death, that person's set of moral codes for living, and the nature of rewards or punishments for the life that person has, in fact, led. Given the profound nature of these issues, it is not surprising that individuals, families, and communities react strongly to perceived threats to their religious beliefs.

At the same time (and perhaps paradoxically), in a religiously heterogeneous society such as the United States, people often switch from one religion to another, and an increasing number of people—estimated at about 14% by some surveys—declare no religion at all. The move from one religious affiliation to another may involve a formal conversion process, or it may be a move from a conservative to a more liberal branch of the same church (or vice versa). It may occur as the result of marriage between people of two faiths, or it may occur in an individual as an outgrowth of intellectual analysis. According to a poll by the Pew Research Center's Forum on Religion and Public Life (2009).

Large numbers of Americans engage in multiple religious practices, mixing elements of diverse traditions. Many say they attend worship services of more than one faith or denomination—even when they are not traveling or going to special events like weddings and funerals. Many also blend Christianity with Eastern or New Age beliefs such as reincarnation, astrology, and the presence of spiritual energy in physical objects. And sizeable minorities of all major U.S. religious groups say they have experienced supernatural phenomena, such as being in touch with the dead or with ghosts (p. 1).

©Mcraw-Hill Education

Those who declare no traditional religious affiliation may, in fact, be members of one of a growing number of religious bodies led by charismatic leaders such as Rick Warren (Saddleback Church in California) or Joel Osteen (Lakewood Church in Houston, Texas). Many of these so-called Megachurches (those having memberships of over 2,000 people) are employing television and the Internet to reach more and more potential congregants who would otherwise not be involved in any religious enterprises.

Clearly, the fastest growing churches in the United States tend to be conservative, sometimes evangelical or pentecostal, Protestant denominations, with an accompanying decline in membership of so-called mainline churches. There are probably a variety of reasons for this trend, not least among them the desire of many people for a solid, unquestioning, and dependable religious orientation at a time when change in all institutions means a dissolution of traditional rules for living. Observers might also argue that the trend toward conservatism reflects, in part, the shrinking of the middle class and the increasing economic gap between those who are wealthy and those who are not. If switching to liberal religious affiliations is a function of upward mobility, then the opposite is perhaps also true. For the first time in American history, there is a general perception that children may not "do better" than their parents, and the real or perceived fact of downward mobility can be related to an increasing desire and need to be a part of a community in which an individual can identify with virtue and righteousness.

At the same time, according to some observers, something new is stirring in all religions around the world, Christianity in particular. Harvey Cox (2009), for example, asserted that **fundamentalism** is dying and is being replaced by a vibrant, functioning kind of pentecostalism in which what he called the coming "Age of the Spirit" is replacing the "Age of Belief". This change can be seen in a number of ways: in people who say, "I'm not religious, but I am spiritual"; in an emphasis on the direct *experience* of religious life rather than on the rules and settings of religious practice; and in the growing number of congregations who do not use the term "church" for their places of worship, but, instead, title their communal gathering places "communities," "centers," "forums," or "life ministries."

And it appears to be a global phenomenon. At the moment, the greatest growth among pentecostals is in South America and Africa, not in North America or Europe. But in those societies struggling to become (or remain) democratic, pentecostalism thinks it has a lot to offer. It is growing in North America as well, and showing up in mainline churches, not always calling itself "Pentecostal." Indeed, Diana Butler Bass (2012) is among those scholars who are chronicling the characteristics of "new" mainline churches that show a spiritual vibrancy based around a serious engagement with faith practices such as prayer, hospitality, and enacting justice. These are active, friendly, and joyful congregations—and they are attracting those who are seeking a new Christian identity.

Organized Religion and the Net Generation

Still another factor in religious affiliation in the United States is the changing role that technology is playing in attracting new generations of members to religious organizations.

Those churches that are attracting large numbers of young people are also quite often those churches that have adopted new forms of worship, especially digital storytelling and contemporary Christian music (Sample, 1998; Wilson & Moore, 2002). Referring, for example, to young Catholics, Arthur Jones (2001) wrote that "the medium that communicates the message of these [religious] traditions has changed radically. Many young adults are pursuing a form of spirituality that is subtle, individual and hence unrecognizable to the older generations."

As it is with other social institutions, religion is having to confront the dawn of a new age, populated with young people for whom the "new age" is not new at all but rather is the context in which they have grown up. Speaking to an older generation, Wilson and Moore (2002) gave some indication of the dimensions of this wired world:

> A whole new digital world is emerging today. Can you see it? If you can, you know it is a world built on emotional, virtual, holographic, decentralized, holistic, empowered, one-by-one, borderless, bottom-up, global/local, and egalitarian characteristics. Such a world will play by totally different rules than the rules of modernity. In the twenty-first century to *not be digital* will be the new form of illiteracy (p. 11).

Others suggest that young people—familiarly known as Millennials—want to return religiously to a more stable time, adopting traditions from very early times. For Christians, this often means more use of ritual and symbol, more spaces for quiet and contemplation, more authenticity, and a convergence of musical styles (Newhouse, 2013).

Ways in which all organized religions will experience transformation in the years ahead, as well as ways in which religious ideas will be played out among the peoples of the world will be the subject of much discussion and debate—as will the role that religion plays in schooling in the United States and around the world.

The Current Status of Religious Practices in American Public Schools

In part because the pattern of public schooling in the United States emerged from the theocratic history of the Massachusetts Bay Colony, there has always been a kind of religious influence on American schooling. While most people would say that schooling is a public phenomenon and religion is a private one, we have seen in this chapter that there are both public and private aspects of religion as it works its way into educational decisions.

In some periods of our history, religion has played a determinedly *political* role in schooling. The selection of primary school books such as *The New England Primer*, which included protestant versions of Biblical language, was intended to inculcate children with the values of New England puritanism and republican government. More recently, electing folks who support conservative beliefs about education to seats on public school boards has been seen as a way to shape the curriculum by directing that anything to do with the theory of evolution be banished. Similarly, efforts have been made by particular religious groups to censor "dangerous" books such as *Huckleberry Finn*, *Of Mice and Men*, and, of course, the *Harry Potter* books.

The tension produced by the constitutional separation of church and state has meant a continual debate regarding the part played by schooling in both protecting religious liberty and enabling religious practice. However, in the past several years, schools have experienced some relaxation of strict separation of religion from schooling. Yet, many people don't know the current status of religion in American schools. The following is a summary of current law with respect to the protection of religious liberty and the prohibition of state-sponsored religious practice.

Fundamentally, the effort of the law is to be fair, to protect individual religious practice while avoiding any idea that the state (public schooling) is giving special status to any existing religion. Clearly, a major difference between public schools and private schools is that public schools are bound to uphold the Constitution is this regard.

The Establishment Clause

Some of the establishment clause issues that have reached the Supreme Court involve school sponsored student prayers over loudspeakers, required listening to and/or participation in Bible reading, belonging to religious clubs in school, providing access to the school to outside organizations that provide after-school religious instruction to young children, requiring moments of silence in lieu of formal prayers, and including the words "under God" to be included in the pledge of allegiance.

Decisions of the Court have been mixed on these matters. Public student prayers over loudspeakers and before sports events are unconstitutional. Student religious clubs enjoy the same status in schools as other student clubs. School districts are required to offer equal access to outside providers of after-school religious instruction to students. Moments of silence in lieu of school prayers are sometimes understood as opportunities for prayer. And it is undecided whether or not the phrase "under God" in the Pledge of Allegiance is unconstitutional. (Center for Public Education,2006).

Other Establishment Clause issues involve teaching about religious sacred texts (e.g., the Bible, the Torah, the Koran). The Court has found that such teaching is constitutional as long as it is not taught in the context of a devotion or as a singular truth. (Center for Public Education, 2006). Similarly, teachers and schools cannot give preferential treatment to believers, nor can they prohibit the wearing of special religious clothing such as yarmulkes for Jewish boys or hijabs for Muslim girls. In addition, tee-shirts, wrist bands, or jewelry that indicate religious belief cannot be forbidden by school districts or individual schools.

Free Exercise Clause

Of all the discussions, not to mention lawsuits, regarding the role of religion or its absence in schools, individual prayer seems to capture the most public attention, as well as perhaps the most attention from the Supreme Court.

In general, students may pray in public schools at will, so long as they are not interrupting or disturbing others. Students may be let out of class for ritual prayer or be dismissed from school early to attend religious instruction in another venue. Teachers may not use religious grounds to refuse to teach a particular section of approved curriculum. A teacher who is a Quaker, for example, cannot refuse to teach about historical or current wars on the grounds that he or she is a committed pacifist.

Free Exercise Clause cases in schools are often paired with First Amendment Free Speech provisions in the Constitution. Thus, students who profess religious ideas in classroom discussion or in written assignments may do so without fear of penalty; religious speech cannot be treated differently by teachers or school authorities just because of its content.

Looking to the Future

As the United States becomes more religiously diverse, one can expect continuing battles over religious issues in schools. The two "religious" clauses in the Constitution are inherently ambiguous. They have been described often as "freedom of religion" (free exercise of) and "freedom *from* religion" (establishment of). Undoubtedly, this ambiguity was purposeful, since many issues arising from the combination of secular schooling and religious beliefs are at best, unpredictable. Moreover, American society appears to be in a period of flux, leaning more toward individual interests and rights and less toward what might be called the common good. Whether than trend continues or becomes more balanced will probably influence the nature of the role of religion in public schools in the future.

Ethical Issues

This chapter has emphasized that teachers who address religious issues in their classrooms must understand their communities and not go too far beyond the values that the community holds. This advice may appear to be common sense and carries with it a certain degree of self-preservation, but it also importantly suggests the belief that *all* deeply held religious beliefs are worthy of respect.

Within the classroom, teachers must be on the lookout for and intercede in instances of religious prejudice, particularly as it might be expressed in the casual name-calling that children do so easily. Like all other forms of prejudice, religious prejudice is learned—and can be unlearned (though not easily). Respectful behavior toward others, however, can and should be insisted upon.

Another ethical issue concerns the responsibility of teachers to be familiar with federal and state laws with respect to religion and schooling. The classroom teacher often must serve in the role of instructor to parents and community members as well as to students and should be knowledgeable about the development of and debates about religious differences that are a part of the fabric of law and judicial decision in the United States.

With respect to relations with parents and the community, teachers should also be knowledgeable about the bases of different religious beliefs and should be as ready and willing as possible to answer questions and discuss objections calmly. There are times when it is not possible to reach consensus, and finding effective ways of agreeing to disagree is both useful and wise.

Critical Incident

Celebrating the Holidays

Allie McNeal was a classmate of Melissa's; the two went through high school and then college together. Allie now teaches third grade at Thomas Edison Elementary School, located in a diverse community in a suburb of Denver. She is a member of the school planning committee for all special events in the school, including the celebration of holidays. Her committee had sent a survey to all the parents, explaining that the school was exploring the possibility of removing "Christmas" from the annual December activities—substituting instead activities having to do with winter—and asking the parents what they thought. The rationale was that because the school has a large number of children from different religious backgrounds, celebrating Christmas spoke to only some of the children, but not all.

Allie has just received an impassioned phone call from one mother, demanding that they not only *keep* Christmas in the holiday schedule, but that they also eliminate Halloween. The mother expressed—in no uncertain terms—the belief that the United States is a Christian country and that other people had just better get used to it. She went on to say that she was the spokesperson for a large number of other parents who would be asking for an appointment with the principal to discuss the matter. She was especially adamant about Halloween, saying that it was a form of devil worship, and that her group did not want their children to participate in any celebration that included pagan signs and symbols.

Allie was quite taken aback at the intensity of the mother's appeal. She knew she had better speak to the principal about the forthcoming visit, and she also knew she had to make some recommendations to her committee.

• If Allie telephoned you asking for advice, how would you suggest she handle this situation?

Critical Incident

Suggested Reading?

George Manson, a seventh-grade English teacher in the middle school just down the road from Melissa, received a call from the father of one of his students, Rema Assadi, a Muslim girl who had brought home a novel she had selected from George's list of recommended books. The novel, one that had been chosen by librarians in the state as among the best modern fiction for middle schoolers, concerned an American girl going to school in London whose 11-year-old brother had been killed by a bomb detonated by a Muslim girl attempting to avoid an arranged marriage to a man in his 50s who already had two other wives. The book contained numerous stereotypes of Muslims, portraying them as abusers of women, anti-Semitic, under the control of their religious leaders, and prone to violence. Both Rema and her family were upset and frightened at the thought that other students in the class would be reading this book. After the violent attacks on September 11, 2001, the family feared a major backlash against Muslims.

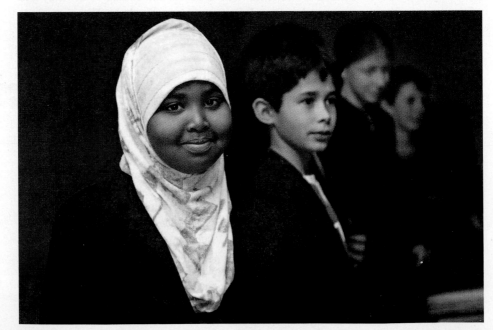

Mr. Assadi told George that his religious community was mounting a letter-writing and e-mail campaign aimed at the publisher of the book, trying to persuade the company to recall it. In the meantime, he asked, would George please take the book off his recommended reading list? And would he talk to his students about the book, making sure they understood how biased it was?

• If you were George, what would you do?

Summary

Because the United States was founded on the principle of religious liberty, the framers of the Constitution built into the First Amendment both a prohibition against a state religion and a prohibition against limiting the free expression of religious beliefs and practices. That ambiguity has led to considerable dispute over the role of religion in American society and particularly in American schools.

The principle of separation of church and state has not prevented many people from believing that schools should be a repository of morality; the question has always been "Whose morality are we talking about?" Because we are a nation of laws, much of the "action" regarding religion and schooling has been in the courts, which have struggled with this issue over the years, often reversing previous decisions, but always trying to come to a reasonable balance between competing views.

This balance has been impeded by the myth that teachers may not talk about religion in schools; this myth is not true. Indeed, the decision that "banned" school prayer explicitly notes that exposure to the story of the world's great religions is necessary for a complete education. This chapter describes the nature of the debate over religion in public schooling and the importance of attending to the diverse religious backgrounds of American students. In an increasingly interdependent world, it is both necessary and prudent that we understand and respect the religious impulse that influences human identity and guides human behavior.

Chapter Review

Go to the Online Learning Center at www.mhhe.com/cushner9e to review important content from the chapter, practice with key terms, take a chapter quiz, and access Active Workbook Exercises.

Key Terms

African religions 277
cultural capital 274
establishment clause
of the First
Amendment 274

Fourteenth
Amendment 274
fundamentalism 292
prohibition clause of the
First Amendment 274

separation of church
and state 283
theocracy 274

Purpose: To assist you with gaining greater understanding and reducing stereotypes of the major religions that may be encountered in schools and communities.
Instructions: Derive a series of interview questions using the guidelines below. Then conduct interviews with individuals who represent religions other than your own.

1. In small groups, generate potential interview questions you could use to help gain greater understanding and reduce misperceptions about religions other than your own.

2. Discuss these questions with the class and determine which among them will help to uncover stereotypes, attitudes, perceptions, and misperceptions of a particular group.

3. Agree as a class upon 5 to 7 questions that will generate the most useful information.

4. Using the same questions, individually or in pairs, interview at least two individuals from religious groups other than your own. You should try to find representatives from at least the five major world religions (Christianity, Judaism, Islam, Buddhism, and Hinduism), as well as any other groups of interest and available in your region.

5. Individually, summarize key points of your interviews.

6. As a class, discuss the following questions:

   a. Did the questions you asked provide you with the information you had hoped for?

   b. Discuss at least one response that you found surprising or interesting. What did you find especially intriguing about this response?

   c. Was there anything the interviewee said that led you to reconsider any of your views?

   d. Did you learn anything significant from the interviewee about the religion?

   e. Were any stereotypes you might have held about this religion challenged?

   f. Now that the interviews are complete, are there any questions you wished you had asked?

   g. What did you learn in this exercise that will influence your teaching?

Classroom Activities

1. In an elementary school classroom, have students research religious holidays for a variety of religious traditions, for example, Jewish, Muslim, Christian, Buddhist, Hinduism, Taoism, and so forth, with the goal of creating an annual calendar of religious festivals and holidays from around the world. Much material for such a study is available online and students will learn, among other things, that the world's major religions probably have as much in common as they have differences.

2. Elementary school students might also be interested in reading stories about world religions; some of these might include both folktales from various religious traditions and explanatory books written for children.

3. High school students might research some (or all!) of the Supreme Court cases discussed in Chapter 9, studying the arguments used in the case and the rationale used by the judges in deciding on the case. A variation of this activity might be for a whole class to study one or two seminal cases and then participate in a mock court in which the arguments are presented and the judges discuss aspects of the case prior to writing their decisions. Students would take the roles of attorneys and each of the judges in the actual case.

4. Organizing, researching, and participating in a debate is an activity that high school students usually enjoy. In this case, students could debate any of a number of "propositions" that are currently matters of debate surrounding religion and schools. For example, Should Public Funding Be Awarded to Support Private, Parochial Schools? Or, What Are the Pros and Cons of Using Christmas as the Focal Point of a Winter Break Holiday for Schools? Or, What Difficulties Are Presented by the First Amendment's Establishment and Free Exercise Clauses Regarding Religion in the United States?

Reflective Questions

Quite unintentionally, indeed with the very best of intentions, Melissa Morgan found herself in the center of a controversy that could have turned into a major issue both in her classroom and in her community. On reflection, it is likely that Melissa might have asked herself the following questions. Think about how you would answer these questions if you were in Melissa's place.

1. Having grown up in a town very much like the one in which she taught and having taught in her school for 5 years, how is it that Melissa didn't think about what she knew to be a streak of deep-seated conservatism present in the community?

2. Once her students' project was under way, are there strategies she could have used that might have forestalled the objections voiced by some parents after they saw the exhibit at the open house?

3. As is evident in other examples in this book, acting as an agent of change can be surprisingly challenging, particularly when the school in which you teach is a very traditional one. Certainly, it is often easier to go with the flow of traditional school culture than to try to change it. It does not appear, however, that Melissa thought of herself as a change agent; rather, she was attempting only to utilize existing human and intellectual resources in a better way for the sake of her students. What are some of the factors that turn a seemingly innocent curricular activity into a potential source of protest?

4. Melissa attempted to resolve the issue by going to a number of community leaders. Are there dangers in this strategy? What might some of those dangers be?

5. Melissa could have simply dismissed the objections raised to her use of religious information in the classroom as ignorant, unenlightened, or prejudiced behavior. How would that view have undermined her strong belief in religious pluralism?

6. When the episode was over, Melissa began to think about some of the long-standing practices of American schooling, such as the way most schools use Christian holidays—particularly Christmas and Easter—as sources for both curricular and extracurricular activities. Are such traditional practices fitting subjects for review and rethinking?

7. In her meeting with the clergy council, Melissa did not mention that, according to the most recent Supreme Court decisions, she was well within her rights to teach *about* religion in her classroom. Should she have raised that issue? Might there have been some negative results if she had?

Endnote

1. This list was adapted and extended from R. Stark & C. Y. Glock, "Dimensions of Religious Commitment," in R. Robertson, *Sociology of Religion,* p. 46; cited in Donna M. Gollnick & Philip C. Chinn, *Multicultural Education in a Pluralistic Society,* 3rd ed. (New York: Macmillan, 1990), p. 175.

References

AARDOC. (2006). African-American religion: A documentary history project. *Atlantic World.* Retrieved from http://www.amherst.edu/˜aardoc/Atlantic_World.html

ACLU. (2017). *Joint statement on current law on religion in the public schools.* Retrieved from https://www.aclu.org/other/joint-statement-current-law-religion-public-schools

Abington Township District School v. Schempp, 374 U.S. 203 (1963).

Ackerman, D. M. (1998). The Religious Freedom Restoration Act: Its rise, fall, and current status." CRS Report for Congress, available at http://digital.library.unt.edu/ark:/67531/metacrs570/

Al-Ani, S. H. (1995). Muslims in America and Arab Americans. In C. L. Bennett, *Comprehensive multicultural education: Theory and practice* (3rd ed.). Boston: Allyn & Bacon.

Bader, C., et al. (2006). *American piety in the 21st century: New insights to the depth and complexity of religion in the US.* The Baylor Religion Survey, Baylor Institute for Studies of Religion. Retrieved from http://www.baylor.edu/content/services/document.php/33304.pdf

Bass, D. B. (2012). Christianity after religion: *The end of church and the birth of a new spiritual awakening.* New York: Harper One.

Berger, P. L., & Berger, B. (1972). S*ociology: A biographical approach.* New York: Basic Books.

Butts, R. F. (1978). *Public education in the United States: From revolution to reform.* New York: Holt, Rinehart, & Winston.

Cochran v. Louisiana State Board of Education, 281 U.S. 370 (1930).

Cox, Harvey. (2009). *The future of faith.* New York: Harper One.

DeVos, Betsy. (2017). Prepared remarks to the Brookings Institution. Washington, DC: *U.S. Department of Education.* Retrieved from https://www.ed.gov/news/speeches/us-secretary-education-betsy-devos-prepared-remarks-brookings-institution

Durkheim, E. (1969). The social foundations of religion. In R. Robertson (Ed.), *Sociology of religion.* Baltimore: Penguin Books.

Everson v. Board of Education, 330 U.S. 1 (1947).

Frieden, T. (2002). Supreme Court affirms school voucher program. Retrieved from http://archives.cnn.com/2002/LAW/06/27/scotus.school.vouchers

Gollnick, D. M., & Chinn, P. C. (2004). *Multicultural education in a pluralistic society* (6th ed.). Upper Saddle River, NJ: Pearson.

Haynes, C. C. (2007) Religious Holidays In Public Schools. (Ch. 8) in Finding common ground: *A guide to religious liberty in public schools.* Washington, DC: First Amendment Center.

Jones, A. (2001, March 30). Engaging, keeping new Catholic generations. *National Catholic Reporter.* Retrieved from http://www.natcath.com/NCR_Online/archives/033001/033001s.htm

Lee v. Weisman, 112 S. Ct. 2649 (1992).

Meyer v. Nebraska, 262 U.S. 390 (1923).

Minersville v. Gobitis, 310 U.S. 586 (1940).

National Center for Education Statistics (2010). Available at http://nces.ed.gov/fastfacts/display.asp?id=16

Newhouse, C. (2013). The forgotten millennials, *Christianity Today,* available at http://www.christianitytoday.com/ct/2013/june/forgotten-millennials.html

Pang, V. O., & Barba, R. H. (1995). The power of culture: Building culturally affirming instruction. In C. A. Grant (Ed.), *Educating for diversity: An anthology of multicultural voices.* Boston: Allyn & Bacon.

Pew Research Center's Forum on Religion and Public Life (2009). Many Americans mix multiple faiths. Retrieved from http://www.pewforum.org/docs/?DocID=490

Pew Forum on Religion and Public Life (2015). The Future of World Religions: Population Growth Projections, 2010–2050. Retrieved from http://www.pewforum.org/2015/04/02/religious-projections-2010-2050/

Pierce v. Society of Sisters, 268 U.S. 510 (1925).

Sample, T. (1998). *The spectacle of worship in a wired world: Electronic culture and the gathered people of God.* Nashville, TN: Abingdon Press.

Santa Fe Independent School District v. Doe, 530 U.S. 290 (2000).

Smith, J. I. (n/d). *Patterns of Muslim immigration.* Bureau of International Information Programs, U.S. Department of State. Retrieved from http://usinfo.state.gov/products/pubs/muslimlife/immigrat.htm

Sowell, T. (1980). *Ethnic America: A history.* New York: Basic Books.

Uphoff, J. K. (1993). Religious diversity and education. In J. A. Banks & C. A. McG. Banks (Eds.), *Multicultural education: Issues and perspectives* (2nd ed.). Boston: Allyn & Bacon.

Van Biema, D. (2007, April 2). The case for teaching the Bible. *Time Magazine,* pp. 40–46.

West Virginia State Board of Education v. Barnette, 319 U.S. 624 (1943).

Wilson, L., & Moore, J. (2002). *Digital storytellers: The art of communicating the gospel in worship.* Nashville, TN: Abingdon Press.

Wisconsin v. Yoder, 406 U.S. 213 (1972).

Yinger, J. M. (1970). *The scientific study of religion.* New York: Macmillan.

Zorach v. Clauson, 343 U.S. 306 (1952).

Developing Gender Inclusive Schools and Classrooms: The Emergence of Gender and Sexual Diversity

Focus Questions

1. If you were buying clothes for a newborn, how would you select the color?
2. What do you think about girls who often use vulgar language? How about boys who do?
3. If you were babysitting for a 3-year-old boy whose favorite toys were dolls, what might you think?
4. How might you feel if your favorite cousin—or your sister—suddenly declared that she was a lesbian?
5. Has anyone (parent, friend, guidance counselor) ever told you that certain subjects were not "suitable" for you because of your gender?
6. What do you think about the increasing number of males who are nurses? What about females who work in construction?
7. Do you think that gender is a spectrum?

" A recent survey of a thousand millennials found that half of them think gender is a spectrum. "

ROBIN MARANTZ-HENIG

Case Study

I Never Expected Such a Firestorm!

Joanne Thomas, high school health teacher in southern South Dakota, walked briskly into the conference room in the Board of Education building. There was quite a crowd in there: all seven members of the School Board, the Superintendent of Schools, the high school principal, about 10 teachers, perhaps 30 parents, 2 reporters from the local newspaper, and 7 high school students. The meeting was to discuss concerns related to the establishment of a Gay-Straight Alliance (GSA) group in the high school, a group that had asked Joanne to be its advisor.

She could feel the tension in the room as she found a seat near the students, all of whom were representing the Alliance.

"What do you people think you're doing?" called out one of the fathers in the room. "I can't believe that you are sanctioning a group for gays and queers!"

"That's my question, too," shouted another father. "Those people defy God's law!"

"I'm afraid my daughter will get wrong ideas from these kids," said one of the mothers, joining in the fray.

"Hold it, everyone, please," said the Board Chair. "We've come to discuss this, not to yell at each other." The room quieted down a bit.

"Now, here's how I'd like to begin. There have been a number of rumors floating around town about this Alliance, and most of them are so over the top as to be outright lies. So, before we open the floor for discussion, which I promise will happen, I'd like to ask Mrs. Thomas to tell us how this whole thing started, to describe the reasons why it got started, and what it's mission is. Is that all right, Mrs. Thomas?"

Joanne, as calm as she could be under the circumstances, smiled at the crowd and stood up, moving to the microphone that had been set up in the front of the room. She looked at the Board Chair and said, "Yes, of course, I'd be happy to do that."

The crowd, still restless, was silent.

"It all began about 6 months ago, right after school started. I was getting ready to leave for the day when two students knocked at the door and asked if they could talk with me for a moment. I knew them from one of my classes, and asked them to come in. I sat down in one of the class chairs and asked them to sit down, too, which they did. They looked a bit uncomfortable to me, so I asked them what was up and how I could help them."

Abby is an African American senior, school leader, and quite a social justice advocate. Zach is also a senior, not quite as in-your-face as Abby, but known throughout the school as someone that any student could talk to and find understanding and support if needed. Abby, as usual, took the lead.

"Well," she said, "we need to start a Gay-Straight Alliance in this high school, and we need to do it now! Do you know, there are students in this school who are being bullied, taunted, called names, and just about shunned because they are gay, or lesbian, or somehow don't fit into traditional gender categories? And nobody does anything about it! Not even people who don't think it's right! The only person I know here who even talks about gender and sexual diversity is you, and you only do it when you're teaching lessons about it! One of these days, one of these kids is going to commit suicide, and then everyone will be appalled, and say, 'Well, I just didn't realize it was that bad for them here, and then it'll be too late!"

Joanne continued, "I have to admit I was startled. But I also have to say that I had seen some evidence of the behavior that Abby was talking about, and, to my shame, I *didn't* do anything about it."

Zach took over in his easy way. "I think maybe Abby is exaggerating just a little bit, Mrs. Thomas. I don't think anyone's ready to kill himself or herself yet. But what she talks about in terms of some other students' behavior toward them is true. I've talked with some of the kids who are being hassled, and they are hurting. They're also getting angry, not only because they're being treated badly with no consequences for the kids who are after them, but because no adults are sticking up for them. And they know that around the country, and around the world for that matter, young people like themselves are rebelling, and asking—even demanding—to be heard."

"So," said Abby, "if we start a Gay-Straight Alliance (GSA), will you be our advisor?"

Joanne looked at her audience of mostly unhappy people. "I was a bit surprised when they asked me to take on starting and advising the group, but the more I thought about it, the more I thought such initiative from these students should be encouraged, so I said "Sure, I think that would be a good idea."

"The students arranged the first brain-storming session, which of course I attended. There were seven students there: Abby and Zach, of course, and one boy who said he was gay, two girls who identified themselves as lesbian, one boy who identified as Questioning, and one girl who said she was trapped in a girl's body but really identified as a boy. I didn't know all of them personally, but they were so eager and so excited—and also so tentative, wondering how I would react to them—that I plunged right in. I had found some resources for starting a GSA, and as I shared them with the students, they began to talk about how they could begin.

"The first thing is to start a GSA the same way you would start any school club or group, by following the rules listed in the students' or school handbook for doing such a thing. And one of those things was talking with the school Principal and getting permission. The next thing was finding an advisor, which they had already done—me." Joanne laughed a little, and got a few smiles from the audience.

"When they had received a go-ahead from the Principal, and made their plans for how the GSA would get off the ground, they spoke with the Principal again, making sure that he knew what was happening all along the way. At the first meeting, which they publicized with flyers and word-of-mouth, 10 students showed up. Some were gay—or, as they informed us—gender non-conforming, and some were straight—most but not all were already friends. All were congenial and spent the meeting time talking about how the group should develop and what it should try to accomplish.

"I told them that Gay-Straight Alliances all over the country had three main missions: social support, education, and advocacy. The *social support mission* was to create a safe space for everyone to find and/or create a support network; the *educational mission* was to provide activities for the group and for all students in the school to raise awareness of the issues; and the *advocacy mission* was to create events that highlight Lesbian, Gay, Bisexual, Transgender and Queer (LGBTQ) contributions and to promote changes that will better protect LGBTQ students through non-discrimination and anti-bullying policies." They were interested in this trio of missions and spent the rest of the first meeting talking about them and what they could do to put them into action.

"It's taken 5 months to get to this point, and the group is ready to do its first event—a kind of Gay-Straight Alliance Fair, in which a number of booths and exhibits will be set up in the gym from 3:30 to 8:00 on a Wednesday afternoon and evening, staffed by members of the GSA, to improve awareness of issues of discrimination, of language (because there are new terms that are used by LBGTQ youth and their allies to describe the variety of ways in which young people are defining their identities), and a series of posters, made by students in the school who may not even be members of the GSA. Anybody in the school or in the community is welcome to come and see what's going on. And, apparently, there will be food!" And that's where we are at the moment."

Mrs. Thomas sat down.

The room was very quiet for a moment. And then it got very loud. Arguments for and against the GSA being allowed to continue were advanced. Bible quotations were used by both sides—sometimes the same scripture used for both pro and con arguments. Some folks wondered if the public school was the right place for such activity. Others noted that all school districts in South Dakota had versions of the federal Office of Civil Rights non-discrimination policy in effect. Some parents were vociferous in their claim that the subject matter underlying this group was only to be done within the family and the school was the wrong place for it. Defenders retorted that if folks thought sex was not alive and well in the high school already, they'd been out of high school too long. A small group of teachers and other community members pointed out that actions on behalf of students who are sexually diverse is not much

(continued)

different than actions on behalf of African Americans, women and girls, and children with disabilities. It had always been a fight to introduce something that seemed to "attack" the dominant society.

Finally, the high school principal asked to be recognized, and spoke to the crowd. "When Abby and Zach came to me about this idea, I, too, was surprised. I really hadn't been aware that there was a problem—and I was a little ashamed that I hadn't. The students were very organized, very thoughtful, and very committed. They were everything we say we want our students to be. They saw a need and sought to fill it. So, I said "yes." I had no idea it would cause such a firestorm. And I'm sorry that it has.

"I can empathize with parents who are shocked and angry. We should have engaged with the community earlier in the planning. But I am hopeful that everyone here would calm down and think a bit more about it. Come to the GSA Fair and learn more about these students and their allies. I would like to meet again with you all after the Fair. And, I would like to propose to the Board that they vote to affirm the establishment of this group in the high school, understanding that we will be doing our best to seek allies among you all as we move forward."

The Principal took his seat One Board member moved to support the establishment of the group. Another seconded the motion.

How do you think they voted?

Case Analysis

The meeting in the Board building in a school district in South Dakota has been and continues to be repeated in communities all across the country. Despite, or perhaps growing out of the women's movement of the past nearly 60 years, a new advocacy is emerging—directed toward issues revolving around gender expression and sexual diversity. The time when life appeared to be simpler, when sexual "diversity" meant only males and females, men and women, guys and dolls, is over. All over the world, including the United States, a growing generation of young people is insisting on being recognized for who they are, or feel they are, sexually, as well as by race, class, or religion. Such insistence has produced a descriptive language, a series of court cases, and a feeling of solidarity among many of those who, for one reason or another, find themselves as people whose gender identity does not match the sex indicators they were born with.

Should you think that only the gender non-conforming youth are part of this movement, think again: girls and boys whose gender *does* match their birth sex indicators are also members in good standing—many of them, anyway. They are allies and they are fighting in their own right, for recognition as women and men who are changing the definitions of male and female to more adequately and accurately what gender means in this and many other societies.

The students in Mrs. Thomas's Gay-Straight Alliance may identify their gender in many different ways. The most familiar are lesbian, gay, bisexual, and transgender (LGBT). Another gender expression is Queer (Q), which in spite of its use as a term of derision, has been taken on by many as a badge of honor and usually is used as an umbrella term for all those who do not identify as male or female, boy/man or girl/woman. So, we have LGBTQ. And still another letter grouping adds (I) Intersexual—those who biologically have some or all of both sex indicators from birth and (2-s) Two-Spirit—those, especially Native American, who have adopted, regardless of how they were born, a special, third gender way of taking roles in the tribe. Historically, they were considered very special, and often became teachers, storytellers, and healers. So, now, students may identify themselves as LGBTQI2-s.

The school, as has often been the case, has become a battleground for some of these issues. The public is at best bewildered and at worst completely hostile both to new gender terminology and to the very reality of students and others who dare to insist on being themselves. The school in South Dakota is fortunate in having a sympathetic and forward-looking Principal. Many are not, or at least would not willingly involve their school in such controversy.

Nationally, there are five aspects of schooling that provide reasons for paying attention to gender and sexual diversity:

1. *Student safety.* Bullying and harassment are common in schools, even though we have recently had a major campaign against bullying. Much of it today is directed toward those children who don't conform to dominant ideas of heterosexual dress, actions, and activities.

2. *Physical and emotional health.* Many students feel isolated and denigrated in school and this has long-term negative effects on them, both physically and emotionally. Finding themselves in a hostile environment, some try to escape by skipping school, or abusing drugs and alcohol, and with the addition of social media bullying, some even commit suicide.

3. *Diversity and Equity.* One of the reasons for public schooling is to educate students to live in a democratic society. As students have become more diverse, in many ways, educators are slowly beginning to realize that they must and can adapt to include voices, experiences, and perspectives of the multicultural society in which we live. It is necessary that all students be able to have the benefits of a "little" democratic society in their high school.

4. *Student engagement and academic success.* It is necessary that educators provide positive school climates for everyone, by developing policies and practices for all school personnel so that they come to know and understand what sexual as well as other types of diversity are all about.

5. In order to increase opportunities for all students to achieve academic success, we have to teach about gender and sexual diversity, an effort that can be done in many kinds of classes, not just health (Meyer, 2010).

These are only some of the ways that schools like the one in South Dakota can provide a healthy environment for all students. There are others, of course, waiting only for school folks and students to think of them. As with any kind of difference, when it is understood, welcomed, and folded into the common human "body" of the school or the society, it enriches everyone.

Rationale for Gender-Inclusive Schools

The rationale for seeing that all schools are gender inclusive is basically the same as it is for making schools inclusive for students representing all other kinds of diversity. First, the students are *there*. Whether it's race, social class, disability, native language, or religion that gives them a little different character, they are there. Whether it's through immigration or migration, they are there. Whether they are 5 years old or 18 years old, whether they've been there from the beginning of kindergarten or moved in last week, they are there. And they cannot be ignored.

Matters of gender have always been part of schooling. In the last century, it was not uncommon for girls and boys to enter the school through different doorways; girls and boys were separated for some subject areas, for example boys took shop and girls took home economics; and certainly, if any sex education classes were in the curriculum, girls and boys were taught separately. Until 1974, pregnant female teachers in many districts were forced to leave their jobs early in their pregnancies and not return until several months after their children were born (*Cleveland Board of Education v. LaFleur*, 1974). It was not until 1978 that Congress passed the Pregnancy Discrimination Act (PL 95-555), which prohibited discrimination on the basis of pregnancy, childbirth, or related medical conditions as unlawful under Title VII of the Civil Rights Act. Furthermore, most teachers were women and most principals and superintendents were men (Strober & Tyack, 1980).

While many of these traditions are no longer in place, the history they represent lives on. Remember that schools have two major purposes: to give students knowledge and skills so that they can manage the society when they grow up, and to socialize them into what it means to be a member of that society. The first is fairly straightforward; the second has all kinds of hidden curricula. Schools have an important, though little discussed, function as socializers to societal norms, particularly those associated with the middle class. Because these norms are so much a part of what most people in schools believe is correct, they seem "normal" and "right" and are usually taken very much for granted. That sense of "normality" is probably the most powerful force operating to encourage obedience to norms. However, other factors are involved in encouraging normative thought and behavior as well. In all societies, there are sanctions, or punishments, for deviation from norms. These sanctions operate in schools on a daily basis, and most of them are particularly social sanctions. Consider again, for example, that girls may avoid taking advanced science or math classes because they don't want boys to think they're "too smart." The assumption of some girls is that the boys will "sanction" them socially for appearing to compete with them academically. Or consider the overt social sanctioning of boys who are gay by those boys who are straight, which is perhaps the most intense sanctioning that occurs. A number of lesser normative rules are broken every day in schools, by both males and females, and it appears that as gender roles change (which they are doing, but slowly), the social sanctions are also becoming less severe. Nevertheless, the power of gender role stereotypes is enormous and frequently costly to both males and females.

Finally, it is also the case that the presence of many different backgrounds among the students of a school adds immeasurably to the character and interest of the school community as a whole. While American public schools have been struggling to turn student diversity into opportunities for all students to share their differences, some colleges and universities have gone to court to defend their Affirmative Action plans, arguing that one reason for implementing such plans is that a diverse student body is, by its very existence, a better learning environment (*Grutter v. Bollinger*, 439 U.S. 306, 2003). While these cases have been about race, the argument is no less true for sexual and all other diversities.

Characteristics of a Gender Inclusive Classroom

The first, and probably most important, characteristic of a gender-inclusive classroom is that all students feel safe in that space. The first statewide legislation explicitly designed to provide such safety was in Massachusetts and is called the Safe Space

Program for LGBTQ students. The seeds of this program were in a 1993 Report called "Making Schools Safe for Gay and Lesbian Youth: Breaking the Silence in Schools and in Families." The report, written to the Massachusetts Commission on Gay and Lesbian Youth, was written by Kevin Jennings, founder of GLSEN (Gay, Lesbian, Straight Education Network) who, in 2009 became part of the Obama administration in the U.S. Department of Education.

In 2015, the state of Massachusetts issued *Principles of Ensuring Safe and Supportive Learning Environments for Lesbian, Gay, Bisexual, Transgender, Queer, and Questioning (LGBTQ) Student,* which can be used as a guide for characteristics of gender-inclusive schools and classrooms. Some of these guidelines include:

- Schools have updated policies which protect LGBTQ students against harassment, violence, and discrimination.

- School personnel must be trained in content about violence and suicide prevention related to LGBTQ students.

- Schools are encouraged to offer school-based groups for LGBTQ and heterosexual students.

- School districts are encouraged to designate a staff member who is proficient in issues related to sexual orientation and gender identity.

- Schools, through their curricula, shall encourage respect for the human and civil rights of all individuals, including LGBTQ individuals.

- Schools are encouraged to provide age-appropriate information about LGBTQ issues in school libraries and in student and faculty resource centers.

- Schools are encouraged to have a diverse workforce.

- Schools are encouraged to review academic and non-academic policies and procedures, and available data, to identify issues or patterns that may create barriers to a safe and successful learning experience for LGBTQ students (Principles, 2015).

Pedagogies: Old and New

Teaching in a classroom that is a safe space where multiple perspectives are encouraged does not require a whole new set of pedagogical ideas and practices. It does require, however, that teachers must be explicit about working toward this outcome. Basic expectations for the class should be given early in the semester, or year, and students should be involved in creating these expectations in order to build a classroom community.

Classrooms in which teachers and students construct the small society they are in a given class relies on what is called "constructivist" ideas; it is student-centered. Learning activities try to engage students in discussion, to encourage them to explore both the subject matter and the differences in their understanding of that subject. Small team projects might be part of the approach, but be careful: many students today have been "small-grouped" to death and shy away from any suggestion that they might actually want to work in groups. What is important is that students have the power to seek answers to their own questions on their own. Conversation is an interesting pedagogical tool; it is not lecturing (although sometimes a *little* lecture is useful, when students need background knowledge that is necessary in order to proceed). Such *little* lectures might cover, for instance, the background of a court case, or a brief history of a social

©PhotoAlto/Alamy Stock Photo RF

movement; think about the connections from civil rights to women's rights to the rights of sexually diverse students. Non-traditional assignments might also play a role in the pedagogy of a safe classroom, for example, interviewing people in the community about the evolution of the meaning of gender, or making a short film to portray the actual gendered lives of students in one's high school.

Another approach might be to create a classroom as a forum, encouraging students to talk about their ideas in a democratic or citizenship framework in which students must try hard to find common ground, for example, make decisions about issues such as how their class would be run. Or, even better, involving students in real-life community issues, for example, letter-writing campaigns, attending school board or city council meetings, or even distributing materials during a political campaign.

A third approach might be to engage students in independent or collective research on a subject chosen by the class (which might also be an activity that teaches democratic citizenship!). What the choices might be depends somewhat on what the class is about, but there are many opportunities for research in any subject. Whether the whole class researches one topic, or each student chooses his or her own topic—or a combination—the important part is the ability to choose within a framework of the subject matter and the need to provide room for everyone's participation.

Roles: Old and New

The traditional roles of teacher as teller and student as listener change in a safe classroom. Rather than always being the expert, the teacher often acts as coach, encouraging and assisting students to complete the assigned tasks. Students also serve as coaches for one another and, not infrequently, find themselves acting as experts in particular areas. One of the most obvious examples of this phenomenon is the native Spanish, French, or German speaker in a foreign-language classroom. There are, however, many other ways in which students of all ages can provide expert knowledge and skills to their fellow students. For instance, the student who is highly tech savvy on all the latest gadgets or one who is proficient in playing a musical instrument can become active as a peer-tutor in these areas.

One of the most important role changes in a gender-inclusive classroom, however, is that of parents. In traditional elementary classrooms, parents ordinarily serve in various "motherly" capacities, such as providing goods for a bake sale, bringing treats on birthdays, and acting as planners for holiday celebrations. Parents also are expected to ensure that homework assignments are completed and to attend open houses and parent-teacher conferences. In traditional middle and high school classrooms, the role of parents is often limited to these latter functions.

In gender-inclusive classrooms, however, parents (and grandparents, and other community members with some interest or expertise) are often central to the instructional program, helping to make and implement curricular and instructional decisions. For example, parents and others may take an important role in normalizing students who are gender non-conforming, for example, demonstrating to other students that their child is loved (and taught and scolded) just like any other child.

To summarize, in gender-inclusive classrooms parents and other community members share with teachers and other school staff the responsibility for educating all children. This partnership model views parents as resources and contributors to the education of their children and helps integrate the school and the community. Oakes and Lipton (2003) suggested that real changes in schools will take place only when the relationships of power begin to change and when the voices and concerns of parents and the community are heard, engaged with, and acted upon.

Place of Content Knowledge: Old and New

In gender-inclusive classrooms where teachers, parents, other school personnel, and students work together, boundaries between academic disciplines tend to become less defined as cooperative teams pool their knowledge in the pursuit of integrated projects. As teachers learn about what other teachers are doing, they begin to see ways of integrating their efforts. In such classrooms, the language arts and social studies may begin to merge, and the arts may be put to use in the service of scientific and geographical knowledge.

It is equally important to note that in gender-inclusive classrooms content about the whole spectrum of gender identity is taught to all students. In elementary schools, this might be part of the study of families that are part of most elementary curricula. Children today live in all kinds of family forms—single-parent families, families with two fathers or two mothers, families headed by grandmothers or grandfathers, families with traditional fathers and mothers. All of these must be made welcome in the classroom and seen as part of a mosaic of families.

Early childhood educator Theresa Bouley said:

> In our efforts to provide the best learning environment possible for all children, we must break the silence, bring visibility to all families, and open up the discourse relating to the inclusion of gay/lesbian issues in elementary schools (Bouley, 2007).

In secondary schools, all subjects can and should include attention to gender identity and sexual diversity. This can be done in a wide variety of ways: select literature that has characters who are gay or questioning, or literature that is about being "different" in the world; use LGBTQ demographics, among other examples, when studying statistics in math; teach the history of the gay liberation movement in social studies; teach gender expression and the male-female binary in biology; and use theatre to explore the experiences of those who are in some way "other". All of these examples and many others can be integrated into regular course work, right along with more traditional content. The idea is to both impart knowledge of gender expression and to normalize it as one more indicator of what it means to be human.

A good example of this "blurring" of disciplinary boundaries was given by Charles Fowler (1994). He wrote:

> If, for example, students are studying the Grand Canyon, and we want to give them a general idea of it without actually going there, we often resort to a verbal description: "The Grand Canyon, the world's largest gorge, is a spectacle of multicolored layers of rock carved out over the millennia by the Colorado River." If we want to convey its vastness, we use measurements: "The Grand Canyon is over 1 mile deep, 4 to 18 miles wide, and more than 200 miles long." Each of these symbolic systems—words and numbers—permits us to reveal important aspects, but a picture or a painting can be equally telling.
>
> The arts—creative writing, dance, music, theater/film, and visual arts—serve as ways that we react to, record, and share our impressions of the world. Students can be asked to set forth their own interpretation of the Grand Canyon, using, say, poetry as the communicative vehicle. While mathematics gives us precise quantitative measures of magnitude, poetry explores our disparate personal reactions. Both views are valid. Both contribute to understanding. Together, they prescribe a larger overall conception of, in this case, one of nature's masterpieces (pp. 4–5).

In a gender-inclusive classroom, content knowledge not only becomes something to be learned but, more important, becomes something meaningful to students who learn to make connections between areas of knowledge that, after all, blend together in the world outside school.

Assessment: Old and New

Methods of evaluating student performance should be compatible with the types of learning activities that characterize a particular classroom. For example, traditional forms of evaluation such as standardized paper-and-pencil tests, answering questions posed by the teacher in a large group format, and student reports all seek to determine what and how much students "know" about a particular subject such as math or English. Each evaluation assumes that subject matter knowledge can be "given" to students who are then able to "give" such knowledge back as a sign that it has been learned. Perhaps the most efficient form of instruction for transmitting subject matter knowledge is that in which teachers talk and students listen, read, and are evaluated on the degree to which they have retained what they have heard and read.

In gender-inclusive classrooms, however, learning is less dependent on teacher talk and more dependent on group activities (projects, problem-solving situations, study groups) that take place over time. In such classrooms compatible evaluation techniques are those that measure performance over time, such as the creation of artifacts and portfolios and demonstrations of individual and group problem-solving ability. Although all these evaluation techniques will be discussed in more detail in Chapter 13, the point to make here is that these forms of assessment are a good match with instructional methods that emphasize collaborative teaching and learning.

Although there is still some political debate about the wisdom of the Common Core Standards and their attendant, and much different, kinds of assessments, it is likely that many states will begin assessing students in ways that emphasize the ability to *apply* knowledge rather than simply answer multiple choice questions (See Chapter 13). However, most experts in evaluation and assessment suggest that assessment must go beyond standardized tests. Assessments, for example, should: (1) include a variety of techniques; (2) encourage students to go beyond simple recall of data or facts; (3) close the gap between the classroom and the real world; and (4) include opportunities for students to perform tasks and solve problems.

Indeed, as we move further into the 21st century, models of assessment from around the world are increasingly of interest to American educators. Indeed, a number of high-performing countries have done away with the kind of standardized, relatively low-level testing system used in the United States and replaced it with "highly trained teachers and curriculum and assessments focused on problem solving, creativity, independent learning, and student reflection" (Sahlberg and Hargreaves (2011); Lavonen, (2008). As states in America seek to create world-class educational systems, the kind of gender safe classroom described in this chapter may become more the norm than the exception, and both teaching and assessments in those classrooms will change.

New Perspectives on Gender Identity

One of the earliest and most important learning experiences in any society is the development of a sense of self-identity—the knowledge that one is separate from mother, father, and family. This perception begins when an infant is 7 or 8 months old and continues throughout an individual's life. It is not unusual for a person's sense of identity to undergo significant changes as new experiences are encountered during the course of that person's life. An extremely important part of an individual's identity, and one that begins at least at birth, is gender. It is thought that identification in terms of sex begins at about 18 months of age and by age 3 is clearly internalized. But sexual identity is more complex than simply "knowing" that you are male or female. More important to your sense of self is your identification as a member of a gender group.

Sex and Gender: Different but Related

Although we often use the terms sex and gender interchangeably, they are different—but related. Sex is a biological characteristic and is generally identified at birth by the presence of differentiated genitalia. This is no small thing because a baby's sex is related to his or her gender in the following way. Based on the knowledge of whether the new baby is a boy or a girl, parents, grandparents, other relatives and friends begin to socialize this baby into his or her **gender role**—what colors to wear, what toys to play with, what games to play, what sports to practice—indeed, what life expectations to have.

Thus, gender is a psychological and social characteristic. *Gender* is what it *means* to be male or female in a particular society. In all culture groups, *gender identity* includes knowledge of a large set of rules and expectations for what males and females should wear, how they should speak and act, what tasks they should perform in the society, and their "place" in the overall social structure. Knowledge of these rules is

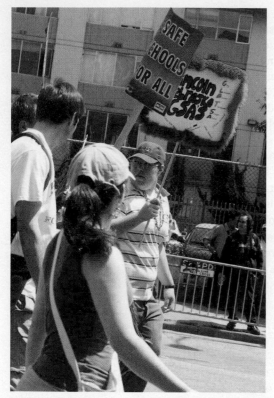

©McGraw-Hill Education/John Flournoy, photogrpaher

knowledge of one's role as a member of a particular gender group and provides us with the ability to deal with many social situations without having to stop each time to figure out what to do. Gender identity, however, also limits us in terms of our range of choices and, sometimes, the very quality of our lives.

Gender Expression and Gender Identity

There are two problems with this system. First, it does not take into account the very many possible variations that can exist in the bodies of these babies. There are four different sex categories that can be used to understand and describe bodies: male, female, intersex, and transsexual (Meyer, 2010).

Males and females are both relatively straightforward in terms of sex. A person is known as *intersex* when they are born with some characteristics of both sexes. A person is known as *transsexual* when his or her physical characteristics are male or female, but that person's gender identity doesn't align with the biological sex. As adults, these folks often go through extensive hormone treatment and surgery to transform their bodies to match their social identity.

Second, the limitations that gender identity can put on individuals are one reason, in an age when focus on the individual is so important, why young people around the United States and abroad are rebelling against the "convention that when it comes to gender and sexuality, there are only two options for each: male or female, gay or straight" (Steinmetz, 2017). Quite the contrary, many of the young who do not accept these limitations have created a lexicon that seeks to extend the possibilities of sex and gender (Killerman & Bolger, 2016). A few brief examples will give the idea:

- *Cisgender.* A person whose biological sex and gender identity are aligned.

- *Bigender.* A person who identifies with both traditional "man" and "woman" in behavior and expression

- *Gay.* Individuals who are primarily emotionally, physically, and/or sexually attracted to members of the same sex and/or gender. The term is more commonly used in reference to men, but can be applied to women as well.

- *Gender expression.* The way in which one displays one's gender identity through dress, demeanor, and social behavior, generally along traditional male/man or female/woman dimensions. Gender expression may or may not align with actual biological sex.

- *Gender fluid.* A gender identity best described as a dynamic mix of boy and girl; those who identify themselves as gender fluid may move between male and female behavior more or less often and to a greater or lesser degree.

- *Lesbian.* A woman who has the capacity to be attracted romantically, erotically, and/or emotionally to another woman.

- *Queer.* Used as an umbrella term for those who do not identity as straight. Sometimes used politically in the sense of taking a negative term and turning it into a positive one by embracing it.

- *Questioning.* An individual who is uncertain about or exploring his or her own sexual orientation or identity.
- *Transgender or Trans.* A person who lives (or feels internally that he or she should/must live) as a gender other than the one that corresponds to one's anatomical sex.
- *Two-spirit.* An umbrella term traditionally used among Native American tribes to recognize individuals who have qualities or fulfill roles of both genders.

The Millennials and Beyond

The generation loosely identified as millennials is especially interested or open to some degree of experimentation with and expressing a wide variety of genderized statuses. Indeed, at last count, Facebook offers more than 60 options for gender identity (Steinmetz, 2017) and a GLAAD/Harris poll in 2015 found that among millennials, 20% identify as something other than strictly straight and 27% know or work with someone who is transgender (Gonella, 2017).

Young people pushing for the freedom and opportunity to define their own gender may have a point. A 2015 study from Tel-Aviv University in Israel, for example, looked for differences in the brain between biological males and females along a number of dimensions. Analyzing more than 1,400 brain scans of men and women, researchers stated:

> Sex/gender differences in the brain are of high social interest because their presence is typically assumed to prove that humans belong to two distinct categories not only in terms of their genitalia, and thus justify differential treatment of males and females. Here we show that, although there are sex/gender differences in brain and behavior, humans and human brains are comprised of unique "mosaics" of features, some more common in females compared with males, some more common in males compared with females, and some common in both females and males. Our results demonstrate that regardless of the cause of observed sex/gender differences in brain and behavior (nature or nurture), human brains cannot be categorized into two distinct classes: male brain/female brain (Joel, 2015).

Interviewed for an article on the growing number of young people who are living the "mosaic" of sex/gender, a 26-year-old who grew up in Florida felt that he didn't "fit" the then-available options of male or female. He was born female, identifies as *agender*, meaning having no gender at all, identified as a transgender male at age 20, had hormone treatments for 2 years, and now says:

> After testosterone I was like O.K., my body is more where I want it to be. People can't really pinpoint me anymore, and that is comforting to me. I really like being neutral. I don't like having to identify with either binary gender. I like being beyond (Steinmetz, 2017).

Gender in a Global Context

In 2016, *National Geographic Magazine* commissioned a survey of 9-year-olds around the world (Conant, 2017). Researchers went into 80 homes on four continents to find out what children in a variety of countries thought about gender and how it affected their lives. A subhead on the resulting article reads: "If you want candid answers about how gender shapes destiny, ask the world's nine-year-olds" (p. 32).

All the children were asked the same questions. Here are a sample of the questions and their answers:

- What is the best thing about being a boy/girl?
  - *For a girl in Canada:* "There isn't anything I can't do because I'm a girl. Everyone is equal. There is always the same amount of opportunities for everyone, but in the olden days everyone wasn't equal." (p. 37).
  - *For a girl in Brazil:* "I like to be a girl because girls take better care of themselves than boys." (p. 40).
  - *For a boy in the West Bank:* "Being a boy, you're stronger, and you can lift things like refrigerators . . . As a girl, you have to comb your hair and put on clothes and make sure you're modest and everything." (p. 45).
- What is the worst thing about being a girl/boy?
  - *For a boy in India:* "The worst thing about being a boy is that they steal stuff and do Eve-teasing [harassing females]." (p. 34).
  - *For a girl in Kenya:* "You are seduced wherever you go. You are chased by men. If you go to fetch water, you are chased; you go to collect firewood, you are chased." (p. 36).
  - *For a girl in China:* "Sometimes I secretly help my older brother [on the farm]. Mom whacks me when she finds out. She says that girls who do these things will grow calluses on their hands; then they will become ugly." (p. 35).
  - *For a girl from the Pine Ridge Reservation in South Dakota:* "The worst thing about being a girl is that you just can't do things that boys can do; like, it kind of bothers me how there was not one girl president." (p. 47).
- How might your life be different if you were a girl instead of a boy (or a boy instead of a girl)?
  - *For a girl in Kenya:* "The difference between boys and girls is that girls are gentle and boys are rough, and some of them call people names, and they are not kind or self-controlled." (p. 43).
  - *For a girl from India:* "We won't get an education in school, but boys will be educated, and therefore they can travel anywhere but girls can't." (p. 44).
  - *For a boy in the Gaza Strip:* "Boys play with each other. And girls play with each other. They play something different from what we play, and we play different from them." (p. 46).
- What do you want to be when you grow up?
  - *For a boy from the Pine Ridge Reservation in Idaho:* "When I grow up, I want to be in the Navy SEALs to protect my country, because other bad people have killed my people." (p. 41).

Clearly, these children are aware of gender differences and speak forthrightly about their own socialization to gender roles. But they are aware that times are changing, as well. Conant (2017) notes that there is agreement among both boys and girls about some things: "boys get in trouble more often than girls, and girls have to spend a lot of time on their hair" (p. 33). These children are demonstrating the power of gender to offer or withhold opportunities, and the limitations on behavior for boys and girls observed by both. Yet, says, Conant, they are aspirational.

The aspiration mentioned most often, across lines of geography and gender, was summed up by a Kansas City native who, living as a transgender girl since she was four, says that "if the world were hers to change, there would be no bullying. Because that's just bad" (p. 33).

Gender Role Socialization in the United States

The rules associated with a person's gender role may vary by race, ethnicity, social class, gender, religion, and even geographical region. Such socialization takes place in a variety of different ways, many of them small and incremental—simple routines of daily life and language. Early in the study of gender roles, Weitzman (1975) described the process of such learning as having three parts:

1. The child learns to *distinguish* between men and women, and between boys and girls, and to know what kinds of behavior are characteristic of each.
2. The child learns to express appropriate gender role *preferences* for him- or herself.
3. The child learns to *behave* in accordance with gender role standards. (p. 109).

Although this process of internalizing knowledge of and identification with gender role is a part of all children's lives, it has been most studied in the lives of middle-class white children, especially girls. This concentration is significant for at least two reasons. First, it reflects the predominant characteristics of the researchers themselves, many of whom are not only white, middle-class university scholars but also feminists interested in documenting the reality of women's lives. Because the focus has been on girls, the consequences of **gender role socialization** on boys, which are great, often have been minimized.

Second, studies primarily located in the white middle class have reflected the dominant social group in the United States. Because dominance is often equated with universality, norms related to the gender role socialization of middle-class whites are often thought to apply to *all* American girls and boys—indeed, to *all girls* and boys everywhere. Researchers who have looked at gender role socialization in terms of racial, ethnic, religious, and national groups over the last 35 years have discovered significant differences in value and orientation between white, middle-class socialization practices and those of other groups. This finding is important because the role of the school in teaching gender role attitudes and behavior is second only to the role of the family. Schools normally represent the **dominant culture,** and gender role is no exception. Thus schools often unconsciously attempt to "mold" boys and girls into dominant (white, middle-class) gender roles while ignoring or trying to eliminate the different orientations and behaviors regarding gender that students bring with them to school.

Socialization to Gender Role in the Middle Class

Despite changing attitudes and values with respect to gender, in the United States, differences in socialization practices for boys and girls are many and obvious. More than 45 years ago, Howe (1974) described some of them in the following way. See whether you think things have changed all that much:

We throw boy babies up in the air and roughhouse with them. We coo over girl babies and handle them delicately. We choose sex related colors and toys for our children from their earliest days. We encourage the energy and physical activity of our sons, just as we expect girls to be quieter and more docile. We love both our sons and daughters with equal fervor, we protest, and yet we are disappointed when there is no male child to carry on the family name (p. 27).

Kramer (1988) suggested a number of socialization agents in early childhood that reflect middle-class values, and these, too, have remained relatively constant. The first, of course, is parents. Studies have demonstrated not only that infant boys are handled more roughly than their sisters and that infant girls receive more verbal attention, but also that young boys are given more freedom to explore than are young girls, who are often kept closer to the supervising parent. In addition, girls receive more help on tasks than do boys, who are encouraged to "figure it out for yourself." Research also shows that parental reaction to the behavior of their children tends to be more favorable when girls and boys are behaving in ways traditionally associated with their gender (Zosuls et al., 2011). Thus parents shape the expectations and abilities of their children not only by overt behavior but also by rewarding them with approval when they behave "appropriately" (McHale, Crouter, & Tucker, 1999).

Socialization to Gender Role in Popular Culture, Books, and Toys

In contrast to the usually more traditional socializing influence of the family is another powerful socializing agent—electronic media. Although there is much that is still stereotypical about the images of boys and girls and women and men on television and the Internet—there has been a significant change in the nature of gender role images to be found in cable TV, platforms like Netflix and Amazon, and on YouTube. Not only are traditional gender roles often reversed, but we are learning about non-conforming gender roles as well. In addition, music—popular, country, rock and roll, rap—has its own messages about sex and gender on computers and hand-helds of many kinds.

It is still the case, however, that images of girls and boys on television, in video games, on music videos, and in movies provide strong messages about gender. In May 2007, the National Organization for Women (NOW) surveyed parents, other caregivers, teachers, and, indeed, anyone who cares about children, looking for feedback on the influence of media and pop culture on raising children today (Grunberg, 2007). The survey suggested five major challenges related to the gender socialization of both boys and girls:

1. Media's sexualization of young female performers/celebrities.

2. Marketing of unrealistic beauty standards through fashion magazines and the beauty/diet industry.

3. Video games that promote violence and negative stereotypes.

4. Music lyrics and music videos that promote negative stereotypes and violence.

5. Sex stereotypes in kids' TV programs and movies.

At the very least, we can say that media messages regarding gender are mixed. If young children don't have their very own devices (and many do, from the age of 5 or so), there are always those that belong to Mom or Dad (or both). Used by both boys and girls, this entry into technology adds another layer of media-mediated socialization to gender that is, perhaps, a bit more equitable than much of the media itself. In all cases, popular culture has a lot to say about gender roles.

Another influence on young children's development of gender role identity is children's books. There is good news on this front: many more children's books tell stories of people of many cultures, including books about non-traditional families, as well as contemporary dilemmas of childhood. The classic fairy tales and nursery rhymes are falling into disuse: no more strong princes rescuing helpless (but beautiful) ladies in distress. Instead, the princess is likely to be rescuing the prince!

Still another gender socializer of children is toys. If the inclination of parents and relatives to buy "gender-appropriate" toys is not sufficient to the task, manufacturers provide on their packaging useful clues to the gender of the child expected to use the toy. This influence also extends to the placing of such toys in store aisles. Go to any large toy store and observe the placement of toys (and colors of the signs) for girls and boys. Ordinarily, blocks, cars, trains, manipulative games, chemistry sets, doctor's kits, work tools, building games, and of course, balls of all kinds show boys on the package. Dolls, kitchen or cleaning toys, needlework, craft, or sewing equipment, and nurse's kits show girls on the package. No matter how many Barbie dolls come with briefcases, astronaut helmets, and computers, Barbie is still a *very* well-endowed young lady who is very much into clothes, and who at one time was known to say that "Math is hard!"

Boys' toys are relatively more complex, more varied, and more expensive than girls' toys and frequently have no counterpart for girls. Consider, for example, the range of remote-control cars, boats, and airplanes for sale as well as electronic sports and adventure games that are marketed for boys. Take a look at a store that sells electronic games for boys and girls in the preteen years: there are a wide variety of action-oriented games (jungle adventures, space travel, Power Rangers, Transformers, Captain America) for boys and a good many Barbie dress-designing games, Disney Princess games, Fashion Girls, and, for the Wii, Cooking Mania, and the Just Dance series, plus the occasional Nancy Drew mystery game for girls of the same age. There is no *law* preventing parents and others from buying cross-gender toys, but most people still feel a bit uncomfortable doing so. Even in the 21st century, we buy toy lawn mowers for little boys and toy shopping carts for little girls, and seldom do the reverse.

Other socializing influences of young children may be found in a variety of everyday places and activities. From nursery rhymes we learn that young girls are frightened of spiders and that young boys are nimble and quick. In Bible stories we observe that young boys are brave and able to do away with giants, whereas women have a tendency toward evil actions such as cutting off a man's hair and robbing him of his strength. From familiar proverbs and sayings we become aware that objectionable behavior on the part of boys sometimes must be excused on the grounds that "boys will be boys" (did you ever hear "girls will be girls"?) and that "it's a man's world."

Masculine and Feminine Behavior

If middle-class gender roles seem to limit girls more than boys, it may be only that our society favors the active, the adventurous, and the aggressive and that those traits are largely associated with boys. However, there is a high price to be paid by boys for all their "freedom." First of all, boys are socialized much earlier to what is perceived to be "manly." A girl who participates in boys' activities, plays with boys' toys, is impatient with dresses and ribbons and lace, and in general eschews "girlish" things is called a "tomboy" and is regarded with some tolerance by most adults, at least until adolescence. At that point, according to conventional wisdom, chances are good that she will "grow out of it." At the same time, from age 3 onward, boys who want to play

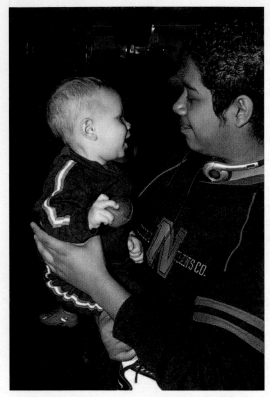

©McGraw-Hill Education/Andrew Resek, photogrpaher

with dolls, spend time with their mothers in the kitchen, cry easily, like to stay clean, and avoid contact sports are called "sissies"—a much more negative label. Adults viewing such behavior even in very young boys often become enormously uncomfortable and worried that "he is moving in the wrong direction." Adult intervention in these "girlish" activities is usually swift, direct, and unmistakable.

Second, boys are punished much more harshly for deviation from the norms of "masculine" behavior. Moreover, such punishment occurs at an age when they are too young to really understand the source of their "problem" or the reasons for adult distress. To make matters more difficult, the desired behavior is rarely defined positively as something the child *should* do; rather, undesirable behavior is indicated negatively as something he should *not* do or be—anything, that is, that the parent or other people regard as "sissy." Thus very early in life the boy must either stumble on the right path or bear repeated punishment without warning when he accidentally enters the wrong one.

One result of this socialization is that boys very early come to regard anything having to do with girls' play and behavior as something to be avoided at all costs, and this attitude increases during the elementary school years until most boys would rather "drop dead" than play with girls. Thus little is done to alter practices that lead to separation of the sexes and the masculine disdain for the "feminine," which often lasts a lifetime.

That such lessons are well learned is without doubt, and little has changed in the responses of a representative group of boys (8 and 10 years old) when asked to describe what boys and girls have to be able to know and do (Hartley, 1974). Boys, they said:

> have to be able to fight in case a bully comes along; they have to be athletic; they have to be able to run fast; they must be able to play rough games; they need to know how to play many games—curb-ball, baseball, basketball, football; they need to be smart; they need to be able to take care of themselves; they should know what girls don't know—how to climb, how to make a fire, how to carry things; they should have more ability than girls . . . they are expected to be noisy; to get dirty; to mess up the house; to be naughty; to be "outside" more than girls are; not to be cry-babies; not to be "softies"; not to be "behind" like girls are; and to get into trouble more than girls do (p. 90).

Thinking about the roles boys must assume, it is hard not to question, with Hartley, "not why boys have difficulty with this role, but why they try as hard as they do to fulfill it" (p. 27).

Gender and the Law for Schools

As with laws and court cases involving issues of race, language, and later, of disability, gender, and sexual diversity has become a legal issue in state governments, Congress, and the courts.

Early Legislation

Inspired by the civil rights movement during the 1960s and early 1970s, members of the women's movement began to pressure Congress to enact legislation that would guarantee equitable educational experience for girls and women. The result was Title IX of the Education Amendments of 1972. This statute was intended to prohibit discrimination in elementary and secondary schools on the basis of sex; its preamble reads:

> No person in the United States shall, on the basis of sex, be excluded from participation in, be denied the benefits of, or be subjected to discrimination under any education program or activity receiving federal financial assistance.

Not until 1975, however, were the rules and regulations enforcing Title IX published and sent to state departments of education and to school districts. In the interim, there was heated controversy; several bills were introduced in Congress to take the teeth out of the legislation (all of which were defeated); and many thousands of citizens sent in written comments. The initial government agency responsible for enforcing Title IX was the Department of Health and Human Services (HHS).

In 1980, the U.S. Department of Education was created, and the responsibility for Title IX was given to them through the Office of Civil Rights. All was not smooth sailing, however. In the now-famous *Grove City v. Bell* (1984) case, Grove City College in Pennsylvania attempted to evade compliance with Title IX (and all other civil rights mandates directed toward schools and colleges receiving federal funds) on the grounds that the college took no money from the federal government (although their students did receive college loans from the federal government). In 1984, the Supreme Court agreed with Grove City College and removed the applicability of Title IX in athletics programs by finding that only those programs or activities that receive *direct* federal assistance can be held accountable to Title IX.

The victory was short-lived because Congress passed the Civil Rights Restoration Act in 1988, overriding President Reagan's veto. This act overrode the decision in *Grove City v. Bell* by establishing that all educational institutions that receive *any* federal funding—direct or indirect—are bound by Title IX legislation. By 1990, the Office of Civil Rights of the U.S. Department of Education had published an investigation manual to aid in enforcement. In 1994, Congress passed the Equity in Athletics Disclosure Act, which requires coeducational institutions of higher education to disclose, on an annual basis, information regarding its intercollegiate athletics program.

More Recent Legislation and Court Cases

For the most part, regulation and interpretation of Title IX has affected middle school, high school, and college athletics programs. Lower courts have seen numerous cases involving the participation of girls in athletics, the requirement that expenditures on male and female athletic programs be "substantially" the same, and the canceling of boys' athletics programs to better balance expenditures on athletics. In most cases, Title IX has been enforced.

Other cases have been brought in the area of sexual harassment—both adult-and-student cases and student-and-student cases. Court decisions have been mixed in this area. For example, in two cases involving sexual harassment by teachers of students, the decisions were opposite. In *Franklin v. Gwinnett County Public Schools* (1992), the Supreme Court ruled that petitioners may claim punitive damages under Title IX when intentional action to prevent Title IX compliance is established. In *Alida Star Gebser and Alida Jean McCullough v. Lago Vista Independent School District* (1998), a California court denied compensatory and punitive damages from both the teacher involved and the school district. However, in the first student-on-student sexual harassment case to be decided successfully under Title IX in federal court—*Doe v. Petaluma Unified School District* (1995)—the plaintiff was awarded $250,000. Clearly, the whole story of unequal educational opportunity for girls has not been written, but progress has been made, particularly in athletics, under Title IX.

In 2005, the liability under Title IX was extended by the Supreme Court, allowing those who report violations of Title IX (usually school personnel) to sue for remedy against retaliation by school districts. In 2006, in an interesting reversal of position, however, the federal government—through the U.S. Department of Education—relaxed the rules governing single-sex education so that public school classes (and sometimes whole public schools) can create and maintain single-sex populations. Title IX has always allowed single-sex education under certain circumstances, but this ruling broadens those circumstances.

In 2010, the Obama administration sent a letter to 15,000 school districts clarifying that Title IX forbids gender-based harassment. Several courts have agreed that the sex discrimination prohibited by Title IX not only includes discrimination for being a girl or a boy, but also includes sexual harassment and discrimination for failing to conform to gender stereotypes. LGBTQ targets of sex discrimination and harassment have successfully relied on Title IX's protections in several court cases involving schools (G-Safe, 2017). While this clarification is, so far, in force, there is some concern that it will eventually be rolled back along with other Obama efforts to strengthen Title IX protections (Misulonas, 2017).

Who Decides, Federal or State?

While both the U.S. Constitution and most state constitutions have "equal protection for all citizens" language under the Fourteenth Amendment of the Constitution, it is sometimes quite difficult for LGBTQ students who are being bullied, harassed, and otherwise mistreated to benefit from those protections while their cases make slow progress to the Supreme Court.

Although the federal government has been quite active in school affairs in recent years, responsibility for public schooling has been a state function since 1789, when it became an example of the Tenth Amendment in the Bill of Rights that says "all powers not delegated to the United States by the Constitution are reserved to the States respectively or to the people." Thus, states, as well as local school districts have the right to pass legislation protecting any or all students from discrimination because they are in some way gender non-conforming.

Two types of state safe school laws are being promoted by supporters. The first are laws that specifically prohibit bullying and harassment of students based on sexual orientation and gender identity. Eighteen states and the District of Columbia currently have such laws. The second type is non-discrimination laws to protect LGBTQ students in schools from discrimination based on sexual orientation and/or gender identity. Currently, 13 states and the District of Columbia have such laws (GLSEN, 2017).

As the current government moves more and more toward sending power and funds back to the states, it is likely that more states will pass this kind of legislation. Clearly, there is a need for it.

Major Debates at the Local Level

Perhaps the most heated debate with respect to gender and sexual diversity has been the debate about the right of transgender students to use the school restrooms that correspond to their gender identity rather than the sex they were assigned at birth. Currently, there are 13 states with so-called "bathroom bills" pending in their legislatures: Alabama, Arkansas, Illinois, Kansas, Kentucky, Minnesota, Missouri, Montana, New York, South Carolina, South Dakota, Tennessee, Texas, Virginia, Washington, and Wyoming have all introduced legislation that would make it illegal to use a public restroom that is not the one that "matches" the sex on one's birth certificate. Ten of these bills effect only public schools; the other three also apply to all public buildings.

To date, one has passed. The North Carolina law was passed in 2016 and has caused the state to lose a good deal of money with the withdrawal of business offices, sporting events, and entertainment shows. Because of this response, the North Carolina legislature repealed parts of the bill in March 2017. The new law "overturns restrictions on public bathrooms but prohibits local governments from passing non-discrimination laws that affect private employment or public accommodation" (Brabaw, 2017).

Interestingly, the separation of restrooms by sex only began in 1887: Massachusetts passed the first such law and the rest of the states followed. But it wasn't so much an effort to separate men and women because of physical differences as it was because there was reluctance to fully include women in the workplace. The creation of "women's reading rooms" in public libraries and special train cars for women are examples of this view. While this attitude is largely gone from society today, the laws on segregated restrooms remain (Rhodan, 2016).

A number of cities in the United States have legislated various solutions to the problem. Gender neutral restrooms and family restrooms, have emerged as alternatives to segregated restrooms, and numbers of churches, schools, airports, and other public buildings are quietly installing these kinds of facilities in new and old buildings.

New Perspectives on Gender and Schooling

One reason why issues of gender in schools are so difficult to solve is that gender roles are **normative**—that is, the ideas about what attitudes, values, and behavior are associated with sex or gender have been coded by the social group into norms or, often, stereotypes. A *norm* is a rule of conduct based on attitudes and values that are usually internalized through socialization until they become "of course" statements.

Schools as Socializing Agents

Schools have an important though little discussed function as socializers to societal norms, particularly those associated with the middle class. Because these norms are so much a part of what most people in schools believe is correct, they seem "normal" and "right" and are usually taken very much for granted. That sense of "normality" is probably the most powerful force operating to encourage obedience to norms. However, other factors are involved in encouraging normative thought and behavior as well. In all societies, there are *sanctions*, or punishments, for deviation from norms.

These sanctions operate in schools on a daily basis, and most of them are particularly *social* sanctions. Consider again, for example, that girls may avoid taking advanced science or math classes because they don't want boys to think they're "too smart." The assumption of some girls is that the boys will "sanction" them socially for appearing to compete with them academically. Or consider the overt social sanctioning of boys who are gay by those boys who are straight, which is perhaps the most intense sanctioning that occurs. A number of lesser normative rules are broken every day in schools, by both males and females, and it appears that as gender roles change the social sanctions are also becoming less severe. Nevertheless, the power of gender role norms is enormous and frequently costly to both males and females.

While the public school, as a socializing agent, is relatively slow to change, the permanent and increasing presence of students from all kinds of places, cultures, abilities and disabilities, and gender identities makes it nearly inevitable that the norms schools teach and enforce will also change. In a discussion of the relation between power and conformity in schools, Saldana (2013) noted:

> If the education system seeks to empower rather than constrain it needs to focus on genuine autonomy and it needs to encourage public debate about the nature of democracy and the rights and responsibilities of citizenship (p. 232).

This is happening now, more and more, in schools where open and thoughtful teachers and administrators are working to change school cultures and school climates so that, in fact, all will be welcome and all will be able to contribute their unique experiences to the whole.

Rethinking Gender and Sexual Diversity

It is often said that in order to really get rid of a deep-seated bias against a person or a group, one has to get to know that person, work with him or her, play with him or her. Schools are excellent places to do that, if there is some little crack in the defenses that norms create.

Another way to begin is to look at some statistics and ask whether or not they can be denied. Questioning the gender binary (only two sexes—male and female) has become a small but growing theme in reporting and popular culture. Some children as young as 3 years of age are announcing in the strongest terms that they are other than their birth sex, some preteens and teenagers are questioning their gender identity, and all of these young people are at serious risk for bullying, harassment, even assault as they go about their daily lives. For teachers and administrators, these are changes they face often, sometimes on a daily basis. If there is a future that includes rethinking sexual diversity, it probably will begin with people in schools, many of whom are already working on changing the culture of schooling.

Changing the Culture of Schooling

Elizabeth Meyer (2010) offered a number of suggestions for those who are serious about changing the culture of schooling. Addressing the multiple factors (external influences, internal influences, perceptions of behaviors, and responses to behaviors) that affect school cultures, Meyer noted that external influences are the most formal, and consist of "administrative structures, school policies, teacher education, and curriculum and workload demands" (p. 122).

Internal influences "include the accepted norms and values in the school community and are absorbed from superiors (administration), peers (colleagues), students, and families/community members" (p. 122). Internal influences interact with external influences to give shape to the school culture. Generally speaking, school principals are key actors in setting school cultures. Specifically, their administrative style, personal values, professional priorities, and ways of implementing policy can make all the difference in whether the culture of the school is open or closed, humanistic or totally rule-governed, welcoming to only the "best" students or welcoming to all students.

©Realistic Reflections RF

Teachers, too, can make a difference in the school culture. In Meyer's study of schools in Canada and the United States, however,

> teachers reported that every aspect of these external influences communicated to them that sexism, homophobia, and transphobia were accepted and endorsed in their school communities and proactive responses against these forms of bias were not supported" (p. 123).

This is consistent with the response Joanne Thomas received to the idea of forming a Gay-Straight Alliance in her school as presented in the Case Study. As presented in Chapter 1, changing school culture as well as changing classroom climates is not an easy process.

One approach is to begin the process of expanding the way teachers are prepared by including study of the changing ideas of gender and the characteristics of gender-inclusive schools and classrooms. Once young teachers are in schools, they can look for allies among veteran teachers in beginning to engage the whole school community in conversations about all kinds of diversity, including gender and sexual diversity. It will undoubtedly be a long road, but as noted earlier, the children of diversity are in school—and they cannot be ignored.

The Importance of Alliances

When Joanne Thomas was asked to be the advisor of a Gay-Straight Alliance in her high school, she began a journey that many others have traveled and are traveling today. Part of that journey is getting used to constant change—in vocabulary, in titles of organizations, in the focus of social justice. Joanne's group of students began by calling themselves a Gay-Straight Alliance (GSA); by the time they were ready for their first activity the national Gay-Straight Alliance Network had changed its name to the Genders and Sexualities Alliance Network. But they are still GSAs and still offer enormous support to GSAs all over the country.

Of all the benefits a GSA provides, perhaps the most important is that it is an **alliance**. It's hard to overestimate the degree to which creating alliances for change will help advocates for a welcoming school culture or classroom come into being. A GSA can be a catalyst for reaching out to all the stakeholders in the school community—creating alliances with community members, businesses, and groups; with teachers and administrators; and with students who have not really been paying attention to the reformation of gender identities.

As an example, an effort called The Research Alliance for New York City Schools wanted to transform the school experience for Black and Latino young men (Klevin & Villavicencio, 2016). Strategies included:

- Developing culturally relevant curriculum.
- Adopting restorative approaches to discipline.
- Promoting strong relationships in schools not only between students but between students and school staff.
- Providing early support for postsecondary goals, including shifting their expectations from high school graduation to college readiness.

Work in these four areas can be applied to students who represent every diverse characteristic found in America's public schools. All require the forming of alliances, formal and informal, aimed at one set of students or all students, started on a very small scale or coming out as a schoolwide initiative. One way or another, it's up to Joanne Thomas, Abby, Zach, all their colleagues and friends, and all of us.

Ethical Issues

Clearly, there are many ethical issues involved in the consideration of gender and sexual diversity in the classroom. One important issue has to do with the degree to which all students, regardless of their beliefs and attitudes, are encouraged to be open, reflective, and critical thinkers. Children and adolescents are all in various stages of physical, intellectual, and moral development. It is unwise and unfair for teachers either to impose their own judgments on students or to differentially favor those students whose beliefs and attitudes are most nearly like their own. Rather, students should be enabled and encouraged to discuss all aspects of these issues in a context of thoughtful inquiry.

A second and related issue is the degree to which such inquiry may place students in direct conflict with the values of their families or the communities in which they live. Teachers should exercise a great deal of judgment in this regard, particularly when the family and community context is fairly rigid. It is quite possible for teachers to insist on an equitable set of language and behaviors while still recognizing and affirming contrary beliefs. To do otherwise is to set up a climate of "political correctness" that usually does more harm than good and does not do anything at all to promote self-reflection or inquiry.

Equity as a value is consistent with democracy, but so is pluralism. In a society as diverse as the one in the United States, it is not possible—nor is it useful—to insist on a single set of attitudes, beliefs, and values. Rather, the role of the school should be to help students negotiate differences, to understand their origins, and to appreciate what is valuable about them. One of the goals of a gender-inclusive classroom is to nurture *both* similarities and differences among people by enabling them to work together in ways that benefit everyone.

Summary

In this chapter, we explained the importance of gender role socialization to a person's identity through discussion of the ways in which children learn to "become" members of a gender group. The part played by the school and by teachers, administrators, and other adults as socialization agents was also discussed, as was the particular *type* of socialization—generally middle class—exercised by the school and the relation of that socialization to mainstream American values.

Traditional gender role stereotypes are both harmful and changing. Indeed, it is the very *change* in the nature of gender roles, as exemplified by Title IX, that is likely to cause some difficulties for students and teachers. In the same way, collaborative classrooms are particularly good vehicles for engendering understanding among both male and female students.

Finally, the issue of sexuality was addressed, in part as a studentwide phenomenon—at least in middle and high schools—and in part in terms of an increasing need to attend to issues raised by students who are gay and lesbian, and to issues created by the relations between homosexual and heterosexual students.

Chapter Review

Go to the Online Learning Center at www.mhhe.com/cushner9e to review important content from the chapter, practice with key terms, take a chapter quiz, and access Active Workbook Exercises.

Key Terms

dominant culture 317   gender role socialization 317
gender role 313   normative 323

Sexual Orientation: A Matter of Experience?

Purpose: To examine potential classroom situations that reflect others' as well as your own responses to issues surrounding sexual orientation.

Instructions: The term sexual orientation refers to the preference one exhibits in terms of sexual partners. There is increasing evidence that one's sexual orientation is genetically based; that is, it may be "hard-wired" into the individual, and therefore resistant, if not impossible, to change. Other beliefs attribute early experience to later sexual preference. Regardless of the explanation you are most comfortable with, in your role as an educator you will encounter situations that will require your action and intervention on behalf of a child, either in making accurate attributions concerning a child's behavior at a given moment, or on behalf of a child who is experiencing strained relationships with her or his peers.

1. How would you explain the following scenarios to the concerned individual?

   a. Four-year-old Jeremy heads right to the doll corner as soon as he arrives at the day-care center each morning. His father is concerned that this behavior is not appropriate for a little boy. How would you respond to the father?

   b. Seventeen-year-old Patricia (who prefers to be called Pat) wears her hair cut very short and tends to dress like the boys. You walk by a group of her female classmates and hear them refer to her as a lesbian. How would you respond to this group of girls?

   c. Five-year-old Suzanne plays with blocks and trucks during most of her free time in kindergarten. Her mother asks you if this is "normal" behavior? How would you respond to the mother?

   d. In addition to his theater performances, 13-year-old Robert takes ballet classes 3 days a week after school. Other boys often ridicule him in class. He comes to you and asks you to intervene. What would you suggest to Robert? What would you say to the other boys in Robert's class?

   e. Fifteen-year-old Shauna, who has few friends, lifts weights and seeks out all the opportunities she can to play typical boys sports. She has also been having conflicting and confusing sexual feelings. She comes to you after school one day, initially to seek your advice about what to do about friends, but soon begins to talk about her confusion and fear of talking to her parents. What advice would you give her?

   f. Sixteen-year-old Joseph's stated goal in life is to become a nurse. You overhear a group of boys teasing him and laughing about his "gay" behavior. You find Joseph sulking in a corner of the room and approach him. What do you say to him?

Reflect on your responses to the above scenarios. Do you notice any patterns in the way you answered the questions? Did you respond differently to the scenarios involving girls than you did for the scenarios involving boys? Did you respond differently to parents than you did to the child? If so, to what do you attribute this?

Classroom Activities

1. Ask elementary school students who their "heroes" are—both male and female. Who do they look up to? What characteristics do these "heroes" have? Do the female "heroes" have different characteristics than the male "heroes"? Do they have some of the same characteristics? Students can then make posters about their "heroes" with a written description of who they are and why they are "heroes," putting the posters up around the classroom as a "Hall of Fame Display."

2. In an elementary school classroom, have students read the language of Title IX: "*No person in the United States shall, on the basis of sex, be excluded from participation in, be denied the benefits of, or be subjected to discrimination under any educational program or activity receiving federal financial assistance.*" Discuss with students the implications of Title IX in their school: Should girls and boys both play sports? What other areas of school life could Title IX be applied to? Ask students to write a short essay describing their ideas about gender equity in school.

3. Using two flip charts, in a high school class, ask students to brainstorm characteristics that demonstrate manly behavior and ladylike behavior. On one flip chart, write students' suggestions for "manly" behavior and draw a box around the responses. Write "Manly Characteristics" at the top of the chart. On the other flip chart, write students' suggestions for "ladylike" behavior, again drawing a box around the responses, and writing "Ladylike Characteristics" at the top of the chart. Discuss the two sets of responses in terms of stereotypes and

ask students where they think they learned these ideas, where in society we find these messages, and to what extent they think these "characteristics" reflect reality in their lives.

4. Ask high school students to be "gender detectives," visiting large local toy stores or big box stores with large toy departments. Students should take notebooks and pencils with them. In the store, or toy department, look for sections that display boys' and girls' toys and describe what kinds of toys are in each section. Then look at the packaging around the toys and describe what words and figures are on the packaging. Finally, see if the store (or department) has a section of "gender neutral" toys (e.g., blocks, stuffed animals) and describe what kinds of toys are in that section. Ask students what they conclude about toys as gender socializers.

Reflective Questions

1. If you had witnessed harassment and bullying against gay, lesbian, or gender non-conforming students in your high school, would you have taken any action against it? What kind of action?

2. All people feel that they need to belong. Do you think a Gay-Straight Alliance (GSA) in your high school would have helped in that regard? If your school had a GSA, did it help students feel part of a community?

3. Some students, and some faculty as well, might have sincere religious beliefs about students who do not conform to the gender binary. What might you say to them as you reached out for allies?

4. Do you think Mrs. Thomas did the right thing in agreeing to be an advisor to a GSA without knowing too much about it? What would you have done?

5. Do you think the school Superintendent handled the meeting of concerned citizens well? Poorly? Would you have handled it differently? How?

References

Alida Star Gebser and Alida Jean McCullough v. Lago Vista Independent School District, 524 U.S. 274 (1998).

Brabaw, K. (2017). Everything you need to know about "bathroom bills." Refinery29. Retrieved from http://www.refinery29.com/2017/03/148085/anti-transgender -bathroom-bills-what-you-need-to-know

Bouley, T. (2007). The silenced family: Policies and personal literature depicting gay /lesbian families in public elementary schools. In Killeran, Isabel, & Jiminez, Karleen Pendleton, (Eds.), *"Unleashing the Unpopular": Talking about sexual orientation and gender diversity in education.* Association of Childhood Education, International, 140–147.

Cleveland Board of Education v. LaFleur, (1974). United States Supreme Court, No. 72-777.

Conant, E. (2017) I am nine years old. *National Geographic Magazine 231* (1), January 2017, 30–47.

Doe v. Petaluma Unified School District, 54 F.3d 1447 (9th Cir., 1995).

Fausto-Sterling, A. (2000). *Sexing the body: Gender politics and the construction of sexuality.* New York: Basic Books, 1. 31.

Franklin v. Gwinnett County Public Schools 503 U.S. 60 (1992).

GLSEN (2017). State maps. Retrieved from https://www.glsen.org/article/state-maps

Gonella, C. (2017). Survey: 20% of millennials identify as LGBTQ. NBC News. Retrieved from http://www.nbcnews.com/feature/nbc-out/survey-20-percent-millennials-identify-lgbtq-n740791

Grove City v. Bell, 465 U.S. 555 (1984).

Grunberg, J. (2007). *Media's influence on raising kids: Moms sound off.* National Organization for Women. Retrieved from http://www.now.org/issues/media/070802momresults.html

Grutter v. Bollinger, 439 U.S. 306 (2003).

Hartley, R. E. (1974). Sex role pressures and the socialization of the male child. In J. Stacey, S. Bereaud, & J. Daniels (Eds.), *And Jill came tumbling after.* New York: Dell.

Howe, F. (1974). Sexual stereotypes start early. In O. L. Johnson (Ed.), *Nonsexist curriculum materials for elementary schools.* Old Westbury, NY: Feminist Press.

Human Rights Resource Center, University of Minnesota. (2004). *Lesbian, gay, bisexual, and transgendered rights: A human rights perspective.* Activity 7. Retrieved from http://www1.umn.edu/humanrts/edumat/hreduseries/TB3/act7/act7f.html

Joel, D. et al. (2015, December 15). Sex beyond the genitalia: The human brain mosaic. *Proceedings of the National Academy of Sciences of the United States of America, 112* (50).

Killermann, S. & Bolger, M. (2016). Comprehensive list of LGBTQ+ vocabulary definitions. Retrieved from http://itspronouncedmetrosexual.com/2013/01/a-comprehensive-list-of-lgbtq-term-definitions/#sthash.pmuTTClq.dpbs

Klevin, S. & Villavicencio, A. (2016). Strategies for improving school culture. New York University. Retrieved from http://steinhardt.nyu.edu/research_alliance/publications/esi_school_culture

Kramer, S. (1988). Sex role stereotyping: How it happens and how to avoid it. In A. Carelli O'Brien (Ed.), *Sex equity in education* (pp. 5-23). Springfield, IL: Charles C Thomas.

Marantz-Henig, R. (2017). Rethinking gender. *National Geographic Magazine 231* (1), 48-72.

Meyer, E. J. (2010). *Gender and sexual diversity in schools.* Springer Netherlands.

McHale, S. M., Crouter, A. C., Tucker, C. J. (1999). Family context and gender role socialization in middle childhood: Comparing girls to boys and sisters to brothers. *Child Development,* July–August, *70*(4); 990-1004.

Misulonas, J. (2017). How Trump can undo everything Obama did for title IX. *Good Sports.* Retrieved from https://sports.good.is/articles/title-ix-trump-obama

Principles of Ensuring Safe and Supportive Learning Environments for Lesbian, Gay, Bisexual, Transgender, Queer, and Questioning (LGBTQ) Students. (2015). Massachusetts Department of Elementary and Secondary Education. Retrieved from http://www.doe.mass.edu/sfs/lgbtq/LearningEnvironments.pdf%20on%20April%2020 http://www.doe.mass.edu/sfs/lgbtq/Learning Environments.pdf

Rhodan, M. (2016, May 16). Why do we have men's and women's bathrooms, anyway? *Time.* Retrieved from http://time.com/4337761/history-sex-segregated-bathrooms/

Safe Schools Program for LGBTQ Students. (2017). Retrieved from http://www.doe.mass.edu/sfs/lgbtq/

Saldana, J. (2013). Power and Conformity in Today's Schools. *International Journal of Humanities and Social Science*, *3* (1), 228-232.

Steinmetz, K. (2017). Infinite identities. *Time 189* (11), 48-54.

Strober, M. H., & Tyack, D. (1980). Why do women teach and men manage? A report on research on schools. *Signs 5* (3), 494-503.

Weitzman, L. J. (1975). Sex-role socialization. In J. Freeman (Ed.), *Women: A feminist perspective.* Palo Alto, CA: Mayfield.

Zosuls, K. M., Miller, C. F., Ruble, D. N., Martin, C. L., & Fabes, R. A. (2011). Gender development research in sex roles: Historical trends and future directions. *Sex Roles, 64*(11-12); 826-842. Retrieved from http://www.apa.org/pi/women/resources/newsletter/2011/06-08/gender-development.aspx

Creating Developmentally Appropriate Classrooms

The Importance of Age and Developmental Status

Focus Questions

1. How can culture and schooling affect students' development?
2. Are there really stages in children's and adolescents' development? If so, are some of those stages critical?
3. How do teachers determine what is developmentally appropriate for their students?
4. How can teachers reconcile demands for educational performance standards and accountability with the goal of education for understanding?

" The blunt fact is that the American high school was designed for 15 to 18 year-olds who were children only beginning their journey to adulthood. It is now filled with young adults of the same age. One does not have to subscribe to a Freudian theory of human development to accept the sharp distinction between the years before and after sexual development. And likewise, one does not need to be a professional psychologist to recognize that the way in which one deals with a prepubescent youngster is quite different from the way in which one deals with one in the early stages of puberty. "

LEON BOTSTEIN

" Much of the story of human development must be written in the light of cultural influences in general and of the particular persons, practices, and paraphernalia of one's culture. And chief among these, of course, in any complex culture will be such educational institutions as apprenticeships or formal schools. "

HOWARD GARDNER

Case Study

Age in Developmentally Appropriate Classrooms

It was a coincidence that Sally Dougherty and Tony Stuart—both recent graduates of the same midwestern university—were hired in the same month at Garfield Elementary School in Asheville, West Virginia.[1] What was not a coincidence was that both Sally and Tony had wanted to come back to the Appalachian Mountains where they had been born.

Settled in waves of people moving westward, Appalachia is ordinarily defined as a set of 397 counties in 12 states, running from southern New York to Mississippi, with a population of some 18 million people. Its population has been comprised predominantly of a mixture of English, German, Welsh, Scots-Irish, and French who, upon their arrival, met major civilizations of Iroquois and Shawnee in the north and Creek, Cherokee, Choctaw, and Chickasaw in the south.

Historically, Appalachia has been a hiding place for Native Americans, runaway slaves, and whites escaping from indentured servitude in the early colonies or from privation and persecution in Europe. Cut off from the rest of the world by geography, traditional conservatism, economic hardship, and fear, the people of Appalachia have developed a culture that values kinship, independence, and tradition. They tend to distrust and avoid involvements with social institutions, such as schooling. Strangers are often regarded with suspicion or disinterest, including all those outsiders who had recently descended upon the area in an effort to "fix" it.

Sally and Tony, however, were not outsiders. They knew that out of the experience of poverty and the pride of independence (some might say the curse of individualism) has come a people who are accustomed to making do or doing without, whose experience with the outside world has been largely one of repeated disappointment, who refer to themselves proudly as "highlanders" or "mountain people," and who have produced beautiful folk art in wood carvings, quilts, dulcimer and fiddle music, baskets, and pottery. Indeed, it was because of their sense of loyalty to and admiration for the people and places in which they had grown up that the two new teachers wanted to return to bring the best education they had to offer to a new generation of mountain children.

Garfield Elementary School, with about 350 children in grades K–8, is typical of many schools in the region. Constructed of cement block, it was built in 1968 as part of a "modernization" effort. It has 12 classrooms painted in pastel colors, tiled floors, a cafeteria with a kitchen, a library, modern restrooms, dependable heating, and adequate lighting. It serves a number of surrounding communities, has about a 10% absentee rate, and has a small budget for books and materials. About 40% of its children qualify for free lunches. Most teachers in the school have been there for 20 or more years, and many are nearing, or have reached, retirement, accounting for Sally and Tony being hired at the same time.

Other changes had occurred as well, perhaps the most important one being the conversion of the sixth, seventh, and eighth grades into a middle school housed in the same building as K–5. Sally was hired to teach kindergarten, and Tony had been hired to teach music to the sixth, seventh, and eighth graders. Although they had known one another slightly in college, neither realized that they were going to be teaching in the same school until the week before school began, when they met at the trash bins behind the school. Each was there getting their rooms ready for the first day of school.

Surprised and excited by their meeting, the two neophyte teachers compared notes. "I've been planning all summer for this," confided Sally. "I didn't get to see much of the place when I came to be interviewed, but I wanted to get here early so I could arrange my room the way I wanted it. Come and see!"

She practically dragged Tony to her classroom, where she was beginning to organize furniture into activity centers like those she had used in student teaching. Already discernible was a block area, with several kinds of blocks for construction; a part of the room for active games and other large muscle activity; a science center, with a terrarium; an area for counting, sorting, and measuring; a listening center; and also a quiet area, where children could stretch out with picture books. "I had hoped to have a computer and a sand table," she said, "but maybe I can figure out how to get those later. At least I have a sink in my room for cleaning up after painting, washing hands, and getting water for our classroom pets."

Not to be outdone, Tony was also eager to show off his room. One of the first at their university to graduate with licensure in middle childhood, Tony knew that the concept of middle school had been devised in part to allow young people more time to explore before committing themselves to futures foreordained by the type of curriculum they chose to pursue. For this reason, there were a lot of things to explore in Tony's room. He had arranged the usual chairs in a semicircle at one end of the room for choral rehearsals and singing, thereby leaving the rest of the rather large room available for bookshelves, tables, and—his pride and joy—a large workbench on which were tools and materials for making and repairing musical instruments.

"I got a lot of these from my grandfather," he explained, pointing to the tools. "He makes both hammered and lap dulcimers and knows just about everything there is to know about mountain music. I'm going to have him come in several times this year and help teach the kids how to play and repair them."

"That's great!" exclaimed Sally. And then, thinking about her own situation, she asked, "Is that part of your curriculum? I didn't get to talk with the principal about the school philosophy, and the kindergarten curriculum is certainly laid out without a lot of room for extra stuff!"

"Well, I'm supposed to do both vocal and instrumental music, and many of these kids are already familiar with the sound of dulcimers, even if they don't know how to play them. And I thought that dulcimers and flutes could be good introductions to other stringed and woodwind instruments. And the songs of the mountains are also familiar, and I hope they'll get the kids interested in other kinds of singing."

"Sounds good to me," said Sally as she headed back to her room. But she wondered what these folks will think about "developmentally appropriate practice" as she thought about the district's goals, which were clearly spelled out for the subjects comprising the kindergarten curriculum, the scope and sequence of which left little to the teacher's, or the children's, imagination.

On the first day of school it was hard to tell who was more excited, Sally and Tony or the new kindergartners. In the kindergarten room, there were a few difficult separations and some tears. Although several children had had preschool experience, most had not. Familiarizing herself with background information that was available, Sally had learned that four of the boys were "late starters" whose kindergarten entry had been delayed based on readiness testing. She wondered fleetingly whether the tests had been accurate assessments. During her student teaching experience, she had witnessed an incident in which a young boy had failed a reading readiness test, although he was fully able to read, because the teacher had never used workbooks or dittos and her students had not had much practice in what she called "the skills test makers want—filling in small dots, sitting for hours." When the teacher had gone to the administrator with samples of the boy's work and the books he was reading in class, the administrator had again referred her to the boy's test scores, which indicated that he wasn't ready to learn to read. When the teacher pointed out that there was no reading on the "reading readiness" test, the administrator retorted that perhaps she should spend more time getting her students ready to read than in having them read!

Looking across the hall at the other kindergarten classroom, Sally saw that Mrs. Conrad had already passed out worksheets to the quietly waiting children seated around five rectangular tables. She also saw a gaily decorated but otherwise empty bulletin board with the words GOOD WORK at the top ready to receive the children's efforts. Principal Wilson had told Sally that Mrs. Conrad would be a good mentor for her. "She's an excellent teacher," the principal had said. "She always has things under control and she has a quiet, friendly manner with the children."

As she invited her charges to look around their room, Sally spent some time observing them as a group. Three other children, two girls and a boy, had "borderline birthdates," but their parents were adamant that they not be held back. Altogether, the group represented more varied ethnicity than Sally had expected, certainly more than she had experienced in

(continued)

her own elementary schooling. This class included four African American and two Asian American pupils; the latter's families had recently immigrated to the United States. Both were just beginning to speak a little English, and one girl spoke scarcely at all. As Sally quickly learned, this girl was by no means the only child in the group that would be difficult to bring out. And that small boy with the sad expression—David; what could be on his mind?

Meanwhile, in Tony's room was a kind of organized chaos. Because Tony was a "special" teacher, his students came to him on a rotating basis. His first group was seventh graders, scheduled for music three times a week, and they were definitely not yet ready to settle into any kind of routine! Remembering his own alarming entry into puberty, Tony grinned at the interplay between boys and girls. Like most young people at this age, the girls were well ahead of the boys in all domains, though most obviously physical development. And like all preteens and early teens, they came in all shapes and sizes and were at diverse points along the road to being grown up. He also knew that some had already tried out "adult" behaviors, including sexual and substance-related ones.

As the year progressed, Sally's room acquired a variety of children's art work, some of it not perfect by any means, some of it unlike anything anyone had ever seen before, but all of it respected and valued because it had been produced by the children's own imaginations. In one corner was the class fairy-tale museum complete with a gingerbread house, and on a low table was a carousel with photographs of each child riding a horse. By January, there was also a list of rules for the classroom hanging on the wall, developed by the children. Rule 1 was "No smoking," and Rule 2 was "No throwing books at the lights." Mrs. Conrad had commented more than once that the list of rules seemed a little silly, but Sally believed that the room was the children's space as well as hers and that the experience of deciding what rules should be followed by everyone was an important step toward building the sense of community she wanted in her class.

Knowing that play is the young child's work and natural mode of expression, Sally had developed a schedule that balanced child-selected activity in especially arranged interest centers with whole-group circle activities. Following opening circle routines—who was here, who would be helpers, today's weather—she introduced a theme through an intriguing "lesson" based on a story or finger play. Afterward, each child was asked to choose from among various centers where that theme could be pursued in different ways, as Sally became a participant-observer, moving from center to center and encouraging children to explore with different media. As new themes were introduced, centers were changed accordingly, but they always enabled children to have experiences with language and other modes of expression, quantities and physical attributes, cause-effect relationships, social interactions, and other curriculum content appropriate for 5-year-olds. Noting what each child chose and how each child played, Sally supported mutual helping and other prosocial behavior, intervening as unobtrusively as possible. Then, bringing the children back to the circle, she returned to the theme, urging them to talk about what they had done, often helping them frame this activity in the form of a story in which each child was an important character.

Tony also was learning about his students, and as he was quick to point out to Sally, he had a much wider age range to deal with than she did. Even in a single class, students' interests and needs were far from uniform. Furthermore, while Tony had anticipated needing to establish his own authenticity (and authority), the students at first had seemed to him to be compliant but apathetic. After the first week they had little apparent interest in either the workbench or any of the other activities he planned. Even their singing of familiar songs had a tendency to be dirge-like. Clearly, he thought, he was failing to connect with their concerns and their priorities.

Toward the end of September, a tragic fire in a cabin up in the hills brought the children out of their lethargy. Two children had died in the fire, and a third child was very badly burned. The family had little money, nothing to wear, and no place to live except with cousins down the road who already had cramped quarters. Help came from all the communities in the school district: a hundred families met to fell trees and raise a new cabin, clothes were provided, and money was collected to tide the family over. But the burned child faced months of hospitalization, and her parents were faced with not only medical bills but also the expenses of traveling back and forth to the city in which she was hospitalized, 60 miles away.

As his students continued to talk about the family's plight, Tony got an idea. Perhaps his classes could raise some money for the family themselves by staging a country music fair, performing in a musical review, and selling space for local musicians and craftspeople to sell their wares. Why not?

Tony's classes were excited by the idea. He formed a grade 6 to grade 8 chorus and organized students into groups to write the review, decide on the music, make costumes and build sets, talk with Principal Wilson and other community leaders about finding space for the fair, write an article for the local newspaper to publicize the event, take orders from craftspeople for booth space, and attend to all the other necessary details. Soon most of the school was involved one way or another: middle school teachers were using the event to teach English, social studies, and math, and even Sally's kindergartners were drafted to help paint large pieces of scenery. The event itself was scheduled to be held just before Thanksgiving in a local church.

The students decided to write a pageant about the history of the community, which enabled them to choose from a wide variety of music—colonial church hymns, patriotic anthems, and 200 years' worth of folk music from many countries that had been adopted and adapted over the years until it became true "mountain music."

Tony found himself stretched to provide enough music history—let alone the music itself—for the students' eager needs. He very quickly learned who in the community could be called upon to help (his own grandfather was, of course, one of the first to be asked), and the project became a community effort. Nearly every minute of Tony's time was devoted to advising, guiding, rehearsing, and teaching his students what they needed to know. Everyone had a job (most had several!), and all the students felt that they were participating in something important.

When the music fair was all over, Tony's students had raised $5,000 to help the stricken family. By the end of that first year, both Sally and Tony were tired. Sally still did not have a computer or a sand table, the district curriculum was still confining, and Mrs. Conrad was still using photocopied worksheets. Tony had a hard time coming up with activities that were as interesting and exciting as the music fair had been, and his students were still afflicted with adolescent moods and quick mouths. Still, Sally's students had discovered that school was a happy and productive place to be, that they could, in fact, learn to read, and that first grade was something to look forward to. Tony's students had learned a great deal about the history of Appalachian music and instruments and quite a bit about themselves as caring, collaborating, and capable people, which, as the two teachers agreed, is what developmentally appropriate practice is all about.

Rationale for Developmentally Appropriate Educational Practice

Age is one of the two most obvious dimensions of diversity among human beings, and clearly Sally's kindergartners and Tony's "middlescents" are at very different points on the journey to adulthood. In fact, although Tony's specialization of music education is a multiage field (preschool through high school), his middle school licensure identifies him also as an age-specialist, as is Sally (whose licensure in fact qualifies her to teach children from preschool to Grade 3). Both of these novice teachers were fortunate in being assigned to children of an age group, and within a cultural context, for which they felt a particular affinity. The teachers also recognized that, those commonalities notwithstanding, each of their students was a unique person making her or his own way along that journey to becoming an adult.

During the 20th century, patterns of schooling were radically influenced by increased knowledge of distinctive phases of human development. A striking example was the emergence of junior high schools, a trend greatly influenced by G. Stanley Hall's *child study movement*. Based on questionnaires, interviews, and teacher observations, Hall had argued that early adolescence is a particularly vulnerable and malleable period and that schooling for that age group ought to be quite different from that provided in high schools. The first American "intermediate school," as it was called, was established in 1909, and by 1930 there were about 4,000 junior high schools in the United States.

The attempt to apply what is known about children's development to school organization is even more sharply reflected in today's middle schools, a refinement of the concept of a transitional school experience between primary and secondary schooling. It is also reflected in those local school districts that have established early childhood centers, often housing child care and Head Start programs, as well as school-administered kindergarten, prekindergarten, and early childhood special education services.

In brief, **developmentally appropriate practice (DAP)** involves providing learning environments, instructional content, and pedagogical practices that are responsive to the major attributes and salient needs and interests that characterize a given life period in order to facilitate continuing developmental progress. Whatever learners of a given age and stage may have in common, however, the principle of developmentally appropriate practice recognizes both each child's uniqueness and the diversity of the social and cultural contexts that affect children's socialization. This recognition is captured in the definition that follows.

Developmentally appropriate practices result from the process of professionals making decisions about the education and well-being of children based on at least three important kinds of information or knowledge:

1. *what is known about child development and learning* (*knowledge of age-related human characteristics*)—to permit general predictions within an age range about what activities, materials, interactions, or experiences will be safe, healthy, interesting, achievable, and also challenging to children;

2. *what is known about the strengths, interests, and needs of each individual child in the group*—to be able to adapt for and be responsive to inevitable individual variation; and

3. *knowledge of the social and cultural contexts in which children live*—to ensure that learning experiences are meaningful, relevant, and respectful for the participating children and their families.

"Furthermore, each of these dimensions of knowledge—human development and learning, individual characteristics and experiences, and social and cultural contexts—is dynamic and changing, requiring that teachers remain learners throughout their careers" (Bredekamp & Copple, 1997, p. 9).

Striking examples of such changes in knowledge have involved the preadolescent and adolescent years. Neuroscientists have long known that the first years of life are characterized by amazingly rapid brain development, with the brain attaining about 95% of its adult size by age 6. It has also been recognized that this early development is characterized by an *overproduction* of cells and neural connections, followed by a period of "pruning," during which the brain continues to be highly malleable.

But what neuroscientists have recently discovered is that a "second wave" of overproduction occurs prior to puberty, making the teen years a period of continuing development in the refinement, and malleability, of higher cognitive processes. This suggests an explanation of the neural substrates underlying marked changes in the way adolescents think as described by developmental psychologists such as Jean Piaget. Yet, although adolescent learners may *appear* to be "full-grown," their decision-making, planning, judgment, and organizational skills are very much "works in progress." Moreover, as in the early childhood years, continued development of areas of skill requires use of these skills, and brain malleability is also highly vulnerable to harmful influences such as drugs or alcohol, the long term effects of which may be more serious than had been previously thought (Jensen & Nutt, 2015). This unevenness in cognitive development helps to account for teenagers' engaging in other high-risk behaviors, such as texting while driving, daredevil stunts, and unprotected sex, despite "knowing" the consequences (Steinberg, 2014).

A second area of new understanding involves adolescent sleep patterns. Although altered circadian timing patterns at puberty, as well as social expectations, result in later bedtimes for most teens, adolescents have been found to require *more,* not less, sleep than either younger children or adults. Consequentially, many—perhaps most—high school students arrive at school and move through their school day—especially if theirs

©McGraw-Hill Education/Jill Braaten, photogrpaher

is a school that starts early in the day—in a state of sleep deprivation (e.g., Wolfson & Carskadon, 1998). The situation becomes even more serious when we consider that accidents, the leading cause of death among American adolescents, are often directly or indirectly attributable to sleep deprivation, and suicide, a second leading cause of adolescent death, is often precipitated by depression, to which sleep deprivation may be a contributing factor.

What implications do these areas of new and emerging knowledge have for educational policy and practice? Better understanding of adolescent sleep needs and patterns should, at the very least, influence teachers and parents to be less judgmental, but it has also encouraged many high schools to experiment with later start times, despite the complications (e.g., for after-school sports or jobs) that may entail. Better understanding of adolescent brain structure and function implies a renewed conviction that teachers indeed can play a highly influential role, not only in their students' acquisition of knowledge but also in their continuing cognitive development.

We must also ask what impact cultural changes, notably the pervasive presence of electronic technology in children's lives, have on their development. How are young learners of the 21st century cognitively and socioemotionally *different* from those of the 20th?

Economic Aims for Schooling

Leon Botstein (1997), president of Bard College, offered the "modest proposal" of replacing the American high school and ending secondary education with what is now the 10th grade. If schooling were more age-appropriate, he argued, it could be more efficient as well as far more effective. His argument is essentially for faith in the potential of the American educational system—for, in his phrase, "the language of hope"—but his critique of what's wrong with the system essentially concerns developmentally inappropriate curriculum and pedagogy. "The challenge," he writes, "is to find ways to engage the early onset of adolescence and its attendant freedoms and habits" (p. 85). Botstein maintained that if we are able to do that and also to capitalize on the learning potential of younger children, what today's 18-year-olds have imperfectly learned most students can master by age 16, when they can move on to postsecondary academic or technical preparation.

Today, American high schools address Botstein's concerns through a variety of programs, such as significantly expanded Advanced Placement opportunities, and "early college" arrangements with higher education institutions. While such provisions may have contributed to improved high school graduation rates, however, Grade 9 continues to be the point at which most American school dropouts occur, arguably implying the need for greater attention to developmental appropriateness of learning opportunities at that level.

The currently high profile of early childhood education can be attributed to a combination of factors, especially mounting evidence of the critical importance of early educational experiences in influencing children's subsequent development. Recognition of such evidence was reflected in Goal 1 identified by the National Education Goals Panel (1996) that, by the year 2000, all American children would enter school "ready to learn." Although there is evidence of progress in reducing the glaring discrepancies in participation in quality preschool programs between high- and low-income families, no one would assert that that goal was achieved, especially for the nearly one American child in five who lives in poverty (CDF, 2014). Moreover, as the Children's Defense Fund 2001 report, *The State of America's Children,* stressed, the discrepancy persists when children enter school, reflected in "the dramatic disparity in resources provided to the poorest children" (p. 62). Jonathan Kozol (1991) depicted this disparity as reflecting "savage inequalities" in the educational opportunities provided in American schools.

Some early 20th-century Progressive reformers had considered kindergarten "the one thing needful" to redress societal inequities and equalize opportunity. The growth since the 1960s of prekindergarten programs has arguably been directed toward that same goal. Yet despite the call for all children to have access to developmentally appropriate preschool programs as an important means for achieving the goal of entering school "ready to learn," do educators attempting to meet this goal face a danger of placing developmentally *inappropriate* cognitive, perceptual-motor, and social-emotional demands on young children?

Concerned observers cite two sources of danger. The first is an economic view of educational aims; that is, the view that the major purpose of schooling is to prepare students to enter the workforce. The second concern emerges from higher education, which now enrolls many students who might otherwise not have considered college but have found that a college degree is required for an increasing number of jobs. Such a view begins with the business community and the professorate, and the sequence of attribution goes something like this: employers concerned about workers' literacy skills, and professors concerned about students' "readiness" for college work, blame high school teachers, who attribute responsibility to middle school teachers for failing to prepare students for the rigors of concentrated academic study. Those teachers in turn think intermediate-level instruction must have

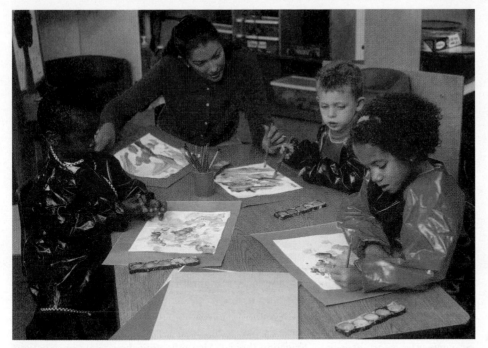

©Ingram Publishing/SuperStock RF

been weak, for students lack grounding in the basics (mathematical operations, paragraph construction, reading for meaning), but those problems, alas, are the fault of primary instruction. The ultimate blame doesn't stop with the kindergarten teacher (who ought to better ensure children's readiness for first grade); it gets passed on to parents.

If the ultimate goal is international competitiveness and if American graduates fare poorly when compared to their counterparts in other industrialized nations, one kind of logic argued for "more! earlier! faster!" And that logic inevitably, as advocates for young children maintain, results in inappropriate practices that actually impede children's development in the attempt to accelerate the notion that "more" will speed up children's development and adolescents' readiness for college has been very evident in connection with homework, as many parents will attest. However, what is known about development suggests to experts like Cathy Vatterot (2009) that "more" isn't necessarily better. In addition to out-of-school factors that differentially affect children's lives, she stressed the differential readiness of each successive developmental level, endorsing the "10-Minute Rule": 10 minutes per night per grade level.

Early Childhood Education and Developmentally Appropriate Practice

Although the principle is relevant to all levels of schooling, *developmental appropriateness* emerged in the 1970s and 1980s as a particular concern in the rapidly growing field of early childhood education. This field encompasses infant and toddler services, preschool programs, kindergarten, and primary grades; that is, from birth through about age 8. As Rebecca New and Bruce Mallory (1994) summarized, the resulting publication of the National Association for the Education of Young Children (NAEYC), *Developmentally Appropriate Practice*, was—like many other reform ideas—an important political statement:

> The NAEYC effort was motivated primarily by the need to respond to the increasingly pervasive pressure for early childhood programs to conform to an academic model of instruction typical of programs designed for older children. Throughout the document, there is also evidence of the intent to advocate for the field's long-standing core values of respect for and nurturing of young children as among the necessary means to achieve the democratic goals of a just and compassionate society (p. 1).

Constructivist Thought in Developmentally Appropriate Practice

The resulting document and its subsequent revisions have a scientific as well as an ideological basis. Developmentally appropriate practice (DAP) is not itself a theory of education (or of child development); it reflects a tradition of child pedagogy that, while centuries old, gained scientific support in the 20th century largely because of Jean Piaget's highly influential theory of cognitive development. Thus developmentally appropriate practice is often described as based on, or at least congruent with, *cognitive developmental theory,* especially Piagetian theory. Also reflecting the social constructivist theory of Lev Vygotsky, DAP is clearly congruent as well with the ideas of cross-cultural psychology, which posits that the ways in which individuals construct their world are strongly influenced by cultural factors. Rebecca Williams (1994) described the pedagogical implications of the theoretical orientation intended by the term **constructivism** in this way:

> Children are understood to be active constructors of their own knowledge. Mental activity is enhanced by wide experience with people, materials, and events, through which children form concepts and develop perceptions. Children's skills also are refined through repeated experience. Curriculum is therefore expected to provide multiple opportunities for children's direct and concrete engagement. This view of children's learning places the locus of control of the process within children themselves. Adults are not the pivotal factor in the process. They can provide a conducive setting, but it is the children's inner structures that impel them to learn (p. 158).

The word *structure* in this context refers to the concepts, ideas, and understandings that children *construct* through their transactions with their social and physical environment. Some scholars call this a *frame* or a *lens* or—after Vygotksy—a *scaffold,* but all agree that it is through this construction that individuals filter information and make sense of the world in which they live.

Thus, from a constructivist perspective, knowledge is "made" by the knower, who, like a person adapting to a new culture, and to use Piaget's term, assimilates new experiences within knowledge structures already present and accommodates to experiences that do not fit neatly into those structures. Imagine the cognitive manipulation that takes place when a small child who knows the class "dog" as four-legged creatures with bushy tails and so on encounters a stub-tailed or pointy-tailed dog . . . or a pony!

Motivation to learn emerges from the fact that children's **cognitive structures** are continuously challenged, and the child's inherent need to understand—*epistemic curiosity,* in philosophical terms—provides the impetus for acquiring new knowledge. Note that this need to understand is an *internal* motivating factor and is significantly different from such external factors as the praise of adults or the awarding of candy and gold stars or stickers. Since some conditions are more likely than others to elicit that motivation, the teacher's task is to solve "the problem of the match" between what each child is ready, cognitively and motivationally, to learn and what is made available to the child to learn. (Vygotsky [1978] called the range of experiences that are sufficiently challenging yet manageable the **zone of proximal development.**)

Although the NAEYC's DAP guidelines emphasize the uniqueness of the early childhood years, both the concept of developmentally appropriate teaching and its underlying constructivist theory of learning and knowing are relevant to the instruction of older children, adolescents, and even adults. Many (most?) college students, experiencing a small epiphany of understanding of some concept or idea, remember that it was introduced in a high school course, but they "didn't get it" then. Many also remember lack of interest and boredom with material presented in high school classes that was already too familiar.

The constructivist view differs from the traditional notion of readiness—used as a criterion for determining when a child should enter kindergarten, move on to first grade, and so on—in that constructivists emphasize that cognitive readiness is not determined simply by biological maturation, a kind of natural unfolding. It is rather an interactional—better, a *transactional*—matter. At any point in time, every individual is ready to learn, if learning experiences are at an optimal level of novelty or incongruity. Clearly, what is optimal for one learner is not necessarily optimal for another, even among learners of the same age. Though each of us functions within a particular social-cultural context, everyone undertakes as an individual the *tasks* of development (Havighurst, 1972) associated with each successive life stage.

Characteristics of a Developmentally Appropriate Classroom

Pedagogies: Old and New

Though they have historical antecedents, constructivist notions gained scientific support and integrity as a coherent theory through the work of Piaget and other theorists, notably Vygotsky and Jerome Bruner, both of whom placed greater emphasis than did Piaget on the social-cultural context of children's development.[2] Constructivist ideas were actually advanced much earlier by a succession of educational theorists and reformers, including Comenius in the 17th century, Condillac and Rousseau in the 18th century, Pestalozzi and Parker in the late 19th century, and John Dewey in the 20th century. Sharply critical of the old methods used to teach reading in the schools—memorization based on recitation from the *New England Primer*—Horace Mann argued that children could best master reading and writing if instruction were guided by, and built on, the language base a child had. (Does that argument sound like today's *whole language* approach?) Pestalozzi's *object teaching* emphasized the child's experience and perceptions as the basis for organizing knowledge and developing powers of reasoning—a "faculty" the authoritative educational psychology of his day considered not available to young children!

In Francis Parker's *child-centered approach*, school subjects and practical arts were correlated—that is, integrated—as pupils worked eagerly, without coercion or control by the teacher, at their individual and cooperative jobs. In contrast to the traditional faculty psychology, which portrayed the mind as comprised of a number of discrete faculties, and pedagogy as mental discipline to strengthen them, Parker viewed children's learning as holistic and, like Piaget, inseparable from development. Yet, turn-of-the-century classrooms—with few exceptions, such as Parker's Quincy (Massachusetts) System and Dewey's laboratory school at the University of Chicago, and kindergartens (which were still quite separate from public schools)—were as described by Larry Cuban (1993):

> Generally, teachers taught the entire class at the same time. Teacher talk dominated verbal expression during class time. Classroom activities revolved around teacher questions and explanations, student recitations, and the class's working on textbook assignments. Except for laboratory work in science classrooms, teachers sought uniformity in behavior. The social organization of the turn-of-the-century classroom, then, was formal, with students sitting in rows of bolted-down desks facing the teacher's desk and chalkboard, rising to recite for the teacher, and moving about the room or leaving it only with the teacher's permission. The academic organization of the classroom hinged upon the whole class's moving as one through the course of study, text, recitations, and homework. Those who worked, succeeded; those who didn't, failed (p. 37).

Does that picture sound familiar to you? Based on his study of American classrooms from 1880 to 1990, Cuban concluded that teacher-centered instruction continued to be the dominant pattern, although at the elementary level and in some secondary schools "a hybrid version of student-centered practices, begun in the early decades of this century, has spread and is maturing" (p. 272). Such practices have included the use of small group organization, activity centers, projects, more provision for student choice, joint teacher–student planning of learning activities, and integration of content.

The notion of intrinsically motivated, *child-directed learning* is, for many, epitomized in the approach developed by Maria Montessori, whose injunction, "Don't *tell*, *teach*!" summed up her view of how classrooms for students of any age should be conducted: The teacher planfully arranges, models, and monitors, as students, within limits defined by the learning materials, follow their inborn inclination to discover and to understand. Yet Montessori's tardy popularity in the United States, in contrast to many other nations, has been attributed to its proposal of a highly individualized approach at a time when Dewey, Kirkpatrick, and other leaders in the American progressive education movement stressed cooperative projects and group problem solving. Paradoxically, since her work had begun with children considered intellectually deficient or living in the slums of Rome, the relatively few Montessori programs in the United States by the 1950s were viewed by many as desirable for exceptionally capable or (perhaps because only privately available) more privileged children. Today, some American public schools and a number of independent schools offer Montessori education, some at least through the eighth grade.

A few other educational approaches have, like Maria Montessori, maintained that teaching the *whole* child must not only take account of characteristics associated with major stages of development but also of the child's *spiritual* nature. Among the best known of these, *the Waldorf approach*, evolved from a school Rudolph Steiner established in 1919 for the children of workers in the Waldorf Astoria cigarette factory in Stuttgart, Germany. Waldorf schools, while not presently as numerous as Montessori programs, are similar in certain respects, but strikingly different in others. Each reflects a pedagogical theory inseparably linked to its founder, views learning holistically and of a piece with development, attempts to respond to the learner's spiritual nature, and

©Randy Faris/SuperStock RF

purposefully eschews competitiveness, but there is much greater emphasis in the Waldorf approach on such areas as art, music, and foreign language, and on the critical role in human development of *imagination*. Although both systems provide for secondary schooling, most Montessori and Waldorf schools in the United States are limited to prekindergarten through Grade 8.

One fairly coherent constructivist model that has attracted much interest among American educators is *the Reggio Emilia approach*. Rather than having a philosophy linked to a single founder, it is named for the town in the Emilia Romagna region of northern Italy where it has been developed and refined from its post–World War II origins (Edwards, Gandini, & Foreman, 1993). The system's distinctive qualities include some familiar constructivist ideas: learning occurs within the context of an emergent curriculum organized around projects carried out over extended periods of time (determined by children's activity and choice rather than adult-controlled time schedules) that integrate diverse areas of learning and elicit children's expression, in all of their "hundred languages," including words, movement, drawing, painting, building, sculpture, shadow play, collage, dramatic play, and music. Leading children to surprising levels of symbolic skills and creativity, the approach takes place not in an elite and sheltered setting of private education but rather in a municipal system of full-day child care open to all, including children with special needs (Edwards et al., pp. 3–4).

Perhaps the most striking feature of Reggio Emilia may be the most difficult to translate from one cultural setting to another: the view, shared by parents and educators, of the school as an extension of the home. This deeply embedded understanding is a legacy of its origins in a parent cooperative movement that emerged in the region during the years of post–World War II reconstruction. A second distinctive feature perhaps difficult to translate is, as in the Waldorf approach, the centrality of artistic expression. Although this approach, like DAP and the progressive and open education movements, was explicitly designed for preprimary and primary schools, some of the key concepts seem valid and applicable with older learners:

- Conscious awareness of the important role of physical space and especially of aesthetic properties of the physical environment in inviting learning
- Not holding students' motivation and accomplishment hostage to the tyranny of the clock, curriculum guide, or textbook
- The importance of true team collaboration, over time, marked by shared ownership of the educational process and continued inquiry on the part of teachers, learners, families, and leaders (principals, supervisors)
- Elimination of artificial compartmentalizations among subjects and between science and the arts, knowledge and creativity, effort and enjoyment
- Trust in and respect for students, expressed through responsibility combined with empowerment, opportunity to work cooperatively as well as independently, and valuing of diverse modes of expression
- A concept of development as a dynamic process rather than as static levels

The shift from the traditional junior high to the **middle school** is another example of DAP being put into practice and uniting an understanding of development of young people with principles of learning. Each age level seems to have a set of characteristics that distinguishes it from all others, and one of the most marked is that of children who are in the transition into adolescence. Actually, as discussed in Chapter 7, the transition begins well before the onset of puberty for most Western children, with increased cognitive flexibility and awareness of perspectives of others. Whereas administrative organization and grade-level content are the focus in secondary schools, in middle schools a focus on broadly defined needs of the learner that, as in Waldorf education, encompasses the full range of intellectual as well as social, emotional, and other developmental needs is fundamental. Moreover, the challenge of middle school education is, as the National Middle School Association (1992) states, "to develop an educational program that is based on the needs and characteristics of a most diverse and varied population" (p. 4).

Although *middle childhood* is usually defined as spanning the years from about age 8 to age 12, American middle schools are generally intended to address developmental issues associated with early adolescence. The publication, *This We Believe: Keys to Educating Young Adolescents* (AMLE, 2010), identifies 16 research-based characteristics of effective middle grades education, dividing them into three areas: Curriculum, Instruction, and Assessment; Leadership and Organization; and Culture and Community. Characteristics under Curriculum, Instruction, and Assessment include: educators value young adolescents; engage in active, purposeful learning; offer a challenging curriculum; employ multiple teaching and learning approaches designed to accommodate a variety of learning skills and abilities; and use varied approaches to assessment. Under Leadership and Organization in effective middle schools, all stakeholders: share a common vision; are committed to the needs of young adolescents; are collaborative in their approach; engage in ongoing professional development; and organize teachers in such a way as to foster purposeful learning and meaningful relationships. Finally, under Culture and Community, effective middle schools: establish a school environment that is inviting, safe, inclusive, and supportive of all; provide adult advocates to guide student development; provide comprehensive guidance and support services to meet the needs of young adolescents; attend to student health needs and education; encourage family involvement; and engage the community-at-large.

Persistent concerns about drops in academic performance among students, as well as declining self-esteem, bullying, and other antisocial behavior have prompted some educators to favor eliminating middle schools and returning to the K–8 and 9–12 grade structure. Others believe children of this age group would benefit from older role models. Modifying school structures is a continuous process as communities attempt to respond to perceived local needs. Increasingly, you may find preschool through primary age groupings served in early childhood centers, or Grades 5 and 6 housed separately from Grades 7 and 8, or schools returning to a K–8 structure, or a return to the grades 7–9 junior high model, or—as Leon Botstein proposes—a two-tiered (K–6 and 7–10) structure. However, differential organizational structures represent but one way in which schools respond to developmental diversity among students.

Roles: Old and New

Although constructivism (in both its old and new forms) places the student at the center of the learning process and acknowledges that much important learning is done by students entirely on their own or with peers, the teacher's role is of key importance. In the 1997 revision of the NAEYC DAP guidelines, Bredekamp (1997) affirmed the basic responsibility of teachers as well as the principle that a child's sense of competence and worth is the essential foundation for learning and development:

> The goal is for teachers to support the learning and development of all children. To achieve this goal, teachers need to know children well and use everything they know about each child—including that individual's learning styles, interests and preferences, personality and temperament, skills and talents, challenges and difficulties. Children are more likely to achieve a positive sense of self if they experience more success than failure in the early school years. The teacher must support a positive sense of self-identity in each child (p. 40).

The one word that best captures the most fundamental change in the teacher's role is *collaboration*. Because the field of early childhood education has been a major influence in bringing about a reexamination of the teacher's role, another look at its history may be instructive.[3]

Soon after Friedrich Froebel's notion of "child-gardening" was brought to America by Margarethe Meyer Schurz in the wake of the great German immigration, Elizabeth Peabody described the role of kindergartner (the term referred to the kindergarten teacher) as a partner and adviser for parents in nurturing young children. Although kindergartens have been around since the mid-19th century, prekindergartens as such have been in existence only about half as long. The common school (not exactly "common," considering that most 19th-century American children received very little instruction, and many none at all) enrolled pupils as young as 3 years old, but they were mixed in with older brothers and sisters with no provisions for early childhood's uniqueness. Nursery schools, like those Margaret MacMillan started for English children of poor families, and kindergartens spread as a facet of the British and American settlement movements of the early 20th century, and they had a particular focus on health and nutritional concerns.

Two other important movements fostered the expansion of early childhood education in the United States: child study and mental hygiene. G. Stanley Hall, often called the founder of child psychology, was a key influence in both movements. He influenced the latter by introducing to American intellectuals and professionals psychoanalytic theories of the formative significance of early childhood experiences (including introducing them to Freud himself at the historic conference at Clark University in 1909).

Arnold Gesell, Hall's student, had by 1930 led the growth of nursery education, in his words, "from a no man's land to an every man's land" (p. 143), although nursery teachers, like "kindergartners," were invariably women. What Gesell meant was that a broad range of professionals—psychologists, physicians, social workers, public health workers—had become involved. Universities had established laboratory programs, like Gesell's own Guidance Nursery at Yale, as centers for child development research and teacher training. He and other professionals viewed programs for young children as important both in identifying problems early in life so that timely ameliorative measures could be provided and in promoting the healthy development of mind and body.

The Great Depression halted the spread of nursery education, but when World War II called multitudes of women to defense industry work, the Lanham Act created another role for such programs: day care. The years since World War II and especially since the 1960s have witnessed an enormous increase in the need for outside-the-home child care in many industrialized nations. In the United States, this need was exacerbated by welfare reform requirements instituted under the Clinton administration, which created a crisis for many families, as well as providers and policymakers. Parents and child advocates insist that child care, including before- and after-school care for school-age children, must be more than custodial, but is it "education"? In the United States, the NAEYC joined forces with other major child advocacy groups such as the Children's Defense Fund in working for policies to ensure that child care is accessible and affordable yet also adheres to high-quality standards of professional nurture and guidance that are in the interests of children and, consequently, of society itself. That is, whether provided in a center or in someone's home, child care must be *developmentally appropriate.*

Growth in families' need for child care led to new discoveries about young children and, consequently, to a redefinition of adult roles. Conventional wisdom in the burgeoning field of child psychology had held that group experiences were of no value for children until at least age 3. But as necessity truly became the mother of invention, caregivers (and psychologists) discovered that toddlers were quite interested in each other, and even babies were, in their fashion, social creatures. Such discoveries implied a (developmentally appropriate) teacher role for adults caring for infants and toddlers, and a number of roles (model, partner in parallel play, friend, leader) for very small children themselves. These new roles became ever more influential in the course of children's development through and beyond the early childhood years. Educators who observed the ways children learn from and with each other sought to reapply Parker's and Dewey's less teacher-centered concepts through such strategies as cooperative learning and small-group activity. From birth through all the years of schooling, learners have a central role in their own learning and an instrumental role in the learning of their peers.

Early childhood programs, especially Project Head Start and Early Start, emphasize collaborative relationships with families to promote optimal development during the most formative years. For school-age children and youth, the teacher's role has increasingly become a collaborative one in other respects. Rather than being expected to function on their own, teachers can anticipate the support of peers through building-level planning and problem-solving teams and actual team teaching. And, of course, working collaboratively with others—fellow professionals, parents and other family members, and community resource persons—requires a unique set of sensitivities and skills.

Place of Content Knowledge: Old and New

Developmentally appropriate practice means a change in the place of content knowledge in schooling that involves rediscovery of some old wisdom undergirded by new knowledge about human development. What is often called the "cognitive revolution" in American psychology that began in the 1950s and 1960s brought new respect for children's intellectual resources and for the potential of schooling to influence the course of development. But it also contributed to an unduly narrow emphasis and raised what Piaget called the "American question": How much can we accelerate the pace of children's cognitive learning in order to create smarter adults?

The discourse concerning DAP is more concerned with process than with content, which Bernard Spodek (1991) attributed to the fact that "early childhood educators are more concerned with the effects of early childhood education on a child's development than with what a child comes to know as a result of that education" (p. 1). What Piaget called "social knowledge" (information)—imparted by parents, teachers, *Sesame Street,* siblings, and peers—is important, but cognitive development is an active, transactional process, not a passive one. The deductive reasoning basic to mathematical understanding and the inductive questioning that is the hallmark of scientific inquiry are inherent capabilities of children as they strive to reconcile incongruities and impose structure on their constantly expanding experiential world. In related fashion, literacy learning begins in early childhood—in fact, in earliest infancy—and is fostered to the degree that the child's active and creative use of language, and pleasure in its use, continue to be encouraged (Vacca, Vacca, & Gove, 1987). However, to put basal readers or phonics worksheets in the hands of all 3-year-olds would be developmentally inappropriate.

In the constructivist perspective, learners of any age generate content knowledge, not just receive it. As Howard Gardner (1991) emphasized, the goal of effective education is not merely transmitting information, but ensuring understanding. Moreover, Gardner emphasized that since understanding is itself a developmental process—proceeding from sensorimotor, to intuitive, to application of logical reasoning—school instruction must support this progression if learners are ultimately to gain mastery of content disciplines.

Assessment: Old and New

When we consider assessment in the context of learners' developmental status, we need to distinguish different purposes of assessment. Statewide proficiency or graduation tests and international comparisons of educational achievement indeed reflect urgent American concerns for accountability and a national effort to identify and maintain educational standards as essential for educational reform. "Setting the bar" higher, some educators argue, will only widen the gap between the more and the less advantaged children and schools. Yet conversely, several decades of research have demonstrated the strong link between adult expectations and student (and school) performance: expectancy becomes a self-fulfilling prophecy (Botstein, 1997). Whatever standards are agreed upon for progression through the educational system and ultimate graduation, there must be some means of assessing the status of individual students in terms of those standards. Although often it may be imperfectly implemented, assessment is essential to educational accountability.

But assessment of student progress vis-à-vis performance standards should not be confused with sorting, a questionable and potentially invidious use of assessment. In the past, assessment often was used to validate beliefs about the limited learning potential of children of poor and low-income families and immigrants, children of color, and children with disabilities. Although inappropriate assessment procedures also have been used to identify which children are ready for school and which ones are not, the DAP guidelines are quite explicit about the responsibility of schools to be "ready" for all children. As Samuel Meisels (1981) wrote, screening and assessment should never be used to close educational doors for a child but to open them.

A 21st-century view of educational assessment goes beyond reliance on narrow and fallible tests in linking knowledge about individual learners with instructional planning and decision making. This view is frequently identified by the term **authentic assessment.** Noting the limited value of traditional, norm-referenced assessment procedures with young children, DAP guidelines emphasize the importance of observation of children in natural activity contexts, collections of children's work, and ongoing communication with parents "for the purpose of improving teaching and learning" (Bredekamp & Copple, 1997, p. 17). To Gardner (1991), with students of any age, understanding can only be meaningfully assessed through opportunities to apply learning to new situations:

> Whereas short-answer tests and oral responses in classes can provide clues to student understanding, it is generally necessary to look more deeply if one desires firm evidence that understandings of significance have been obtained. For these purposes, new and unfamiliar problems, followed by open-ended clinical interviews or careful observations, provide the best way of establishing the degree of understanding that students have obtained (p. 145).

Perspectives on Age and Development

School experiences both profoundly influence and are influenced by people's development as human beings. That statement may seem on the surface so obvious that it scarcely deserves mention. But consider it more closely. What is "development," and precisely what implications does it have for learning and teaching in schools? As David Shaffer (1993) summarized, "Simply stated, development refers to systematic changes in the individual that occur between the moment of conception . . . and the moment the individual dies" (p. 4). You are probably familiar with important concepts involving patterns of change that humans experience over time, such as nature versus nurture, sensitive or critical periods, individual differences, and developmental stages and domains. What implications do such concepts have for schooling?

Sensitive Periods and Developmental Crises

Since critically important systematic changes occur before schooling begins (indeed, from the moment of conception) as well as afterward, it may appear that development proceeds relatively independently of schooling. While the so-called **nature versus nurture debate** has revolved more around what young children experience at home than what older children and youth experience in school, major social programs, such as Project Head Start, have reflected the awareness that education can indeed alter the course of children's development. Moreover, as described in Chapter 7, middle childhood is also a period of heightened receptiveness to developmental influence, when teachers can encourage children's desires to process new experiences and foster their awareness of the perspectives of others. As noted previously, recent neuroscientific findings confirm that the adolescent years also constitute a period of significant cognitive change, and thus it is a period of sensitivity and responsiveness to the influence of others, teachers as well as parents and peers. Probably most people believe their own lives have been affected in crucial ways by school experiences that occurred at some point in their lives when they were particularly receptive or particularly vulnerable.

Although those points of receptivity and vulnerability are to a great extent an individual matter—associated with a major change in an individual's family situation like parental divorce, separation, or death; a person's own or a family member's illness; a move to a new community and a new school; a new friendship; even a certain teacher or coach—some are fairly universal. In Erik Erikson's (1963) familiar formulation, the development of *ego identity* is a lifetime enterprise, involving eight stages of psychosocial development, each marked by a conflict to be resolved. The adolescent identity crisis is preceded by successive childhood crises, or turning points, emerging from conflicting influences or needs: basic trust versus mistrust, autonomy versus shame and doubt, initiative versus guilt, industry versus inferiority. Everyone remembers—happily, painfully, or ruefully—their own adolescent years and the changes they brought. For centuries, in fact, adolescence, though not identified as such, was assumed to be the critical period for learning, and schooling often didn't begin until then. Infancy, traditionally the first 7 years of life, was accorded little importance.

Clearly, the kinds of experience that are critical will change in the course of development. Yet, as Howard Gardner (1991) noted in *The Unschooled Mind,* formal instruction often fails to challenge students to move beyond the intuitive modes of knowing that served them well as young children and use the cognitive resources they have acquired. Matching instruction to the developmental level of learners requires, he reminds us, challenging students to demonstrate understanding by applying knowledge to new situations.

Socioemotional Implications of Body Size and Body Image

An older adult standing in a middle school corridor as classes change cannot help but be struck by the signs of near physical maturity of many of the students passing by. Through most of the 20th century, successive generations of young people entered puberty, on average, earlier than their predecessors, a phenomenon termed **secular trend**. Among today's American girls, although there is considerable variability in its onset, puberty can begin as early as age 7, with early onset, coupled with other stressors, increasing emotional liability, and even the likelihood of debilitating anxiety or depression (Steinberg, 2005). Rapid physical changes, coupled with heightened attention to social messages conveyed through the media and heightened concern for peer approval, combine to make adolescence a "critical period" with respect to self-esteem as well as, especially for girls, susceptibility to serious eating disorders. Subject to these factors, a young girl may have a distorted body image, perceiving herself as different from the perceived ideal conveyed in women's and teen magazines and music videos.

Complicating these concerns about the harmful effects of distorted body image is the campaign championed by, among others, former American First Lady Michelle Obama to combat childhood obesity, which has increased at alarming rates since the 1980s. Since this increase has occurred across ethnic and socioeconomic lines, no doubt many aspects of contemporary society, rather than simply cultural attitudes concerning food and body size, poor diet associated with poverty, or, conversely, affluence, have contributed to this phenomenon. Among its many social functions, the public school has assumed or been given a role in this campaign, especially in the form of increased attention to lunchroom fare and provision for physical exercise during the school day.

In addition to the physical deleterious effects associated with less physically active lifestyles and unwholesome diets, overweight and obese youngsters are often victims of teasing or bullying. Although bullying is certainly not a new concern among school children, recent events such as school shootings and highly publicized teen suicides have dramatically increased public awareness of some young people's extreme responses to being teased or bullied. Again, while being verbally or even physically tormented by peers on the playground, in the halls or locker room, or on the school bus has long placed many children and adolescents, especially early adolescents, at serious risk, driving some to taking their own lives, **cyberbullying** may today be an even greater concern, since it typically occurs outside of the school's purview and may afford the bully the cloak of anonymity. While earlier generations of teens expressed opinions of their peers through "slam books" circulated surreptitiously in school, postings on various social media outlets, compromising photos, or other uses of technology have virtually revolutionized the ways in which young people can be seriously harmed by their peers or by adults who prey on the young.

Individual Differences and Developmental Domains

Developmentally appropriate practice is based not only on age and stage differences but also on another key concept in the psychology of human development: individual differences. Many such differences are culture-related; others are situational, influenced by circumstances in a person's life and quite idiosyncratic. Wide variations, even within cultures, are to some degree attributable to built-in factors, certainly including biological heredity. Arnold Gesell (1949), well-known for his detailed descriptions of nearly universal characteristics of infants, children, and youth that are virtually programmed in humans as in other species, asserted, "No two infants were ever born alike" (p. 530). While the nature side of the nature versus nurture debate involves both common (i.e., maturational) and highly idiosyncratic (i.e., hereditary) influences, development involves the subtle interaction of these influences with a host of environmental influences, many cultural and many specific to the individual. All the characteristics or traits that distinguish everyone's unique personality reflect some interactive mix of biological and environmental influences. This impact is true even of some physical attributes, such as skeletal structure, although others (e.g., eye color) are entirely biologically influenced.

Human development proceeds on many fronts, often referred to as *developmental domains* (e.g., motor, cognitive, language/communication, social/emotional). The notion of domains in some ways involves arbitrary distinctions, for babies, children, youth, and adults are whole beings, not just composites of discrete parts. Language development, for example, is virtually inseparable from cognitive and social development. During the critical period for language acquisition—the first 3 years of life—language is also mightily influenced by sensory and motor development. But language can be analyzed on the basis of domain-specific concepts (phonology, morphology, syntax, semantics, and pragmatics). Appropriate educational practice requires knowledge of such concepts and patterns of change associated with major domains. It is not developmentally appropriate to expect 3-year-olds to cut expertly with scissors or know (in the adult sense) what clouds are, to expect 5-year-olds to be physically inactive for extended periods or argue the merits of a bicameral legislature, or to expect 10-year-olds to do grueling labor or solve algebraic equations. Nor is it developmentally appropriate, Gardner reminded us, to fail to challenge learners to apply their developing powers of understanding.

Because milestones, such as first words and independent walking, as well as transitions from one stage to another are reached by different children at different times, it is necessary to be aware of normal ranges of variation in the timing and sequencing of developmental changes. Such variations are attributable to many factors, including gender, geography (e.g., climate), genetics, specific environmental influences, and differential cultural values and expectations. For some children, such as a child who is blind or one who has cerebral palsy, developmental processes may differ qualitatively, rather than quantitatively, from their typical peers. It makes no sense to say, for example, that a child who cannot see has "delayed" visual development or that a child with cerebral palsy who cannot walk independently has "delayed" motor development. The first child learns to complement functional vision with other sensory information more than do most children; the second child may accomplish mobility with the aid of adaptive equipment, such as a wheelchair.

The Importance of Developmental Knowledge

What should teachers know about children and adolescents in order for their instruction to be developmentally appropriate? Until the latter half of the 19th century, most American and European teachers and school officials knew very little because not much attention was paid to the unique features of successive stages. In some common schools, children as young as age 3 or 4 were instructed along with older students, even adolescents, seated on hard benches inappropriate for all, awaiting their turn to recite. Age-grading supplanted such arrangements, however, and though instruction could be more age-appropriate, it rarely took into account individual variations. Pupils who deviated considerably from the norm—who didn't "fit"—presented problems that were addressed through grade repetition or ungraded classes and classes for "unrulies" (forerunners of special education classes, which are discussed in Chapter 12).

The **child study movement,** while promoting more positive awareness of differential rates of development among children, mainly inspired more age-appropriate practices, such as the introduction of the junior high school. From the child study tradition, through the work of Gesell and his associates, a generation of aspiring teachers who were trained in the 1940s and 1950s also learned about the terrible 2s, trusting 3s, and general attributes characteristic of successive ages and stages of childhood and adolescence. What they didn't always learn about development was the extent to which, and the ways in which, it is influenced by experience and the wide variability among children that can be expected within each of the successive stages. Nor did they learn about variability associated with diverse cultural norms, expectations, and values.

Stage theories of human development emphasize the universality of developmental milestones and the manifestations of specific attributes of successive stages. In addition to Gesell's normative descriptions, some well-known theorists have focused on personality development (Sigmund Freud, Anna Freud, Erik Erikson), on cognitive development (Jean Piaget), on language (Noam Chomsky), and on moral development (Lawrence Kohlberg). Although many of these aspects of development may emerge in much the same way among the world's children, it is also the case that they may be differentially valued and expressed in different cultural settings.

One instance of culturally different values placed on developmental skills involves the notion of *independence,* or autonomy, and developmental domains labeled on assessment scales as *self-help, adaptive,* or *social-emotional.* Noting aspects of the Reggio Emilia early childhood approach that may be culture-specific, Rebecca New (1994) commented on a standard routine that children in American day-care centers quickly learn: how to put on one's jacket when it's time to go home or for outdoor play by flipping it, arms in sleeves, over one's head. This maneuver may require concentration and involves occasional mistakes, but the pleasure in accomplishment and sense of mastery youngsters experience is apparent in their expression. "Few Italian 2-year-olds have been taught how to put their coats on unassisted," she notes, for "adults . . . enjoy the opportunity to assist children, even as they encourage children to also help one another" (p. 72). This example illustrates a difference in culturally valued independence versus cooperation that is expressed in various ways. What implications do such differences have for developmentally appropriate expectations concerning children?

The concept of *developmentally appropriate practice* emerged in a political context, with a certain agenda, of establishing consensus concerning the uniqueness of early childhood, defined as the first 8 years of life. But age, stage, or developmental status cannot be the sole determinant of *educational* appropriateness, in the early childhood years or beyond. The guidelines as they were originally formulated and generally understood may have been insufficiently responsive to diverse cultural values, a concern addressed in the revised version of DAP. For example, Leslie Williams (1994) contrasted widely shared Native American traditions of interconnectedness, interdependence, and respectful listening with DAP's original strong emphasis on individualism, independence, and overt expression of language. The constructivism underlying DAP guidelines, as originally formulated, has thus been criticized as being ethnocentrically narrow and inadvertently legitimizing social and educational inequities by expressing a preconceived and prescribed version of what is developmentally appropriate.

A broader social constructivism, on the other hand, implies a more inclusive and collaborative perspective of educational practices that not only considers family and culture but recognizes their primacy in the lives of children and respects children in both their uniqueness and interconnectedness. In the Reggio Emilia educational approach, for example,

> the child is understood as having not only needs but competencies and rights as well. . . . Implicit in this view is the recognition of the child's embeddedness in a family, a community, a culture, and a society. It is thus the responsibility of the teachers, in active collaboration with parents and other members of the community, to acknowledge and respect those rights, to identify and understand those competencies, and respond collectively to those needs. In order to fulfill this role, teachers in Reggio Emilia become researchers in their own classrooms, regularly making and sharing hypotheses about learning and development rather than reifying existing conceptions (Williams, 1994, p. 158).

There are in fact different "constructions" of what constructivism entails, ranging from those that encompass applied behavior analysis and direct instruction to those that consider teaching, if the term implies adult direction and management of children's learning, a "dirty word" (Harris & Graham, 1994). Exclusive commitment to any doctrinaire approach in teaching risks blinding a teacher to the differences among students at any particular stage of development or level of schooling. In its essence, constructivist teaching recognizes that learning, though it occurs in and is supported by social contexts, is an individual affair. Developmentally appropriate practices are those that respond to each student's uniqueness.

Critical Incident

Responding to a Concerned Board Member

Things seemed to take a positive turn for Tony once he and his students began planning for the music program; many of the students seemed to be actively engaged and interested in the program planning and in the variety of preparatory activities that needed to occur. Then one morning, about 3 weeks before the scheduled program, Tony was called into Principal Wilson's office. One of the members of the school board, a rather influential individual who was quite supportive of the existing school band, had complained that Tony might be setting a bad example for other teachers—especially ones new to the school. While this board member acknowledged that it was of benefit to raise money to assist the family with their expenses, it was pretty clear to him that this activity was outside the standard music curriculum and that it was setting a bad precedent. Besides, he reasoned, there was a pretty good music curriculum in place that was approved by the state. The principal wanted to let Tony know of the concern because the board member was coming in to discuss the issue in 2 days, and he had asked to speak with Tony. The principal asked Tony to think about how he might best present his argument and rationale for the activities in which he and the students were presently engaged.

- If you were Tony, how would you best structure your meeting with the board member?
- Given the developmental status of the students involved, what particular justification do you see for such an activity that would make it worth advocating for?

Critical Incident

The Disgruntled Parent

A few weeks into the school year, Mrs. Johnson, a parent of one of the children in Mrs. Conrad's class, stopped Sally in the hallway after school, sounding both excited and concerned. It seemed that her son, Ronald, had complained to her about school, saying that it was boring and hard and that he didn't want to go anymore. Mrs. Johnson seemed certain that her son's unhappiness in school was related to Mrs. Conrad's reliance on worksheets and excessive seatwork, and the mother was going to ask for a meeting with Principal Wilson to discuss the issue. Mrs. Johnson wondered if Sally might have a talk with the principal with the hope of encouraging Mrs. Conrad to have a greater variety of activities in her teaching.

- If you were Sally, how would you respond to Mrs. Johnson?
- If you were, in fact, called in to speak with the principal, what would you say?

Summary

The concept of developmentally appropriate practice, or structuring an educational program that is sensitive to factors of age, individual differences, and culture-influenced life experience, is introduced in this chapter. In particular, the concept of constructivist learning is introduced as a pedagogical approach that integrates both development of the learner and practice of the teacher.

Chapter Review

Go to the Online Learning Center at www.mhhe.com/cushner9e. to review important content from the chapter, practice with key terms, take a chapter quiz, and access active workbook exercises.

Key Terms

authentic assessment 350
child study
  movement 353
cognitive structures 342
constructivism 342

cyberbullying 352
developmentally
  appropriate
  practice (DAP) 338
middle school 346

nature versus nurture
  debate 350
secular trend 351
zone of proximal
  development 343

Active Exercise

Additional Active Exercises are available online at www.mhhe.com/cushner9e.

Childhood Experiences

Purpose: To identify early socialization experiences that have influenced one's cultural values, beliefs, and practices held today.

Instructions: For culture to be a shared phenomenon, it must be effectively transmitted to the young. There oftentimes exist clear childhood experiences that individuals can identify that help to develop and teach particular values and practices. Identify three examples of cultural beliefs, values, and practices that are expected of "successful" representatives of American culture (or another culture with which you are familiar). Your list will include desirable beliefs, values, and behaviors.

Beliefs	Values	Behaviors
_____	_____	_____
_____	_____	_____
_____	_____	_____

Next, consider an example from each column. What childhood experiences did you have that may have helped you to develop the cultural traits that are expected of you? (For instance, a paper route helps one develop responsibility, individuality, business sense, initiative, and so forth.) Describe early childhood experiences that may have helped you to achieve the desired and expected outcome.

Classroom Activities

1. Ask each (primary-grade) student to choose a character in a story (book, TV cartoon) they especially like (or assign a character familiar to the student) and use any, or several, of various media (crayon drawing, descriptive words, mime, cooperative role-playing) to illustrate some of the character's important characteristics. Ask other class members to interpret their classmate's representation of what the character is like, is feeling, and so on, or (if appropriate) guess who the character is and why they think so.

2. In assigning tasks or activities to be carried out at home, try to apply the "10-minute rule." Let parents (and students) know what you are attempting and why. Reflect to determine whether or how this affects your efforts to achieve instructional objectives, including objectives imposed by state or district standards or requirements, such as standardized achievement testing.

3. Ask high school students, perhaps in an English or social studies class, to write brief descriptions of fairly specific ways they are different now than they were as a young children. Ask volunteers to share their descriptions or examples with the class. Encourage discussion of similarities or differences. As a follow-up—or as an alternative—ask students to do this individually or in groups of 3 or 4 based on real or fictional characters from their own or common reading.

Reflective Questions

1. Consider for a moment what it might mean to integrate developmentally appropriate practice into a variety of content-area disciplines. Give an example of developmentally appropriate practice when considering (a) a physical education class on basketball for students in grades 3, 7, and 10; (b) a social studies class discussion related to the topic of slavery in the United States for children in Grade 6 versus Grade 10; and (c) basic literacy and reading readiness activities for a class of nonreading 6-year-olds compared to a class of nonreading adults in a basic literacy evening class.

2. How does the more recent development of middle schools address developmentally appropriate practice differently than the more traditional junior high schools, even though they both are designed to serve children of similar ages?

Endnotes

1. The setting for Garfield Elementary School as well as elements of Sally Dougherty's classroom have been incorporated from a true story related by George Wood about a first-grade classroom in southern Ohio in *Schools That Work: America's Most Innovative Public Education Programs* (New York: Penguin Books, 1992, pp. 9–12).

2. Unless otherwise noted, the source consulted for historical background information discussed in this chapter is Philip L. Safford and Elizabeth J. Safford, *A History of Childhood and Disability* (New York: Teachers College Press, 1996).

3. See Lillian Weber, *The Kindergarten: Its Encounter with Educational Thought* (New York: Teachers College Press, 1969), for an excellent analysis of the impact of the progressive movement on the philosophy and goals of the American kindergarten.

References

AMLE (2010). *This we Believe: Keys to Educating Young Adolescents*. Association for Middle Level Education. Retrieved from http://www.amle.org/AboutAMLE/ThisWeBelieve/tabid/121/Default.aspx#122516-the-16-characteristics

Bredekamp, S. (1997). Developmentally appropriate practice: The early childhood teacher as decisionmaker. In S. Bredekamp & C. Copple (Eds.), *Developmentally appropriate practice in early childhood programs*. Washington, DC: National Association for the Education of Young Children.

Bredekamp, S., & Copple, C. (Eds.). (1997). *Developmentally appropriate practice in early childhood programs* (Rev. ed.). Washington, DC: National Association for the Education of Young Children.

Botstein, L. (1997). *Jefferson's children: Education and the promise of American culture*. New York: Doubleday.

Children's Defense Fund. (2001). *The state of America's children: A report from the Children's Defense Fund, Yearbook 2001*. Boston, MA: Beacon Press.

Children's Defense Fund. (2014). The State of America's Children: Retrieved from http://www.childrensdefense.org/library/state-of-americas-children /2014-soac.pdf?utm_source=2014-SOAC-PDF&utm_medium=link&utm _campaign=2014-SOAC

Cuban, L. (1993). *How teachers taught: Constancy and change in American classrooms, 1890-1990* (2nd ed.). New York: Teachers College Press.

Edwards, C., Gandini, L., & Foreman, G. (Eds.). (1993). *The hundred languages of children: The Reggio Emilia approach to early childhood education.* Norwood, NJ: Ablex.

Erikson, E. H. (1963). *Childhood and society* (2nd ed.). New York: Norton.

Gardner, H. (1991). *The unschooled mind: How children think and how schools should teach.* New York: Basic Books.

Gesell, A. (1930). A decade of progress in the mental hygiene of the preschool child. *The Annals of the American Academy of Political and Social Sciences 151*, 143.

Gesell, A. (1949). Human infancy and the ontogenesis of behavior. *American Scientist, 37*, 529-553.

Harris, K. R., & Graham, S. (1994). Constructivism: Principles, paradigms, and integration. *Journal of Special Education 28*(3), 233-247.

Havighurst, R. J. (1972). *Developmental tasks and education* (3rd ed.). New York: David McKay.

Jensen, F., & Nutt, A. E. (2015). *The teenage brain: A neuroscientist's guide to raising adolescents and young adults.* New York: HarperCollins.

Kozol, J. (1991). *Savage inequalities: Children in America's schools.* New York: Crown.

Meisels, S. J. (1981). Testing four- and five-year olds: Response to Salzer and to Sheppard and Smith. *Educational Leadership 44*(3), 90-92.

National Education Goals Panel. (1996). *Profile of 1994-95: State assessment systems and reported results.* Washington, DC: Author.

National Middle School Association (NMSA). (1992). *This we believe.* Columbus, OH: Author.

New, R. S. (1994). Culture, child development, and developmentally appropriate practice: Teachers as collaborative researchers. In B. L. Mallory, & R. S. New (Eds.), *Diversity and developmentally appropriate practice: Challenge for early childhood education.* New York: Teachers College Press.

New, R. S., & Mallory, B. L. (1994). Introduction: The ethic of inclusion. In R. S. New, & B. L. Mallory (Eds.), *Diversity and developmentally appropriate practice: Challenges for early childhood education.* New York: Teachers College Press.

Safford, P. L., & Safford, E. J. (1996). *A history of childhood and disability.* New York: Teachers College Press.

Shaffer, D. R. (1993). *Developmental psychology: Childhood and adolescence* (3rd ed.). Pacific Grove, CA: Brooks/Cole.

Spodek, B. (1991). Early childhood curriculum and cultural definitions of knowledge. In B. Spodek, & O. N. Saracho (Eds.), *Issues in early childhood curriculum: Yearbook in early childhood education* (Vol. 2, pp. 1-20). New York: Teachers College Press.

Steinberg, L. (2005). Cognitive and affective development in adolescence. *Trends in Cognitive Sciences, 9*, 69-74.

Steinberg, L. (2014). *Age of opportunity: Lessons from the new science of adolescence.* New York: Houghton-Mifflin.

Vacca, R., Vacca, J., & Gove, M. (1987). *Reading and learning to read.* Boston: Little, Brown, 1987.

Vatterot, C. (2009). *Rethinking homework: Best practices that support diverse needs.* Washington, DC: American Society for Curriculum Development.

Vygotsky, L. S. (1978). *Mind in society: The development of higher psychological processes.* Cambridge, MA: Harvard University Press.

Weber, L. (1969). *The kindergarten: Its encounter with educational thought.* New York: Teachers College Press.

Williams, L. R. (1994). Developmentally appropriate practice and cultural values: A case in point. In B. L. Mallory, & R. S. New (Eds.), *Diversity and developmentally appropriate practice: Challenges for early childhood education.* New York: Teachers College Press.

Wolfson, A. R., & Carskadon, M. A. (1998). Sleep schedules and daytime functioning in adolescents. *Child Development, 69,* 875–887.

Wood, G. (1992). *Schools that work: America's most innovative public education programs.* New York: Penguin Books.

Chapter

12

Creating Inclusive Classrooms

The Ability/Disability Continuum and the Health Dimension

Focus Questions

1. What determines which students are "exceptional"?
2. What is meant by the term *inclusion* of exceptional students?
3. What is the philosophical basis of inclusion? Its legal basis?
4. What is the educational basis of inclusion?

" Wow! I would love to be able to show yesterday to others and say, THIS is inclusion! . . . I really enjoyed visiting Tim's class. . . . It's good to see him in the classroom environment, so mature and confident. "

A PARENT

Case Study

Schools That Include All Students

Located in Burlington, a suburb of a large midwestern city, John Dewey Elementary School serves the children of predominantly middle- and upper-middle-class families.[1] The community is relatively conservative, but its citizens want what is best for their children and have shown they're willing to pay for it through consistent passage of operating levies. Inspired by a state initiative encouraging schools to develop alternative models to include students with disabilities in the regular school program, the John Dewey faculty, with the administration's blessing, developed a plan designed to enhance the educational opportunities of all students.

The program initially focused on including primary-age children with suspected or identified **specific learning disabilities** in regular classrooms with their same-age peers. Planning for this was accomplished through regular meetings of the participating classroom teachers and a special educator, who was present in each classroom during the 75 minutes scheduled daily for the Language Arts block, the area of greatest difficulty for most of the identified students.

In subsequent years, all John Dewey students with disabilities, including those with significant delays and multiple impairments as well as those with disabilities requiring less intensive intervention, were served in inclusion classes. These classes comprised typical pupils experiencing no particular difficulties, pupils considered at risk for learning or behavior problems, and pupils with identified disabilities ranging from mild to severe. For each student eligible for special education, the instructional goals and most related services identified in the student's **individual education program (IEP)** would be implemented within the context of regular classroom activity. Joint planning is continuous, and each Inclusion Team meets once each month to review progress and consider needs to modify strategies. All teams come together for periodic Building Inclusion Meetings, joined by the school psychologist, counselor, speech-language pathologist, art and physical education teachers, and school librarian.

All classes reflect a common philosophy and basic strategy of collaboration and individualized adaptation, but each is a unique community in many respects, including the specific needs presented by its members who have disabilities. The extent to which a special educator participates directly in instruction is determined by individual students' needs for varying degrees of support, which also determines class size, ratio of typical students to those with special needs, and whether a classroom aide is assigned. **Related services** are integrated within ongoing class routines (e.g., physical therapy in the context of physical education, occupational therapy in art and other activities), except where certain objectives (e.g., self-care for a child with **cerebral palsy**) suggest the need for brief, unobtrusive pullout for work with a therapist.

Carol is a fully accepted member of Mr. Tom Beeman's first-grade class, even though her IEP indicates a label of "multihandicapped." The supports she needs have also become an integral part of the classroom routine; that is, as Carol needs assistance, everyone knows help will be provided, whether by a classroom aide, by Mr. Beeman, or by another student.

On this day, the class is learning about units of measurement. Working in small learning groups, the children are engaged in such tasks as determining how many "hands" it takes to measure the width of a doorway or length of a table. Today's lesson also involves walking heel-to-toe across the room to determine its length and width in "feet." Mr. Beeman instructs the students in the group with Carol, who uses a wheelchair, to place a piece of tape on the wheel of her chair and determine the number of rotations required as she moves from one side of the room to the other. The children view this simply as part of their lesson on units of measurement, and Carol is happy to have yet another opportunity to participate with her peers in the ongoing classroom activities. Mr. Beeman considers such an adjustment "no big deal. Isn't that what being 'included' should be?"

Carol's parents have been gratified by her teachers' willingness to regard her as just another one of the students. Prominent in her file is the letter they wrote last year to the principal:

Watching our daughter go off to kindergarten was the beginning of a new adventure. The anticipation of riding the "big yellow school bus" and entering a world of all new learning was thrilling! As the year progressed, each day brought much joy. She loved making new friends and learning new skills. Carol's confidence and willingness to learn is only enhanced by the surrounding of real life with real children of all walks of life. It has been fulfilling to watch her grow in a classroom where the teacher reaches out to all the children's potential. All children deserve to discover their abilities and develop their talents regardless of their circumstances. It has been a positive experience for Carol to be given the opportunity to expand her mind in an exceptional classroom . . . where all children are encouraged to pursue their academic and social challenges.

Since teachers' participation has been voluntary, some negotiation has been involved. Elizabeth Sims, a first-grade teacher with 19 years of experience, recalls being "very apprehensive" when Sheila Marks, a special education colleague, approached her. "She assured me it would be fun and listed the benefits: a full-time aide's help with running off papers and monitoring recess, a hand-selected class with fewer children, specials such as art and gym at the time we would choose, and the largest classroom in the building. After listening to her litany, being one who does not say no easily, I agreed." Mrs. Sims continues,

It was a wonderful decision. . . . I am a teacher who has done a 180-degree turn! I had always felt "those children" needed to be in a class by themselves with teachers who were trained to meet their needs. I saw no benefit to including them in regular classes and felt a disservice was being done to the typical child. Now, I see the advantages far outweigh the disadvantages for everyone involved. The children are accepting of differences and very helpful to each other, whether they are typically developing or have special needs. I also feel that the children with special needs try more challenging things when seeing what their peers can do.

Margaret Burns stresses the importance of meeting the needs of the children in her kindergarten class.

My one overview special education course gave me little specific knowledge about the children our inclusion program might serve. As it has turned out, my preparation as a regular teacher, combined with the expertise of the specialist I'm privileged to work with, has combined to create an effective and positive learning environment for all of the children.

Our class is composed of 20 typical children and 4 with disabilities identified as **"low-incidence."** The teaching team this semester includes a student teacher, as well as the special education teacher, a classroom aide, and myself. Several factors are critical to the success of this type of program, most basic of which is having a team with the same philosophy and vision for all the children served. Since hands-on time is fundamental at the kindergarten level, where every child has very immediate needs, a workable teacher–pupil ratio is essential. Specific numbers would vary as do the profiles of the children from year to year. Having an experienced and knowledgeable special educator on the team is important, but our greatest strength as a team is the flexibility visible every single day in our classroom. Knowing that our bottom line is meeting the emotional and educational needs of each of our students gives us the freedom to exchange roles, modify plans, and adapt as situations warrant.

Ms. Burns emphasizes that "It is critical that the class be a truly representative sample of a normal population distribution. Placing many identified children in one room and calling it

(continued)

'inclusion' would defeat its most important purpose—to be a model for the world we live in outside the school walls." To underscore this point, she shares a letter expressing the feelings of parents about their boys' experiences:

> Our fourth grade son was in a homeroom with several multiple-handicapped children last year. This year our first grade son has been in an inclusion room. Both boys have had wonderful learning experiences as a result of being involved directly on a day-to-day basis with special children. We as adults have not been exposed to this! Imagine how great it has been for their learning environment to know that not all people are alike. Everyone has special gifts, and at such a young age my children have been able to realize this! I think it has brought out in them responsibility, increased sensitivity to others, and a sense of pride in being involved with these special children. As parents we have been very pleased with the inclusion environment for all these reasons. Our children are receiving an excellent education . . . both scholastically and socially.

As the Burlington inclusion program progressed, the model was extended to the middle and high schools. As anyone familiar with middle schools knows, defining what is "normal" can be difficult. In 15-year-old Marty's school, 800 students are grappling with the developmental tasks of adolescence. Prior to his family's move to Burlington, Marty had spent his elementary school years in a self-contained, special class with other similarly labeled children, where much professional effort had been invested in implementing **behavior management plans** to address his displays of inappropriate social behaviors and incessant drooling, and to ensure that Marty made it to the bathroom and avoided accidents. On entering middle school, with the inclusion program in place, his school experiences changed dramatically. Interestingly, within a short time the drooling lessened significantly, and his ability to monitor his own bathroom schedule improved markedly, both greatly enhancing Marty's social success.

One of the intended by-products of being included in typical classroom settings is involvement in the ongoing social milieu of the school and community, an outcome truly realized for Marty the day he was hanging out with other students after lunch. When an exchange of taunting and teasing with members of the opposite sex escalated, he and several of his "regular" classmates were taken to the assistant principal, who determined that all involved would be subject to in-school suspension. Neither Marty's parents nor his resource teacher viewed this negatively, but instead were gratified that he was an integral member of the group being disciplined.

James, whose various diagnoses over the years have included **autism spectrum disorder**, spent much of his childhood in segregated residential facilities and special schools, but his life had recently changed dramatically. Now 17, James lives in a foster home and attends Burlington High, where he is enrolled in regular classes. One of the first assignments in his Public Speaking class required reciting a poem, a challenge for James, but a resourceful teacher turned into a teaching strategy using James's tendency to repeat phrases or sentences addressed to him. James's poem was recorded by another student, who left a pause between each line and stanza. When the time came to recite, he was given the tape recorder and a headset, and as the voice on the tape recited a line into James's ears, he repeated it flawlessly. This continued until he had recited the entire poem. As he finished reciting, the classroom erupted into applause and cheers, his classmates sharing in the joy of his accomplishment.

It would be misleading to suggest there have been no problems, or that Burlington's inclusion program has been greeted with universal enthusiasm. The first 2 years, in fact, saw some heated exchanges at Board of Education meetings, and two families, concerned that classmates with special needs would detract from their own children's learning, opted for home schooling. And Marty, the middle-schooler, wasn't always just "one of the guys," certainly not at first; his acceptance by peers was hindered by the fact that he was older and bigger, as well as "different."

©wavebreakmedia/Shutterstock.com RF

Moreover, in Burlington as throughout the United States, legislation brought with it special academic proficiency concerns involving students with disabilities. Some tension is inevitable between the requirement that the educational progress of most students with disabilities must be assessed based on the same benchmarks as for their peers and the Individuals with Disabilities Education Act (IDEA) philosophy of assessments tailored to individualized goals and objectives. Since, by definition, students eligible for IEPs have disabilities that adversely affect educational performance, a concern for schools that welcome student diversity, including diversity reflected in the ability/disability and health dimensions, involves meeting aggregated student performance criteria. However, assessment requirements for these students are not affected by placement, and inclusion in regular classrooms is intended to increase their access to curricular content addressed in general performance measures.

Rationale for Inclusive Classrooms

From its inception, a fundamental characteristic of American schooling has been its intended inclusiveness, across social boundaries of gender, class, and—belatedly—race. Today, the term **inclusion** refers to the practice of including another group of students in regular classrooms: students with physical, developmental, or social-emotional disabilities, and those with chronic health problems.

Educational inclusion has both a philosophical and legal basis. Philosophically, proponents believe that groups of learners are ideally inclusive communities—cohesive groups with common goals, each of whose members is a unique individual, different from every other member, but sharing with every other member the characteristics that distinguish the age (e.g., middle school), affinity (e.g., computer club), or other basis for forming that particular community. All members have their individual contributions to make, and each derives his or her own benefits from membership. The philosophical basis of inclusive education does not rest on the manifestly wrong notion that everyone

365

is the same or learns in the same way. It rests, instead, on the principles that heterogeneity within a group is both unavoidable and desirable and that differences in ability—to read printed material or use Braille, to speak or use signs, to walk or use a wheelchair, to acquire skills rapidly or slowly, to express thoughts with pen and paper or with a keyboard—are not marks of greater or lesser worth.

Another key philosophical basis for inclusive education is the concept of **normalization,** an idea that emerged in work with persons with cognitive disabilities in the Scandinavian countries in the 1960s. It was originally defined as "making available to all mentally retarded people patterns of life and conditions of everyday living which are as close as possible to the regular circumstances and way of life of society" (Nirje, 1969, p. 231; see also, Wolfensberger, 1972). Subsequently extended to all areas of disability, normalization means that the lives of exceptional individuals of any age should be characterized as much as possible by the same kinds of experiences and daily routines and rhythms as those of persons who do not have disabilities.

For a person living in an institution, rather than with a family in the community, that implied radical changes in practice—a shift from institutional care to community-based services, such as **group homes** and **supported employment.** This principle also has had important implications for exceptional children and youth in school, not in suggesting they do not need supportive services, but concerning *how* assistance is provided. The idea is to provide whatever adaptations are needed as unobtrusively as possible, ensuring that the student can participate in all classroom experiences and, as much as possible, in the same manner as everyone else.

While philosophical principles transcend the letter of the law, civil rights legislation represents their expression in public policy. In the legal sense, an inclusive classroom is one from which no "otherwise qualified" student, who would ordinarily be a member, has been *excluded* because of a disability if the student's needs can be addressed through "reasonable accommodations." Those key phrases—"otherwise qualified" and "reasonable accommodations"—were contained in two pieces of civil rights legislation. First, Section 504 of the Rehabilitation Act of 1973 prohibited discrimination based on disability on the part of agencies receiving federal funds (including public schools). This mandate was extended to the private sector by the Americans With Disabilities Act (ADA) of 1990.[2] As a practical matter for schools, that means no *a priori* policies can be adopted consigning pupils who have, have had, or have been thought to have a certain "type" of disability to a certain "type" of program. It means pupils with impairments affecting major life functions cannot be deprived of access to learning opportunities by architectural or attitudinal barriers, and that all pedagogical decisions, including placement, must be based on individual, rather than categorical, considerations. This legal protection from discrimination also affects pupils who have disabilities but who have not been found eligible for special education (including many with special health care needs, such as asthma, sickle cell disease, and HIV/AIDS) as well as those who are eligible for special education.

The other legal cornerstone of inclusive education is the principle of **least restrictive environment (LRE),** expressed in Public Law 94-142, federal legislation that was reauthorized in 1990 as the Individuals with Disabilities Education Act (IDEA) and subsequently as IDEIA, with the addition to its title of the word *Improvement*.[3] While recognizing a continuum of potential school placements, this principle states that, to the maximum extent appropriate, students with disabilities must be educated in a regular classroom, with nondisabled peers, and be removed from such settings only if the student's needs cannot be met there, even with supportive aids and services. Moreover, each student's individual education program (IEP) must include a statement of the extent to which the student will participate in regular education and an explanation of why any needed services cannot be provided in a regular class. Although this law, like Section 504 and the ADA, was most compellingly based on the need to prohibit *exclusion,* in this instance of children from public schooling, its intent was also to promote *inclusion* of exceptional children in the learning experiences shared by other children. Congress clearly meant to ensure that each student found eligible receive specialized instruction and related services (e.g., speech, physical, or occupational therapy; adapted physical education; counseling; and **adaptive equipment** or technology) appropriate to his or her individual needs in the most normal setting considered feasible for that student.

Although the legal basis for inclusion—nondiscrimination and LRE—has not changed, changes in language used by educators, advocates, and exceptional individuals themselves reflect philosophical changes. *Mainstreaming,* a term used in the 1970s, implied movement out of a special placement, often for limited periods of time, and into regular school experiences—the "mainstream." In the 1980s, reflecting the legacy of the civil rights movement, the word on the lips of many educators and parents was *integration,* sometimes merely physical, preferably social, and ideally instructional.

Like societal *inclusion,* inclusive education implies shared participation of diverse individuals in common experiences. As one might expect, this concept is interpreted somewhat differently by different people and, therefore, is implemented with varying degrees of inclusiveness. The most straightforward interpretation of *full inclusion,* which many educators and parents endorse as the standard, is that a pupil, like those in the Burlington School District, should attend the school she would attend if she did not have a disability, with her neighbors and siblings, and be enrolled with whatever groups of learners she would be part of if she did not have a disability. A key proviso is that any needed supportive aids or services are provided, including those requiring the direct service or consultative expertise of specialists, so that special education is defined as a *service,* not a *place.*

Also like societal inclusion, educational inclusion has, since the 1990s, been a worldwide movement. While inclusion may be implemented differently in different schools and different societies, its primary intent is to reduce, if not eliminate, the distance, physical and psychosocial, between students who have disabilities and their peers who do not. While some national policy statements, like those of the United States, Ireland, and Great Britain, refer to a continuum of placement arrangements to provide individually-determined least restrictive learning environments, others, like those in the Scandinavian countries, aim to reduce if not eliminate the "regular-special" distinction altogether, while assuring that each individual student's needs are addressed. Indeed, virtually all educational inclusion policy statements stress the importance of providing whatever supports, modifications, or adaptations each individual student may need, wherever the student is placed.

What Is Exceptionality?

Ability/disability and health are distinct dimensions. They do not necessarily overlap except in certain conditions, such as **muscular dystrophy,** which entail high risks for health problems. People who are in any way "exceptional" with respect to ability/disability—such as those with cerebral palsy, a hearing loss, impaired vision, or who are intellectually gifted or cognitively impaired—are not necessarily "exceptional" with respect to health. Like everyone else, these people may experience health problems.

As stated, the inclusive classroom is one in which class members *include* some who are considered exceptional on either of these two dimensions; they have not been *excluded* because of their exceptionality.

The Ability/Disability Continuum

Defining childhood exceptionality is a circular affair: exceptional children and youth are those eligible for special educational services, which in turn are services provided for exceptional pupils. However, this definition restricts the scope of human differences, which may include the following factors:

- Sensory differences (vision and hearing)
- Other physical differences (e.g., those affecting mobility or other voluntary control of motor activity, vitality, and such basic life functions as eating)
- Communication differences (speech and language)
- Cognitive, or intellectual, and information processing differences
- Emotional and behavioral differences

Federal guidelines under IDEA delineate 13 disability categories based on these dimensions (e.g., *deaf* is distinguished from *hard of hearing*; some children are both deaf and blind or are otherwise multiply impaired; and autism spectrum disorder and **traumatic brain injury (TBI)** are now distinct categories).

Explicit definitions of each classification are important because allocation of financial resources is involved, and schools must ensure that eligible pupils receive services to which they are entitled. But since many such differences occur along a continuum (e.g., cognitive, social–emotional, communication, as discussed in Chapter 11), differentiating exceptionality from normality in the course of children's development is often a matter of judgment and somewhat arbitrary. Although some disabilities, and some special health care needs, involve qualitative differences that must be considered and addressed, most exceptional children have the same needs, interests, and concerns that their "typical" peers have, and the same right to public education.

Historical Perspectives on Special Education

Horace Mann believed the goal of education as preparation for citizenship in a democracy applied to all children.[4] Accordingly, Massachusetts's compulsory attendance law of 1851 explicitly encompassed "crippled" children, and Boston's Horace Mann School was named in recognition of Mann's efforts to provide day classes so that deaf children could live at home and interact with hearing children. His staunch ally, Samuel Gridley Howe, was 19th-century America's most influential special educator. Though he founded the world-renowned Perkins Institute, now located in Watertown, Massachusetts, and was an important figure in the spread of residential institutions, Howe later wrote that such segregated facilities could be justified only, in his words, as "a last resort. The practice of training . . . blind and [deaf] children in the common schools . . . will hardly come in my day; but I see it plainly with the eye of faith and rejoice in the prospect of its fulfillment" (as cited in Richards, 1909, p. 25).

Special education's history is studded with tales of pioneers like Howe, the first to teach a pupil (Laura Dewey Bridgman) who was both deaf and blind; like Jean-Marc

Gaspard Itard, the physician who taught Victor, the "wild boy of Aveyron"; and like Edouard Seguin, who defied received wisdom by undertaking to instruct persons who were thought unable to learn, fated to be beggars, dependents, or a threat to society.

Significantly, the historical record also reveals that many of the key breakthroughs were made by persons who themselves had disabilities. Arguing that in blindness lay a key to understanding human reason, the Enlightenment philosopher Denis Diderot advised that to understand blindness one must consult blind persons themselves. Valentin Hauy, who founded the world's first school for blind students in Paris in 1784, heeded Diderot's counsel and learned from his first pupil, Francois Lesueur, how reading could be accomplished through touch. Since then, the pantheon of "greats" has included persons with visual impairment such as J. W. Klein, Louis Braille, Helen Keller, Thomas Cutsforth, and Robert Irwin. Deaf persons have had a critical role in gaining recognition of Deaf culture and the legitimacy of signed languages. Although deaf education has had hearing pioneers, their own "teachers" were their deaf pupils, many of whom, most notably Laurent Clerc, became influential leaders in that field.

Special education emerged in the context of social reform, inspired by belief in natural rights and individual worth, and the conviction that, through education, every person can contribute to society. In important respects, it began as a rescue mission. In 1860 nearly two thirds of the countless "unfortunates" who languished in American almshouses were children with sensory or other physical or cognitive impairments. By the 1870s, state Boards of Charities, supporting the work of local benevolent societies, had undertaken a major "child-saving" effort, organized nationally as the National Conference of Charities and Corrections. In some families of more privileged circumstance, parents advocated for schooling for their children, a tradition of parent advocacy that since has been pivotal in bringing about major policy reforms.

Early programs based in centralized residential facilities represented an important step in enabling children with disabilities "to share in the blessings of education," as Howe (1848) eloquently persuaded the Massachusetts legislature in 1848. Although early reformers' most urgent concern was to provide proper care and at least rudimentary instruction, the goal then, as now, was to achieve maximum independence and integration in society (a goal sadly for a time abandoned for many persons with mental or physical abnormality, such as epilepsy, as attitudes toward deviance became less accepting). Although 19th-century facilities were often called asylums, they were originally intended as extensions of the common schools. But they were training schools, employing a highly utilitarian pedagogy to enable pupils to become, as much as possible, able to support themselves through certain prescribed trades, such as boot-making.

Specialized instruction had begun its gradual move into the Common Schools by the beginning of the 20th century. At the same time, school officials, pressed by Settlement leaders like Lillian Wald and Jane Addams, were struggling to meet the challenge of pupil diversity compounded by massive immigration from southern and eastern Europe. Special classes were a facet of a more general diversification effort: so-called "steamer classes" to expose immigrant youngsters to the English language (which led to programs for children with actual speech impairments); separate classes for "unrulies" or troublesome students; "fresh air" schools for pupils with tuberculosis or who were "physically weak" (which led to classes for children with other health impairments); and "ungraded classes" for those who "just didn't fit" (from which classes for pupils with cognitive disabilities evolved). Excepting deafness and blindness, and speech training for "young stammerers," special pedagogy was usually secondary to the perceived need to separate pupils who were different as a way of making schooling more manageable.

By the first decades of the 20th century, day classes were increasingly a component of the Common School. The first public day school program for blind children, in Chicago, involved them in many ways with seeing peers, a model emulated in other cities. In rural areas, because blindness is a low-incidence impairment, many children, even those using Braille, have long been enrolled in regular classrooms, receiving periodic assistance from itinerant specialists. Many schools made "reasonable accommodations" for pupils with other physical impairments long before that was legally mandated. But as American attitudes toward differentness grew increasingly negative, special education increasingly became a system within a system, separated physically and administratively. Segregating students who "didn't fit" in special classes, and excluding altogether those who "didn't fit" in those classes, schools seemingly tried to manage pupil diversity by making it go away.

By the 1930s, with widespread adoption of IQ testing, the basis for separation of students who had difficulty learning presumably became more scientific and less arbitrary. However, the specialized instruction provided differed from regular instruction mainly because classes were somewhat smaller and comprised pupils of various ages: urban versions (in most instances) of the one-room schoolhouse. However, an emphasis on practical life skills emerged in these programs. For children with physical impairments, chronic health problems, and (by the 1960s) serious emotional disturbance, special pedagogy was truly an afterthought, decidedly secondary to the medically oriented *treatment* focus. Until the parent-led learning disability movement gathered force in the 1960s, special education was more likely to mean special place than special pedagogy. With implementation of systematic exclusionary policies, the place was often likely to be somewhere other than public school: home, an expensive private facility if families could afford it, or an institution.

Yet even as special education expanded, most students with special needs who were not excluded from schooling altogether were "mainstreamed" because their problems had not been identified or services were not available. For those who had difficulty learning, and also those who were exceptionally capable, there was a downside. Pupils who needed more time, or less time, than their peers, or who could succeed only with some adaptation in the way material was taught or assignments could be completed, often paid a considerable price for being treated like everyone else. In 1975, a watershed year from the standpoint of social policy, the Education of All Handicapped Children Act (P.L. 94–142) required schools to identify all students whose disabilities adversely affected their educational functioning and provide them, excluding none, with a Free Appropriate Public Education (FAPE). Even earlier, some special educators (and parents) questioned whether special education must mean special placement, and many regular educators and parents were concerned about students who experienced difficulties but were not found eligible for special education.

In the 1920s, a few leaders, like Leta Hollingworth (1924), were concerned also that gifted children were not being challenged to realize their potential. During this period, some large urban school districts initiated provisions, such as Cleveland's Major Work Program, for students identified as academically gifted using the special class model. Since then, support for special programs for gifted students has waxed and waned, with advocates concerned that the brightest students are insufficiently challenged in inclusive classrooms, while many opponents argue that what is presented as appropriate for gifted students would be desirable for *all* students. Two other major concerns involve gifted students who are hard to identify, including ethnic and linguistic minority students and students with disabilities who are also gifted, and each schools', or each state's, definition of giftedness. The latter is problematic not only with respect to determining criteria for academic giftedness (usually based on measures of school learning ability, or IQ, and of academic achievement) but also because giftedness can take various forms, including leadership, artistic endeavors, motor performance, and creativity—which are not necessarily reflected in academic measures.

What constitutes an appropriate education for a student who is identified as gifted? Most programs involve enrichment, acceleration, "pull-out," specialized tracking strategies, or combinations thereof. For students with disabilities, IDEA defines *appropriate* on the basis of the IEP developed for each student, stipulating that the student's educational placement must be in the least restrictive environment. In some states, such as Pennsylvania, identification and education requirements for children and youth who are gifted are the same as those with disabilities, although federal legislation addresses only the latter.

Subsequent amendments to the original federal legislation (P.L. 94-142) extended the law's provisions to children as young as age 3 who demonstrate significant delays in one or more areas of development; added a family-focused early intervention component for infants and toddlers; stipulated a required **transition plan** (by age 14) in anticipation of a student's leaving school and entering the adult world of work and community living; clarified definitions; and distinguished autism and traumatic brain injury as distinct areas of disability. No doubt the legislation will continue to be amended as it is revisited by the Congress for periodic reauthorization. Many advocates for gifted and talented students hope that eventually an *individually appropriate education* will be mandated on a national basis for these students as well.

New Perspectives: Being "Neuro-Atypical" and the Mental Health Continuum

Reports that autism, long believed to be among the rare, "low-incidence" forms of developmental disability, may occur today in as many as 2% of American children causes us to revise our thinking about human differences. Ongoing research seeking to understand this alarming change focuses on the interaction of genetic and environmental factors that may cause autism; however, while promising findings are reported, adding to our understanding of human brain structure and function, the increase remains a puzzle.

While nearly all professionals acknowledge that the increase is real, there are other contributory factors. The fact that we now speak of *autism spectrum disorder* (ASD) suggests a broad range, from individuals who present somewhat unusual linguistic, sensory, or social characteristics to a much smaller number with severe impairment in these areas. No doubt many individuals considered today "on the spectrum" would, in the past, not have been considered to have a disability. Similarly, the level of awareness of autism among both professionals and the general public is much higher than in the past, increasing the likelihood of early identification and early intervention.

The autism spectrum encompasses conditions characterized by regression following typical early development, such as **Rett's disorder,** as well as **Asperger's syndrome,** which is often characterized by strong intellectual interests and aptitude accompanying challenges in the areas of self-regulation and social interaction. It has been the community of persons experiencing Asperger's syndrome and their family members who have promulgated the descriptor "neuro-atypical," to help "neurotypical" people understand differences in the ways sensory and social phenomena can be experienced.

Sometimes likened to a tapestry, ASD can encompass a wide range of presenting behaviors as development proceeds during childhood and adolescence. Accordingly, children with autism sometimes present with behaviors associated with other clinical conditions, such as **attention deficit hyperactivity disorder (ADHD).** Another, which only in recent years has been thought to be present in childhood, **bipolar disorder,** is characterized by varying degrees of atypical mood, ranging from debilitating depression to difficult-to-regulate exhilaration or excitability. The most effective treatments for children, as well as adolescents and adults, with ADHD or bipolar disorder are generally believed to involve medication in combination with counseling. Again, recognizing the reality of atypical rather than typical neurological functioning is helpful in understanding these as other areas of human difference.

As we know, anyone can experience illness; although illness may occur as a result of factors beyond one's own control, avoiding harmful substances and sources of infection and maintaining personal hygiene, proper sleep and diet, and physical exercise, are important factors in achieving and maintaining physical health. We now speak of "wellness" with respect to such behavioral patterns. The term mental health, like physical health, also implies the absence of illness, but both concepts also suggest a positive state of thriving and relative well-being. While both reflect a range, rather than an absolute state, qualities or characteristics that have been associated with positive mental health include such attributes associated with psychological well-being as reasonable self-confidence and optimism about the future; ability to maintain satisfying interpersonal relationships; and ability to employ productively one's cognitive and creative abilities. As with physical well-being, mental hygiene encompasses practices and conditions conducive to achieving and maintaining such qualities.

As with physical health and illness, virtually anyone may potentially be subject to challenges with respect to mental health, whether associated with life events (e.g., loss of a friend or loved one, family crisis, work- or school-related change, or other critical event), genetic or other constitutional factors, or these in combination. One's success in coping with such challenges, even with therapeutic support, is in no small measure a reflection of one's mental health.

In children, as noted in the previous section, mood disorders, such as bipolar disorder, and many attentional and/self-regulatory issues, such as ADHD, are now generally considered to be biologically based, as are most personality disorders, such as schizophrenia. But debilitating depression, general anxiety, or specific fears or worries can be associated with a combination of causal factors, environmental as well as biological. Many children and youth who engage in self-injurious behavior, such as cutting or, most tragically, suicide, have manifested pervasive sadness, loneliness, or feelings of low self-worth. Children and adolescents may also experience seriously affected life functions, as in sleep disorders and eating disorders. A great many children and adolescents present serious acting-out behaviors which, if recurrent, are collectively termed **conduct disorders**. These include conditions associated with physical aggression directed at others or fantasies or acts of destruction of property, as well as less serious norm-violating behavior, such as truancy or petty theft.

Teachers, school administrators, and parents have understandably expressed grave concerns about inclusion in regular classrooms of students believed likely to present serious classroom management issues. Consequently, specific policies have been formulated and intervention practices recommended to protect the rights, and safety, of all students, as well as those of the student with challenging behavior.

The Health Dimension

Although certain forms of disability may involve greater vulnerability to health problems (e.g., many people with **Down syndrome** tend to experience cardiac difficulties and middle ear and upper respiratory infections), health is a dimension encompassing everyone. Some disabilities, such as **spina bifida,** may involve health services such as **clean intermittent catheterization (CIC).** A child with cerebral palsy may have significant motor, sensory, communication, and possibly cognitive impairment, yet experience no health problems, whereas a child with no such neuromotor involvement may experience, for example, chronic asthma. Most of us enjoy reasonably robust good health most of the time, but all of us will probably, at some times in our lives, experience debilitating illness. Were it not for anticonvulsants or other forms of medication, special diets, or other adaptations, some of us would experience continuous, significant disruption in our daily lives or impairment of critical life functions of self-care, working, and going to school. And for some of us, supplemental oxygen, kidney dialysis, or adaptations make it possible to take in nourishment or eliminate waste, which are essential life functions. Children with leukemia or other forms of cancer may experience times of great fatigue; those with **sickle cell disease** may experience times of excruciating pain.

Although they represent a very small proportion of students eligible for special services, children with significant health care needs are often a matter of concern in discussions of inclusion. In fact, a great many American children, estimated at more than 1 in 10, experience some form of chronic illness, although the number with relatively severe conditions is much less. However, several factors have led to increased prevalence in recent years: interventions that sustain life in utero and facilitate the survival of newborns at very low birth weight and with related biological risk factors, such as respiratory distress; medical advances in bringing certain childhood diseases that were once fatal into remission during the vulnerable first year of life; marked increases in drug-affected pregnancies; and HIV transmission to newborns. Given these factors, the National Center for Health Statistics (2000) estimated that at least 2% of all surviving American newborns were likely to have conditions implying special health care needs, with the risk factors twice as great for babies born to African American mothers than for babies born to European American mothers.

Some conditions involve *established risk* (that is, the condition is known to involve lasting impairment), but much more often the future of a newborn at *biological risk* (e.g., very young gestational age at birth, very low birth weight)

©Wavebreakmedia/Getty Images RF

cannot be reliably predicted, for much depends on the quality of nurture the child will have. Although many of the great numbers of children born each year who were prenatally exposed to alcohol, lead, crack or powder cocaine, or other toxic agents continue to have special needs, biology is not destiny. These and other biological factors interact in subtle ways with environmental ones, most crucially the quality of nurture and of health care.

After a brief period of time in the neonatal intensive care unit, a still tiny infant is likely to come home, dependent on life-support equipment parents will need to manage as they attempt to normalize the baby's life and their own. Many young children soon cease to be technology dependent, but some will continue to need a respirator, perhaps, or require nasogastric or gastrostomy tube feeding. Although the term *medically fragile* is really inappropriate considering the struggle a newborn may need to put forth just to survive, some children who may require no special adaptations to support life functions may be particularly susceptible to infection, experience debilitating allergies, or have other special health care needs throughout their school careers, and perhaps throughout their lives.

Historically, the belief that children with special health care needs needed special school arrangements originated with efforts to contain the spread of tuberculosis. Fresh air classes were first established in the United States in Providence, Rhode Island, in 1908. In Europe open air schools were often located, like adult sanitoriums, in the mountains or forests. However, American fresh air schools were usually in large cities where the disease was epidemic, with classes sometimes conducted on tenement roofs. (Tragically, little effective intervention was done in the reservations and boarding schools established for Native Americans, where tuberculosis decimated tribal populations.) In eastern states, siblings of infected children were often removed to "preventoriums." Where children were thus gathered, school districts collaborated with charity groups and health agencies to provide arrangements for instruction, mild exercise, and rest. Although worldwide public health measures eventually halted the spread of tuberculosis, reducing the need for segregated programs, the special class or special school model established in response to tuberculosis was adopted for children with other health care needs, such as heart defects.

Also, for children experiencing lengthy hospital stays for any reason, the convention of establishing a hospital school, introduced in Europe, was adopted in the growing number of pediatric hospitals and pediatric units in general hospitals. Increasingly, public education agencies assumed operation of such schools, especially in large metropolitan communities. For many children believed unable to manage the physical demands of school attendance, whether hospitalized or at home, state departments of education or local school districts established tutoring for "homebound and hospitalized children."

Health needs of children and youth have changed with the presumed conquest (in industrialized nations) of tuberculosis, poliomyelitis, and a number of diseases, such as smallpox, scarlet fever, and diptheria, to which children had been particularly vulnerable. Philosophies of medical care have changed also. Extended periods of hospitalization are now rare for children (as for adults), and while that has been influenced by crass realities of cost and insurance coverage limits, it also reflects awareness of the importance for children to experience conditions of growing up that are as normal as possible. Most children who in times past would have been excluded, either by formal policy or assumed dependency, weakness, or vulnerability, now go to school with their siblings, neighbors, and friends.

What are the implications for inclusive education? We should remember three basic, and obvious, principles: (1) we can all expect to experience serious health problems at some time in our lives, for they are part of the universal human condition; (2) serious health impairment in childhood is certainly not a new phenomenon, historically speaking, evidenced in epidemics and pandemics of the past to which children were especially vulnerable; and (3) a health problem is, for a child or an adult, certainly not a person's only, or primary, identifying characteristic or need.

Our own vulnerability helps explain an element of fear, particularly of contagion, that for centuries focused on leprosy, a century ago on tuberculosis, then on poliomyelitis, and today on AIDS even though other conditions (e.g., hepatitis B) are more readily transmitted than is the HIV virus. Today, all school personnel are advised to employ **universal health precautions** to lessen the risk to themselves or to pupils of any form of infection, especially if there is possible exposure to blood or any body fluids. The need for such precautions is not affected by whether or not a school adopts an inclusive education philosophy. While contagious disease is understandably feared, it is conquered not by avoidance, ignorance, or blaming the victim. This point is certainly the message of AIDS awareness.

Another source of fear has to do with a different type of vulnerability, implied by terms such as *medically fragile.* Teachers neither want a child to be endangered nor want themselves to be vulnerable to guilt feelings or even to a lawsuit should a pupil in their charge incur injury or even die. As with many human fears, these are best allayed by information, availability of appropriate resources and supports, and most important, personal experience. Teachers can feel vulnerable whether they are dealing with a child who has a condition that is actually life threatening or has no chronic special health care needs per se but significant physical impairment. A fourth-grade teacher participating in an inclusion project in Virginia spoke of "fear of the unknown. . . . You're afraid they might hurt you or you might hurt them" (Janney, Snell, Beers, & Raynes, 1995, p. 436). Rachel Janney and her co-authors, reporting on the success of that project, summarized:

> Teachers who initially had been hesitant to get involved . . . judged that their original fears and expectations were based on inaccurate perceptions about the integrated student's needs and abilities. By getting to know the students with disabilities on an individual basis, they had gained knowledge of the student's unique abilities and a new perspective on disabilities in general. "I guess we just really had never thought about them being 'normal.' They really are," explained the junior high math teacher in District C. These general education teachers' attitudes toward integration also had been changed by finding that it was personally and professionally rewarding to work with the integrated students, a sentiment expressed in these words by the high school physical education teacher in District A: "These kids seem to appreciate you a lot more . . . and that's a little pat on the back for the teacher" (p. 438).

Characteristics of an Inclusive Classroom

The discussion in the preceding section, although it gives a sense of what inclusion in this specific sense means, is likely to raise questions in a teacher's, or prospective teacher's, mind about how, or even whether, inclusion actually works. Inclusive schools and classrooms do not just happen, nor do they require each individual teacher to be "all things to all students." Some of the major ideas reflected in this chapter's Case Study are based on legal requirements, but most derive from or are congruent with emerging principles and practices in general pedagogy and in the way many schools now operate.

Inclusion and Human Diversity

One fundamental idea is an old one, and it is that a major purpose of schooling is to prepare the young for citizenship in a democracy that is increasingly heterogeneous. Another idea is relatively new: that the young must be prepared for successful participation in a global economy. The fact that the world children will enter is not one in which everyone is like themselves has important implications for the necessary learning experiences of any child, with or without a disability or health impairment. The former will not live in a society comprised only of other people with cerebral palsy, mental retardation, autism, dyslexia, diabetes, and so forth; the latter will not live in a society comprised only of people who do not have these conditions or characteristics. Related to that societal reality is another that can be seen in any school and in any classroom: even if it were desirable to eliminate heterogeneity in a group of learners by putting anyone who is "different" in another group, it is impossible, for every group is necessarily heterogeneous; *all* children are "different."

Another major idea emerging in general pedagogy, *collaboration*, involves new kinds of teacher–specialist relationships and team models, more mutually supportive school-family relationships, and new awareness of the important role of interactions among learners. Each of these sets of relationships is multifaceted. For example, Marlene Pugach and Lawrence Johnson (1995) described four different roles—*supportive, facilitative, informative,* and *prescriptive*—underlying relationships of adults within schools. The IDEA legislation implies such relationships with respect to the education of students with disabilities, but the concept of collaboration goes beyond the legal requirements:

1. The law requires multidiscipline participation in assessing a student's current functioning and planning and monitoring the student's IEP, but collaboration suggests continuing *interdisciplinary* teamwork on the part of regular and special educators and other specialists in implementing the student's program.

©wavebreakmedia/Shutterstock.com RF

2. The law requires parents' **informed consent** prior to multifactored evaluation, participation in developing the IEP, and right to procedural due process in the event of disagreement; collaboration suggests going beyond these bare legal requirements to ensure that a student's IEP reflects the family's concerns and priorities, that a student's home and school expectations and experiences are mutually supportive, and that professionals respect the primacy and continuing influence of families on children's development.

3. The law requires that students with disabilities be educated as much as is appropriate with peers who do not have disabilities; collaboration implies optimizing the potential benefits for both by fostering positive classroom interactions and creating opportunities for students to respect and learn from each other and to develop feelings of group identification.

Policy requirements have a critical role in determining how students with disabilities are educated, but as in all aspects of schooling, other factors such as research findings influence pedagogical practices. The next sections summarize some contrasts between old and new characteristics. Keep in mind that, in one sense, everything before the IDEA legislation was enacted is "old," and what is "new" continues to emerge.

Pedagogies: Old and New

Although traditional methods of teaching are incorporated in pedagogies for inclusion, a major influence on inclusive pedagogy is *constructivism,* a way of understanding students' learning as a process of cognitive development influenced, but not controlled, by adult instruction. Constructivist perspectives are fundamental to current conceptions of developmentally appropriate practices for young children,[5] but they are also reflected in current discussions of elementary, middle school, and even high school curriculum and instruction, especially in the areas of literacy, mathematics, social studies, and science. Is all genuine and meaningful learning—though externally influenced by family and peers, as well as teachers and textbooks—internally motivated and internally organized? And if so, is it true of all learners? Beliefs about *how* children learn are key determinants of *what* is taught.

This issue is critical with respect to the pedagogy of inclusion because special education, strongly influenced both by a *medical model* of treatment and a *behavioral model* of learning, has traditionally placed great emphasis on skill acquisition through training strategies employed by teachers and therapists. The assumption has been that most children "naturally" learn important skills, such as language skills, and generalize what they have learned to new situations, but that children with developmental delays or disabilities for which they must learn to compensate require more direct adult intervention. This is far from a simple issue considering the wide variation among children with disabilities, and such distinctions have certainly been unduly emphasized; generally speaking, children with disabilities, and certainly children with health impairments, are more *like* other children in the way they learn, and in what they need to learn, than they are *different* from their peers.

Moreover, some constructivist practices were actually introduced or readily adopted by special education pioneers like S. G. Howe, Seguin, and early educators of deaf children. Edouard Seguin, Maria Montessori, and Ovide DeCroly were convinced that the experiential methods they developed in working with children with cognitive disabilities based on faith in every child's ability and motivation to learn, should be extended to instruction of all children. Some learners do require more adult direction and adult-imposed structure than others, but the same can be said of many students who do not have disabilities. Arguably, the diverse needs present in any learning group can more effectively be accommodated with constructivist approaches than those that assume all pupils learn the same things at the same pace. Individualized pedagogy represents an important legacy of special education that is applicable for all students.

Roles: Old and New

The most dramatic difference between old and new affecting the education of children with disabilities is that today most live at home with their families and attend public schools, which was not the case in the era of centralized, residential institutions. That fact implies fundamental changes in the roles of both families and educators, and critically important changes in their relationships. Moreover, the increasing number of students with disabilities who participate to some degree or totally in regular education suggests fundamental changes in the roles of both special and regular educators, and critically important changes in their relationships. To appreciate the significance of these changes, consider other contrasts between old and new roles of regular and special educators.

The special educator of the past was indeed a specialist, not only as a special educator but as a teacher of a specific category of students. As children were segregated, so too were their teachers. Early special educators were trained in residential schools, following a medically oriented, preceptor model, which was quite unlike the preparation their counterparts were provided in normal schools. Even as preparation for both types of educators moved to degree-granting colleges and universities, special and general educators were most often prepared separately and taught different content by different instructors. Those barriers, like those separating regular and special education in schools, have been gradually receding.

Except in schools for deaf students, which had a strong pedagogic tradition, the special educator was a clinician, albeit a junior one, increasingly likely to be a woman, as Edouard Seguin (1880) insisted, "supervised by a competent [male] physician." In school and in clinical settings, special education teachers were (and are today) members of teams, collaborating with (or carrying out the recommendations of) psychologists; sometimes physicians or social workers; and physical, occupational, and speech-language therapists. In medical settings—hospitals, rehabilitation centers, and residential treatment facilities—the team was often led by a physician, and in schools by a school psychologist or special education supervisor. Because team members were expected to work together, each applying her or his own expertise, the model was termed *multidisciplinary.* To the extent diverse perspectives on the child as patient, or client, were integrated within a unified plan (difficult because members had been trained in their respective disciplines in relative isolation from each other), teams increasingly evolved an *interdisciplinary* approach. In clinical settings a social worker often provided the only link teachers had with parents, but in schools home–school cooperation and consistency were often seen as critical. A more integrated, *transdisciplinary team* model has emerged, characterized by *role exchange* and *role release,* in which professionals share and synthesize perspectives on an ongoing basis (Rainforth, York, & Macdonald, 1997).

Like their fellow team members, then, and quite unlike regular education teachers, special educators were imbued with a clinical orientation influenced more by a medical than an educational model. Just as their preparation was relatively distinct from that of elementary and secondary school teachers, their work environment was often in relative isolation from other teachers. Older special educators recall that their classrooms were located next to the boiler room. Their pupils were usually transported on separate buses, used the playground at separate times, and often ate lunch in their classrooms, with their teachers, rather than the cafeteria. Like their students, many special educators perceived themselves as outsiders, and in fact were more likely to be accountable to a central office supervisor, or "inspector," than to the building principal.

Regular educators, for their part, were often the first line of identification of children experiencing difficulty in school, as well as those who might be gifted. Their principal role vis-à-vis exceptional students was to identify suspected problems and, as IDEA stipulates, to attempt to address such problems within the regular classroom. Only if their attempts are unsuccessful should a referral be made for **multifactored evaluation**, with parents' informed consent, to determine whether a student is eligible for special education. However, the federally mandated **placement continuum** of possible school arrangements implies that nearly all exceptional pupils would have varying degrees of involvement in regular education, either pulled out for special help or provided supportive aids and services within the regular education program.

Place of Content Knowledge: Old and New

As suggested in the previous section, *what* was to be learned has long been a key issue in special education, and it is a key issue in discussions of inclusion. Generally, content issues have involved the same fundamental question, posed by Herbert Spencer (1963) /(1859, original edition), that has been raised for all learners: What knowledge is of most worth? In the case of blindness, deafness, and other physical impairment, the answer to that question was knowledge that could enable one to be maximally independent and self-supporting as an adult. In the past, such knowledge generally implied training in a trade. Although their societal role later shifted from instruction to containment, facilities for persons with cognitive disabilities and epilepsy also originally were intended to be training schools, a designation that was maintained even though residents were "trained" based on the expectation of lifelong institutionalization. As the European day class model was introduced in the United States, at first in the form of ungraded classes for relatively undifferentiated low achievers, the goal of economic self-sufficiency shifted to imply that pupils with cognitive disabilities needed to develop habits that would make them reliable workers as well as good citizens. Consequently, the distinctive curricular tradition that emerged in special classes focused on relatively generic and social *employability skills*. With extension of schooling under the **zero exclusion mandate** of P.L. 94-142, a "criterion of ultimate functioning" was advanced as the basis for curriculum for students with severe disabilities, including severe cognitive disability. This criterion means that what is taught must be age-appropriate, future-oriented, functional, and community-referenced (Snell, 1993).

The advent of the concept of specific learning disabilities (SLD), which today comprises more than half the special education enrollment, brought a greater focus on differential instructional strategy than on curricular content. Based on an educational diagnostic profile showing specific areas of strength and of difficulty, or intra-individual differences—differences *within* an individual student—a plan of remediation or compensatory instruction could be devised for each pupil, usually within the context of the standard curriculum. This distinctive feature, individually tailored instruction, was subsequently mandated for all eligible students with disabilities, through the Individualized Educational Plan (IEP), which specifies individual annual goals and short-term objectives for each area in which a student is to receive special education. Although not required by federal law, as noted previously, in some states an IEP and other provisions also are required for students identified as gifted.

Assessment: Old and New

With respect to children with disabilities, assessment has both a general and a specific meaning. Emerging trends in educational assessment (general) are relevant for all learners, but two assessment concerns (specific) have unique importance: the determination, as a result of assessment, of eligibility for special education services, and the determination of how accountability for those services is demonstrated. The former concern also pertains to possibly gifted and talented students, but for those with "suspected handicaps" The Individuals with Disabilities Education Act (IDEA) requires that, to be eligible for special education services, a pupil must have a disability (as defined in the law) that adversely affects educational functioning. Such determination cannot be based on only one measure, or one criterion, but is based instead on a multifactored evaluation, conducted with informed parental consent by appropriately qualified, multidisciplinary professionals, using appropriate and nondiscriminatory procedures.

IDEA broadly defines criteria for each disability "category," but individual state standards may specify what types of assessment must be carried out, such as medical or psychological evaluations. In the case of gifted and talented programs, mandated in some states but not in others, state or local district policies stipulate criteria and identification processes. In both cases, norm-referenced, standardized tests (e.g., IQ tests) play an important role but must be used in combination with other appropriate procedures (e.g., criterion-referenced tests of academic skills, teacher reports, and ratings).

With respect to outcome as well as process, the IEP is an accountability document. It states what services the pupil will be provided, and for each goal that is listed it delineates the evaluation procedure that will be used and who is responsible. These two key functions reflect the legacy of a medical and of a behavioral model, the former in such concepts as *screening* (to identify indications of need for thorough diagnostic evaluation) and *diagnosis*, the latter in stipulating that objectives must be stated in the form of observable, measurable behavior. Although medically oriented diagnostic evaluation may be essential in determining eligibility, it has limited value as a guide to the individualized instruction that is the hallmark of special education.

Although the term *diagnostic/prescriptive teaching,* a legacy of the medical model tradition, has been closely associated with special education, more instructionally relevant types of assessment have been developed. Moreover, whether special learning difficulties are believed to reflect underlying *process* differences (e.g., in information processing or visual-motor coordination) or are viewed as specific *skill* deficiencies to be identified and remediated, the most useful types of assessment are criterion-referenced rather than norm-referenced. The purpose of such assessment is to ascertain a pupil's current status and progress on the basis of age or stage expectations (developmental assessment), the school's or state's curricular expectations (curriculum-based assessment), systemic observation of functioning in the classroom (behavioral assessment), skill acquisition (task-analytic assessment), or in accomplishing skills required to function in present and/or future environments (ecological assessment).

Increasingly, educators have been implementing an alternative method to determine a student's need for special education services, called *response to intervention* (RTI). This approach is intended to address key concerns associated with past practice, specifically with reference to the identification of specific learning disabilities by means of an *ability/achievement discrepancy model*: (1) that model's inability to identify children's learning problems early in their school careers; (2) an overreliance on standardized tests, which may be subject to cultural bias or other limitations; (3) inconsistency in determining eligibility criteria; and (4) overidentification and labeling of students as SLD who could respond to regular instruction more attentively tailored to their individual learning characteristics. While RTI may be variously implemented and its effectiveness is still being researched, the approach has certain common elements, all of which are associated with "new" assessment practices:

- It involves "tiers" of assessment rather than a single decision point and continuous monitoring of the individual student's progress.
- It involves curriculum-based, criterion-referenced assessment.
- It is collaborative, usually assigning a major role to regular education personnel in the initial stage, with increasing specialist participation in successive tiers.
- It ensures continuing instruction for students as they are being assessed.
- It requires implementation of evidence-based instructional practices at each successive tier.

With young children diagnostic profiles are often based on *developmental domains,* as described in Chapter 11. For older students and those with severe or multiple impairments, diagnostic profiles often are based on *functional domains*; that is, important life functioning areas, such as work and leisure skills. For children with visual impairments, assessing how the child uses his or her vision, orients in space, and progresses in achieving independent mobility are critical concerns. For those with hearing impairments, use of residual hearing or of compensatory (hearing aid augmentation, lipreading) or alternative (sign language) communication modes are critical. In both instances, progress in communication and literacy, as well as in general curricular areas, are continuously assessed. For children with impaired mobility or communication, specific assessment concerns involve possible needs for adaptive equipment or procedures.

Each student is unique, and some indeed have differences that require certain adaptations or support services in order to receive an appropriate education as required under federal law. Can these be provided within normalized classroom settings in which they learn side by side with typical peers? That is the challenge of inclusive education.

Making Inclusive Teaching Work

The Importance of Collaboration

Students with and without disabilities are intended to benefit from participation in inclusive classrooms. Perhaps the greatest benefits are the positive self-esteem of all the students and the fact that more students have their needs met than in a conventional classroom. The special education student doesn't experience the stigma and confusion associated with the daily journey to a "special" room for "special" instruction. The day is less fragmented, and the student doesn't feel different or left out. Also, special education teachers have hands-on experience with their interventions—applying them to real, daily learning situations—and can make more precise changes in those interventions as they are needed. With a co-teaching situation, there is always a teacher available to help a student. Also, co-teaching provides two perspectives on any situation and increases creativity in teaching.

Mutual understanding and respect are essential elements in any true collaboration. The teachers at John Dewey Elementary agreed that the special educator and the regular educator should acknowledge that both have specialized knowledge and skills but that their perspectives and knowledge bases may differ. For example, special educators should recognize that the regular educators' instructional and behavior management techniques often can be effective in working with students with special needs. They must also understand that teachers in regular classrooms must respond to the needs of many students and cannot devote disproportionate time and attention to any one student. They must also recognize that some techniques that may be successful in a separate special education class may not be appropriate for the regular classroom environment.

At the same time, the regular educator should recognize that his or her special education colleagues may be responsible for supporting many students in a variety of settings and therefore have a limited amount of time to devote to each student. She or he must also realize that a new intervention strategy is unlikely to have an immediate effect and that a fair trial is needed before judging it ineffective. Acknowledging that students differ in the extent of instructional adaptations they need, regular classroom teachers should understand that many of the adaptations that the specialist recommends will be extensions of regular education techniques. They should also maintain familiarity with each exceptional student's IEP, sharing responsibilities for determining how goals and objectives can be reinforced during the course of classroom activities.

Accordingly, the teachers at John Dewey Elementary developed the following set of principles to guide their collaborative team functioning:

- Establish a system for ongoing communication.
- Discuss each placement together.
- Assist each other in individualizing instruction.
- Work together to adapt subject matter.
- Share materials.
- Assist each other in adapting evaluative procedures.
- Exhibit characteristics of flexibility, dedication, reliability, organization, imagination, energy, initiative, and enthusiasm.
- Involve others by sharing plans and ideas.
- Seek support and suggestions from others.
- Set realistic goals.
- Work to improve interpersonal relations.
- Be happy and proud about working with students with special needs.
- Remember that presenting a positive attitude will change attitudes about inclusion both inside and outside the school.

What Does Flexibility Involve

Burlington teachers often use the word *flexibility* in describing their inclusion programs. While flexibility is important in any teaching situation, as they note, it is critical to the success of inclusion of students whose learning characteristics and needs may require adaptations, both planned and spontaneous, in the instructional program. They concluded that classroom adaptations to accommodate differential needs among *all* students can be delineated in terms of four basic parameters: curriculum materials, instructional strategies, classroom organization, and behavior management.

Curriculum Materials

Within the context of the regular curriculum, learning experiences can be adapted in a wide variety of ways, as suggested by these examples:

- When working with fractions, provide recipes that include measurements and have student identify all the fractions on the recipe.

- When teaching about time, help student develop a personal schedule showing daily activities matched to a clock face showing the time of the activity.

- When working with adding two columns of numbers and regrouping, help student practice balancing a checkbook or compile a shopping list with prices, using a calculator to add.

- When administering a spelling test, have student practice identifying functional words.

- When identifying U.S. presidents, have student practice keyboarding skills by locating letters of presidents' names.

Instructional Strategies

Examples of instructional adaptations include the following:

- The way instruction is delivered (e.g., visual or auditory aids, learning centers, cooperatively structured activities, cooperative learning, small group instruction).

- The way the learner can demonstrate knowledge (e.g., oral vs. written response, pictures that can be pointed to, using a computer, augmentative communication devices such as picture boards, tape recorder, language master, calculators).

- Modifying the number of items the learner is expected to complete (e.g., spelling words, math problems).

Classroom Organization

Adaptations can be made in aspects such as the following:

- The skill level, problem type, or rules on how the learner may approach the work (e.g., using calculators or computer, simplifying task directions, changing rules to allow for participation, breaking a task down to sequential steps, providing more planned opportunities to achieve success).

- The amount of individual instruction with a specific learner (e.g., peer partner, use of teaching assistant).

- The time allotted (e.g., extra time to practice new skills, individualized timelines for work completion, flexible class schedules) and/or the location (e.g., specific classroom area, home, school library, or media center) for completing a task.

Behavior Management

Examples of adaptations that can be used to anticipate and prevent inappropriate or disruptive behavior include the following:

- Have student assist with visual aid equipment while some other students are being instructed.
- Have student take on a teacher role by sharing a favorite activity or interest.
- Individualize goals or outcome expectations while using the same materials (e.g., a language arts activity of diagramming a sentence can be, for some students, a verbal language activity of hearing and speaking in full sentences).

As a way of conceptualizing variations in individual students' needs for instructional adaptation or curricular modifications, the Burlington teachers devised a continuum of levels, each defined by a question for the team to resolve through discussion.

Level I. What can the student learn in the regular program of instruction with the same performance standards as nondisabled peers?

Level II. What can the student learn with nondisabled peers, but with adjustments in performance standards according to the student's needs as identified through curriculum-based assessment?

Level III. What can the student learn with adjustments in pacing, method of instruction, or special materials or techniques provided with consultant support to the teacher?

Level IV. What can the student learn with adjustments in pacing, method of instruction, or special materials or techniques provided jointly with regular and support or ancillary staff?

Level V. What can the student learn with adjustments in the content of the classroom curriculum to be taught jointly by regular and special support or ancillary staff?

Level VI. What classroom curriculum content must be modified significantly and taught by special staff?

Level VII. In what situation is some or all of the content of the classroom curriculum inappropriate for this student? What alternative curriculum program will be used to address this student's educational needs?

Ethical Issues in Inclusive Education

Federal legislation does not mandate inclusion, as defined earlier in the chapter, although it does forbid exclusion. The legal basis for inclusion continues to be the least restrictive environment (LRE), the requirement that education occur "as much as appropriate" in a regular classroom setting, with supportive aids and services, as may be needed. Some professionals, organizations, and also parents have reservations about any concept that could be interpreted to suggest "one size fits all," especially if legislators and school officials construe inclusion to mean less costly services. (Although individual needs differ widely, the cost per year of educating a student with disabilities is, on average, about twice the cost of educating other pupils, only a part of which is provided through IDEA.)

The American Federation of Teachers, in fact, had called for a moratorium on inclusion until all schools were provided with the kinds of supports (resource specialists and classroom aides) and other provisions (such as manageable class size) that they needed. But advocates compare such proposals to similar situations in the civil rights movement, in which a moratorium on school de-segregation was suggested until all European Americans fully "accepted" their African American fellow citizens. The question in both situations is, Should the crucial years of childhood be allowed to pass irretrievably while children's elders await optimal conditions?

Can every individual child with special needs receive an individually appropriate education without having to be segregated in a special place? Can these students still get the services they need? And what about the typical students? As such questions are debated in local schools like those in the Burlington Case Study, many teachers in collaboration with parents are making inclusive education a reality. From such examples, the Advocacy Board for the Center on Human Policy (1994) at Syracuse University developed the following statement:

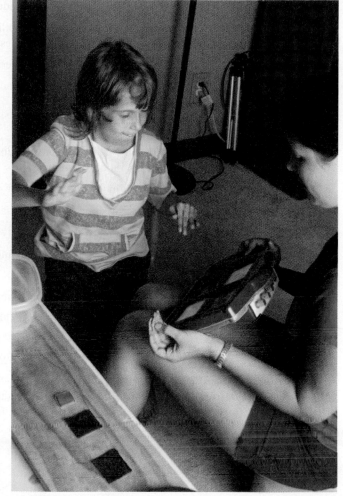

©Kim Gunkel/Getty Images RF

Inclusion Means

1. Educating all children with disabilities in regular classrooms regardless of the nature of their disabling condition(s).

2. Providing all students enhanced opportunities to learn from each other's contributions.

3. Providing necessary services within the regular schools.

4. Supporting regular teachers and administrators (e.g., by providing time, training, teamwork, resources, and strategies).

5. Having students with disabilities follow the same schedules as nondisabled students.

6. Involving students with disabilities in age-appropriate academic classes and extracurricular activities, including art, music, gym, field trips, assemblies, and graduation exercises.

7. Students with disabilities using school cafeteria, library, playground, and other facilities along with nondisabled students.

8. Encouraging friendships between nondisabled and disabled students.

9. Students with disabilities receiving their education and job training in regular community environments when appropriate.

10. Teaching all children to understand and accept human differences.

11. Placing children with disabilities in the same schools they would attend if they did not have disabilities.

12. Taking parents' concerns seriously.

13. Providing an appropriate individualized educational program.

Inclusion Does Not Mean

1. "Dumping" students with disabilities into regular programs without preparation or support.

2. Providing special education services in separate or isolated places.

3. Ignoring children's individual needs.

4. Jeopardizing students' safety or well-being.

5. Placing unreasonable demands on teachers and administrators.

6. Ignoring parents' concerns.

7. Isolating students with disabilities in regular schools.

8. Placing students with disabilities in schools or classes that are not age-appropriate.

9. Requiring that students be "ready" and "earn" their way into regular classrooms based on cognitive or social skills.

Perhaps the most important ethical issues involved in inclusion, however, are the degree to which it benefits an individual student and the degree to which educators are committed to seeing that positive effect occur. Consider the case of Stevie, a student in Burlington Elementary School, and his school experience as described by his parents:

> Stevie ends each day by asking if it's a school day tomorrow. When it is, he picks out his clothes promptly for the next day so that he won't be late. . . . We believe that his eagerness reflects his joy in being included in a kindergarten classroom just like every other child in his neighborhood. In so many ways, Stevie is just like all of the other children. But he does face extra challenges due to his Down syndrome. We recognize that Stevie's learning style and ability does differ when compared to his typically developing peers. What we have found critical, though, is not the differences in style and ability, but the desire to do what his peers are doing. We believe that this desire is shared by all children. And for Stevie, this desire becomes his greatest source of motivation and thereby his success.
>
> In an inclusive classroom, Stevie's classmates become his positive role models. In the last six months, Stevie has made considerable progress in his academic and fine motor skills. He is now able to write his name with minimal prompting, count to five with meaning and begin to identify the beginning letters of words by their sounds. His speech, self-help and social skills continue to improve because he wants and expects to interact with the other children. . . . Probably one of the most important benefits of an inclusive classroom is that our life is just *more normal*. As parents, we volunteer in the classroom and participate in school-sponsored events just like every other parent. Thus, we are constantly talking to other parents about mutual parenting concerns. For Stevie's younger brother, it gives him the opportunity to follow the footsteps of his big brother just like other siblings do. And, for Stevie, he has *friends*. Stevie's friends include classmates who are both typically developing and others who have special needs. This too we believe will become the norm for all children because of inclusion. Thus, inclusion leads us to focus our attention on the *child* first and his disability second. Stevie needs that focus. We will always strive to maintain it.

Critical Incident

Integrating the New Student With a Disability

As a new second-grade teacher in Burlington Elementary School, you are assigned to a classroom that is directly across the hall from Mr. Beeman's. You have been watching him closely throughout the year and are particularly intrigued by the degree of comfort he seems to have with Carol, the student who uses a wheelchair. At mid-year, a new student is assigned to your classroom. Stephen is a boy from out of state who has a degenerative orthopedic disorder that requires him to use a walker on most days and a wheelchair on some of the more difficult days. You are not certain how you will integrate him into the classroom, but you are concerned that his first day is most positive.

- How will you go about introducing Stephen to other students in your class?
- What will you do to familiarize your students with disabilities in general and with Stephen's in particular?

Critical Incident

The Reluctant Parents

Not long after Stephen moves into your classroom, several parents approach you expressing concerns that their children may be missing out on valuable time with you as the primary teacher and may not themselves develop as fully as the parents expect. You, of course, are concerned that all students receive the education to which they are entitled.

- How will you go about addressing the parents' concerns?
- What issues would you want to be certain they understood?
- In what kinds of activities might you engage them so they become better informed and more positive about the opportunities their children will have?

Summary

This chapter has described both the historical foundations of the field of special education and current practices in the inclusion of children with disabilities or who may be identified as gifted in regular education programs. In addition, it addresses issues related to the health of children and the responsibility of teachers and schools to consider the means by which children with a variety of special health care needs can be integrated into the regular classroom. Of most importance is the critical role the teacher can play in ensuring that all children are fully integrated into the life and activities of today's classroom while they develop the skills necessary to function effectively in the society at large.

Chapter Review

Go to the Online Learning Center at www.mhhe.com/cushner9e to review important content from the chapter, practice with key terms, take a chapter quiz, and access active workbook exercises.

Key Terms

adaptive equipment 367

Asperger's syndrome 371

attention deficit hyperactivity disorder (ADHD) 372

autism spectrum disorder 364

behavior management plans 364

bipolar disorder 372

cerebral palsy 362

clean intermittent catheterization (CIC) 373

conduct disorders 372

Down syndrome 373

group homes 366

inclusion 365

individual education program (IEP) 362

informed consent 377

least restrictive environment (LRE) 366

low-incidence 363

multifactored evaluation 379

muscular dystrophy 367

normalization 366

placement continuum 379

related services 362

Rett's disorder 371

sickle cell disease 373

specific learning disabilities 362

spina bifida 373

supported employment 366

transition plan 371

traumatic brain injury (TBI) 368

universal health precautions 375

zero exclusion mandate 379

The Student With Special Needs

Purpose: To assist future teachers in gaining greater understanding and insight into the probable expectations and responsibilities toward children with special needs.

Instructions: Full inclusion of all children in all classrooms is likely to be a major emphasis in the years to come, thus making it essential that all teachers are well-versed in ways to accommodate the needs of children with special needs. The following exercises will assist you in developing a greater understanding of your role and responsibilities.

1. Arrange to do an observation of a classroom that has children who have special needs. What do you notice about the manner in which the teacher interacts with the children who have special needs compared to those without special needs? What needs do the children seem to have that are unique to this group? Common to other children? What modifications in instructional approach are evident?

2. Interview a parent of a child who receives special educational services. In what ways has the child been helped? What improvements are still needed in the education the child receives? What recommendations does the parent have for you, as a future teacher, regarding what you might provide for children who have special needs?

3. Interview a teacher, focusing on how she or he has been affected by educational policy directed at children with special needs. What modifications has the teacher made in teaching? What special preparation has she or he received to help make the necessary changes? What does the teacher still feel is needed?

4. Ask to observe a conference where an individual educational plan (IEP) is developed for a student with special needs. Analyze the perspectives and needs of each of the parties at the meeting. What concerns did parents

address? Teachers? Administrators? Psychologists? Students? What concerns did you have that were not addressed?

Classroom Activities

1. Aided by information you are able to obtain, describe what, if any, adaptations you would want to make to enable any of the following students to participate fully and most successfully in a lesson you plan to implement:

   - A class member whose *low vision* often requires the use of high-contrast or otherwise-adapted print materials in order for her to participate optimally.

   - A class member who is an avid and generally successful achiever, even though his behavioral characteristics are consistent with the autism spectrum disorder/Asperger's disorder diagnoses he has received.

   - A class member who uses a wheelchair.

   - A class member who, although experiencing no hearing loss, demonstrates particular difficulty processing auditory information.

2. Depending on the instructional level at which you plan to teach, begin a bibliography or resource file (e.g., films) that will help your future students better understand and interact comfortably with others, including their peers, who experience special health care needs, difficulties in learning or social behavior, mobility or sensory impairments, or other special needs. For each item, describe your possible classroom use.

Reflective Questions

1. Can every student with special needs receive an individually appropriate education without having to be segregated in a special place? Using information about these conditions accessible via the Internet or other sources, suggest how a teacher might endeavor to accomplish this for:

   - Madeline, a 13-year-old middle school student whose *Asperger's syndrome* involves difficulties in social interactions and sometimes in self-control, along with strong, although sometimes atypical, intellectual interests.

   - Marcus, age 7, who is one of a growing number of young children given a diagnosis of *bipolar disorder* and whose parents and pediatrician rely on his teacher's communication in order to monitor his medication and guide the therapeutic counseling he receives.

2. How can Madeline's and Marcus's teachers make certain that these students' classmates not only are not detrimentally affected but derive benefit from their inclusion in regular education?

Endnotes

1. The Case Study in this chapter is a composite that reflects the experiences of children, parents, and educators in two communities. The authors extend appreciation to the educators who, with parents' consent, provided material for this Case Study. The names of all children and adults are pseudonyms.

2. Vocational Rehabilitation Act of 1973 § 504, P. L. 93–112, 29 U.S.C. § 794 (1973); Americans With Disabilities Act of 1990, 42 U.S.C. § 12101 (1990).

3. Individuals With Disabilities Education Act of 1990, P. L. 101-476, 20, U.S.C. §§ 1400-1485 (1990, reauthorized in 1995).

4. The source for this and subsequent historical information in this chapter is Philip Safford and Elizabeth Safford, *A History of Childhood and Disability*. (New York: Teachers College Press, 1996).

5. See Chapter 11 for a comprehensive discussion of constructivism as reflected in the concept of developmentally appropriate practice.

References

Advocacy Board, Center on Human Policy. (1994). Inclusion (Inclusion in education: A choice for your child). *Newsletter, TASH: The Association for Persons with Severe Handicaps, 20*(9), 27.

Hollingworth, L. S. (1924). Provisions for intellectually superior children. In M. V. O'Shea (Ed.), *The child: His nature and his needs* (pp. 277-299). New York: The Children's Foundation.

Howe, S. G. (1848). *Report of Commission to Inquire into the Conditions of Idiots of the Commonwealth of Massachusetts.* Boston, MA: Senate Document No. 51.

Janney, R. E., Snell, M. E., Beers, M. K., & Raynes, M. (1995). Integrating students with moderate and severe disabilities into general education classes. *Exceptional Children, 61*(5), 425-439.

National Center for Health Statistics. (2000). Births: Final data for 1998. *National Vital Statistics Reports 48*(11).

Nirje, B. (1969). The normalization principle and its human management implications. In R. B. Kugel & W. Wolfensberger (Eds.), *Changing patterns in residential services for the mentally retarded* (pp. 179-188). Washington, DC: President's Committee on Mental Retardation.

Pugach, M., & Johnson, L. (1995). *Collaborative practitioners, collaborative schools.* Denver, CO: Love.

Rainforth, B., York, J., & Macdonald, C. (1997). *Collaborative teams for students with severe disabilities: Integrating therapy and educational services* (2nd ed.). Baltimore, MD: Paul H. Brookes.

Richards, L. E. (1909). *Letters and journals of Samuel Gridley Howe, the servant of humanity* (Vol. 2). Boston: Dana Estes.

Safford, P. L., & Safford, E. J. (1996). *A history of childhood and disability.* New York: Teachers College Press.

Seguin, E. O. (1880). *Report on education (U.S. Commissioner on Education at the Vienna Universal Exhibition).* Washington, DC: U.S. Government Printing Office.

Snell, M. (Ed.). (1993). *Instruction of students with severe disabilities* (4th ed.). New York: Macmillan.

Spencer, H. (1963). What knowledge is of most worth? *Education: Intellectual, Moral & Physical* [Essays, 1854-1859] (pp. 21-96). Patterson, NJ: Littlefield, Adams, & Co. (Original work published 1859)

Wolfensberger, W. (1972). *The principle of normalization in human services.* Toronto, Ontario: National Institute of Mental Retardation.

Improving Schools for All Children

The Role of Social Stratification in Teaching and Learning

Focus Questions

1. Do you believe that all children can learn?

2. Do you believe that all children should be educated to the same level?

3. What factors do you think may hinder reforms that promote learning for all children?

4. What role do you think social class and social status might have had in your own education?

5. Are you the first in your family to go to college?

6. Can you think of some examples in which a person might have high status but not be a member of a higher social class?

7. Do you believe that those who are born into the lower classes can rise in the U.S. class system if they really work hard? If not, why not?

> " An imbalance between rich and poor is the oldest and most fatal ailment of all republics. "
>
> PLUTARCH

Case Study

Climate Change and Economic Distress in the Northeast Kingdom[1]

Encompassing three counties in northeastern Vermont (Caledonia, Essex, and Orleans), the Northeast Kingdom is bordered 20 miles to the north by Quebec, Canada and to the east by northern New Hampshire. It has almost no industry but is a region of glacial lakes, rugged forests, small towns, dairy farms, a surprising lack of quaintness, a statistical lack of sunshine in the winter, and a noticeable degree of poverty.

It was given its name, the Northeast Kingdom, by then Vermont Senator George Aiken, who said: "You know, this is such beautiful country up here—it should be called the Northeast Kingdom." And so it has been and still is. Over time, the richness of its landscape has stood in contrast with the degree of economic development in the area. Still, a wide variety of people have called this area home, including a fair number of French Canadian descendants, some residents of communes founded by counterculture folks in the 1960s and 1970s, farmers, artists, entrepreneurs, and a few fugitives from the fast life in cities down the Eastern Seaboard.

Ben Webster, high school science teacher and sometime consultant for the Northeast Vermont Development Association (NVDA), knows all this in his very soul, for he was born and brought up on a dairy farm in the Kingdom. On this day, he is on his way to yet another meeting of folks who are interested in working with his science students to undertake research projects on climate change in the area. It is May, the mountain laurel and wild azalea are in bloom all over the hillsides, and his small corner of Vermont had never looked more beautiful. But Ben is worried.

Two years ago, the National Science Foundation awarded $20,000,000 to the Vermont Experimental Program to Stimulate Research (Vermont EPSCoR) for studies related to climate change in Vermont. Ben's alma mater, Lyndon College, is one of the participants in the study, and through the college, he involved himself and some of his students. It is great experience for them all, and it also is leading to information that can help not only the local ecology, but also the economy.

Changing climate conditions are having a particularly negative effect on Vermont: it is getting wetter, especially in northern Vermont. Overall precipitation has increased 9 inches per year in the past century. It has also become warmer—approximately 2.5 degrees over the same period of time. Because of this phenomenon, Ben's dad, and all the other dairy farmers, can expect damaging floods and more days of higher temperatures, which increases stress to cows and decreases milk production. This hurts the dairy industry, which accounts for 70–80% of the agricultural sales in the state (UVM Extension Center, 2014). Decreasing milk production means decreasing profits, which translates into fewer farms and less income for Vermont's dairy farmers.

Ben is quite aware of the back-and-forth talk between those who think climate change is both real and dangerous, and those who believe it is "fake news." He talks at length with his dad and other farmers to monitor what seems to be happening on family farms around his dad's. He knows that his father and other farmers are, indeed, seeing the results of some of these changes in climate. They are worried, too.

While Vermont isn't the poorest state in the Union, parts of it—including the Northeast Kingdom—are in need of some help. The three counties in the Kingdom are the lowest in the

[1]This Case Study was enriched by several primary sources. One is the work of Garret Keizer, a teacher and minister who wrote of his experiences teaching in northeastern Vermont, an area popularly referred to as the "Northeast Kingdom" (see Keizer, 1988, *No place but here: A teacher's vocation in a rural community*. New York: Penguin Books. Other works important to the Case Study are: an article on a real $20,000,000 grant from the National Science Foundation to the Vermont Experimental Program to Stimulate Research (Vermont EPSCoR) in 2015 (retrieved from http://www.nvda.net/regional-plan.php on April 12, 2017); Climate change and agriculture (retrieved from https://www.uvm.edu/~susagctr/whatwedo/farmingclimatechange/FarmCCQuickFacts.pdf on April 12, 2017; the Vermont Department of Labor (2015). Economic/demographic profile series (retrieved from http://www.vtlmi.info/profile2015.pdf on April 12, 2017.

state in per capita income and it is getting harder and harder for agricultural workers to stay in the middle class. Indeed, the percentage of people living below the poverty line in the three counties is higher than the national average (Center for Poverty Research, 2015).

Ben sees the results of poverty every day: most of his students have lived in the Kingdom all their lives, mostly on farms. And they're all a bit isolated, both because of the circumstances of their lives and because the rest of America is woefully ignorant of, not to say indifferent to its rural populations. Even some of his students' real deprivations don't "count" in the larger scheme of things, he thought, because "real" poverty is most often equated with urban poverty. But he knows that Emily spent last winter living in an unheated trailer behind her grandma's house, and that Tom missed a week of school because of all the fleas he picked up at his father's house.

For Ben, the combination of a changing climate, reduced circumstances for many of the folks in his corner of Vermont, and real poverty, require action. His way of acting has been to become involved as a consultant with the Northeast Vermont Development Association and with his college's new Bachelor's degree in Climate Change Science (Lyndon State College, 2017). Two of his students were accepted into this program after graduation last year, and many of his students are currently working as support people to researchers in the broader effort supported by the large NSF grant.

Now, two of the five years of the NSF grant have passed, and research seems to be going well. Teams from the college are collecting data from lakes, rivers, and land as well as information on adjacent land use by farms and developers. When there is sufficient data, probably next year, researchers will develop computer models to test various ways of managing water resources, as well as identifying and trying out scenarios for preserving infrastructure, environmental health, and drinking water quality in the case of intense storms.

Even better, his students—the ones actively engaged in research and those who aren't—are seeing that maybe they can do something to better their own lives and those of their friends and neighbors. They don't have to let things just "happen" to them; they can actively try to change their world.

At the meeting Ben is about to attend, the agenda concerns the proposed 31% cut in the federal Environmental Protection Agency budget. It is uncertain whether or not such cuts would affect the NSF funding that already supports their work, because the National Science Foundation is an independent agency of the government. But Vermont receives about 35% of its $5.7 billion state budget in federal dollars and the NSF grant is intertwined with the work of a variety of agencies. In terms of Vermont's environmental work, if this budget were fully implemented it would affect enforcement of the state's clean air and drinking water laws, support for the Lake Champlain basin clean-up, and grants to Vermont's Fish and Wildlife Department among many other departments and projects (Craven, 2017).

The federal budget has not yet been debated in Congress, so changes in those cuts can still be made. But Ben and his colleagues need to have plans ready in case they all pass as they are currently projected.

At the moment, Ben is thinking about the new **Every Student Succeeds Act (ESSA),** which replaces The No Child Left Behind Act in the fall of 2017. He heard that there were some provisions in the new law that opened the door to project-based assessment. It seems that seven states can apply for permission to pilot new forms of testing, one of which is project-based. New Hampshire has already received permission, largely because that state acquired permission to experiment with performance-based assessments under the No Child Left Behind law, and is being allowed to continue. Vermont is one of six other states to attend a webinar given by the Council of Chief State School Officers in May 2016 to talk about the pilot's potential (Klein, 2016). Ben didn't know if that had led to plans for a Vermont application, but he meant to find out. If Vermont received such permission, his students could continue to develop projects on climate change and be evaluated on their work in this area. They would still take paper and pencil tests, of course, but at least some of their work to date could continue.

So much depends on what happens at the federal level—both with the Environmental Protection Agency (EPA) and with the new education law. As he parked his car, he thought to himself, "Maybe, someday, I'll have to run for office so that I have some say in all this!"

In 2001, with the passage of the **No Child Left Behind Act,** the federal government of the United States entered into the most far-reaching, controversial, and potentially expensive effort to reform public education in the history of the country. Actually a reauthorization of the Elementary and Secondary Education Act of 1965 (ESEA), No Child Left Behind (NCLB) has imposed a whole series of conditions on public schooling, with sanctions if those conditions are not met. These conditions are based on two major ideas: (1) that the nation's education system needs subject area standards for what students should know and be able to do, and (2) that the nation's students, teachers, and schools should be held accountable for reaching those standards.

Under No Child Left Behind, accountability has been enforced by testing all children in Grades 3 to 8 in reading and mathematics, with some other subject area testing done in middle and high school. Indeed, it is this assessment of progress that is believed by proponents to be the engine of reform—serving both to measure achievement and to compel it.

Other aspects of the law included: the provision that every classroom would be staffed by a "highly qualified" teacher; that further support for reform would be aided by introducing competition into education by encouraging parental choice through the establishment of charter schools and through school voucher programs for low-income families; that all schools must meet "adequate yearly progress" toward the goals of proficient education; and that such progress (or lack of it) must be reported to the public in the form of a state "report card."

Increasing criticism of NCLB over time settled into three basic arguments. First, it was argued that the law was too much intrusion by the Federal government into education, which was a responsibility of the state. Second, that it became an unfunded mandate, forcing costs to move from the federal to the state and local level. And finally, that it placed too much emphasis on assessment by standardized tests. Teachers agreed with all of these arguments and, in addition, asserted that the law took all the joy out of teaching and learning.

In the end, the biggest criticism was about assessment, both the number of assessments each school year and the kind of assessments—e.g., standardized tests. Some of the questions that critics wanted addressed were: What kinds of assessment? Who should be assessed, and how often? How much time should be given to assessments? How is the implementation of assessments affecting the curriculum at the state level? Who decides the answers to all of the above?

In this chapter, we ask—in addition—what role does social class and social status play in the outcomes, not only of assessments but of teaching and learning as well? Indeed, it has long been somewhat wryly acknowledged that the best predictor of student achievement is the student's zip code; where one lives (and how much one's home is worth as an indicator of social class) is still too often the determiner of how well one does in school. How that comes to be the case is a major subject in this chapter. Also how does stratification work in other areas of the world?

Case Analysis

Ben's experience in the Northeast Kingdom is typical of many teachers who work in schools where there is significant poverty, but it is somewhat different from those whose students live in urban areas. Rural poverty is just as devastating, but it often doesn't get the attention that urban poverty does. The counties of the Northeast Kingdom are 3 of 1,976 such counties defined as rural by the federal census; these counties comprise about 72% of the nation's land. In 2013, 46.2 million people lived in rural areas—about 15% of the total population of the United States (Yen & Dreier, 2013). Rural child poverty rates have been rising in the United States since 2003, reaching their highest level of 26.7% in 2012. Rising income inequality rather than lower average incomes is the major driver of child poverty (Farrigan & Hertz, 2016).

Residents of the Northeast Kingdom, like other residents of rural areas, are also keepers of important American history and traditions, and significant caretakers of the environment. What is difficult for many residents is their isolation, which often contributes to a lack of access to well-paying jobs and to education and health care. Small farmers, largely dairy farmers, often have a hard time too, especially as they are being squeezed by "megafarms" in other parts of the country. Indeed, in the United States over half a million small farmers have incomes below the poverty level. In Vermont, there's an old joke about the farmer who won the lottery. "What are you going to do now?" he was asked. "Well, I guess I'll just keep on farming till it's gone!"

Over the years, Ben has tried in many different ways to adapt his own ideas about education and his science curriculum to the needs of the students of the Northeast Kingdom and to ways in which their work can benefit the entire region.

Pedagogies: Old and New

Like many teachers of rural children, Ben has always been determined not to "dumb down" his curriculum. He introduces his students both to a variety of scientific content and scientific methods of research as well as to the real problems in the world that science can address.

But a good science curriculum is not enough if it means the same old pedagogies. One of the ideas that often prevents innovative teaching of poor students is a belief in deficit models—that is, that children from low-income families are perceived as culturally deprived or disadvantaged and cannot be taught the same things in the same ways as middle-class children.

> By characterizing the environment of lower-class children as deprived, disorganized, or pathological, the cultural deprivation argument [shifts] attention away from the failings of the schools and of biased testing instruments to the supposed failure of poor people to bring up their children correctly (Hurn, 1993, p. 152).

Such attitudes are counterproductive at best and harmful to both students and teachers at worst. Not surprisingly, low expectations of students quite often produce low performance, thus engaging in what is called a "self-fulfilling prophecy" (see below). And research has demonstrated that:

> The instruction available to students lower down on (any) social-class scale is, on average, academically less challenging, more repetitive, and more dominated by a concern for social control than that offered to students of higher-social-class background (Knapp & Woolverton, 2003, p. 672).

In contrast, when teaching is respectful, exciting, engaging, and challenges the real and human needs of the learner, great things often happen as they do in Ben's class where hands-on research and other forms of scientific practice occur on a daily basis.

Roles: Old and New

Social class influences the nature of the teaching force just as it influences the nature of the student population in any school. Teaching as a profession occupies a middle rung in the hierarchy of occupations, and, in fact, many teachers come from middle-class backgrounds. But not all do, and for those from working-class backgrounds, teaching offers the possibility of "moving up" the social ladder a bit. This upward mobility differs somewhat, however, for men and women, as there is a long history in U.S. schools of what is often called the "feminization of teaching" (Knapp & Woolverton, 2003). This phenomenon divides the labor market of school people into a kind of within-the-profession stratification in which men manage and women teach (Tyack, 1981).

Not surprisingly, teachers bring their own class-based knowledge, attitudes, and values with them into the profession, just as students do. Metz (1990) studied variations in teachers' social class backgrounds and found the following:

> Teachers participate in communities and in kinship and friendship networks that also are part of the social class system. While teachers have formally similar educational credentials. . . . they not only come from a range of social class backgrounds but participate as adults in networks that vary significantly in their social class (p. 94).

In this study, this variance had an effect on how teachers defined their work. Those whose background was more middle and upper-middle class tended to think of their responsibilities in terms of being sure to do a good job. Those from lower-class backgrounds tended to think of their work in terms of "conscientiously putting in required hours" (Metz, 1990, p. 95).

There is also some evidence that social class helps to subtly shape faculties within and between schools (Anyon, 1980, 1981; Metz, 1990). As Knapp and Woolverton (2003) pointed out, while social class is not the most powerful variable influencing where teachers are assigned or find work, and while teachers are not passive participants in their search for employment, it is still the case that:

> Teachers are likely to gravitate to teaching situations in which their colleagues' social class sensibilities resemble their own. . . . Thus, the cadre of teachers at a typical working-class school and those serving predominantly upper-middle-class students are likely to look very different (p. 666).

When teachers—regardless of their own social class backgrounds—are consciously prepared to be aware of, to think, and to act in multicultural ways, they are more likely to be effective in teaching students from a variety of backgrounds. This will be the case even more in the years ahead as student populations in the United States become more and more diverse.

Place of Content Knowledge: Old and New

In her now-classic study of the work fifth-grade children do in schools representing different social classes, Jean Anyon (1980) documented the role of curriculum in preparing students for different roles in life based on their social class. In general, for children in working-class schools, work is procedural and teacher-directed and involves little choice or decision making. For children in middle-class schools, work is demonstrated by getting the right answer, which is usually based on following directions. Accumulating right answers results in good grades. However, in middle-class schools, following directions often includes some figuring out, some choice, and some decision making. In upper- or professional-class schools, work is quite often carried out independently and involves creative and/or critical thinking. Suggesting that her study (and others) finds the nature of schoolwork is "tacit preparation for relating to the process of production in a particular way," she noted that by emphasizing different cognitive and behavioral skills related to academic content, children are learning the expectations the society has with respect to their relation to authority and to work.

In many ways, these distinctions are part of a "hidden" curriculum. The *formal* curriculum teaches little about the experiences of people living at either end of the social class scale, and teaches quite a bit about the experiences and worldview of middle-class America. The public school is, after all, a middle-class institution.

What does seem to be the case, however, is a differentiation of actual content by social class along several dimensions: emphasis on "advanced" versus "basic" skills, emphasis on conceptual understanding, range and variety of academic tasks, degree of repetition, extent of topical coverage, and attention to "practical" or vocational knowledge (Knapp & Woolverton, 2003, p. 673). By the time students reach high school, selection into various "tracks" (e.g., college-bound, vocational, commercial), can be fundamentally related to social class patterns, with the result that students from different social class backgrounds often leave public schooling with quite different educations. It is, in part, this phenomenon that the No Child Left Behind Act failed to effectively address. When there is so much emphasis on testing, no one has time (or incentive!) to individualize schooling on the basis of the many kinds of diversity, including social class.

Assessment: Old and New

Similarly, the goal of measuring student achievement in terms of standardized testing is, in part, an effort to avoid the kind of differentiation of assessment by class that has allowed many lower-class students to fall through the cracks of public education. For example, in Anyon's (1980, 1981) study of fifth-grade classrooms in schools catering to different social classes, students in working-class schools tended to be evaluated on whether or not they had followed the correct steps rather than on whether or not their answers were right. Middle-class students tended to be evaluated on whether they had done the assignment and "understood it." In contrast, students in upper-class schools tended to be evaluated on their ability to think critically, express themselves well, and apply ideas and concepts.

One criticism of the one-size-fits-all use of standardized tests, as articulated by many critics (see, for example, Meier & Wood, 2004), is that judgments are made by comparing how much students know in one year (e.g., the fourth grade *this* year) with how much a different group of students (e.g., the fourth grade *next* year) know in other years. Increasingly, however, educators and planners are becoming interested in different approaches. Such changes are suggested, in part, because it is becoming increasingly clear that the skills needed in the 21st century may very well not be amenable to paper-and-pencil tests. For example, a government report even two decades ago ("What Work Requires of Schools," 1991) suggested that the following skills would be needed in the workforce in the future: the ability to identify, analyze, plan, and allocate resources; the ability to work effectively with others; the ability to acquire and evaluate

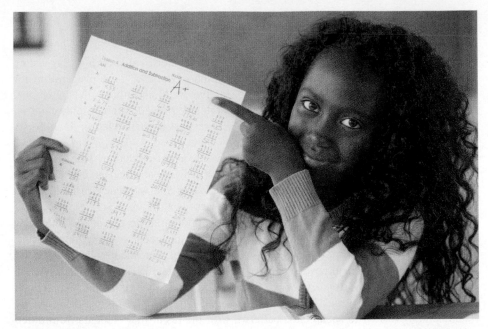

©JGI/Jamie Grill/Blend Images LLC RF

information; the ability to understand complex interrelationships; and the ability to work with a variety of technologies.

An analysis of six frameworks for 21st century skills lists 13 skills that the authors think are going to be necessary in this century: collaboration and teamwork, creativity and imagination, critical thinking, problem solving, flexibility and adaptability, global and cultural awareness, information literacy, leadership, civic literacy and citizenship, oral and written communication skills, social responsibility and ethics, technology literacy, and initiative (Potter, Whitener, & Sikorsky, 2014). These kinds of skills have several attributes in common:

1. They are not easily measured by standardized tests.

2. They are skills that are necessary when the society is changing rapidly and there are fewer familiar ways of responding to problems.

3. We, as a society, are unsure what life will be like in 10 years, or 5 years, or even 1 year.

Similarly, in her book, *The Flat World and Education*, Linda Darling-Hammond (2010) listed six sets of skills that are already required in the work world of the 21st century—the capacity to: design, evaluate, and manage one's own work so that it continually improves; frame, investigate, and solve problems using a wide range of tools and resources; collaborate strategically with others; communicate effectively in many forms; find, analyze, and use information for many purposes; and develop new products and ideas.

As more and more educators and policymakers have observed the need to create assessments that will better align with curriculum needs and will also provide students and teachers with deeper knowledge and more flexible approaches to the demonstration of that knowledge, teachers and learners are beginning to craft new ways of evaluating students' work. Hopefully, this movement will gain strength, results will be shared, and the Every Student Succeeds Act will serve as a support for this effort.

Perspectives on Stratification: Social Class and Social Status

Previous chapters have suggested that differences in school achievement may be attributed to a variety of cultural influences. Two of those influences are the cultural aspects of social class and social status.

For much of our recent history, at least since the major expansion of the American middle class in the early and middle parts of the 20th century, Americans have believed that they live in a relatively classless, egalitarian society. In addition, American ideology promotes the idea that through proper attention, diligent effort, and some luck (which Americans also believe in), an individual may "rise above" the social class into which he or she is born. Part of what has been called an "American religion" (Bellah, 1976), this faith in the reality of upward mobility may partially account for the relative lack of attention given to the concept of social class in much of the educational and psychological literature in the United States (Brislin, 1988).

Certainly it accounts for the difficulty encountered by history, sociology, and education professors in helping young people understand the bases of class differences in this society. Nevertheless, as we all know, there are significant variations in economic standard of living, status of occupation, and extent of expectations for upward mobility among U.S. citizens. And, as we have learned recently, there is growing inequality among America's people: indeed, in today's society, it appears that "the top 1% of Americans are now taking in nearly 52% of the nation's new income every year" (Qiu, 2016).

Definitions of Social Class

Social class has been defined in a number of ways, all of which refer in some sense to a hierarchical stratification or "layering" of people in social groups, communities, and societies. Assignment to social class categories is one of several stratification systems that can be used to distinguish one individual or group from another in such a way as to assign "worth." The urge to organize people in layers almost appears to be a human characteristic. Indeed, it has been said that whenever there are more than three people in a group there will be stratification; someone will be more respected, more powerful, or more "worthy" than the rest. Although many Americans would identify class membership in terms of income (Gilbert & Kahl, 1982), it is important to understand that money alone does not determine a person's social class. Rather, social class standing depends on a combination of prestige, power, influence, and income (Webb & Sherman, 1989).

Traditional class markers in the United States include family income, prestige of one's father's or mother's occupation, prestige of one's neighborhood, the power one has to achieve one's ends in times of conflict, and the level of schooling achieved by the family head. Among other nations and cultures, markers of one's social class may include such determiners as bloodline and status of the family name, the caste into which one was born, the degree to which one engages in physical labor, and the amount of time that one might devote to scholarly or leisurely activities of one's choosing (Brislin, 1988).

One reason that social class is so difficult to talk about and truly understand is that while class distinctions are real and observable in concrete daily experience, they are also highly abstract. It is no accident that social class categories are mostly "assigned" by others (often sociologists), for social class in the real world is often in the eyes of the beholder.

Nevertheless, for purposes of analysis, American society can be divided into five social classes. At the top is a very small upper class, or social elite, consisting of people who have generally inherited social privilege from others. Second is a somewhat larger upper-middle class whose members often are professionals, corporate managers, and leading scientists. This group usually has benefited from extensive higher education, and while family history is not so important, manners, tastes, and patterns of behavior are. The third (or middle) social class is generally comprised of people employed in white-collar occupations earning middle incomes—small business owners, teachers, social workers, nurses, sales and clerical workers, bank tellers, and so forth. This class has been the largest of the social classes in the United States (at least until now) and encompasses a wide range of occupations and incomes. Central to the values of the "typical" middle class is a "desire to belong and be respectable . . . friendliness and openness are valued and attention is paid to 'keeping up appearances'" (Webb & Sherman, 1989, p. 407).

Fourth in the hierarchy of social class is the working or lower middle class, whose members have been largely blue-collar workers (industrial wage earners) or employees in low-paid service occupations. Working-class families often have to struggle with poor job security, limited fringe benefits, longer hours of work, and more dangerous or "dirtier" work than people in the classes above them. It is not surprising, then, that members of the working class often feel more alienation from the social mainstream. Finally, fifth in the hierarchy is the lower class, which includes both the so-called **working poor** and those who belong to what has been termed the **underclass**—a designation that refers to people who have been in poverty for so long that they seem unable to take any advantage at all of mobility options and thus lie nearly outside the class system. Clearly, poverty is both the chief characteristic and the chief problem of this group.

Changes in the Definition of Social Class

As the American economy has become more and more global, as many of the manufacturing jobs that once powered the growth of the middle class are moved abroad, and as new technologies have both eliminated traditional kinds of work (think of the small dairy farmer in the Northeast Kingdom of Vermont, now being replaced by agribusiness dairy farms) and created the need for highly skilled people who can use technology to solve problems on a global scale and with global collaboration, new possibilities of social stratification have come into play. These have not been set in stone as yet, but there are interesting conceptions being put forth by economic thinkers.

Robert B. Reich, former secretary of labor under President Clinton, was one of the first to set out some new categories similar to class, but based on what work they did (Reich, 1992). His three categories were:

- *Routine producers*, which included not only manufacturing (or "blue collar" workers) but also "white collar" data processors, and primary care physicians who provided "routine" medical care and sent more complicated cases to specialists.

- *In-person servers*, which included not only restaurant, hotel, and retail workers, but also librarians, and those who serve the rapidly growing elderly population as nurses, home health care workers, and nursing home staff.

- *Symbolic analysts,* which included a relatively new group of people, knowledge workers who manipulate symbols for a living, such as scientists, engineers, journalists, investment people, bankers, consultants, and (maybe) college professors.

While these three categories do not easily replace traditional social class categories, they do suggest a major shift in thinking about stratification systems that may very well lead to new definitions of social class. Furthermore, the notion of the precariat as an emerging 'class-like' global phenomenon may help to explain some of the social disruption that we see on the front pages of our newspapers today. It seems well worth watching.

The Precariat

A much more recent view is taken by the British economist, Guy Standing, who not only changes the names of identified classes, but asserts that the world is witnessing the emergence of an altogether new class. He calls this class "the precariat" (Standing, 2016).

Observing enormous structural changes brought about by globalization, Standing proposes six levels of stratification in contemporary societies:

- At the very top, a tiny number of wealthy *elite* global citizens able to influence governments everywhere and to indulge in munificent philanthropic gestures (p. 8).

- Next to the *elite* is the *salariat,* concentrated in large corporations, government agencies, and public administration, living in stable, full-time employment, with pensions, paid holidays, and other benefits, often subsidized by the state (p. 6).

- Next to the *salariat* comes the *proficians,* a term that combines the traditional ideas of 'professional' and 'technician' but covers those with bundles of skills that they can market, earning high incomes on contract, as consultants or independent own-account workers. They live with the expectation and desire to move around, without an impulse for long-term, full-time employment in a single enterprise. Contemporary examples might be college professors, or information technologists who move from employer to employer, or work for themselves (p. 7).

- Below the *proficians* is a shrinking "core" of manual employees, the essence of the old "working class". Built for them were the welfare states and systems of labor regulation. But the millions of industrial laborers who formed great unions have shriveled and lost their sense of solidarity (except perhaps, in the United States; teachers who still support and are supported by teachers' unions, although they are under continual attack from other sectors in the society).

- Below these four groups is emerging the growing *precariat,* which has class characteristics. It consists of people who lack both employment and job security, and income vulnerability. In addition, they lack a work-based identity. Examples of the varied people who occupy the precariat might be the teenager who flits in and out of the Internet café while surviving on fleeting jobs; or the migrant who uses his wits to survive, networking feverishly while worrying about the police; the single mother fretting where the money for next week's food bill is coming from; or the man in his 60s who takes casual jobs to pay his medical bills (pp. 11–15).

- *Standing* refers to those "below" the precariat as more traditional observers might refer to an *underclass*—those unemployed, and thus detached from the social structure entirely (p. 9).

Both the stratification concepts of Reich and Standing break down or interrupt the traditional notion of upper, middle, and lower class designations that have been very popular and relatively accurate ways of describing class in industrial societies. But in a "knowledge" society, a "global society," a "post-industrial" society—these designations may be fluid—growing or diminishing as social circumstances change. What is reasonably clear is that our ideas of social class are changing, along with our ideas about most things that we've grown up with. Neither Reich nor Standing has succeeded in re-naming or re-describing social class in the 21st century, but they are probably harbingers of those to come.

Furthermore, it is quite likely that the prospects for individuals to move up or down in the social structure have themselves declined, thus placing an arrow at the heart of one of the most treasured American ideas—that the next generation will do better than the current one. Indeed, a 2015 Pew Research Poll brought the news that the proportion of the American population in the middle class has declined; while membership in both the lower and upper classes has grown. According to the Pew study, In 2015, 20% of American adults were in the lowest income tier, up from 16% in 1971. On the opposite side, 9% were in the upper tier, more than double the 4% share in 1971. At the same time, the shares of adults in the lower-middle or upper-middle income tiers were nearly unchanged (Pew, 2015).

Given the changes in both ideas of social class and changes in family structure, it is well for teachers and other educators to think seriously about what a rise in poverty, the diminishing of optimism, and the very real threat to the American consumer economy in lower consumer confidence and the absence of discretionary income means for the educational enterprise.

Social Stratification in a Global Context

Perhaps the best way to think about global stratification is to envision three categories of nations, organized by their degree of wealth or poverty, their level of industrialization and the size of their economies, and other related factors (Barkan, 2017).

After World War II, the favorite way of classifying the nations of the world was First World, Second World, and Third World. The *First World* consisted of the nations of North America, Europe, Japan, and other English-speaking countries around the world. The *Second World* consisted of the nations of the Soviet Union. The *Third World* consisted of all the rest, nearly all of them from Central and South America, Africa, and Asia. After the disintegration of the Soviet Union in 1991, these terms fell into disuse.

Subsequently, for a while the classification system labeled all nations either *developed, developing,* or *undeveloped,* but these terms were deemed too hierarchical, and have also begun to fall out of favor. Today, a growing terminology ranks nations into the classification system as *Wealthy (or high-income) nations, middle-income (upper and lower middle) nations,* and *poor (or low-income nations.* In the end, most important differences among nations—military might, economies, educational and cultural production, scientific status—come from the degree of wealth they have.

Wealthy nations are the most industrialized nations. Although wealthy nations constitute only about one-fifth of the world's population, they hold about four-fifths of the world's entire wealth. They are the leading nations in industry, high finance, and information technology. Although each of the world's wealthy nations is internally stratified to a greater or lesser degree, these nations as a group live a much more comfortable existence than middle-income nations and, especially, poor nations. People in wealthy nations are more educated and healthier, and they enjoy longer lives.

At the same time, wealthy nations use up more than their fair share of the world's natural resources, and their high level of industrialization causes them to pollute and otherwise contribute to climate change to a far greater degree than is true of nations in the other two categories (Barkan, 2017).

Middle income nations have less industry than wealthy nations but more than poor nations. Much of Central and South America, Eastern Europe, and parts of Africa and Asia constitute the upper and lower middle income nations, and they make up about one-third of the world's population. Poor nations have the least industry, and are the largest agricultural nations. This category encompasses much of Africa and parts of Asia, and consists of about half of the world's population.

The effects of global stratification are many, including the differences it makes in health and illness, infant mortality, life expectancy, and other life chances. As the distribution of resources becomes more and more unequal the well-being of human beings also becomes unequal. As it does with individuals, when nations experience inequality in resources, their populations suffer. Access to necessary resources—food, housing, the stories of their heritage, work, and particularly, education has life-long consequences for both individuals and societies (Global Stratification and Inequality, 2017).

Social Status

As discussed in Chapter 3, the term **social status** refers to a hierarchical position determined not so much by one's wealth (or lack of it) but by the prestige, social esteem, and honor accorded one within one's own social milieu. It is quite possible, in fact, to have high social status without having commensurate income. Members of the clergy are good examples of this condition, as are, quite often, teachers. Conversely, it is also possible to have a great deal of money but occupy a low-status position, at least in terms of general community norms, for example, drug lords and leaders of gangs.

In the social hierarchy of schools, individual students usually achieve high status because of roles they assume, such as star athlete, academic achiever, cheerleading captain, and so forth. Interestingly, the social status of a particular student often differs from the point of view of students and of teachers. Thus students may often accord athletes with high status, whereas teachers generally accord high status to students who achieve well academically. In neither case are economic considerations necessarily predominant, or even present.

While social status has never been thought to be particularly important—indeed, it has been largely hidden!—in schools, there is a new definition of status that may have some bearing on students and teachers. On Facebook, Twitter, and Instagram, "status" seems to mean something like "the state you (or one of your friends) is in at the moment of posting." And, in any case, most school-age students have left Facebook to their parents and moved on to Instagram. But the idea of status is still temporary at best.

Thus, the meaning of status shifts from being a social, collective, shared set of characteristics to being an individual, always changing, relatively whimsical action, belief, feeling, or thought. Given the ubiquity of Twitter and Instagram among students, however, one can speculate that the notion of a static "status" based on social prestige may be losing traction in favor of a dynamic, self-renewing, self-defining individual state that is, nevertheless, shared by countless "friends"—perhaps all over the world.

All of which, of course, is not to say that social class and at least several degrees of social status don't necessarily go hand in hand. To the extent, for example, that teachers believe that middle- and upper-middle-class students will achieve more than working and lower-class students, such expectations are often reflected in reality.

Perspectives on Teaching and Evaluation in the Context of Social Class

As noted in Chapter 4, students in schools not only bring their class identities to school with them, but also define themselves by creating in-school groups with which they identify. Like social class, these in-groups are usually hierarchical—which ones are "on top," and which are lower on the social ladder vary from school to school, but they are very powerful. Indeed, one way to help students understand the concept of social class in the larger society is to ask them about these groups in their school. Further, ask them how easy or difficult it is to move from one group to another. Teachers, too, are aware of their students' "place" in the social hierarchy, both in-school and out-of-school, and—often unwittingly—associate a student's "place" with their own expectations.

The Importance of Teacher Expectations

Teacher expectations regarding the possibilities and potential of academic success for individual students are a critical factor in student achievement. **Teacher expectation** refers to the attributions that teachers make about the future behavior or academic achievement of their students, based on what they presently know about them. *Teacher expectation effects* refer to student outcomes that occur because of the actions taken by teachers in response to their own expectations (Good & Brophy, 1987).

An important type of teacher expectation is the *self-fulfilling prophecy*. In this effect, a false or untrue belief leads to specific behavior that causes that expectation to become

©Erik Isakson/Blend Images LLC RF

true. For instance, if false rumors begin to spread that the stock market is going to crash and if millions of people then rush to sell off their stock holdings, the market may in fact crash. The outcome, however, is not due to any event that was predicted accurately but because people responded to the false information that was rumored.

In the classroom setting, teachers may tell themselves about the potential for success or failure of the students in their charge. For instance, assume that a teacher looks at her roster for the upcoming year and sees that she will have in her classroom a particular student, named Sasha, whose sister, Kristina, was in her classroom 2 years earlier. Assume further that Kristina had a difficult year. Not only did she struggle academically, but (perhaps as a result of academic failure) she also had behavior problems. This teacher, vividly remembering her problems with Kristina, may expect that Sasha will repeat the pattern. When Sasha walks into the classroom at the start of the year, the teacher may greet her in a cool manner, may be hesitant to approach her, and may even avoid personal contact with her as much as possible. Such behavior on the part of the teacher may alienate Sasha, may make her feel as if she doesn't belong, and may generate many feelings of anxiety and uncertainty. These feelings may, in turn, result in certain acting-out behaviors on Sasha's part. The teacher may then have set the stage for a self-fulfilling prophecy.

Just the opposite can also be true. A teacher may, for whatever reason, believe a certain child will be a good student when in fact he or she may be just about average. This belief may translate into particular actions on the part of the teacher that demonstrate care and concern and an expectation of success to the student. The teacher may call on this particular student to read more than other students, may trust this student with particular responsibilities, and may afford greater attention and privilege to this student, which may, in turn, result in increased gains in achievement. This outcome may not have happened if the teacher did not have high expectations for this student.

The Culturally Responsive Teacher

Although Americans are not used to thinking (or talking) about social class as a cultural category, it is relatively easy to think about the relationship between social class and school achievement because there is so much data on the subject, particularly with respect to poverty. Nevertheless, there is a class aspect of culture observable in different forms in both rural and urban settings around the world. In the United States, we might think of all but middle-class children as living in "another country," from which, at age 5, they are suddenly transported every day to a highly middle-class setting—the school—where they are expected to not only have but also honor the knowledge, attitudes, and values of this new place. This conception is as true for upper-class children as it is for lower-class children, although many upper-class children attend private rather than public schools, in part for this very reason.

For the culturally responsive teacher, however, any aspect of a student's social context—class, race, ethnicity, gender, language, and so forth—is important to note and to take into consideration when planning instruction as well as assessment. Villegas and Lucas (2007) listed six characteristics of a culturally responsive teacher:

- *They understand how their learners construct knowledge.* They are interested in how students connect new knowledge to prior knowledge and beliefs, and help students "build bridges between what they already know about a topic and what they need to learn about it" (p. 29).

- *They learn about their students' lives.* To understand how learners construct knowledge, culturally responsive teachers make it a point to learn about their students' family makeup, their interests, concerns, strengths, and problem-solving strategies.

- *They are socioculturally conscious,* defined as "the awareness that a person's worldview is not universal but is profoundly influenced by life experiences, as mediated by a variety of factors, including race, ethnicity, gender, and social class" (p. 31).

- *They hold affirming views about diversity* rather than having a deficit perspective. This is especially important when it is related to the idea of self-fulfilling prophesies because the expectations of teachers are critical to student success.

- *They use appropriate instructional strategies* such as "asking them to discuss what they know about a given topic . . . embedding new ideas and skills in projects that are meaningful to the students . . . and . . . using pertinent examples and analogies from students' lives" (p. 32).

- *They are advocates for all students,* thus "seeing themselves as part of a community of educators working to make schools more equitable for all students" (p. 32).

As Villegas and Lucas (2007) noted, "Teaching is an ethical activity and teachers have an ethical obligation to help all students learn" (p. 32).

The Debate on Multiple Forms of Assessment: Demand vs. Support

The belief that *all* children can and should learn is, in essence, at the heart of the idea of multiple forms of assessment. A number of scholars have looked at ways in which this philosophical position can be translated into classroom practice.

Kohn (1999) suggested that certain classroom orientations distinguish between what we as educators expect that students ought to be able to do and how we as educators can support students' development, thereby helping them to learn. He called these opposing approaches "demand" versus "support."

In the *demand model,* students are perceived as workers who are obligated to do a better job. Students who do not succeed are said to have chosen not to study or not to have earned a given grade. Under such an approach, responsibility is removed from the teacher and attention is deflected away from the curriculum and the context under which learning is meant to occur. In reporting to parents, teachers state whether students did what they were supposed to do. Even programs that reportedly emphasize performance objectives often adopt such an approach under the guise of the common buzzword—outcomes. Unfortunately, in the context of the demand model, many working- and lower-class students *appear* to choose not to study and thus earn lower grades.

The *support model,* on the other hand, assumes that students are active contributors to the learning process, or as Nichols and Hazzard (1993) put it, the "adventure of ideas." Under such an approach, the teacher has a major responsibility to guide and stimulate all students' natural curiosity and desire to learn and explore the unfamiliar, to construct meaning in their world, and to develop the competence for using words, numbers, and ideas. Teaching and learning become child-centered or student-centered, and the goal becomes helping students build on their desire to make sense of, and to become competent in, their world. Student evaluation becomes, in part, a way to determine how effective we have been as educators. We seek to measure improvement in students because it indicates that we have been successful in engaging students and in creating a context in which they become motivated. Assessment, then, becomes supportive.

Kohn (1999) offered five principles of assessment that follow a supportive model:

1. Assessment should not be overdone. The United States seems to be a test-happy nation, and American young people are the most tested in the world. When students become preoccupied with how they are doing, they begin to lose interest in what they are doing. An excessive concern with performance can erode curiosity and thus reduce the quality of performance. Students excessively concerned with their performance may tend to avoid difficult tasks so they can avoid any negative evaluation.

2. The best evidence we have of whether we are succeeding as educators is to observe the behavior of children. Test scores only tell us if students perform well on that specific test. Most tests are not true indicators of a student's subsequent ability to perform a specific task. When we observe children actively engaged in dialogue or conversation about a given topic, seeking out answers to their own questions, or reading on their own, we know that we have sparked their interest and that skills are often subsequently acquired.

3. Schools must be transformed into caring, safe communities. Such characteristics are critical for helping students become good learners willing to take risks and seek guidance and support. Only when there is no fear of humiliation or punitive judgment will children be free to acknowledge their mistakes and take the guidance of others. When the environment stresses grades and standardized testing or when teachers feel that a certain amount of curriculum must be covered, pressures increase and, subsequently, learning diminishes.

4. Any responsible discussion about assessment must attend to the quality of the curriculum. The easy question to answer is whether the student has learned anything. The more difficult question to answer is whether the student has been given something worth learning. Research has supported the notion that good teachers already know. That is, when students have interesting things to do, artificial inducements to boost their achievement are not necessary. If the need to evaluate students has directed the design of the curriculum, students will not be actively engaged in their learning.

5. Students must become part of the discussion in determining the criteria by which their work will be judged and then play a role in that judgment. Such participation gives students greater control over their own education, makes evaluation feel less punitive, and provides an important learning experience in and of itself.

To the extent that educators consider adapting both instructional and assessment strategies in such a way that all children are encouraged and supported in their learning, the public schools will truly continue to be what they have always been in the United States—a place where doors open to children who may not even know those doors are there, and a boost up the social class ladder. As Lugg (2005) noted about the theme of *The American Dream and the Public Schools* by Jennifer Hochschild and Nathan Scovronick, "regardless of the numerous flaws, public schools are essential to maintaining a vital U.S. democracy, as well as ensuring that the pursuit of the American dream is available for all."

Social Class and School Funding

One of the most visible ways in which social class in American schooling plays itself out is the way public schools are funded. Public schooling is a responsibility of the states, and the states have traditionally turned over control of school finances to local districts, which generally fund schools through taxing property. As local districts vary widely in the value of their property, the ability to raise money for education also varies widely. Although most states also have some sort of funding formula through which state money is allocated to local districts, and although federal funding is still available for specific programs in schools (e.g., Title I, special education), it is still the case that the value of local property sets the parameters for how much funding is available for public schools at the local level.

In the past 35 years, numerous court cases have been filed in both state and federal courts seeking in one way or another to change the way in which schools are funded. In one of the earliest cases, *Serrano v. Priest* (1971), the California Supreme Court declared that the state's dependence on property taxes to support schools was a violation of equal protection principles in the state constitution. In response, the state legislature put a cap on potential revenues in wealthy districts and increased state aid to poorer districts. Some say that this decision contributed to the California tax revolt of 1978, which resulted in the passage of Proposition 13, an amendment to the state constitution that reduced property taxes by 57% and drastically cut funding for public services, notably, public schools.

In the *Rodriguez* case in Texas (*San Antonio Independent School District v. Rodriguez*, 1973), the school district argued that using the property tax as the basis for school funding disadvantaged poor children because poor districts didn't have the tax base that wealthier districts had. Thus, the Fourteenth Amendment, which guarantees equal protection under the law, had been violated. The U.S. Supreme Court disagreed, stating that since there is no federal constitutional right to education, and since the Texas system did not discriminate systematically against all poor people, the equal protection clause of the Fourteenth Amendment was not violated. The amendment, it was noted, did not require absolute equality.

These cases did not end the battle for changes in school funding policy. As of 2014 (National Association of State Legislators, 2017), only five states have not filed court cases challenging school funding policies, and only seven have not had such cases decided. In general, these cases have had decidedly mixed results. A more successful outcome was experienced in Kentucky (*Rose v. Council for Better Education,* 1989), when the Kentucky Supreme Court affirmed a lower court decision that found:

> that the system of school financing provided for by the General Assembly is inadequate; places too much emphasis on local school board resources; and results in inadequacies, inequities, and inequalities throughout the state so as to result in an inefficient system of common school education in violation of Kentucky Constitution, Sections 1, 3, and 183 and the equal protection clause and the due process of law clause of the 14th Amendment to the United States Constitution. Additionally the complaint maintains the entire system is not efficient under the mandate of Section 183.

Moreover, since the start of the recent recession, many states have made steep budget cuts in state funding and continued to do so in the 2011–2012 academic year. Such cuts have resulted in the loss of 328,000 jobs—many of them teaching jobs—nationally since 2008. And 31 of the 50 states surveyed provided less per-student funding for K–12 education in the 2015 fiscal year than they did in fiscal year 2008 (Center on Budget and Policy Priorities, 2015). Largely, this has happened because while the recession caused a major reduction in state revenues, state legislatures have been unwilling (and sometimes ideologically opposed) to raising new revenues through taxation.

Such cuts have had serious consequences not only for schools but for the economy at large. They slow the pace of economic recovery by ensuring that people don't have extra money to spend. They require the cancellation of contracts with suppliers that are normally made by both businesses and schools. They discourage businesses from making new investments. They undermine education reforms such as the provision of professional development to improve teacher quality, cutting needed interventions for young children that might prevent learning problems later on, and reducing summer and other ancillary instructional programs for students. As school district funding decreases, schools are less able to provide what Jonathan Kozol wistfully asks for: a beautiful, healthy, vibrant, well-stocked school for every child in America.

Hopes for the Every Student Succeeds Act (ESSA)

In 1965, when the original Elementary and Secondary Education Act was passed as part of President Lyndon Johnson's Great Society legislation (also known as the War on Poverty), there was great excitement among the population that schools would have the opportunity to really address the effects of poverty on poor children. *Title I* provided major funding for special reading and math teachers. *Title II* provided funding for school libraries, particularly audio-visual resources, textbooks, and other instructional materials (and perhaps the beginning of the conversion of school libraries into media centers). *Title III* provided funds for innovation, at its time the greatest federal investment in innovation ever made in the United States. The idea of Title III was to develop innovative ways of teaching and curriculum development that improved learning and then sharing those ideas with other schools through the National Diffusion Network. That idea also appeared in the form of charter schools in the 1980s, which were originally envisioned as schools that were free to innovate and share new models and methods (Elementary and Secondary Education Act—ESEA, 2001).

Through a succession of reauthorizations, culminating in the No Child Left Behind Act of 2002, there has been a steady growth in federal funding and federal authority associated with the original law. There has also been a continuing debate about the value of such federal involvement. President Johnson thought that only the deep resources of the federal government were sufficient to make meaningful changes in learning for poor children. Others thought from the beginning that such governmental largess was welfare and would not only greatly enlarge the size of the government but also start a cycle of dependence among the American population. They also pointed out that there is no provision in the Constitution for education: it "belongs to the states."

In the 52 years since the first Elementary and Secondary Education Act, provisions have been added (programs for migrant, neglected, or delinquent children, the Bilingual Education Act), changed (Title I, various regulations involving funding requirements), and removed (the Bilingual Education Act). Over time, the policies governing the relationship between the federal government and schooling have been susceptible to political winds—sometimes taking funding directly from the federal government and sometimes moving it to the states. Today, the Every Student Succeeds Act is more fully controlled by local districts and states rather than the federal government.

According to summaries of the law (*Education Week*, 2016), the Every Student Succeeds Act lifts much of the federal government's "heavy" hand on education policy. States still have to submit accountability plans that include a variety of goals, both long and short term, and several kinds of indicators that those goals have been met. However, states will decide how much each indicator will be weighted.

States still have to test students in reading and math in grades 3 to 8, once in high school, and break down data by sub groups of students. Districts can use nationally recognized tests such as the ACT or the SAT for the high school test. Initially, up to seven states may apply to the U.S. Department of Education for permission to try out local tests (or other kinds of assessments) for a limited time.

States are required to adopt "challenging" standards; those might be the Common Core State standards but do not have to be. In addition, the U.S. Secretary of Education cannot force, or even suggest, a particular set of standards for any state. Accountability for English-language learners moves from Title III to Title I, where all other accountability measures are. Only 1% of students overall can be given alternative tests, which is about 10% of special education students.

Teachers will no longer be evaluated on the basis of student outcomes. There will be specific funds to support experiments with a variety of teacher improvement measures, and resources to help teachers receive further education in literacy and STEM.

Finally, ESSA has consolidated many separate programs into a $1.6 billion block grant to states, turned the Preschool Development Grant into law, and created a new evidence-based research and innovation program similar to one that already existed.

All in all, there seems to be hope that ESSA will correct the excesses of No Child Left Behind, and, at the same, provide considerably more flexibility for teachers, schools, districts, and states to adjust curriculum, teaching, and assessments to local culture and local conditions. Clearly, High School Science teacher Ben Webster is holding out a lot of hope for the future!

Ethical Issues

Regardless of the specific means of communicating performance to others, assessment is inherently a subjective process. Ornstein (1994) suggested that the more detailed the reporting method and the more analytic the process, the more likely it is that subjectivity will influence the results. Subjectivity, however, is not always a negative factor. After all, teachers who truly know their students understand their progress in far greater detail than any test might uncover.

It is when subjectivity turns into bias that educators get into trouble. Teachers' perceptions and subsequent expectations can significantly influence their judgments of scholastic performance. Students with behavior problems, for instance, often face the obstacle that their infractions will overshadow their performance. These effects are especially evident with boys. Such aspects as a student's handwriting, dress, family background, and so forth can all influence a teacher's judgment.

The official labeling of children and identification of cognitive difficulties happens chiefly in the elementary years. Public schools typically label children as mentally retarded when their measured IQ is below 79. Children with African American and Spanish surnames are more likely to score below 79 than are European American counterparts and subsequently are more likely to be placed in special education classes. Children with African American and Spanish surnames are overlabeled as mentally retarded by public agencies; European Americans are underlabeled when compared to the general population. Such a situation suggests that educators are using tools of analysis that favor some students over others or that actively discriminate against some groups. The special education literature is replete with evidence of individuals wrongfully identified as in need of special education services when all that was really at issue was their inability to communicate as expected in the English language at the time the exam was administered. How many children have been cheated or wrongfully labeled as failures because of an inadequate means of assessment?

Imagine, for a moment, that you are viewing the files of the following two students. What kinds of judgments would you make about these children? What kind of academic program would you recommend? Would you expect them to fit in with your regular class program? Would you suggest any special intervention, such as special classes for gifted or handicapped students? Would you recommend any extracurricular activities that would help develop special skills in these children?

Sam Edder did not begin speaking until he was 3 years old. He has always had trouble with school, often remaining withdrawn and unsociable. He was even removed from school at one time because of his emotional instability. Sam's test scores are well below average except for his performance on creativity measures. In this area he shows some potential. Other than reading intently and playing a musical instrument, Sam seems to have few interests and expresses little in the way of personal or vocational goals. Sam's parents are of European descent, with high school educations.

Bill Ridell has never spent much time in school. He started late because of an illness and was withdrawn several times because of continued sickness. Bill has been labeled "backward" by school officials. He has suffered from a variety of ailments and is going deaf. Although his creative performance shows some promise, Bill's IQ score is low (81), as are his scores on other achievement indices. However, Bill enjoys building things and mechanical pursuits, has good manual dexterity, and would like someday to be a scientist or railroad mechanic. Although Bill's mother is well educated, his father has no formal schooling and is unemployed.

What do you think? What judgments are you able to make about these two children, given this descriptive information? As a teacher, what other information would you like to have? How might you go about working with these children?

This exercise can be used to check the accuracy of your attributions as well as the assumptions you are making. The descriptions of Sam Edder and Bill Ridell are actually case studies of real people. Sam Edder's file is that of Albert Einstein and Bill Ridell's is that of Thomas Edison. How quickly did you make faulty attributions about the potential for success of these students? How many other potential geniuses have been overlooked or have slipped through the cracks because of our narrow approaches to assessing and judging students?

Increasingly, teachers are searching for more effective ways to communicate performance to both students and parents. Many issues converge as we consider what it is, exactly, that we wish to communicate to others. Clearly, it is well to remember that—as is the case with all forms of student and teacher differences—social class differences require that attention be paid to subtle and often relatively invisible beliefs and values. Because the United States *professes* to be a classless society doesn't make it so; indeed, the combination of ethnicity and social class may, in the end, give us our most perplexing and most important problems.

Critical Incident

The Pull of Home

Beth Thomas, one of Ben's students who had gone on to the university in Burlington to major in Environment Science, was homesick for her small town life and confused by all the strange ways of the university. She was ready to leave the place that enormous amounts of student loans had let her leave home to attend. The last straw had been when her roommate's car had been broken into and robbed of nearly $500 of clothing, cosmetics, and cash. Beth's roommate told her father that she'd lost $1,000 worth of belongings, and her dad had quickly sent her a check to cover the losses. The check arrived just as Beth was leaving for her job waiting tables in one of the university dining halls, and her roommate was leaving to buy a satisfyingly large batch of new clothes.

Beth's younger sister came to see Ben, begging him to write to Beth to encourage her to stay in college. He agreed to write, although he didn't think it would mean much.

- If you were Ben, what would you say in such a letter?

Critical Incident

Too Much Traveling[2]

Tommy's dad is a career Army soldier, and Tommy is a quintessential "Army brat," having lived in 10 places in 20 years. Although he has gotten used to the traveling, he has had a hard time adjusting to the sharp changes in his social status that come with each move. Until the age of 10 he was oblivious to class differences, but when he hit middle school, he began to notice how he was perceived by others.

For a while the family lived in a small town in western Pennsylvania, where Tommy's father, a colonel, was considered part of the local elite. Tommy fondly remembers country club parties with his friends who were the sons and daughters of the local banker and lawyer. But then his father was posted to the Pentagon, where colonels are a dime a dozen. He moved to rental housing in a Virginia suburb and felt excluded from the golden inner circle at his new high school. The family couldn't get into the "best" country club, his clothes seemed out of fashion, and he developed a sense of resentment that had begun to erode his relationship with his parents.

Tommy struck up the beginnings of a friendship with his social studies teacher, Mr. Gordon. One day after school, he told Mr. Gordon some of what was bothering him.

- If you were Mr. Gordon, what might you do to help Tommy understand what he is experiencing?
- What advice might you give Tommy to help him feel that he "belongs" in the new environment?

Summary

In this chapter we explored the concepts of social class and social status nationally and globally in terms of their relation to schooling—to its curriculum, both hidden and explicit, to the ways in which schools are funded, and to its implications for the Every Student Succeeds Act, particularly in terms of assessment. Social class is difficult to discuss in the United States because the American "story" presupposes that one's social class is not important—one can always rise up the social ladder by keeping one's "nose to the grindstone."

The degree to which this is not as easy as it sounds is a pervasive theme in the chapter, and the role of assessment is presented as a critical part of both the debate and the substance of school reform issues today. Arguments for and against standardized testing and the arguments for the use of multiple forms of assessment are presented as subjects for discussion, and suggestions are made for a model of supportive assessment as an approach that will help all students learn.

Chapter Review

Go to the Online Learning Center at www.mhhe.com/cushner9e to review important content from the chapter, practice with key terms, take a chapter quiz, and access active workbook activities.

Key Terms

Every Student Succeeds Act (ESSA) 395	social status 405	working poor 402
social class 401	teacher expectations 406	underclass 402

Active Exercise

Additional Active Exercises are available online at www.mhhe.com/cushner9e.

Institutional Discrimination: Social Class in Focus

Purpose: To distinguish between individual and institutional practices that may discriminate against certain social classes.
Instructions: Institutional discrimination refers to policies and practices of institutions that allow certain discriminatory practices to persist. In this exercise you are presented with a number of situations and are asked to determine if these policies or practices systematically privilege members of certain groups while discriminating against members of other groups. Complete the three questions that follow for each situation that you determine to be an example of institutional discrimination.

1. Children of teachers employed in this private school receive free tuition. Is this an example of discrimination?

    a. Against which groups, if any, might this policy discriminate?
    b. What is the purpose of the policy?
    c. If the purpose is valid, how else might it be achieved?

2. A local religious school offers reduced tuition for members of its faith. Is this an example of discrimination?

    a. Against which groups, if any, might this policy discriminate?
    b. What is the purpose of the policy?
    c. If the purpose is valid, how else might it be achieved?

3. Because a recent school levy failed, a new school policy states that children who wish to participate in sports or musical performing groups must pay for their own uniforms. Is this an example of discrimination?

    a. Against which groups, if any, might this policy discriminate?
    b. What is the purpose of the policy?
    c. If the purpose is valid, how else might it be achieved?

4. A teacher awards 10 points out of 100 to boys who wear a jacket and tie and to girls who wear a full-length dress during an oral presentation as part of the final grade in a business speech class. Is this an example of discrimination?

    a. Against which groups, if any, might this policy discriminate?
    b. What is the purpose of the policy?
    c. If the purpose is valid, how else might it be achieved?

Classroom Activities

1. Engage elementary school students in a discussion of what they understand about a classmate's circumstances from looking at what they wear. In order to make it less "personal" in the class, a teacher might want to use pictures of students of the same age in various kinds of dress. List their reactions on the board, and discuss, being sure to include in the discussion the notion that some students really don't pay much attention to what they wear, or don't much care what others think. Then, ask students whether or not a school dress code might be helpful to children whose families could not afford to buy them many clothes, or to follow the "in" styles that change so often in children's clothing. Ask students to list pros and cons of a dress code.

2. Ask students in a high school classroom to discuss the assessments they are familiar with from their own experiences in school. Do they think these assessments actually measure what they know? Which of the various types of assessments (e.g., multiple choice, essay, short answer questions) they think produce a good representation of their knowledge and skills. Ask them "why" or "why not"? Engage students in a discussion of alternate forms of assessment, for example, portfolio, oral, knowledge application. Do students think alternate forms of assessment should be included in the assessment mix? Ask students to

research various forms of assessment and bring findings back to the classroom. What do they conclude?

3. It is very difficult to discuss social class in the United States, because most people believe that they are "middle class" or will soon become so. One way to get the idea of social stratification across to high school students is to ask students to describe the informal but identifiable social "groups" in their school and who "belongs" to each group. Write the names of these groups on the board as they come in from the students. Then ask students to rank these groups in terms of which are "better" or "worse" to be identified with. Then ask students how easy or difficult it would be for a member of a "lower" group to "move up" to a more prestigious group. Discuss this phenomenon in terms of social class and social status in the wider society.

Reflective Questions

1. How is poverty in rural Vermont different from what you know about urban poverty?

2. How might tests be an impediment to effective instruction (i.e., instruction that results in student learning)?

3. A common criticism of multiple forms of assessment is that two teachers using the same assessment procedures may arrive at different evaluations of students' achievement. Assuming that this criticism has some validity, how might conditions be set so that variation in teachers' evaluations might be minimized?

Endnotes

This Case Study was enriched by several primary sources. One is the work of Garret Keizer, a teacher and minister who wrote of his experiences teaching in northeastern Vermont, an area popularly referred to as the "Northeast Kingdom" (see Keizer, 1988, *No place but here: A teacher's vocation in a rural community.* New York: Penguin Books). Other works important to the Case Study are: an article on a real $20,000,000 grant from the National Science Foundation to the Vermont Experimental Program to Stimulate Research (Vermont EPSCoR) in 2015 (retrieved from http://www.nvda.net/regional-plan.php); Climate change and agriculture (retrieved from https://www.uvm.edu/~susagctr/whatwedo/farmingclimatechange/Farm CCQuickFacts.pdf; https://www.uvm.edu/~susagctr/whatwedo/farmingclimat echange/FarmCCQuickFacts.pdf; Vermont Department of Labor (2015). Economic /demographic profile series (retrieved from http://www.vtlmi.info/profile2015.pdf; http://www.vtlmi.info/profile2015.pdf).

References

Anyon, J. (1980). Social class and the hidden curriculum of work. *Journal of Education, 162*(1), 67–92.

Anyon, J. (1981). Social class and school knowledge. *Curriculum Inquiry, 11*(1), 3–42.

Barkan, S. E. (2011). *Sociology: Understanding and Changing the Social World, Brief Edition.* Irvington, NY: Flatworld Knowledge, Inc. Retrieved from http://catalog.flatworldknowledge.com/bookhub/reader/4306?e=barkbrief-1.1-ch06_s05

Bellah, R. N. (1976). Civil religion in America. In A. Wells (Ed.), *American society: Problems and dilemmas* (pp. 351–368). Pacific Palisades, CA: Goodyear.

Brislin, R. (1988). Increasing awareness of class, ethnicity, culture, and race. In I. Cohen (Ed.), *The G. Stanley Hall lecture series* (Vol. 8, pp. 137–180). Washington, DC: American Psychological Association.

Carle, David. (2016). Vermont EPSCoR wins $20,000,000 award from National Science Foundation to study and promote resiliency in Lake Champlain basin. Retrieved from https://www.leahy.senate.gov/press/-vermont-epscor-wins-20-million-award-from-national-science-foundation-to-study-and-promote-resiliency-in-lake-champlain-basin

Center for Poverty Research, University of California at Davis. (2015). What is the current poverty rate in the United States? Retrieved from http://poverty.ucdavis.edu/faq/what-current-poverty-rate-united-states

Craven, J. (2017, March 17). Trump budget cuts would gut federal funds to Vermont. *VTDIGGER,* Retrieved from https://vtdigger.org/2017/03/17/trump-budget-cuts-would-gut-federal-funds-to-vermont/

Darling-Hammond, L. (2010). *The flat world and education: How America's commitment to equity will determine our future.* New York: Teachers College, Columbia University, p. 2.

Elementary and Secondary Education Act (ESEA). (2001). Association for Educational Communications and Technology. Retrieved from http://aect.site-ym.com/?page=elementary_and_secon

Farrigan, Tracey; Hertz, Thomas. (2016) Understanding the rise in rural child poverty, 2003–2014) United States Department of Agriculture, Economic Research Service. Retrieved from https://www.ers.usda.gov/publications/pub-details/?pubid=45543

Faulkner, Joshua. (2014). Climate change and agriculture. University of Vermont, Extension. Retrieved from "https://www.uvm.edu/~susagctr/whatwedo/farmingclimatechange/FarmCCQuickFacts.pdf%20on%20April%2012" https://www.uvm.edu/~susagctr/whatwedo/farmingclimatechange/FarmCCQuickFacts.pdf

Gilbert, D., & Kahl, J. (1982). The American class structure: A new synthesis. Homewood, IL: Dorsey.

Global Stratification and Inequality. *Boundless Sociology,* 26 May 2016. Retrieved from https://www.boundless.com/sociology/textbooks/boundless-sociology-textbook/global-stratification-and-inequality-8/global-stratification-68/global-stratification-and-inequality-401-10459/

Good, T., & Brophy, J. (1987). *Looking in classrooms* (4th ed.). New York: Harper & Row.

Hurn, C. (1993). *The limits and possibilities of schooling* (3rd ed.). Boston: Allyn & Bacon.

Keizer, G. (1988). *No place but here: A teacher's vocation in a rural community.* New York: Penguin Books.

Kharas, H. (2017). The unprecedented expansion of the global middle class: An update. Washington, DC: The Brookings Institution. Retrieved from https://www.brookings.edu/wp-content/uploads/2017/02/global_20170228_global-middle-class.pdf

Klein, A. (2016, March 31). The Every Student Succeeds Act: An ESSA overview. *Education Week*. Retrieved from http://www.edweek.org/ew/issues/every-student-succeeds-act/

Klein, A. (2016, June 30). How Will ESSA's Innovative Assessment Pilot Work? *Education Week* Blogs, Politics K-12. Retrieved from http://blogs.edweek.org/edweek/campaign-k-12/2016/06/how_will_essas_innovative_asse.html

Knapp, M. S., & Woolverton, S. (2003). Social class and schooling. In J. A. Banks & C. A. McG. Banks (Eds.), *Handbook of research on multicultural education* (2nd ed.). San Francisco: Jossey-Bass.

Kohn, A. (1999). *The schools our children deserve: Moving beyond traditional classrooms and "tougher standards."* Boston: Houghton Mifflin.

Lugg, C. A. (2005, May). *The American dream and the public schools* [Book review]. *American Journal of Education, 423.*

Lyndon State College. (2017). New climate change science degree: LCS to tackle global problem. Retrieved from http://lyndonstate.edu/atmospheric-sciences/new-climate-change-science-degree/

Meier, D., & Wood, G. (Eds.). (2004). *Many children left behind: How the No Child Left Behind Act is damaging our children and our schools.* Boston: Beacon Press.

Metz, M. H. (1990). How social class differences shape teachers' work. In M. W. McLaughlin, J. E. Talbert, & N. Bascia (Eds.), *The context of teaching in secondary schools: Teachers' realities* (pp. 40-107). New York: Teachers College Press.

National Conference of State Legislatures. (2017). State role in education finance. Retrieved from http://www.ncsl.org/research/education/state-role-in-education-finance.aspx%20on%20April%2022 http://www.ncsl.org/research/education/state-role-in-education-finance.aspx

Nichols, J. G., & Hazzard, S. P. (1993). *Education as adventure: Lessons from the second grade.* New York: Teachers College Press.

Northeastern Vermont Development Association (NVDA). (2015). Northeast kingdom regional plan. Retrieved from http://www.nvda.net/regional-plan.php

Ornstein, A. C. (1994). Grading practices and policies: An overview and some suggestions. *NASSP Bulletin, 78,* 55-64.

People's Daily Online. (2004). Retrieved from http://english.people.com.cn/90833/90836/review/

Pew Research Center. (2015). The American middle class is losing ground. Retrieved from http://www.pewsocialtrends.org/2015/12/09/the-american-middle-class-is-losing-ground/

Potter, A., Whitener, A., & Sikorsky, J., Jan. (2014). 13 essential 21st century skills for today's students. Retrieved from https://www.envisionexperience.com/blog/13-essential-21st-century-skills-for-todays-students%20on%20April%2020 https://www.envisionexperience.com/blog/13-essential-21st-century-skills-for-todays-students

Reich, R. B. (1992). *The work of nations.* New York: Vintage.

Rose v. Council for Better Education, 790 S.W.2d 186 (1989).

San Antonio Independent School District v. Rodriguez, 411 U.S. 1 (1973).

Serrano v. Priest, 487 P.2d 1241 (Cal. 1971).

Standing, G. (2016). *The precariat: The new dangerous class.* London: Bloomsbury Academic Revelations Series.

Tyack, D. B. (1981). *Women and men in schools: A history of the sexual structuring of educational employment.* Washington, DC: National Institute of Education.

Villegas, A. M., & Lucas, T. (2007, March). The culturally responsive teacher. *Educational Leadership,* 28–33.

Webb, R. B., & Sherman, R. R. (1989). *Schooling and society* (2nd ed., pp. 397–398). New York: Macmillan.

What work requires of schools: A SCANS report for America 2000. (1991). Washington, DC: Secretary's Commission on Achieving Necessary Skills (SCANS), U.S. Department of Labor, U.S. Department of Education.

World Bank. (2015). Rural population. Retrieved from http://data.worldbank.org /indicator/SP.RUR.TOTL.ZS%20on%20April%2022

Glossary

A

Ability/disability A dimension encompassing the range of individual differences with respect to the physical, cognitive, socio-emotional, and other (e.g., aesthetic) domains characterizing human behavior.

Accent The pronunciation habits of the standard language acquired by people from a particular geographic region.

Acceptance Acceptance is the first ethnorelative stage of the Developmental Model of Intercultural Sensitivity and represents an individual's ability to recognize and appreciate cultural difference in terms of both people's values and their behavior.

Acculturation The changes that take place as a result of continuous firsthand contact between individuals of different cultures; usually refers to the experiences of adults.

Adaptation The ability of organisms, including human beings, to successfully negotiate the requirements of their environment.

Adaptive equipment The range of electronic, mechanical, and other devices that may enable a child or adult with a sensory, motoric, or other disability to perform tasks, such as those required for self-care, mobility, and classroom and work participation.

Affirmative action Policies that take factors such as race, color, religion, sex, or national origin into consideration in order to benefit an underrepresented group in areas of employment, education, and business.

African American Vernacular English A variety (dialect) of American English spoken by urban, working class African Americans.

Age The chronological index of developmental change from conception to death.

American Sign Language (ASL) Recognized as a distinct and legitimate language employing manual signs, facial expression, and other visual information according to a shared system of symbols and rules, ASL is the official signed system of communication in North America.

Anglo-conformity The belief that all immigrant children must be socialized into the culture and worldview of the dominant Anglo society in the United States.

Asperger's syndrome An autism spectrum disorder that is characterized by significant difficulties in social interaction and nonverbal communication, along with restricted and repetitive patterns of behavior and interests. It differs from other autism spectrum disorders by its relative preservation of linguistic and cognitive development.

Assimilation The process whereby an individual or group is absorbed into the social structures and cultural life of another person, group, or society.

Assimilationist ideology The practices by which children were socialized into the culture and worldview of the dominant Anglo society.

Attention Deficit Hyperactivity Disorder (ADHD) A psychiatric disorder in which there are significant problems of attention and/or hyperactivity and impulsive actions that are not appropriate for a person's age.

Authentic assessment A form of assessment in which students are called upon to perform real-world tasks that demonstrate understanding and application of essential knowledge and skills.

Autism spectrum disorder (autism) A brain disorder that to varying degrees typically affects a person's ability to communicate, form relationships with others, and respond appropriately to the environment.

B

Behavior management plan A formal plan for classroom organization and instruction designed to elicit good behavior on the part of all students, as well as to plan for adaptations required for children with disabilities.

Bidialectalism The ability to speak and understand two (and sometimes more) dialects and to switch back and forth among them.

Bilingual A person who speaks two languages fluently.

Bilingual education An education program for children whose native language is not English. Children are taught for some portion of the day in their native language, with the goal of moving them into mainstream English classes as quickly as possible, usually within two to three years.

Bipolar disorder A mental illness classified by psychiatrists characterized by abnormal mood shifts, as well as fluctuations in energy, activity levels, and the ability to complete everyday tasks.

C

Categorization The process of dividing stimuli into classes or groups according to a particular system. In the cultural context, the manner by which one's culture teaches one to view the world around him or her.

Cerebral palsy An administrative term for a range of impairments caused by nonprogressive damage to the brain incurred pre-, peri-, or post-natally and reflected in impaired voluntary use of specific muscle groups.

Child study movement Pioneered by G. Stanley Hall at the turn of the 20th century, the child study movement was an aspect of the (then) new discipline of psychology, which defined childhood as a distinct stage of life and set about to study it.

Clean intermittent catheterization (CIC) A process by which a hollow plastic tube (catheter) is inserted into the bladder to drain it. CIC is normally done on a regular schedule during the day and night to assist children and adults who, for one reason or another, cannot control bladder function.

Code-switching The ability to alternate between two or more languages in conversation.

Cognitive structures The ways in which individuals organize or scaffold knowledge so as to learn, remember, think, and otherwise use it.

Conduct disorder A psychological disorder diagnosed in childhood or adolescence that often presents itself through a repetitive and persistent pattern of antisocial behavior in which the basic rights of others or major age-appropriate norms are violated.

Constructivism The belief that all knowledge is built or "constructed" by individual learners; it is thus important when teaching and learning *new* knowledge to connect it to knowledge already known.

Cross-cultural awareness Perception of significant differences among cultural groups that leads to greater understanding and ability to interact effectively with members of different groups.

Cultural capital The accumulation of both subjective and objective cultural knowledge that one uses to advance or be a leader in one's society.

Cultural pluralism A system of social or political organization that stresses and promotes mutual understanding and respect among disparate ethnic, religious, and racial groups existing in a society.

Culture The totality of socially transmitted behavior patterns, arts, beliefs, institutions, and all other products of human work and thought characteristic of a community or a population.

Culture-general approaches Cross-cultural concepts that apply to the kinds of interactions and experiences people are likely to encounter regardless of the groups that are interacting.

Culture-specific approaches Cross-cultural concepts that apply to people who live and/or work with people of a particular culture or group.

Cyberbullying Use of the Internet and related social media technologies to harm other people in a deliberate, repeated, and hostile manner.

D

Defense Defense is the second stage of the Developmental Model of Intercultural Sensitivity and is characterized by a recognition of cultural difference coupled with negative evaluations of those whose culture is different from one's own.

Demographics Vital statistics that characterize human popu-lations, including age, gender, ethnicity, and so forth. Demographics, often generated from population census data, can be used to project future trends and needs of relevance to educators.

Denial Denial is the first stage of the Developmental Model of Intercultural Sensitivity and refers to an inability to see cultural differences, usually evidenced when individuals isolate or separate themselves in homogeneous groups.

Developmentally appropriate practice (DAP) Instructional practices that are organized and designed on the basis of the age and development of the student.

Dialect A variation of some "standard" language form that includes differences in pronunciation, word usage, and syntax; such differences may be based on ethnicity, religion, geographical region, social class, or age.

Dominant culture The culture of the social/political group that holds the most power and influence in a society.

Down syndrome A genetically inherited condition caused by extra genetic material (genes) from the 21st chromosome, resulting in a combination of features including some degree of mental retardation, or cognitive disability, and other developmental delays.

E

Empathy A psychological sense of understanding and "feeling for" another person's situation.

Enculturate The process of raising a child to be a member of a particular culture or culture group.

Establishment clause of the First Amendment The clause that prohibits the government from establishing a state religion.

Ethnic group A group that shares a common heritage and reflects identification with some collective or reference group, oftentimes in a common homeland. A feeling that one's own destiny is somehow linked with others who share this same knowledge.

Ethnicity/nationality Ethnicity is culturally defined according to the knowledge, beliefs, and behavior patterns shared by a group of people with the same history and perhaps the same language. Nationality is culturally defined on the basis of a shared citizenship, which may or may not include a shared ethnicity.

Ethnocentrism The tendency people have to evaluate others from their own cultural reference point.

Every Student Succeeds Act (2015) The latest iteration of the Elementary and Secondary Education Act of 1965.

F

Fourteenth Amendment Constitutional amendment prohibiting states from abridging rights granted to all U.S. citizens, born or naturalized in the United States. It also guarantees that no person shall be deprived of life, liberty, or property without due process of law, and that all persons shall be guaranteed equal protection under the law.

Freedmen's Bureau Officially known as the Bureau of Refugees, Freedmen, and Abandoned Lands, the Freedmen's Bureau was established by Congress on March 3, 1865, to supervise all relief and educational activities relating to refugees and freedmen, and to assume custody of confiscated lands in the former Confederate States, border states, District of Columbia, and Indian Territories.

G

Gender inclusion The practice of welcoming students who express their gender differently in a classroom or school in the same way as one welcomes other differences among students.

Gender role A set of social norms dictating the types of behaviors generally considered acceptable, appropriate, or desirable based on the sex they were assigned at birth.

Gender role socialization The process by which young children acquire the knowledge and internalize the values of socially determined sex roles.

Generalization The tendency of a majority of people in a cultural group to hold certain values and beliefs, and to engage in certain patterns of behavior. Thus, this information can be supported by research and can be applied to a large percentage of a population or group.

Genotype The whole complex of genes inherited from both parents and determines the potentials and limitations of an individual from embryonic formation through adulthood.

Geographic location/region Geographic location and region are culturally defined by the characteristics (topographical features, natural resources) of the ecological environment in which a person lives. Geographic location may include the characteristics of a neighborhood or community (rural, urban, suburban) and/or the natural and climatic features of a region (mountains, desert, plains, coastal, hot, cold, wet, dry).

Global perspective A worldview that takes into account the fact that individuals and societies are a part of a larger, worldwide system.

Globalization The process by which nations of the world become connected and interdependent through ties created by electronic communication, rapid means of travel, and interlocking economies.

Group homes Supervised, family-style residential arrangements accommodating small numbers of adults with disabilities.

Growth measures An approach to assessment of students that uses computerized tests in several subjects to identify where individual students are at a particular time, for the purpose of intervening exactly where the student is in mastering a particular subject. The test questions "adjust" to each student and, when given to that same student again, can measure growth.

H

Health The dimension encompassing acute and chronic physical and psychological illness, on the one hand, and physical and psychological vigor, stamina, and general well-being on the other.

Hypodescent A way to categorize racial membership in which any amount of biological inheritance from a group considered to be a socially "lower" or minority group automatically places one in that group.

I

Immigrants People who voluntarily move to a country of which they are not a native with the purpose of taking up permanent residence.

Inclusion The belief in and practice of creating heterogeneous classrooms; more particularly, the practice of teaching students with disabilities in "regular" classrooms.

In-context learning Learning that takes place through direct participation in real-world events.

Indigenous people Those living in an area generally since prehistoric (or pre-European contact) times. Related terms include aboriginal people (particularly in Australia) and first nation people (particularly in Canada).

Individual education program (IEP) A formal plan for instruction mandated by laws governing special education that sets forth the educational needs of a student, the goals and objectives that direct his or her program, the educational programming and placement, and the evaluation and measurement criteria that have been agreed upon by a team encompassing appropriate school personnel, parents, and when appropriate, the individual student her- or himself.

Informed consent The legal requirement for parents' informed consent prior to multifactored evaluation, participation in developing an IEP, and right to procedural due process in the event of disagreement.

Institutional racism Any kind of system of inequality based on race that can occur in institutions such as schools, universities, government entities, or corpora-

tions that systematically discriminates against one or more groups.

Integration The coming together of ideas, things, people, or objects in such a manner to form a common unit that cannot be distinguished from the original parts. In the educational context, it refers to the positive interaction of all people along equal lines of power, authority, status, and involvement in the school process.

K

Kinesics The study of nonverbal communication in the form of body movements, often called "body language"; kinesics includes gestures, posture, facial expressions, and eye contact.

L

Language Language is often defined as a system of shared vocal sounds and/or nonverbal behaviors that enables members of a particular group to communicate with one another.

Least restrictive environment (LRE) The requirement of federal special education legislation that requires that students with disabilities be educated as much as is individually appropriate in "regular" or "typical" learning environments along with peers who do not have disabilities.

Limited English proficient (LEP) Those individuals who do not speak English as their primary language and who have a limited ability to read, speak, write, or understand English.

Low-incidence A type of disability that does not occur very often, for example, blindness.

M

Marginalization The practice of excluding a social group from the mainstream of the society; placing that group—legally or socially—on the "margins" of the society.

Microculture A social group that shares distinctive traits, values, and behaviors that set it apart from the parent macroculture of which it is a part. Microculture seems to imply a greater linkage with the parent culture and often mediate the ideas, values, and institutions of the larger political community.

Middle schools Schools at a level between elementary and high school; middle school can include grades 5 through 8, but more typically includes grades 6 through 8; devoted to enhancing the education of young adolescents, who are perceived to have particular needs apart from either elementary or high school students.

Minimization The last ethnocentric stage in the Developmental Model of Intercultural Sensitivity begins when people recognize and accept superficial cultural differences such as eating customs, money, and so forth, yet continue to hold the belief that all human beings are essentially the same.

Mountain English A dialect of English spoken largely in Appalachia.

Multicultural education An education that is designed and shaped by several cultural perspectives.

Multifactored evaluation An evaluation that looks at many possible aspects of the learning problems of children with disabilities; may include cognitive, physical, social, and psychological factors.

Muscular dystrophy An inherited disease that causes increasing weakness in muscle tissue. The muscles affected are the skeletal muscles and, occasionally, the muscles of the heart.

N

Nativist religions Religions practiced by native peoples, often based on a sense of oneness with the earth.

Nature versus nurture debate A long-standing argument about whether a set of inborn and immutable characteristics or education is more important in the outcome of an individual's development.

No Child Left Behind Act of 2001 (NCLB) The name given the reauthorization of the Elementary and Secondary Education Act of 1992.

Normalization A philosophical view that the lives of exceptional individuals, of any age, should be characterized as much as possible by the same kinds of experiences, daily routines, and rhythms as those of persons who do not have disabilities.

Normative The norms of a society influence and regulate an individual's beliefs and behavior.

Norms Accepted ways of agreed-upon behavior that enable similar groups of people to function in a similar manner.

O

Objective culture The tangible, visible aspects of a culture, including such things as the artifacts produced, the foods eaten, and the clothing worn.

Out-of-context learning Learning that typically occurs in the abstract as opposed to learning using concrete objects and references.

P

Paralanguage A form of nonverbal communication that is concerned with vocalizations that are not words.

People of color Nonwhite minority group members, but reflects recent demographic realities of the United States. The phrase *people of color* refers to groups such as African Americans, Mexican Americans, Puerto Ricans, and Native Americans and is often preferred over *ethnic minority* because these groups are, in many schools and communities, the majority rather than the minority.

Perception The process by which people are aware of stimuli in the world around them.

Perspective consciousness The awareness (consciousness) of the perspectives of others who are different from oneself.

Phenotype All the observable characteristics of an organism, such as shape, size, color, and behavior, that result from the interaction of its genotype (total genetic inheritance) with the environment. The common type of a group of physically similar organisms is sometimes also known as the phenotype. The phenotype may change constantly throughout the life of an individual.

Placement continuum The degree to which students with disabilities are involved in "regular" education.

Prejudice Nonreflective judgments about others that are harsh, discriminatory, or involve rejection.

Prohibition clause of the First Amendment The clause that says that Congress shall make no laws "prohibiting the free exercise" of religion or religious beliefs.

Proxemics The normal physical distance between speakers when they are communicating with one another, which is normally acquired as part of one's culture. It is sometimes referred to as "social space."

Pseudoscience A set or system of beliefs claiming to be "scientific" without the benefit of the scientific method used to make further inquiries that might suggest that the belief system is wrong in any particular way.

R

Race Race is an imprecise term: biologically, it is defined as the clustering of inherited physical characteristics that favor adaptation to a particular ecological area; culturally it is defined according to the particular set of physical characteristics emphasized by different cultural groups.

Racial profiling The practice of constructing a set of characteristics or behaviors based on race and using that set of characteristics to decide whether or not an individual might be guilty of some crime and therefore worthy of investigation or arrest.

Racism Discriminatory or abusive behavior toward members of another race; and/or the belief that members of one race are inherently superior to members of other races.

Refugees People who flee for safety to another country.

Related services Defined in the Individuals with Disabilities Education Act (IDEA) as services an eligible student between the ages of 3 and 22 requires to benefit from special education. These services, such as transportation, adapted physical education, counseling, speech-language pathology, or occupational or physical therapy services, are identified in the student's IEP and provided by the school at no cost to the student's family.

Religion/spirituality Religion and spirituality are culturally defined on the basis of a shared set of ideas about the relationship of the earth and the people on it to a deity or deities and a shared set of rules for living moral values that enhance that relationship.

Rett's disorder A neurodevelopmental disorder that almost exclusively affects females that results in small hands and feet and a deceleration of the rate of head growth (including microcephaly in some). Repetitive stereotyped hand movements, such as wringing and/or repeatedly putting hands into the mouth, are often observed. People with Rett's syndrome typically have no verbal skills, and about 50% of individuals affected do not walk.

Rural English A dialect of English, sometimes called "mountain English," spoken primarily in Appalachia and derived from the language of early English settlers in the area.

S

Secular trend The term used to refer to the recognition that the average age of puberty has decreased over time. Since the 1900s in the United States, puberty seems to have occurred about 4 months earlier with each passing decade.

Segregation The act of separating or setting apart from others. In the educational context, it may refer to the establishment of separate schools for students of different races or abilities/disabilities.

Separation Situations in which two social groups voluntarily decide that it is of value for each to maintain its own cultural identity but not considered a value to maintain relationships with other groups.

Separation of church and state The philosophical belief that religion and government should not be conjoined. In the United States, this belief is codified in the First Amendment to the Constitution.

Sex/gender Sex is a biological category referring to a set of human reproductive physical characteristics. Gender, on the other hand, is culturally defined on the basis of what it means to be male or female in a given society or cultural group. Thus, gender is expressed in terms of socially valued behaviors of males and females.

Sexuality Sexuality is culturally defined on the basis of particular patterns of sexual self-identification, behavior, and interpersonal relationships.

Sickle cell disease A genetic abnormality, affecting more individuals of African descent than other groups, causing intermittent or chronic severe and debilitating pain and impaired physical functioning.

Social class A way to categorize individuals in a stratified social system; social class characteristics are often related (but may not be limited) to child-rearing practices, beliefs, values, economic status, prestige and influence, and general life chances.

Social institution A formal, recognized, established, and stabilized way of pursuing some activity in society.

Social status The degree to which an individual has power, influence, or leadership in his or her social group.

Socialization The process whereby individuals learn what is appropriate to be a functioning member of a particular group, such as a family, work, or social group.

Sojourner A person who stays in a place for a relatively brief period of time; often used in reference to tourists or short-term visitors or strangers to a country.

Specific learning disabilities (SLD) A significant difficulty in one or more areas of school achievement, such as reading, writing, mathematical calculation, spelling, or listening, that is not caused by general cognitive disability (mental retardation); hearing, vision, or motor impairment; emotional disturbance; or social or cultural disadvantage. SLD is reflected in a discrepancy between intellectual ability and academic achievement that may be caused by impairment in one or more basic neurological processes underlying linguistic functioning.

Spina bifida A condition in which there is a congenital cleft or opening in the vertebral column.

Standard English A dialect of the English language, usually taken to mean that version of the English language most acceptable or most "correct," used by educated middle and upper classes, and thus the dialect taught in public schools; standard English may vary by geographical location, but in general it is the dialect used in formal writing and in the broadcast and print media.

State of the planet awareness Awareness (consciousness) of the ways in which human beings are acting in ways that endanger the ecological life of the planet as well as knowledge of ways in which such dangers can be averted.

Stereotypes Beliefs about the personal attributes of a group based on the inaccurate generalizations used to describe all members of the group, thus ignoring individual differences.

Subculture A social group with shared characteristics that distinguish it in some way from the larger cultural group or society in which it is embedded. Generally, a subculture is distinguished either by a unifying set of ideas and/or practices (such as the corporate culture or the drug culture) or by some demographic characteristic (such as the adolescent culture or the culture of poverty).

Subjective culture The invisible, intangible aspects of a group, including such things as attitudes, values, norms of behavior—the things typically kept in people's minds.

Supported employment A range of methods used to enable individuals with significant disabilities to engage in regular productive and remunerative employment in various work settings in the community, rather than within traditional, segregated settings.

T

Teacher expectations The relation between what a teacher believes a student can do and what the student can actually do; generally, the more a teacher believes a student can do, the higher the achievement of the student, without respect to such factors as measured intelligence, social class, or family background.

Theocracy A system of government in which a particular set of religious beliefs, or an organized religion, is completely intertwined with the processes of government.

Transition plan A formal education plan, mandated by federal special education legislation, that elaborates the steps to be taken to move a student with disabilities into adult and working life.

Traumatic brain injury An injury to the brain causing subsequent cognitive or psychomotor disability; usually the result of an accident, but sometimes can be sustained at birth.

U

Underclass The class of people belonging to the lowest and least privileged social stratum or a group that is in some sense outside the mainstream of society.

Universal health precautions Observing common hygienic practices as precautions against contracting infection or disease, especially frequent handwashing and avoiding skin contact with human bodily fluids. These precautions should be observed whether or not it is known that a communicable disease is present.

W

White privilege A set of societal privileges that white individuals may not recognize they have, such as cultural affirmations of one's own worth; greater presumed social status; and freedom to move, buy, work, play, and speak freely wherever they wish. It also implies the universality of one's own experiences, judging others as different or exceptional while perceiving oneself as the norm. It can be compared and/or combined with the concept of male privilege.

Working class Most often refers to the social class of those who work for wages rather than salaries, who do manual or manufacturing work, and who, in the United States at least, also can be perceived (and perceive themselves) as lower middle class.

Working poor This usually refers to that group of people in a society who, although gainfully employed, do not earn enough to rise out of poverty.

Z

Zero exclusion mandate The section of Public Law 94-142 that requires that all children with disabilities be provided a free, appropriate, and public education because local school systems do not have the option to decide whether to provide needed services.

Zone of proximal development Russian psychologist Lev S. Vygotsky used this phrase to refer to learning experiences that allow an individual learner to build upon what is already familiar, yet sufficiently novel to be interesting and challenging.

Name Index

Subject Index

Note: The letter 'f' followed by the numbers denotes the 'figures'.